Lecture Notes in Computer Science   13302

More information about this series at https://link.springer.com/bookseries/558

Masaaki Kurosu (Ed.)

Human-Computer Interaction

Theoretical Approaches and Design Methods

Thematic Area, HCI 2022
Held as Part of the 24th HCI International Conference, HCII 2022
Virtual Event, June 26 – July 1, 2022
Proceedings, Part I

 Springer

Editor
Masaaki Kurosu
The Open University of Japan
Chiba, Japan

ISSN 0302-9743   ISSN 1611-3349 (electronic)
Lecture Notes in Computer Science
ISBN 978-3-031-05310-8   ISBN 978-3-031-05311-5 (eBook)
https://doi.org/10.1007/978-3-031-05311-5

This Springer imprint is published by the registered company Springer Nature Switzerland AG
The registered company address is: Gewerbestrasse 11, 6330 Cham, Switzerland

Foreword

Human-computer interaction (HCI) is acquiring an ever-increasing scientific and industrial importance, as well as having more impact on people's everyday life, as an ever-growing number of human activities are progressively moving from the physical to the digital world. This process, which has been ongoing for some time now, has been dramatically accelerated by the COVID-19 pandemic. The HCI International (HCII) conference series, held yearly, aims to respond to the compelling need to advance the exchange of knowledge and research and development efforts on the human aspects of design and use of computing systems.

The 24th International Conference on Human-Computer Interaction, HCI International 2022 (HCII 2022), was planned to be held at the Gothia Towers Hotel and Swedish Exhibition & Congress Centre, Göteborg, Sweden, during June 26 to July 1, 2022. Due to the COVID-19 pandemic and with everyone's health and safety in mind, HCII 2022 was organized and run as a virtual conference. It incorporated the 21 thematic areas and affiliated conferences listed on the following page.

A total of 5583 individuals from academia, research institutes, industry, and governmental agencies from 88 countries submitted contributions, and 1276 papers and 275 posters were included in the proceedings to appear just before the start of the conference. The contributions thoroughly cover the entire field of human-computer interaction, addressing major advances in knowledge and effective use of computers in a variety of application areas. These papers provide academics, researchers, engineers, scientists, practitioners, and students with state-of-the-art information on the most recent advances in HCI. The volumes constituting the set of proceedings to appear before the start of the conference are listed in the following pages.

The HCI International (HCII) conference also offers the option of 'Late Breaking Work' which applies both for papers and posters, and the corresponding volume(s) of the proceedings will appear after the conference. Full papers will be included in the 'HCII 2022 - Late Breaking Papers' volumes of the proceedings to be published in the Springer LNCS series, while 'Poster Extended Abstracts' will be included as short research papers in the 'HCII 2022 - Late Breaking Posters' volumes to be published in the Springer CCIS series.

I would like to thank the Program Board Chairs and the members of the Program Boards of all thematic areas and affiliated conferences for their contribution and support towards the highest scientific quality and overall success of the HCI International 2022 conference; they have helped in so many ways, including session organization, paper reviewing (single-blind review process, with a minimum of two reviews per submission) and, more generally, acting as goodwill ambassadors for the HCII conference.

This conference would not have been possible without the continuous and unwavering support and advice of Gavriel Salvendy, founder, General Chair Emeritus, and Scientific Advisor. For his outstanding efforts, I would like to express my appreciation to Abbas Moallem, Communications Chair and Editor of HCI International News.

June 2022   Constantine Stephanidis

HCI International 2022 Thematic Areas and Affiliated Conferences

Thematic Areas

- HCI: Human-Computer Interaction
- HIMI: Human Interface and the Management of Information

Affiliated Conferences

- EPCE: 19th International Conference on Engineering Psychology and Cognitive Ergonomics
- AC: 16th International Conference on Augmented Cognition
- UAHCI: 16th International Conference on Universal Access in Human-Computer Interaction
- CCD: 14th International Conference on Cross-Cultural Design
- SCSM: 14th International Conference on Social Computing and Social Media
- VAMR: 14th International Conference on Virtual, Augmented and Mixed Reality
- DHM: 13th International Conference on Digital Human Modeling and Applications in Health, Safety, Ergonomics and Risk Management
- DUXU: 11th International Conference on Design, User Experience and Usability
- C&C: 10th International Conference on Culture and Computing
- DAPI: 10th International Conference on Distributed, Ambient and Pervasive Interactions
- HCIBGO: 9th International Conference on HCI in Business, Government and Organizations
- LCT: 9th International Conference on Learning and Collaboration Technologies
- ITAP: 8th International Conference on Human Aspects of IT for the Aged Population
- AIS: 4th International Conference on Adaptive Instructional Systems
- HCI-CPT: 4th International Conference on HCI for Cybersecurity, Privacy and Trust
- HCI-Games: 4th International Conference on HCI in Games
- MobiTAS: 4th International Conference on HCI in Mobility, Transport and Automotive Systems
- AI-HCI: 3rd International Conference on Artificial Intelligence in HCI
- MOBILE: 3rd International Conference on Design, Operation and Evaluation of Mobile Communications

List of Conference Proceedings Volumes Appearing Before the Conference

18. LNCS 13319, Digital Human Modeling and Applications in Health, Safety, Ergonomics and Risk Management: Anthropometry, Human Behavior, and Communication (Part I), edited by Vincent G. Duffy

19. LNCS 13320, Digital Human Modeling and Applications in Health, Safety, Ergonomics and Risk Management: Health, Operations Management, and Design (Part II), edited by Vincent G. Duffy

20. LNCS 13321, Design, User Experience, and Usability: UX Research, Design, and Assessment (Part I), edited by Marcelo M. Soares, Elizabeth Rosenzweig and Aaron Marcus

21. LNCS 13322, Design, User Experience, and Usability: Design for Emotion, Well-being and Health, Learning, and Culture (Part II), edited by Marcelo M. Soares, Elizabeth Rosenzweig and Aaron Marcus

22. LNCS 13323, Design, User Experience, and Usability: Design Thinking and Practice in Contemporary and Emerging Technologies (Part III), edited by Marcelo M. Soares, Elizabeth Rosenzweig and Aaron Marcus

23. LNCS 13324, Culture and Computing, edited by Matthias Rauterberg

24. LNCS 13325, Distributed, Ambient and Pervasive Interactions: Smart Environments, Ecosystems, and Cities (Part I), edited by Norbert A. Streitz and Shin'ichi Konomi

25. LNCS 13326, Distributed, Ambient and Pervasive Interactions: Smart Living, Learning, Well-being and Health, Art and Creativity (Part II), edited by Norbert A. Streitz and Shin'ichi Konomi

26. LNCS 13327, HCI in Business, Government and Organizations, edited by Fiona Fui-Hoon Nah and Keng Siau

27. LNCS 13328, Learning and Collaboration Technologies: Designing the Learner and Teacher Experience (Part I), edited by Panayiotis Zaphiris and Andri Ioannou

28. LNCS 13329, Learning and Collaboration Technologies: Novel Technological Environments (Part II), edited by Panayiotis Zaphiris and Andri Ioannou

29. LNCS 13330, Human Aspects of IT for the Aged Population: Design, Interaction and Technology Acceptance (Part I), edited by Qin Gao and Jia Zhou

30. LNCS 13331, Human Aspects of IT for the Aged Population: Technology in Everyday Living (Part II), edited by Qin Gao and Jia Zhou

31. LNCS 13332, Adaptive Instructional Systems, edited by Robert A. Sottilare and Jessica Schwarz

32. LNCS 13333, HCI for Cybersecurity, Privacy and Trust, edited by Abbas Moallem

33. LNCS 13334, HCI in Games, edited by Xiaowen Fang

34. LNCS 13335, HCI in Mobility, Transport and Automotive Systems, edited by Heidi Krömker

35. LNAI 13336, Artificial Intelligence in HCI, edited by Helmut Degen and Stavroula Ntoa

36. LNCS 13337, Design, Operation and Evaluation of Mobile Communications, edited by Gavriel Salvendy and June Wei

37. CCIS 1580, HCI International 2022 Posters - Part I, edited by Constantine Stephanidis, Margherita Antona and Stavroula Ntoa

38. CCIS 1581, HCI International 2022 Posters - Part II, edited by Constantine Stephanidis, Margherita Antona and Stavroula Ntoa

39. CCIS 1582, HCI International 2022 Posters - Part III, edited by Constantine Stephanidis, Margherita Antona and Stavroula Ntoa
40. CCIS 1583, HCI International 2022 Posters - Part IV, edited by Constantine Stephanidis, Margherita Antona and Stavroula Ntoa

http://2022.hci.international/proceedings

Preface

Human-Computer Interaction is a Thematic Area of the International Conference on Human-Computer Interaction (HCII). The HCI field is today undergoing a wave of significant innovation and breakthroughs towards radically new future forms of interaction. The HCI Thematic Area constitutes a forum for scientific research and innovation in human-computer interaction, addressing challenging and innovative topics in human-computer interaction theory, methodology, and practice, including, for example, novel theoretical approaches to interaction, novel user interface concepts and technologies, novel interaction devices, UI development methods, environments and tools, multimodal user interfaces, human-robot interaction, emotions in HCI, aesthetic issues, HCI and children, evaluation methods and tools, and many others.

The HCI Thematic Area covers three major dimensions, namely theory, technology, and human beings. The following three volumes of the HCII 2022 proceedings reflect these dimensions:

- Human-Computer Interaction: Theoretical Approaches and Design Methods (Part I), addressing topics related to theoretical and multidisciplinary approaches in HCI, design and evaluation methods, techniques and tools, emotions and design, and children-computer interaction
- Human-Computer Interaction: Technological Innovation (Part II), addressing topics related to novel interaction devices, methods and techniques, text, speech and image processing in HCI, emotion and physiological reactions recognition, and human-robot interaction.
- Human-Computer Interaction: User Experience and Behavior (Part III), addressing topics related to design and user experience case studies, persuasive design and behavioral change, and interacting with chatbots and virtual agents.

Papers of these volumes are included for publication after a minimum of two single-blind reviews from the members of the HCI Program Board or, in some cases, from members of the Program Boards of other affiliated conferences. I would like to thank all of them for their invaluable contribution, support, and efforts.

June 2022   Masaaki Kurosu

Human-Computer Interaction Thematic Area (HCI 2022)

Program Board Chair: **Masaaki Kurosu,** The Open University of Japan, Japan

- Salah Ahmed, University of South-Eastern Norway, Norway
- Valdecir Becker, Federal University of Paraiba, Brazil
- Nimish Biloria, University of Technology Sydney, Australia
- Zhigang Chen, Shanghai University, China
- Yu-Hsiu Hung, National Cheng Kung University, Taiwan
- Yi Ji, Guangdong University of Technology, China
- Tsuneo Jozen, Osaka Electro-Communication University, Shijonawate, Japan
- Masanao Koeda, Okayama Prefectural University, Japan
- Hiroshi Noborio, Osaka Electro-Communication University, Neyagawa-shi, Japan
- Michiko Ohkura, Shibaura Institute of Technology, Japan
- Katsuhiko Onishi, Osaka Electro-Communication University, Shijonawate, Japan
- Vinícius Segura, IBM Research, Rio de Janeiro, Brazil
- Mohammad Shidujaman, American International University-Bangladesh, Bangladesh

The full list with the Program Board Chairs and the members of the Program Boards of all thematic areas and affiliated conferences is available online at

http://www.hci.international/board-members-2022.php

HCI International 2023

The 25th International Conference on Human-Computer Interaction, HCI International 2023, will be held jointly with the affiliated conferences at the AC Bella Sky Hotel and Bella Center, Copenhagen, Denmark, 23–28 July 2023. It will cover a broad spectrum of themes related to human-computer interaction, including theoretical issues, methods, tools, processes, and case studies in HCI design, as well as novel interaction techniques, interfaces, and applications. The proceedings will be published by Springer. More information will be available on the conference website: http://2023.hci.international/.

General Chair
Constantine Stephanidis
University of Crete and ICS-FORTH
Heraklion, Crete, Greece
Email: general_chair@hcii2023.org

http://2023.hci.international/

Contents – Part I

Design and Evaluation Methods, Techniques and Tools

Emotions and Design

Children-Computer Interaction

Contents – Part II

Text, Speech and Image Processing in HCI

Human-Robot Interaction

Contents – Part III

Design and User Experience Case Studies

Persuasive Design and Behavioral Change

Interacting with Chatbots and Virtual Agents

Theoretical and Multidisciplinary Approaches in HCI

Non-destructive Interaction. Embracing Mistakes as an Activity Theoretical UX-Design Approach

Sturla Bakke[✉] (iD)

Kristiania University College, Oslo, Norway
sturla.bakke@kristiania.no

Abstract. With increasing technological complexity, especially within the field of computer mediated interaction, possibilities for user mistakes, and security risks, follows.

This paper presents an interaction design pattern for anticipating mistakes in a computer mediated context by letting the users store their actions and current state of 'object fulfilment' as a temporary action status.

This paper presents parts of an empirical material from a doctoral research project, and a case study of designing a planning software in a shipping company. The interaction design approach involved facilitating a "safe place" for errors in order to anticipate and use the mistakes as learning points. By developing a function for temporary storing current activity states, the users could work on [multiple] preliminary scenarios.

Based on the literature and the empirical findings, the paper suggests that this interaction design pattern of "iterative interaction" for anticipating and embracing user-errors adds a layer of security, and an experience of mastery and an emerging sense of development and might contribute to a perceived good user experience.

Keywords: Interaction design · User experience · Activity theory

1 Introduction

The information technological revolution in the industrialised parts of the world, at least the part of it with stable and abundant access to electric power, has penetrated almost all aspects of modern society. Manuel Castells describes this process as a 'technological transformation that expands exponentially because of its ability to create an interface between technological fields through common digital language in which information is generated, stored, retrieved, processed, and transmitted' [8].

Our everyday life has become technology saturated by apps and online services, affecting on a variety of fields, like e.g. health, education, media consumption, communication and privacy, public services and what might be described as overall interactive societal practice [10, 16, 21, 37], conceivably with the digitalisation of the Estonian public service into an all-encompassing online service [1, 20, 22, 43] as an extreme example.

© The Author(s), under exclusive license to Springer Nature Switzerland AG 2022
M. Kurosu (Ed.): HCII 2022, LNCS 13302, pp. 3–17, 2022.
https://doi.org/10.1007/978-3-031-05311-5_1

Ordinary users are increasingly expected or required to perform tasks that earlier were performed by specialised personnel, and using somewhat complicated technological information infrastructures, as these are described by e.g. Hanseth and Lyytinen [18], with all the possibilities for user mistakes, and security risks, this entails.

Usability and user experience are obvious and important elements in modern ICT development, which in its heterogeneity have become more and more complex [17, 19]. There's no secret that information systems might be difficult to learn and cumbersome to use [47].

Steep learning curves and certain degrees of awkwardness will eventually lead to a proneness to make mistakes and a difficulty to correct them, quite the opposite of the ideal user-experience. It should be difficult to make mistakes and if mistakes are made, they should be easy to correct [40]. As the complexity and technological connectedness increase, these are key elements in the fields of human-computer interaction and interaction design, and central when working with usability and user experience.

1.1 Motivation

"We should deal with error by embracing it, by seeking to understand the causes and ensuring they do not happen again. We need to assist rather than punish or scold."[1]

Research work within the HCI field and its historical significance in the socio-technical area play an important part in the subject of bringing technology to the public [2, 7, 11, 30, 36, 41, 44, 48], in parallel, the literature on human error in technological systems is comprehensive [6, 24, 45].

The perspective of use is important, and the many areas of technological development, makes this a complex area - from the field of information systems in working life to elements of design and user experience. The ubiquitousness of computer technology in societal life is increasingly mirrored in the business sector, but the focus of good user-experiences we might find in online services, may not have been equally evident in the same manner and volumes in business systems, as described by e.g. Söderstrøm [47].

"If the system lets you make the error, it is badly designed. And if the system induces you to make the error, then it is really badly designed."[2]

What if user mistakes would not lead to crashes, loss of data or [significant amounts of] time, but were absorbed or even anticipated by the application or service, and used with intent as learning elements in the user experience? Smoothing out the societal gap in the digital skills needed in mastering the current digital everyday life by regarding and preparing the user experience as a continuous learning process, treating mistakes and

---

[1] Don Norman, 2013. The Design of Everyday Things. Revised and expanded edition. New York: Basic Books. p. 216 [42].

[2] Don Norman, 2013. The Design of Everyday Things. Revised and expanded edition. New York: Basic Books. p. 167 [42].

breakdowns as sources of development rather than something that is unwanted and has to be avoided.

1.2 Research Question

In this paper, we ask: what interaction design patterns could we design and use in the development of apps or services where the user experience would not deteriorate when users make mistakes? Where the users would still reach the objective of the activity.

1.3 Paper Structure

This paper is structured as follows: Sect. 2 presents the literature and theoretical framework, while chapter three and four presents the research methods and findings. Parts of the material in these sections contains edited excerpts from my doctoral thesis [3]. Discussion follows in Sect. 5 and concludes from findings and discussion, in Sect. 6.

2 Literature: Activity Theory and UX

Since the mid-nineties, Activity Theory has become a growing and central post-cognitivist approach and concept in HCI research [4, 5, 27, 29, 31, 39].

Activity theory developed from the Soviet psychology of Lev Vygotsky and his colleagues Rubinshtein, Leontiev, Luria and other Russian researchers [26]. It provides a framework for analysing individual and organisational action as a reflective and goal-directed sequence of mediated activity that evolves over time rather than a single, static act.

The primary object of activity theory is to comprehend and explain the unity of consciousness and activity within a complex setting of motives and activities, goals and actions, conditions and operations, within a hierarchical activity structure which shows how we mediate our interactions with the world. According to Leontiev [34], an activity theoretical approach to human activity acknowledges and incorporates cultural and contextual factors into human actions, with process development as a core element. This approach seeks to understand how we interact with the outside world by focusing on the interplay between our goals and actions, as well as the interplay between our thoughts and our actions [34].

As a theoretical framework it comprises a comprehensive collection of analytical tools and methods analysing the relationship between humans as subjects acting towards an objective in the external world, not as a momentary, static doing, frozen in time, but as a goal-directed, developing sequence of mediated activity, evolving over time.

2.1 Basic Principles

Through a set of fundamental principles, activity theory enables the exploration of human use of technology as a conscious, purposeful activity via an abstracted or metaphorical tool, such as a graphical user interface. This enables the exploration of key areas for what activity theory regards as the basic unit of analysis: human activity and its three primary characteristics of being goal oriented, mediated by artefacts, and situational within societal practises (Fig. 1).

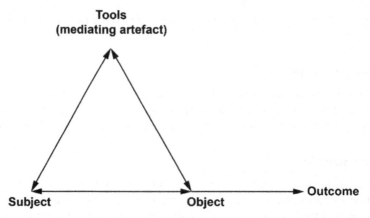

Fig. 1. The subject of an activity has a need, which entails that activities have a specific direction - a purpose. The subject transforms the objective of an activity into an outcome through mediated interaction with the world.

Subject, Object, and Tools. Within activity theory, the relationship between a *subject* and an *object* is mediated by tools. A *subject* is a living entity with intentions and agency to act upon things and objectives, to fulfil its needs or goals, as opposed to other elements within a particular context, that are, however, useful, graspable - physical or cognitively, without agency.

Within this context, the concept of agency points to the capability of an individual subject to act independently upon an object in the world, and change the context within which the objective is situated. Collectively, the unity of subject and object is part of the framework of activity, as defined by e.g. Davydov et al. in their analysis of Leontiev's activity approach:

> "[…] human activity is characterized not only by its objectiveness but also by its subjectiveness: the activity of the subject is always directed toward the transformation of an object that is able to satisfy some specific need. Activity brings together in a unity such opposing principles as object and subject." [9]

The Hierarchical Structure of Activity. Activity is defined by the contextual motive and necessitated by the objective, in the subject-object interaction, and can be represented as a hierarchical structure [34].

In Leontiev's three-levelled hierarchical structure, the mid-level is relating to goals being the objective of actions that, together with other actions, can form a group of actions, each with their own goals connected to each action in the group. While actions result from conscious doings, they are composed of single operations that might be undertaken in a kind of automatic approach [31, 34] (Fig. 2).

Internalisation and Externalisation. *Internalisation* is presented as a simulation process that takes place in the internal plane of action, without actually performing them in reality. This planning process - of *what* is going to be done, *why* it is needed, the simulation of *how* it is going to be done, and the consideration of the potential outcome

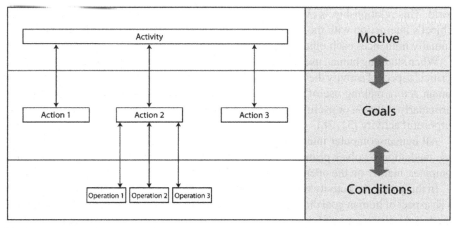

Fig. 2. Hierarchical structure of activity. as continuous reciprocal transformation between the parts of activity [9, 34, 35]. Illustration derived from Davydov et al. [9] and is visually based on Fig. 2.3 in Kuutti [31]. We see that an activity is initiated by a motive, and is comprised by a set of actions based on a conscious direction for each specific action, for which undertaking depends on a sequence of operations that is not goal directed, but related to the conditions for the operations.

of the activity, is done prior to actually performing an action in the real world [33]. *Externalisation* is the reverse action of internalisation, and is the unique human ability to transform ideas, objects, procedures, and possibilities simulated in the internal plane into external activities with the help of tools, is called externalisation. When conditions change and mental processes in the internal plane need adjustments, externalisation is a necessary action.

Mediation. The principle of mediation is a central concept that human activity originates from having an objective that is fulfilled by being mediated by the conscious use of tools as an intermediate link between the subject and object. Kaptelinin et al. argue that activity theory is "built upon the concept of mediation", which makes it particularly suitable for HCI "exploration" [26]. This notion of socially and culturally mediated actions would lean on the principle of internalisation, where external mediation develops into actions based on internally mediated psychological tools [28, 34, 50].

Development. Within Activity Theory, it is required that all activity must be contextually related to development. Leaning on Vygotsky [50], the cultural aspect of human actions, the knowledge that accumulates from being a member of a culture and the human use of cultural artefacts that naturally follows, this would, necessarily, inform the analysis of computer mediated human activity [25].

2.2 Activity Theory and Human-Computer Interaction

In an HCI research context, activity represents a relational context in which a [human] subject [34], interacts, physically or mentally, with an object, observably existing in the world. This relationship is characterised by the subject's needs being met through the subject's interaction with the world, where the subject's activity towards an objective - mutually influences each other [28].

When studying human use of technology, i.e. human activity mediated by a computer, a critical aspect of activity theory is to comprehend the concept that activity emerges from human actors making use of consciously chosen artefacts [34]. This understanding is particularly valuable or useful when exploring human use of technology as a conscious, purposeful activity [31, 38].

All human-computer interactions are mediated by a user interface; thus, user interface mediation revolves primarily around the contextual relations between human and computer, mainly on the operations and actions level.

In this paper, the activity theoretical framework with its strong focus on development as an aspect of human goal directed activity, is used to analyse the specific design pattern which is the starting point for all interaction in the program that is the target for the case study; that almost all actions/interactions are exploratory, and preliminary in nature, and are collected in - a temporarily stored iteration.

2.3 UX

In the modern and, according to Don Norman, rather misused description of user experience, this paper connects the term user-experience with the experience of using an application, and not the total range of experiences that Norman initially put into its definition [42].

User Experience in the context of this study leans on the activity theoretical framework, where we analyse the user's experience related to the hierarchical structure of activity [31, 34] within the field on computer mediated interaction [25], i.e. focusing primarily on the interaction between a user and a computer as the mediating tool [14, 15], and also the perception of user experiences as an emerging quality by building skills and competence over time [32], and as such, more than the sequences of single interactions.

3 Method

The paper reports from a longitudinal case study [52]. The empirical material has been gathered in three stages; first, among the designers/developers and users, on site, during the software development process lasting approximately 15 months; second, during the implementation phase lasting about 5 months. Throughout the research period, we observed user participants reflect on their requirements and activities, convert tasks into actions, and undertake operations within the vocational environment into which the system was launched, and intended to mediate.

The empirical material consists of semi-structured interviews with designers, developers and users, in addition to observations of the users' interaction with the system, where participants carried out typical, vocational tasks, in demonstration contexts during the testing period, actual tasks within a production context during and after the implementation period. The observation sessions varied in length, from 30 min to three hours, depending on the number of work tasks. Semi-structured interviews have lasted for a period of 45 min–1,5 h.

The respondents comprise five designers/developers, and seven operators/users, of whom three were also regarded as participant users. Two years after the system's deployment, the initial empirical material was supplemented with follow-up interviews and observation sessions with users who then had had nearly two years of experience with the system. The study period lasted four years in total.

3.1 Research Context

The paper presents a part of the empirical material from a doctoral research project [3] that aimed at addressing contexts of perceived intuitive interaction in user-interfaces, and how the subjective perception of intuitive interaction might *emerge* during an interaction process rather than being solely grounded in *momentary* action. *This* paper points at an additional characteristic that emerged from the findings; that of the developmental character of stored states of interactions within an activity sequence.

The findings are collected from a case study undertaken at the headquarters of Odfjell Shipping, one of the world's largest shipping companies within the field of sea transport of chemical liquids. During the case study, we followed the development and design, implementation and subsequent use-phase of the new stowage planning software, ORCA[3].

4   Using the ORCA Software

The design pattern of interaction aimed at supporting the vocational planning best-practice of temporality i.e. sketching plans in variants and as iterations, sketching out possible mistakes, postponing a final, irreversible interaction by iteratively test, simulate, and store in-real-life use-scenarios as copies or stored snapshots. Following this primary action pattern, the software was designed to facilitate the utilisation of errors as learning points, and to mediate the causal grounds, and the sequence of interactions and error states, in order to avoid errors or breakdowns in the final 'decision', presented in the discussion chapter.

The users never work with 'originals,' and all operations, actions, and even activities are, from an activity theoretical perspective, internalisations until the motive of the activity is fulfilled by finalising and then 'promoting' the plan as the final stowage iteration into a published final plan.

4.1 Simulation and Probing

The simulation and probing paradigm in ORCA is manifested on two levels;

1. all stowage plans are tentative as default and must be actively promoted to valid prior to being used as an actual stowage plan.

---

[3] Odfjell Resource Control Application.

Fig. 3. Duplicate stowage plans. The operator can make as many duplicates as needed. Here, the operator can try out three different stowage plans: the initial plan (1), that the operator preserved by making a copy (2), which could be used to explore other stowage constellations. This copy was, in turn, preserved by making yet another copy (3), providing the operator with an extended number of possibilities to mediate the internalisation process.

2. externalising stowage solutions as a chain of actions, and the operations of which they are constituted, by distributing simulation capacity to the user interface, extending the internal plane of action.

During observation sessions, operators probing various stowage configurations in the abstracted tank models in the user interface, made possible by the risk-free, default 'work-on-copies' approach in the ORCA system (see Figs. 3 and 6).

4.2 Simulation as Individual Expansive Learning

During use of ORCA, the simulation functionality situates the dialectical relationship between internalisation and externalisation as a long-term perspective on learning intro-duced by Engeström [13]. Generally beginning with an emphasis on internalisation, working to learn new skills, or changing work methods, for example, in the context

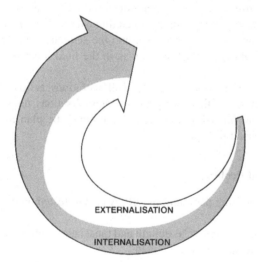

Fig. 4. Engeströms expansive cycle of learning, and the relation between internalisation and externalisation during the development process [12].

of introducing new software in an organisation, gradually, through experiencing break-downs reflecting and becoming competent users. However, in ORCA, it is the expectation of breaks in a planned sequence of actions and making workarounds by storing them in a safe place, as a copy, leads to an evolutionary kind of development facilitated by the system (Fig. 4).

4.3 Mediating Practice

ORCA facilitates or even seeks possible contradictions in an attempt to visualise incompatibilities in an action (see Fig. 5). In the dialectical logic-perspective often associated with activity theory, contradictions are regarded as a means of development.

During an interview, one of the operators explains how the program responds to a mistake, and warns about a mix of cargo, "Illegal commingling". Previously, the operator had to find out about commingling cargo manually.

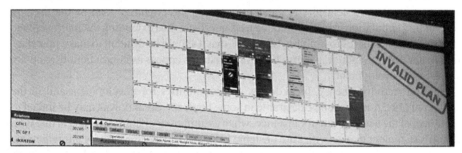

Fig. 5. In addition to the storage functionality, the system also presents more common warning feedbacks when an action is illegal, which could be stored in a "safe" copy for later investigation, and subsequent learning.

5   Design Decisions

The design of the model software developed in the case study was based on a historically established best practice. It lets the user work in intermediate states or sequences of externalisation in a pattern where the GUI mediates the internalisation process is a system that can facilitate embracing mistakes and ruling them out.

A result of the design choices made in the development of the ORCA system is that one of the main features facilitates simulating and iteratively store different scenarios, and test whether the performed interaction is valid or correct. In ORCA, there is no limit to the number of stored simulations beyond what is convenient for the users to keep track of.

5.1 Hierarchical Structure of Iterative Interaction

In an activity theoretical approach, the user's motivation and goals for success will be the same, but the system includes functionality to copy and store all "current" states of the interactions, in the form of actions and operations, that a user does in a temporarily fulfilled objective.

By linking the findings to the activity theoretical hierarchical structure, described in the literature [31, 34], we see that the motivation that initiated the activity in the first instance can accommodate parallel, temporary activities. Each of these activities can, interaction-wise, be similar, with identical or partly identical sets of actions and operations, in that the user creates copies of the result of the set of interactions so far.

5.2   Activities as Stored Explorative Simulations

All interactions are tentative as default and can be stored as sets of actions for explorative simulation. One set, of several, is then chosen and verified as valid prior to being used as an actual stowage plan.

Utilising the possibility of iteratively store multiple intermediate state of interactions containing the chain of actions, and the operations of which they are constituted, the system achieves two central UX ideals: it lightens the cognitive load of the user by distributing simulation capacity onto the user interface, thus extending the internal plane of action, and it adheres to usability rule no. 1, that it should be difficult to make mistakes. In *this* iterative interaction pattern, however, mistakes appear as contradictions, and are a source of development.

Within Activity Theory, breakdowns are possibilities for development and in the context of ORCA may even be desirable in some contexts. Breakdowns may be linked to the object of the activity that, for instance, when assumptions change, which is in line with Kuutti's statement that activities are unstable [31], making the use-activity unpredictable and situational. During observations, it seemed like this lack of predictability also was handled by the system's default state of tentativeness, that the unpredictability was taken care of by the possibility of making non-destructive revisions.

5.3   User Experience as a Continuous Personal Development Process

Breakdowns and contradictions are viewed as a means of development in the dialectical logic-perspective within activity theory, and ORCAs approach to seeking out contradictions and visualise them in a temporal space contributes to this development perspective in a way that might be perceived as safe and somewhat risk-free, to the extent that risk-free is viable. This approach informs the developers in designing systems that would facilitate development through 'dialectical' error handling. In ORCA, a user's cognitive load can be unloaded into the system and stored as a potential solution. This approach would support our understanding of UX as comprising a series of momentary user experiences into what Roto et al. describe as cumulative UX, where the user recollects multiple sessions of use [46], facilitating a sense of the user experience as an emerging and compounded process, and thus may comprise all, or most, aspects of a development process in the activity theoretical sense.

Ambiguities. Within activity theory, the systemic causes for involuntary breaks or stops in the sequence of actions are labelled as contradictions, i.e. events that manifest themselves as complications and mismatches - breakdowns. This kind of misalignment could be represented by, e.g. a not sufficiently trained user or inadequate system functionality that fails to support the goal-directed interaction. According to Virkunnen and Kuutti, "Contradictions are fundamental tensions and misalignments in the structure that typically manifest themselves as problems, ruptures, and breakdowns in the functioning of the activity system" [49].

The traditional Western logic regards contradictions as indications of problems that have to be solved, while this "eastern" Activity Theoretical framework regards contradictions as problems which must be overcome in a process that is dynamically and dialectically transforming use-activities and tools related to the hierarchical structure, and varying cognitive actions on the internal plane over time [23, 29, 34, 51]. In ORCA, this is facilitated by the design pattern of temporary storage of the current state of activity as a safe place to vary action choices.

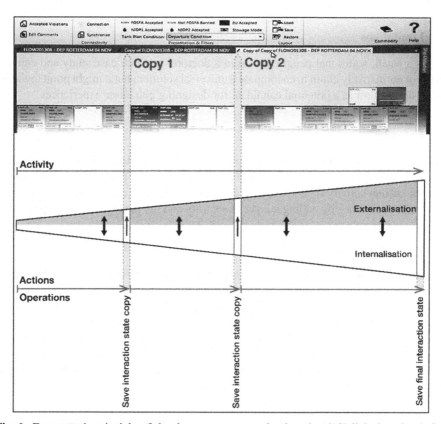

Fig. 6. Engeström's principle of development as expansive learning [12] linked to the design pattern of iterative interaction in ORCA. A current state of activity saved as a copy in a tabbed-browsing pattern in the user interface.

6 Concluding Remarks

In this approach to UX, one can see that the exploratory aspect of human-computer interaction which was one of core interaction paradigms in the ORCA project meant that even inexperienced users were able to solve rather complex tasks, and that the difference between beginners and experienced users were diminished by the fact that a mistake was not defined as a mistake, but as a risk-free contradiction, in the form of a stored set of interactions. A user interface designed for taking advantage of deliberate, simulated user "mistakes" could possibly be a redemptive design approach.

The lack of risk lies in temporarily saved copies. In the case of a full breakdown, the user only needs to return to the last stored action state copy. In this design pattern of designing for anticipation of errors lies a paradox in that designing for error-anticipation the software is also designed to handle contexts that cannot be anticipated.

6.1 Limitations

This is a small, additional perspective from a doctoral research case study and can, as such, not normatively claim to encompass a universal solution, but it might point towards this design pattern as a potential candidate for designing good user experiences.

6.2 Contributions

This paper contributes to practise by suggesting that software which facilitates the handling or even anticipation of contradictions as opportunities for progress, by letting users store the current activity state as a temporary copy or snapshot, could lead to an assumed better user experience by adding a layer of security and the perception of competence.

6.3 Further Work and Direction

This paper primarily presents an interaction design pattern in the design of a single system and the idea that, in some contexts, this can also be a pattern for UX design outside a skilled worker environment. Human access to, and understanding of, computers have a far wider impact on societal life than possible to cover here. For that, books are needed. Further research should include what impact such a purely technical design pattern prototypical concepts might have at a public level. In ORCA, a saved current state of activity becomes a copy in a familiar tabbed-browsing pattern. Exploring this approach, and how it could translate to other computer-mediated contexts, would be a natural direction within our continued research on user experience.

References

1. Anthes, G.: Estonia: a model for e-government. Communications of the ACM **58**(6), 18–20 (2015)
2. Baecker, R.M., Buxton, W.A.S.: Readings in Human-Computer Interaction: A Multidisciplinary Approach. Morgan Kaufmann Publishers (1987)

3. Bakke, S.: Mediating thoughts and streams of actions. Complex intuitive interactions in a skilled worker environment. Dissertation, University of Oslo (2018)
4. Bertelsen, O.W., Bødker, S.: Activity theory. In: Carroll, J.M. (ed.) HCI models, theories, and frameworks: toward a multidisciplinary science multidisciplinary science, pp. 291–324. Morgan Kaufmann, San Francisco (2003)
5. Bødker, S.: Through the interface - a human activity approach to user interface design. Dissertation, Lawrence Erlbaum (1991)
6. Brodbeck, F.C., Zapf, D., Prümper, J., Frese, M.: Error handling in office work with computers: a field study. J. Occup. Organ. Psychol. **66**(4), 303–317 (1993). https://doi.org/10.1111/j.2044-8325.1993.tb00541.x
7. Bush, V.: As we may think. In: Packer, R., Jordan, K. (eds.) Multimedia: From Wagner to Virtual Reality, pp. 141–159. W.W. Norton & Company, New York (2001)
8. Castells, M.: The Information Age: Economy, Society, and Culture Volume I. The Rise of the Network Society, 2nd ed. Wiley-Blackwell, Chichester (2010)
9. Davydov, V.V., Zinchenko, V.P., Talyzina, N.F.: The problem of activity in the works of A. N. Leont'ev. J. Russ. East Eur. Psychol. **21**(4), 31–42 (1983). https://doi.org/10.2753/RPO 1061-0405210431
10. Dourish, P.: Commentary: interactivity as cultural. Hum. Comput. Interact. **32**(3), 153–154 (2017). https://doi.org/10.1080/07370024.2016.1257388
11. Engelbart, D.: Augmenting human intellect: a conceptual framework. In: Multimedia: From Wagner to Virtual Reality, pp. 64–90. W.W. Norton & Company, New York (2001)
12. Engeström, Y.: Activity theory and individual and social transformation. In: Engeström, Y., Miettinen, R., Punamäki, R.-L. (eds.) Perspectives on Activity Theory, pp. 19–38. Cambridge University Press, Cambridge (1999)
13. Engeström, Y.: Expansive visibilization of work: an activity-theoretical perspective. Comput. Support. Coop. Work (CSCW) **8**(1–2), 63–93 (1999)
14. Forlizzi, J., Battarbee, K.: Understanding experience in interactive systems. In: Proceedings of DIS2004, pp. 261–268. (2004)
15. Garrett, J.J.: The Elements of User Experience: User-Centered Design for the Web and Beyond. New Riders, Berkeley, CA (2010)
16. Gillen, J.: Digital literacies. Routledge (2014). https://doi.org/10.4324/9781315813530
17. Hanseth, O., Ciborra, C.: Risk, Complexity and ICT. Edward Elgar Publishing, Northampton, MA (2007)
18. Hanseth, O., Lyytinen, K.: Theorizing about the design of information infrastructures: design kernel theories and principles. Sprouts: working papers on information environments. System. Organ. **4**(4), 207–241 (2004) 10.1.1.93.8163b
19. Hanseth, O., Lyytinen, K.: Design theory for dynamic complexity in information infrastructures: the case of building internet. J. Inform. Technol. **25**(1), 1–19 (2010). https://doi.org/10.1057/jit.2009.19
20. Hartleb, F.: E-estonia—"Europe's silicon valley" or a new "1984"? In: Feldner, D. (ed.) Redesigning Organizations, pp. 215–228. Springer, Cham (2020). https://doi.org/10.1007/978-3-030-27957-8_16
21. Helbing, D., Pournaras, E.: Society: build digital democracy. Nature **527**(7576), 33–34 (2015)
22. Heller, N.: Estonia, the digital republic. In New Yorker. https://www.newyorker.com/magazine/2017/12/18/estonia-the-digital-republic. Accessed 20 Dec 2020
23. Ilyenkov, E.V.: Dialectical Logic; Essays on its History and Theory. marxist.org, (Republishing of version from 1977 by Progress Publishers, Moscow) (2009)
24. Im, G.P., Baskerville, R.L.: A longitudinal study of information system threat categories: the enduring problem of human error. ACM SIGMIS Database: the DATABASE for Adv. Inform. Syst. **36**(4), 68–79 (2005). https://doi.org/10.1145/1104004.1104010

25. Kaptelinin, V.: Computer-mediated activity: functional organs in social and developmental contexts. In: Nardi, B.A. (ed.) Context and Consciousness: Activity Theory and Human-Computer Interaction, pp. 45–68. The MIT Press, Cambridge, MA (1995)
26. Kaptelinin, V., Kuutti, K., Bannon, L.: Activity theory: basic concepts and applications. In: Blumenthal, B., Gornostaev, J., Unger, C. (eds.) EWHCI 1995. LNCS, vol. 1015, pp. 189–201. Springer, Heidelberg (1995). https://doi.org/10.1007/3-540-60614-9_14
27. Kaptelinin, V., Nardi, B.: Post-cognitivist HCI: second-wave theories. In: Proceedings of CHI '03, pp. 692–693. (2003)
28. Kaptelinin, V., Nardi, B.: Activity Theory in HCI: Fundamentals and Reflections. Morgan & Claypool Publishers, San Rafael (2012)
29. Kaptelinin, V., Nardi, B.A.: Acting with Technology: Activity Theory and Interaction Design. The MIT Press, Cambridge (2006)
30. Kay, A.: User interface: a personal view. In: Jordan, K., Packer, R. (eds.) Multimedia: From Wagner to Virtual Reality, pp. 121–131. W.W. Norton & Company, New York (2001)
31. Kuutti, K.: Activity theory as a potential framework for human computer interaction research. In: Nardi, B.A. (ed.) Context and Consciousness: Activity Theory and Human Computer Interaction, pp. 17–44. MIT Press, Cambridge (1995)
32. Kuutti, K., Bannon, L.J.: The turn to practice in HCI. In: Proceedings of Proceedings of CHI '14, pp. 3543–3552. (2014). https://doi.org/10.1145/2556288.2557111
33. Leont'ev, A.N.: The problem of activity in psychology. Sov. Psychol. **13**(2), 4–33 (1974). https://doi.org/10.2753/RPO1061-040513024
34. Leontiev, A.N.: Activity, Consciousness, and Personality. Prentice-Hall, Englewood Cliffs (1978)
35. Leontyev, A.N.: The Development of Mind. Marxist Internet Archive, Pacifica, CA (2009)
36. Licklider, J.C.R.: Man-computer symbiosis. IRE Trans. Hum. Factors Electron. **HFE-1**(1), 4–11 (1960)
37. Lindgren, S.: Digital Media and Society. Sage Publications Limited (2017)
38. Nardi, B.A.: Activity theory and human-computer interaction. In: Nardi, B.A. (ed.) Context and consciousness: Activity theory and human-computer interaction, pp. 7–16. The MIT Press, Cambridge (1995)
39. Nardi, B.A.: Context and Consciousness: Activity Theory and Human-Computer Interaction. The MIT Press, Cambridge, MA (1995). https://doi.org/10.5860/choice.33-5756
40. Nielsen, J.: 10 Usability heuristics for user interface design. https://www.nngroup.com/articles/ten-usability-heuristics/. Accessed 21 Nov 2021
41. Nielsen, J., Loranger, H.: Prioritizing Web Usability. New Riders Press, Berkeley, CA (2006)
42. Norman, D.: The Design of Everyday Things. Revised and expanded edition. Basic Books, New York (2013)
43. Papp-Váry, Á.: A Successful Example of Complex Country Branding: The 'E-Estonia' Positioning Concept and Its Relation to the Presidency of the Council of the EU. Acta Universitatis Sapientiae, European and Regional Studies. Scientia (14), 87–115 (2018)
44. Raskin, J.: The Humane Interface: New Directions for Designing Interactive Systems. Addison-Wesley Professional (2000)
45. Rasmussen, J., Vicente, K.J.: Coping with human errors through system design: implications for ecological interface design. Int. J. Man-Machine Studies **31**(5), 517–534 (1989). https://doi.org/10.1016/0020-7373(89)90014-X
46. Roto, V., Law, E.L.-C., Vermeeren, A.P.O.S., Hoonhout, J.: User experience white paper: Bringing clarity to the concept of user experience (2011)
47. Söderström, J.: Jävla skitsystem!: hur en usel digital arbetsmiljö stressar oss på jobbet - och hur vi kan ta tillbaka kontrollen. Stockholm, Karneval förlag (2015).In Swedish
48. Tidwell, J.: Designing Interfaces. O'Reilly Media Inc., Sebastopol, CA (2006)

49. Virkkunen, J., Kuutti, K.: Understanding organizational learning by focusing on "activity systems." Account. Manag. Inform. Technol. **10**, 291–319 (2000)
50. Vygotsky, L.S.: Mind in society: The development of higher psychological processes. Harvard University Press, Cambridge, MA (1978)
51. Vygotsky, L.S.: The Collected Works of L. S. Vygotsky, vol. 2. Springer Science+Business Media, New York (1993). https://doi.org/10.1007/978-1-4615-2806-7
52. Yin, D.R.K.: Case Study Research: Design and Methods (Applied Social Research Methods). Sage Publications Inc, Thousand Oaks (2008)

Immersive Sims: A New Paradigm or a New Game Genre?

Myles Blasonato$^{(\boxtimes)}$, Cinzia Cremona, Manolya Kavakli, and Dan Staines

AIE Institute, Macquarie University, Sydney, Australia
myles.blasonato@aie.edu.au, Cinzia.Cremona@mq.edu.au,
{manolya.kavakli,dan.staines}@aieinstitute.edu.au

Abstract. In this paper, first we discuss how sets of common principles constitute paradigms in HCI and what creates a paradigm shift; second, we analyse characteristics of immersive sims and examine if they qualify as a new paradigm. The first HCI paradigm, an amalgam of engineering and human factors, accepts interaction as a form of man-machine coupling in ways inspired by industrial engineering and ergonomics. The second HCI paradigm, in contrast, hinges on a metaphor of mind and computer as symmetric, coupled information processors. The third HCI paradigm focuses on embodied interaction, meaning and meaning construction, situated knowledge, an explicit focus on values and the centrality of context. In this paper, we build a rigorous speculative set of concepts to test our hypothesis that immersive sims present a paradigm shift. We align this conceptual clarity with a structured and systematic analysis of the high and low-level characteristics of immersive sims based on Samoylenko's description of the five pillars of immersive sim design. We propose more refined low-level characteristics within the three high-level characteristics of immersion, simulation, and interaction. This methodical analysis of principles and practices results in a set of reliable tools supported by examples drawn from the full history of immersive sims. Using these principles, we develop an immersive sim and conduct a usability test to verify the low-level characteristics listed above in a UX case study. Finally, we conclude by stating that the immersive sim design principles constitute a paradigm shift in HCI, rather than a new genre.

Keywords: Immersive sims · HCI paradigms · Design principles · Characteristics of immersive sims

1 Introduction

As we continue to interact with the products of Virtual and Augmented Reality technologies, we also see an increase in our expectations. As suggested by Dalladay-Simpson (2020), harnessing these technologies requires HCI systems than move more from the computer towards the human than the previous generation of screen-based interactive media. With these technologies becoming pervasive, designers must find creative answers to ensure that systems not only work, but also fit in more comfortably with people's lives. What the next design paradigm is and what challenges we need to overcome will become increasingly important questions.

© The Author(s), under exclusive license to Springer Nature Switzerland AG 2022
M. Kurosu (Ed.): HCII 2022, LNCS 13302, pp. 18–39, 2022.
https://doi.org/10.1007/978-3-031-05311-5_2

We believe that the design principles of immersive sims – exemplified by games like *Ultima Underworld: The Stygian Abyss, Deus Ex*, and *The Legend of Zelda: Breath of the Wild* – constitute a viable candidate for a new design paradigm in HCI. While immersive sims have existed for almost three decades, there is little in the way of academic and critical discourse about them. The literature (e.g., Jørgensen 2015) tends to focus on specific examples, with little discussion about how immersive sims fit into the broader ecology of the genre and medium. Our goal in this paper is to, in part, start that discussion and begin identifying design patterns and principles common to immersive sims. Whether these principles and patterns make immersive sims a genre or meta-genre or something else altogether is an interesting question, but one beyond the remit of this paper.

In the following sections we will first present what constitutes paradigms in HCI, then we will review characteristics of immersive sims. We will validate these characteristics with a usability test in an immersive sim designed by our team. Finally, we will evaluate the results and discuss what creates a paradigm shift and if immersive sims qualify for this.

1.1 Paradigms in Human Computer Interaction

The concept of shifting paradigms was first applied to scientific research by Thomas Kuhn (1962), who defined paradigms as "universally recognized scientific achievements that, for a time, provide model problems and solutions for a community of practitioners" (p. 48). These achievements are the result of a structured approach to research founded on specific questions, methods, assumptions and models privileged for a period of time. Harrison et al. (2007) describe this approach to different research paradigms within a discipline as 'a model of successive and overlapping waves in which ideas are fundamentally re-framed. New paradigms do not disprove the old paradigms, but instead provide alternative ways of thinking'.

The concept of three waves in Human Computer Interaction (HCI) has been widely accepted (e.g., Grudin 2005; Harrison et al. 2007). The first paradigm reflects the relationship between machines and people found in industrial engineering and ergonomics. Consequently, the first paradigm focuses on identifying practical issues and developing pragmatic solutions in the pairing of humans and machines. (Harrison et al. 2007). The second paradigm, in contrast, is organized around a central metaphor of mind and computer as symmetric, coupled information processors. HCI has been dominated by the second wave (Grudin 2005), influenced by the cognitive revolution centrally captured in Card et al.'s (1983) human information processing model, which demonstrates similarities between human cognition and computational signal processing and cycle times. This has deeply affected the ways HCI researchers conceive design and evaluation.

A paradigm shift is accompanied by a shift in the examples which are considered standard and central to the field. As proposed by Harrison et al. (2007), 'paradigm shifts in HCI can be traced by tracing shifts in the underlying metaphor of interaction'. For example, the metaphor underlying cognitive science accepts human minds as information processors and proposes methods for solving problems such as how humans process the input, how they represent information internally, how they access memory, etc.

Over the last three decades a wide variety of technologies such as affective computing and motion tracking emerged that appear to poorly fit the models and methods derived from the cognitive revolution. Embodiment, situated cognition and affect studies are not new perspectives in the analysis of HCI, but under the dominant cognitive paradigm they had been pushed to the margins (see for example Boehner et al. 2005; De Paula and Dourish 2005; Shami et al. 2008). As suggested by Harrison et al. (2007), 'some of these approaches can be seen as elements of a third paradigm, which treats interaction not as a form of information processing but as a form of meaning making'. The artifact and its context are subject to multiple interpretations and the meaning is defined on the fly by the users and other stakeholders in the situation of use. While this brings ambiguity into meaning making, it also provides freedom and flexibility to accommodate various types of interaction.

Interrogating technologies and approaches that resonate with the third paradigm using analytic criteria derived from the second does not constitute a suitable evaluation approach. Instead, evaluation and development methods that incorporate a 'wholistic, reflective understanding while staying open to the possibility of simultaneous, conflicting interpretation' can reveal design directions for third paradigm HCI systems (Harrison et al. 2007). Drawing directly on this work, in the next section we outline the main characteristics of the third paradigm before suggesting some adjacent philosophical concepts that we think will enrich it. In this framework, we will then explore if and how immersive sims belong to and extend this third paradigm as, in our opinion, contexts, meaning making and the nature of interactions in immersive sims resonate with and, possibly, add to the principles of this third wave.

2   Characteristics of the Third HCI Paradigm

According to Harrison et al. (2007), we are moving from the second paradigm towards a third where embodied interaction, situated meaning making, affect, values, context and social issues come to the forefront. Taking as a starting point ideas about embodied interactions first discussed by McCullough (2004) and Dourish (2001), Harrison et al. (2007) state that these emerging interests present forces that constitute a third wave in HCI. The authors call this a "phenomenological matrix" (Harrison et al. 2007) and identify a set of high-level characteristics of emerging HCI practices that form a coherent approach.

In the third wave of HCI, 'all action, interaction, and knowledge is seen as embodied in situated human actors' and meaning is constructed on the fly (Harrison et al. 2007). Situated knowledge (Haraway 1988) justifies a shift to recognize a plurality of perspectives, as it refers to the idea that people's understanding of the world and their interactions are influenced by their contexts. In other words, the human actor has agency to make sense of a situation from a subjective perspective, and make decisions on the basis of past experiences, emotions and personal ethics. In this third wave, accommodating multiple understandings of what is happening in a relationship between human and computer is necessary. It is this primacy of individual experience, affect and subjective positioning that motivates Harrison et al. (2007) to reference phenomenology, even though in their own approach to the third paradigm echoes of post-phenomenological thinking can be detected.

Based on this discussion, we can summarise the characteristics of a new HCI paradigm as follows:

1. Embodied interaction with its material, affective and social dimensions
2. Plurality of perspectives and multiple interpretations
3. Context-driven design space
4. Meaning making and meaningful engagement

2.1 Embodied Interaction

In Dourish' (2001) analysis, embodied interaction emerges as one of the principles that underlies the third paradigm. His definition of embodiment is based on a central stance drawing on phenomenology, and it entails that interaction is informed by our location in a material and social world as embodied actors – our contexts. 'Embodiment is not a property of systems, technologies, or artifacts; it is a property of interaction…. In contrast to Cartesian approaches that separate mind from body and thought from action, embodied interaction emphasizes their duality.' (Dourish 2001).

Barrett and Lindquist (2008) note that 'historically, almost all psychological theories of emotion have proposed that emotional reactions are constituted by the body in some fashion'. Eickers et al. (2017) take this perspective in an interesting direction when they claim that emotions are embodied states and thus play a role in registering and generating social affordances. They disagree with the argument that emotions are directly presented to the world via facial expressions or gestures, and thereby universally understandable (Gallagher 2008). Rather they state that body changes prepare people for culturally tuned actions and that these changes can be interpreted through cultural learning and affect culturally sanctioned responses. Therefore, context and embodiment are tightly linked and from an observer's perspective this changes affordances. If an observer perceives facial expressions or other physical signals in others, their choices are influenced and may change to more closely match the choices of others (Eickers et al. 2017). Similarly, according to transactional theories (Griffiths and Scarantino 2009; Scarantino 2012, 2015), emotions are a kind of meaningful engagement with the world, highly influenced by and dynamically related to the social environment and the situation we are in (e.g., the context, as described in Dourish 2004).

This expanded understanding of embodiment suggests that the boundaries of a body are always blurred as bodies are shaped by – and therefore encompass – natural and cultural contexts. On this basis, it becomes clear that subjective experience is not contained within the individual but exists in a dynamic assemblage with everything else (Braidotti 2013). Just as embodiment and subjectivity continually emerge renewed in interactions, so do subjective perspective and experience. From this point of view, phenomenology does not suffice to articulate conceptually the complexity that characterises the third paradigm and immersive sims.

2.2 Plurality of Perspectives and Multiple Interpretations

Harrison et al. (2007) describe the third paradigm as 'a multidimensional characterization of concerns' and highlight the 'complexities of multiple perspectives at the scene of action'. Adopting a phenomenological perspective allows observers to follow a momentary individual interpretation and avoid a false objective reading of a complex set of interactions. Although we understand the value of this shift, we argue that this does not aid a wholistic understanding of the material complexity that emerges in the third paradigm.

Seen from a posthuman perspective, the third paradigm puts human and non-human actors on a comparable level of agency and in continuous becoming (Braidotti 2013; Latour 2007). Fox and Alldred (2019) describe 'a material world that is plural, complex, heterogeneous and emergent'. Multiple perspectives are not simply a way of approaching HCI but are already real and present. As evolving HCI technologies and systems increasingly attempt to approximate the material world they inevitably increase in complexity and require different theoretical and epistemological tools. We propose that immersive sims push the third paradigm in this direction by multiplying the dimensions and interpretations that are at play in HCI. When applied to HCI, and in particular to the third paradigm, these concepts move the phenomenological matrix into a new phase that encompasses the materiality of the digital context, the narrative context within immersive sims and any intersecting context.

2.3 Context-Driven Design Space

Dourish (2004) observes that 'ubiquitous computing proposes a digital future in which computation is embedded into the fabric of the world around us.' On the basis of the same definition of context, we propose that in immersive sims the world around us is embedded into the fabric of computation. For Dourish, contextuality is relational, it is defined dynamically, it emerges between activity and object, and it is 'relevant to particular settings, particular instances of action and particular parties to that action' (Dourish 2004). In other words, 'context isn't something that describes a setting; it's something that people do' (Dourish 2004).

This analysis is foundational of the third paradigm and the author themself observes its phenomenological nature. Nevertheless, similarly to what we observed about the phenomenological matrix that Harrison et al. (2007) propose, a post-phenomenological approach can already be detected in his statements. In fact, Dourish's words resonate with a new materialist 'embodied and embedded, empirical and grounded, situated and accountable modality of thinking' (Cremona 2020). Itself an umbrella term for a number of attuned perspectives, New Materialism and Posthumanism (we use these terms interchangeably) constitute a dynamic response to phenomenology itself, post-psychoanalytic approaches (particularly Judith Butler) and post-structuralism (particularly Jacque Derrida). Posthumanism reflects 'a scientific paradigm that takes its distance from the social constructivist approach' (Braidotti 2013) and in this sense it is aligned with the third paradigm. It is a non-dualistic understanding of context as an emergent nature-culture continuum in constant transformation (Braidotti 2013).

2.4 Meaning Making and Meaningful Engagement

Having acknowledged the complexity of being embodied in a nature-culture continuum of shifting and overlapping contexts, it follows that we are constantly making sense of our own identity, roles, position and surroundings in "a continuous process of being-with and becoming-with" (Cremona 2020). In the third paradigm, the construction of meaning is a collaborative activity conducted 'by people in specific contexts and situations, and therefore that interaction itself is an essential element in meaning construction' (Harrison et al. 2007). Similarly, the construction of subjectivity (i.e., who am I in this situation?) remains fluid.

According to Latour (2007), the process of making meaning consists of disentangling emerging forms of interactions between human and non-human actors as they happen. Latour's Actor-Network-Theory (ANT) is a practice of observation and recording of shifts in the relay of interactions to track the formation and transformations of associations as they happen, acknowledging a continuous state of flux and the artificiality of the perceived solidity of context or identity (Latour 2007). ANT may be a suitable epistemological tool to analyse if immersive sims and HCI systems fit with the third paradigm.

3 Analysis of Immersive Sims

The first game generally considered an immersive sim is *Ultima Underworld: The Stygian Abyss*, a first-person fantasy game developed by Blue Sky Productions in 1992. Other examples include *Thief* and *Thief 2*, *System Shock* and *System Shock 2*, the *Deus Ex* series, *Arx Fatalis* and *Prey*. These are what we might call "traditional" immersive sims, i.e., immersive sims designed by Looking Glass Studios or their successors at Ion Storm, Eidos Montreal, Arkane, and elsewhere. However, there are other examples that might not fit the traditional mould such as *The Legend of Zelda: Breath of the Wild* and *Half-Life Alyx*. This diversity indicates that the principles and patterns associated with immersive sims have gained traction in the broader development community and are now being applied to games quite unlike anything produced by Looking Glass and its successors.

3.1 High Level Characteristics of Immersive Reality Sims

Samoylenko (2021) describes five pillars that characterise immersive sims: message of the narrative (moral argument), focused design, system design, tools, and choices. We categorise these in three main groups under immersion, simulation, and interaction:

Immersion

- Multi-dimensional solution space open to a plurality of interpretations of the message of the narrative and moral argument (Truby 2007): Traditional immersive sims use mature storytelling features for meaning making and meaningful engagement, conveying ideas and messages through advanced narrative mechanisms without limiting player's interactions. The narrative is told in such a way that significant, story-changing choices are often left to the player, who then must deal with the consequences of their decisions. A single moral argument may not always be present in more contemporary immersive sims such as *The Legend of Zelda: Breath of the Wild*, but in such cases the game's flexible physics engine and open-ended scenario design allows players to approach problems in different ways rather than trying to find a single, developer-ordained solution. In this way, *Breath of the Wild* offers dimensional multiplicity to explore solution space.

- Focused Design space: Design space immerses players in believable locations that approximate actual places beyond game levels and emphasises production values and design aspects that matter for creating highly immersive experiences. Being "an inch wide and a mile deep" (Samoylenko 2021), the design space constrains game levels to relatively small areas but remains full of rich simulation to allow a multitude of interactions. Even in large, open-world games like the aforementioned *Breath of the Wild,* a large portion of gameplay takes place in condensed, self-contained environments like "puzzles shrines" and enemy encampments, where players are free to experiment with the game's systems to achieve specific objectives.

Simulation

- Systemic Design: A context-sensitive system is designed to be an interplay of many complex systems, including AI, physics, level design, etc., which result in emergent and occasionally unpredictable gameplay situations, and ensure that each playthrough is unique to an extent. A defining element of immersive sims is that systemic design extends to the whole game world, or as much of it as practically feasible.
- Rules: The world has rules in place that allow for emergent gameplay. Rules can be thought of as the low-level principles that interact to produce higher order systems. For example, in *Deus Ex,* a rule stating that certain enemies explode upon death and another rule stating that doors can be destroyed with explosions combine to produce a systemic interaction in which players may use enemies to blow open doors.
- Tools: The system provides multitudes of meaningful tools players can use, primarily through interactivity in the game world and physics-based systems that further personalize gameplay experience, interpretation and meaning making.

Interaction

- Choices: Embodied interaction with simulated physical dimensions to allow plurality of perspectives and multiple interpretations. In a reactive world, choices are designed from the ground up to provide the players various ways of completing objectives and offer significant gameplay-defining differences in character progression.
- Problem solving: Players have no specified outcome, and they are presented with a variety of options to choose from.

As demonstrated in the high-level characteristics, immersive sims possess the qualities of a new HCI paradigm (i.e., embodied interaction, plurality of perspectives and multiple interpretations, context-driven design space, and meaning making and meaningful engagement) incorporated into the concepts, principles and practices of immersion, simulation, and interaction.

3.2 Low-Level Characteristics of Immersive Sims

Immersive sims have low-level characteristics that can be categorised under the 3 main high-level groups discussed above:

Immersion

- **Realistic or symbolic meaning-making design space:** Typically, immersive sims are perceived as realistic. For example, *Ultima Underworld* (fantasy), *Deus-Ex* (cyberpunk) and *Prey* (sci-fi) 'feel' realistic, although they are set in worlds quite unlike our own. The realism in these cases is a product of consistent world and system design emphasizing predictable interactions and outcomes. Casting a fire spell in *Arx Fatalis*, for example, not only ignites torches, but anything else flammable within the vicinity. This gives us a sense that this world, like our own, is governed by consistent, predictable laws.
- **Player's agency and interaction based narrative:** In immersive sims, a large portion of storytelling is done in-game or emerges from gameplay. Outside of a few cut-scenes needed to establish the game's fiction, such as the opening "walk and talk" at the start of *Deus Ex: Human Revolution*, control is seldom taken away from the player in a non-contextual way due to the risk of breaking immersion. Narrative is told through the environment (Mise-en-scène) or world and its rules (e.g., through emails in computer terminals or audio logs merged with emergent narrative via encounters and NPC sequences that occur around the player). There is no breaking of the figurative "fourth wall" in a theatrical sense. Characters in immersive sims do not address the audience directly.
- **Focused design and mechanics:** Focused design puts players in believable locations with highly recognisable action-oriented and cognitive-oriented mechanics. One of the key arguments for immersive sims being a paradigm is that each handles their mechanics in the same way even though their genres are different and unique. For example, in *Half-Life*, players can grab boxes and use them as shields against specific aliens. This is an action-oriented dynamic. In *Prey*, players can grab boxes, like in Half-life, but to reveal entrances to new locations instead. This is a more cognitive-oriented dynamic. It is the same mechanic but used with two different meanings.

Simulation

- **Systemic context and context-driven design space:** Systemic context refers to the correspondence between the context within the game (narrative, mechanics, etc.) and the context outside the game (geographical location, social and financial circumstances, health/gender/ embodied context). This informs, for example, moral choices and meaning making when the player has agency within the game. Context-driven design gives meaning to players' actions when it is linked to a similar context that exists outside the game. For example, in *Prey* the player gains quests from finding prompts in emails, audio logs, videos and sometimes in interactive cutscenes. The player seeks out their own experience through context, rather than having it spoon fed at different checkpoints. The experiences currently available in VR in *Boneworks* and *Half-life Alyx* are designed as immersive sims, with player agency and systemic design taking centre-stage.

- **Systemic world:** An immersive sim generally consists of either one large open world or several self-contained levels. Each environment provides a sense of scale on a micro and/or macro level while facilitating multiple playstyles (Restrepo 2017). Regardless of how a player chooses to build their character, immersive sims are designed from the ground up to allow each objective to be completed in a multitude of ways.

  - **Rules:** Covered above: rules that apply to one object in the game should apply equally and consistently to all similar objects. Being able to pick up a crate and move it around is not enough on its own. The crate must interact with the world in a consistent, predictable way too. If one moves the crate through a window, the glass should shatter. If it is flammable and moved over fire, it should burn. In these two cases we have two cohesive rules: "Glass breaks when a force impacts it" and "Fire burns whatever collides with it". With these two world rules in place, we allow for emergent gameplay to occur.
  - **Systemic gating in level design:** Immersive sims use systemic rules to gate players out of interactions and locations in the world. System rules can be modelled with statistics such as strength or physical attributes. In *Prey*, players who invest in the "Leverage" ability can use their preternatural strength to force open a locked door blocking the way to the next level. Alternatively, players who have the Boltcaster toy bow can open that same door by shooting foam darts to press the "unlock" button on a distant computer terminal. This open way in dealing with a gate makes system gating a valuable level design tool in immersive sims.
  - **Systemic game elements:** Immersive sims tend to blend simulation elements, immersive design, and traditional (or not so traditional) game design concepts (as an example, see Spector's (2013) list of rules for *Deus Ex*). Game elements must also work with one another to ensure systemic integration with the world rules. If a player can pick up rigid bodies as a game element, systemically they could grab a bucket filled with water, carry it over to some fire and pour it over the fire to extinguish it. *Prey* and *Minecraft* utilise grab mechanics in this way. This also includes AI systems such as the Typhons in *Prey*, where all aliens can be scanned with the Psychoscope and their abilities obtained. Therefore, the enemy design was intrinsically tied to the Psychoscope system. (See O'Dwyer's (2021) documentary). Even the AI is built with system design in mind since the players can scan and take their abilities.
  - **Systemic tools (items):** Weapons, items and abilities in immersive sims are built with the world and AI rules in mind to ensure emergent gameplay. In *Prey*, the glue gun can be used to reach high places or to freeze enemies. It can also be used to stop electrical charges from broken computers. Immersive sims employ abstract elements to allow the player's imagination to fill in the blanks.

- **Illusory design and scripting:** Slater (2009) addressed the question as to why participants tend to respond realistically to situations and events portrayed within an immersive virtual reality system. He suggested that the concepts of plausibility illusion and place illusion contribute to a sense of presence. Place illusion (PI) refers to the qualia of having a sensation of being in a real place. Plausibility illusion (Psi) refers to the illusion that the scenario being depicted is actually occurring. While PI is constrained by the sensorimotor contingencies afforded by the virtual reality system, Psi is determined by the extent to which the system can produce events that directly relate to the participant – the overall credibility of the scenario in comparison with expectations. Slater (2009) argued that when both PI and Psi occur, participants will respond realistically to the virtual reality. Illusory design builds a believable space and achieve presence. Illusory design and scripting in an immersive sim should support both PI and Psi. Therefore, game elements must either be executed in an unscripted/simulated manner or scripted with illusory design to come across as organic/natural to the player. Everything from the heads-up display, AI behaviour and presentation, level design, to storytelling, and often even execution of RPG systems, are variably simulated or illusory scripted.

3.3 Embodied Interaction with its Material, Affective and Social Dimensions

- **Choices:** In stealth focused immersive sims like *Thief*, a defining aspect of player choice is non-linear and open level design, and the fact that players can complete missions by freely navigating through space. Although there are linear fragments to certain *Thief*'s missions, most of the time levels are very open. For example, in *Thief 2*'s "First City Bank & Trust" there are many ways to get inside the bank building, and the sprawling level can be explored freely. Non-linearity and an abundance of alternative ways through spaces are inherent to the core concept of stealth gameplay. If one cannot bypass a guard undetected, they can find another way. This open approach to level design in immersive sims has been later adopted by other stealth focused and hybrid games in this school of design, such as *Deus Ex* and *Dishonored*.
- **Problem solving:** In their postmortem for the original *Deus Ex,* creative lead Warren Spector discusses the distinction between puzzles and problems. According to Spector, a puzzle is an obstacle with a single, developer-ordained solution; a problem, on the other hand, permits any number of viable solutions, even ones the developer did not anticipate (Spector 2000). Immersive sims are defined by problems, which players are challenged to overcome using the tools at their disposal. For this reason, even relatively open-ended puzzle games like *Myst* do not qualify as immersive sims.
- **Emergent gameplay:** As a result of simulated and highly dynamic elements, the systemic design of immersive sims is deep enough to work in ways the developers never feasibly predicted. While this engenders player freedom and expressivity, the downside is that bugs and glitches are all too common in immersive sim, as they are in many sufficiently complex, system-driven games. It's also worth noting that emergent gameplay is not a concept unique to immersive sims. Any game with moderate complexity is bound to feature it in some form.
- **Flexible gameplay:** In all immersive sims, players can engage in encounters in any way the system and world rules allow in a non-binary way. For example – the grab mechanic has a lot of range because grabbed items can be placed in a lot of different

places and not just a single specific spot. This approach to system design can be seen in games such as *Legend of Zelda: Breath of Wild*, *Thief* and *Half-life*.

- **Embodiment:** Immersive sims are always primarily played in first person perspective. They use cutscenes only occasionally (mostly in introduction and ending) so that they don't disconnect the player from the protagonist's shoes. Game-over states are rarely, if ever, triggered because of plot failures (e.g. failing to protect a specific NPC). Currently, this direct form of embodiment utilises two strategies:

  - **Character controller:** All immersive sims have the player embody a vessel that lives in the simulation. With this vessel they can move around the world and interact with it.
  - **Grab action:** All immersive sims allow players to grab items and manoeuvre them around the world.

- **Seamless direct manipulation:** Blasonato in 2021 conducted an experiment during the production of *Beyond the Box*. In Unity, Blasonato tested two implementations of the grab mechanic. In the original implementation the player held down a button to hold an object. If the player released this button, they would drop the object. The next iteration had the player simply press a button to toggle between grabbing and dropping. The comparison showed that even though the first method is closer to direct manipulation and to the metaphor of holding an object, the player's finger was not free to do anything else. This impaired the character's capacity to act in the immersive sim in ways not related to its internal context and immediately made the experience less immersive. This discovery led Blasonato to believe that when thinking about direct manipulation in the future, the seamlessness of integration with the character controller is imperative as immersion is king and not realism. This is the same conclusion that Damion Schubert, Lead Design of Star Wars: The Old Republic came too (Schubert 2010)

4   Immersive Sim Prototype

We have developed an immersive sim prototype to test if the listed low-level characteristics of immersive sims are validated by users. Our hypothesis is that all of the characteristics mentioned above, if added to a game, will make it an immersive sim. For example, the principle of direct manipulation is incorporated in the game through the grab and inspect mechanics. One could argue that this game is an adventure game – not really an immersive sim however, we hexpect that players would feel that it is an immersive sim due to the design choices we have made using the principles listed in this paper.

The game takes place in a single small-scale open environment. This is an important design pattern of the immersive sim paradigm as the consistency in rules this pattern offers sets the foundation of the systemic gameplay such as the open world in *Breath of the Wild* or the Talos 1 Space Station in *Prey*. There are 10 photos hidden throughout the house in drawers, cabinets, under objects and other locations the player can directly manipulate to investigate. The player must find all 10 photos to complete the game (Fig. 1).

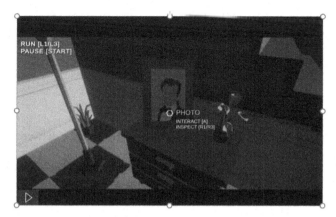

Fig. 1. Immersive sim prototype - lockwood

Player Arthur Lockwood awakes with no memory of the last 24 h. He cannot see his reflection in windows or mirrors. As he explores his home, he discovers questionable photos taken the night before shedding more light on his true nature. He may find out that he is a vampire with amnesia who lives in the suburbs.

The controller consists of first-person movement and look along with:

– **Grab**: players can grab and freely move any object that seems light enough.
– **Inspect**: players can fully rotate grabbed objects to investigate or to line objects up in the world.
– **Interact**: turn on the jukebox or the lamp.

Using the features defined in the paper, the small sample of key design patterns listed above along with the open world and goal creates the smallest immersive simulation example meeting the following criteria:

Immersion

- *Realistic or symbolic meaning-making design space:* Through the environmental storytelling and level design, the projected context will add meaning to actions.
- *Multi-dimensional solution space for interactive narrative systems supporting plurality of perspectives and multiple interpretations:* The photos will show how having open and diegetic narrative systems built into the consistent rules of the world enhances the immersion of the experience.
- *Focused design and mechanics:* A small subset of design patterns that we have confirmed as being part of the immersive simulation paradigm: Free-move and free-look (camera perspective is not important), Grab, Inspect, Interact
- *Systemic range:* All these patterns or mechanics grant something powerful to the experience. They all are in the systemic range and their useability defines the range of mechanics. For example – when a player grabs an object and moves it, there are a multitude of options to solve encounters. They could pick up a box and move it over

to a wall and climb on it to reach a higher space. The same goes for inspect. They can rotate objects in any direction and place them back into the world in that orientation giving range to the options.

Simulation

- *Systemic context and context-driven design space*: This will be delivered through the level design and environmental storytelling.
- *Illusory design and scripting:* This will be delivered through the systemic rules of world such as real-time lighting and diegetic audio along with direct manipulation to achieve presence.

Embodied interaction with its material, affective and social dimensions

- *Choices:* Through multiple objects placed in the house and the freedom to access any part of the house if the right choices are made.
- *Problem solving:* Each randomly presented photograph helps reveal the identity of the player.
- *Emergent gameplay:* Players freely move, grab, inspect and interact with any object they see to come up with solutions to encounters in the level.
- *Flexible gameplay:* All mechanics have range to provide flexibility in the systemic design of the mechanics and world.
- *Embodiment:* Players freely move, look, grab, inspect and interact with any object.
- *Seamless direct manipulation:* Players do not just press some buttons to rotate, but click and drag to directly rotate an object. They do not just press a button to grab and place an object in their inventory; instead they directly grab an object in the world and drag it to where they need it.

4.1 Usability Testing

We tested the immersive sim in a playtesting session using a questionnaire with 20 questions. 11 people participated in the testing sessions. Majority were males (90.9%), primarily from game art (27.3%) and design (36.4%) backgrounds, and the others from programming, business, sound design and other fields (9.1% each). 54.5% of the participants were in their 20s, 27.3% in 30s, and 18.2% were in 40s. Majority of participants (72.7%) were highly experienced in playing games. After the playtesting session, the players were asked to fill in an online questionnaire, indicating their agreement to a range of sentences in a 7-point Likert scale.

The first task for the players was to download and install and set up Open Broadcast Software (OBS). Once OBS is ready to record, the second step was to play the game - Last Night - over on Simmer.io: https://simmer.io/@mylesblasonato/last-night. Players could use an XBOX controller or mouse and keyboard. The third and final step was to fill in the Google Form questionnaire at: https://forms.gle/NDWT2dwaCewcJoCr7.

4.2 Test Results

Overall, players state that they are satisfied with this immersive sim (81.8%). Table 1 demonstrates the distribution of the results for each feature listed above to qualify the game as an immersive sim. Each parameter below was tested by asking two or three questions to verify the range, as some overlaps with other parameter domains. We used the following sentences which indicate the sum for high Likert points 5–7:

Meaning making

I can control the storytelling with my choices in the immersive sim (45.5%).
I feel I can make sense of the story in the immersive sim (91%).

Focused design

I feel totally immersed in the story while playing this immersive sim (54.6%).
This immersive sim immerses players in believable, meticulously designed locations which make sense as actual places beyond game levels (91%).
I can complete my missions efficiently using this immersive sim (63.7%).

Systemic design

This immersive sim provides multitudes of meaningful tools players can use (63.7%).
The immersive sim allows emergent gameplay when the player moves an object to interact with the world (81.9%).

Interaction

The immersive sim provides the players various options to overcome challenges and completing objectives (54.6%).
The immersive sim offers significant gameplay-defining differences in character progression with no preconceived notion of the specified outcome (45.5%).

Direct manipulation

Player mechanics in this immersive sim allows me to perform any action, such as Free-move and Free-look, Grab, Inspect and Interact (72.8%).
This immersive sim has all the functions and capabilities I expect it to have (63.7%).
My interactions feel natural within the immersive sim (63.7%).

Embodiment

I feel in control when I am controlling my avatar (54.6%).
My avatar is responsive to the actions I initiated (54.6%).

Interface design

I feel my senses are efficiently engaged in this immersive sim (63.7%).
The visual aspects of the immersive sim are satisfactory (72.8%).
The auditory aspects of the immersive sim are satisfactory (81.9%).
The organization of information on the immersive sim screen is clear (72.7%).
The interface of this immersive sim is pleasant (91%).
Overall, I am satisfied with this immersive sim (81.8%).

As Table 1 indicates, design and solution space, mechanics and direct manipulation offered by the sim have very high ratings, as it allows emergent gameplay. However, the choices are still problematic as the level design lacks more fleshed out encounters or problems. This affects problem solving and embodiment and causes low rankings for flexible gameplay.

5 Evaluation of Immersive Sims as a New Paradigm

In the following sections, we analyse if immersive sims fit into the third paradigm definition in Harrison et al. (2007). As one of the most important characteristics of the third wave in HCI, the meaning of an object in immersive sims depends largely on the context in which it is used and the player's current goals. For example, the situational meaning of a crate object in *Deus Ex* can be an object to hide behind, a way to get to a high place, a weapon (with the strength mod), a container for valuable ammo, a floating island in a body of water, and a piece in a larger structure (like an impromptu bridge) – all depending on the context and the player's capabilities/goals. Because of the systemic design of immersive sims, the wider intersecting contexts of player, technology and anything else at play at the time outside the immersive sim influences meaning making and gameplay. This reinforces the characteristic of plurality of perspectives and multiple interpretations for the use of a game object and gameplay more widely.

The context-sensitivity is an important characteristic of the third wave in HCI paradigms. In immersive sims, as described in Harrison et al. (2007), players are not simply 'users' of information/fun, but the creators of fun. Immersive sims allow creative player expression with a more embodied, situated view of the game world in a systemic context.

The ability to construct fun, and in particular the ability to construct solutions to problems that emerge from the game's systems and narrative, makes immersive sims especially well-suited to ethical gameplay (Sicart 2013). In games, there is a tendency to reduce moral dilemmas to an information/response dynamic: give player dilemma; give

Table 1. Low-level characteristics of immersive sims

	Meaning-making design space	Multi-dimensional solution space	Focused design and mechanics	Context-driven design space	Illusory design and scripting	Choices	Problem-solving	Emergent gameplay	Flexible gameplay	Embodiment	Direct manipulation
Immersion	91	91	54.6	72.8–81.9	63.7						
Simulation			63.7	63.7	63.7					54.6	91
Interaction		91				45.5	54.6	81.9	45.5	54.6	72.8

player facts about dilemma; present obvious choice in form of dialogue tree. The much more interesting dilemmas, however, are the ones where the player is placed within a specific context and given the tools to act in morally meaningful ways that the system recognises as legitimate, and – crucially – that players themselves decide are morally meaningful.

The focus on embodied interaction and on situated action in the world in the third paradigm gives rise to a series of questions around how to integrate computational representations and actions within complex situations, such as those identified by Harrison et al. (2007). These questions, together with the analysis of practices we presented above, form the basis of a set of epistemological tools suitable for conducting rigorous investigations of immersive sims within the conceptual framework of the third paradigm.

- *What existing situated activities in the world should we support?*

If we look at a good selection of immersive sims in the framework of the third a paradigm – for example *Ultima Underworld, Deus Ex, System Shock, Bioshock, Prey,* and *Breath of the Wild*, we find that they all share similar embodied activities that tie the game world to the player's wider context via the character controller, such as: Movement, Orientation, Jump, Crouch, Grab, Drop, Attacking, Using (as in: pushing a button, opening a cupboard etc.), Inventory, Systemic Items (tied to Action), Systemic World, Systemic Game Elements.

These activities do not happen in a vacuum, but in complex contexts that ask users to appeal to their situated embodied dynamic meaning-making skills. From this perspective, the connection to the character control expands embodiment to encompass the simulated vessel and conversely expands the immersive sim into the wider material context of the user's life. The ethical boundaries of which existing situated activities should or should not be considered in immersive sims is a wider ongoing debate that goes beyond the scope of this research and deserves further investigation.

- *How do users use appropriate technologies, and how can we support those appropriations?*

The systemic design of immersive sims allows users to discover gameplay possibilities via trial and error and have agency in ways the developers could not have predicted. We suggest that this is a mode of appropriation of physics engines and character controller technologies. Moreover, we see this as a first step towards building players' agency comparable to newer interaction possibilities, such as motion controls in VR. If we observe the types of interactions users are currently performing in VR, we notice similarities with the mechanics listed above. We propose that emerging technologies such as VR and AR aim to make computer interactions more intuitive and immersive as discussed by Karnes (2021) in similar ways to what we observe in the design principles of immersive sims. In other words, there is an alignment between emerging technologies and design principles. This concept also applies to the *Metaverse*, an integrated way to interact with the internet.

- *How can we support interaction without constraining it too strongly by what a computer can do or understand?*

Immersive sims adopt systemic design and physics engines that approximate material contexts and dynamics in virtual simulations. It could be argued that, qualitatively, the outcomes of those computational operations create interactions that go beyond what the human user might expect a computer to do or 'understand'. The most intense recent HCI research work revolves around head mounted devices (HMD), body recognition and haptics. It is evident that peripherals are being designed to make interactions more immersive. This resonates with the third paradigm, as the design aims to enable interactions that feel more intuitive, embodied and situated beyond something that a computer can do or 'understand'.

- *What are the politics and values in interaction, and how can we support those in design?*

As we begin to make simulations more immersive, increasingly more ethical values from the social contexts of players and designers come into play within interactions. In other words, political and ethical issues emerge in context-driven simulations and call into play the situated understanding and decision-making skills of users based on meaningful interactions. This is increasingly perceived as natural and intuitive due to the systemic nature of the design. Most ethical issues arise from *social,* or quasi-social, gameplay systems that offer the opportunity to exercise agency and engage meaningfully. Immersive sims facilitate exactly this kind of meaningful engagement, which may explain why prominent examples of the form (e.g. *Deus Ex, Prey*) tend to emphasise moral themes in their narratives. This is a topic to explore further, as ethical values influence player behaviour and impacts the immersive design of the gameplay and, possibly, situated choices beyond the immersive sims.

6   Conclusion

In the second half of this paper, we have adopted a pragmatic approach to evaluating if immersive sims present characteristics that resonate with the third paradigm as delineated by Harrison et al. (2007). We have relied on our extended experience in game design, research and education as well as on relevant conceptual apparatus proposed by Samoylenko (2021). We argue that these valuable methods enable researchers to ask useful questions related to the third paradigm.

The conceptual analysis of the third paradigm we conducted in the first part of this paper expands the 'phenomenological matrix' proposed by Harrison et al. (2007) towards a post-phenomenological, new materialist and posthuman approach. We discussed several principles proposed by these authors and demonstrated that they already resonate with these philosophical developments, including direct references to Donna Haraway. We have also referenced Latour's (2007) ANT as a practice of observation of associations in the making and as foundational of the flat ontology that characterises new materialism and posthumanism. In other words, a view of everything as material and equally meaningful in a nature-culture dynamic continuum, including bodies, machines, concepts, social structures, material *things* and digital *things*.

A paradigm shift occurs when technology, new findings or a radical turn in research perspective completely change the way stakeholders think about or interact with an object or a world. New paradigm ideas create a fundamental shift in how we think and act from that point onwards, even if older paradigms do not necessarily disappear. Could immersive sims constitute a new paradigm in HCI?

Harrison et al. (2007) derive from Kuhn (1962) four essential elements that identify a scientific paradigm in HCI:

- *'a common understanding of the salient properties of interaction*
- *types of questions that appear to be both interesting and answerable about those properties of interaction*
- *a set of broad procedures which can be used to provide warrantable answers to those questions*
- *a common understanding of how to interpret the results of these procedures'*

In this paper, we have analysed the characteristics of immersive sims and found that they shift all four elements in a scientific paradigm and therefore correspond to the third paradigm in HCI. We listed the characteristics of a new HCI paradigm as embodied interaction with its material, affective and social dimensions; plurality of perspectives and multiple interpretations; context-driven design space; meaning making and meaningful engagement, and provided examples from a range of immersive sims for each characteristic. We developed a game to validate if these characteristics are conceived as an immersive sim. Our experimental findings state that the immersive sim design principles constitute a paradigm shift in HCI, rather than a new genre.

As computer technology advances, one element remains constant – interactions with computer technology must become more intuitive and immersive. By continuing to discuss and clarify the principles of immersive design, we believe that we will enable a strong foundation for design on emerging forms of computer technology and HCI in the future.

6.1 Future Work

We believe that the next step in this research is to identify a list of design principles for this new paradigm.

'As we push people out of unnatural patterns such as apps, screens and key-boards, into more natural modes of interaction like gestures and voice, designers become even more important than the technologists because over time, the technology becomes commoditized, but, conversely, the design principles become more relevant'

(Peter Rai, Principal Engineer at Cisco quoted in Dalladay-Simpson 2020).

In addition to the analytical tools we employed to explore immersive sims high level and low level characteristics, we suggest that Actor–network theory offers one possible rigorous methodology for analysing interactions in the making motivated by matters of concern, keeping into account the agencies of different actors and multiple perspectives (Latour 2007). Actor–network theory is a theoretical and methodological approach to social theory where everything in the social and natural worlds exists in constantly shifting networks of relationships. Stating that 'what is acting at the same moment in any place is coming from many other places, many distant materials, and faraway actors', Latour (2007, p. 200) advocates a practice of observation and recording of shifts in the relay of interactions to track the formation or transformation of "associations" as they happen. Understanding the combinations and interactions of elements that make it successful, rather than saying it is true and the others are false supports plurality of perspectives and problem solving, which are key characteristics of immersive sims. We believe that further research and testing of this method as a suitable epistemological tool for third paradigm HCI systems and immersive sims would be interesting and fruitful.

In addition to iterating on our research model to use ANT, further exploration of the prototype is desired with a stronger focus on providing more mechanics through a genre layer. After synthesising the results and noticing a common notion of players wanting more mechanics to allow for even more options, an original hunch was confirmed. The prototype we are presenting to players includes the base design patterns for an immersive experience which is the result of using this new paradigm however the genre specific design patterns, such as shooting mechanics like in Prey or Role-playing mechanics in Breath of the Wild, still need to be layered on top to provide an adequate range using the flexible gameplay principle defined in this paper.

The flexible gameplay principle is a concept that revolves around giving each mechanic more than just a binary state of on and off such as a door that can only be opened and closed. In games such as Layers of Fear or Amnesia: The Dark Descent the player can open doors slightly to peek through first, in fact they have full control over the door through the direct manipulation principle allowing for a full range in flexible gameplay for the door system. In addition to the results shining a light of players wanting more genre-specific mechanics which we can add a layer on top of the base patterns to validate this theory. The optimum range and thresholds for flexible gameplay hasn't been defined yet and in our attempts to do that, further exploration is necessary to define the optimum range and where the experience ends up being too realistic and therefore is no longer engaging for the players.

References

Barrett, L., Lindquist, K.: The embodiment of emotion Blasonato, M. Beyond the box, Simmer I.O. https://simmer.io/@mylesblasonato/beyond-the-box (2008). Accessed on 21 Oct 2021

Braidotti, R.: The Posthuman. Polity, Cambridge (2013)

Boehner, K., de Paula, R., Dourish, P., Sengers, P.: Affect: from information to interaction. In: Proceedings of the 4th Decennial Conference on Critical Computing: Between Sense and Sensibility, pp. 59–68. Aarhus, Denmark, 20–24 Aug 2005

Card, S.K., Moran, T.P., Newell, A.: The Psychology of Human-Computer Interaction. L. Erlbaum Associates, Hillsdale, N.J. (1983)

Cremona, C.: Networked commensals: bodily, relational and performative affordances of sharing food remotely. In: Whatley, S., Racz, I., Paramana, K., Crawley, M.-L. (eds.) Art and Dance in Dialogue, pp. 19–38. Springer, Cham (2020). https://doi.org/10.1007/978-3-030-44085-5_2

Dalladay-Simpson, J.: Deep design: the next paradigm of human-computer interaction, BCG digital ventures. https://medium.com/bcg-digital-ventures/deep-design-the-next-paradigm-of-human-computer-interaction-8bbe9a4c17e2. Accessed 18 Oct 2021 (2020)

DePaula, R., Dourish, P.: Cognitive and cultural views of emotions. In: Proc. HCIC (2005)

Dourish, P.: Where the Action Is: The Foundations of Embodied Interaction. MIT Press, Cambridge, MA (2001)

Dourish, P.: What we talk about when we talk about context. Pers. Ubiquitous Comput. **8**(1), 19–30 (2004)

Eickers, G., Loaiza, J.R., Prinz, J.: Embodiment, context-sensitivity, and discrete emotions: a response to moors. Psychol. Inq. **28**(1), 31–38 (2017)

Fox, N.J., Alldred, P.: New materialism. In: Atkinson, P.A., Delamont, S., Cernat, A., Sakshaug, J.W., Williams, M. (eds.) SAGE Research Methods Foundations. Sage, London (2019) https://methods.sagepub.com/foundations/new-materialism

Gallagher, S.: Direct perception in the intersubjective context. Conscious. Cogn. **17**, 535–543 (2008)

Griffiths, P.E., Scarantino, A.: Emotions in the wild: the situated perspective on emotion. In: Robbins, P., Ayede, M. (eds.) Handbook of Situated Cognition, pp. 437–454. Cambridge University Press, Cambridge, UK (2009)

Grudin, J.: Three faces of human-computer interaction. IEEE Annals Hist. Comput. **27**(4), 46–62 (2005)

Haraway, D.: Situated knowledges. Fem. Stud. **14**(3), 575–599 (1988)

Harrison, S., Tatar, D., Sengers, P.: The three paradigms of HCI. In: Proceedings of CHI 2007, 28 Apr – 3 May 2007, ACM, San Jose, CA (2007)

Jørgensen, K.: Dark play in dishonored. In: Mortensen, T.E., Linderoth, J., Brown, A.M.L. (eds.) The Dark Side of Game Play Controversial Issues in Playful Environments, Chapter 13, pp. 210–225, Routledge, New York (2015)

Karnes, K.C.: What is an immersive experience and how do you create one? https://clevertap.com/blog/immersive-experience/ (2021). Accessed 19 Oct 2021

Kuhn, T.S.: The Structure of Scientific Revolutions. University of Chicago Press, Chicago (1962)

Latour, B.: Reassembling the Social: An Introduction to Actor-Network-Theory. Oxford University Press, Oxford (2007)

McCullough, M.: Digital Ground. MIT Press, Cambridge, MA (2004)

O'Dwyer, D.: How arkane studios designed prey – documentary. https://www.youtube.com/watch?v=kXLxaKrcFZ0&t=3135s (2021). Accessed 19 Oct 2021

Restrepo, D.: Editorial: the modern immersive sim. https://gamelust.com/news/editorial-modern-immersive-sim/ (2017). Accessed 21 Oct 2021

Samoylenko, M.: Five pillars of immersive sims. https://maximsamoylenko.medium.com/five-pillars-of-immersive-sims-7263167e7258 (2021). Accessed 19 Oct 2021

Scarantino, A.: How to define emotions scientifically. Emot. Rev. **4**, 358–368 (2012)

Scarantino, A.: Basic emotions, psychological construction, and the problem of variability. In: Barrett, L.F., Russell, J.A. (eds.) The Psychological Construction of Emotion, pp. 334–376. Guilford Press, New York, NY (2015)

Schubert, D.: How Realistic is Too Realistic? Game Developer Informa PLC Ltd., UK (2010)

Shami, N.S., Hancock, J., Peter, C., Muller, M., Mandryk, R.: Measuring affect in hci: going beyond the individual. In: Extended Abstracts of the ACM Conference on Human Factors in Computing Systems (CHI 2008). ACM Press, New York (2008)

Slater, M.: Place illusion and plausibility can lead to realistic behaviour in immersive virtual environments. Philos. Trans. R Soc. Lond B Biol. Sci. **364**(1535), 3549–3557 (2009)

Sicart, M.: Beyond Choices, The Design of Ethical Gameplay. MIT Press (2013)

Spector, W.: Warren spector's commandments of game design. https://www.gamesindustry.biz/art icles/2013-09-04-warren-spectors-commandments-of-game-design (2013). Accessed 18 Oct 2021

Spector, W.: Deus ex postmortem. https://www.gamedeveloper.com/design/postmortem-ion-storm-s-i-deus-ex-i- (2000). Accessed 4 Feb 2022

Truby, J.: The Anatomy of Story: 22 Steps to Becoming a Master Storyteller. Faber and Faber, New York (2007)

Hybrid Spaces, Hybrid Methodologies: Finding Ways of Working with Social Sciences and Humanities in Human-Computer Interaction

Claude Draude[(✉)] and Goda Klumbytė

Faculty of Electrical Engineering and Computer Science, University of Kassel, Kassel, Germany
`claude.draude@uni-kassel.de`

Abstract. Starting from the need for responsible research and innovation in computing, this paper addresses the challenges that come from working with the social sciences and the humanities in human-computer interaction. In this paper, we attempt to move beyond interdisciplinarity towards transdisciplinarity. In particular, we explore concepts of hybridity and third spaces that are used in HCI participatory design practices. We trace back the postcolonial, decolonial and feminist scholarship basis of these concepts and look at how their critical potential can inform a conceptualization of what we call hybrid methodology in its own right. For this, we present three case studies. The first two work with experimental spaces in artistic research and research through design, the third works with intersectional critical and speculative methodologies in machine learning systems design. The first two case studies center around the discussions of disciplinary openness through experimentation as a way of moving beyond interdisciplinarity towards transdisciplinarity; the third zooms in on the role of critical theoretical knowledge from the social sciences and the humanities as knowledge that enables new orientations in research and design of IT systems.

Keywords: HCI methods and theories · Computing and humanities · Computing and social sciences · Transdisciplinarity · Hybridity

1 Introduction

Computing technology increasingly impacts all areas of life. Products, services, logistics and infrastructure, as well as processes of knowledge, information and communication organization are being significantly shaped through IT. Computing is often seen as a driver of innovation, but the field is also under pressure to rethink its research and development practices and to respond appropriately to societal challenges [1].

In recent years, AI-driven IT systems with problematic societal impact have been reported, such as those that have discriminatory effects and reinforce social inequalities, like racist or sexist autocompletions or photo classifications in search engines or facial recognition [2, 3]; incorrect translation software [4] or race and gender biases

M. Kurosu (Ed.): HCII 2022, LNCS 13302, pp. 40–56, 2022.
https://doi.org/10.1007/978-3-031-05311-5_3

in algorithm-based decision-making aids, such as the assessment of recidivism rates of convicts [5] or the allocation of training measures on the labor market [6]. Counteracting this, responsible research and innovation in computing should enable the broadest possible participation in society for all, comply with democratic values and norms, and be socially and ecologically sustainable [7].

Taking up this entanglement of the social and the technological, seven grand challenges have been formulated for human-computer interaction (HCI): human-technology symbiosis; human-environment interactions; ethics, privacy and security; well-being, health; accessibility and universal access; learning and creativity; social organization and democracy [8]. To implement value-orientation in IT systems design and address the challenges posed, computing increasingly relies on working with knowledge from the social sciences and the humanities (SSH).

In HCI, design approaches exist that focus on ethical and social issues in IT research and development; value-sensitive, participatory, inclusive, reflective design all seek to foster responsibility and fairness [9]. Hence, while HCI already has developed approaches to build upon, the pervasiveness of IT and the increase in AI technologies bring new challenges and are calling for new qualities and methodologies in interdisciplinary work. Considering power relations, social inequalities and diversity in people and contexts is one major task. Embedded, ubiquitous and intelligent IT, however, also lead to a crisis in values, norms, and concepts of traditional responsible design. With machine learning systems, humanist democratic values, such as participation, empowerment, agency, accountability become fragile. Questions like who is responsible for choices that have been supported through algorithmic decision making and who can be held accountable, call for new approaches to respond to hybrid intelligence systems where human and machine agency are tightly coupled [10, 11].

This paper takes up these challenges and explores working with knowledge from the social sciences and the humanities in HCI through the concept of "hybridity." Postcolonial scholar Homi K. Bhabha developed the notion of a "third space", an in-between hybrid space, that allows for the creation of something new rather than assuming the coexistence of predetermined entities or ways of doing, thinking, knowing or being [12]. In the HCI methodology of participatory design (PD) this idea of the third space is already taken up and serves as a collaborative means for end users and software developers. We follow up on this, seeking to work with the critical, postcolonial stance of Bhaba's work as well as the work of science and technology studies scholar Donna Haraway and decolonial and postcolonial feminist thinker Gloria Anzaldúa. With this, our paper presents a more meta-methodological reflection that goes beyond specific methods such as value-sensitive design and reflective design and conceptualizes the idea and practice of hybrid methodologies and their development in HCI as a broader principle.

After a more theoretical discussion of hybridity and what it could bring as a conceptual foundation of rethinking interdisciplinary exchange between SSH and HCI, we provide practical examples selected from our own research practice between the two fields. These examples started out as interdisciplinary endeavors but managed, at least in parts, to move towards trans- or cross-disciplinarity. Specifically, we will discuss examples of research that worked with experimental spaces in artistic research and research through design (sect. 3.1), and intersectional critical and speculative methodologies in machine learning systems design (sect. 3.2). The first two cases center around the discussions of disciplinary openness and looks at experimentation as a way of moving beyond interdisciplinarity towards transdisciplinarity; the third zooms in on the role of critical theoretical knowledge from SSH as knowledge that enables new orientations in research and design of IT systems.

From this discussion of practical examples, we follow up on the moments and findings where new ways of working, knowing, and constructing emerged – eventually formulating the need for *hybrid methodologies*. While employing various approaches in HCI that originate in SSH is not new, this discussion tends to focus on the validity and use of such methods in HCI [13]. In this paper we offer instead a conceptualization of hybrid methodologies as a category in its own right, suggesting that in some cases it might be appropriate to not simply incorporate SSH methodologies in HCI but, treating research as a *hybrid space*, creating genuine *hybrid methodologies*. We will also highlight the significance of retaining critical potential of such methodologies and the importance of retaining critical political and ethical orientations in working with them.

2 Third Spaces and Hybridity

The concept of the "third space" finds its entry into the field of HCI in Participatory Design (PD) approaches. Here, a third space that allows for productive exchange between software developers and end-users is incremental. Third space ideally opens up a space where neither developers nor end-users are at home initially and where all participants can encounter one another open-mindedly [9, 14]. It is as much a methodological concept as it describes a physical space.

2.1 Theoretical Background of Hybridity: Bhabha, Anzalduá, Haraway

The notion of third space in PD is derived from postcolonial scholar Homi K. Bhabha relating closely to his understanding of "hybridity". The third space is a noteworthy example of how concepts from SSH are taken up in HCI and how their connotations change through this transfer.

Bhabha developed the concepts of third space and hybridity against the background of colonialism, oppression, colonial antagonism, and unequal power relations. He employs literature and cultural theory to explore the emancipatory and innovative character of what hybridity could entail. This potential is tied to carving out an epistemological space that allows to move beyond essentialist, fixed notions of "pure cultures" that encounter one another. His conception of cultural identities opposes a simplified and dichotomic thinking and singular direction of influence: from colonizers imposing their culture unto a colonized group. Instead, and based on poststructuralist thinking, apart from the power struggle and forces of oppression, there is an in-between space that emerges where new meanings, cultures and identities are constructed. This is theoretically grounded through linguistics and semiotics – the third space is a "place of enunciation" [12].

In wider postcolonial discourse, however, the prominence of hybridity is discussed quite controversially and even deemed as a fetishization of a vulnerable position of not-belonging [15, 16]. This, of course, is not Bhaba's intention. He does not negate the interdependencies and inequities between colonizer and colonized but deconstructs any take on essentialist "pure" culture and hence dismantles normalized discourses of "the other." This makes agency of the subaltern in oppressive contexts possible and allows to grasp that both, colonizer and colonized, change, or are affected in such contexts.

We suggest taking up Bhabha's work on third space alongside ideas around hybridity proposed by science and technology studies scholar Donna Haraway and feminist post-colonial thinker Gloria Anzaldúa[1]. Anzaldúa in her work on Chicana cultural belonging introduces the idea of hybrid identity and forms of belonging that navigate multiple marginalizations, power dynamics, languages, and politics. Speaking of her own experience as a Chicana growing up at the US-Mexican border, Anzaldúa theorizes and re-appropriates – through literary, scholarly, and experimental work – the position of a *mestiza*: a racial colonial category developed by the Spanish Empire to refer to people (in this case, women) of mixed White and Indigenous American ancestry. By re-appropriating the term *mestiza*, Anzaldúa invites to consider the complex intersecting inequalities of race, gender, class, culture and proposes to think about politics and ethics in ways that focus on crossing, multiplicity and situated accountability instead of politics of ethical, moral, national, and other "purity." She calls such thinking-in-between "border thinking" [21].

In a similar vein, Donna Haraway also focuses on interconnections, inter-dependencies and co-definitions of bodies and technologies in her early work that re-appropriates *cyborg* as a feminist figure [22, 23]. Haraway proposes cyborg as a concept and a figure for challenging dichotomies between human and machine, nature, and culture, organic and inorganic. However, cyborg also necessitates to consider the inequalities that are entrenched in technological production (such as underpaid labor in the value chain, digital divide across and within regions, gender disparities in technological production and consumption, to name a few). Thus, much like the figure of *mestiza* and the method of "border thinking," Haraway's cyborg thought also proposes to look for hybrid ways of generating knowledge in order to account for the multiple, often contradictory circumstances in which knowledge is created and objects that it is created about. Such knowledge, as Haraway explains in her other work, needs to be situated and partial in order to remain responsible and accountable [24]. Ethically, like Anzaldúa, she suggests moving away from universal moral values and focus on ethics that is sensitive to different embodied agencies and power dynamics in different contexts.

2.2 Third Space and Hybridity in PD and HCI

Bhabha's theory makes its way into diverse contexts such as Educational Studies [25] or Library and Information Studies [26], while Haraway's work has been influential in HCI research too [27–30]. How much recourse there is on the postcolonial and political background that these theories were conceived in, varies. As noted above, in PD the

---

[1] It is important to note that other postcolonial theories have been taken up in HCI and interaction design [17], as well as decolonial theories [18] and Indigenous approaches [19,20] These theories do not necessarily contradict, but they do have significant divergences. For this paper, we will focus on Bhabha's, Anzaldúa's and Haraway's work as theories to genealogically and politically root the notion of "hybridity" in.

third space is an important concept and hence finds its way into HCI/computing [31]. Reviewing application examples of the approach, Muller collects characteristics of third spaces across various fields. Noteworthy, the table of Fig. 1 presents knowledge from SSH in a format which mirrors checklists and criteria more common in technology design.

The overview starts by naming sites where in-between spaces could occur; a cross-cutting theme is the ability to be open for other perspectives and reflect upon and challenge one's own assumptions. Furthermore, collective practices and a sense of co-creation are helpful. Important here is to make room for working with differences. Also, shared understandings, meanings and languages need to be established first keeping in mind that differences do not need to be dissolved. In the table this shows in the claim of "potential site of conflicts between reference/among reference fields." Potential conflicts, however, exceed the confrontations between disciplinary cultures and reference fields, and also relate to the central question of PD: "who has a say?" in the design and usage of IT systems[2]. This means that power relations and social inequalities always must be acknowledged when working with concepts of third spaces.

Overlap between two (or more) different regions or fields (inbetweenness)
Marginal to reference fields
Novel to reference fields
Not "owned" by any reference field
Partaking of selected attributes of reference fields
Potential site of conflicts between/among reference fields
Questioning and challenging of assumptions
Mutual learning
Synthesis of new ideas
Negotiation and (co-)creation of…
Identities
Working language
Working assumptions and dynamics
Understandings
Relationships
Collective actions
Dialogues across and within differences (disciplines)
Polyvocality
What is considered to be data?
What are the rules of evidence?
How are conclusions drawn?
Reduced emphasis on authority – increased emphasis on interpretation
Reduced emphasis on individualism – increased emphasis on collectivism
Heterogeneity as the norm

Fig. 1. "Summary of claims relating to third spaces" [31]

---

[2] For a deeper discussion on the need of PD to adapt to current and future digital transformations, see [32].

Questions of power and inequality are the background from which Bhabha's, Anzaldúa's and Haraway's conceptualizations of hybridity necessarily evolve. This is important in order to understand the political dimension of Bhabha's conception of the third space, Anzaldúa's border thinking and Haraway's cyborg and the role hybridity plays. It is only through hybridity that third spaces occur and therefore new cultural forms and expressions emerge. This newness can also reflect or come at the cost of oppression and on-going power struggles and should not be idealized. Therefore, hybridity does not mean a clean slate, a third space where the rest of the context disappears. Instead, notions of hybridity have to include considerations of power and social positionality. We will come back to the problematic connotation this holds when Bhaba's and other postcolonial thinkers' critical concepts are taken up in other fields. Now, we want to point out a couple of things in the discussion of third space in PD and HCI.

2.3 Potential of Hybrid Methodologies in HCI

First, the world of software development and the world of tech usage are commonly viewed as two different cultures with different languages, customs, interests, and expertise. The broader field of HCI typically is engaged with bringing together and aligning affordances of these two worlds to create tech devices and services. So, one could see HCI already as a third space that enables exchange between the two cultures. In academia, knowledge on application or life domains – or methods on how such knowledge is gained – usually is located in SSH fields whereas computing corresponds with expertise on tech development. But, following Bhaba's, Haraway's and Anzaldúa's work, and as shown in Fig. 1, the third space necessarily needs to move beyond traditional exchange practices. For HCI, Muller states that: "Most of the traditional methods are relatively one-directional – e.g., we analyze the requirements *from* the users; we deliver a system *to* the users; we collect usability data *from* the users. While there are many specific practices for performing these operations, relatively few of them involve two-way discussions, and fewer still afford opportunities for the software professionals to be surprised – i.e., *to learn something that we didn't know we needed to know.*" [31] The latter points at innovations that could happen through exploring the characteristics of third spaces and hybridity.

Second, hybridity can be substantiated through the disciplinary foundation of computer science. This foundation has been controversially discussed – spanning from positions that locate computer science within engineering to positioning it as a design science [33]. Among other aspects, these discussions are motivated by perspectives that view computer science as a semiotic discipline [34] highlighting the special character of computing machinery as sign-processing [35]. Furthermore, any application or digital service must comply with the formal logic and core functional principles of computers, while they are at the same time situated in sociocultural contexts [36]. This means that the artefacts themselves have got a "double character" and can be regarded as hybrid objects leading to phenomena that transgress dichotomic boundaries [37].

Both aspects – the positioning of HCI in-between and the discussions on the disciplinary basis provide the grounds for addressing the important third aspect: hybridity in methods and approaches – or, as we call it, hybrid methodology as a category in its own right. To develop the notion of hybridity in PD further, Muller [31] first of all understands methods in HCI in their positioning on a continuum that spans between the two cultures of usage and development. On each outer edge respective methods and tools are used: on the usage end, these are qualitative methods from SSH like ethnographic field work; on the development end, these are tools like rapid prototyping. Put differently, either the developers have to adapt to SHH methods, or the users or user representatives have to adhere to tools close to technology design. When it comes to the physical space where encounters between end-users and developers happen this means that either the developers visit the usage context, entering literally the world of the user, or that the potential end-users get invited to the developers' lab, e.g., taking part in a focus group or do usability tests. Hybridity in methods would then mean to broaden the space in-between those poles.

In this section, we highlighted PD as a place where hybridity and third spaces prominently are discussed in HCI. The examples we revisit in the following Sect. 3 are not strictly PD practices although questions of participation, in- and exclusions and boundary making certainly do play a significant role. The claims/characteristics found above (Fig. 1) can serve nonetheless as guiding principles for conditions in which hybridity in HCI research practices can emerge. As overarching themes spaces and modalities that enable *negotiation, shared construction, collective discovery,* and *polyvocality* are useful. Furthermore, facilitating *process-orientation* and attentiveness to *situatedness, contexts* and *materialities* is important.

3 Exploring Hybridity

In this section we revisit examples of our research and try a review of our practices through the lens of hybridity developed above. For a better understanding it is important to note that our research group itself presents a space of interdisciplinarity between computer science and SSH. While the group[3] is located within an engineering department it is also affiliated with the Social Sciences faculty. The composition of the group with researchers from both fields mirrors this. Furthermore, we are part of a research center for information systems design[4] where disciplines such as computer science, psychology, sociology, economics, law, and mechanical engineering work together.

In computer science it is not unusual to work with researchers from other disciplines such as mathematics, physics, engineering, cognitive or behavioral Sciences. Collaborating with people from the social or political sciences and employing critical theory, gender studies or artistic research as part of a work group is still rather unusual in the German academic context. Hence, the examples we discuss already were made possible through this interdisciplinary location. In the following, we want to trace where they managed, at least in parts, to move beyond and establish third spaces and find new ways of working.

---

[3] For more information see https://www.uni-kassel.de/go/GeDIS/.

[4] See website of the Research Center for Information System Design (ITeG), https://www.uni-kassel.de/forschung/en/iteg/home.

3.1 Experimental Spaces Through Artistic Research and Research Through Design

The examples in this sub-section center disciplinary openness and look at experimentation as a way of moving beyond interdisciplinarity towards transdisciplinarity. Hence, both case studies were set up as experimentations: the first one following a physical object and experiential phenomena, the second one investigating a social question against a technological background. Experimentation here is informed by the SSH fields science and technology studies and philosophy of science. We use the term experiments deliberately keeping in mind that it invokes lab contexts of the natural sciences. Philosopher and biologist Hans-Jörg Rheinberger formulates that experimental set-ups form a systemic structure where new knowledge becomes possible. Experiments in themselves are in-between spaces oscillating between knowing and not-knowing. He describes experimental systems as "places of emergence", "generators of surprise" and even "machines to fabricate the future" [38]. While, of course, in scientific experiments reproducibility, generalization and controllability are important, in artistic research and research through design the innovative quality and the process of experimenting is the main focus.

In the following, we explore how in our case studies experimentation contributes towards establishing a third space and trace where hybrid constellations might lead to new findings.

Experiencing Screens. The first example refers to a three-part series of artistic research experiments that aimed at drawing attentiveness to screens and displays. Artistic research allowed to approach screens as objects beyond their use in technological systems.

Artistic research holds the potential of third spaces, respectively can be seen as a contested zone between the arts and academia [39, 40]. Artistic research transgresses the art and theory dichotomy and can be viewed as being neither fully at home in the art world nor in academic research. It leaves logics of production and exhibitions, and moves more towards process-orientation, retracing where and what kind of knowledge and experiences materialize. For academia, however, the openness of artistic processes, the importance of materiality and performative function of artistic research which also only insufficiently translates to scholarly texts, is a challenge. Experimenting with materials, the constructive character of arts, is closer to computing and engineering than to SSH. For technological production affordances, however, the fact that artistic experiments elude clear functionality and use is demanding.

The experiments started from the finding that although screens as interfaces are omnipresent in everyday life, as phenomena and in their experiential quality as objects themselves they are rarely the center of attention[5]. So, of interest were questions like what is unseen or unattended to in computer screen culture and what kind of surfaces are enacted as screens and in what way? For this, a retranslation from digital screens as technology to analog screen experiments was undertaken. Here, we present only a short recap of one of the experiments[6].

---

[5] For exceptions see [41].

[6] For an extensive account of the screen experiments please look at [42].

Window Displays in Former Warehouse. Figure 2 shows a site-specific installation in a former warehouse in Berlin, Germany, which had been temporarily used as a space for artistic practice before the building was torn down. The space was also open for the public.

For this experiment, the double-glazed windows were turned into display cases. The bottom half of the outer window-parts was glazed to produce translucency. Collected plant parts, were arranged between the two glass panels. The upper parts of the windows were filled with sand from the construction site. Over time, the sand gradually shifted, altering the amount of light that got through, as well as the pattern it produced.

There was no electric lighting, therefore the shapes that the display cases cast, differed depending on weather conditions and time of the day. On sunny days, the display projected multicolored shapes onto walls and floor. On cloudy days, the colors of the display itself seemed to disappear. Starting at sunset, the patterns began to dissolve, resulting in their disappearance when it was a dark, moonless night. From outside of the building, the plant parts appeared blurred; details were hardly visible due to the glazing.

The windows formed a three-dimensional display, which from the outside looked like a flat screen. From inside the room, the plant parts invited a closer observance of the display. They motivated touching, but the glass served as a barrier for touch – only light got through. When the sun illuminated them, images were projected onto walls and floor that subsequently became screens as well. Thus, the windows served both as a barrier and as link between the inside and the outside of the building, as well as they provided a space themselves and functioned as projection devices. Turning them into display cases altered their visibleness: From something we ordinarily look through, they became something which was looked at.

Fig. 2. Mixed-media installation

The artistic research approach made it possible to recontextualize and defamiliarize screens. The experiments obfuscate the typical roles of screens and displays in HCI as interfaces and instead interrogate screens as phenomena. Furthermore, for visitors of the space, attentiveness towards screens and how they comport themselves towards screens became more tangible. All screen experiments were highly site-specific, context-dependent and used simple, readily available, materials. These were mostly organic and prone to decay, alteration or fading.

Artistic research and experimentation contribute to enabling third spaces due to their in-between positioning. In these experiments, furthermore, hybridity in methodology emerges through recontextualizing the experiments in computing and HCI. At various intersections then new aspects come up. The warehouse windows had a double quality as screen and projector which depended on the time of the day and the weather condition. Transferred to computer technology, this invokes question of access and availability – on screens being always on(line). What screens and displays were only available at certain times or in specific environments? What if their transparency depended on context? And beyond the immediate screen context – is this something with which, for example, transparency in algorithmic systems experience could be rethought through? Artistic research here established a hybrid open space to ask questions about the logic, function and definition of digital artefacts and computing.

Social Privilege Estimator. This experiment brought together the social sciences concept of social privilege with the workings and impact of machine learning systems. The idea for this project started from the rather provocative question of whether social privilege could be inferred from the human face alone, against the background of facial recognition technology. The "Social Privilege Estimator" (SPE) allowed us to look into the potentials of algorithmic user experience (AX) to increase digital literacy and invoke reflections on both social inequality as well as on facial recognition technology[7]. We followed a research through design approach which, like artistic research, is oriented on the process and knowledge gains that materialize through design artefacts [43].

The SPE was set up as a live technological demonstrator at a public AI convention consisting of a PC, camera, screen and additional explanatory posters and human facilitators for assistance and discussion. The visitors' faces were captured by camera, evaluated, and a social privilege score was estimated, which then they could discuss with each other or with the facilitators. The demonstrator used pre-trained deep neural networks for facial recognition and derived social categories such as age, gender, and ethnicity from the image feed. The social privilege score, an additional category we invented to be displayed, was calculated in a simple additive manner depending on which age, gender, and ethnicity the SPE attributed to a person. The function of these categories in relation to social privilege was backed by intersectional gender research and statistical data from Germany and Europe. The goal was not so much to invoke or suggest that social privilege can be quantified with a single score, but instead to provoke critical thinking and reflection around questions of social inequalities and privilege, algorithmic scoring and evaluation, and facial recognition technologies.

---

[7] For more detail, please note the full paper on the Social Privilege Estimator [11].

In reviewing the SPE against the background of this paper, we want to point out several aspects. First and most obvious, we worked with a concept from SSH in computing. The aim of the SPE, however, was not to smoothly transfer this concept to machine learning and enhance facial recognition technology. Instead, we deliberately sought to produce a field of tension where critical digital literacy as well as an understanding of societal inequalities could emerge. Frictions that occurred in the use of the demonstrator were not dissolved but actively explored for educational purposes.

In the technical set-up the ambiguity of automated classification became quite clear because participants could gain at least a basic understanding of how the end results were calculated. The demonstrator provided a diffractive mirror for how social privilege might affect a person on an individual as well as on a societal level and what role AI technology might play in this.

Furthermore, the experimentation encouraged us to understand AX not mainly as a property of service but as a property of the interactional setting itself. This means including socio-cultural norms, educational level, other humans, and non-human agents as well as ethical and normative dimensions. This necessarily invokes the need to think with different conceptual metaphors for designing responsible and inclusive AI systems. AX then corresponds less with fixed settings and properties and more as something which is actively co-created in a specific setting.

SPE was created and deployed through and in a hybrid cross-disciplinary space, where research through design, AX, critical algorithm studies, interaction design, digital literacy, and social studies of structural inequalities as they relate to technologies, came together. It required collaborative work of social and computer scientists and openness to understanding different vocabularies, as well as building a shared practice for materializing knowledge of algorithmic systems and social inequalities through a concrete project. This collaborative work was crucial for SPE design space as a hybrid space and SPE design as a hybrid method.

3.2 Intersectional Critical and Speculative Methodologies in Machine Learning Systems Design

This example zooms in on the role of critical theoretical knowledge from SSH as knowledge that enables new orientations in research and design of IT systems. While more pertinent to algorithmic systems design, this example however also addresses human-algorithm interaction and algorithmic experience (AX) as a sub-field of HCI [11].

critML project entailed a series of workshops[8] on working with concepts from critical theories in SSH in machine learning (ML) systems design. The premise of the workshops was that approaches to fairness, accountability, justice, and ethics in ML could benefit from insights from critical SSH study fields. Critical theories, particularly feminist and postcolonial as well as anti-racist critical theories, have developed rigorous tools to address systemic bias and its embeddedness in sociotechnical systems, and to trace how

---

[8] Workshops were conducted in different contexts: four as a longer four-workshop course at the Centre for Human-Computer Interaction Design at City, University of London (in collaboration with Prof. Alex Taylor), and one at the CHITaly'21 conference – see [44].

these systems (re)produce power hierarchies. critML workshops thus aimed to create a hybrid space to experiment with critical concepts towards more inclusive, contextualized, and accountable ML systems design.

The project introduced four concepts from SSH, specifically intersectional critical feminist theories: *situated knowledges/situating* [24, 45], *figurations/figuring* [21, 46], *diffraction* [47], and *critical fabulation/speculation* [48, 49]. All these concepts can be seen as methodological and conceptual tools that address different aspects of inclusivity, contextualization, and accountability. Situated knowledges point to the embeddedness of any knowledge claims – and, by extension, design – in material, historical, socio-political, and other conditions, and advocates for partial situated perspectives instead of striving for "pure" objectivity. Figurations or figuring help generate structuring metaphors and concepts-to-think-with (such as aforementioned *mestiza* or *cyborg*) as nodes that connect technical systems and socio-cultural imaginaries and thus generate fruitful design directions. Diffraction as a concept provides a lens to address the multi-faceted effects of ML systems as diffraction apparati that affect, re-configure, disrupt, and construct the sociotechnical environments in which they operate. Last but not least, critical fabulation and speculation propel forward questions of whose perspectives are missing in design and encourage to take historically grounded, power-sensitive view towards ML systems, their design, and operations.

Each workshop entailed introduction to the concept and a series of exercises that "actualized" the concept by suggesting ways that participants could explore it further and then to work with it in their design projects. The participants were primarily from the fields of HCI and ML, and the design projects they were working on were speculative. All activities were carried out in small design teams (approx. five people per team), thus encouraging collaboration, co-creation, and collective discussion.

In terms of hybridity, the workshops exemplified the creation of hybrid methodological approaches. On the one hand, the workshops were framed as co-creation and speculative design workshops – thus employing methods traditional to HCI and situated in a clearly computing and design oriented disciplinary space. On the other hand, the introduction of critical concepts as design methodologies productively confused this disciplinary space by introducing ways of thinking and analysis employed in SSH.

However, most importantly the workshop series allowed participants to create hybrid methodologies in their own right by providing an experimental space to put the critical concepts to work in a design context. The exercises that were designed in order to facilitate this work did precisely that – they *facilitated* and perhaps *guided* the process without prescribing formal rules for how concepts are to be applied. This means that working with critical concepts necessitated participants to develop their own understanding and ways of working with them through personal reflection, collective discussion, and putting their interpretations to practice in speculative design projects. Such methodological and interpretative openness was crucial for hybrid space and hybrid approaches to emerge. Furthermore, this hybridity did not eliminate the critical political and explicitly ethical orientation and genealogy of the concepts themselves but rather required the participants to ask critical and ethical questions in the context of their design projects.

Last but not least, the fact that there were no fool proof, pre-set formalized rules on how to work with concepts, participants had to constantly engage in collaborative discussion and interpretation. This in turn, re-oriented the idea of accountability of and in ML systems as something that is limited to fixed criteria and flowcharts of who is responsible for what in which case. Instead, the idea of accountability was re-defined as a capacity that is process-based: it is only through asking ethical questions, investigating the implications, and deliberating about choices that one becomes response-able (able to respond for) those choices.

4 Towards Conceptualizing Hybrid Methodologies

Starting from the grand challenges that computer science faces, this paper took up the question of how to work with the social sciences and the humanities in human-computer interaction. We are, of course, aware of the manifold approaches that exist at the intersection of SSH and HCI and that are incremental to the field's history and current work. Our goal was to contribute to moving forward with how this working in-between, and given the heterogeneity in approaches, could be methodologically conceptualized.

How to navigate disciplinary boundaries is subject to a broad range of discussions evolving around interdisciplinarity, multidisciplinarity and transdisciplinarity [50–52]. Without going into detail of these debates, our aim with this paper was to move beyond shifting from interdisciplinary practices towards transdisciplinary ways of working, knowing, and constructing. If for interdisciplinary ways of working we usually ask how can a certain method or approach from SSH be made fruitful and integrated in HCI, for transdisciplinarity we ask where and how a transposing of expertise happens and something genuinely new emerges [40]. This is expressed in PD practice when we *"learn something that we didn't know we needed to know."* [31].

For exploring and cultivating the grounds for these *moments of newness*, we took up postcolonial and feminist scholarship on concepts such as hybridity, border thinking and third spaces. The attempt to conceptualize hybrid methodologies in their own right also brings the tension that occurs in translating critical theories into usable concepts for HCI. As we pointed out, taking over concepts from SSH runs the risk of losing their critical potential in the process. Hybridity and the third space, we showed, are taken up in computing since they are foundational for participatory design practices. The postcolonial and feminist basis of these concepts, however, makes it indispensable to not just center newness but to always address question of power relations and uphold the critical potential that these concepts are rooted in. This is important not least for socially-responsible research and design and education [53]. Doing justice to this strong political-ethical orientation and context of concepts such as hybridity and third space are also crucial for allowing truly fruitful crossovers to emerge, as the concepts were designed to challenge not only power hierarchies, but also of epistemological hierarchies and create space for diverse ways of knowing.

In our examples, we tried to trace both – hybridity as a space for learning something new while also acknowledging questions of power, in- and exclusion and border thinking. The artistic research example does this in a more abstract way. It provides a conceptual case study on how to explore a computing object and phenomena through recontextualizing and focusing on materiality, context, and tangible experiences. The Social Privilege Estimator forms a third space for educational purposes that transgresses existing approaches of algorithmic experience and digital literacy. Last not least, the critML workshop series demonstrates how a political-ethical space can be established through working with intersectional feminist concepts in machine learning.

The examples, different as they are in approaches and contexts, share as overarching theme an attentiveness towards the conditions from which collaborative spaces and practices could emerge. Designing these conditions through attentive open collaboration and allowing sufficient time and space for bringing different knowledges together, instead of simply exchanging the views, is crucial. Furthermore, the emergent quality of hybrid methodologies is central – the third space is not the result of simply combining different methods or approaches as in a construction kit. This means that some institutionalized practices of collaboration will need to be challenged, and others invented so that emergent hybrid methodologies can be situated not simply in one disciplinary field, but in the third space as such. We suggest, nonetheless, that hybrid methodologies – i.e., methodologies that emerge in and through collaboration, which are rooted in the third space, and that challenge epistemological hierarchies – are worth pursuing to embrace and further the agenda of responsible research and innovation in computing and design.

References

1. Schwab, K.: The fourth industrial revolution: what it means and how to respond. https://www.weforum.org/agenda/2016/01/the-fourth-industrial-revolution-what-it-means-and-how-to-respond/ (2016). Accessed 29 July 2021
2. Buolamwini, J., Gebru, T.: Gender shades: intersectional accuracy disparities in commercial gender classification. In: Proceedings of the 1st Conference on Fairness, Accountability and Transparency, pp. 77–91 (2018)
3. Noble, S.U.: Algorithms of Oppression How Search Engines Reinforce Racism. New York University Press, New York (2018)
4. Schiebinger, L., Klinge, I., Paik, H.Y., Sánchez de Madariaga, I., Schraudner, M., Stefanick, M.: Gendered Innovations in Science, Health & Medicine, Engineering, and Environment. http://genderedinnovations.stanford.edu/ (2011–2020)
5. Angwin, J., Larson, J., Kirchner, L., Mattu, S.: Machine bias. There's software used across the country to predict future criminals. And it's biased against blacks. ProPublica. https://www.propublica.org/article/machine-bias-risk-assessments-in-criminal-sentencing (23 May 2016). Accessed 29 July 2021
6. Fanta, A.: Datenschutzbehörde stoppt Jobcenter-Algorithmus. https://netzpolitik.org/2020/oesterreich-ams-datenschutzbehoerde-stoppt-jobcenter-algorithmus/ (2020). Accessed 29 July 2021
7. WBGU: Politikpapier: Transformation unserer Welt im digitalen Zeitalter. https://www.wbgu.de/de/ (2019). Accessed 30 July 2021
8. Stephanidis, C., et al.: Seven HCI grand challenges. Int. J. Hum.–Comput. Interaction (2019). https://doi.org/10.1080/10447318.2019.1619259
9. Simonsen, J., Robertson, T. (eds.): Routledge International Handbook of Participatory Design. Routledge, London, New York (2012)
10. Draude, C., Klumbyte, G., Lücking, P., Treusch, P.: Situated algorithms: a sociotechnical systemic approach to bias. OIR, 325–342 (2020)

11. Klumbyte, G., Lücking, P., Draude, C.: Reframing AX with critical design: the potentials and limits of algorithmic experience as a critical design concept. In: Lamas, D., Sarapuu, H., Šmorgun, I., Berget, G. (eds.) Proceedings of the 11th Nordic Conference on Human-Computer Interaction: Shaping Experiences, Shaping Society. NordiCHI 2020: Shaping Experiences, Shaping Society, Tallinn Estonia, 25 10 2020–29 10 2020, pp. 1–12. ACM, New York, NY, USA (2020). https://doi.org/10.1145/3419249.3420120

12. Bhabha, H.K.: The Location of Culture. Routledge, London, New York (1994)

13. Dourish, P.: Implications for design. In: Grinter, R., Rodden, T., Aoki, P., Cutrell, E., Jeffries, R., Olson, G. (eds.) Proceedings of the SIGCHI Conference on Human Factors in Computing Systems. CHI06: CHI 2006 Conference on Human Factors in Computing Systems, Montréal Québec Canada, 22 04 2006–27 04 2006, pp. 541–550. ACM, New York, NY, USA (2006). https://doi.org/10.1145/1124772.1124855

14. Muller, M., Druin, A.: Participatory design: the third space in HCI. Handbook of HCI, pp. 1–71 (2002)

15. Mitchell, K.: Different diasporas and the hype of hybridity. Environ. Plan. D: Soc. Space (1997). https://doi.org/10.1068/d150533

16. Twine, F.W., Werbner, P., Modood, T.: Debating cultural hybridity: multi-cultural identities and the politics of anti-racism. Contemp. Sociol. (2000). https://doi.org/10.2307/2654960

17. Irani, L., Vertesi, J., Dourish, P., Philip, K., Grinter, R.E.: Postcolonial computing: a lens on design and development. In: Mynatt, E., Schoner, D., Fitzpatrick, G., Hudson, S., Edwards, K., Rodden, T. (eds.) Proceedings of the 28th International Conference on Human Factors in Computing Systems – CHI 2010, Atlanta, Georgia, USA, 10 4 2010–15 4 2010, pp. 1311–1320. ACM Press, New York, New York, USA (2010). https://doi.org/10.1145/1753326.1753522

18. Ali, S.M.: A brief introduction to decolonial computing. XRDS (2016). https://doi.org/10.1145/2930886

19. Proceedings of the 31st Australian Conference on Human-Computer-Interaction. OZCHI2019, Fremantle, WA, Australia, 02 12 2019–05 12 2019. ACM, New York, NY, USA (2019)

20. Winschiers-Theophilus, H., Bidwell, N.J.: Toward an Afro-centric indigenous HCI paradigm. Int. J. Hum.-Compt. Interaction (2013). https://doi.org/10.1080/10447318.2013.765763

21. Anzalduá, G.: Borderlands/La frontera: The new Mestiza, 4th edn. Aunt Lute Books, San Francisco (2012 [1987])

22. Haraway, D.J.: A cyborg manifesto. Technology and socialist feminism in the late twentieth century. In: Simians, Cyborgs and Women. The Reinvention of Nature, pp. 149–181. Routledge, New York (1991)

23. Haraway, D.J.: Simians, Cyborgs and Women. The Reinvention of Nature. Routledge, New York (1991)

24. Haraway, D.: Situated knowledges: the science question in feminism and the privilege of partial perspective. Fem. Stud. (1988). https://doi.org/10.2307/3178066

25. Gutiérrez, K.D., Baquedano-López, P., Tejeda, C.: Rethinking diversity: hybridity and hybrid language practices in the third space. Mind Cult. Act. **6**, 286–303 (1999)

26. James, K.: Elmborg: libraries as the spaces between us: recognizing and valuing the third space. Ref. User Ser. Quar. **50**, 338–350 (2011)

27. Ismail, A., Karusala, N., Kumar, N.: Bridging disconnected knowledges for community health. Proc. ACM Hum.-Comput. Interact. (2018). https://doi.org/10.1145/3274344

28. Westerlaken, M., Gualeni, S.: Becoming with. In: Mancini, C. (ed.) Proceedings of the Third International Conference on Animal-Computer Interaction. ACI 2016, Milton Keynes United Kingdom, 15 11 2016–17 11 2016, pp. 1–10. ACM, New York, NY, USA (2016). https://doi.org/10.1145/2995257.2995392

29. Hsu, A., Kemper, S.. The hybrid body and sonic cyborg performance in why should our bodies end at the skin? In: Kuznetsov, S., Saakes, D., Wakkary, R., Geurts, L., Hayes, L., Lau, M. (eds.) Proceedings of the Thirteenth International Conference on Tangible, Embedded, and Embodied Interaction. TEI 2019, Tempe, Arizona, USA, 17 03 2019–20 03 2019, pp. 547–551. ACM, New York, NY, USA (2019). https://doi.org/10.1145/3294109.3301255

30. Wagman, K.B., Parks, L.: Beyond the command: feminist STS research and critical issues for the design of social machines. Proc. ACM Hum.-Comput. Interact. (2021). https://doi.org/10.1145/3449175

31. Muller, M.J.: Participatory design: the third space in HCI. In: The Human-Computer Interaction Handbook: Fundamentals, Evolving Technologies and Emerging Applications, pp. 1051–1068. L. Erlbaum Associates Inc., USA (2002)

32. Bannon, L., Bardzell, J., Bødker, S.: Reimagining participatory design. Interactions (2018). https://doi.org/10.1145/3292015

33. Hellige, H.D. (ed.): Geschichten der Informatik. Visionen, Paradigmen, Leitmotive. Springer, Berlin (2004)

34. Andersen, P.B., Nake, F.: Computers and signs. Prolegomena to a Semiotic Foundation of Computing Science, 1st edn. Digital Horizons, vol. 3. Synchron, Heidelberg (2007)

35. Nadin, M.: Semiotic machine. Pub. J. Semiotics (2007). https://doi.org/10.37693/pjos.2007.1.8815

36. Wulf, V., Pipek, V., Randall, D., Rohde, M., Schmidt, K., Stevens, G. (eds.): Socio-informatics. A Practice-based Perspective on the Design and Use of IT Artifacts. Oxford University Press, Oxford (2018)

37. Draude, C.: "Boundaries do not sit still". From interaction to agential intra-action in HCI. In: Kurosu, M. (ed.) Human-Computer Interaction. Design and User Experience. Thematic Area, HCI 2020, Held as Part of the 22nd International Conference, HCII 2020. HCII 2020, Copenhagen, Denmark, July 19–24, pp. 20–32. Springer International Publishing (2020)

38. Rheinberger, H.-J.: Experiment, Forschung, Kunst. Jahreskonferenz der Dramaturgischen Gesellschaft, Oldenburg. https://dramaturgische-gesellschaft.de/wp-content/uploads/2020/06/Hans-Joerg-Rheinberger-Experiment-Forschung-Kunst.pdf (2012). Accessed 4 Feb 2022

39. Borgdorff, H.: Artistic practice and epistemic things. In: Schwab, M. (ed.) Experimental Systems – Future Knowledge in Artistic Research, pp. 112–120. Leuven University Press, Leuven (2013)

40. Britton, L., Klumbyte, G., Draude, C.: Doing thinking: revisiting computing with artistic research and technofeminism. Digital Creativity (2019). https://doi.org/10.1080/14626268.2019.1684322

41. Ziewitz, M.: How to attend to screens? Technology, ontology and precarious enactments. Encounters **4**, 203–228 (2011)

42. Draude, C.: "Everything will be screen." Readdressing screenness through art-based experiments. In: Borgdorff, H., Peters, P., Pinch, T. (eds.) Dialogues Between Artistic Research and Science and Technology Studies, pp. 139–154. Routledge, London/New York (2019)

43. Bardzell, J., Bardzell, S., Koefoed Hansen, L.: Immodest proposals. In: Begole, B., Kim, J., Inkpen, K., Woo, W. (eds.) CHI 2015. Proceedings of the 33rd Annual CHI Conference on Human Factors in Computing Systems/sponsored by ACM SIGCHI. CHI 2015, Seoul, Republic of Korea, 18 04 2015–23 04 2015, pp. 2093–2102. The Association for Computing Machinery, New York, New York (2015). https://doi.org/10.1145/2702123.2702400

44. Klumbytė, G., Draude, C., Taylor, A.: Critical tools for machine learning: situating, figuring, diffracting, fabulating machine learning systems design. In: Angeli, A., et al.: (eds.) CHItaly 2021: 14th Biannual Conference of the Italian SIGCHI Chapter. CHItaly 2021, Bolzano, Italy, 11 07 2021–13 07 2021, pp. 1–2. ACM, New York, NY, USA (2021). https://doi.org/10.1145/3464385.3467475

45. Hill Collins, P.: Black Feminist Thought. Knowledge, Consciousness, and the Politics of Empowerment. Routledge, New York (1991)
46. Braidotti, R.: Nomadic subjects. Embodiment and Sexual Difference in Contemporary Feminist Theory, 2nd edn. Columbia University Press, New York, Chichester (2011)
47. Barad, K.: Meeting the Universe Halfway: Quantum Physics and the Entanglement of Matter. Duke University Press, Durham (2007)
48. Hartman, S.: Venus in two acts. Small Axe: Caribbean J. Criticism (2008). https://doi.org/10.1215/-12-2-1
49. Rosner, D.: Critical Fabulations. Reworking the Methods and Margins of Design. MIT Press, Cambridge, MA (2020)
50. Frodeman, R., Klein, J.T., Pacheco, R.C.S. (eds.): The Oxford Handbook of Interdisciplinarity. Oxford Handbooks. Oxford University Press, Oxford, United Kingdom (2017)
51. Liinason, M., van der Tuin, I. (eds.): Practising feminist interdisciplinarity. Special Issue. Graduate J. Soc. Sci. **2**(4), 1–10 (2007)
52. Moran, J.: Interdisciplinarity, 2nd edn. The New Critical Idiom. Routledge, London (2010)
53. Ratto, M., Rosner, D., Boeva, Y., Taylor, A.: Special issue on hybrid pedagogies editorial. Digital Creativity (2019). https://doi.org/10.1080/14626268.2019.1699576

A Survey on Automated Machine Learning: Problems, Methods and Frameworks

Dohyung Kim[ID], Jahwan Koo[(✉)][ID], and Ung-Mo Kim[ID]

College of Software, Sungkyunkwan University, Seobu-ro, Suwon, Gyeonggi-do 2066,
South Korea
{shape1248,jhkoo,ukim}@skku.edu

Abstract. Automated Machine Learning (AutoML) is a research field
that automates machine learning processes and optimizes their costs.
As machine learning begins to be widely used, many users in industry and academia are paying attention to AutoML. However, to satisfy
the different demands in their various fields, the AutoML systems have
been defined and studied differently according to several requirements.
This paper classifies various characteristics of the AutoML systems into
Hyperparameter Optimization (HPO), Combined Algorithm Search and
Hyperparameter Optimization (CASH), and Machine Learning Pipeline
Creation (MLPC) problems, and formulates their problem statements
in a similar fashion. Moreover, we review the methods and frameworks
widely used in the AutoML field in order to improve the practical understanding of the future direction of AutoML.

Keywords: Automated machine learning · Automl · Hyperparameter
optimization · Neural architecture search · Meta learning

1 Introduction

Automated Machine Learning (AutoML) system is a tool that assists data scientists by automating and optimizing repetitive tasks in the process of training a
machine learning (ML) model. The scope of automation has been extended from
hyperparameter optimization through grid search [23] in the 1990 s s to algorithm
selection [43] and pipeline generation [36]. Although most early AutoML frameworks explored classical machine learning techniques, recently studied Neural
Architecture Search (NAS) [50], which builds artificial neural network models
on their own and optimizes the learning process, is also part of AutoML. Beyond
helping data scientists, finding a novel architecture optimized for specific data
and tasks is also proposed through NAS [19].

Because of the great utility of automating the machine learning process in the
real world, various companies such as Google [31], H2O.ai [27], and Microsoft [42]
have deployed commercial AutoML tools. These commercial tools often add functions such as data collection and ML model deployment. On the other hand,

M. Kurosu (Ed.): HCII 2022, LNCS 13302, pp. 57–70, 2022.
https://doi.org/10.1007/978-3-031-05311-5_4

Neural Architecture Search [50] uses methodologies of AutoML to automatically create a neural architecture optimized for specific tasks like image classification, and aims to compete with architectures created by human experts. As a result, some NAS models show state-of-the-art performance for a specific image classification data set [6]. This paper aims to generalize several problem definitions and methodologies of AutoML used in various fields and formulate them, identify the differences and characteristics of each method, and review the major open-source AutoML frameworks and researches.

In Sect. 2, we formulate the hyperparameter optimization, CASH problem, and machine learning pipeline creation problem in the flow of expanding the searching space. Section 3 deals with the main methodologies that make up AutoML. Section 4 introduces the major existing AutoML frameworks. And in Sect. 5, we propose the future direction of AutoML research.

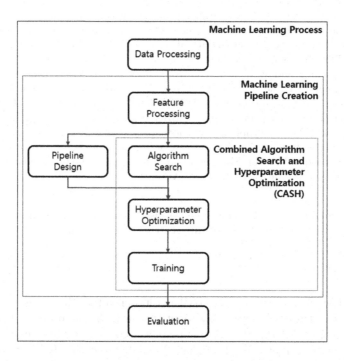

Fig. 1. AutoML problem definitions with machine learning process components.

2   Problem Statement

Zoller and Huber [49] viewed AutoML as a problem that combines Structure Search, Algorithm Selection, and Hyperparameter Optimization. Figure 1 shows the scope of these problems in a typical machine learning process from Data Processing to Evaluation. Early AutoML studies tried to treat the algorithm selection [13,24,43] or algorithm selection with structure selection problem [32,36] as an extension of the HPO problem and then solve them using HPO meth ods [2,45]. However, several studies on AutoML have their own problem defini- tion depending on whether some optional processes are applied such as feature extraction [24], pipeline generation [36], cell-based architecture [51], and super- model [30]. Therefore, in this section, we formulate a general problem definition that can cover most AutoML studies, from hyperparameter optimization to neu- ral architecture search.

2.1 Hyperparameter Optimization (HPO) Problem

Let a machine learning algorithm $\mathcal{A}$, data D consisting of feature x and tar- get y, and loss function $\mathcal{L}$ for evaluating the performance of the algorithm be given. The configuration space Λ is a domain space of the hyperparameter set λ that algorithm $\mathcal{A}$ can have. When the algorithm defined by λ is called $\mathcal{A}_\lambda$, the hyperparameter optimization problem is defined as Eq. 1.

$$\lambda^* = \arg\min_{\lambda \in \Lambda} V(\mathcal{L}, \mathcal{A}_\lambda, D_{train}, D_{valid}) \tag{1}$$

$$V(\mathcal{L}, \mathcal{A}_\lambda, D_{train}, D_{test}) = \mathcal{L}(y_{valid}, \mathcal{A}_\lambda^*(x_{valid}))$$

where $\mathcal{A}_\lambda^*$ is machine learning algorithm $\mathcal{A}_\lambda$ trained with D_{train}.

Each hyperparameter included in λ can be a real value, an integer value, or a categorical value. In addition, real and integer value hyperparameters can be distinguished whether the distances in the configuration space are uniform or log scale.

It is necessary to build a validation set D_{valid} based on given data D to estimate the distribution of D_{test}. Also, cross validation method is often used as a method to generate D_{train} and D_{valid}.

2.2 Combined Algorithm Selection and Hyperparameter Optimization (CASH) Problem

CASH problem [43] is a problem that combines hyperparameter optimization and algorithm selection. In CASH problem, unlike the HPO's problem defi- nition, data D, loss function $\mathcal{L}$, and a set of K different domain algorithms $A = \{\mathcal{A}^{(1)}, \mathcal{A}^{(2)}, \cdots, \mathcal{A}^{(k)}\}$ are given. Algorithm $\mathcal{A}^{(i)}$ has its own configuration space $\Lambda^{(i)}$. CASH problem can be formulated as an extension of HPO problem, becomes the following Eq. 2.

$$\mathcal{A}_{\lambda^*}^* = \arg\min_{\lambda \in \Lambda, \mathcal{A} \in A} V(\mathcal{L}, \mathcal{A}_\lambda, D_{train}, D_{valid}) \tag{2}$$

A CASH solving method should find the optimal algorithm in the domain algorithm set A, and at the same time find the optimal hyperparameter set λ^* for the optimal algorithm.

In addition, suppose that the algorithm $\mathcal{A}^{(a)}$ is determined by one categor- ical hyperparameter a having a value between 1 and K. In this case, the new configuration set λ_{CASH} is the combination of algorithm selection hyperparameter a and the algorithm's hyperparameter set λ_A, and the configuration space $\Lambda_{CASH} = \Lambda \times \{1, 2, \cdots, K\}$, and the formula Eq. 2 has the same form as Eq. 1. However, there is a problem that Λ changes depending on the selected algorithm. One solution is constructing global configuration space that combines all the configuration spaces of all algorithms [13, 24, 43].

2.3 Machine Learning Pipeline Creation (MLPC) Problem

A full machine learning process is not limited to training single or parallel algorithms. As a view of the data flow, ML pipeline can be a sequential flow of preprocessing, machine learning model, and evaluation. To describe this sequential flow, the ML pipeline can also be expressed in the form of a graph in which several ML algorithms are connected in parallel or sequentially. Assume that the ML pipeline $\mathcal{P}$ is a graph in which has N nodes and directed edges are defined as $\mathcal{G}$. The content of each node is an ML algorithm, selected by an N-dimensional algorithm selection vector $\vec{a}$. And when edge $(p, q) \in \mathcal{G}$, the output y_p of $\mathcal{A}^{(a^{(p)})}$ is used for the input x_q of $\mathcal{A}^{(a^{(q)})}$. Except for some studies using the concatenation operator[36] and the fixed output operator of cell structure-based NAS[6,30], the input and output of each node are defined as Eq. 3 and Eq. 4. With given $\vec{\lambda}, \vec{a}, A$,

$$y^{(i)} = \mathcal{A}^{(a^{(i)})}_{\lambda^{(i)}}(x^{(i)}) \tag{3}$$

$$x^{(i)} = \sum_{(j,i)\in\mathcal{G}} y^{(j)} = \sum_{(j,i)\in\mathcal{G}} \mathcal{A}^{(a^{(j)})}_{\lambda^{(j)}}(x^{(j)}) \tag{4}$$

In addition, the ML pipeline does not have cyclic structure so the ML pipeline graph is a directed acyclic graph (DAG), and there are no edges pointing to the start node $\mathcal{A}^{(1)}$ and no edges pointing to the end node $\mathcal{A}^{(n)}$. Therefore, when defining the ML pipeline $\mathcal{P}$ as $y = \mathcal{P}_{\vec{a}, \mathcal{G}, \vec{\lambda}}(x)$, input value of the starting node $\mathcal{A}^{(1)}$ is $x^{(1)} = x$ and $y^{(n)} = y$. Note that the feature extraction method that does not require training and the activation function can also be viewed as an algorithm with weight $w = \emptyset$.

Now, MLPC problem is defined as a extension of CASH problem, which is the problem of finding $(\vec{a}^*, \mathcal{G}^*, \vec{\lambda}^*)$ that satisfying Eq. 5

$$\mathcal{P}^*_{\vec{a}^*, \mathcal{G}^*, \vec{\lambda}^*} = \underset{\vec{a}, \mathcal{G}, \vec{\lambda} \in \Lambda}{\arg\min} V(\mathcal{L}, \mathcal{P}_{\vec{a}, \mathcal{G}, \vec{\lambda}}, D_{train}, D_{valid}) \tag{5}$$

Following the form of this equation, the HPO problem is a special case where $\dim \vec{a} = 1$ and number of candidate algorithm $n(A) = 1$. And the CASH problem corresponds to the special case of the MLPC problem where $\dim \vec{a} = 1$, and if the preprocessing methods are also included in optimization object[13, 24], it can be interpreted as a pipeline creation problem with $\dim \vec{a} = 2$ with fixed graph $\mathcal{G}$.

Since the entire domain space of the graph shape $\mathcal{G}$ is too large to search, there are some techniques that define each node as a layer with different roles (e.g. data preprocessing layer, feature extraction layer, classification layer) and fix the graph [13,35], or a method to perform pipeline creation by reducing the domain space of $\mathcal{G}$ [30,51] to frequently used neural network architectures such as cell-based architecture with skip-connection [18,20] are being used.

3 Methodology

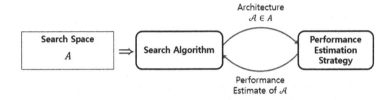

Fig. 2. The components of neural architecture search [10].

Elsken, et al. [10] described the methodology of NAS as Fig. 2, which can be similarly applied to AutoML. Both algorithm selection and pipeline generation in the CASH and MLPC problems are determined by configuration parameters, so every search space that can be created in the AutoML framework is given as a set of hyperparameter. From this search space, a search algorithm selects one configuration, and the performance of the configuration will be given by the performance estimation strategy. By the observations, the search algorithm chooses a better-performed configuration. One different thing is that NAS has some gradient descent-based search strategy [30], while hyperparameters of traditional ML algorithms that AutoML uses are often non-differentiable, so sequential model-based optimization methods (SMBO) [2,45], genetic algorithm [36], and random search [27] are used.

3.1 Search Space

The most commonly used search space definition is the CASH problem, which is expressed as a set of algorithms and their hyperparameters [43]. The most considered additional configuration is a set of preprocessors [24]. There also exist optional operations such as a set of ensemble methods [13], optimizers and schedulers [32].

Preprocessors are divided into data processing method and feature extraction method, and data processing can be divided into cleaning and transformation. The components to be considered in each step are shown in Table 1.

Table 1. Components of preprocessor in AutoML architecture.

Phases	Components	Methods
Data cleaning	Error data detection	Null value, Anomaly detection
	Error data repairing	Univariate feature imputation
		Feature prediction, Deletion
Data transformation	Encoding	One-hot encoding, Label encoding
	Scaling	MinMax Scaling, Standard Scaling
		RobustScaling, Normalization
		Whitening
Feature extraction	Numeric	PCA, Backward/forward elimination
	Textual	TF-IDF, Word Embedding

Data cleaning is very important when dealing with real data, but in the field of AutoML, only a few systems [13] provide hard-coded data cleaning.

Meanwhile, data transformation methods such as scaling and normalization are mainly considered in AutoML systems [13,24,32] because machine learning methods have different sensitivity to scaling according to their characteristics. For example, methods such as Naïve Bayes and Random Forest are not significantly affected by the scale difference between features, whereas Support Vector Machine (SVM) and Multi Layer Perceptron (MLP) are sensitive to scale and require preprocessing. Since most supervised machine learning methods require numeric values as input data, it is necessary to convert textual features into categorical data through one-hot encoding.

Automatic optimization of feature engineering methods is also provided in most AutoML frameworks. Most frameworks only provide PCA method for unsupervised feature engineering, but some frameworks consider feature extraction for text data through TF-IDF [13,24], or word embedding methods [27] such as Word2Vec [34].

Most AutoML systems and studies have been focused on classification and regression tasks. Therefore, algorithms that are mainly considered as ML models are divided into classifiers and regressors. Except for neural architecture, the classical ML algorithms that are often considered are shown in Table 2. Since many Automl frameworks are based on existing open-source machine learning tools such as WEKA [16], Scikit-learn [38], Pytorch [37], and Keras [7], classifiers and regressors that frameworks provided are dependent on their machine learning tools.

3.2   Search Algorithm

The main methods, algorithms, and studies used to solve CASH problem are shown in Table 3.

Table 2. Components of machine learning models in AutoML architecture.

Phases	Components	Methods
Classifier	Statistical method	KNN, Naïve Bayes
	Tree-based method	Decision tree, Random forest
	Ensemble	Bagging, Boosting
	Others	SVM, SGD, Gaussian Process Classifier
Regressor	Statistical method	KNN
	Tree-based method	Decision tree, Random forest
	Ensemble	Bagging, Boosting
	Others	SVM, SGD, Gaussian Process Regressor

Table 3. Methods, algorithms and studies for solving CASH problem.

Method	Algorithm	Studies
Random search	Random Search	[27],[3]
Population-based search	Genetic Algorithm	[36]
	Evolutionary Algorithm	[1],[17]
Sequential Model-based Optimization(SMBO)	Gaussian Processing	[43],[5],[11],[48],[13]
	Tree-based Parzen Estimator	[2],[4],[24]

Random Search is a method that randomly chooses a configuration from a search space. Since vanilla random search algorithm [3] is the simplest search algorithm, it is used as a baseline algorithm. Random search often gives better results than grid search algorithm, because it tests more various configurations freely, while grid search sets strict small set of variation on each hyperparameter and test every combinations [12]. Fig. 3 shows an example of how grid search and random search work. When a total of 9 searching chances are provided on a search space in which two hyperparameters exist, grid search can search only 3 values for each hyperparameter, whereas random search can search 9 different values and can find more optimal solution. Moreover, in the neural architecture search field, there is a study that even a model trained with complex algorithms such as reinforcement learning and the evolutionary algorithm does not show a significantly better performance than a random search-based NAS model with early stopping [28].

Population-Based Search. In population-based search, genetic algorithms and evolutionary algorithms are mainly used. TPOT [36] used a genetic algorithm to ML pipeline creation for the first time. It generates a tree-like ML pipeline and grows the tree by genetic programming. On the other side, the evolutionary algorithm like CMA-ES [17] construct a generation that contains several different configurations selected by random search. After training and

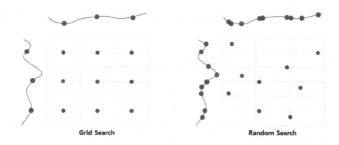

Fig. 3. Comparison between grid search and random search algorithm.

evaluating them in parallel, the distribution of the next generation is generated based on highly performed configurations. The next generation is generated by a weighted random search according to the distribution obtained.

Sequential Model-Based Optimization (SMBO). Since the cost of model training and evaluation process is high, SMBO builds a surrogate model to predict the evaluation result of the model and chooses the next observation point by an acquisition function based on the result of the surrogate model. Representative SMBO methods used in HPO include Gaussian Process (GP) and Tree-based Parzen Estimator (TPE). However, since the search space of AutoML is much larger than that of HPO, a modified form to respond to high-dimensional HPO such as SMAC framework with random forest [13,43] is used.

Other Approaches Used in Neural Architecture Search. In neural architecture search, in addition to random search and SMBO, reinforcement learning (RL) based methods [9,50,51] are also used. The RL-based method is a method that can be used to solve non-differentiable optimization problems such as HPO. Since the objective of the RL algorithm is to find the best policy by training the policy controller with simulating a given environment, we can use the RL approach in AutoML by setting a search algorithm as the controller, a generated ML pipeline as the environment and evaluation result $V(\mathcal{L}, \mathcal{P}_{\vec{a},\mathcal{G},\vec{\lambda}}, D_{train}, D_{valid})$ as the reward of simulation. The reinforcement learning-based methodology has a problem that it took too long to learn, but ENAS [39] improves the learning speed to be competitive through a weight sharing technique.

In the case of gradient descent-based neural architecture search methods [6, 30], instead of letting the categorical hyperparameter selects the algorithm, they define a supermodel in which all algorithm candidates are connected in parallel, train this supermodel, and finally select the best candidate for each node. This also obtained a competitive speed through the weight sharing technique, but there is a study that the weight sharing-based model is greatly affected by the random initial value, and thus the performance variation is high [47].

3.3 Cost Efficiency

As the number of data gets increases and the number of data features get increases, the cost of training an ML model sometimes requires tens of days even if the computation is accelerated using GPU [26,50]. In particular, except for using warm-starting methods using meta-learning [13,15], the AutoML system should consider the training and evaluation cost more important than normal supervised learning because they require at least dozens of training and performance observations. One good solution is the consideration of multi-fidelity methods, which is a method of giving different times for each configuration, allocates computing resources differently according to the potential performance estimation of different configurations [8,41].

First of all, the simplest way to deal with the cost efficiency is to add a time limit, which is a method that the AutoML system runs until the time limit given by the user and returns the best model searched. Many AutoML frameworks simply adopt the time limit method and do not consider optimization (See Table 4).

As a method to consider multi-fidelity, there is a method that estimates the final performance by learning curve in the stage of model training, and terminates the configuration if the estimated final performance is lower than the existing best observation [8]. Auto-Sklearn has a similar approach in the validation stage, which terminates the configurations that are evaluated as poor performance while cross-validation is running.

Successive Halving (SH) [21], another method that considers multi-fidelity, is a bandit-based approach. This is a method while parallel training is ongoing, which leaves only the model with the best learning curve and excludes the rest. The SH algorithm has a problem that large and heavy models with poor initial learning curves can be ignored, but it can observe the performances on much more configuration sets with low fidelity evaluations compared to the existing timeout method. AutoNet2.0 [33] and AutoPytorch [48] use BOHB [11], which combines one of the SH methods, Hyperband [29] and Bayesian Optimization, to implement AutoML including neural network architecture with a large search space. In NAS, there is another method that uses short-term fine-tuning [46], which trains a lot of models with a small subset of the data set and only a small number of iterations, and then only the model with the highest evaluation accuracy remains for long-term fine-tuning.

4 Frameworks

Many AutoML studies are developed as open-source frameworks to take scalability and productivity. This section introduces the major AutoML Frameworks. The summary is shown in Table 4 below.

Table 4. Popular AutoML frameworks. "explicit" means the framework can support the type, but requires explicit user input. The meaning that the framework can get image type as an input is the framework supports some computer vision algorithms.

Framework	Available Input Types	Preprocessing	Model Structure	Strategy	Cost Optimization
AutoWEKA	Numeric Categorical	-	Fixed +Ensemble	SMAC+random forest	Time limitation
Hyperopt-Sklearn	Numeric Text(explicit)	Automatic Optimization	Fixed	Hyperopt	Time limitation
Auto-Sklearn	Numeric Categorical(explicit) Text(explicit)	Automatic Optimization	Fixed +Ensemble	SMAC+random forest Meta-learning based warm starting	Time limitation
H2O	Numeric Categorical Text(explicit)	-	Fixed +Ensemble	Random Search	Time limitation
TPOT	Numeric	Automatic Optimization	Automatic Generation	Genetic Programming	Time limitation
Auto-Keras	Numeric Categorical Image(explicit) Text(explicit)	Fixed	Automatic Generation	Network Morphism + Bayesian Optimization	Time limitation
Auto-Pytorch	Numeric Categorical Text(explicit)	Automatic Optimization	Automatic Generation	BOHB	Hyperband

AutoWEKA [43] is a framework that first proposed the CASH problem, and therefore it is considered the first AutoML framework. AutoWEKA is based on WEKA [16], a JAVA data mining software, and is continuously updated [25]. AutoWEKA solves the CASH problem with Bayesian optimization and random forest and finds the optimized algorithm and its hyperparameters with several ensemble methods.

Hyperopt-Sklearn [24] is based on Scikit-learn [38], a widely used python ML library, and at the same time solves the CASH problem by using Hyperopt [4], a python HPO library. Hyperopt-Sklearn divides the ML pipeline into a preprocessing layer and an ML layer to search for an optimal pair of preprocessors and models.

Auto-Sklearn [13] is based on Scikit-learn. Bayesian optimization is solved using SMAC with random forest like AutoWEKA, and the most powerful differentiator of Auto-Sklearn is that it has a method to predict an initial configuration optimized for a given data set using meta-learning to enable warm starting.

H2O [27] is one of the most widely used AutoML frameworks and solves the CASH problem using only a simple random search. Although several preprocessing methods are given, there is no function to automatically optimize them. H2O supports several ensemble methods that automatically optimize the model.

TPOT [36] is an AutoML framework that supports machine learning pipeline creation by utilizing genetic programming. TPOT builds the pipeline in a way that creates a tree with all nodes such as preprocessing operation, hyperparameter, machine learning model, and ensemble operation.

Auto-Keras [22] is an AutoML library based on Keras [7], a deep learning library of python, and is particularly oriented to NAS. It builds a pipeline in the form of stacking neural network kernels using network morphism [44]. Like

NAS-related studies [30,50], It has a fixed preprocessing method and does not consider traditional ML algorithms.

Auto-Pytorch [48] is based on Pytorch [37], a deep learning library of python, and is a successor of Auto-Net [32,33]. It is NAS-oriented, and at the same time, it implements a cost efficient training process by optimizing multi-fidelity using BOHB [11]. In addition, the pre-processing method can also be optimized by optimizing the preprocessors.

5 Future Direction

So far, many AutoML studies have been carried out and have provided useful solutions to hyperparameter optimization and CASH problems. However, existing AutoML frameworks have only automated a small portion of the overall machine learning pipeline. Most frameworks can only handle numeric data and categorical data without additional user specifications. Also, there are various data cleaning methods that have to consider such as data deletion, substitution (e.g. mean value, mode value, zero, KNN), and prediction (e.g. regression, interpolation).

The problem of cost efficiency has not been considered much yet in AutoML. Most frameworks use the time limitation method, which does not affect the learning algorithm separately, so optimization for a given time, computing resource, etc. is not performed. On the other hand, in neural architecture search, there are some studies that propose the algorithm to improve training speed [39], but cost management has not received attention.

In addition, many NAS frameworks have a clear different search space from the traditional ML algorithm-based AutoML, so studies on deep learning-based AutoML corresponding to various data types are few. Traditional AutoML systems usually consider dozens of different machine learning algorithms and their different hyperparameters while does not consider pipeline creation. On the other hand, NAS considers pipeline creation, but only about 5 to 7 operations, which are mostly convolutional neural networks (CNN), are considered for search efficiency. This limitation makes the NAS study focus on a single specific task(e.g. image classification) and hard to apply in other tasks as much as the existing generalized traditional ML algorithm-based AutoML. It is necessary to study how to efficiently reduce the search space while responding to various tasks.

When labeled data is insufficient in reality, methods such as semi-supervised learning and a few shot learning are used, but autoML is currently oriented only to supervised classification and regression, so it is necessary to expand the task. Like meta-learning-based few-shot learning approaches [14,40], meta-learning-based pre-processing methods such as data augmentation could be considered in the AutoML system.

Acknowledgements. This research was supported by Basic Science Research Program through the National Research Foundation of Korea (NRF) funded by the Ministry of Education (2021R1I1A1A01052299).

References

1. Angeline, P.J., Saunders, G.M., Pollack, J.B.: An evolutionary algorithm that constructs recurrent neural networks. IEEE Trans. Neural Networks **5**(1), 54–65 (1994)
2. Bergstra, J., Bardenet, R., Bengio, Y., Kégl, B.: Algorithms for hyper-parameter optimization. Adv. Neural. Inf. Process. Syst. **24**, 2546–2554 (2011)
3. Bergstra, J., Bengio, Y.: Random search for hyper-parameter optimization. J. Mach. Learn. Res. **13**(2), 281–305 (2012)
4. Bergstra, J., Yamins, D., Cox, D.D., et al.: Hyperopt: a python library for optimizing the hyperparameters of machine learning algorithms. In: Proceedings of the 12th Python in Science Conference, vol. 13, p. 20, Citeseer (2013)
5. Bergstra, J., Yamins, D., Cox, D.: Making a science of model search: hyperparameter optimization in hundreds of dimensions for vision architectures. In: International Conference on Machine Learning, PMLR, pp. 115–123 (2013)
6. Cai, H., Zhu, L., Han, S.: ProxylessNAS: direct neural architecture search on target task and hardware (2018). arXiv preprint arXiv:1812.00332
7. Chollet, F., et al.: Keras (2015). https://github.com/fchollet/keras
8. Domhan, T., Springenberg, J.T., Hutter, F.: Speeding up automatic hyperparameter optimization of deep neural networks by extrapolation of learning curves. In: Twenty-Fourth International Joint Conference on Artificial Intelligence (2015)
9. Drori, I., Krishnamurthy, Y., et al.: AlphaD3M: machine learning pipeline synthesis. arXiv preprint arXiv:2111.02508 (2021)
10. Elsken, T., Metzen, J.H., Hutter, F.: Neural architecture search: a survey. J. Mach. Learn. Res. **20**(1), 1997–2017 (2019)
11. Falkner, S., Klein, A., Hutter, F.: BOHB: robust and efficient hyperparameter optimization at scale. In: International Conference on Machine Learning, PMLR, pp. 1437–1446 (2018)
12. Feurer, M., Hutter, F.: Hyperparameter optimization. In: Hutter, F., Kotthoff, L., Vanschoren, J. (eds.) Automated Machine Learning. TSSCML, pp. 3–33. Springer, Cham (2019). https://doi.org/10.1007/978-3-030-05318-5_1
13. Feurer, M., Klein, A., Eggensperger, K., Springenberg, J., Blum, M., Hutter, F.: Efficient and robust automated machine learning. Adv. Neur. Inf. Process. Syst. **28**, 2755–2763 (2015)
14. Finn, C., Abbeel, P., Levine, S.: Model-agnostic meta-learning for fast adaptation of deep networks. In: International Conference on Machine Learning, PMLR, pp. 1126–1135 (2017)
15. Guerra, S.B., Prudêncio, R.B.C., Ludermir, T.B.: Predicting the performance of learning algorithms using support vector machines as meta-regressors. In: Kůrková, V., Neruda, R., Koutník, J. (eds.) ICANN 2008. LNCS, vol. 5163, pp. 523–532. Springer, Heidelberg (2008). https://doi.org/10.1007/978-3-540-87536-9_54
16. Hall, M., Frank, E., Holmes, G., Pfahringer, B., Reutemann, P., Witten, I.H.: The weka data mining software: an update. ACM SIGKDD Explor. Newsl **11**(1), 10–18 (2009)
17. Hansen, N.: The CMA evolution strategy: a tutorial. arXiv preprint arXiv:1604.00772 (2016)
18. He, K., Zhang, X., Ren, S., Sun, J.: Deep residual learning for image recognition. In: Proceedings of the IEEE Conference on Computer Vision and Pattern Recognition, pp. 770–778 (2016)
19. Howard, A., et al.: Searching for MobileNetV3. In: Proceedings of the IEEE/CVF International Conference on Computer Vision, pp. 1314–1324 (2019)

20. Howard, A.G., et al.: MobileNets: efficient convolutional neural networks for mobile vision applications. arXiv preprint arXiv:1704.04861 (2017)
21. Jamieson, K., Talwalkar, A.: Non-stochastic best arm identification and hyperparameter optimization. In: Artificial intelligence and statistics, PMLR, pp. 240–248 (2016)
22. Jin, H., Song, Q., Hu, X.: Auto-Keras: an efficient neural architecture search system. In: Proceedings of the 25th ACM SIGKDD International Conference on Knowledge Discovery & Data Mining, pp. 1946–1956 (2019)
23. Kohavi, R., John, G.H.: Automatic parameter selection by minimizing estimated error. In: Machine Learning Proceedings 1995, pp. 304–312. Elsevier (1995)
24. Komer, B., Bergstra, J., Eliasmith, C.: Hyperopt-sklearn: automatic hyperparameter configuration for scikit-learn. In: ICML Workshop on AutoML, Citeseer, vol. 9, p. 50 (2014)
25. Kotthoff, L., Thornton, C., Hoos, H.H., Hutter, F., Leyton-Brown, K.: Auto-WEKA: automatic model selection and hyperparameter optimization in WEKA. In: Automated Machine Learning, pp. 81–95. Springer, Cham (2019)
26. Krizhevsky, A., Sutskever, I., Hinton, G.E.: ImageNet classification with deep convolutional neural networks. Adv. Neur. Inf. Process. Syst. **25** (2012)
27. LeDell, E., Poirier, S.: H2O AutoML: scalable automatic machine learning. In: Proceedings of the AutoML Workshop at ICML, vol. 2020 (2020)
28. Li, L., Talwalkar, A.: Random search and reproducibility for neural architecture search. In: Uncertainty in Artificial Intelligence, PMLR, pp. 367–377 (2020)
29. Li, L., Jamieson, K., DeSalvo, G., Rostamizadeh, A., Talwalkar, A.: Hyperband: a novel bandit-based approach to hyperparameter optimization. J. Mach. Learn. Res. **18**(1), 6765–6816 (2017)
30. Liu, H., Simonyan, K., Yang, Y.: Darts: differentiable architecture search. arXiv preprint arXiv:1806.09055 (2018)
31. Lu, Y.: An end-to-end automl solution for tabular data at kaggledays (2019). https://ai.googleblog.com/2019/05/an-end-to-end-automl-solution-for.html
32. Mendoza, H., Klein, A., Feurer, M., Springenberg, J.T., Hutter, F.: Towards automatically-tuned neural networks. In: Workshop on Automatic Machine Learning, PMLR, pp. 58–65 (2016)
33. Mendoza, H., et al.: Towards automatically-tuned deep neural networks. In: Hutter, F., Kotthoff, L., Vanschoren, J. (eds.) Automated Machine Learning. TSSCML, pp. 135–149. Springer, Cham (2019). https://doi.org/10.1007/978-3-030-05318-5_7
34. Mikolov, T., Sutskever, I., Chen, K., Corrado, G.S., Dean, J.: Distributed representations of words and phrases and their compositionality. Adv. Neural. Inf. Process. Syst. **26**, 3111–3119 (2013)
35. Nguyen, P., Hilario, M., Kalousis, A.: Using meta-mining to support data mining workflow planning and optimization. J. Artif. Intell. Res. **51**, 605–644 (2014)
36. Olson, R.S., Moore, J.H.: TPOT: a tree-based pipeline optimization tool for automating machine learning. In: Workshop on Automatic Machine Learning, PMLR, pp. 66–74 (2016)
37. Paszke, A., et al.: PyTorch: an imperative style, high-performance deep learning library. Adv. Neural Inf. Process Syst. **32**, 8026–8037 (2019)
38. Pedregosa, F., et al.: Scikit-learn: machine learning in Python. J. Mach. Learn. Res. **12**, 2825–2830 (2011)
39. Pham, H., Guan, M., Zoph, B., Le, Q., Dean, J.: Efficient neural architecture search via parameters sharing. In: International Conference on Machine Learning, PMLR, pp. 4095–4104 (2018)

40. Snell, J., Swersky, K., Zemel, R.: Prototypical networks for few-shot learning. Adv. Neural Inf. Process. Syst. **30** (2017)
41. Sparks, E.R., Talwalkar, A., Haas, D., Franklin, M.J., Jordan, M.I., Kraska, T.: Automating model search for large scale machine learning. In: Proceedings of the Sixth ACM Symposium on Cloud Computing, pp. 368–380 (2015)
42. Team, A.: AzureML: anatomy of a machine learning service. In: Conference on Predictive APIs and Apps, PMLR, pp. 1–13 (2016)
43. Thornton, C., Hutter, F., Hoos, H.H., Leyton-Brown, K.: Auto-WEKA: combined selection and hyperparameter optimization of classification algorithms. In: Proceedings of the 19th ACM SIGKDD International Conference on Knowledge Discovery and Data Mining, pp. 847–855 (2013)
44. Wei, T., Wang, C., Rui, Y., Chen, C.W.: Network morphism. In: International Conference on Machine Learning, PMLR, pp. 564–572 (2016)
45. Williams, C.K., Rasmussen, C.E.: Gaussian Processes for Machine Learning, vol. 2, no. 3. MIT Press, Cambridge (2006)
46. Yang, T.J., et al.: NetAdapt: platform-aware neural network adaptation for mobile applications. In: Proceedings of the European Conference on Computer Vision, ECCV, pp. 285–300 (2018)
47. Yu, K., Sciuto, C., Jaggi, M., Musat, C., Salzmann, M.: Evaluating the search phase of neural architecture search. arXiv preprint arXiv:1902.08142 (2019)
48. Zimmer, L., Lindauer, M., Hutter, F.: Auto-PyTorch: multi-fidelity metalearning for efficient and robust AutoDL. IEEE Trans. Pattern Anal. Mach. Intell. **43**(9), 3079–3090 (2021)
49. Zöller, M.A., Huber, M.F.: Benchmark and survey of automated machine learning frameworks. J. Artif. Intell. Res. **70**, 409–472 (2021)
50. Zoph, B., Le, Q.V.: Neural architecture search with reinforcement learning. arXiv preprint arXiv:1611.01578 (2016)
51. Zoph, B., Vasudevan, V., Shlens, J., Le, Q.V.: Learning transferable architectures for scalable image recognition. In: Proceedings of the IEEE Conference on Computer Vision and Pattern Recognition, pp. 8697–8710 (2018)

Blending Learning Practice and Research for STEAM Education

Ming Ma, Yi Ji[✉], Yutong Liu, Sean Clark, and Dongjin Lin

School of Art and Design, Guangdong University of Technology, Yuexiu District of Dongfeng East Road No. 729, Guangzhou 510000, China
jiyi001@hotmail.com

Abstract. With the development of educational technology, the way of learning is changing at amazing high speed, and the traditional classroom is gradually shifting to the way of blending learning. In order to remove the dependence of STEAM education curriculum on offline teaching and the single online teaching content and form, this paper summarizes the present situation and advantages of blending teaching and STEAM education, and then expounds the necessity and importance of the combination of these two options. Therefore, based on the framework of STEAM education and the characteristics of blending teaching, this paper affords practical referenced implementation paths for the blending teaching model of STEAM education.

Keywords: Blending teaching mode · STEAM education · Cantonese porcelain

1 Introduction

In 2002, American scholars Smith J and Elliot Masier put forward the concept of blending learning, whose essence is combining traditional classroom teaching with online education to achieve complementary advantages [1]. After more than 20 years of development, domestic and foreign blending learning has been widely used in all kinds of education in our country. The paper named *The Education Informatization 2.0 Action Plan* as well as *the opinions on speeding up the Construction of High-level undergraduate Education and improving the ability of Talent training in an all-round way (2018)* promulgated by the Ministry of Education of China all clearly put forward that colleges and universities should actively explore the blending learning model. The focus of its research has risen from the level of technical support and application to the level of students' knowledge and ability acquisition [2]. There are mainly three implementation paths of blending learning: the construction and quality assurance of online curriculum resources, the organization and implementation of offline teaching as well as the identity and promotion of online teaching, and the feedback and evaluation of students' learning [3]. In terms of teaching content, domestic scholars prefer the research on the mixture of resources, mainly in the fields of higher education and vocational education [4]. The teaching form is mainly combined with other teaching methods or modern information technology, such as the combination of blending learning and MOOCs, the combination of blending learning and cloud classroom, the combination of blending learning and flipped classroom [5].

Generally speaking, the current blending learning model is still in the exploratory stage and exists some problems. The reform theory and practice need to be deepened. The incentive system has not yet been established or perfected. There is a general lack of overall planning and construction standards. Teachers' education and teaching ability needs to be improved, and teaching quality evaluation indicators lack of pertinence and so on.

2 The Necessity of the Application of Blending Learning in STEAM Education

2.1 Present Situation and Characteristics of STEAM Education

STEAM education, which originates from the educational concept of multidisciplinary integration in the United States, is the most characteristic educational theory at the beginning of the 21st century. As early as in 1986, the United States launched the STEAM education program, which focused on cultivating the comprehensive disciplinary ability of talents, including science, technology, engineering and mathematics. After that, the content of arts was added. Thus, STEAM education evolved [6]. STEAM education is characterized by the integration of multidisciplinary content, comprehensively using the knowledge and skills of different disciplines to solve practical problems, and adopting practical project-oriented team cooperation teaching form, independently inquiring learning teaching method, and paying attention to the feasibility of project achievement transformation and project practice, so as to cultivate students' ability of practice, innovation and inquiry [7]. It can be seen that the educational theory and characteristics of STEAM education pay too much attention to the offline practice.

At present, most of the STEAM education courses are mainly implemented in two places: educational and teaching institutions, innovative courses in school are the main bearing objects of offline teaching; online teaching is mainly based on online software skills such as Code mao [8], scratch [9] and so on. According to the literature research and desktop investigate and survey, this paper obtains the present situation and characteristics of STEAM education in the Chinese online and offline teaching market (Fig. 1).

	Online(experience based on skill operation)	Offline(practice based on subject inquiry learning)
learning goal	By learning visual programming(or the teaching and application of tools with interdisciplinary characteristics), we can enhance the understanding of different disciplines and improve the comprehensive literacy.	Through the practice based on subject inquiry learning, we can enhance the understanding of different disciplines and improve the comprehensive literacy.
learning form	Open community resources,online course teaching, and the practice of completing online multimedia projects through skills learning and application.	Theme exploration and comprehensive design project practice.
learning content	Thematic multimedia display design based on tool applications, such as games, animations, interactive posters, etc.	Exploratory preatice of cultural and creative products, experimental design and application, etc.
learning evaluation	Learner communication in an open community.	Work evaluation, teacher evaluation, process evaluation.

Fig. 1. Present situation of online and offline teaching in STEAM education.

2.2 The Advantages of Blending Learning

"Blended teaching" is a combination of multiple learning methods, mainly combining the advantages of traditional teaching and digital online teaching, making the two complementary advantages. Traditional offline learning is mainly teacher-centered, and students passively listen to lessons and have weak subjective initiative; however, online learning cannot implement face-to-face communication and practical guidance [10].

Enrich the Course Content and Improve the Ability of Autonomous Learning. The Internet-based learning platform of blending learning can greatly enrich the course content and make online courses become systematic learning resources that integrates text, animation, video, project practice and so on [9]. In teaching activities, teachers design relevant questions and tasks according to the curriculum teaching objectives. Students determine the learning content, define the learning process, think and explore independently and cooperate with their peers to find solutions to form personalized learning cognition. Students can learn how to consult relevant information and communicate effectively, and internalize the knowledge, so as to improve the ability of autonomous learning and lifelong learning [11].

Enrich the Form of Curriculum and Expand the Time and Space of Teaching. Blending learning can transcend the limitations of time and space under the utilization of internet technology [12] and expand learning content from textbooks to the internet; in the process of learning, teachers and students can interact online across time and space, point out the existing problems in time and share experience; At the end of online and offline teaching activities, teachers can get timely teaching feedback through diversified evaluation methods, so that students can better understand their own advantages and disadvantages [13].

Summary. To sum up, there are still limitations in the main teaching forms of STEAM education. Lack of practice in the online teaching form leads to the lack of multidisciplinary, interdisciplinary comprehensiveness and richness of the curriculum content. Meantime, the offline teaching form pays too much attention to the importance of hands-on practice, resulting in part of the content cannot be shown in an appropriate way. This over-dependent offline teaching form is limited by time and space. It is difficult to popularize on a large scale and lead to the phenomenon of education unfairness. Therefore, this paper will design the course content according to the thematic inquiry of STEAM education, combined with the advantages of blending learning, and put forward a spiral blending learning model. Based on the STEAM educational framework combined with meaningful learning goal classification, thematic learning content is classified, corresponding learning forms and teaching strategies are formulated according to different teaching objectives, and teaching evaluation is made.

3 The Design of Blending STEAM Education Mode

3.1 Set Curriculum Objectives

According to the degree of integration of curriculum content, the educational framework of STEAM is divided into: the lowest level is composed of courses such as specific science, technology, engineering, mathematics and so on, which are the basic disciplines of the whole STEAM curriculum; the second level is the specific discipline, which empha-sizes the inherent logical relationship between science, technology, engineering and mathematics; the third level is the discipline integration, that is, based on the integration of the four disciplines to form an independent STEM curriculum system and infiltrate arts and other humanities disciplines; the fourth level is the STEAM layer, that is, to cul-tivate interdisciplinary thinking and innovation ability on the basis of further integration of multiple disciplines; the top level is the overall integration, that is, beyond a single discipline, integrate all kinds of interdisciplinary knowledge, and apply it flexibly to cultivate interdisciplinary literacy and comprehensive ability to solve specific problems in complex situations [14].

According to the division standard of STEAM education framework, and combined with meaningful learning objectives, the learning objectives of knowledge are classi-fied into aspects of knowledge, application, integration, human, value and learning [15]. For the different requirements of knowledge classification, formulate different contents. Based on the concept of STEAM education, integrating cross-disciplinary and cross-disciplinary blending learning, creating a new normal of students' blending learning, new development ideas and models for current STEAM education are provide. The combination of blending learning improves the time and space limitation of STEAM education, enriches the educational form of STEAM, promotes innovation through edu-cational technology media, strengthens students' innovative consciousness and the abil-ity of self-exploration, induction and summary, analyzing and solving problems, as well as communication skills such as communication and expression, self-expression, evaluation of others and teamwork (Fig. 2).

	Explain	Common verbs	Teaching strategy	Evaluation method
Knowledge dimension	Understand and remember knowledge and information	Remember, understand, identify, list.	Make full use of extracurricular time to provide different types of resources related to classroom activities.	Traditional paper-and-pencil exams ask questions in class
Application dimension	Skills, thinking skills, project management	Use, criticize, manage, resolve, acquire, judge, imagine, analyze, calculate, manufacture, coordinate, solve problems, make decisions.	Provide sufficient practice to provide counter-indignation for practice.	Simulated situation Project(case) presentation Writing The activities of classroom test
Integration dimension	Connect ideas, learning experiences and real	Connect, determine the gap between the network, determine the similarities between the two, connect, compare, integrate.	Study different topics/subjects, Reflect on the relationship between different themes.	Reflective writing, Case analysis, interdisciplinary case Problem-based research, real situation
Human dimension	Know yourself and others, know society	Began to think of themselves as. Decided to start. It has something to do with communicating with others. Understand others at the level of... and be able to cooperate with others at...	Let students be in it and experience. the feelings of themselves and others. Talk to others and discover how they feel Combining feelings to reflect on personal growth and cooperation with others.	Personal reflection activity. Standardized questionnaires, such as self-confidence. Peer evaluation. Study portfolio (case study).
Value dimension	Develop new feelings and values	Be interested in..., ready to start..., become interested in..., value...	Ask students to think about the relationship between their feelings and the topic. Let students determine the next action plan	Personal reflection activity. Standardized questionnaires, such as self-confidence. Study portfolio (case study)
Learning dimension	Learn to learn better, subject learning ability, self-learning ability	Develop future learning plans and determine important sources of information, feel useful	Help students to learn better, but the knowledge structure of specific topics becomes self-directed learners	Reflection activities after learning activities, reflection activities after learning knowledge, learning portfolio (case study), including performance of learning projects

Fig. 2. Knowledge goal classification of meaningful learning objective.

3.2 Design of Blending Learning Mode

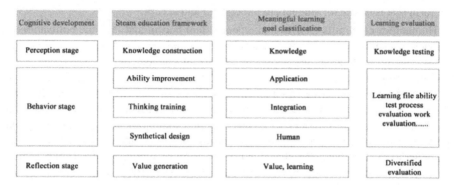

Fig. 3. Design of blending learning mode for STEAM education.

According to the different levels of requirements of knowledge and the attributes of teaching activities, students' cognitive development can be summarized and reduced to perception, behavior and reflection. Guided by the curriculum objectives [16], systematically designs the teaching content, learning situation and teaching methods. As shown in the table, the teaching content consists of five ladder modules: knowledge, application, integration, human, value and learning. Sort out the knowledge points of each module and create learning tasks for each teaching content module. Finally, according to the learning tasks to select project teaching methods, students independently explore to complete the learning tasks online and offline in the form of group cooperation, by using theoretical knowledge to solve design problems, and finally achieve the curriculum objectives (Fig. 3 and Fig. 4).

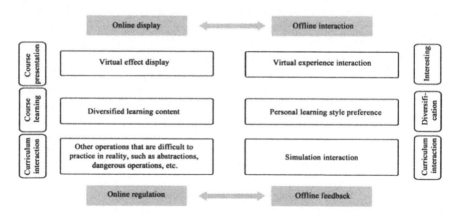

Fig. 4. Blending learning design in perceptual stage.

Perception: Cognitive Teaching Activities (Knowledge). In the perception stage, teaching activities should combine different types of content and characteristics, make full use of the advantages of blending learning, and show different types of knowledge in a form that is easier for students to understand and accept.

Humanities content is easy to make people feel boring and lack the cultivation of innovative practical ability [2], which is suitable to combine interdisciplinary content to enhance the understanding and application of social science content. The relationship between information can be visualized in the form of mind map and knowledge graph, such as technical engineering and mathematics. However, due to the strong practicality of some technologies and projects, or the contents with higher risk coefficients and conditions, they can be presented by means of digital simulation and virtual display and operation. The contents of art appreciation usually pay more attention to visual effects and experience. It is generally displayed in the form of pictures and text and should be combined with new forms to break through the display effect of art content. In the perceptual stage, the knowledge requirement is to remember, understand and identify. The knowledge test questionnaire is usually used to evaluate the learning results.

The effect of online display is not limited by objective conditions, and can be simulated, repaired and reproduced. Consequently, students can accept abstract knowledge more intuitively. In addition, digital virtual display can also enhance students' interest in learning [7] through the design of visual effects, interactive experience, emotional atmosphere and so on. Virtual reality products such as AR/VR can integrate offline interaction with display effects to enhance the cognition and understanding of the conveyed content [1]. Online learning content is not limited by time and space, thus students can freely control their own learning time and frequency, which helps to improve learning efficiency and effectiveness (Fig. 5).

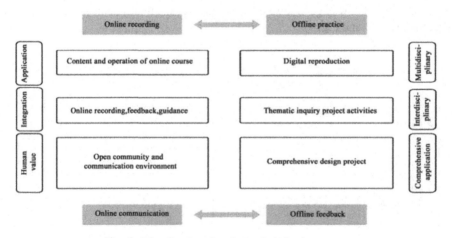

Fig. 5. Blending learning design in behavior stage.

Behavior: Application Practice Activities (Applications, Integration, People). In problem-oriented project-based learning, through the application of knowledge of different disciplines, students can find the inherent logical relationship between different disciplines and find new feelings and values.

This stage is mainly through the application of practical learning activities to integrate the contents of different disciplines in the project tasks. Therefore, the teaching tools and media with more inclusiveness and richer content should be selected in the project setting. Combined with the degree of discipline integration of STEAM education framework, the project content should be refined to these three behaviors tomography: subject content understanding and reproduction, exploration and analysis, and comprehensive application. Completing the study and understanding of STEAM topics step by step in these three different project tasks.

The knowledge requirement in the behavior stage is to use, connect, integrate and understand from the perspective of self, usually by means of learning files, focus groups, interviews, questionnaires and so on, but at present, it is mainly based on qualitative analysis. There is still a lack of a unified evaluation method for this kind of learning content.

However, the offline teaching of STEAM education pays too much attention to practice and relies on tools to complete the setting and development of multidisciplinary content, which leads to the limited popularity of STEAM education. To be specific, STEAM education mainly distributed in first-and second-tier cities [2]. Real-time communication can be carried out with the help of online communication tools for basic content, course Q & A, group discussion and other behaviors. Offline students can complete their learning tasks through hands-on practice, and record and share their experiences and experiences in the online community. The online community can provide rich learning resources, create a good atmosphere for discussion and learning and promote communication and learning among students in a way that conforms to the behavior habits of young people (Fig. 6).

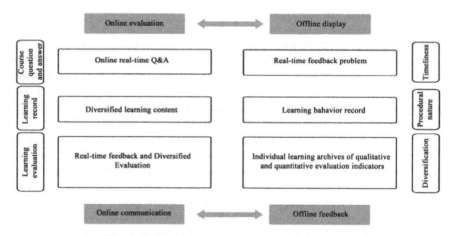

Fig. 6. Blending learning design in reflection stage.

Reflection: Evaluation and Reflection Activities (Value, Learning). By integrating all kinds of interdisciplinary knowledge through diversified evaluation combined with experience in the project, thinking about the relationship between individuals and topics is triggered among students.

The interdisciplinary characteristics of STEAM education and the problem-oriented form of project-based learning require that the perspectives of evaluation should be diversified, process-oriented and comprehensive. The learning achievements of opinion class and feeling class should be observed and evaluated through personal reflection activities, personalized questionnaires and interview case studies and so on.

Due to lower threshold and conditions of online teaching, more resources can be obtained more easily. In the process of evaluation, more experts related to the project should be invited to put forward suggestions from different angles to help students fill gaps and broaden their horizons and knowledge. At the same time, the online community is also the data of offline learning behavior to help teachers understand the offline learning situation of students. Teachers can combine the questionnaire test results, behavioral data, project process to establish a curriculum evaluation system as well as students' personal learning files to make up for the lack of learning evaluation in STEAM education.

4   Teaching Practice

After a wealth of practice and research, this course sorts out and arranges the course content respectively. Based on the previous research, our research group choose the appropriate teaching method according to the characteristics of the course content, analyzes and organizes the course content from the following aspects: the formulation of learning objectives, the planning and formulation of content, the selection and implementation of teaching tools, the transformation of course content and the formulation of learning evaluation.

4.1   Set Curriculum Objectives

We have integrated geographical advantages, resource advantages, and professional advantages of the team, with Cantonese porcelain (Cantonese porcelain is an important representative of traditional Chinese handicrafts and is included in the second batch of intangible cultural heritage) as the theme. In November 2020, a four-week smart crafts innovation workshop (32 class hours in total) was launched. There are 30 undergraduates and graduate students from different majors (Fig. 7).

In order to achieve the practical effect of the hybrid teaching model, questionnaire surveys and interviews were conducted with the students in the workshop. Bang-Hee Kim divided the evaluation indexes of steam education and teaching ability into 35 evaluation indexes through literature review and evaluation indexes. This article selects five perspectives: subject setting, teaching method, learner participation in learning, learner understanding, learning environment and environment to evaluate the course effect. This study will use this indicator to evaluate the STEAM online teaching mode. The process of evaluation is set up as follows: This article takes the cultural theme as an example, and separately analyzes the following ten indicators (each indicator is divided into four

	Learning content	Learning activity	Learning evaluation
knowledge	Origin and development Subjects, shapes, patterns, color classification and standards Craft production process Understanding and function of tools	Teacher explanation visit the museum Online research Multimedia formats such as Web AR, applets, etc.	Knowledge Test (50 questions in Guangcai Knowledge Test) Adopt the method of learning before and after testing
application	Matching of common elements such as theme, style, pattern, etc. Digital reproduction of history, tools and craftsmanship	Optional Cantonese porcelain theme game design	Work evaluation + process evaluation
Integration	Cultural meaning and connotation	Cultural inquiry theme design (pattern, theme innovation, etc.)	Process evaluation can appropriately adjust the evaluation content in the questionnaire according to the characteristics of the subject.
people	The Semantic Transformation of Traditional Culture in Modern Society	Cultural and creative product theme design (Deepen the understanding of Guangcai through the design of function, appearance, material, etc.)	
value, Learn	Function and significance in modern society development trend	Show report, evaluation and reflection	User interview + STEAM teaching ability questionnaire

Fig. 7. The blending teaching practice based on STEAM education with Cantonese porcelain as the theme.

levels according to different levels, allowing students to self-evaluate): problem analysis, information analysis, knowledge application, tools Application, program design, practical operation, cultural expression, cooperation, and independent learning.

In the aspect of course content display: in addition to the explanation in class, teachers can use multimedia and digital forms to assist in learning. For some of the knowledge categories of wide-color porcelain that are relatively difficult to understand, such as production technology, the team develops an augmented reality APP, for wide-color porcelain learning, which is unable to present the content in two-dimensional plane through three-dimensional, dynamic and procedural form. The interactive way of three-dimensional model is used to refine the flow of traditional handicrafts, so that users can dynamically simulate the technological process of traditional handicrafts through the mobile end before production. It can also enhance the current situation that learners only learn this kind of knowledge from the traditional two-dimensional perspective, breaks the limitations of time and space in traditional handicraft learning and promotes learners' interest in participation (Fig. 8).

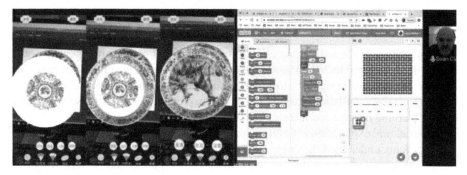

Fig. 8. Online teaching activity display chart.

In the aspect of course content learning: through the learning results and interviews of online learning, it is found that for the course activities of software operation and content display, students are more inclined to online learning. Online screen sharing can make the transmission of display content be more clear and intuitive. In addition, after discovering points of interest and problems, students can search and understand them in real time, so as to improve the efficiency of course learning and the utilization rate of time.

In the aspect of learning evaluation: for the analysis of quantitative questionnaire, online evaluation can easily collect and analyze learning results. According to the learning situation of different students to carry out personalized learning program planning, so as to help students accurately check and fill gaps, improve learning efficiency and effect. For qualitative research, students' learning files can also be established through keywords, semantic analysis and other methods to facilitate teachers to understand students' learning process. The online environment has obvious advantages in providing persistent recording information, which students can use for reflection. Self-assessment can stimulate and improve meta-awareness.

4.2 The Content and Effect of Offline Learning

Fig. 9. Game design with the theme of Cantonese porcelain.

The combination of Cantonese porcelain and scratch visual programming enables students to digitally reproduce the knowledge they have learned in the process of creation. Through the detailed design of story background, music, lines, personas and so on, transform passive instillation learning into active exploratory constructivist learning to improve learning interest and learning efficiency (Fig. 9).

In the cultural exploration activities with the theme of the pattern innovation project, let the students understand the composition of the colorful pattern and grasp the constituent elements and connotation of the pattern in essence. As can be seen from the comparison in the picture, the students' works have made innovations such as the change of the form of the original pattern as well as the way of organization, the reorganization of units and so on (Fig. 10).

Fig. 10. Offline work display.

In the practice of the comprehensive project, students complete the determination of theme, scheme design, scheme screening, model making, lamp interaction pattern design, product display and reflection of the whole design process in the form of a group. In the process, students improve the cognitive depth of subject knowledge and carry out personalized self-expression.

5 Conclusion

Through process assessment and steam teaching ability assessment, you can get: In order to achieve the practical effect of the blending learning mode, questionnaires and interviews were conducted among the students in the workshop. The results show that the advantages of implementing blending learning are obvious, and the learning effect of students has been significantly improved.

First of all, the blending learning mode is recognized by students. By asking all 30 students about "do you like and approve the blending learning mode?" "What is the reason?", according to the online questionnaire survey, 92% of the students said they liked and approved the blending learning mode. As for the reasons, 89% of the students thought that they could break through the limitation of time and space to complete the study; 86% of the students thought that the classroom learning atmosphere was good; 86% of the students thought that the interdisciplinary teaching content courses were interesting; 81% of the students thought that the teamwork ability had been significantly improved; and 79% of the students thought that their communication, expression and presentation ability had been improved. In addition, interviews with two students with low acceptance of this learning mode are mainly due to the fact that they are not accustomed. Besides, concentration and high input are required in class as well as great pressure on interdisciplinary tasks. Generally speaking, the mixed teaching of steam education has brought greater gains to students and has been recognized by students.

In a word, introducing the concept of blending learning and modern information technology into STEAM education makes the blending learning reform of STEAM education have rules to follow and a way to go. Through empirical research, this paper proves that this teaching mode can improve students' spirit of exploration, practical ability and innovative consciousness.

Acknowledgments. This research was supported by Guangzhou University Innovation and Entrepreneurship Education Project(2020kc007) and Ministry of education production university cooperation education project (201802148006).

References

1. Wang, Y., Zhang, X., Zhang, L., Wang, G., Sun, Y.: Take the course of Digital signal processing as an example to explore and practice the progressive hybrid teaching mode. Experimental Technol. Management (12), 244249 (2020). 29 Dec 2020. https://doi.org/10.16791/j.cnki.sjg. 2020.12.053
2. Wei, Z., Luo, Z.: Cuckoo: Research on mixed teaching aiming at improving students' learning initiative. Educ. Theory Prac. **40**(33), 59–61 (2020J).
3. Zhang, J.: Exploration and innovation of online and offline mixed teaching – comment on mixed teaching design and practice. Chinese J. Educ. **11**, 136 (2020)
4. Zhai, M., Zhang, R., Liu, H.: Research on formative evaluation indexes of mixed teaching in colleges and universities. Mod. Educ. Technol. **30**(09), 35–39 (2020)
5. Ma, Y.: Online and offline hybrid teaching action research– the integration and innovation of information technology and ideological and political teaching. Month. J. Educ. Learn. **07**, 97–105 (2020)
6. Zhang, H., Ran, Y.: The landing of the educational concept of stream: the construction of learning model and case development of mathematical culture project. Audio-visual Education in China **07**, 97–103 (2020)
7. Sun, T.: Stream education: humanistic turn and realistic orientation. Shanghai Educ. Sci. Res. **04**, 27–30 (2020)
8. Hofmann, J.: Blended Learning. Association for Talent Development(ATD)Press, Alexandria, p. 95 (2018)
9. https://hi.codemao.cn/
10. https://www.scratch-cn.cn/
11. Cao, Y.: A probe into the mixed teaching mode from the perspective of "three metaphorical Culture." Teaching and Management **12**, 20–22 (2020)
12. Yang, Q., Yang, F.: Research on the innovation of "mixed teaching" mode in higher vocational education from the perspective of "Creator"– comment on the exploration of mixed teaching practice based on "one flat and three ends." Leadership Science **08**, 126 (2020)
13. Hu, Y., Jiang, Q.: The integration of mathematics education and STEM (STEAM) education: opportunities and challenges– based on the international symposium on mathematics education and STEM (STEAM) education. J. Maths. Educ. **28**(06), 92–94 (2019)
14. Euphrásio, P.C.S., Faria, L.A., Germano, J.S.E., Hirata, D.: Improving teaching-learning process in MIL-STD-1553B bus classes using a new hybrid web-lab methodology. IEEE Trans. Educ. **63**(4), 291–298 (2020). https://doi.org/10.1109/TE.2020.2984882. Nov.
15. Li, Y., Peng, Y.: The development, value orientation and localization construction of stream curriculum. Mod. Educ. Technol. **29**(09), 115–120 (2019)
16. Ding, J., Zhu, Y.: Flipped classroom design based on cognitive development. Vocation. Tech. Educ. China (17), 37–41 (2018). 46

The Status of Human-Machine Communication Research: A Decade of Publication Trends Across Top-Ranking Journals

Heidi Makady(⊠) ⓘ and Fanjue Liu

University of Florida, Gainesville, USA
{Makady.h,fanjueliu}@ufl.edu

Abstract. This study explores the trends in Human-Machine Communication (HMC) scholarship in the past decade. We examined 444 peer-reviewed empirical studies published between 2010 and 2021 across journals with highest impact factor according to Social Sciences Citation Index (SSCI). Through a systematic review, we looked at theoretical frameworks, methodological approaches, studied technologies, funding sources, and contributing countries in HMC studies. Using an LDA topic modeling on article abstracts, we further explore the top topic composition in the field and topic distribution across the journals in the past decade. Our analysis revealed diversity among contributing countries. The United States-led studies saw the highest share in HMC research, followed by Asia and Europe. Funding saw a dominant contribution from government and university. A diversity in thematic focus was observed with some topics' dominance among domain-specific journals. Significant differences among journals in terms of theory, method, investigated technology and contributing disciplinary affiliation were also found.

Keywords: Systematic review · Human-machine communication · LDA topic modeling · Affiliation · Funding · Technology · Method · Theory · Research trends

1 Introduction

In the past decade, the field of Human-Machine Communication (HMC) has been witnessing continuous epistemological and methodological growth as well as becoming increasingly interdisciplinary [1]. With this progress, there's a corresponding demand to identify HMC's key trends and advance its research agenda [2]. Field publications, including cross-disciplinary journals, have been serving as fundamental resources for HMC scholars and practitioners and providing a microcosm for the status of this maturing field. Nevertheless, systematic reviews of communication studies may often overlook emergent subfields such as HMC in portraying an overarching picture [3]. Thus, it is our role to identify trends in HMC research and assess its literature balance [4] to map out directions for promoting future HMC scholarship discussions in peer-reviewed journals.

© The Author(s), under exclusive license to Springer Nature Switzerland AG 2022
M. Kurosu (Ed.): HCII 2022, LNCS 13302, pp. 83–103, 2022.
https://doi.org/10.1007/978-3-031-05311-5_6

Today, the technologies under HMC investigation are the outcomes of the efforts to emulate human-human communication with machines [5]. For instance, studies explored users' perception of AI in journalism [6], behavioral response towards the use of AR in medicine [7], and emotional response towards robots [8]. In this context, several scholars [e.g., 1, 9] recommended focusing on delineating the ontological gap between people and machines in HMC and setting a research agenda to further understand how people perceive, relate with, and interact with machines. Therefore, it is fundamental to establish a picture regarding the status quo of HMC research, depicting the functional, relational, and metaphysical dynamics through which people associate with emerging technologies.

Towards this end, we contribute to the exploration HMC research trends in terms of thematic focus, differences between publication outlets in terms of methods and theory, investigated technology, contributing affiliations, countries, and research funding. We first look at the definitions and establishment of HMC field and its history from inception towards evolution, review the past literature investigating relative field trends, then further describe the rationale of our study.

2   Literature Review

2.1   HMC: Technology as Communicators in Communication

Human-machine communication (HMC) has been proposed as an emerging and distinct area of research in the communication discipline in response to the growing number of technologies designed to function as message sources rather than message channels [10, 11]. Although the conceptualization of HMC is derived from human-human communication, HMC research charts the ontological divide between human-machine communication and human-human communication [5]. While in human communication, when interacting with other humans, people rapidly consider multiple aspects pertaining to their communication partner, and this assessment ultimately shapes their communicative behavior [12]. However, in human-machine communication, the ontological assessment made when interacting with machines is not as straightforward as in human-human communication [13]. To communicate effectively with machines, during initial communications, people must first determine the nature of machines as the communicator, what it is, which then determines subsequent communication behavior [14]. Within HMC, communication is not defined based on an ontological understanding of communicators, which assumes that communication is a process exclusive to humans [15]. Instead, communication is conceptualized as meaning creation, and human communication and human-machine communication represent distinct types of communication [11]. Taken together, in human-machine communication, people's judgments and interactions with machines depend significantly on how they interpret the nature of the communicative technology [16].

Enhanced by artificial intelligence and more sophisticated and powerful software [17], emerging media technologies are characterized as fostering more autonomous, more personalized, and more human forms of communication [11]. The definition of "machine" in human-machine communication is multi-facet. As a meta-ontological category, machines encompass a wide range of technologies [18]. The onus of human-machine communication thus falls on people deciphering the nature of these communicative technologies [5]. HMC research [2] suggested that the unique feature of HMC is its focus on people's interactions with technologies designed as communicative subjects rather than mere interactive objects. In response, as a distinct field of research, human-machine communication aims to illuminate how machines start to assume the role of communicator and how people conceptualize machines in such a role [5]. The shift in the machine's role redefines the boundaries of human communication from traditional perspectives of human-human interactions studied in communication studies to a new paradigm where machines are capable of establishing meaningful interactions with humans [10]. In this vein, HMC draws on theories of media equation and computers are social actors' paradigm (CASA), source orientation, social presence, and human-computer interactions (HCI) to understand the role of machines as communicators [19–22].

Historically, communication scholars started with studying Information Communication Technologies (ICTs) without giving attention to the leading "manufacturing technologies" that are essentially designed to be social and to hold similar anthropomorphic features like robots [15]. Today, with the repositioning of the machines from being the channel to the communicator within the information flow and social processes [11], the emerging research studies grounded in HMC eventually started to investigate various types of technologies and the cognitive, emotional, and behavioral dimensions associated with them in the process.

2.2 The Present Study

The rationale for our study is based on the following. First, 2010 to 2020 has signaled dramatic technological advancements, especially the ubiquity of artificial intelligence [23]. There have been notable increases in the use of emerging technologies, AI, and big data, leading to near-saturation levels of use among significant segments of the population [24]. Given that patterns and outlets may function as indicators of developments occurring in new communication technology research [25], this study aims to better understand what was occurring within the emerging HMC research area's published record during the 2010s decade. Second, although extant trend studies have acknowledged the importance of new communication technologies and applications [e.g., 25, 26], little research has analyzed the publication and thematic patterns of studies that focus on emerging artificial intelligence-based technology such as robots, virtual agents, VR, and AR. Moreover, as most previous trend research draws upon the 1990s and 2000s decade, the development of new communication technology research during the 2010s decade remains to be explored. Third, the 2010s are deemed the early evolution of HMC research when the field of HMC started to be known with the launch of its first conference in 2016 as a part of a post-conference at the International Communication Association (ICA). Therefore, the 2010–2021 period was considered appropriate as it made possible a gauge on how HMC has taken shape before it has been officially defined and how this field has flourished after. Taken together, this study seeks to map out the development of HMC by 1) examining HMC studies in top publishing outlets over a timely timeframe, 2010 to 2021; 2) focusing on the trends and thematic patterns of HMC research; 3) providing insights into where HMC as an emerging research area has been, is at present, and where it may yet lead. Specifically, we examined the following:

RQ1: What is the topic composition and distribution in HMC articles published in peer-reviewed journals over the past decade?

RQ2: Are there significant differences in theory use, methodologies employed, disciplinary affiliations, technologies investigated, and the journals in which they are published?

RQ3: How are the main theories employed in HMC research related to the methodological design and disciplinary affiliations over the past decade?

RQ4: What are the significant trends regarding funding in HMC studies over the past decade?

RQ5: What are the significant trends regarding diversity (contributors' country) in HMC studies over the past decade?

3   Data and Methods

To address the raised research questions, the researchers conducted a systematic review of high impact journals with the highest impact factor, according to Social Sciences Citation Index (SSCI), in the field of communication and interdisciplinary journals focusing on media technologies, i.e., Computers in Human Behavior, International Journal of Human-Computer Studies, Digital Journalism. A total of 18 journals were identified for this study. To collect data, we completed a content analysis of research articles in each journal from January 2010 to May 2021. Following the Preferred Reporting Items for Systematic Reviews and Meta-Analyses (PRISMA) guidelines for inclusion criteria [26], a total of 444 articles were identified for final analysis – See Table 1. Based on existing definitions of HMC studies, we considered any academic article focusing on communication with and about machines, which may include robots, smart devices, virtual agents, computers, etc. To identify relevant studies, we employed search terms "human-machine communication", "human-computer interaction", "human-robot interaction", "human-agent interaction". All articles were retrieved from EBSCOhost Web, ScienceDirect, and SpringerLink databases. The full articles were reviewed for theoretical frameworks, methods, technologies investigated, affiliations, first author country of affiliation, and funding sources.

Table 1. Reviewed journals and their abbreviations with article count.

Journal title (abbreviation)	Count	Percent (%)
Computers in Human Behavior (CHB)	120	27.0
International Journal of Human-Computer Studies (IJHCS)	65	14.6
Cyberpsychology Behavior & Social Networking (CBSN)	39	8.8
International Journal of Human-Computer Interaction (IJHCI)	38	8.6
International Journal of Social Robotics (IJSR)	36	8.1
New Media & Society (NMS)	35	7.9
Journal of Computer-Mediated Communication (JCMC)	22	5.0
Digital Journalism (DJ)	22	5.0
Communication Research (CR)	21	4.7
Media Psychology (MP)	10	2.3
Human-Machine Communication (HMC)	10	2.3
Journal of Communication (JOC)	7	1.6
Journal of Broadcasting & Electronic Media (JBEM)	7	1.6
Technology, Mind, and Behavior (TMB)	6	1.4
Information, Communication & Society (ICS)	3	0.7
Human Communication Research (HCR)	1	0.2
Communication Theory (CT)	1	0.2
Journalism Studies (JS)	1	0.2
Total count	444	100

4 Analytical Strategy

Our analyses proceed in three segments. First, we employed a Latent Dirichlet Allocation (LDA) topic modeling using R statistical programming language version 4.1.2 to our corpus of 444 articles' abstracts to identify the significant research topics and their distribution over the past decade (RQ1). Abstracts comprise central keywords and themes of each study [28, 29]. Second, we ran a series of chi-square tests to determine whether the 18 journals were significantly different from one another and the relationship between employed theoretical frameworks with methodological designs and disciplinary affiliations (RQ2 & RQ3). Finally, we conducted a series of frequency analyses to estimate the top trends in funding and diversity over the past decade (RQ4 & RQ5).

4.1 LDA Topic Modeling

Discovering the topics underlying the research structure is the first step towards discovering meaningful trends in the content [28]. LDA is a probabilistic model approach that determines the probability of topics' distribution in documents using a generative algorithm to extract topics based on set of words that best describe documents [28, 30, 31]. In this study we employ an LDA Gibbs sampling algorithm for topic modeling considering its advantages in terms of speed in generating sample distributions of data sets and its efficiency in identifying associations between scientific papers from distinctive disciplines [28]. Previous studies [28, 32] attempting to discover addressed topics in corpora of scientific studies proved the efficiency of Gibbs sampling approach in discovering meaningful structure and high-quality topics among documents. To perform our LDA sampling, we proceeded in three steps.

First, upon extracting article abstracts ($N = 444$), text was converted to a Document Term Matrix (DTM) corpus using a tidytext package for processing with an LDA modeling. Each abstract comprised a single document in the corpus. The corpus was cleaned by removing stop words, punctuation, numbers, dates, white spaces, and word-stemmed using tm_map function from tm package. The final DTM comprised of 444 documents, 4274 terms and had a sparsity of 99%.

Second, we established the required set of LDA hyperparameters *[K, N, α, β]*; where k represents the number of topics, N represents the number of iterations, α represents the topic distributions per document, and β represents the term's distribution per topic [33]. To determine the best fitting number of topics K for our LDA modeling, we applied the ldatuning package ldatuning::FindTopicsNumber()(Nikita, 2020) to the corpus of abstracts. LDA tuning yields higher quality topics for modeling [31]. As Fig. 5 depicts, the FindTopicsNumber_plot metrics, Griffiths [28], CaoJuan [34], and Arun [35] indicated an optimal number of topics within the range of 15 to 20 topics. The minimization and maximization panels of each metric indicate a divergence among the number of topics until topic 20, which stabilize by topic 50. Thus, we reported the top 20 topics, $K = 20$ for this study. Our LDA hyperparameters *[N, α, β]* were set at $\alpha = 0.25$, $\beta = 0.1$ with $N = 1000$ iterations. For each hyperparameter, previous LDA approaches on finding scientific topics from abstracts [28] suggested an $\alpha = 50/k$ (if T > 50) and $\beta = 0.1$. A higher α yields a better topic distribution for each document [33]. A small β value is recommended for scientific topics to yield the highest number of topics with specific research areas where β impacts model granularity [28]. Since our T < 50 and alpha score should be set between 0 and 1, we settled for the recommended default $\alpha = 0.25$ [36].

Finally, we subset the corpus of abstracts by journal to detect the topics of central focus among each journal. Using textmineR, for each set of abstracts, we created an LDA Gibbs modeling with the highest quality of topics indicated by textmineR metrics for quality of topics. We evaluated each set's overall goodness of fit and then extracted the top topics with the highest phi value (term distribution in a topic). Finally, we inspected the topics using probabilistic coherence and prevalence metrics for each journal and extracted the top 5 topics with the highest coherence and prevalence probability score. Coherence indicates the probability of word co-occurrence per topic [31, 32], and prevalence indicates the probability of topic distribution within documents [28]. We extracted the top topic and corresponding terms for the journals of *Communication Theory (CR), Journalism Studies (JS), and Human Communication Research (HCR)* separately since their sets comprised single studies.

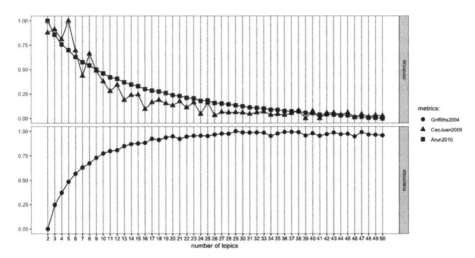

Fig. 1. Suggested number of topics using as defined by LDA metrics

5   Results

5.1   Research Topic Composition and Distribution

An LDA Gibbs sampling with top 20 topics among the corpus of abstracts generated the topics and corresponding words with the highest posterior probability of alpha size as illustrated in Fig. 1. First term implies a higher phi value representing the word distribution over a topic. The size of each word is in proportion to its coherence and prevalence probability. As seen in Fig. 1, the word distributions in the top 20 topics' trend reveal significant topic clusters linked with distinctive research areas in the field. The top topic terms with the highest phi values indicate the following themes robot (15%), emotion (8%), social (9%), agent (8%), news (6%), game (6%), and communication (6%). For instance, sub-themes for "robot" in Topic #4 suggest a focus on human behavior and perception in Human-Robot Interaction (HRI). Sub-themes for the term "emotion" in Topic #2 indicate a focus on studying responses, facial expressions, and stress. We also see Topics #5 and #6 commonly emphasize the term "social" when studying computer, phone, and mobile communication. While Topic #5 emphasizes the use of CASA and politeness theory to investigate effects and responses for computer and phone communication, terms in Topic #6 suggest a focus on understanding relationships and challenges in mobile technologies. Relevant to the focus on mobile devices, we observe an association with developing valid measurements and using the technology acceptance model in Topic #11. A noticeable theme in Topics #7, #9, #13, and #20 was virtual agents, chatbots, and avatars. The top terms among the three topics suggest a specific interest in the social cues, trustworthiness, privacy, intentions, behavior, and social presence in Human-Agent Interaction (HAI).

Furthermore, we observe a set of distinctive focal themes among topics. For example, Topic #19 suggests a central focus on journalism, emphasizing automated journalism, algorithms, and bot within news production. We also see a focus on video games and prosocial behavior among older adults in Topic #16; interactions in messages and online conversations in the context of CMC in Topic #1; student and children learning, engagement, and motivation within teaching with computerized systems in Topic #3; uncanny valley, face animation and aggressiveness in Topic #15; and video humor, audience perception and exposure in Topic #10.

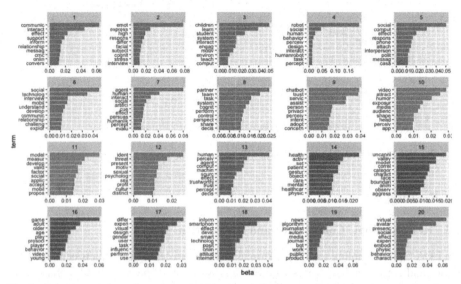

Fig. 2. Top 10 terms in topics 1 through 10 in the whole corpus of articles. (First term implies a higher phi value).

Journal-topic analyses also indicated distinctive distributions for research topics among journals. Table 2 summarizes top topic distributions with the highest phi value of coherence and prevalence for each journal. Concerning space limitations, we only report the first top topic for each. Table 3 summarizes the top terms for *CT, HCR & JS,* which comprised single studies during this period. By comparing the topic word distribution among all journals in Fig. 2 with specific journal topic distribution in Table 2, we find the corresponding focal themes for each journal with more depth. For instance, the topic term distribution in Table 2 suggests that each of *IJSC* and *JCMC* shared unique focus in HRI (Topic #4, Fig. 2). While *IJCR* emphasized gaze, gesture, robot-persuasiveness and related implications and strategies, *JCMC* focused on users' experience, embodiments, haptics, and age factors. We also notice the shared interest in HRI, focusing on uncanny valley (Topic #15, Fig. 2) among *CBSN* and *CHB*. Similarly, each seemed to have a distinctive thematic focus examining the uncanny valley. While *CBSN* investigated perceptions of voice (talking, pitch) and appearance (head, face) characteristics, *CHB* addressed emotions, feelings, and behavior. We also notice that the emphasis on virtual assistants (Topics #7, #9, #13, and #20, Fig. 2) seems to mainly emerge from *JCMC, CHB, IJSR,* as in Table 2.

In gaming studies, we notice a focus on two sub-themes: gaming and violence, which was a prevalent focus for *MP*, and gaming and AR, which was more dominant in *IJHCI*. Moreover, as term prevalence values indicate, the *IJHCS* focused on user engagement, interaction, emotions, attitudes, and wearable devices, i.e., Google Glass. Aside from devices and technologies, we notice that the thematic focus on "emotions" (Topic #2, Fig. 2) seemed to emerge from *IJHCS, CHB, HMC, and JC* studies. It is notable that the emphasis on this theme predominantly emerged from media technology-oriented journals (i.e., *IJSR, CHB, HMC*) over communication journals (i.e., *CR, HCR, CT*), and media psychology-oriented journals (i.e., *MP, TMB, CBSN*). Interestingly, the latter *MP, TMB, CBSN* emphasized impacts, exposure, trust, and experience more than other aspects. However, there seemed to be a common thematic focus among the three categories of journals beyond technologies solely. For instance, a focus on health emerged among *HMC, HCR*, and *TMB*. The latter mainly focused on mental health. Finally, the prevalent thematic focus on "news" among *JS, DJ*, and *JBEM*, emphasized algorithmic transparency and trust, news bots, and automation in news writing. A prominent recurring term among two of those journals was "power," indicating their emphasis on the critical role of AI in journalism. Focusing on Twitter, messages, citizens, and audiences, *JC* and *CT* seemed to be the only communication journals sharing interests in news and audiences with journalism journals.

Table 2. Journals focusing on specific topics.

Journal	Topic	Coherence	Prevalence	Words
IJHCS	t_5	0.504	4.829	older, adults, emotions, character, text, attitudes, social, google_glass, potential, interface, engagement
IJHCI	t_3	0.908	5.282	ar, camera, players, reality, augmented, single, single_ar, sense, game, presentation, stereoscopic_ar, vr_camera
JCMC	t_14	0.809	4.549	embodiment, haptic, feedback, robot, avatar, mediated, experience, understanding, users, activated, advanced, advanced_age, affect, agent, ai
CR	t_97	0.952	4.152	birth, private, family, parents, privacy, adoptive_parents, disclosures, management, information, media, users, communication, acquaintanceship
CHB	t_14	0.317	4.447	uncanny, effect, avatars, correlated, pain, real, confusion, motion, feelings, interacting, behavior, predictions, body
CBSN	t_2	0.801	2.820	head, talking, face, exposure, affectbased_trust, trust, exposure_talking, pitch, uncanny, valley, strangers, perceptions
DJ	t_12	0.750	4.309	technologies, icts, revolution, newsrooms, development, changing, communication, information, new, algorithm, algorithmic_transparency, algorithmwritten_news, attention, bot
HMC	t_20	0.730	11.885	identity, gender, individuals, users, role, social, age, artificial_intelligence, attributes, complex, demonstrability, emotional, eyetracking, functional, health

(continued)

Table 2. (*continued*)

ICS	t_5	0.667	29.762	moral, violation, ai, attribute, decisionmaking, joint, less, human, control, effect, impact, information, information_communication, interactions, internet_users
IJSR	t_5	0.667	2.435	persuasive, gazing, gestures, strategies, used, robots_persuasiveness, story, robot, evaluate, agent, implications, theory, accept
JBEM	t_11	0.857	8.756	processes, ai, algorithmic, trust, algorithm, perceive, heuristic, user, artworks, attractive, avatar, cognitive, influence, interactions, power
JC	t_6	0.800	8.819	tv, interview, twitter, messages, affect, bots, changes, citizens, cmc, complex, conductance, disclosing, effects, emotional
MP	t_4	0.90	5.448	interpersonal, game_violence, interpersonal_trust, longterm, video_game, violence, trust, video, players, game, activation, body, computers, design, experienced
NMS	t_9	0.765	4.123	music, ai, intelligence, artificial, expectancy, violation, evaluation, advertising, better, brand, experiment, design, implications
TMB	t_4	0.833	7.470	smartphone, estimates, objective, logs, mental, health, attributes, communication, copresent, development, different, effective, evaluate

*Top topics with the highest probability of quality (coherence) and (prevalence) for each journal. Words in each topic with the highest value of phi (distribution of words over topics).

Table 3. Top terms in topics for CT, HCR and JS.

Journal	Terms	Beta
CT	interactivity	0.26
	Human	0.13
	attitude, audience, intention, visit	0.08
HCR	communication	0.11
	attitude, conversational, tone	0.08
	health, influence, perceived, users	0.06
JS	news	0.17
	journalists, news workers, production	0.06
	automation, increasingly, power, role, writing	0.05

5.2 Associations Between Theory, Methods, Affiliations, and Technologies Among Journals

Chi-square tests of independence (RQ2) revealed statistically significant differences among theoretical perspectives χ^2 (170, n = 433) = 280.92, p < .001, Cramer's V = .26 methodological designs χ^2 (153, n = 444) = 293.29, p < .001, Cramer's V = .27, disciplinary affiliations χ^2 (136, n = 444) = 302.47, p < .001, Cramer's V = .29, and the investigated technologies χ^2 (102, n = 433) = 393.85, p < .001, Cramer's V = .39, across the eighteen journals. Table 4 summarizes frequency counts in each journal. Chi-square test results (RQ3) also revealed significant associations between 1) the employed theory and method χ^2 (90, n = 434) = 148.47, p < .001, Cramer's V = .20; and 2) the employed theory and disciplinary affiliations χ^2 (80, n = 433) = 112.51, p = .010, Cramer's V = .18.

Table 4. Theoretical frameworks, methods, technologies and affiliations by journals

	Journals																		Total
	IJSR	HMC	ICS	HCR	TMB	CBSN	IJHCI	IJHCS	CHB	CR	MP	CT	JCMC	JOC	NMS	JBEM	DJ	JS	
Theoretical Perspectives																			
CASA	5	4	0	0	1	8	2	4	26	1	0	0	1	1	3	1	2	0	59
Theory of Mind	3	1	0	0	1	2	0	12	13	1	0	0	3	1	1	0	0	0	38
Communication Theories	0	0	0	0	0	1	3	3	7	2	0	1	4	1	5	3	6	0	36
Presence	3	0	0	0	0	5	1	5	3	3	1	0	2	1	0	0	0	0	24
CMC Theories	0	0	1	1	0	1	0	0	2	7	2	0	2	0	5	1	0	0	22
Other Comm Tech Theories	0	1	0	0	1	2	1	4	1	2	0	0	2	0	2	1	0	0	17
Uncanny Valley	2	0	0	0	0	1	2	3	7	0	0	0	0	0	0	1	0	0	16
Technology Acceptance Model	3	0	0	0	0	3	3	1	4	0	0	0	0	0	1	0	0	0	15
Anthropomorphism	4	0	0	0	0	0	3	1	3	0	0	0	0	0	1	0	1	0	13
Theories from other fields	10	2	1	0	1	10	10	21	37	5	5	0	5	3	13	0	1	1	125
Methods																			
Experiment	23	3	2	1	3	29	20	40	84	16	7	0	9	4	8	5	7	0	261
Survey	4	2	0	0	1	6	10	8	20	3	1	1	4	0	5	2	0	0	67
Interviews	5	1	1	0	0	0	0	2	5	0	0	0	4	0	12	0	7	1	38
Mixed	3	1	0	0	1	6	4	6	5	0	0	0	1	0	3	0	2	0	26
Physiological	0	1	0	0	0	2	1	5	5	1	1	0	0	1	0	0	0	0	17
Computational	0	1	0	0	0	0	0	2	1	0	1	0	1	2	1	0	2	0	11
Field Observation	0	1	0	0	0	0	0	0	0	0	0	0	1	0	6	0	0	0	8
Content Analysis	0	0	0	0	0	2	0	1	0	0	0	0	0	2	0	2	0	0	7
Case Study	0	0	0	0	1	0	0	1	1	0	0	0	0	0	0	0	2	0	5
Discourse Analysis	1	0	0	0	0	0	0	0	0	1	0	0	2	0	0	0	0	0	4
Technologies																			
Robot	36	3	0	0	4	7	5	14	44	0	0	0	1	0	4	0	1	0	119
Virtual Agent	0	3	0	0	1	14	16	20	39	3	3	0	4	3	5	3	4	0	118
Computer Software	0	1	1	1	0	1	4	12	18	11	4	1	4	1	10	2	1	0	72
Smartphones & Apps	0	0	0	0	1	6	2	7	12	4	2	0	10	3	12	0	0	0	59
Other AI Technologies	0	2	2	0	0	3	3	1	5	1	0	0	2	0	4	2	16	1	42
VR	0	1	0	0	0	5	2	4	1	0	1	0	0	0	0	0	0	0	14
AR	0	0	0	0	0	3	3	2	0	0	0	0	0	0	1	0	0	0	9
Affiliations																			
Communication	2	8	2	1	3	22	3	7	24	20	7	1	15	7	23	7	21	1	174
Psychology	7	0	1	0	2	10	3	9	30	1	0	0	0	0	2	0	0	0	65
Business	1	1	0	0	0	1	8	3	14	0	0	0	0	0	2	0	0	0	31
Engineering	5	1	0	0	0	1	5	4	10	0	1	0	1	0	0	0	1	0	29
Information Technology	3	0	0	0	0	0	4	6	9	0	0	0	2	0	2	0	0	0	25
Computer Science	3	0	0	0	0	0	4	11	2	0	0	0	0	0	3	0	0	0	23
HCI Research Center	8	0	0	0	0	0	1	2	4	0	1	0	0	0	1	0	0	0	17
Medicine	1	0	0	0	1	0	1	2	3	0	0	0	0	0	0	0	0	0	8
Other affiliations	7	0	0	0	0	5	7	21	24	0	1	0	4	0	4	0	0	0	73

5.3 Trends Associated with First Country Affiliations

A total of 40 countries were involved in publishing 444 articles in HMC research from 2010 to 2021. The articles reflect diversity in geographical contributions ranging from America, Europe, Asia, and the Middle East. All contributing countries are listed in Table 5 according to article count between period 1 (2010–2015) and period 2 (2016–2021). As Table 5 illustrates, the top five countries were the United States who led with a contribution of 174 articles (39.2%), followed by Netherlands (7.9%), Korea (7.2%), China (6.5%), and Germany (6.3%). All 5 countries cumulatively accounted for (67.1%) of the total HMC research in the last decade. Figure 3 depicts the trend across the years among the top 20 countries which accounted for (93%) of the research. Geographically, the United States-led studies had the highest proportion of HMC research with a significant progressive trend reflecting a 105.2% increase from period 1 to period 2. The trend for Europe-led studies also saw a 113% increase between both periods while Asia-led studies saw a 75.8% increase with China seeing a 271.4% increase alone. Countries (i.e., Denmark (2, 0.5%), Ireland (2, 0.5%), Malaysia (2, 0.5%), Poland (2, 0.5%), Portugal (2, 0.5%), Brazil (1, 0.2%), India (1, 0.2%), Iran (1, 0.2%), Qatar (1, 0.2%), Slovenia (1, 0.2%), Taiwan (2, 0.5%), Turkey (1, 0.2%), Vietnam (1, 0.2%)) cumulatively contributed for 4.3% of total HMC research studies during the last decade.

Table 5. Trends associated with first authors' country of affiliation over the past decade

Country	Period 1 2010–2015		Period 2 2016–2021		Total	
	Count	%	Count	%	Count	%
The United States	57	12.8	117	26.4	174	39.2
Netherlands	13	2.9	22	5.0	35	7.9
Korea*	18	4.1	14	3.2	32	7.2
China	6	1.4	23	5.2	29	6.5
Germany	10	2.3	18	4.1	28	6.3
UK	6	1.4	12	2.7	18	4.1
Australia	3	0.7	10	2.3	13	2.9
Japan	6	1.4	4	0.9	10	2.3
Singapore	2	0.5	7	1.6	9	2.0
Italy	1	0.2	8	1.8	9	2.0
Israel	2	0.5	6	1.4	8	1.8
Spain	3	0.7	5	1.1	8	1.8
Austria	4	0.9	3	0.7	7	1.6
Canada	3	0.7	4	0.9	7	1.6
New Zealand	2	0.5	5	1.1	7	1.6
Finland	2	0.5	4	0.9	6	1.4
France	0	0.0	4	0.9	4	0.9
Greece	1	0.2	2	0.5	3	0.7
Belgium	1	0.2	2	0.5	3	0.7
Hungary	0	0.0	3	0.7	3	0.7
Norway	1	0.2	2	0.5	3	0.7
Sweden	1	0.2	2	0.5	3	0.7

(*continued*)

Table 5. (*continued*)

Country	Period 1 2010–2015		Period 2 2016–2021		Total	
	Count	%	Count	%	Count	%
Switzerland	1	0.2	2	0.5	3	0.7
UAE	0	0.0	3	0.7	3	0.7
(Denmark, Ireland, Malaysia, Poland, Portugal, Brazil, India, Iran, Qatar, Slovenia, Taiwan, Turkey, Vietnam)	3	0.7	16	3.6	19	4.3

*Includes South Korea (4 articles: 0.90% from 2010 to May 2021).

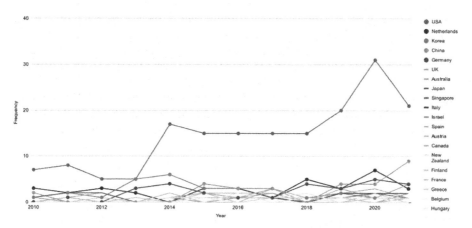

Fig. 3. Trends associated with top 20 countries over the past decade.

5.4 Trends Associated with Funding

The examination of HMC research funding during the last decade indicated a progressive growth across the years. As shown in Table 6, while more than half of the studies (238, 53%) haven't reported receiving financial support, the proportion of funded studies over the last decade grew by 104% from period 1 (2010–2015) (146 studies, 32.9%) to period 2 (2016–2021) (298 studies, 67.1%). As Fig. 4 presents, trends in government funding (125, 28.2%) played a larger role across the years, followed by university (40, 9.0%). Private (10, 2.3%) and public (3, 0.7%) funding had the least contribution share in HMC research funding but remained steadily constant across the years. However, private and public funding sources slightly peaked between 2019 and 2020, respectively when university funding trends saw a brief drop. Interestingly, about (28, 6.3%) of HMC studies received funding support from multiple sources (i.e., government & university, government & public, government & private, or all).

Overall, there seemed to be a significant difference between countries χ^2 (185, n = 444) = 401.41, p < .001, Cramer's V = .43 as well as affiliation with funding support χ^2 (40, n = 444) = 56.612, p = .043, Cramer's V = .20. In terms of countries, the United States (56, 27%), China (21, 10.3%), Korea (18, 8.9%), Netherlands (18, 8.9%), and Germany (15, 7.4%) were the top five countries to receive funding. Each was more likely to receive government funds than other sources. Private funding was more common among Germany-led studies (3, 20%); meanwhile, university funding was prevalent among the United States-led studies (14, 25%). Interestingly, studies led by the United States (7, 12.5%) and China (4, 19%) were more likely to receive multiple source funding. Public funding was most common among France-led studies (2, 67%). In terms of affiliation, communication (66, 40%), psychology (38, 23%), and computer science (17, 10.3%) were the three top-funded affiliations. Communication and psychology were more likely to receive government and university funding. Computer science and industrial engineering were more likely to receive government and multiple source funding. Figure 5 presents the overall shares of funding sources among top 10 funded countries over the past decade.

Interestingly, there was no statistically significant difference in terms of funding whether studies were theory-driven or non-theory driven, χ^2 (1, n = 444) = .03, p = .90, Cramer's V = .01. Of the funded research, theory-driven studies were (171, 46.2%) and non-theory-driven studies were (35, 47.3%). Similarly, there was no significant difference between the employed method and funding χ^2 (4, n = 444) = .76, p = .94, Cramer's V = .04. Out of those funded, quantitative studies were (155, 46.3%), qualitative studies were (24, 43.6%), physiological methods studies were (8, 47.1%), computational methods studies were (5, 45.5%), and mixed methods studies were (14, 53.8%).

Table 6. Trends associated with funding over the past decade

Funding source	Period 1 2010–2015		Period 2 2016–2021		Total	
	Count	%	Count	%	Count	%
Government	41	9.2	84	18.9	125	28.2
University	12	2.7	28	6.3	40	9.0
Multiple	9	2.0	19	4.3	28	6.3
Private	3	0.7	7	1.6	10	2.3
Public	0	0	3	0.7	3	0.7
Unfunded	81	18.2	157	35.4	238	53.6

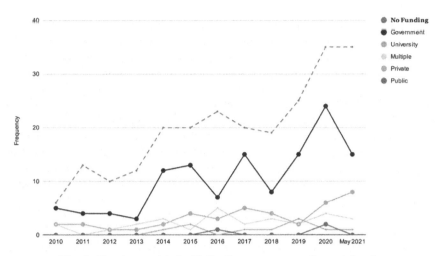

Fig. 4. Trends associated with funding sources over the past decade.

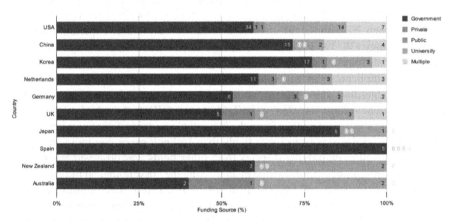

Fig. 5. Overall shares of funding sources by country over the past decade.

6   Discussion

This paper sought to explore the overarching trends in research themes, methods, theoretical frameworks, technologies, affiliation, and funding sources in the HMC research field over the last decade. First, an LDA topic modeling analysis of article abstracts reflected a trend of diverse thematic focus in HMC literature across the previous decade (RQ1). Second, we identified significant distinctions in methods, theoretical frameworks, studied technologies, and contributing affiliations (RQ2). Third, we found associations between employed theories, methods, and affiliations (RQ3), which corroborated our identified thematic trends. Finally, patterns that merit attention for *HMC* funding trends (RQ5) and contributing countries (RQ6). We expand on these trends below while addressing potential underlying reasons for the observed patterns.

First, in terms of the topic composition and distribution, we noticed diversity in focal areas among domain-specific journals. Communication journals (i.e., *CR, HCR, CT*) emphasized critical themes to the users and the society, such as privacy disclosure, information, moral violation, and social media messages with interest in impacts, perceptions, and attitudes. Meanwhile, most technology-oriented journals (i.e., *IJSR, JCMC, IJHCS*), which predominantly emphasized specific technologies, focused on users' experience, engagement, interaction, and persuasion rather than users' concerns. However, there were anomalies to this pattern. *CHB* seemed to maintain a balanced distribution in addressing user experience and concerns while focusing on specific technologies. *HMC* was among few technology-oriented journals that appeared to focus on the user (i.e., gender, age, children, and health) over any type of technology. The above trends are explained by the prominent developments in research and practice during the past decade. In 2018, HMC scholars [15] drew attention to the aspects receiving less consideration in communication with technology involving social aspects and cultural implications. Recent studies [37] examining the nature of HCI research also revealed that the field focused on behavioral aspects until 2012 and methodological designs between 2017–2020 with a brief attention to critical aspects to the user such as health and privacy only during 2013–2016. Simultaneously, the exponential growth of the user experience industry between 2010 and 2020 saw a significant interest in user experience research to inform strategy [38, 39]. Perhaps this explains the thematic trend among technology-oriented journals focusing on experience, engagement, and interaction more than users' concerns and implications as with communication journals.

Second, regarding the differences between each journal, we find that most technology-oriented journals: *IJSR, IJHCI, IJCS*, and *CHB* had the highest proportion of theory-based studies than other journals. Nevertheless, a significant number of these studies employed theories from other fields than technology or communication. The highest proportion of employing theories from other fields was observed among *CHB* which is attributed to their central scope in addressing the "psychological impact of computer use in human behavior" [40]. Thus, this high proportion may be streaming from the field psychology. Nevertheless, such a trend still reflects a shortage in field-specific frameworks addressing HMC thematic topics. Indeed, at a closer look our analysis indicated an association between using theories from outside the field of communication, technology, or CMC among all affiliations – including communication affiliations. This echoes previous findings [25] on emerging communication technology research which signaled a lack of theoretical frameworks to advance the field.

Third, in terms of methodological trends, technology and psychology-oriented journals were more likely to employ quantitative methods. Communication journals were more likely to employ qualitative approaches. Computational methods were almost absent among all journals except for a marginal use in *JCMC*. Regarding publishing affiliations, although we noticed a significant diversity in affiliations, the dispersion of those affiliations across the publishing journals during the past decade was sparse. *CHB* had the highest diversity rate compared to other journals followed by *IJHCI, IJSR, IJHCS,* and *NMS*.

Fourth, the analysis of HMC research trends among countries revealed an exponential growth at a competitive rate across the United States, Europe, and China over the past decade which is attributed to their leading positions across the globe in talent, research, development, adoption, and hardware acquisition in the field of AI technologies [41]. Over the past decade, each had their unique growth trend. While the United States-led studies saw highest share of contributions overall, China and Europe-led studies were the fastest growing. The United States leading position is attributed to its National AI Research & Development (R&D) Strategic Plan with the highest (R&D) expenditure, highest talent and research acquisition among all countries, and the increasing international collaborations of United States-affiliated researchers [41, 42]. The rapid growth of Europe-led studies in HMC may be attributed to the EU's efforts to implement its strategic plans towards a leading position in secure and ethical AI deployment [43] and the diversity of AI research agendas and specialties among EU countries [41]. Notably, HMC's growth in Europe is significantly led by the Netherlands which is deemed a hub for the EU's biggest technology businesses and research [44]. Meanwhile, China's fourfold increase between both periods is attributed to its highest AI adoption and availability of big data that is key for developing AI technologies [41, 45].

Finally, the proportion of government and university funded HMC research saw a twofold increase in the last five years. A trend that could be attributed to the high global expenditure on R&D in 2019 alone [46] which included the top 10 funded countries in this study. This also explains the steadiness and incremental growth in 2020 regardless of potential COVID-19 economic repercussions. The brief drops in government and university funding in 2013, 2016 and 2018 are also synchronous with the global economy recessions in the respective years [47]. Nevertheless, public and private funded HMC studies saw a significant drawback across the years among all countries despite the industry sector's increased investment in research globally [47]. Perhaps this trend is associated with public distrust and concerns about biases of industry-sponsored studies [48, 49]. Recent Pew research findings among US adults alone revealed a public skepticism of findings' reliability for industry-backed research in science and technology [48]. Even industrial engineering-affiliated studies were either predominantly government-funded or funded by sources other than the private sector. Meanwhile, it was refreshing to see that communication-affiliated studies were among top-funded disciplines signaling a trend in backing social sciences vis à vis STEM fields. Nevertheless, the percentage of HMC research (53.6%) receiving no funding support portends further future attention. Interestingly, our results indicated that neither tendency to employ a specific method nor reliance on theoretical lenses (theoretical vs. atheoretical studies) were significant drivers for funding likelihood.

7 Limitations and Future Directions

This study is not without limitations. First, as with any topic modeling approach, our investigation is limited to the statistical structure of the data and the authors' inference and interpretations of the topic-term distributions. However, it provides a preliminary overview in identifying the elements of HMC topic composition. Second, the study aimed at drawing an overarching picture for HMC research by looking at various journals. In this context, for space limitations, we only reported the first top topic incoherence and prevalence among the top five generated for each journal. Thus, there may be further topics – though of less coherence – reflecting a broader picture of the topic-term distribution for each journal. Future studies might look at each journal extensively. Third, the topic distribution results only reveal an overall trend during the past decade. Future studies may investigate how each theme evolved. Finally, our articles' screening included only English-language HMC studies, which may have affected the percentage and frequency of each country's distribution. Thus, the results presented in our study pertain to English-language HMC studies only. Future studies may investigate HMC studies in other languages.

8 Concluding Remarks

In conclusion, our study illustrated the diverse composition of HMC research and the unique scopes that each domain-specific journal comprised. The thematic focus of HMC literature exhibited a balanced focus among communication journals and technology-specific journals. However, more diversity is needed in terms of the studied technologies. The past decade trend comprised a limited set of devices and saw marginal attention to others such as wearables. Echoing previous emerging technology research, additional efforts are equally needed towards developing theoretical HMC-focused frameworks. Finally, HMC funding trends suggest more attention to the proportion of unfunded studies.

References

1. Fortunati, L., Edwards, A.: Moving Ahead with Human-Machine Communication (2021)
2. Guzman, A.L., Lewis, S.C.: Artificial intelligence and communication: a human-machine communication research agenda. New Media Soc. **22**(1), 70–86 (2020). https://doi.org/10.1177/1461444819858691
3. Song, H., Eberl, J.-M., Eisele, O.: Less fragmented than we thought? Toward clarification of a subdisciplinary linkage in communication science, 2010–2019. J. Commun. **70**(3), 310–334 (2020). https://doi.org/10.1093/joc/jqaa009
4. Duke, N.K., Mallette, M.H.: Critical Issues: Preparation for New Literacy Researchers in Multi-Epistemological, Multi-Methodological Times (2001). https://doi.org/10.1080/10862960109548114
5. Guzman, A.L.: Ontological boundaries between humans and computers and the implications for Human-Machine Communication. Hum.-Machine Commun. **1**, 37–54 (2020). https://doi.org/10.30658/hmc.1.3
6. Johanssen, J., Wang, X.: Artificial intuition in tech journalism on AI: imagining the human subject. Hum.-Machine Commun. **2**, 173–190 (2021). https://doi.org/10.30658/hmc.2.9
7. Wołk, K.: Emergency, pictogram-based augmented reality medical communicator prototype using precise eye-tracking technology. Cyberpsychol. Behav. Soc. Netw. **22**(2), 151–157 (2019). https://doi.org/10.1089/cyber.2018.0035
8. Guo, F., Li, M., Qu, Q., Duffy, V.G.: The effect of a humanoid robot's emotional behaviors on users' emotional responses: evidence from pupillometry and electroencephalography measures. Int. J. Hum.-Comput. Interaction **35**(20), 1947–1959 (2019). https://doi.org/10.1080/10447318.2019.1587938
9. Edwards, C., et al.: Communicating with machines: interventions with digital agents. International Communication Association (ICA) 2017 Pre-Conference (2017)

10. Gunkel, D.J.: Communication and artificial intelligence: opportunities and challenges for the 21st century. Communication+1, **1**(1), 1–25 (2012). https://doi.org/10.7275/R5QJ7F7R

11. Lewis, S.C., Guzman, A.L., Schmidt, T.R.: Automation, journalism, and human–machine communication: rethinking roles and relationships of humans and machines in news. Digit. J. **7**(4), 409–427 (2019). https://doi.org/10.1080/21670811.2019.1577147

12. Pavitt, C., Braddock, K., Mann, A.: Group communication during resource dilemmas: 3. Effects of social value orientation. Commun. Quarterly **57**(4), 433–451 (2009). https://doi.org/10.1080/01463370903320856

13. Dautenhahn, K.: Socially intelligent agents in human primate culture. In: Payr, S., Trappl, R. (eds.) Agent Culture: Human-Agent Interaction in a Multicultural World, pp. 35–51. CRC Press (2004). https://doi.org/10.1201/b12476

14. Edwards, A.P.: Animals, humans, and machines: interactive implications of ontological classification. In: Guzman, A.L. (ed.), Human-Machine Communication: Rethinking Communication, Technology, and Ourselves, pp. 29–50. Peter Lang (2018). https://doi.org/10.3726/b14399

15. Guzman, A.L.: Human-Machine Communication. https://www.peterlang.com/document/1055458 (2018)

16. Sundar, S.S.: The MAIN model: a heuristic approach to understanding technology effects on credibility. In: Metzger, M.J., Flanagin, A.J. (eds.), MacArthur Foundation Series on Digital Media and Learning, pp. 73–100. Cambridge (2008). https://doi.org/10.1162/dmal.9780262562324.073

17. Smith, R.G., Eckroth, J.: Building AI applications: yesterday, today, and tomorrow. AI Mag. **38**(1), 6–22 (2017). https://doi.org/10.1609/aimag.v38i1.2709

18. Human-Machine Communication: https://stars.library.ucf.edu/hmc/ (2020)

19. Lombard, M., Ditton, T.: At the heart of it all: the concept of presence. J. Comput.-Mediated Commun. **3**(2), JCMC321 (1997)

20. Nass, C., Moon, Y.: Machines and mindlessness: social responses to computers. J. Soc. Issues **56**(1), 81–103 (2000)

21. Sundar, S.S., Nass, C.: Source orientation in human-computer interaction: programmer, networker, or independent social actor. Commun. Res. **27**(6), 683–703 (2000)

22. Picard, R.W.: Affective computing: challenges. Int. J. Hum. Comput. Stud. **59**(1), 55–64 (2003). https://doi.org/10.1016/S1071-5819(03)00052-1

23. Palandrani, P., Little, A.: A decade of change: how Tech evolved in the 2010s and what's in store for the 2020s (2020)

24. Auxier, B., Anderson, M., Kumar, M.: 10 tech-related trends that shaped the decade. Pew Research Center. https://www.pewresearch.org/fact-tank/2019/12/20/10-tech-related-trends-that-shaped-the-decade/ (2019)

25. Borah, P.: Emerging communication technology research: theoretical and methodological variables in the last 16 years and future directions. New Media Soc. **19**(4), 616–636 (2017). https://doi.org/10.1177/1461444815621512

26. Tomasello, T.K., Lee, Y., Baer, A.P.: 'New media' research publication trends and outlets in communication, 1990–2006. New Media Soc. **12**(4), 531–548 (2010). https://doi.org/10.1177/1461444809342762

27. Page, M.J., et al.: The PRISMA 2020 statement: an updated guideline for reporting systematic reviews. Syst. Rev. **10**(89), 1–11 (2021). https://doi.org/10.1186/s13643-021-01626-4

28. Griffiths, T.L., Steyvers, M.: Finding scientific topics. Proc. Natl. Acad. Sci. **101**(Suppl. 1), 5228–5235 (2004)

29. Sun, L., Yin, Y.: Discovering themes and trends in transportation research using topic modeling. Transport. Res. C: Emerg. Technol. **77**, 49–66 (2017)
30. Blei, D.M., Ng, A., Jordan, M.: Latent Dirichlet allocation. J. Mach. Learn. Res. **30** (2003)
31. Panichella, A.: A systematic comparison of search-based approaches for LDA hyperparameter tuning. Inf. Softw. Technol. **130**, 106411 (2021). https://doi.org/10.1016/j.infsof.2020.106411
32. Mimno, D., Wallach, H., Talley, E., Leenders, M., McCallum, A.: Optimizing semantic coherence in topic models. In: Proceedings of the 2011 Conference on Empirical Methods in Natural Language Processing, pp. 262–272. https://aclanthology.org/D11-1024 (2011)
33. Panichella, A., Dit, B., Oliveto, R., Di Penta, M., Poshyvanyk, D., De Lucia, A.: How to effectively use topic models for software engineering tasks? An approach based on genetic algorithms. In: 2013 35th International Conference on Software Engineering (ICSE), pp. 522–531 (2013). https://doi.org/10.1109/ICSE.2013.6606598
34. Cao, J., Xia, T., Li, J., Zhang, Y., Tang, S.: A density-based method for adaptive LDA model selection. In: Neurocomputing — 16th European Symposium on Artificial Neural Networks, 2008, vol. 72, no. 7–9, pp. 1775–1781 (2009)
35. Arun, R., Suresh, V., Veni Madhavan, C.E., Narasimha Murthy, M.N.: On Finding the Natural Number of Topics with Latent Dirichlet Allocation: Some Observations. In: Zaki, M.J., Yu, J.X., Ravindran, B., Pudi, V. (eds.) PAKDD 2010. LNCS (LNAI), vol. 6118, pp. 391–402. Springer, Heidelberg (2010). https://doi.org/10.1007/978-3-642-13657-3_43
36. Schwarz, C.: Ldagibbs: a command for topic modeling in Stata using latent Dirichlet allocation. Stata J.: Promot. Commun. Stat. Stata **18**(1), 101–117 (2018). https://doi.org/10.1177/1536867X1801800107
37. Shibuya, Y., Hamm, A., Pargman, T.C.: Mapping HCI Research Methods for Studying Social Media Interaction: A Systematic Literature Review. https://www.sciencedirect.com/science/article/pii/S0747563221004544 (2022)
38. Collum, M.: The State of UX Research in 2019. Medium. https://uxdesign.cc/the-state-of-ux-research-in-2019-4ba797c09b2f (31 Jan 2019)
39. Nielsen, J.: A 100-Year View of User Experience. Nielsen Norman Group. https://www.nngroup.com/articles/100-years-ux/ (2017)
40. Computers in Human Behavior Journal, Aims & Scope, Elsevier: https://www.journals.elsevier.com/journals.elsevier.com/computers-in-human-behavior
41. Castro, D., McLaughlin, M., Chivot, E.: Who Is Winning the AI Race: China, the EU or the United States? 106 (2021)
42. AI Report: Artificial Intelligence: How knowledge is created, transferred, and used Trends in China, Europe, and the United States. Elsevier. https://www.elsevier.com/research-intelligence/resource-library/ai-report (n.d.). Retrieved 10 Feb 2022
43. Member States and Commission to work together to boost artificial intelligence "made in Europe": European Commission – European Commission. https://ec.europa.eu/commission/presscorner/detail/en/IP_18_6689 (n.d.). Retrieved 10 Feb 2022
44. Techleap.nl.: Netherlands Emerging as "Hottest Tech Hub" in Europe, but not Reaching its Full Potential yet. https://www.prnewswire.com/news-releases/netherlands-emerging-as-hottest-tech-hub-in-europe-but-not-reaching-its-full-potential-yet-301438925.html (n.d.). Retrieved 10 Feb 2022
45. Li, D., Tong, T.W., Xiao, Y.: Is China Emerging as the Global Leader in AI? Harvard Business Review. https://hbr.org/2021/02/is-china-emerging-as-the-global-leader-in-ai (18 Feb 2021)
46. Global Research and Development Expenditures: Fact Sheet 2022 [online]. Congressional Research Service. https://sgp.fas.org/crs/misc/R44283.pdf
47. Kose, M.A., Sugawara, N., Terrones, M.E.: Global Recessions. World Bank (2020). https://doi.org/10.1596/1813-9450-9172

48. Johnson, C.: Most Americans are wary of industry funded research. Pew Research Center. https://www.pewresearch.org/fact-tank/2019/10/04/most-americans-are-wary-of-industry-funded-research/ (2019). Retrieved 7 Feb 2022
49. Fabbri, A., Lai, A., Grundy, Q., Bero, L.A.: The influence of industry sponsorship on the research agenda: a scoping review. Am. J. Public Health **108**(11), e9–e16 (2018). https://doi.org/10.2105/AJPH.2018.304677

A Descriptive Model of Passive and Natural Passive Human-Computer Interaction

Andreas Mallas[1]([⊠]) [iD], Michalis Xenos[1] [iD], and Christos Katsanos[2] [iD]

[1] Computer Engineering and Informatics Department, Patras University, Patras, Greece
{mallas,xenos}@ceid.upatras.gr
[2] Department of Informatics, Aristotle University of Thessaloniki, Thessaloniki, Greece
ckatsanos@csd.auth.gr

Abstract. System invisibility is a common aim for various computing types such as context-aware and ubiquitous computing. We argue that to achieve invisibility, one must examine the user interactions from a user experience point of view. In this paper, we focus on non-intentional human-computer interactions and discuss the term Passive Interaction, starting from its theoretical background. We present a descriptive model where we define Passive Interaction as an interaction initiated by the system without the user's intention that is triggered by a change in the physical or mental state of a user aiming at adjusting the system status to provide a consistent user experience in an ongoing task. Consequently, we define Natural Passive Interaction as a specific case of Passive Interaction in which the system response is undetected by the user. Finally, we present the requirements that must be satisfied for a Passive Interaction to qualify as a Natural Passive Interaction, and we discuss Passive Interaction effectiveness related to system response time followed by examples of real and envisioned cases/scenarios where such interactions can occur.

Keywords: HCI theories and methods · Passive interactions · Implicit interactions

1 Introduction

From the introduction [1] and the popularization [2] of the term Human-Computer Interaction (HCI) until recently, the "I" in HCI implied a typical action and reaction. In this action-reaction sequence(s) the human was either actively initiating this sequence (e.g., the human selects an icon, and the computer responds) or the human was actively responding to a change of the computer status (e.g., the computer shows a message, and the human responds with a follow-up action).

Recent innovations in HCI-related technology have changed a lot of how humans interact with computers. Nowadays, the "C" in HCI has broadened from the narrow perspective of the term when HCI was introduced and includes a plethora of devices that are part of everyday life such as tablets, pocket-carried smartphones, Internet of things (IoT) devices, Head-up displays (HUDs), etc. Interactions can be as casual as playing a

M. Kurosu (Ed.): HCII 2022, LNCS 13302, pp. 104–116, 2022.
https://doi.org/10.1007/978-3-031-05311-5_7

game on a smartphone, to as important as to intervene to relinquish control of a semi-automated vehicle [3]. From hereinafter we use "system" to refer to the computer for all such interactions between humans (equivalently referred to as "users") and a system.

Furthermore, contemporary interactions involve more modalities. Examples of such modalities include users who talk to digital voice assistants for complex tasks such as crowdsourcing [4], touch and blink to their smartwatches [5], interact with tangible interfaces based on fluidic mechanisms [6], receive haptic feedback when interacting with objects in virtual reality [7], and participate in a training session moderated by a robot [8]. What all these examples have in common is the fact that the interaction is considered active and intentional (i.e., the user intentionally acts, either responding to a change of the system status or initiating an action-response sequence).

Recently, an increased interest in human-computer interactions that deviate from the norm of intentional interactions is observed. These interactions are often called "implicit interactions" and are encountered in different domains such as attentive interfaces [9, 10], physiological computing [11], and ubiquitous computing [12]. The basic principle of such interactions is that the system uses the information available in the environment and acts without the user's intention to achieve a specific goal. Serim and Jacucci [13] define implicit interactions as "interactions in which the appropriateness of a system response to the user input (i.e., an effect) does not rely on the user having conducted the input to intentionally achieve it."

In this paper, we focus on non-intentional human-computer interactions that are initiated by context-aware systems. We present a descriptive model, where we propose and define a subcategory of such interactions called "Passive Interaction" aiming to provide a consistent user experience in an ongoing task. Consequently, we present the theoretical background of Passive Interaction and its definition and define a subcategory of Passive Interactions, the "Natural Passive Interaction", as a specific case in which the system response is undetected by the user. The combination of the unintentionality of the interaction -in terms of the system response- and the non-detectable nature of the system response – that aims to provide a consistent user experience – results in a non-intrusive, distraction-free user experience making Natural Passive Interactions invisible to the user. Afterward, we present the requirements that must be satisfied to ensure an undetected response followed by a breakdown of Passive Interaction effectiveness related to system response time. Finally, we provide examples of real and envisioned cases/scenarios where such interactions can occur.

2 Related Work

HCI is challenging because rapid changes in technology run up against negligible changes in human nature [14]. These rapid changes in technology allowed us to present the concepts of Passive and Natural Passive Interactions. The term "passive" has also been used in Brain-Computer Interfaces (BCI) but in a different context. BCI does not focus on the direct control of computer interfaces (e.g., mouse cursors or text input systems) but instead focuses on brain-sensing for passive or background access into the cognitive and affective state [15]. BCI is classified as active, reactive, and passive, with passive being the "one that derives its outputs from arbitrary brain activity arising without the purpose of voluntary control, for enriching a human-machine interaction with implicit information on the actual user state" [16]. There are 3 main differences when comparing passive BCI to Passive Interactions. First, the primary input in passive BCI is brain activity, whereas in Passive Interactions it is the physical or mental state of a user that includes other forms of input methods (brain activity is not required). Second, passive BCI system response aims at enriching a human-machine interaction (i.e., changing the user experience), whereas, in Passive Interactions, the focus is on providing a consistent user experience (i.e., keeping the user experience the same). Third, Passive Interactions narrow the scope of interactions to only those that support an ongoing task.

Multiple visions of context-aware computing have been introduced, including ubiquitous/pervasive computing, invisible computing, proactive computing, ambient intelligence, sentient computing, etc. [17]. Context-aware applications provide less distraction to the users by adapting their outputs to contextual information with regards to the user and the surrounding environment.

The term proactive computing was introduced [18] as moving from human-centered computing to human-supervised computing. In this research strand, the envisioned goal of getting humans out of the operational loop even in tasks such as the software-creation process is still a vision, but our work suggests that it is now feasible for other specific interactions.

The concept of seamless and destruction-free support of users is a vision of pervasive computing [19] that leads towards smart homes. In such cases, the system automatically adjusts the environment based on what anticipates the user's desire is. For example, in [20] the system automatically adjusts the lighting of the environment, and in [21] the system controls automated mini-blinds by predicting user needs. In such cases, as stated in [22], from a user's perspective, the proactive adaptation is usually preferable over the reactive adaptation as it results in an uninterrupted execution. However, from a system developer's perspective, proactive adaptation is only possible with sufficiently accurate predictions for the future states of the system. Therefore, due to the difficulty of developing such predictions for complex systems that involve users, most existing systems are focusing primarily on reactive adaptation.

What most types of context-aware computing have in common is the aim of making the systems invisible to the user: Weiser mentions the disappearance of pervasive computing technology from a user's consciousness [23], invisible computing argues for minimal distraction to the users [24], proactive computing suggests that the system should take action on users behalf so that they can focus on higher-level tasks [18], and ambient intelligence focuses on providing unobtrusive and invisible services [25]. However, there does not seem to exist a concrete framework that provides the conditions and guidelines to achieve system invisibility. In all these works, a reasonable approximation to the ideal of the disappearance of computing from user's consciousness is minimal user distraction [26].

To investigate the conditions where interactions with content-aware systems are invisible to the user, one must examine those cases from a user experience point of view. We argue that such interactions should be non-intended by the user, which is similar to the concept of implicit interactions [13]. Contrary to the definition of implicit interactions, we must limit the scope of such interactions and also specify the response type in order to achieve invisibility. To this end, the aim of the system response should be to achieve a consistent user experience and be undetected to the user. When both conditions are fulfilled, the interaction should be invisible to the user.

Achieving system invisibility is not an easy task, and with the existing technological possibilities, it might not be feasible for every human-computer interaction. Nevertheless, there are enough existing technologies that can facilitate Passive Interactions and are already incorporated in everyday devices (e.g., cameras and microphones) or becoming part of everyday life (e.g., smartwatches with multiple sensors such as accelerometer, gyro, heart rate monitor, barometer, compass). For instance, there are existing applications that detect emotions such as stress from a camera [27], or even using the newly available 3D-sensing cameras on smartphones [28], applications that can predict stress from user's galvanic skin response [29, 30], smartwatches that predict stress [31], or smartwatches that can be used to detect complex human activities [32], car steering wheels that monitor blood pressure [33], and wearables that transmit information from the body to the mind on a subconscious level [34]. Furthermore, as these technologies evolve and existing technologies such as eye-tracking mature, they are becoming more affordable and more accessible to everyday life.

In this paper, we present the definition of Natural Passive Interaction that represents the cases where particular interactions with context-aware systems can remain hidden from the user bringing us a step closer to accomplishing the goal of achieving system invisibility.

3   Natural Passive Interaction

Every individual has a unique way of interacting with computer systems. Some differences occur naturally from users' physical characteristics, and some depend on their habits and preferences. Even in the traditional context in which a user uses a computer on a desk, the conditions that depend on the user continuously fluctuate. For example, unintentional minor ergonomic changes (e.g., chair and body movements) directly influence the distance of the user from the screen, and consequently, the efficiency of the interaction. To counteract those changes, users must actively adjust the system to maintain the ideal conditions (e.g., zoom in/out the content of the screen), although these adjustments can severely interrupt their workflow. Some modern systems are capable of monitoring the user's physical and mental state and attempt to maintain consistent conditions unshackling the user from the burden of unintended system adjustments that do not offer any value towards their intended use of the system.

In the following section, we introduce the terms "Passive Interaction" and "Natural Passive Interaction". The latter aims to define a subcategory of unintentional interactions that result in system responses that are imperceptible to the user and thus do not interrupt their workflow. Henceforward by system status, we refer to the variables of the system that can be configured by the user or automatically configured by the system.

3.1 Definition

We define Passive Interaction as "*an interaction initiated by the system without the user's intention that is triggered by a change in the physical or mental state of a user aiming at adjusting the system status to provide a consistent user experience in an ongoing task*".

The basic premise of Passive Interactions is that an unintended change in the user state would result in an unintended variation in the user experience that the system counteracts by adjusting the system status accordingly to provide an uninterrupted user experience in an ongoing task.

The term "passive" in the previous definition refers to interactions that are not actively and intentionally initiated by the user. These Passive Interactions occur when the user is occupied with an ongoing task, and changes in the user's physical or mental state require adjustments to the system status to maintain a consistent user experience. Considering that the required adjustments are made by the system, these interactions can be characterized as passive – from the user's perception – while the user actively focuses on their ongoing task.

The term "consistent user experience" refers to maintaining the user's workflow by eliminating interruptions that would otherwise occur by changes in the user's state as time passes. These interruptions can fall under two categories: a) the changes per se that would ensue by the adjustments in the user's state (e.g., changes in the distance between the user and the system result in differences in perceived sound volumes and potentially the sound's characteristics), and b) the actions that the user would have to perform to counteract those adjustments, for instance, breaking their workflow to adjust the volume.

We denote the system status as $S(U(t))$, which is a function of the user state U, and the user state is a function of time t. With system response, we refer to the time it takes for the system to modify its status given a change in the user's state. In an ideal system, where the system response is instant, the $S(U(t))$ function should be enough to determine the system status, but in actual conditions, the system response can never be equal to zero.

When the actual system status is S, then the relation between the ideal system status S_i and actual system status S in Passive Interactions is:

$$S(U(t)) = S_i(U(t - T_s)) \tag{1}$$

where t measures time and T_s is the actual system response time.

Consequently, we define the Natural Passive Interaction as "*a specific case of Passive Interaction in which the system response is undetected by the user*".

Two critical requirements must be satisfied to ensure an undetected response:

1. The system response time (T_s) must be less than the time the user needs to perceive the response (T_p).
2. The type of response must ensure that from the user's perspective, the system status is perceived as unchanged.

3.2 System Response Time

The system response time is a crucial factor for the Natural Passive Interactions. A Natural Passive Interaction requires that $T_s < T_p$. Several factors can affect the system's response time T_s. The most significant of them are the time that the system needs to perceive a change in the physical or mental state of a user, the time required to process and determine the needed response to this stimulus (this can greatly vary from nearly instantly for simple algorithms to a significant time if the system is using machine learning techniques), and finally, the time for the system to manifest the response.

The user's perceived time T_p can be dependent on the type of stimulus. Recent advancements suggest that visual perception may also depend on a movement controlling region of the brain [35]. However, for the scope of this paper, we can approach the user factor of Passive Interaction based on the engineering models of human performance [36]. The Human Processor Model assumes that a simple user reaction to a computer stimulus is the sum of perceptual cycle time (T_p which depends on the complexity of the signal being perceived), followed by cognitive cycle time T_c and motor processor time T_m. It should be noted that the T_p value in the case of Passive Interactions might be different from the one used in the Human Processor Model [37] because, in the case of Passive Interactions, the user must notice a change in an existing element already in their perception (e.g., the volume level of a sound system increasing or decreasing), which might take them more time to notice. Assuming that the type of response is such that from the user's perspective the system status can be perceived as unchanged we distinguish four categories only for the system's response time T_s with regards to the user in Passive Interactions. These categories are a) optimal, b) efficient, c) lazy, and d) inefficient. For the first requirement to be satisfied and for the interaction to qualify as a Natural Passive Interaction, the system response time must be in the optimal category. The categories are explained as follows.

Optimal. In the Optimal category, the system response is less than the time the user needs to perceive the change. Hence, the change in the system status is not perceived by the user, as shown in (2). Every Natural Passive Interaction should have a response time that is in the optimal category.

$$T_s < T_p \tag{2}$$

Efficient. In the case of Efficient Passive Interaction, on one hand, the system response can be perceived by the user, but on the other hand, that change that was initiated by the system is still useful for the user because it is always faster than the time the user needs to realize what their own response to this change should be, as shown in (3).

$$T_p < T_s < T_p + T_c \tag{3}$$

Lazy. In the case of Lazy Passive Interaction, the system response is always faster than a user response to the stimulus, the change of the system status can be perceived by the user, and they certainly feel a delay from the time there is a change in their physical or mental state to the time the machine responds resulting in a "laggy" feeling, as shown in (4).

$$T_p + T_c < T_s < T_p + T_c + T_m \tag{4}$$

Inefficient. In the case of Inefficient Passive Interaction, the system response is slower than the user's response to the stimulus, as shown in (5).

$$T_s > T_p + T_c + T_m \tag{5}$$

System responses that do not fall in the optimal category are still beneficial for the user and can qualify as Passive Interactions, but the system response cannot be undetected by the user even if the second requirement regarding the type of response for Natural Passive Interaction is satisfied, which is described in the next section.

3.3 Type of Response

To better understand the second requirement, we illustrate an example of a Natural Passive Interaction that satisfies it and explain the case where it might not.

Let us assume an ongoing task where a user is listening to music in a stationary sound system while the user is moving around a room (e.g., cleaning the room). In a Passive Interaction, the sound system tracks the user's position in the room and adjusts the volume output (i.e., lowers the volume when the person moves nearer and raises it when they move farther) to provide the same volume level regardless of the user's location in the room. Let us assume that the first requirement is satisfied, and the system response is optimal.

To fulfil the second requirement, one should also examine the sound characteristics of the audio that the user perceives and not only the volume level. In a simplified case where the user can only move in a straight line (one degree of freedom) and only for a few meters away from the system, with no obstacles in between, then, the first requirement should reasonably be enough for the system response to be undetected. In a more realistic case where the user has more degrees of freedom to move around the room, the direction of the sound should always face the user for the experience to be consistent. An off-axis direction of the audio source (e.g., behind the speaker) would provide different sound characteristics making the change detectable by the user. In that case, to achieve a Natural Passive Interaction, the system can employ a 360-degree speaker or speakers that physically rotate towards the user.

4 Sample Cases

To supplement the descriptive model, we present sample cases based on existing and envisioned future implementations that conform to our definitions and could be distinctive utilization of our model. The sample case of the earbuds is based on existing technologies, and the research mentioned in the example demonstrates that this implementation can be a Natural Passive Interaction. The envisioned future cases include a display that adapts its image based on the user position and an exoskeleton that adjusts the level of assistive power to maintain the same level of user effort even when the user is fatigued. The suggested future cases (Display and Exoskeleton) are based on technologies that are available today but have not been implemented as we envisioned Passive and Natural Passive Interaction. The sample cases aim to be discussion points on how to materialize systems that adhere to the requirements of Natural Passive Interactions.

4.1 Earbuds with Spatial Audio that Maintain the Ideal 3D Audio Image Regardless of Head Rotation

Spatial audio is a way to create an immersive audio experience by providing sound in 360° around a listener, as shown in Fig. 1 (left side). Recent technological advances implemented spatial surround sound on headphones and earphones, bringing the technology away from the home theaters into our everyday lives. Users can now have unique experiences while viewing videos and other media, playing games, and in the future, even conference calls that provide audio spatial awareness.

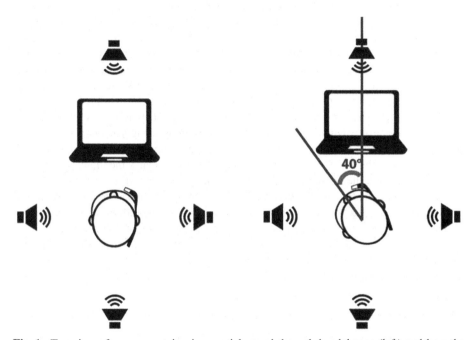

Fig. 1. Top view of a user experiencing spatial sound through headphones (left) and how the system maintains the audio image despite changes in head orientation (right); icons made by Pixel perfect (www.flaticon.com).

Being free from the spatial restrictions of a living room means that the user can now move more freely around the environment – including head movements – and this factor might influence the ideal audio experience. A rotation of the head by a few degrees to the left results in a sound that – should originally be heard from the right side of a user – is now being heard from the front side. A system that adjusts the spatial sound image to the head's orientation fast enough – and keeps the position of the sound sources in their intended place irrelevant of the head's orientation (Fig. 1, right side) – could qualify as Natural Passive Interaction because the type of response will not be detected by the user.

Zotkin and colleagues [38] presented a headphone system for rendering localized spatial audio in a virtual auditory space with head tracking that captures the user position and head orientation and adjusts the spatial sound accordingly. The researchers concluded that "the latency of our system falls within the limits of perceptually unnoticeable latency" and since the user does not intend to change the orientation of the audio image by moving their head (the movement happens for unrelated reasons) the interaction can be characterized as Natural Passive Interaction.

4.2   Display System that Adjusts Naturally to User Position

Following the current developments in display technologies, manufacturers aim to transform every surface into a screen. This includes but is not limited to projectors that can be utilized on ordinary objects like desks, glass windows that also act as information hubs, to head-up displays on cars. The addition of more and larger viewing devices in our daily experiences does not appear to stop anytime soon. In the past, the limited availability of screens meant that they were carefully placed at optimal conditions regarding the user, e.g., a monitor on a desk, or a laptop on the user's lap. However, the broad utilization of viewing devices in non-conventional situations suggests that users must forgo – to some degree – the optimal conditions that they have previously been accustomed to.

In this sample case, we suggest a system with a large display that is aware of the user's position and viewing angle relative to the screen by using sensors and cameras. The system can then adjust the displayed image size to the appropriate zoom level based on the distance of the user. The system's aim is for the user to view the image at the ideal size, independent of their distance. Additionally, the system can offset the user's off-axis viewing angle by controlling the perspective of the image, similarly to [39], providing a perceived image that would be identical to what the user would view in front of the screen. If the system response is fast enough, the image being displayed will always appear to the user, at the same size with no tilt independent of the user's movement, providing a consistent user experience. Such an experience can be characterized as a Natural Passive Interaction.

4.3   Exoskeleton with Adaptive Assistance Power

An exoskeleton is an external structural mechanism for human power amplification utilized in different settings, including medical (e.g., for patient rehabilitation) and industrial (e.g., to assist workers in carrying heavy equipment) [40]. In this sample case, we suggest a powered exoskeleton system that adapts the level of assistive power based on the user's physical and mental status.

In a powered exoskeleton used to enhance worker carrying capacity, the system could infer the user fatigue by monitoring – for example – the user's difficulty in performing particular motions that would incur after a period of time. The basic premise of this example is that user fatigue can increase the level of effort to perform a motion, and the system suggested would aim to sustain the same level of user effort by adjusting the level of assistive power when needed. A weary user would be slower (e.g., by applying less power, slower responses, etc.) in performing the same motions repeatedly and the system – after deducing that the user is fatigued – can increase the level of assistance aiming at a consistent user experience. The proposed system could also adjust the level of assistive power on a per motion basis, meaning that a tired user that is performing poorly In a certain hand motion would have the assistive power adjusted only in this particular motion.

A similar system can be used for rehabilitation, for example, utilized by an injured individual that is starting to regain muscle power. In this case, the system would provide more assistive power at the start of the rehabilitation process, and as the patient progresses, the level of assistive power would minimize.

In both cases, to accurately infer the effort level (not force) a user is applying at any given time, the system can monitor multiple inputs such as human input characteristics (applied force, speed, reflexes, etc.) and physiological signals and then use machine learning technics to calculate the assistance level.

5 Discussion, Conclusions and Future Work

This paper presented the Passive and Natural Passive Interactions as forms of implicit interactions that focus on the user experience perspective, aiming at providing a consistent user experience regardless of the changes in the user's physical or mental state. Natural Passive Interaction, in addition, states that the system response should be undetected by the user and specifies two requirements regarding the system response time and the type of the response. Assuring that the system's response time is fast enough alone does not ensure that the interaction would not be noticed by the user. The type of system response plays a crucial role in maintaining concealment regarding the user.

In a Natural Passive Interaction, a system that maintains the same conditions for the user, if it is not correctly configured it would result in a very poor user experience. Let's take the example of an audio system that adjusts the volume level based on the user distance from the system -higher volume when the user is further away and lower when near- aiming at a listening experience where the volume level is perceived as invariable by the user. In this case, the user relinquishes the natural method of increasing the perceived volume by going near the audio source, e.g., to hear better someone -that is speaking more quietly than the others- in a discussion. This factor alone suggests that it is crucial for some systems to adopt a calibration method for learning the specific user's preferences and eliminate such cases. Furthermore, all systems should have an override method that is easily accessible to the user to disengage or recalibrate them.

Moreover, a system designed for Natural Passive Interaction requires careful consideration of the characteristics of the user state that it will be monitoring. For example, a system that is changing the brightness of a screen based on the user's pupil dilation (e.g., if the pupil is too small in diameter the screen should be dimmer to reduce fatigue) should also take into account that the pupil diameter might change by other factors such as changes in the emotions, etc. Therefore, some systems might require a combination of user characteristics to determine the user state. Furthermore, the task of defining the $S(U)$ function might not be as clear as in most of the sample cases provided in this paper. More complex systems, in addition to user calibration, might require the use of machine learning and a training period before the system determines the $S(U)$, as in the exoskeleton case presented as an example.

Concerning the system response time, adopting the Human Processor Model [37] allowed us to categorize the responses regarding the level of effectiveness. Nevertheless, in an actual system, the time that the user needs to perceive a change might be dependent on the modalities involved, and further experimental research is required to accurately determine the factors that influence this quantity.

We believe that in the near future, many of the functions that are now user-initiated in order to sustain a good user interaction experience will naturally fade into the background, with the user not even noticing how the system is adjusting to their needs. The context-aware systems that adopt these technologies will bring us a step closer to the dream of system invisibility that had – so long ago – been envisioned by types of context-aware computing. For example, a child born into such a future might not even know affordances that are available today, such as "pinch to zoom" because the system would take care of this need for them. In such cases of Passive and Natural Passive Interactions, the model presented in this paper and the levels of effectiveness discussed could play a meaningful role in guiding new designs and applications.

References

1. Carlisle, J.H.: Evaluating the impact of office automation on top management communication. In: Proceedings of the June 7–10, 1976, National Computer Conference and Exposition, pp. 611–616. Association for Computing Machinery, New York, NY, USA (1976). https://doi.org/10.1145/1499799.1499885

2. Card, S.K., Moran, T.P., Newell, A.: The keystroke-level model for user performance time with interactive systems. Commun. ACM. **23**, 396–410 (1980). https://doi.org/10.1145/358886.358895

3. Mallas, A., Xenos, M., Rigou, M.: Evaluating a Mouse-Based and a Tangible Interface Used for Operator Intervention on Two Autonomous Robots. In: Kurosu, M. (ed.) HCII 2020. LNCS, vol. 12182, pp. 668–678. Springer, Cham (2020). https://doi.org/10.1007/978-3-030-49062-1_46

4. Hettiachchi, D., et al.: "Hi! I am the Crowd Tasker" Crowdsourcing through Digital Voice Assistants. In: Proceedings of the 2020 CHI Conference on Human Factors in Computing Systems, pp. 1–14. Association for Computing Machinery, New York, NY, USA (2020). https://doi.org/10.1145/3313831.3376320

5. Wang, B., Grossman, T.: BlyncSync: enabling multimodal smartwatch gestures with synchronous touch and blink. In: Proceedings of the 2020 CHI Conference on Human Factors in Computing Systems, pp. 1–14. Association for Computing Machinery, New York, NY, USA (2020). https://doi.org/10.1145/3313831.3376132

6. Mor, H., Yu, T., Nakagaki, K., Miller, B.H., Jia, Y., Ishii, H.: Venous materials: towards interactive fluidic mechanisms. In: Proceedings of the 2020 CHI Conference on Human Factors in Computing Systems, pp. 1–14. Association for Computing Machinery, New York, NY, USA (2020). https://doi.org/10.1145/3313831.3376129

7. Huang, H.-Y., Ning, C.-W., Wang, P.-Y., Cheng, J.-H., Cheng, L.-P.: Haptic-go-round: a surrounding platform for encounter-type haptics in virtual reality experiences. In: Proceedings of the 2020 CHI Conference on Human Factors in Computing Systems, pp. 1–10. Association for Computing Machinery, New York, NY, USA (2020). https://doi.org/10.1145/3313831.3376476

8. Carros, F., et al.: Exploring human-robot interaction with the elderly: results from a ten-week case study in a care home. In: Proceedings of the 2020 CHI Conference on Human Factors in Computing Systems. pp. 1–12. Association for Computing Machinery, New York, NY, USA (2020). https://doi.org/10.1145/3313831.3376402

9. Vertegaal, R.: Designing attentive interfaces. In: Proceedings of the 2002 Symposium on Eye Tracking Research and Applications. pp. 23–30. Association for Computing Machinery, New York, NY, USA (2002). https://doi.org/10.1145/507072.507077

10. Zhai, S.: What's in the eyes for attentive input. Commun. ACM **46**, 34–39 (2003). https://doi.org/10.1145/636772.636795

11. Fairclough, S.H.: Fundamentals of physiological computing. Interact. Comput. **21**, 133–145 (2009). https://doi.org/10.1016/j.intcom.2008.10.011

12. Schmidt, A.: Implicit human computer interaction through context. Pers. Technol. **4**, 191–199 (2000). https://doi.org/10.1007/BF01324126

13. Serim, B., Jacucci, G.: Explicating "implicit interaction": an examination of the concept and challenges for research. In: Proceedings of the 2019 CHI Conference on Human Factors in Computing Systems, pp. 1–16. Association for Computing Machinery, New York, NY, USA (2019). https://doi.org/10.1145/3290605.3300647

14. Grudin, J.: HCI history and today's challenges — what was anticipated, what was not. In: Extended Abstracts of the 2020 CHI Conference on Human Factors in Computing Systems, pp. 1–3. Association for Computing Machinery, New York, NY, USA (2020). https://doi.org/10.1145/3334480.3375058

15. Cutrell, E., Tan, D.: BCI for passive input in HCI. In: Proceedings of CHI, pp. 1–3. Citeseer (2008)

16. Zander, T.O., Kothe, C.: Towards passive brain–computer interfaces: applying brain–computer interface technology to human–machine systems in general. J. Neural Eng. **8**, 025005 (2011). https://doi.org/10.1088/1741-2560/8/2/025005

17. Loke, S.: Context-Aware Pervasive Systems: Architectures for a New Breed of Applications. CRC Press (2006)

18. Tennenhouse, D.: Proactive computing. Commun. ACM **43**, 43–50 (2000). https://doi.org/10.1145/332833.332837

19. Weiser, M.: Hot topics-ubiquitous computing. Computer **26**, 71–72 (1993). https://doi.org/10.1109/2.237456

20. Vainio, A.-M., Valtonen, M., Vanhala, J.: Proactive fuzzy control and adaptation methods for smart homes. IEEE Intell. Syst. **23**, 42–49 (2008). https://doi.org/10.1109/MIS.2008.33

21. Cook, D.J., et al.: MavHome: an agent-based smart home. In: Proceedings of the First IEEE International Conference on Pervasive Computing and Communications, 2003 (PerCom 2003), pp. 521–524 (2003). https://doi.org/10.1109/PERCOM.2003.1192783

22. Handte, M., Schiele, G., Matjuntke, V., Becker, C., Marrón, P.J.: 3PC: system support for adaptive peer-to-peer pervasive computing. ACM Trans. Auton. Adapt. Syst. **7**, 10:1–10:19 (2012). https://doi.org/10.1145/2168260.2168270

23. Weiser, M.: The Computer for the 21st Century. Sci. Am. **265**, 94–105 (1991)

24. Borriello, G.: The challenges to invisible computing. Computer **33**, 123–125 (2000). https://doi.org/10.1109/2.881699

25. Aarts, E.: Ambient intelligence: a multimedia perspective. IEEE Multimedia **11**, 12–19 (2004). https://doi.org/10.1109/MMUL.2004.1261101

26. Satyanarayanan, M.: Pervasive computing: vision and challenges. IEEE Pers. Commun. **8**, 10–17 (2001). https://doi.org/10.1109/98.943998

27. McDuff, D.J., Hernandez, J., Gontarek, S., Picard, R.W.: COGCAM: contact-free measurement of cognitive stress during computer tasks with a digital camera. In: Proceedings of the 2016 CHI Conference on Human Factors in Computing Systems, pp. 4000–4004. Association for Computing Machinery, New York, NY, USA (2016). https://doi.org/10.1145/2858036.2858247

28. Scherr, S.A., Kammler, C., Elberzhager, F.: Detecting user emotions with the true-depth camera to support mobile app quality assurance. In: 2019 45th Euromicro Conference on Software Engineering and Advanced Applications (SEAA), pp. 169–173 (2019). https://doi.org/10.1109/SEAA.2019.00034

29. Liapis, A., Katsanos, C., Xenos, M.: Don't Leave Me Alone: Retrospective Think Aloud Supported by Real-Time Monitoring of Participant's Physiology. In: Kurosu, M. (ed.) HCI 2018. LNCS, vol. 10901, pp. 148–158. Springer, Cham (2018). https://doi.org/10.1007/978-3-319-91238-7_13

30. Liapis, A., Katsanos, C., Sotiropoulos, D., Xenos, M., Karousos, N.: Recognizing Emotions in Human Computer Interaction: Studying Stress Using Skin Conductance. In: Abascal, J., Barbosa, S., Fetter, M., Gross, T., Palanque, P., Winckler, M. (eds.) INTERACT 2015. LNCS, vol. 9296, pp. 255–262. Springer, Cham (2015). https://doi.org/10.1007/978-3-319-22701-6_18

31. Ciabattoni, L., Ferracuti, F., Longhi, S., Pepa, L., Romeo, L., Verdini, F.: Real-time mental stress detection based on smartwatch. In: 2017 IEEE International Conference on Consumer Electronics (ICCE), pp. 110–111 (2017). https://doi.org/10.1109/ICCE.2017.7889247

32. Shoaib, M., Bosch, S., Scholten, H., Havinga, P.J.M., Incel, O.D.: Towards detection of bad habits by fusing smartphone and smartwatch sensors. In: 2015 IEEE International Conference on Pervasive Computing and Communication Workshops (PerCom Workshops), pp. 591–596 (2015). https://doi.org/10.1109/PERCOMW.2015.7134104

33. Arakawa, T.: Recent research and developing trends of wearable sensors for detecting blood pressure. Sensors 18, 2772 (2018). https://doi.org/10.3390/s18092772

34. Jain, A., Horowitz, A.H., Schoeller, F., Leigh, S., Maes, P., Sra, M.: Designing interactions beyond conscious control: a new model for wearable interfaces. Proc. ACM Interact. Mob. Wearable Ubiquitous Technol. 4, 108:1–108:23 (2020). https://doi.org/10.1145/3411829

35. Guitchounts, G., Masís, J., Wolff, S.B.E., Cox, D.: Encoding of 3D head orienting movements in the primary visual cortex. Neuron 108, 512-525.e4 (2020). https://doi.org/10.1016/j.neuron.2020.07.014

36. John, B.E., Kieras, D.E.: The GOMS family of user interface analysis techniques: comparison and contrast. ACM Trans. Comput.-Hum. Interact. 3, 320–351 (1996). https://doi.org/10.1145/235833.236054

37. Card, S., Moran, T., Newell, A.: The model human processor – an engineering model of human performance. Handbook Percept. Hum. Perform. 2 (1986)

38. Zotkin, D.N., Duraiswami, R., Davis, L.S.: Rendering localized spatial audio in a virtual auditory space. IEEE Trans. Multimedia 6, 553–564 (2004). https://doi.org/10.1109/TMM.2004.827516

39. Nacenta, M.A., et al..: E-conic: a perspective-aware interface for multi-display environments. In: Proceedings of the 20th Annual ACM Symposium on User Interface Software and Technology, pp. 279–288. Association for Computing Machinery, New York, NY, USA (2007). https://doi.org/10.1145/1294211.1294260

40. Perry, J.C., Rosen, J., Burns, S.: Upper-limb powered exoskeleton design. IEEE/ASME Trans. Mechatron. 12, 408–417 (2007). https://doi.org/10.1109/TMECH.2007.901934

Engagements² as 'HCI Material': Propagating Community Agency, Through Embedded Technologies

Rob Phillips[1]([✉]), Nick Gant[2], Mel Jordan[3], Sarah Teasley[4], Gail Ramster[1],
Katie Gaudion[1], Katie Spragg[1], Hannah Franklin Stewart[1], and Mel Brimfield[1]

[1] Royal College of Art, Kensington Gore, London SW7 2EU, UK
`robert.phillips@rca.ac.uk`
[2] University of Brighton, 68 Grand Parade, Brighton BN2 0JY, UK
[3] Coventry University, Priory Street, Coventry CV1 5FB, UK
[4] RMIT University, GPO Box 2476, Melbourne, VIC 3001, Australia

Abstract. HCI has material attributes. As a sociotechnical assemblage, HCI mediates and/or translates technologies to public(s) and vice versa. It is malleable, 'made' and crafted and as a material media technology changes our relationships to 'things', each other and our surrounding world. Thinking through HCI as material allows us to unite disciplines with technologies, ensuring that how we conceptualise work is tangible and applicable. Working from this understanding of HCI, allows the authors to contextualise Engagements² as an emerging 'material' space uniting art, design and other practices often fractured through disciplinary conventions. Traditionally, public engagement encompasses ways organisations engage with external parties. HCI contemporaries, Public Interest Technologies (PITs) empower public stakeholders and municipalities. PITs unravel intractable problems, through design, data, and delivery, thus providing user agency and yields wider societal benefit(s).

We question how digital technologies can transition 'public(s)', to sustainable approaches. In time, Engagements² will be commonplace as technologies (PITs, augmented reality, IoT sensing and more) are embedded into public environment(s), if engagement can be defined as a 'craft-able', material concern. The article unites contemporaries in: the public realm, social design, and public engagement methods to identify the: pitfalls, benefits, and opportunities. There is a need for creating a 'best practice' roadmap to creative, active engagement. These values go well beyond designing for inclusion and seek for more sustainable and integral interactions, impacts and culture creation.

Keywords: Engagement · Creative practice · Human computer interaction

1 Research Objective(s)

Opening a creative space beyond 'participation', comprehending Engagements² as an HCI material. Answering: *How should carefully curated 'Engagements²' form new embedded practice(s), transitioning sustainable actions, through HCI?*

© The Author(s), under exclusive license to Springer Nature Switzerland AG 2022
M. Kurosu (Ed.): HCII 2022, LNCS 13302, pp. 117–136, 2022.
https://doi.org/10.1007/978-3-031-05311-5_8

1.1 Introduction

In the past decade, 'engagement' has become an increasingly expected – and often measured – aspect of research practice in multiple national and disciplinary contexts. People "do not only purchase and use products; they design, appropriate and innovate" [1]. Despite the growing literature and body of practice on research engagement, widely and within HCI, art and design, the concept remains unstable and is subject to interpretive flexibility depending on the context. Put simply, 'engagement' means different things to different people. [1] Furthermore, 'engagement' can range from [first order dissemination/communication to communities] to [third order integrally interrelated, contributive, in which engagement upstream in the research process shapes research questions and objectives] [1]. Public engagement is often seen as a 'bolt-on', a dissemination activity, passive and not commonly an active process. Many approaches have included 'the public' in art and design disciplines. One exemplar is Open Design (OD). OD encompasses "on-and offline design and making activities, describ[ing] a design process allowing for the participation of anybody (novice or professional) in the collaborative development of something" [2]. OD enables design to move beyond professional realms as designing *"has to be made present as an activity that extends well beyond the rubric of designers"* [3]. In contrast, engagement can enable participants to transition beyond consequence mitigation to active activities. This model for engagement is gaining increasing traction amongst research stakeholders including funding bodies. In Britain, UK Research, and Innovation (UKRI) states that "research and innovation should be responsive to the knowledge, priorities, values of society and open to participation from all backgrounds" [4]. Authors of a 2020 report by UKRI highlight two concerns: "[to] nurture a future generation passionate about research and innovation" and, "[to] listen to public concerns and aspirations" [4]. Aligned with this third order expectation for the possibilities of engagement, we propose a model of engagement. Authors propose our treatment of engagement should be inclusive, respectful, and ethical. As funding bodies, reviewers, hiring, tenure and promotion committees, clients and wider publics alike in many national and disciplinary contexts increasingly expect research not only to demonstrate social, environmental and economic value to communities but to engage and engage with communities within the research process, not only defining 'engagement' but understanding its valences and possibilities becomes increasingly important. This paper adds to the literature setting out best practice for engagement in HCI, design and art research through the proposition of Engagements[2] as a conceptual approach for undertaking research with civic and environmental value. By Engagements[2], we understand an emerging 'material' space that unites art, design, and other practices through [what] [to do what].

The paper substantiates and articulates Engagements[2] as a social or community technology for this purpose. Authors see 'technologies' as having the potential to support civic empowerment, enabling and catalysing citizens. Citizenship advocate Hess defines 'Community Technology' *[1]* as resources "enabl[ing] scientists, engineers, and craftspeople to re-think the roles of their skills and talents, to become part of everyday life" [5]. Hess summarises the "need to shift from focusing on single issues, toward taking holistic approaches" [5]. Authors propose the concept of Engagements[2] as transdisciplinary materials that provide people with agency beyond HCI experiences. The article reports on interdisciplinary literature, key stakeholder interviews, analysis, and expert symposium findings. The article frames pitfalls, benefits, and opportunities to the combined territory. Engagement approaches need to be embedded within communities as we look to: deployable, repairable, and more citizen-led technological HCI. Authors frame the HCI, design and arts space, share lessons from leading practitioners and then translate insights that can be applied to HCI contexts for deeper active engagement of audiences. *Engagements² as 'HCI Material'* guides readers through literature, projects, lessons, and analysed insights for repeatability and scalability. It is valuable to territories overlapping HCI, design and arts-based communities; intent on tackling contemporary sustainable issues.

1.2   Material Engagements as Political Acts

Both HCI and Design (as a practice) communicate making interactions usable and tangible. However, some methods or approaches allow researchers and practitioners to move beyond dissemination for more meaningful engagement upstream with communities of interest. The argument in this paper derives in part from the authors' shared commitments to careful, critical art, design, and creative practice for social good, with awareness of the power relations at play in any such claim. Within this commitment lies an understanding that design can generate agency for both those that produce it and those that use it; it is a tool which is being used as a pervasive means to address issues of our time. 'Good' design is often engaging utilising design to engage and captivate viewers and users; using aesthetics, technology, materiality and meaning to stimulate social interactions; and providing compelling experiences. Creative practitioners use the powerful language and culture of objects, technologies and products and the potency of services and systems to change behaviour, provoke protests and empower communities as well as to develop consumer material and visual literacy. Designers *"have become more engaged as citizens and more conscious of the roles they play in culture, politics and society, both serving and creating"* [6]. Art's function is a contested subject. Rivalries exist between those that believe it is art's autonomy that generates its agency - thus providing an ability to maintain a distance from society to challenge it; and those that want to utilise it to deliver a different type of society (Arte Util). Others are committed to its expressive, formal, and decorative qualities [7]. Creative cultures reflect upon social problems and can intervene and act on the world through changing the way things are and producing new futures and imaginaries. Art's relationship to its audiences and users are based on a different type of encounter to designed products and systems, although what both art and design practices have in common is the ability to work on the world through actualising ideas and presenting new alternatives to existing problems. As we transition to what we will call a creative approach to living where travel, health, food, materials, and interactions with the natural world will require greater political, economic, and ecological transparency. Authors believe that 'engagement' is a definable commodity and material force to enact sustainable transitions and to develop a new paradigm of Arts and Design Practice; to this end the numerous versions of how we might engage with things and others deserve to be explored. The intention highlights the need for producing art & design research with appropriate communities whilst acknowledging the criticality of publicly embedded outputs, enacting change, and producing *impactful alternatives*. Examples of pervasive technologies (being disruptive) include online shopping [8], Arduino {7} [9] and IoT monitoring without data safeguards [10].

As technologies become more pervasive, Public IoT, accessibility, cost, proliferation of smartphones, drones now publicly owned, these routes to engagement will become more possible. A second commitment shared by authors concerns the politics of agency. Authors believe in providing agency to groups, as a form of democratic empowerment. Citizen *"engagement is not only a basic element of democratic systems, but it is also crucial for other elements of democratic systems"* [11] and is written into statutory processes, for example in the UK's 'neighbourhood planning' mechanism, which gives communities more involvement in decisions around local development strategies. A lack of tools and processes for engagement processes can hinder people's capacity to engage in visioning processes [12, 13] & [14]. The Creative Citizens project {8} co-designed participatory technology with community groups, including the use of digital maps that enable comment threads around specific issues and locations, to gather wider local engagement with the development of neighbourhood planning proposals [15]. Public "disengagement with democracy can provide fertile ground for populism", i.e., a broader concept such as 'designed engagements can enable democratic participation, to explore new, rich territories' [11]. Citizens have a major role to play in addressing the challenges to a sustainable future. For example, 'Doing It Together' Science (DITOs) "implements many innovative participatory events across Europe focusing on the active involvement of citizens in two critical areas: the cutting-edge topic of bio design and the pressing area of environmental monitoring" [16].

Whilst there are challenges for how we engage the natural world, there are also challenges in how we engage each other within it. To achieve active Engagements[2] with the public and stakeholders, we are compelled to design for humans and communities, not scenarios and personas. Designing "products to support users' behaviour change is becoming one of the most popular trends in design research at the moment. To achieve the desired results, design for behaviour change, and in particular, Design for Sustainable Behaviour exploits a variety of approaches" [17]. [whilst behaviour change is one potential impact of engagements within these civics and sustainable? space, Engagements[2] has broader intent. It aims to provide communities with….], as this practice is intent on providing communities with agency and empowerment through art and design interventions, in effect as a form of 'citizenship'. Prior author work has discussed "ecological citizenship" and questioned our role within sustainable society, giving people agency over their environment [18]. A third commitment concerns material practice. *Public Interest Technologies* (PITs) empower public stakeholders and municipalities. PITs unravel intractable problems, through design, data, and delivery, thus providing user agency and yielding wider societal benefit(s). Authors question how digital technologies can transition 'public(s)', to 'sustainable approaches'. Current challenges and opportunities include: material consumption; climate change; circular economies and product life extension; ecological citizenship (citizens benefiting local ecologies / environments); re-naturing and transitioning to more sustainable behaviours. Engagements[2] can create and foster similar longevity to that of the longevity of conventional material infrastructure and its smart form, including emergent PITs. Mechanisms for Engagements[2] require rethinking; the materials are not solely 'digital' or wood, metal, plastic etc. They are embedded; systems, ticket machines, cultural institutions, digital bus stop signage, maker spaces, distributed materials, off-the-shelf parts, builders' merchants, community spaces, vending machines, recycle stores, service station leaflet displays, accessible resources, local non-government organisations, community resources, downloadable plans, broadcasters, social media, WhatsApp groups, radio stations, tear, and share signs etc.… and digital resources. Engagements[2], operates beyond participation, as a deployable material for mutual citizen, community, and practitioner gain [19]. Engagements can be designed, are designable and can be co-defined and sculpted (with adequate creative consideration) to stimulate and foster collaborative envisioning, consensus building, creative co-operation, and community cohesion [20].

Figure 1 (Pg 127) is a visual map communicating how authors frame example projects, with numbers e.g. {x} providing cross referencing. Practice exemplars demonstrate the authors' conceptual framework of Engagements[2]. Design practitioners *Blast Theory {2}*, leverage various technologies for active participation [21]. Their project *I'd hide you* is an example of real world public IoT games, authors see the 'product' as the engagement [22]. Virtual reality is now used on cruise ships to sell diving experiences of far flung and or inaccessible spaces to amateur divers {3} [23]. Sensor networks that were once under the ownership of municipalities and councils are now established by amateur, even created through DIY kits and processing power, for example the *smart citizen's {4}* project [24]. Quitmeyers' Digital Naturalist {5}, creates engagements with leading ecologists, fabricating custom technologies live within the amazon basin, transforming expert's capabilities [25]. Finally, the pandemic shift saw institutions offering digital experiences whilst their buildings remained inaccessible. Authors see this territory as creating custodians of sustainable interventions and preparing the field of HCI to build on it appropriately and ethically. In *Design as Politics,* Fry presents a rigorous review of transitioning beyond dichotomies of sustainable practice, to 'sustainment' i.e., embedding adjustments within community life [3]. The challenge is 'instilling agency' and designing engagement(s), to achieve embedded buy-in from participants, creating empowered citizens and custodians, rather than traditional HCI 'users'. Authors frame an 'engagement space' (through HCI) enabling participants to become empowered and direct the use of technology within their lives. One contextual example is a 'technologically enabled' rock pooling net used by amateur/expert stakeholders. The net could explore and feedback details on water quality, biodiversity, lichen etc. The net could be borrowed from a tourist office, wildlife trust etc. The nets gathered data can be used at source, to invoke public experiences. Employing these pervasive technologies within the frame of Engagements[2] can catalyse a more informed public and transform our actions to more sustainable approaches.

1.3 Defining Active Engagement

A grounded example of Engaging Design (ED) is *The Nursery Garden* {29}, a collaborative public artwork by SUPERFLEX. Designed for three public hospitals in the French islands of Réunion and Mayotte located in the Indian Ocean. Nursery Garden facilitates knowledge exchange between medicine cultures, challenging boundaries of 'modern' and 'traditional' medicine. "Each hospital courtyard, [hosts a] plant nursery and surrounding garden, containing medicinal plants growing on each island. The nursery gardens provide a neutral setting where patients, visitors and hospital staff can take a break, meet each other, learn about botany, join a workshop, or nurture the growing plants. As the plants grow larger, they are replanted onto the outer hospital grounds" [3]. As plants are grown and archived, local culture and knowledge of the medicinal plants is maintained for future generations. The project goes well beyond 'participatory' models and cultivates new roles, new communities, educational value, and new relationships, both inside and outside the hospital. Authors question what happens when we employ engagement methods and techniques, as part of an explicit process of art and design practice and what types of engagement(s) generate productive results? Engagements have different scales and levels of engagement from DIY movements and people creating their own technologies, through to garden observation. During the collaborative *'My Naturewatch'* {9} project between Goldsmiths Interaction Research Studio Northumbria and the Design Products Programme at the RCA, the design research element became the notion of 'citizenship' that was produced when participants engaged in the collective event of using technology and watching nature. The emphasis on citizenship and community provided a more comprehensive involvement transcending the technical use of a camera and establishing a community of interest. The *My Naturewatch* work identified a new potential in engagement providing citizen authorship and transformation [26]. This 'Engagements[2] agenda' will be a trajectory for the blending of disciplines enacting change and can be used to transition to sustainable means. Engaging Design: "showcases creative material, models and methods for transformative action. Sustainability is arguably a human construct born from a necessity to re-engage with our relationship to a range of issues" associated with our biosphere dependency [19]. Active Engagement Definition: when are facilitated to become actively engaged in a product, service, social issue, through an interaction that can provide solutions to themselves and other physical or digital communities.

1.4 Design-Led Frame

In *Research into Art and Design*, Frayling identifies three approaches: Research into Design, Research for Art, and Design and Research Through Design [27]. Our agenda falls into Research Through Design as the process of including stakeholders and communities can often yield interesting and unpredictable results. The act of including people within the design process is traditionally Human Centred Design. This has taken many forms: Participatory Design; Co-design; User Centred Design and more, each having unique subtleties and nuances. Authors see a point of difference, is that Engagements[2] is 'intent on actively engaging audiences' informing their agency. The emergence of *Society Centred Design* forms principles: *Design for sustainable development, Confront uncertainty* and more *(societycentered.design)*. As a discipline Planet Centred Design refocuses our attentions.

> "Our planet is threatened by human activity, propagating a human centric worldview is no longer adequate. Agency in design becomes ever more important, to include secondary users, affected bystanders or non-users, or non-human beings affected by design interventions" [28].

Sevaldson highlights 'systems thinking' approaches to proposed solutions and over-time builds resilience by using discursive methods. We need to surpass Human Centred design principles and centre ourselves around the environment, the wildlife, materials, impact etc. The Engagements[2] approach values serendipity through engagement, building a research through design approach. Design should "do less harm to leaving things better" [28]. Thackara endorses the 'art of hosting' and reciprocity:

> *"Empower[ing] local people:* any design action that rearranges places and relationships is an exercise of power. A good test for sensitivity of a design proposal is whether it enables people to increase control over their own territory and resources [i.e., reciprocity]. The principle of reciprocity: anyone who takes from the commons has to contribute [to] the commons" [29].

In totality, Thackara sees grassroots and bottom-up opportunities as a form of citizenship and form of human rights, which is the material language of Engagement. These two principles are paramount as they proliferate agency and a notion of collaboration, no matter how small. We "must end this obsession with perpetual growth, change is most likely to happen when people reconnect – with each other, and with the biosphere – in rich, real-world contexts" [29]. We are living at a time of transition from Human to Planet centred design and engage communities within that challenge. We still need to understand challenges within context by and for communities, whilst moving beyond sustainability to empower sustainment. Design practices are converging dictated by materials, track record and expertise not just by someone's training:

> *"Research Engagement as Activity:* understood as an activity, initiative or event.
> *Research Engagement as System:* unfolds through a more complex set of relationships between people, things, and places.
> *Research Engagement as Relationship:* the idea of a relationship between two parties.
> *Research Engagement as Process:* linear or cyclical processes of research or knowledge-to-action.
> *Research Engagement as Affect:* A final configuration" [30].

1.5 Design-Led Field Exemplars

Engagement as Activity: *an activity, initiative, or event. Virtual Snorkelling {3};* allows water parks to transform any pool into a vibrant attraction allowing guests a full-body sensory experience through coral reefs, shipwrecks, and underwater caves in exotic locations. Guests "swim alongside turtles, manta rays and massive whales seeing a world previously accessible to advanced scuba divers in remote international dive spots" [23]. *The Urban Barley Field* [31] *{10};* Estonian design/agricultural installation, encouraged locals to change their neighbourhood. The grassroots crowdfunded project was built and cut by volunteers. Harvested crops were gifted to funders; with some laboratory tested, calculating the area's pollution levels. The "project inspired locals and authorities to enliven the traffic channel with 38 flowerbeds" [32]. The impacts were encouraging local government into funding pilots for urban food in the area. The *Crochet Coral Reef {11} (crochetcoralreef.org)* responds to climate change. It is an exercise in applied mathematics, and a woolly experiment in evolutionary theory. *"Living reefs are dying from heat exhaustion and awash in plastic, the Crochet Coral Reef offers an impassioned response. The Reef project is a condensation of human labor, hundreds of thousands of hours of stitching quietly performed"* [33]. *Crochet Coral Reef* contributes to Engagements[2] as it creates a direct link between people, scientific materials, the act of making and textile materials. Encouraging the creation of artefacts, spaces, and public exhibits that all can engage with.

Engagement as System: *complex relationships between people, institutions, ideas, places etc. Living Sea Wall {12};* manufactured structures mimicking the root structure of native mangrove trees, the Living Seawall adds complexity to existing structures providing a habitat for marine life. Aiding *"biodiversity and attracts filter-feeding organisms that actually absorb and filter out pollutants – such as particulate matter and heavy metals – keeping the water 'clean"* [34]. *30 Days Wild {13};* Annually in June, thousands of people participate in the Wildlife Trusts nature challenge, 30 Days Wild. By participating in one *"wild thing a day throughout the whole month: for your health, well-being and for the planet in 30 simple, fun and exciting Random Acts of Wildness"* [35]. These examples are tied into specific locations, times, networks and are interconnected by stakeholders, interdependencies, and systems.

Engagement as Relationship: the idea of a relationship between two parties.

The *'Crime Prevention' Occasional Badge {14};* produced by West Yorkshire Police and the University of Huddersfield. It "engage[s], educate[s] and empower[s] Cub [scouts] in relation to the importance of crime prevention, specifically the prevention of domestic burglary and online safety" [36]. The project formed a positive relationship within an existing context leveraging the desire to obtain recognition and working with a local constabulary, i.e., engaging relationships with communities. *Public Lab Balloon mapping {15};* Balloon mapping is a low-cost way to take aerial photos using a camera, attached to a balloon, on a spool of string "from a few hundred feet up all the way to over 4,000 feet in the air" [37]. Both examples form a link between users, makers, communities and collected data, the relationship becomes intertwined relying on all parties. Both examples contribute toward 'Engagement as Material' as they both form a relationship between communities, methods and people's homes.

Engagement as Process: processes of research or knowledge-to-action. *Zooniverse {16};* a citizen science platform that enables everyone to take part in real cutting-edge research in many fields across the sciences, humanities, and more. The Zooniverse creates opportunities for you to unlock answers and contribute to real discoveries [38]. These projects provide a two-way framework and process between initiatives and communities, providing a voice to disparate and underfunded communities. Creative Citizens {8} co-designed digital tools with community-led projects for the projects to use as part of their own processes of engaging wider participation. Participatory civic technology was used within neighbourhood planning, whilst digital media tools were included within the aesthetics and activities of a community centre, to develop storytelling about the space. These digital engagements sought to boost participation, capture value, and increase belonging [39]. These examples open a dialogue between parties, within a tight process that transfers knowledge-to-action.

Engagement as Affect: A final configuration. The My Naturewatch (NW) project [9], is "[an] inexpensive wildlife camera designed for people to make themselves promoting engagement with nature and digital making. It aligned to the interests of the BBC's Natural History Unit. Since June 2018, the BBC featured the camera on a SpringWatch broadcast, over 2,500 [at time of writing] NW Cameras are constructed using instructions, software and commercially available components" [40]. NW enabled participants grow beyond the original intention providing serendipity to research. NW can provide unity across communities and be adapted by novice or expert. It contributes to Engagements[2] by going beyond participation, is open to public response, enables others to build their own resource at rapidly diminished economic cost.

1.6 Art-Led Frame

Practice-led research in art is conducted primarily through the medium of practice. It is situated at the confluence of practice, theory and history and requires that the practitioner-researcher is fluent in all these fields [41]. As a scientist turned creative practitioner, Skains notes, 'that artist researchers offer insights into art and the practice of art as it occurs, but can throw new and unexpected light onto a range of topics including cognition, discourse, psychology, history, culture, and sociology' [42]. The artist-researcher seeks to understand things in the world through action and reflection. A rationale for the production of an artwork which reflects the site, context, theory, and previous practices is established, the researcher works towards to final outcomes by adapting their ideas and responding to any insights or new knowledge they acquire on the way [43]. The means by which the artefact is realised, and its content is developed together by the researcher, thus the outcome is not usually illustrative of the content and process [44]. Although contemporary art has embraced participatory methods as a form of social art practice, seeking contributions towards shared authorship as a way of overturning the canonical artist. Some artist - researchers use participation as a part of collaborative processes seeing contemporary art as a form of opinion formation rather than a way to enact public engagement [45]. Whilst artists do not consider their audiences as users as is the case of design, they do share social and community principles. "Socially Engaged Art Practice" [46] shares an ethos with Socially Centred Design as outlined above and many would also align with what Thackara has described as "Empowering Local People" [29]. The author's approach to Engagement as Material correlates to the theories of civic engagement. Vaughan and Jacquez [47] note that the Spectrum of Public Participation describes a continuum of engagement. The 'inform' phase provides information to help communities relate to complex topics, this leads to 'empower', in which decisions made by participants are implemented into practice. One outcome of Engagement [2] is to aid the formation and communication of participants' own opinions through engaging in affective and aesthetic processes of knowledge acquisition [48]. This positions art and design engagement as research through the process of hypothesis, testing and reflection in collaboration.

1.7 Art-Led Field Exemplars

Engagement as Commoning: care and sharing for an egalitarian society. The art collective, SUPERFLEX, inquired into the problems of power, both through the way in which global capital operates and in relation to high culture [49]. For example, their project 'Free Sol Lewitt {17}', for the Van Abbemuseum, in 2010, saw them set up a metal workshop to produce copies of a work by Sol Lewitt, Untitled {18} (Wall Structure), 1972. Replicas of the artwork were made and then 'set free', given away to the museum's public, free of charge. This sharing of cultural artefacts becomes a type of intellectual property commoning [50], which not only extends Sol Lewitt's ideas of reproduction – he specified artworks and others produced them – but emphasises the shared ownership of objects held in museum collections. SUPERFLEX member, Christiane Berndes, says, '[i]f the museum's role is to collect and preserve artworks then maybe the next step is for it to distribute artworks, to open up new levels of use, access and ownership' [51]. Their approach offers 'propositions' to ingrained problems rather than overturning the condition of the problem. Moreover, their projects have consistently utilized design and engineering processes to produce responses to social problems typically developing new systems over single products. For example, the Supergas project {19} in which they developed a biogas energy production system developed with European and African engineers. 'Supergas is a simple biogas unit that can produce sufficient gas for the cooking and lighting needs of a typical family living in rural areas of the Global South' [52]. The 'care' in their work is demonstrated by the way in which they produce tools to engage critically with systems of 'social and cultural production and distribution, with financial and political institutions, with the law, with renewable energy and with urban space' [53].

Engagement as Activity: At its most basic, research engagement is understood as an activity, initiative, or event. *On Space Time* {20} is a floating structure composed of three levels of clear film accessible to the public, inspired by the cubical configuration of the occupying exhibition space. The work is a giant instrument with movement creating reverberations and acoustics [54]. *Trolley Reef* {21} is a long-term project and artwork creating a new oyster reef in North Kent, using supermarket trolleys. The idea plays with the common sight of seeing the legs of dumped trolleys sticking out of waterways, a symbol of society's disconnect and disregard for nature. Supermarket trolleys are also the end point of an industrial and global agricultural system that is destroying ecosystems worldwide. The trolleys will be used in the same way as the traditional *oyster culture* cages which grow new reefs, holding the oysters while they grow [55] and will be passed over to teenage custodians to benefit from over time.

Engagement as System: Engagement unfolds through a more complex set of relationships between people, institutions, things, ideas, and localities. *Project Row Houses* {22} site encompasses 39 structures and is home to community enriching initiatives, art programs, and neighbourhood development activities. PRH programs touch the lives of under-resourced neighbours, young single mothers, small enterprises, and artists interested in enriching people's lives [56].

Engagement as Relationship: Probably the most common manifestation of engagement in the literature is the idea of a relationship between two parties. *Chicken Town* {23}, Assemble worked with Chicken Town to create a not-for-profit social-enterprise restaurant serving healthy fried chicken to Tottenham [57]. In *A designer's approach how can autistic adults with learning disabilities be involved in the design process?* creating activities for engagement was paramount in building trust and creating meaningful connections between the designer and autistic participants [58].

Engagement as Process: Linear or cyclical processes of research or knowledge-to-action. *Climavore: On Tidal Zones {24}*. Humans eating can Change Climates. CLIMAVORE is a long-term project that sets out to envision seasons of food production and consumption that react to man-induced climatic events and landscape alterations. The project engaged with local restaurants that removed farmed salmon off their menu and introduced a CLIMAVORE dish instead. CLIMAVORE reviews forms of eating, addressing environmental regeneration and promotes more responsive aqua-cultures in an era of man-induced environmental transformations [59]. *Feast on the Bridge {25}* for one Saturday each September Southwark Bridge (London) was closed to traffic for an urban harvest meal enjoyed by over 35,000 people. The project's emphasis wasn't on spectacle, or even entertainment, it was simply to explore the cyclical story of food production, reclaim the space from traffic and invite people to engage, sharing food and conversation [60].

Engagement as Affect: A final configuration. The *Tele-present Wind {26}, when* the wind blows it causes the stalk outside to sway. The accelerometer detects this movement transmitting the motion to the grouping of devices in the gallery. Therefore, the stalks in the gallery space move in real-time and in unison based on the movement of the wind outside [61]. *For Forest {27}* unifies the 'unending attraction of nature', a temporary art intervention that transformed the Wörthersee football stadium in Klagenfurt into Austria's largest public art installation in 2019. Around 300 trees, some weighing up to six tons each, were carefully transplanted over the existing football pitch to give the impression of a central 'European forest' [62].

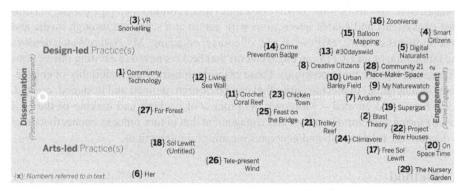

Fig. 1. Contextual map; locating examples for Engagements[2] contexts, each project {no.}.

1.8 Engagement[2] (Common Frame)

The difference between arts practice and design practice has long since been contested. The authors align to (Frayling's) advance "learning, knowledge and professional competence, in the principles and practice of art and design in their relation to industrial and commercial processes and social developments" [27]. We know the multitude of differences between Art and Design and how long it's been discussed and strategically avoided here. Authors are interested in the positive crossovers of working with 'people' for new practices in engagement through learning, knowledge, and professional competence. This common field not only informs how we create, but its impact, its practice, and projects 'sustainability' outside of researchers circles for positive ecological transformation. We fully respect the differences and believe we can learn from each other creating Engagements[2]. Fundamental to all art and design education and training is the consideration of the user, consumer, audience, and spectator therefore it is not surprising that this is applied to art and design research.

1.9 Engagement Making

The Hackspace and the maker movement have been identified as means to (potentially) widen access to technology (ref) and craft and making (within makerspaces, repairs cafés and clubs) provide opportunities to promote social engagement and well-being benefits of making (together). Hence the opportunity to co-design spaces in which to hack technologies as a means to accentuate and deliberately foster, fabricate, and facilitate engagement as a both means and ends. The Brighton Place-Maker-Space {28} [63] 'hacked' the notion of hackspaces and deployed HCI's and making, using technology as a means to enact and craft engagement relating to the participants' community and local environment. The use of technologies and making themselves provide the basis for engagement around topics that generally disengage and disenfranchise such as environmental, urban and community planning. 'Hacking' the use of animation and augmented reality apps provides space and place-based media, to express unheard voices, generating empathy with nature and envision how nature might thrive in cities through augmented-town-tapestries and gamified, virtual landscapes. Minecraft is used to engage collaborative visions of more biodiverse cities (Blockbuilders), engage people in complex ecosystems and enable interactions with nature at a scale and through media and making that is creative, expressive and, of course, engaging. My NatureWatch deploys the fabrication of an HCI (as an engagement) that brokers new and exciting interactions with nature (not formerly possible). These cases demonstrate the materiality of engagement as a tangible, malleable entity that can be desired, defined and designed, created, constructed, and curated – Moreover the process of hacking and making of the HCI (itself) forms the seminal catalyst and engagement that in turn unlocks connectivity that is deepens the relationship and generates meaningful interactions.

2 Method

The work draws from; interdisciplinary projects and case studies of the authors, working across HCI, design, arts practice, history of design and industry. 'Nature engagement' workshops, round table discussions and semi-structured participant interviews were documented and provided feedback. The participants represented organisations and bodies tasked with engagement within their public contexts making them key stakeholders (e.g., engagement directors and volunteer coordinators). Key informant interviews "allow[ed] a free flow of ideas and information, interviewers frame questions spontaneously, probe for information and takes notes, which are elaborated on later" providing information directly from experts [64]. The key informant interviews "provide flexibility to explore new ideas and issues not anticipated during planning" [64]. Interviewees included science engagement researchers, designers, and artists. Participants were interviewed individually, avoiding the "*Hawthorne effect*" where participants behave differently when they know they are being observed" [65]. The interviewers were briefed, initiating from an identical script "enabl[ing] strict comparison between interviews" as it "is easier for a novice to follow" [65]. Interviews were clustered and thematically analysed into; clarity topics and emerging practices "covering key themes, concepts and ideas" [64].

– *How can carefully curated 'engagement(s)' form a new practice that is embedded, transitioning actions and communities?*
– *What are the opportunities and benefits for art and design practices to actively engage audiences, communities, users, viewers, spectators, and passers-by?*
– *How can these actions and outcomes affect long-term mutual benefit, and sustainable living?*
– *Can you offer any best practice examples of practice-based engagements and or comment on a code-of-ethics or code-of-conduct?*

3   Results

The following are excerpts from the interview series and then summaries from experts and literature.

1) *How can carefully curated 'engagement(s)' form a new practice that is embedded, transitioning actions and communities?*

"What social change might your participants want to see? How can projects help participants achieve that? Working together, and intertwining engagements is key, with community members and instigators of your engagement. There's different terms for that, co-production, co-design, etc. If they're genuinely an equal partnership, understanding both parties' aims, and working together is critical". **Expert 001**

"Within engagement practises, there are spaces for other species, using things we have, until now reserved for humanity. A massive question as 99.9% of what humanity does, puts humanity first and foremost. How can anything from an airport to the military, our homes to bridges become places for other species?" **Expert 003**

Authors summarise the criticality of; Comprehending all agendas, within projects so they meet those needs but also do not counteract alternate or unknown objectives, they might not be obvious. Ensure equality in all means, from inclusion, attribution, and dissemination. Create outputs holistically considering species/ecological impacts.

2) *What are the opportunities and benefits for art and design practices to actively engage audiences, communities, users, viewers, spectators, and passers-by?*

"Open communication with participants, [i.e,] everybody communicating. [It] is the only reason people say, 'you know that is not cool'. It's often research's problem, you get funded for fixed time periods. You're expected to co-design projects and build trusted relationships, where people can identify challenges. Ethics are really complicated and understanding what people mean. These things [all] take time, so we need longer term community relationships". **Expert 001**

"Part of Trolley Reef is its ability to let the oysters grow on top of each other, this makes oyster reefs a keystone species. The problem is that with 98% of oyster reefs gone and rebuilding a new reef means elevating the oysters away from silts. The project will set up a community owned oyster company, given to teenagers. By the time they grow up the oyster reef will be in a state where it can be harvested but the structural forms of the trolleys" **Expert 003**.

Authors summarise the criticality of the following elements. Clear communication and unification of terminology ensuring parties are not alienated or excluded. Question how the funding can establish legacies, these take time to establish. Finally thinking about exit and who projects are 'donated' to.

3) *How can these actions and outcomes affect long-term mutual benefit, and sustainable living?*

"Some projects are bleeding into your life, whilst you're cooking tea etc. You're wanting to build trusting relationships, it's hard to say, it's my day off, you can't really do that. It's hard to build those things into funding proposals. [Funders] are not going to give you funding to foster those skills". **Expert 001**

"The Trolley reef is a project that will probably not see complete fruition within my lifetime, so how we develop projects beyond the life of individuals is a critical perspective and opportunity within funding terms". **Expert 003**

Summarising the importance of; clarity on 'all parties' work through attribution and development of that attribution over time. Finally defining, what the "life and activities" of projects span as these need to be fostered through ambassadors.

4) *Can you offer any best practice examples of practice-based engagements and or comment on a code-of-ethics or code-of-conduct?*

"It's important not to forget those rely[ing] on traditional media, newspapers, radio, etc. I appear regularly on our local radio, and people ring me up afterwards or DM me on social media. It's really important not to forget that demographic. The drawback is that you can lose complexities of [some] issues". **Expert 004**

"It's luxurious to communicate with participants on WhatsApp in the evenings. You're on your phone, to keep those relationships going, for many people, you can't do all of that. Unless it's built into projects, or university systems. From an academia perspective, it's not going to change very much. **Expert 005**

"We develop codes of conduct/interdisciplinary working contracts, [through] co-designed workshops. They outline our expectations within the team. In terms of ethics, they need to be considered, on a project-by-project basis. There is psychological harm, or physical harm resulting from your project for both the researchers / practitioners running it and the project participants. Finally, data ethics and attribution of outputs". **Expert 005**

We summarise that; media typologies and how they reflect user groups and demographics are important to remember. Building 'appropriate means' and accessibilities into projects. For example, establishing HR processes that protect individuals and enable them to work when their participants are 'available', outside conventional hours. These could include Interdisciplinary working contracts or / agreements.

4 Discussion

Authors frame the HCI, design and arts space, share lessons from leading practitioners and then translate insights that can be applied to HCI contexts for deeper active engagement of audiences. *Engagements^2 as 'HCI Material'* guides readers through literature, projects, lessons, and analysed insights for repeatability and scalability. It is valuable to territories that overlap HCI, design and arts-based communities; intent on tackling contemporary sustainable and contextual issues. Previous literature [66] explored similarities and lessons learnt from design research projects carried out with geographic communities, within the context of inclusive design for social change. This identified findings such as: ensuring clarity of intent with participants around the brief; inclusive, co-defining and designing accessible engagement methods; matching motivations for a mutual exchange or transaction between designers and participants; and leaving responsibly, in terms of being upfront about the project ambitions, the duration of involvement of designers and meaningful adoption of outputs by the community where possible and appropriate. Designing engagement - contributors articulated perspectives that recognise the role and expectations around engagement without definitive metrics or references to what engagement is, however, common attributes. Authors do not want to polarise with positive and or negative approaches. Authors believe these are challenges within this 'creative space', contextual points defining the backbone of Engagements^2. We view these as different from convention as 'participants' might have more agency and be more deeply involved in decision making processes and potentially outside institutional boundaries. Findings from the interviews and territory present potential frameworks to more creative engagement(s). The following contexts (outlined in research objective) are defined, (but not exclusive to):

Ecological Citizenship: Fostering activities that benefit the local ecology or environment for example, appropriate mapping, reduction in waste or inform behaviours toward more sustainable practices. For example, Google Maps already informs users of the lowest carbon emission impacts to inform journey decisions [67]. These 'actions for more sustainable communities' are transferable and scalable.

Re-naturing: Mapping spaces (accurately) so they can be cultivated to help more species diversity and reduce invasive species. Providing the ability to internationally see food growing conditions that can be replicated, based on facts and data. Finally, document species diversity accurately through community-led digital documentation.

Participant Motivations: Unpick local communities' aspirations to align their contextual motivations, with appropriate goals.

Climate change: A wicked problem that needs unpicking, but could inform our predicted behaviour and make suggestions, or determine our lowest impact choices.

Material Consumption: Digitally showing the provenance of the material(s), informing purchasing decisions and/or its impacts. Demonstrating new methods for how materials can be re-used or disassembled appropriately.

Repair Culture: Leveraging HCI to compliment physical systems with: VR, AR, or digital platforms to share materials. For example, BMW initially explored VR for staff training purposes [68]. With the financial reduction of technologies, these approaches can become more commonplace.

4.1 Value to HCI Practice

Agendas: align what 'success is' for parties, this is common practice in Citizen Science (CS). CS unites 'project design', technologies, accessibility, and science.

Motivation(s): align interests of; participants, municipality, and organisation.

Ethical: issues of paying participants (meeting minimum wage) as it is unethical if participants cannot afford to be involved.

Inclusion: create processes that include participants and potentially can become stakeholders providing, agency: to local communities.

Designing for Exit: build in self-sustainability or resourcing to create legacies.

Over-selling success: do not over promise and/or creating something that is unsustainable for researchers and communities.

Commodities: for academic institutions REF material is paramount, however these can be clarified. For corporations IP and licensing models can be paramount.

Sustainable Legacies: Projects reliant on legacy funding. Build trusted ambassadors, within communities. They should be within resource/financial constraints.

Authorship & IP: when ownership is passed over to social innovation how are initial parties protected? and what happens if engagement has negative consequences?

Social Capital: build the 'personable art' of managing relationships, expectations etc.

New fields: i.e., the opportunity to create social innovations and spread opportunities.

Transparency: projects must fulfil certain criteria and have caveats. Understanding (appropriate) technological adoption. i.e., making the "material" or data that is gathered 'good quality' comparable and usable.

4.2 Summary

These actions and outcomes affect long-term mutual benefit. The authors summarise from the results, literature, and interviews that the following are the key repeatable steps to optimise Engagements[2].

1. **Platform Creation:** Be flexible and create a clear means for all to contribute and have ownership.
2. **Designing for Exit:** Providing transitions i.e., when participant(s) and researchers leave, infrastructure(s) must be self-sustaining.
3. **Leveraging the everyday:** Building embedded interactions in environments (Bus stops, parks), non-embedded, (smartphones).
4. **Cultural Institutions:** A mediator to deliver sustainable practices through HCI / interactions located in/or around them.
5. **Accessibility/affordability:** The tools can be 'a smart phone' and the physical space. We see the material as the process in which creatives use and deploy. This opens the experience, the interactions, the opportunities, and unified experiences.
6. **New areas for interaction(s):** Urban Barley Field, opens up a digital design space of how and where people can grow food, ownership, and its care. Authors see Engagements[2] as a means to open-up new domains and territories.

5 Conclusion

Authors conclude that we must leverage creative practice well beyond problem solving and leveraging communities. For example, NW used serendipity, to open up possibilities for participants. In *Politics of the Everyday* Manzini states we must "create the conditions" [69]. The question is how do you 'set the right conditions', to ensure cross-generational motivations. Authors do not have a 'fix all' position so; place, demographic, inclusion, finance etc. must be quantified. Authors believe *Engagements[2]* is a discipline in its own right. It is not just 'mixed media', service design, or 'raising awareness'. The key is how is it validated academically and by other communities? As the relationship is often backward; for example, funding research you need to know what 'could' happen, however fostering relationships needs to encourage ownership, serendipity and enable choice. Engagement is considered one stage towards impact (UKRI); however, authors assert it is one of the most significant considerations that artists/designers make in the process of cultural production and in this context is part of the research process. Moreover, and importantly for *Engagements[2]* (as material) is that the relationship between parties is an integrated collaborative exchange? I.e., the artist/ designer does not solely rely on the participant to resolve the design problem or interpret the artefact. Rather, they recognise that the spectator is not automatically furnished with the capacity to translate works of art and design - at least not straight away - but needs to engage in a kind of creative labour which is as much about transforming oneself as it is about knowing the work. This entails negotiating the places constructed by the design object, artefact, exhibition, or event, of altering oneself so as to occupy the new place designated by the work [70]. For example, Environmental Design requires both designer and user to transform the current understandings and situate themselves in a paradigm to imagine alternative behaviours, routines, and practises, it is this process we identify in Engagement as Material. In the same way, artefacts are sometimes described as unfathomable. We assert that this act of transformation is the place where art and design research is situated, and we aim to identify this significant methodological contribution to society by articulating it as a type of material. Authors believe that translating practice to audiences, doing good, fostering debate, assisting others is our role as practitioners. The final question is how you design *'Engagements[2]'* that is opaque, ensures safeguarding of; physical-self, mental health, finance with elements protected, even during researcher exit.

Acknowledgements. Funded by: (RCA) Research Office, (RP/CS/157: 800076). Informed by My Naturewatch, EPSRC (Grant EP/P006353/1). Thanks to: Sarah West, Something & Sons, Bailey Richardson, Susan Hamilton & Christie Walker.

References

1. Kohtala, C., Hyysalo, S., Whalen, J.: A taxonomy of users' active design engagement in the 21st century. Des. Stud. **67**, 27–54 (2020)
2. Tooze, J., Baurley, S., Phillips, R., Smith, P., Foote, E., Silve, S.: Open design: contributions, solutions, processes, and projects. Des. J. **17**(4), 538–559 (2014)
3. Fry, T.: Design as Politics. Berg (2010)
4. Johnson, M.T.: The knowledge exchange framework: understanding parameters and the capacity for transformative engagement. Stud. Higher Educ., 1–18 (2020)
5. Hess, K.: Community Technology, vol. 689. HarperCollins Publishers (1979)
6. Heller, S., Vienne, V.: Citizen Designer: Perspectives on Design Responsibility, 2nd edn. Skyhorse Publishing Inc., New York (2003)
7. Beech, D., Hewitt, A., Jordan, M.: Functions, functionalism and functionlessness: on the social function of public art after modernism. In: Miles, M., Jordan, M. (eds.) Art and Theory After Socialism, pp. 113–125. Intellect Books, Bristol (Oct 2008)
8. Krämer, A., Kalka, R.: How digital disruption changes pricing strategies and price models. In: Phantom Ex Machine, pp. 87–103. Springer, Cham (2017)
9. Arduino: Retrieved from: shorturl.at/fimyH (2022). Accessed 19 Jan 2022
10. Alnaeli, S.M., Sarnowski, M., Aman, M., Abdelgawad, A., Yelamarthi, K.: Source code vulnerabilities in IoT software systems. Adv. Sci. Technol. Eng. Syst. J. **2**, 1502–1507 (2017)
11. Dasandi, N., Taylor, M.: Is democracy failing?: A Primer for the 21st Century, 1st ed., Thames & Hudson (2018)
12. Cornwall, A.: Democratising Engagement: What the UK Can Learn From International Experience. Demos, London (2008)
13. Wates, N.: The Community Planning Handbook, How People can Shape their Cities, Towns and Villages in any Part of the World. Earthscan (2014)
14. Collin, P., Swist, T.: From products to publics? The potential of participatory design for research on youth, safety and well-being. J. Youth Stud. **19**, 305–318 (2016)
15. Turner, J., Lockton, D., Dovey, J.: Technology and the creative citizen. In: Hargreaves, I., Hartley, J. (eds.) The Creative Citizen Unbound. Policy Press, Bristol (2014)
16. Hackalay, M.: How Many Citizen Scientists in the World? shorturl.at/hAKM0 (2018)
17. Scurati, G.W., Carulli, M., Ferrise, F., Bordegoni, M.: Sustainable behaviour: a framework for the design of products for behaviour change. Emotion. Eng. **8**, 65–83 (2020)

18. Phillips, R., Anderson, R., Abbas-Nazari, A., Gaver, B., Boucher, A.: 'Urban & suburban nature interactions', impacts and serendipitous narratives of the my naturewatch project. In: Proceedings of the Design Society: DESIGN Conference, vol. 1, pp. 2109–2118. Cambridge University Press (May 2020)

19. Phillips, R., Gant, N.: Engaging design: empowering beyond 'participation' for active engagement. Res. Art Educ. **2021**(1), 23–49 (2021)

20. Gant, N., Duggan, K., Dean, T., Barnes, J.: Encouraging 'young digital citizenship' through co-designed, hybrid digi-tools. In: Proceedings of the 2nd Biennial Research Through Design Conference, pp. 25–27 (2015)

21. Blast Theory: Film. Games. Installation. Performance. Technology. https://www.blasttheory.co.uk/ (2022). Accessed 19 Jan 2022

22. I'd hide you: I'D HIDE YOU, online game of stealth, cunning and adventure. https://www.blasttheory.co.uk/projects/id-hide-you/ (2012). Accessed 19 Jan 2022

23. VR-Snorkel: Virtual reality, underwater! https://vr-snorkel.com/ (2022). Accessed 19 Jan 2022

24. Smart Citizens: We empower communities to better understand their environment. https://smartcitizen.me/ (2018). Accessed 19 Jan 2022

25. Quitmeyer, A.: Digital naturalism: designing holistic ethological interaction. In: CHI 2014 Extended Abstracts on Human Factors in Computing Systems, pp. 311–314 (2014)

26. Superflex: The Nursery Garden. https://tinyurl.com/muamu7dd (2017). Accessed 19 Jan 2022

27. Frayling, C.: Research in Art and Design, Royal College of Art Research Papers, vol. 1(1), 1993/4 (1994)

28. Sevaldson, B.: Beyond User Centric Design (2018)

29. Thackara, J.: How to Thrive in the Next Economy, 1st edn. Thames & Hudson London, London (2015)

30. Fransman, J.: Charting a course to an emerging field of 'research engagement studies': a conceptual meta-synthesis. Res. All **2**(2), 185–229 (2018)

31. Urban Barley field: Student Runner Up, Built Environment Award, Core77 Design Awards 2017. https://tinyurl.com/2p8d8whp (2017). Accessed 19 Jan 2022

32. Parsons, S.: The potential of digital technologies for transforming informed consent practices with children and young people. Soc. Inclusion **3**(6), 56–68 (2015)

33. Wertheim, C.: Evolving Nature-Culture Hybrid. crochetcoralreef.org/ (2020)

34. Volvo: https://tinyurl.com/kf3kyykv (2020). Accessed 19 Jan 2022

35. Wildlife Trusts: https://tinyurl.com/47kny8b2 (2018). Accessed 19 Jan 2022

36. West Yorkshire Police: Cub Scouts Crime Prevention Badge. https://tinyurl.com/mrxfj2k8 (2022). Accessed 19 Jan 2022

37. Warren, J.Y.: Public Lab is a Community and a Non-Profit, Democratizing Science. https://publiclab.org/ (2022). Accessed 19 Jan 2022

38. Zooniverse: People Powered Research. https://www.zooniverse.org/ (2022). Accessed 19 Jan 2022

39. Greene, C., Sobers, S., Zamenopolous, T., Chapain, C., Turner, J.: Conversations about co-production. In: Hargreaves, I., Hartley, J. (eds.) The Creative Citizen Unbound. Policy Press, Bristol (2014)

40. Gaver, W., et al.: My Naturewatch camera: disseminating practice research with a cheap and easy DIY design. In: Paper presented at the Proceedings of the 2019 CHI Conference on Human Factors in Computing Systems, p. 302 (2019)

41. Lilja, E.: Art, research, empowerment. On the Artist as (2015)

42. Skains, R.L.: Creative practice as research: discourse on methodology. J. Media Prac. **19**(1), 82–97 (2018). https://doi.org/10.1080/14682753.2017.1362175

43. Jordan, M.: Rehearsing practice research, unpublished paper. In: Practice Research: Interdisciplinary Methodologies in Cultural Institutions and HEI's, M4C Funded One Day Symposium, 10 June 2021 (2021)
44. Scrivener, S.: The art object does not embody a form of knowledge. Working Papers in Art and Design, vol. 2 (2002)
45. Jordan, M., Hewitt, A.: Misrecognitions in art and ethnography, In: Lígia, F., David, P. (eds.) Learning, Arts and Ethnography in a Contemporary World. Tufnell Press (2018)
46. Sholette, G., Bass, C.: Art as Social Action: An Introduction to the Principles and Practices of Teaching Social Practice. Allworth Press, USA (2018)
47. Vaughn, M., Jacquez, F.: Participatory research methods – choice points in the research process. J. Participatory Res. Meth. 1(1) (2020). https://doi.org/10.35844/001c.1324
48. Beech, D., Jordan, M.: Toppling statues, affective publics and the lessons of the black lives matter movement. Art Public Sphere 10(1), 3–15 (2021). https://doi.org/10.1386/aps_000 45_3
49. Hewitt, A., Jordan, M.: On trying to be collective. Art Public Sphere 9(1 and 2), 63–84 (2020). https://doi.org/10.1386/aps_00033_
50. Von Gunten: Intellectual Property is Common Property: Arguments Abolishing Intellectual Property, Buch & Netz, Zurich. https://tinyurl.com/3f9uye2t (2015). Accessed 5 Jan 2022
51. Berndes, C., Esche, C., McClean, D., SUPERFLEX: 'Discussion' https://tinyurl.com/mpt m3fhr (2010). Accessed 5 Jan 2022
52. Charpenal, P., McClean, D., SUPERFLEX (eds.) The Corrupt Show and the Speculative Machine. Fundacion and Colecccion Jumex, Mexico City, p. 335 (2014)
53. Charpenal, P., McClean, D.: Background, the Corrupt Show, and the Speculative Machine. In: Charpenal, P., McClean, D., SUPERFLEX (eds.) Fundacion and Colecccion Jumex, Mexico City, pp. 15–18 (2014)
54. Saraceno, T.: On Space Time Foam. https://tinyurl.com/25b7hx48 (2012). Accessed 19 Jan 2022
55. Something & Son: Trolley Reef. https://tinyurl.com/54k8sayp (2020). Accessed 19 Jan 2022
56. Anonymous: https://tinyurl.com/yckmeu29 (2021). Accessed 19 Jan 2022
57. Assemble: https://tinyurl.com/4e5zuuxc (2012). Accessed 19 Jan 2022
58. Gaudion, K., Hall, A., Myerson, J., Pellicano, L.: A designer's approach how can autistic adults with learning disabilities be involved in the design process? CoDesign (2015)
59. Cooking-sections: https://tinyurl.com/4rta7vkt (2015). Accessed 19 Jan 2022
60. Patey: https://tinyurl.com/2p8fhj7p (2007). Accessed 19 Jan 2022
61. Bowen: https://tinyurl.com/4dwwjvcm (2010). Accessed 19 Jan 2022
62. Anonymous: https://forforest.net/en/ (2019). Accessed 19 Jan 2022
63. Davies, C., et al.: Exploring engaged spaces in community-university partnership. Metro. Univ. 27(3), 6–26 (2016)
64. Binnendijk, A.: Conducting Key Informant Interviews. United States Agency for International Development (USAID) Center for Development Information and Evaluation, Washington, DC (1996)
65. Chipchase, J., Lee, J.P.: Field Study Handbook. Studio D Store (2017)
66. Ramster, G., Keren, C.: Designing with Communities. Royal College of Art, London. https://rca-media2.rca.ac.uk/documents/201209_dwithc_small_2.pdf (2020)
67. Phillips, R.: Communal response(s): designing a socially engaged nature recovery network. Disegno 22(32), 110–143 (2021). ISSN: 2064-7778 (Print). https://doi.org/10.21096/disegno_2021_1-2rph
68. BMW: https://tinyurl.com/3nwbwabc (2009). Accessed 19 Jan 2022
69. Manzini, E.: Politics of the Everyday. Bloomsbury Visual Arts (2019)
70. Jordan, M.: Towards Critical Practices: Art and Design as Socially Productive Practices. In: King, L., Young, O. (eds.) Transdisciplinary Practice, pp. 14–19. Oonagh Young Gallery (2017)

Multimodal Semantics for Affordances and Actions

James Pustejovsky[1]([✉]) [iD] and Nikhil Krishnaswamy[2] [iD]

[1] Brandeis University, Waltham, MA 02453, USA
jamesp@brandeis.edu
[2] Colorado State University, Fort Collins, CO 80523, USA
nkrishna@colostate.edu

Abstract. In this paper, we argue that, as HCI becomes more multimodal with the integration of gesture, gaze, posture, and other nonverbal behavior, it is important to understand the role played by affordances and their associated actions in human-object interactions (HOI), so as to facilitate reasoning in HCI and HRI environments. We outline the requirements and challenges involved in developing a multimodal semantics for human-computer and human-robot interactions. Unlike unimodal interactive agents (e.g., text-based chatbots or voice-based personal digital assistants), multimodal HCI and HRI inherently require a notion of embodiment, or an understanding of the agent's placement within the environment and that of its interlocutor. We present a dynamic semantics of the language, VoxML, to model human-computer, human-robot, and human-human interactions by creating multimodal simulations of both the communicative content and the agents' common ground, and show the utility of VoxML information that is reified within the environment on computational understanding of objects for HOI.

Keywords: Affordances · HCI · Habitats · Common ground · Multimodal dialogue · VoxML · Embodiment

1 Introduction

In this paper, we argue that, as HCI becomes more multimodal with the integration of gesture, gaze, posture, and other nonverbal behavior [12,25,41,53,76,88], it is important to understand the role played by affordances and their associated actions in human-object interactions (HOI), so as to facilitate reasoning in HCI and HRI environments. We outline the requirements and challenges involved in

This work was supported in part by NSF grant DRL 2019805, to Dr. Pustejovsky at Brandeis University, and Dr. Krishnaswamy at Colorado State University. It was also supported in part by NSF grant CNS 2033932 to Dr. Pustejovsky. We would like to thank Ken Lai, Bruce Draper, Ross Beveridge, Joshua Hartshorne, Mengguo Jing, Iris Ovid, Ricky Brutti, and Lucia Donatelli, for their comments and suggestions. The views expressed herein are ours alone.

M. Kurosu (Ed.): HCII 2022, LNCS 13302, pp. 137–160, 2022.
https://doi.org/10.1007/978-3-031-05311-5_9

developing a multimodal semantics for human-computer and human-robot interactions. Unlike unimodal interactive agents (e.g., text-based chatbots or voice-based personal digital assistants), multimodal HCI and HRI inherently require a notion of embodiment [2,17,37,53,82], or an understanding of the agent's placement within the environment and that of its interlocutor [24,47,49,57,77].

As natural language technology becomes ever-present in everyday life, people will expect artificial agents to understand language use as humans do, in a situated context. Nevertheless, most advanced neural AI systems fail at some types of interactions that are trivial for humans. Certain problems in both human-human communication and HCI cannot be solved without *situated reasoning*, meaning they cannot be adequately addressed with ungrounded meaning representation or cross-modal linking of instances alone. Examples include grounding an object and then reasoning with it ("Pick up *this* box. Put it *there*."), referring to a previously-established concept or instance that was never explicitly introduced into the dialogue, underspecification of deixis, and in general, dynamic updating of context through perceptual, linguistic, action, or self-announcement [1,71]. Without *both* a representation framework and mechanism for grounding references and inferences to the environment, such problems may well remain out of reach for NLP.

This requires not only the robust recognition and generation of expressions through multiple modalities (language, gesture, vision, action), but also the encoding of situated meaning: (a) the situated grounding of expressions in context; (b) an interpretation of the expression contextualized to the dynamics of the discourse; and (c) an appreciation of the actions and consequences associated with objects in the environment. This in turn impacts how we computationally model human-human communicative interactions, with particular relevance to the shared understanding of affordances [28] and actions over objects.

All multimodal human-to-human communicative acts are inherently embodied. Therefore, modeling similar capabilities with computational agents necessitates a notion of "embodied HCI" (EHCI). Agents in this framework are embodied and situated, which affords them the ability to affect the world they inhabit (either real or virtual), but also requires them to have accurate and robust interpretive capabilities for multiple input modalities, which must run in real time. In addition, an artificial agent must be able to communicate with its human interlocutors using all communicative modalities humans may use, including natural language, body language, gesture, demonstrated action, emotional cues, etc. This paper describes the semantics of actions and object affordances and the impact such knowledge has on embodied reasoning [45,71]. While the dynamic semantics of epistemic updating in discourse has been extensively modeled, there has been less development of integrated models of the dynamics of actions and affordances in cooperative or goal-directed discourse. We present a dynamic semantics of the language, VoxML [69], to model human-computer, human-robot, and human-human interactions by creating multimodal simulations of both the communicative content and the agents' common ground [4,19,84,86], which is formalized in a data structure known as a *common ground structure* [70]. A multimodal simulation is an embodied 3D virtual realization of both the situational environment and the co-situated agents, as well as the most salient content denoted by communicative acts in a discourse. VoxML provides a representation for the situated grounding of expressions between individuals involved in a communicative exchange. It does this by encoding objects with rich semantic typing and action affordances, and actions themselves as multimodal programs, enabling contextually salient inferences and decisions in the environment. Underlying this model is a dedicated platform, VoxWorld [44], that is used to create these 3D realizations and deploy embodied multimodal agents.

We believe that the major issues in HCI for situated reasoning involve the multimodal grounding of expressions, as well as contextual reasoning with this information. In particular, we address the question of how to encode the knowledge associated with Human Object Interactions (HOI): how is object-specific behavioral knowledge encoded in our everyday interactions with the entities we encounter?

2   Modeling Human Object Interactions

When humans engage in conversation, the objects under discussion can range from things and events present in their shared communicative space, to entities and situations removed from the present context, and potentially even hypothetical or irrealis in nature [30,50]. Because the focus here is on situated HCI and HRI, we restrict the domain of discourse between the agents to those objects and events that are either present or emergent in an environment shared by the interlocutors. Even with such a seemingly limited context, the objects in a dialogue, either between two humans or between human and computer, carry much more semantic information than conventionally assumed in planning research. This includes knowledge for how the objects can be manipulated and used by an agent in space and time, that is, their *physical and functional affordances* [28,64]. Such information also includes knowledge of how an object is situated in the environment relative to an agent for specific purposes and actions, that is, its *habitat* [65]. These two parameters constitute a kind of *teleological* knowledge [66], and in the discussion below, we describe this information and what role it plays in both reasoning and communication for HCI.

There is currently a disconnect between semantic models that support linguistic analysis and processing of narrative text, dialogue, and image captions, and the interpretation and grounding that is actually required to fully understand how an event is situated in a context. Some recent efforts have been made to provide contextual grounding to linguistic expressions. For example, work on "multimodal semantic grounding" within the natural language processing and image processing communities has resulted in a number of large corpora linking words or captions with images [13,54,92].

Here we argue that language understanding and linking to abstract instances of concepts in other modalities is insufficient; *situated grounding* entails knowledge of situation and contextual entities beyond that provided by a multimodal linking approach (cf. [36]).

Fig. 1. "Woman drinking coffee."

Actual situated meaning is much more involved than aligning captions and bounding boxes in an image: e.g., [34] discuss the contribution of non-linguistic events in situated discourse, and also whether they can be the arguments to discourse relations. Similarly, it is acknowledged that gesture is part of either the direct content of the utterance [85] or cosuppositional content [79]. Hence, we must assume that natural interactions with computers and robots have to account for interpreting and generating language and gesture.

For example, consider the event depicted in Fig. 1. We assume that conventional semantic composition results in a logical form such as that shown in (1b); for convenience, we will also employ a situated representation that takes advantage of contextual Skolemization; that is, "a woman" will be denoted by w, and "coffee" will be denoted by c.

(1) a. A woman drinks coffee.
   b. $\exists x \exists y [\text{woman}(x) \land coffee(y) \land \text{drink}(x, y)]$
   c. $drink(w, c)$

Such representations need to be grounded, hence the recent interest in linking text, and captions in particular, to image-based information (in the form of annotated bounding boxes, etc.). As useful as such cross-modal (image-caption) linking can be for Question Answering tasks [3,51], it does not provide sufficient information to perform situated or embodied reasoning. That is, no true model of the underlying human-object interaction can be extracted from such alignments.

Let's examine just what kind of information would be necessary to have regarding an event and its participants, so that novel inferencing and reasoning can be performed. We begin by creating a verbose gloss or dense paraphrase for the caption in Fig. 1.

(2) a. *A woman drinking coffee.*
   b. A upright seated woman is holding in her hand, a cup filled with coffee while she drinks it.
   c. The cup is upright so the container portion (inside) is able to hold coffee.
   d. She is holding the cup by an attached handle.
   e. The cup is tilted towards her and touches her partially open mouth, in order to allow drinking.

Similarly, the caption for Fig. 2 is perfectly adequate as a description of the situation for a human to interpret. But for a computer to be able to understand the caption by itself or indeed even with the image provided, there needs to be an interpretation of how the human and the objects are interacting.

A similar "unpacking" of the situation would involve a dense paraphrase as shown below, where the semantic and pragmatic presuppositions in the caption are made explicit. As in the previous example in Fig. 1, this spells out: the orientation and facing of the human to the object; touch points (hot spots) on the object, e.g., keyboard; pose and embodied actions, e.g., typing with both hands.

Fig. 2. A man working at a desk.

(3) a. *A man working at a desk.*
    b. A upright man is seated in a chair, typing with both hands on the keyboard of a laptop, which is on the top surface of a table.
    c. The chair he is seated in is close enough to the table for him to reach the keyboard.
    d. The laptop is open, with the keyboard exposed flat and the screen facing the man.
    e. The man is facing the computer and the desk.

Where does this human-object interaction (HOI) information come from? Ideally, it can be learned through multimodal alignment of image and caption embeddings [14,31,73,91], but this is still a difficult problem within the knowledge acquisition community. Explicit representation has been disfavored in modern AI, but typical neural networks that learn implicit representations are treated as passive recipients of data, with the question of context- and situation-sensitive grounding treated as something of an inconvenience [16]. There is less attention paid to letting the current state of the world, as opposed to reams of pre-existing data, be "its own model", per Brooks [9]. In the present work, we start with an initial library of human-object interaction pairs, encoded as affordances in their habitats (cf. next section), and then discuss experiments where such HOI properties can be learned.

3   Modeling Habitats and Affordances

In everyday discourse, when referring to objects and events, humans expect each other to know more than what a word refers to: e.g., a cup is an artifact, coffee is a substance, and a toy is an inanimate object. Such categorical knowledge is typically represented as a type structure, such as that shown in Fig. 3 below.

Such typing is useful in linguistic interpretations so as to ensure that predicates select the appropriate types of arguments in composition, as illustrated in the semantic type derivation in (4), for the caption from Fig. 1, "Woman drinking coffee."

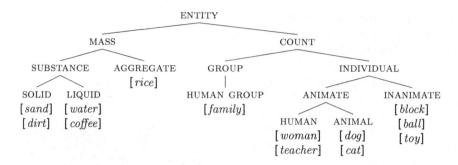

Fig. 3. *Classical* ENTITY *subtyping*

(4)

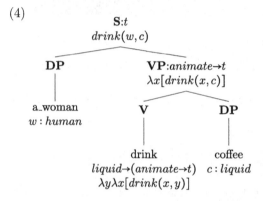

However, as the situated paraphrases from the previous section suggest, there is information missing from conventional semantic representations for deeper reasoning and inferencing about events and situations. In fact, we understand an entire set of object attributes as well as a network of relations concerning how the object appropriately participates in the situation under discussion. Many of these involve human-object interactions (HOIs), and our knowledge of things is predicated on are understanding of how to interact with them. Hence, just as a cup will conventionally have an ontological relationship of a handle to the whole structure, there is a conventional presupposition that the orientation of the cup exposes the concavity of the interior to enable the functioning of the cup. Notice that there are several things mentioned here that are partially spatial and partially teleological. This is what we will call a *teleotopological relationship* [67]. There are aspects of qualitative spatial reasoning that are implicated in this relationship such as orientation of the concavity [26].

In order to create a compositional interpretation from a sentences such as "the cup is on the table" and further "the coffee is in the cup," we must likely have some semantic encoding lexically associated with all these objects as well as compositionally for how they are physically and spatially configured relative to each other.

Consider what some of the relevant parameters from this example are, that may be tied to the way specific objects inhabit their situation. Assuming that an object such as a cup, typed as a container is an asymmetric object, such as a cylinder, it would appear that orientation information is critical for enabling the use or function the object *qua* container. In fact, only when the cup's orientation facilitates containment can the function be "activated", as it were. This references two notions that are critical for reasoning about objects and HOI generally: we encode *what* the function associated with an object is (its affordance), but just as critically, we also identify *when* it is active (its habitat).

Similarly, consider the implicit knowledge we seem to exploit for the way we refer to and interact with an instrument such a spoon, knife, or fork. Each of these can be considered a tool for eating. Each is asymmetric in form with a handle, and "another" end that is associated with the function of eating, or a subevent of eating. Hence when asked to pick up a spoon and start eating from a bowl, we naturally grasp the handle and know where to put the spoon relative to the bowl, etc. This is a simple but telling example of the myriad actions which are afforded by and encoded with specific objects, in order to engage in specific activities.

Fig. 4. Top: *Spoon* in different habitats allowing holding (left) and stirring (right). Bottom: *Knife* allowing spreading (left) and cutting (right).

In the images above, we see roughly the following condition-action pair:

(5) *If* **Habitat** *then* **Action**

For a spoon, we identify at least two functions, associated with distinct actions, each of which is enabled by distinct habitats in Fig. 4 Top:

(6) a. If *spoon's concavity is vertical,* then it can *support containment of a substance;*

   b. If *spoon's major axis is vertical,* then it can *support mixing.*

Similar remarks hold for the orientation of a knife, as illustrated above in Fig. 4 (Bottom):

(7) a. If *knife's zero convexity (sheet) is horizontal,* then it can *support spreading of a substance;*

   b. If *knife's zero convexity (sheet) is vertical,* then it can *support cutting or separating.*

Given the notion of affordance and how we interact with the objects in our environment, we can refactor the classic entity type ontology from Fig. 3 in terms of how it is possible to interact with the objects in our environment. This is shown, in part, below in the modal definition of objects as possible behaviors in (8).

(8) Refactoring Entity Types as Modal Actions (Affordances)

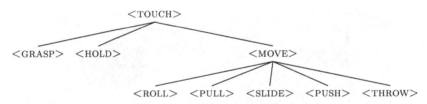

In the next section, we outline a language that captures much of the information missing from conventional semantic models of events, as shown above: in particular, information encoding object geometry, as well as event-participant configuration and orientation constraints. This language, VoxML, encodes knowledge about objects, their attributes, events, and functions to their visual and spatial instantiations, called a "visual object concept", or *voxeme.*

4 VoxML

A significant part of any model for situated communication is an encoding of the semantic type, functions, purposes, and uses introduced by the "objects under discussion". For example, a semantic model of perceived *object teleology,* as introduced by Generative Lexicon (GL) with the Qualia Structure, for example [64], as well as *object affordances* [28] is useful to help ground expression meaning to speaker intent. As an illustration, consider first how such information is encoded, and then exploited in reasoning. Knowledge of objects can be partially contextualized through their *qualia structure* [68], where each Qualia role can be seen as answering a specific question about the object it is bound to:

(9)   a. *Formal*: encoding taxonomic information about the lexical item (the IS-A relation);

   b. *Constitutive*: encoding information on the parts and constitution of an object (PART-OF or MADE-OF relation);

   c. *Telic*: encoding information on purpose and function (the used-for or FUNCTIONS-AS relation);

   d. *Agentive*: encoding information about the origin of the object (the CREATED-BY relation).

In human-human communication, objects under discussion (cf. [30]) can be partially contextualized through their semantic type and their qualia structure: a food item has a TELIC value of *eat*, an instrument for writing, a TELIC of *write*, a cup, a TELIC of *hold*, and so forth. For example, the lexical semantics for the noun *chair* in (10), assuming a Generative Lexicon encoding, carries a TELIC value of *sit_in*, while the concept of *letter* carries a TELIC value of *read* and an AGENTIVE value of *write*. Such object-based information will need to be recognized by computational agents in HCI and HRI, as well, as it is so crucial for situational reasoning is dialogue and discourse.

$$(10)\ \lambda x \begin{bmatrix} \textbf{chair} \\ \text{AS} = \begin{bmatrix} \text{ARG1} = x : e \end{bmatrix} \\ \text{QS} = \begin{bmatrix} \text{F} = phys(x) \\ \text{T} = \lambda z, e[sit\_in(e, z, x)] \end{bmatrix} \end{bmatrix}$$

Notice that, while an artifact may be designed for a specific purpose, this purpose can only be achieved under specific circumstances. To account for this context-dependence, [65, 70] enrich the lexical semantics of words denoting artifacts (the TELIC role specifically) by introducing the notion of an object's *habitat*, which encodes these circumstances. For example, an object, x, within the appropriate habitat (or context) $\mathcal{C}$, performing the action π will result in the intended or desired resulting state, $\mathcal{R}$, i.e., $\mathcal{C} \rightarrow [\pi]\mathcal{R}$. That is, if the habitat $\mathcal{C}$ (a set of contextual factors) is satisfied, then every time the activity of π is performed, the resulting state $\mathcal{R}$ will occur. It is necessary to specify the precondition context $\mathcal{C}$, since this enables the local modality to be satisfied. An illustration of what the resulting knowledge structure for the habitat of a chair is shown in the QS entry below.

$$(11)\ \lambda\mathcal{C}\lambda x \begin{bmatrix} \textbf{chair} \\ \text{F} = [phys(x), on(x, y_1), in(x, y_2), orient(x, up)] \\ \text{C} = [seat(x_1), back(x_2), legs(x_3), clear(x_1)] \\ \text{T} = \lambda z \lambda e[\mathcal{C} \rightarrow [sit(e, z, x)]\mathcal{R}_{sit}(x)] \\ \text{A} = [made(e', w, x)] \end{bmatrix}$$

The habitat for an object is built by first placing it within an *embedding space* and then contextualizing it. For example, in order to use a table, the top has to be oriented upward, the surface must be accessible, and so on. A chair must also be oriented up, the seat must be free and accessible, it must be able to support the user, etc., [21, 23].

The notion of habitat described above and the attached behaviors that are associated with an object are further developed in [69], where an explicit connection to Gibson's ecological psychology is made [29], along with a direct encoding of the *affordance structure* for the object [28]. The affordance structure available to an agent, when presented with an object, is the set of actions that can be performed with it. We refer to these as GIBSONIAN affordances, and they include "grasp", "move", "hold", "turn", etc. This is to distinguish them from more goal-directed, intentionally situated activities, what we call TELIC affordances.

Extending this notion, we define a habitat as a representation of an object situated within a simulation, a partial minimal model [8, 40, 43]; in this sense, it is a directed enhancement of the qualia structure. Multi-dimensional affordances determine how habitats are deployed and how they modify or augment the context, and compositional operations include procedural (simulation) and operational (selection, specification, refinement) knowledge.

The language used to construct this simulation is called VoxML (Visual Object Concept Modeling Language) [69]. VoxML is a modeling language for constructing 3D visualizations of concepts denoted by natural language expressions, and is being used as the platform for creating multimodal semantic simulations in the context of human-computer and human-robot communication [44]. It adopts the basic semantic typing for objects and properties from Generative Lexicon and the dynamic interpretation of event structure developed in [72], along with a continuation-based dynamic interpretation for both sentence and discourse composition [5, 6, 22].

VoxML forms the scaffolding we use to encode knowledge about objects, events, attributes, and functions by linking lexemes to their visual instantiations, termed the "visual object concept" or *voxeme*.

Entities modeled in VoxML can be OBJECTS, programs, or logical types. OBJECTS are logical constants; PROGRAMS are n-ary predicates that can take objects or other evaluated predicates as arguments; logical types can be divided into ATRIBUTES, RELATIONS, and FUNCTIONS, all predicates which take OBJECTS as arguments. ATTRIBUTES and RELATIONS evaluate to states, and FUNCTIONS evaluate to geometric regions. These entities can then compose into visualizations of natural language concepts and expressions. For example, the attributes associated with objects such as *cup*, *chair*, and *block*, include the following:

LEX	OBJECT's lexical information
TYPE	OBJECT's geometrical typing
HABITAT	OBJECT's habitat for actions
AFFORD_STR	OBJECT's affordance structure
EMBODIMENT	OBJECT's agent-relative embodiment

The LEX attribute contains the subcomponents PRED, the predicate lexeme denoting the object, and TYPE, the object's type according to Generative Lexicon.

Voxemes representing humans or IVAs are lexically typed as *agents*, but arti-ficial agents, due to their embodiments, ultimately inherit from physical objects and so fall under objects in the taxonomy. In parallel to a lexicon, a collection of voxemes is termed a *voxicon*. There is no requirement on a voxicon to have a one-to-one correspondence between its voxemes and the lexemes in the associ-ated lexicon, which often results in a many-to-many correspondence. That is, the lexeme *plate* may be visualized as a [[SQUARE PLATE]][1], a [[ROUND PLATE]], or other voxemes, and those voxemes in turn may be linked to other lexemes such as *dish* or *saucer*. Each voxeme is linked to either an object geometry, a program in a dynamic semantics, an attribute set, or a transformation algorithm, which are all structures easily exploitable in a rendered simulation platform.

An OBJECT's voxeme structure provides *habitats*, which are situational con-texts or environments conditioning the object's *affordances*, which may be either "Gibsonian" affordances [28] or "Telic" affordances [64,65]. A habitat specifies how an object typically occupies a space. When we are challenged with comput-ing the embedding space for an event, the individual habitats associated with each participant in the event will both define and delineate the space required for the event to transpire. Affordances are used as attached behaviors, which the object either facilitates by its geometry (Gibsonian) or purposes for which it is intended to be used (Telic). For example, a Gibsonian affordance for [[CUP]] is "grasp," while a Telic affordance is "drink from." This allows procedural rea-soning to be associated with habitats and affordances, executed in real time in the simulation, inferring the complete set of spatial relations between objects at each frame and tracking changes in the shared context between human and computer.

For example, the object geometry for the concept [[CUP]], along with the constraints on symmetry, is illustrated below.

$$(12) \quad \begin{bmatrix} \textbf{cup} \\ \text{TYPE} = \begin{bmatrix} \text{HEAD} = \textbf{cylindroid}[1] \\ \text{COMPONENTS} = \textbf{surface, interior} \\ \text{CONCAVITY} = \textbf{concave} \\ \text{ROTATIONAL\_SYMMETRY} = \{Y\} \\ \text{REFLECTION\_SYMMETRY} = \{XY, YZ\} \end{bmatrix} \end{bmatrix}$$

Consider now the various habitats identified with [[CUP]].

$$(13) \quad \begin{bmatrix} \textbf{cup} \\ \text{HABITAT} = \begin{bmatrix} \text{INTRINSIC} = [2] \begin{bmatrix} \text{CONSTR} = \{Y > X, Y > Z\} \\ \text{UP} = align(Y, \mathcal{E}_Y) \\ \text{TOP} = top(+Y) \end{bmatrix} \\ \text{EXTRINSIC} = [3] \begin{bmatrix} \text{UP} = align(Y, \mathcal{E}_{\perp Y}) \end{bmatrix} \end{bmatrix} \end{bmatrix}$$

Finally, given these habitats, we can identify the associated behaviors that are enabled (afforded) in such situations:

$$(14) \quad \begin{bmatrix} \textbf{cup} \\ \text{AFF\_STR} = \begin{bmatrix} A_1 = H_{[2]} \rightarrow [put(x, on([1]))]support([1], x) \\ A_2 = H_{[2]} \rightarrow [put(x, in([1]))]contain([1], x) \\ A_3 = H_{[2]} \rightarrow [grasp(x, [1])]hold(x, [1]) \\ A_4 = H_{[3]} \rightarrow [roll(x, [1])]\mathcal{R} \end{bmatrix} \end{bmatrix}$$

---

[1] Beginning in [42], voxemes have been denoted [[VOXEME]].

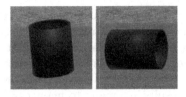

Fig. 5. Cup in different habitats allowing sliding and holding (left) and rolling (right).

Indeed, object properties and the events they facilitate are a primary component of situational context. In Fig. 12, we understand that the cup in the orientation shown can be *rolled* by a human. Were it not in this orientation, it might be able to be only *slid* across its supporting surface (cf. (15)). This voxeme for [[CUP]] gives the object appropriate lexical predicate and typing (a *cup* is a PHYSICAL OBJECT and an ARTIFACT). It denotes that the cup is roughly cylindrical and concave, has a surface and an interior, is symmetrical around the Y-axis and across associated planes (VoxML adopts 3D graphics conventions, where the Y-axis is vertical), and is smaller than and movable by the artificial agent. The remainder of VoxML typing structure is devoted to habitat and affordance structures, which we discuss below.

(15) Objects encoding semantic type, habitat, and affordances:

$$
\begin{bmatrix}
\textbf{cup} \\
\text{LEXICAL} = \begin{bmatrix} \text{PREDICATE} = \textbf{cup} \\ \text{TYPE} = \textbf{physobj} \bullet \textbf{artifact} \end{bmatrix} \\
\text{TYPE} = \begin{bmatrix} \text{HEAD} = \textbf{cylindroid}[1] \\ \text{COMPONENTS} = \textbf{surface, interior} \\ \text{CONCAVITY} = \textbf{concave} \\ \text{ROTATIONAL\_SYMMETRY} = \{Y\} \\ \text{REFLECTION\_SYMMETRY} = \{XY, YZ\} \end{bmatrix} \\
\text{HABITAT} = \begin{bmatrix} \text{INTRINSIC} = [2] \begin{bmatrix} \text{CONSTR} = \{Y > X, Y > Z\} \\ \text{UP} = align(Y, \mathcal{E}_Y) \\ \text{TOP} = top(+Y) \end{bmatrix} \\ \text{EXTRINSIC} = [3] \begin{bmatrix} \text{UP} = align(Y, \mathcal{E}_{\perp Y}) \end{bmatrix} \end{bmatrix} \\
\text{AFF\_STR} = \begin{bmatrix} A_1 = H_{[2]} \rightarrow [put(x, on([1]))]support([1], x) \\ A_2 = H_{[2]} \rightarrow [put(x, in([1]))]contain([1], x) \\ A_3 = H_{[2]} \rightarrow [grasp(x, [1])]hold(x, [1]) \\ A_4 = H_{[3]} \rightarrow [roll(x, [1])]\mathcal{R} \end{bmatrix} \\
\text{EMBOD} = \begin{bmatrix} \text{SCALE} = <\textbf{agent} \\ \text{MOVABLE} = \textbf{true} \end{bmatrix}
\end{bmatrix}
$$

(12–14) respectively show the typing, habitat, and affordance structure of [[CUP]], which are brought together in the complete VoxML encoding in (15). Bracketed numbers (e.g., [1]) are reentrancy indices; terms annotated with the same number refer to the same entitiy. For instance, in habitat 2 ($H_{[2]}$), the intrinsic habitat where the cup has an upward orientation, if an agent puts some x inside the cup's cylindroid geometry ([1]), the cup contains x.

Now let us consider how this model informs the interactions available to agent in a simple environment of a child playing with blocks, as shown in Fig. 6.

Fig. 6. Girl stacking blocks.

Each of these blocks encodes the specific set of affordances associated with its class: namely, given the appropriate habitat, they can be grasped, and then moved (picked up, slid, pushed, puled, thrown, but not rolled!). In the current situation depicted in this image, however, only the top-most blocks are immediately available for these affordances.

As we show in the next section, object properties associated with how an agent can behave or interact with them can be the key towards classification and discrimination of objects in an otherwise homogeneous environment.

5   Reasoning with Affordances

To demonstrate the information that object affordances and situated grounding as encoded in VoxML provides, let us examine a simple object classification example. Humans are efficient at seeking out experiences that are maximally informative about their environment [52,58,60,75,80]. We explore the physical world to practice skills, test hypotheses, learn object affordances, etc. [11,32,33, 59,62,63,83]. Young children, in particular, can rapidl generalize from previous to new experiences with few or even no examples [18,20,87].

Meanwhile, artificial neural networks require large numbers of samples to train. A single cortical neuron may take 5–8 layers of artificial neurons to approximate [7]. Common few-, one-, or zero-shot learning approaches in AI provide at best a rough simulacrum of human learning and generalization [39,61,93]. Recent success in few-shot learning in end-to-end deep neural systems still requires extensive pre-training and fine-tuning, often on special hardware [10] or specific task formulation [78].

In AI, object identification is usually approached as a computer vision task [46]. While convolutional neural nets, the most common method for object identification in modern computer vision, do appear to optimize for a form of invariance [35], and invariance is important for semantic interpretation [48], visual input alone is only one part of how humans learn to identify objects [89].

To examine the different affordances of objects, an artificial agent can interact with various objects and see how they behave differently under the same circumstances. To test this, we trained a TD3 reinforcement learning policy [27] to learn to stack two cubes. We then used a successful cube-stacking policy to make the agent attempt to stack other spheres, cylinders, and capsules (Fig. 7) on a block, forcing it to stack the other objects *as if they were cubes*. This control structure allowed us to identify differences in the behaviors of the different objects in the stacking task. Since these behaviors can be described in terms like "cubes stack successfully," "spheres roll off," etc., they can be described in terms of the object's *affordances*.

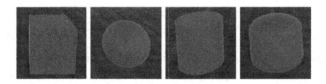

Fig. 7. Test objects.

As the agent executes the trained policy over the various objects, we gather information about each stacking attempt from the VoxSim virtual environment. At each timestep we store the type of the theme object, its rotation in radians at episode start, radians between the world upright axis and the object upright (+Y) axis, the numerical action executed, the object rotation and offset from world upright after the action, the state observation after action completion, the reward for the attempt, the cumulative total reward over the episode, and the cumulative mean reward over the episode. At the end of the action, a small "jitter" is applied to the object, to simulate the small force exerted on an object when it is released from a grasp. We also store the vector representing the magnitude and direction of this small force. This jitter force is applied perpendicular to the major rotational axis of the theme object if one exists, or randomly if the object is symmetric around all axes. Therefore, the jitter applied to cylinder or capsule is applied perpendicularly to the object's Y-axis, while the jitter applied to a cube or sphere is random. Therefore the post-action jitter implicitly encodes information about the objects' habitats, while some other parameters gathered implicitly encode affordances. Compare a subset of parameters extracted from the environment from a single stacking attempt each with a cube and a sphere, and two attempts with a cylinder (Table 1).

Table 1. Observations gathered during stacking task with multiple objects.

Object	Jitter			θ After action	Stack height
Cube	-1.472×10^{-4}	0	2.021×10^{-4}	0.02238165	2
Sphere	8.165×10^{-5}	0	-2.363×10^{-5}	2.134116	1
Cylinder	0	0	2.5×10^{-4}	0.01457105	2
Cylinder	0	0	2.5×10^{-4}	1.570793	1

"Stack Height" indicates the number of stacked objects after the action was complete. 2 indicates the object was stacked successfully, while 1 indicates that it fell off when the action was complete, leaving only the bottom block in the stack. "θ after Action" is the net angle (in radians) of the object space upright $(+Y)$ from the world space upright $(+Y)$ axis. Values close to 0 indicate that the object is upright while values near $\pm\frac{\pi}{2}$ indicate that the object is lying on its side. A cube, which is flat on all sides, can rest stably at any multiple of $\frac{\pi}{2}$ radians. In Table 1, we see that the stacking attempt with a cube results in a stable stack (height 2) with the top object sitting upright. The sphere, which rolls off, does not stack (height 1), and comes to rest at an arbitrary angle.

The cylinder shares properties with cubes (flat ends) and others with spheres (round sides), and this behavior can be seen in the last two rows. In the second-to-last row, the cylinder stacks successfully (height 2), and is resting upright $(\theta \approx 0)$. In the sample shown in the last row, the stacking attempt was made with the cylinder on its side $(\theta \approx \frac{\pi}{2})$. Since this places the cylinder's round surface in contact with its supporting surface, this habitat does not afford sustained support, and the cylinder rolls off (indicated by the height value of 1). We can also see that the direction of the jitter implicitly encodes the axis of symmetry of the object, and therefore the habitat.

We use all the parameters gathered above to train a model that will predict the object type from its behavior in the stacking task. We use a 1D convolutional neural net for this task. Since episodes can be variable length (depending on how successful the policy was at stacking the object in question), we pad out the length of each input to 10 timesteps, copying the last sample out to the padding length. Therefore an episode where the policy stacked the object successfully on the first try will consist of 10 identical timestep representations, while an episode where the agent tried and failed the stack the object 10 times will have 10 different timestep representations, so stackable objects like cubes and (upright) cylinders will have more consistent representations across the 10 timestep sample while less stackable objects will exhibit more variation across the 10 attempts.

The classifier consists of two convolutional layers (256 and 128 hidden units respectively). The filter size in the first layer is c, a variable equal to the number of parameters saved at each evaluation timestep during data gathering ($c = 19$ here) and a stride length of 8, and the second layer uses a filter size of 4 and a stride length of 2. This allows the convolutions to generate feature maps in the hidden layers that are approximately equal to the size of a single timestep sample, and convolving over this approximates observing each timestep of the episode in turn. The convolutional layers are followed by two 64-unit fully-connected layers and a softmax layer. We train for 500 epochs using the Adam optimizer [38], a batch size of 100 (= 10 episodes) and a learning rate of 0.001. Figure 8 shows the classification results over an unseen test set of 100 episodes worth of samples for each object.

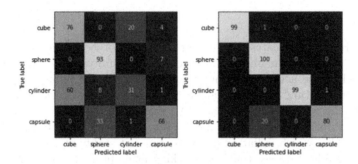

Fig. 8. 1D CNN behavioral features classifier results. First chart shows results without the input of the implicit habitat and affordance information encoded in the post-action jitter. Second chart shows results with those input features.

Not only can the objects be predicted from their behavior, meaning the that affordances encode important information about object type, but the post-action jitter features, that specifically encode the dependency between habitat and affordance by virtue of the object's axis of symmetry, increases classifier performance by *28%*, from 66.5% without the jitter features to **94.5%**. Without the jitter features, most confusions are between the objects that share very broad stacking behavior: cube and cylinder (mostly stackable), and sphere and capsule (mostly unstackable). Implicit information about affordances and habitats makes the difference.

Of course, humans can readily tell that objects are different because they look different. Sometimes interaction is not needed. Therefore we compare the performance of the behavior-based classifier to a 2D CNN CIFAR-10 style object detector. We crop and downsample all images to 84 × 84 pixels, and use 3 2D convolutional layers with a filter size of 16, a 3 × 3 stride, and 2 × 2 average pooling, followed by a 64-unit fully-connected layer before the softmax layer. We train for 500 epochs using the Adam optimizer and a learning rate of 0.01, which are the same learning hyperparameters as the behavior-based 1D CNN.

This classifier achieves a validation accuracy of 97.5%, but when evaluated against an unseen test set of 140 novel images of the four object classes (35 images each), accuracy falls below the behavior-based classifier, to **90.7%** (Fig. 9).

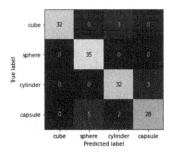

Fig. 9. 2D CNN visual classifier results.

A look at the mistakes this classifier makes (Fig. 10) reveals why. If the object is occluded, as in the top row, or distored due to perspective, the vision classifier naturally fails often.

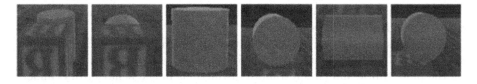

Fig. 10. Sample of misrecognized objects. From left: cylinder misrecognized as cube (1), and capsule (2), cylinder misrecognized as cube (3), sphere (4), and capsule (5), and capsule misrecognized as sphere (6).

Therefore while we can see that some objects are clearly visually distinct, like cube vs. sphere, other object classes are more difficult to distinguish visually. To confirm this, we go inside the 2D CNN and draw out the 64-dimensional embedding vectors from the final fully-connected layer. An embedding vector represents what a sample input is transformed into in the interior of a neural network after being multiplied by the optimized weight matrices in each layer in turn, until it reaches the softmax layer. These can be used to quantitatively assess the similarity of different input samples to each other. Figure 11 shows the cosine similarity of each of the 140 test visual embeddings to each other embedding.

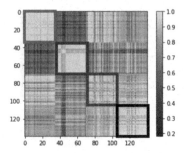

Fig. 11. Cosine similarity matrix of visual embedding vectors from 2D CNN.

The red box indicates the cube embedding vectors, blue the sphere embeddings, purple the cylinder embeddings, and black the capsule embeddings. A brighter color indicates more similarity. We can see that cube embeddings are obviously most similar to each other, as are sphere embeddings, but when we look at the cylinder and capsule embeddings, the similarities are much less obvious, and therefore the softmax layer of the networks makes its final prediction will less confidence in those cases.

Cube and sphere are also the most distinct objects in the behavior-based classifier, and the habitat and affordance information appears to be critical to making the more subtle and circumstantial distinctions in the behavior of cylinders and capsule. These implicit semantics are what VoxML is designed to explicitly encode.

We therefore propose that we can learn and populate VoxML encodings themselves through multiple inputs, such as interactive behavior, communication, and qualitative spatial relation calculi (e.g., [55,56,74]). For example, let A and B be two objects. If the Y-coordinate of A's position is above the Y-coordinate of B's position, and A and B are *externally connected* (touching), then it is likely that *B supports A* or *A is on top of B*. This can be learnable though interaction by learning a correlation between a embedding or vector representation of the resultant state and a symbol that denotes that state, such as a classification label, or ideally a word.

Fig. 12. Roll of tape can be thrown like a *disk*: it can be both "flicked" between thumb and fingers (left) and "released" (right).

6 Conclusion and Future Directions

In this paper, we have outlined the requirements in developing a multimodal semantics for human-computer and human-robot interactions. We presented a model for how to encode, reason with, and learn object affordances in dynamic human-object interactions (HOI). Being able to identify and then perform inferencing from the modal possibilities inherent in the objects one encounters is an essential component of any natural HCI or HRI system. We introduced the language, VoxML, which provides a representation for the situated grounding of expressions between individuals involved in a communicative exchange. By providing a rich semantic typing and encoding of action affordances for objects, and for actions as multimodal programs, contextually salient inferences and decisions are made available in the environment as the interaction unfolds.

One current line of research is to examine how this model can inform the interpretation of student behavior in classroom interactions, as well as subsequent development of curriculum for use in middle school education. This is part of research conducted in the context of the NSF National AI Institute for Student-AI Teaming (iSAT)[2]. The goal is to imagine a range of increasingly sophisticated "AI partners" that a teacher could have as an assistant in a classroom. One particular task for this partner would be the interpretation of student behavior and attention to the lesson at hand. This is a challenging problem for AI but not for a seasoned teacher, since the latter can understand when a student is engaged in on-topic behavior or when they are acting out.

Following developments within the area of embodied cognition [15,81,82,90], it is interesting to see how this plays out. As a case in point, we have examined extensive videos of classroom lessons from an urban public school, while they are engaged in science immersion units. What is immediately clear is the need to distinguish between actions that are associated with an "embodied solution" to a task in the curriculum, from simply random actions performed off-topic. For example, consider the task of determining the characteristics of a *disk*, from a collection of objects. One way is to determine the relative height and diameter of each object. However, another means is to test the objects through experienced play, determining whether, for example, they can be thrown like a disk. In the images below, we see a girl testing a roll of tape, which satisfies the embodied action associated with a disk: *it can be grasped, flicked and then released, and it moves through the air*. That is, the girl is answering the question through actions on the object, using her body and reasoning from the consequences of the actions. This is embodied cognition.

This is an embodied cognitive solution utilizing the notion of affordances as developed in this paper, and is, we believe, an interesting direction for further research [45,71].

---

[2] https://www.colorado.edu/today/ai-education.

References

1. Alikhani, M., Khalid, B., Shome, R., Mitash, C., Bekris, K., Stone, M.: That and there: judging the intent of pointing actions with robotic arms. In: Proceedings of the AAAI Conference on Artificial Intelligence, vol. 34, pp. 10343–10351 (2020)
2. Anderson, M.L.: Embodied cognition: a field guide. Artif. Intell. **149**(1), 91–130 (2003)
3. Antol, S., et al.: VQA: visual question answering. In: Proceedings of the IEEE International Conference on Computer Vision, pp. 2425–2433 (2015)
4. Asher, N.: Common ground, corrections and coordination. J. Semant. (1998)
5. Asher, N., Pogodalla, S.: SDRT and continuation semantics. In: Onada, T., Bekki, D., McCready, E. (eds.) JSAI-ISAI 2010. LNCS (LNAI), vol. 6797, pp. 3–15. Springer, Heidelberg (2011). https://doi.org/10.1007/978-3-642-25655-4_2
6. Barker, C., Shan, C.C.: Continuations and natural language. Oxford Studies in Theoretical Linguistics, vol. 53 (2014)
7. Beniaguev, D., Segev, I., London, M.: Single cortical neurons as deep artificial neural networks. bioRxiv p. 613141 (2020)
8. Blackburn, P., Bos, J.: Computational semantics. Theoria: Int. J. Theory Hist. Found. Sci. 27–45 (2003)
9. Brooks, R.A.: Intelligence without representation. Artif. Intell. **47**(1–3), 139–159 (1991)
10. Brown, T.B., et al.: Language models are few-shot learners. arXiv preprint arXiv:2005.14165 (2020)
11. Caligiore, D., Ferrauto, T., Parisi, D., Accornero, N., Capozza, M., Baldassarre, G.: Using motor babbling and Hebb rules for modeling the development of reaching with obstacles and grasping. In: International Conference on Cognitive Systems, pp. E1–E8 (2008)
12. Cassell, J., Sullivan, J., Churchill, E., Prevost, S.: Embodied Conversational Agents. MIT Press (2000)
13. Chai, J.Y., Fang, R., Liu, C., She, L.: Collaborative language grounding toward situated human-robot dialogue. AI Magazine **37**(4), 32–45 (2016)
14. Chao, Y.W., Liu, Y., Liu, X., Zeng, H., Deng, J.: Learning to detect human-object interactions. In: 2018 IEEE Winter Conference on Applications of Computer Vision (WACV), pp. 381–389. IEEE (2018)
15. Chemero, A.: Radical Embodied Cognitive Science. MIT Press (2011)
16. Chen, C., Seff, A., Kornhauser, A., Xiao, J.: Deepdriving: learning affordance for direct perception in autonomous driving. In: Proceedings of the IEEE International Conference on Computer Vision, pp. 2722–2730 (2015)
17. Chrisley, R.: Embodied artificial intelligence. Artif. Intell. **149**(1), 131–150 (2003)
18. Clark, A.: Language, embodiment, and the cognitive niche. Trends Cognit. Sci. **10**(8), 370–374 (2006)
19. Clark, H.H., Brennan, S.E.: Grounding in communication. Perspect. Social. Shared Cognit. **13**(1991), 127–149 (1991)
20. Colung, E., Smith, L.B.: The emergence of abstract ideas: evidence from networks and babies. Philos. Trans. Roy. Soc. London Ser. B Biol. Sci. **358**(1435), 1205–1214 (2003)
21. Coventry, K., Garrod, S.C.: Spatial prepositions and the functional geometric framework. In: Towards a Classification of Extra-Geometric Influences (2005)

22. De Groote, P.: Type raising, continuations, and classical logic. In: Proceedings of the Thirteenth Amsterdam Colloquium, pp. 97–101 (2001)
23. Dobnik, S., Cooper, R.: Interfacing language, spatial perception and cognition in type theory with records. J. Lang. Model. **5**(2), 273–301 (2017)
24. Fischer, K.: How people talk with robots: designing dialog to reduce user uncertainty. AI Magazine **32**(4), 31–38 (2011)
25. Foster, M.E.: Enhancing human-computer interaction with embodied conversational agents. In: Stephanidis, C. (ed.) UAHCI 2007. LNCS, vol. 4555, pp. 828–837. Springer, Heidelberg (2007). https://doi.org/10.1007/978-3-540-73281-5_91
26. Freksa, C.: Using orientation information for qualitative spatial reasoning. In: Frank, A.U., Campari, I., Formentini, U. (eds.) GIS 1992. LNCS, vol. 639, pp. 162–178. Springer, Heidelberg (1992). https://doi.org/10.1007/3-540-55966-3_10
27. Fujimoto, S., Hoof, H., Meger, D.: Addressing function approximation error in actor-critic methods. In: International Conference on Machine Learning, pp. 1587–1596. PMLR (2018)
28. Gibson, J.J.: The theory of affordances. In: Perceiving, Acting, and Knowing: Toward an Ecological Psychology, pp. 67–82 (1977)
29. Gibson, J.J.: The Ecological Approach to Visual Perception. Psychology Press (1979)
30. Ginzburg, J.: Interrogatives: questions, facts and dialogue. The Handbook of Contemporary Semantic Theory, pp. 359–423. Blackwell, Oxford (1996)
31. Gkioxari, G., Girshick, R., Dollár, P., He, K.: Detecting and recognizing human-object interactions. In: Proceedings of the IEEE Conference on Computer Vision and Pattern Recognition, pp. 8359–8367 (2018)
32. Gopnik, A.: How babies think. Sci. Am. **303**(1), 76–81 (2010)
33. Gottlieb, J., Oudeyer, P.Y.: Towards a neuroscience of active sampling and curiosity. Nat. Rev. Neurosci. **19**(12), 758–770 (2018)
34. Hunter, J., Asher, N., Lascarides, A.: A formal semantics for situated conversation. Semant. Pragmat. **11** (2018)
35. Kayhan, O.S., Gemert, J.C.V.: On translation invariance in CNNs: convolutional layers can exploit absolute spatial location. In: Proceedings of the IEEE/CVF Conference on Computer Vision and Pattern Recognition, pp. 14274–14285 (2020)
36. Kennington, C., Kousidis, S., Schlangen, D.: Interpreting situated dialogue utterances: an update model that uses speech, gaze, and gesture information. In: Proceedings of SigDial 2013 (2013)
37. Kiela, D., Bulat, L., Vero, A.L., Clark, S.: Virtual embodiment: a scalable long-term strategy for artificial intelligence research. arXiv preprint arXiv:1610.07432 (2016)
38. Kingma, D.P., Ba, J.: Adam: a method for stochastic optimization. arXiv preprint arXiv:1412.6980 (2014)
39. Knudsen, E.I.: Supervised learning in the brain. J. Neurosci. **14**(7), 3985–3997 (1994)
40. Konrad, Karsten: 4 Minimal model generation. In: Model Generation for Natural Language Interpretation and Analysis. LNCS (LNAI), vol. 2953, pp. 55–56. Springer, Heidelberg (2004). https://doi.org/10.1007/978-3-540-24640-4_4
41. Kopp, S., Wachsmuth, I. (eds.): GW 2009. LNCS (LNAI), vol. 5934. Springer, Heidelberg (2010). https://doi.org/10.1007/978-3-642-12553-9
42. Krishnaswamy, N.: Monte-Carlo simulation generation through operationalization of spatial primitives. Ph.D. thesis, Brandeis University (2017)

43. Krishnaswamy, N., Pustejovsky, J.: Multimodal semantic simulations of linguistically underspecified motion events. In: Barkowsky, T., Burte, H., Hölscher, C., Schultheis, H. (eds.) Spatial Cognition/KogWis -2016. LNCS (LNAI), vol. 10523, pp. 177–197. Springer, Cham (2017). https://doi.org/10.1007/978-3-319-68189-4_11

44. Krishnaswamy, N., Pustejovsky, J.: VoxSim: a visual platform for modeling motion language. In: Proceedings of COLING 2016, the 26th International Conference on Computational Linguistics. ACL (2016)

45. Krishnaswamy, N., Pustejovsky, J.: The role of embodiment and simulation in evaluating HCI: experiments and evaluation. In: Duffy, V.G. (ed.) HCII 2021. LNCS, vol. 12777, pp. 220–232. Springer, Cham (2021). https://doi.org/10.1007/978-3-030-77817-0_17

46. Krizhevsky, A., Sutskever, I., Hinton, G.E.: Imagenet classification with deep convolutional neural networks. Adv. Neural Inf. Process. Syst. **25** (2012)

47. Kruijff, G.J.M., et al.: Situated dialogue processing for human-robot interaction. In: Cognitive Systems, pp. 311–364. Springer, Heidelberg (2010)

48. Lakoff, G.: The invariance hypothesis: is abstract reason based on image-schemas? (1990)

49. Landragin, F.: Visual perception, language and gesture: a model for their understanding in multimodal dialogue systems. Signal Process. **86**(12), 3578–3595 (2006)

50. Larsson, S., Ericsson, S.: Godis-issue-based dialogue management in a multi-domain, multi-language dialogue system. In: Demonstration Abstracts, ACL-02 (2002)

51. Lin, X., Parikh, D.: Leveraging visual question answering for image-caption ranking. In: Leibe, B., Matas, J., Sebe, N., Welling, M. (eds.) ECCV 2016. LNCS, vol. 9906, pp. 261–277. Springer, Cham (2016). https://doi.org/10.1007/978-3-319-46475-6_17

52. Markant, D.B., Gureckis, T.M.: Is it better to select or to receive? learning via active and passive hypothesis testing. J. Exp. Psychol. Gen. **143**(1), 94 (2014)

53. Marshall, P., Hornecker, E.: Theories of embodiment in HCI. SAGE Handb. Digit. Technol. Res. **1**, 144–158 (2013)

54. Misra, D., Langford, J., Artzi, Y.: Mapping instructions and visual observations to actions with reinforcement learning. arXiv preprint arXiv:1704.08795 (2017)

55. Moratz, R., Nebel, B., Freksa, C.: Qualitative spatial reasoning about relative position. In: Freksa, C., Brauer, W., Habel, C., Wender, K.F. (eds.) Spatial Cognition 2002. LNCS, vol. 2685, pp. 385–400. Springer, Heidelberg (2003). https://doi.org/10.1007/3-540-45004-1_22

56. Moratz, R., Tenbrink, T.: Spatial reference in linguistic human-robot interaction: iterative, empirically supported development of a model of projective relations. Spatial Cognit. Comput. **6**(1), 63–107 (2006)

57. Muller, P., Prévot, L.: Grounding information in route explanation dialogues (2009)

58. Najemnik, J., Geisler, W.S.: Eye movement statistics in humans are consistent with an optimal search strategy. J. Vis. **8**(3), 4–4 (2008)

59. Neftci, E.O., Averbeck, B.B.: Reinforcement learning in artificial and biological systems. Nat. Mach. Intell. **1**(3), 133–143 (2019)

60. Nelson, J.D., McKenzie, C.R., Cottrell, G.W., Sejnowski, T.J.: Experience matters: information acquisition optimizes probability gain. Psychol. Sci. **21**(7), 960–969 (2010)

61. Niv, Y.: Reinforcement learning in the brain. J. Math. Psychol. **53**(3), 139–154 (2009)

62. Piaget, J.: The attainment of invariants and reversible operations in the development of thinking. Soc. Res. 283–299 (1963)
63. Piaget, J., Inhelder, B.: The Psychology of the Child. Basic Books (1962)
64. Pustejovsky, J.: The Generative Lexicon. MIT Press (1995)
65. Pustejovsky, J.: Dynamic event structure and habitat theory. In: Proceedings of the 6th International Conference on Generative Approaches to the Lexicon (GL2013), pp. 1–10. ACL (2013)
66. Pustejovsky, J.: Affordances and the functional characterization of space. In: Cognitive Processing, vol. 16, p. S43. Springer, Heidelberg (2015)
67. Pustejovsky, J.: Computational models of events. In: ESSLLI Summer School, August 2018, Sofia, Bulgaria (2018)
68. Pustejovsky, J., Boguraev, B.: Lexical knowledge representation and natural language processing. Artif. Intell. **63**(1–2), 193–223 (1993)
69. Pustejovsky, J., Krishnaswamy, N.: Voxml: a visualization modeling language. In: Proceedings of LREC (2016)
70. Pustejovsky, J., Krishnaswamy, N.: Embodied human computer interaction. KI-Künstliche Intell. **35**(3), 307–327 (2021)
71. Pustejovsky, J., Krishnaswamy, N.: The role of embodiment and simulation in evaluating HCI: theory and framework. In: Duffy, V.G. (ed.) HCII 2021. LNCS, vol. 12777, pp. 288–303. Springer, Cham (2021). https://doi.org/10.1007/978-3-030-77817-0_21
72. Pustejovsky, J., Moszkowicz, J.L.: The qualitative spatial dynamics of motion in language. Spatial Cognit. Comput. **11**(1), 15–44 (2011)
73. Qi, S., Wang, W., Jia, B., Shen, J., Zhu, S.C.: Learning human-object interactions by graph parsing neural networks. In: Proceedings of the European Conference on Computer Vision (ECCV), pp. 401–417 (2018)
74. Randell, D., Cui, Z., Cohn, A., Nebel, B., Rich, C., Swartout, W.: A spatial logic based on regions and connection. In: Proceedings of the 3rd International Conference on Principles of Knowledge Representation and Reasoning (KR 1992), pp. 165–176. Morgan Kaufmann, San Mateo (1992)
75. Renninger, L.W., Verghese, P., Coughlan, J.: Where to look next? eye movements reduce local uncertainty. J. Vis. **7**(3) (2007). https://doi.org/10.1167/7.3.6
76. Schaffer, S., Reithinger, N.: Conversation is multimodal: thus conversational user interfaces should be as well. In: Proceedings of the 1st International Conference on Conversational User Interfaces, pp. 1–3 (2019)
77. Scheutz, M., Cantrell, R., Schermerhorn, P.: Toward humanlike task-based dialogue processing for human robot interaction. Ai Magazine **32**(4), 77–84 (2011)
78. Schick, T., Schütze, H.: It's not just size that matters: small language models are also few-shot learners. arXiv preprint arXiv:2009.07118 (2020)
79. Schlenker, P.: Gesture projection and cosuppositions. Linguist. Philos. **41**(3), 295–365 (2018)
80. Schulz, L.E., Bonawitz, E.B.: Serious fun: preschoolers engage in more exploratory play when evidence is confounded. Develop. Psychol. **43**(4), 1045 (2007)
81. Shapiro, L.: Embodied Cognition. Routledge, London (2010)
82. Shapiro, L.A.: The Routledge Handbook of Embodied Cognition (2014)
83. Son, L.K., Sethi, R.: Metacognitive control and optimal learning. Cognit. Sci. **30**(4), 759–774 (2006)
84. Stalnaker, R.: Common ground. Linguist. Philos. **25**(5–6), 701–721 (2002)
85. Stojnić, U., Stone, M., Lepore, E.: Pointing things out: in defense of attention and coherence. Linguist. Philos. 1–10 (2019)

86. Tomasello, M., Carpenter, M.: Shared intentionality. Develop. Sci. **10**(1), 121–125 (2007)
87. Vlach, H., Sandhofer, C.M.: Fast mapping across time: memory processes support children's retention of learned words. Front. Psychol. **3**, 46 (2012)
88. Wahlster, W.: Dialogue systems go multimodal: the Smartkom experience. In: SmartKom: Foundations of Multimodal Dialogue Systems, pp. 3–27. Springer, Heidelberg (2006). https://doi.org/10.1007/3-540-36678-4_1
89. Wallis, G., Bülthoff, H.: Learning to recognize objects. Trends Cognit. Sci. **3**(1), 22–31 (1999)
90. Wilson, A.D., Golonka, S.: Embodied cognition is not what you think it is. Front. Psychol. **4**, 58 (2013)
91. Xu, B., Wong, Y., Li, J., Zhao, Q., Kankanhalli, M.S.: Learning to detect human-object interactions with knowledge. In: Proceedings of the IEEE/CVF Conference on Computer Vision and Pattern Recognition (2019)
92. Yatskar, M., Zettlemoyer, L., Farhadi, A.: Situation recognition: visual semantic role labeling for image understanding. In: Proceedings of the IEEE Conference on Computer Vision and Pattern Recognition, pp. 5534–5542 (2016)
93. Zador, A.M.: A critique of pure learning and what artificial neural networks can learn from animal brains. Nat. Commun. **10**(1), 1–7 (2019)

Interaction Designers of the Future: Shedding Light on Students Entering the Industry

Hanne Sørum[⊠]

Kristiania University College, Prinsens gate 7-9, 0107 Oslo, Norway
hanne.sorum@kristiania.no

Abstract. Increasingly more services are being digitized, and the design of user interfaces is important for creating impressive user experiences. Businesses use websites and apps as components of their business model, precisely to interact and communicate with their users and customers. Furthermore, to distribute services, and to provide extended information and digital services. Thus, digital user interfaces need to carry a high level of quality, and interaction designers are key players and vital contributors in this matter. It is therefore important for the industry to employ people with good skills and competence who at the same time have the necessary personal qualities and motivation to perform an outstanding job as interaction designers. This paper draws on qualitative and quantitative data from an online survey conducted among interaction design students enrolled in higher educational programs in Norway. The purpose of the study is to gain an updated understanding of the students' thoughts and expectations relating to a career in interaction design. The findings show that the students are captivated by the fact that interaction design is creative and design-oriented work that allows them to collaborate in teams, and that it provides a combination of technology and design for humans and is an industry with abundant job opportunities.

Keywords: Interaction design · Human–computer interaction · User experience · Higher education · Online survey · Student perspective

1 Introduction

Over the past decade, we have witnessed an ever-increasing degree of digitalization in our society. This has been fueled by huge changes in the use and availability of technology since the year 2000. Such changes have influenced how people communicate, behave, collaborate, and interact with each other, both at times of leisure and in business. Today, mobile phones have become an indispensable life companion for most of us and are used in many of our daily activities, including for communication with family, friends, and business partners. In combination with the rapid development of technology, the rise of mobile phones has brought massive demand for mobile applications (apps) and software to satisfy countless user needs and for professional working lives. From large screens to today's always-available small mobile interfaces, we use mobile devices at any time for almost every purpose possible [1]. Mobile devices are available to most of us

© The Author(s), under exclusive license to Springer Nature Switzerland AG 2022
M. Kurosu (Ed.): HCII 2022, LNCS 13302, pp. 161–172, 2022.
https://doi.org/10.1007/978-3-031-05311-5_10

and are commonplace throughout the world. There are now apps for almost everything, from cooking apps and apps used to start the bike to ones that even provide help for knitting a sweater. Behind all these digital solutions, there is a great deal of work related to development, both technical and in terms of design (user interface). Users are now becoming increasingly picky; they expect effective solutions and inviting designs. Digital interfaces should be easy to use and efficient, and users should not have to search too hard for information and services. Statistics show that Norway is a European leader in digital skills; indeed, 83% of all companies there had their own website in 2021 [2]. This testifies to the skills and knowledge that people in Norway tend to have. With such experience, users expect solutions to be in accordance with their requirements and needs. There are many other countries that are in the same position as Norway, each with a high level of technical knowledge and a wealth of experience in using technology for different tasks. The rising use of digital user interfaces offers many exciting opportunities. To meet the requirements of digital user interfaces for different user groups and individual requirements, the need for quality is paramount. Delivering such quality requires, among other things, interaction designers who possess knowledge, have the right attitude, and enjoy a strong interest in the field. Interaction designers are key players and vital contributors in the design process. Previous studies on interaction design and human–computer interaction (HCI) have found that designers are not necessarily a homogeneous group, and not all possess the same skills and knowledge [3]. Interaction design is about developing interactive products that are usable, easy to learn, effective to use, and also enjoyable, which together create a satisfying user experience [4]. Improving user experiences and enhancing usability are therefore vital, as are the people who develop, design, and bring solutions to life. Many approaches can be taken in interaction design. The purpose of the present paper is to gain an understanding of students' thoughts about and expectations for embarking on a career in the field. The respondents included in this study were students undertaking higher education in interaction design. An online survey (n = 89) was conducted among 1st, 2nd, and 3rd year students enrolled at two different educational institutions in Norway. The survey was designed by using the SurveyMonkey® survey tool and consisted of both qualitative and quantitative questions.

2 Background

Because of the current trend for digitalization, there is doubtless an urgent need for designers with both back-end and front-end knowledge. As users now have ever higher expectations for digital user infaces and technical solutions, and companies are constantly working to create better designs and become more user-friendly, the development of the interaction design field will have importance for the future. Gurcan et al. [5] shed light on research conducted on HCI from 1957 to 2018 and emphasized research themes and trends. The authors revealed a transition from machine-oriented systems to human-oriented ones and indicated a future direction toward context-aware adaptive systems. According to the authors, "three main developmental ages of the evolution of the HCI field can be defined as Legacy Systems Age (1959–1989), Internet Age (1989–2009), and Pervasive Age (2009–2019)" [5, p. 277]. This indicates that HCI has undergone changes over the study period. As a result, the field of interaction design has developed and is constantly gaining ground in new areas. It has also become a key field for user experience, usability concerns, and the experience of successfully performing tasks on digital screens. Interaction design concerns how users interact with products, which in most cases are apps or websites. Its aim is to develop products that enable the user to achieve their goal in the best possible way through the interaction that takes place [6]. Kolko [7] explained interaction design as "the creation of a dialogue between a person and a product, system, or service. This dialogue is both physical and emotional in nature and is manifested in the interplay between form, function, and technology as experienced over time." Interaction design is in many ways an umbrella term that covers a variety of disciplines, including HCI, although its focus is broader than HCI alone, which focuses on the interface between users and computers and interactions that take place there [4]. According to Fallman [8], "Interaction design takes a holistic view of the relationship between designed artifacts, those that are exposed to these artifacts, and the social, cultural, and business context in which the meeting takes place" (p. 4). Interaction design thus throws its net wider by incorporating different disciplines, of which HCI is one. A study by Sørum and Pettersen [9] investigated the skills and qualifications needed by interaction designers versus companies' expectations of them within the industry. The findings showed that interaction designers require a variety of skills, ranging from very technical to soft design and interpersonal skills. Moreover, companies have unrealistic expectations of the qualifications and knowledge that interaction designs should possess, and what they expect is not always covered in educational programs within the field and its related areas.

Due to the increasing degree of digitization and use of technology, chatbots are one example that has replaced humans. They communicate with users without any human physically doing that job. According to Chaves and Gerosa [10], such chatbots have resulted in new challenges for HCI. The growing need to approach conversational interaction styles increases the expectations of chatbots. They must act as human beings to the greatest possible extent and should therefore be designed so that users are taken care of in the best possible way. As we see new technologies appearing, interaction design is constantly gaining ground in new areas. Zhang and Wakkary [11] explored how interaction designers, when engaged in industrial design projects, made use of their own experiences. The findings show that designers used different personal experiences for various aspects of interaction design, and that such experiences could be incorporated in the design process. A study by Begnum, Pettersen and Sørum [3] identified five archetypes of interaction design professionals: 1) front-enders, 2) full-stackers, 3) design tinkers, 4) communicators, and 5) user empaths. These archetypes reflect the interdisciplinary nature of the field, with each one possessing different characteristics and skills that are needed for interaction design, varying from softer (user-oriented) to more technical (programming) skills. This highlights how an interaction design process requires several different skills and competences at different stages of it. The fact that large parts of society are being digitized is reflected by the diversity of interaction design educations in higher educational institutions. Because of the diversified origins of the discipline, various courses of study are offered [12]. It is important to provide strong education and teaching in interaction design and its associated disciplines to meet the need for this knowledge in the years to come. Interaction designers today not only develop apps and websites but also other digital interfaces that users interact with. This means that substantial demands are placed on both the solutions and those who develop them. Wilcox et al. [13] looked at design and HCI teaching, finding that there is a need to research the subject further to meet the demands of the future. Among other things, this would be so that lecturers can see the value and use of different design approaches and how they can be used. Moreover, new pedagogical approaches should be developed so that design education can avoid the institutional limitations of many HCI programs and benefit from knowledge being integrated into teaching design and HCI. Ideally, interaction design is performed by interdisciplinary teams, whereby each has unique expertise for contributing to the team. Who is included in the team will depend on factors such as the size of the project, scope, and available time and resources [4]. Working in multidisciplinary teams is a part of everyday life for many when entering a job as an interaction designer. Therefore, it is important that they are well prepared for their positions and trained in multidisciplinary collaboration during their education [14]. Teams are required to work together to form successful multidisciplinary teams, since teamwork is an essential part of the interaction design process [15]. This suggests that not only is education important when working with interaction design, but so are different forms of collaboration and teamwork. Consequently, personality and preferences are important qualities for designers, beyond a professionally solid competence.

3   Method

3.1 Survey Design

The survey was designed by using the SurveyMonkey® cloud-based survey tool and consisted of 14 questions covering areas such as background information, motivation for studying interaction design, respondents' characteristics, and their preferred job opportunities after graduation. In addition to matrix and rating scale questions, the questionnaire consisted of open-ended questions. This combination provided rich data materials with opportunities for both qualitative and quantitative data analysis. Before the survey was distributed, pilot testing was performed with four respondents. Based on the feedback, minor changes were made. Among these changes, some questions were clarified. The survey was conducted in Norwegian and translated into English for the purpose of this paper. It is worth mentioning that the present study design was inspired by a study conducted in 2016 [16]. The focus was in the same thematic area, the target group (interaction design students) were the same, as well as the author behind the publication. As interaction design is a moving field, it was interesting to continue working with this target group, years after the first study was conducted. Both in terms of what today's students think and experience, but also provide an updated study related to a field that is in an exciting evolving.

3.2 Data Collection

The data collection was carried out between September and October 2021. A link to the questionnaire was generated by SurveyMonkey® and distributed to the respondents. Participation in the survey was voluntary, the answers were anonymous, and the survey was conducted in a classroom setting. Before the respondents started answering the questionnaire, a brief introduction was given on the purpose of the study. The respondents could end the survey at any time if they so wished. The average time to complete the survey was 6.27 min (reported by the survey tool). A total of 89 respondents started answering the survey, and the completion rate (the percentage of respondents who completed the entire survey) was 93%.

3.3 The Respondents

The survey's respondents come from two different higher educational institutions in Norway that had extensive experience in interaction design education and its associated areas for many years. Of the respondents, 24% were 1st year students, 46% were 2nd year students, and 30% were in the 3rd and final year of their bachelor's education. Moreover, 42% of the respondents were male, 55% were female, and 3% did not want to state their gender. In terms of age, most respondents were in the 19–26 year age group and at the start of their career, and 60% had no previous higher education. Of the remaining 40%, 7% of the respondents had a bachelor-level degree whereby all or part of it was focused on design. Furthermore, 15% of the respondents had a bachelor-level degree with no relation to design, and 18% had a different level of higher education. None had a master's degree. Regarding their plans for further studies after graduation from their course, 24% of the respondents intended to continue education that would be relevant to their current course and 46% do not know. The rest of the respondents (30%) had no plans for further studies. Many students had part-time jobs alongside their studies. Of the respondents who participated in this study, 11% had a part-time job relevant to their study area, 17% had a job that was partially relevant, and 72% did not have a relevant part-time job (or no job at all). These numbers show that the majority did not have a part-time job that was relevant to their course in interaction design.

3.4 Data Analysis

Qualitative and quantitative analyses were carried out to explore trends and patterns in the data set. Hence, this work has a mixed method approach [17]. Before analyzing the data, the material was first reviewed using SurveyMonkey's analysis tool to form an overall impression of the data. This was useful for seeing initial trends and patterns in the material and how the answers were distributed on the measurement scale. After this pre-phase, the qualitative comments were exported to Microsoft Word® for review and qualitative analysis. The themes emerging from the data was identified and interpreted to form an understanding of the respondents' views on the various questions asked in the survey. The qualitative findings were identified through an analysis of the open text fields (open-ended answers), precisely quotations provided by the respondents. The quantitative data were analyzed using Microsoft Excel® and reported in the paper through descriptive statistics/diagrams.

3.5 Limitations

There are some limitations to this study that are worth mentioning. The respondents come from two different educational institutions in Norway and the answers may vary if data were collected across countries. Nevertheless, this study provides the students view on preferences, expectations, and views on a career as an interaction designer. None sophisticated analyzes or cross-analyzes based on background variables or other questions in the survey are performed, only descriptive analysis. Further research could also increase the number of respondents, to get a larger dataset and perform more advanced statistics. In addition, go deeper into the qualitative analysis to identify themes and sub-themes, beyond what is presented here. This may be left to a later contribution.

4   Findings

4.1   Quantitative Findings

In the quantitative part of the survey, the respondents were asked to respond on a scale ranging from completely disagree to completely agree. Figure 1 shows the findings for the students' views on a career in interaction design.

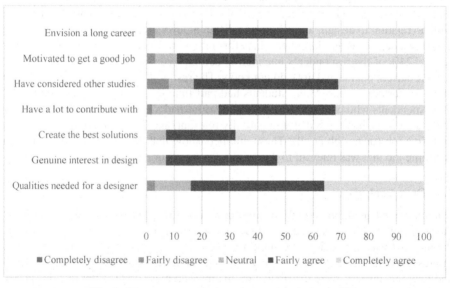

Fig. 1. Views on a career as an interaction designer (%).

The motivation to get a good job in interaction design was strong among the respondents (almost 90%), and over 70% envisaged a long career in the field (while about 20% were neutral or somewhat disagreed). About 15% were unsure whether they would continue in the field in the future. This signifies that most respondents felt that the subject was relevant in terms of their own preferences for work after completing their education. Approximately 70% of the respondents felt they would contribute much within the field, while the rest were neutral (except for a few percent). At the same time, the findings show that over 80% of the respondents had considered other studies that were also of interest. Almost 80% of them somewhat or completely agreed that they had always been iiiteiesled in design, indicating that they were completing a education in an area they found interesting. This was also reflected by the fact that the vast majority had a genuine interest in design and wanted to create the best solutions for the future. At the same time, about 80% of the respondents felt they possessed the qualities needed to become a good designer. Figure 2 shows the respondents' preferences pertaining to work in the field of interaction design.

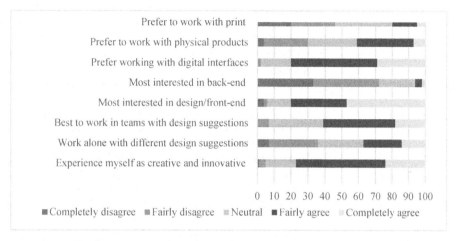

Fig. 2. Preferences regarding work as an interaction designer (%).

The findings in Fig. 2 show that about 15% of the respondents preferred to work with design related to print, while approximately 80% preferred digital interfaces. About 40% answered that they most liked interaction design related to physical products. In relation to the students' interest in front-end work (design and visual expression) and back-end work (programming and coding), the findings show that the interaction design students were clearly most interested in the design aspect. About 80% of the respondents preferred front-end work, while only 6% preferred back-end work. During work as an interaction designer, collaboration (teamwork) is in many cases a key element representing how people work both during education and when entering the design industry after graduation. The findings from this study show that the respondents strongly preferred to work in teams (62%), rather than working alone (37%). Creativity and innovation are advantageous qualities in interaction design work and result in many good solutions and design proposals. About 75% of the respondents said they had these characteristics and that they were creative and innovative.

4.2 Qualitative Findings

Additionally, the survey comprised questions that required the respondents to provide answers using their own words. Such qualitative data contribute to richer findings grounded in the respondents' own words and explanations. Table 1 reports on the themes emerging from the qualitative data analysis.

Table 1. Summary of the qualitative comments provided by the respondents.

Survey topics	Themes	Example quotes
Motivation for studying interaction design	– Combining work with technology and people – Using creativity – Creating great user experiences – Many and varied job opportunities – Future-oriented education	"Great job opportunities, can develop creatively, IT-oriented but not IT" "Work with technology; design and communication in perfect harmony" "A combination of psychology and design"
Interaction design as an exciting field	– Several disciplines are linked together – The discipline is in continuous development – Opportunity to create great user experiences – Opportunity to be creative – Lots of variation in working tasks – A field within a fast growing industry	"A good mix of creativity, understanding problems, problem solving, and development of solutions" "There are no limits to what you can work with" "I feel interaction design is a broad range of designs, whereby you often have to wear several hats"
Job preferences after graduation	– Either a job in an established company or in a consulting company – Teamwork and project-based work – Focusing on front-end work (visual design) – A job with a variety of work tasks – Work with interaction design or UX design	"I hope to be able to work with a large team where we work with revolutionary technology. Being a project manager would be cool" "My dream job is to work with UX in a company with meaningful assignments and then work with a mix of UX and web development"

The overall findings show that the motivation for studying interaction design was anchored in aspects such as the opportunity to combine working with technology and people, creativity, striving for user-friendliness, and the job opportunities it may lead to. Moreover, the respondents showed interaction design to be an exciting field because it links several disciplines together, is a discipline in continuous development, involves interaction between humans and machines, and provides an opportunity to develop satisfying user experiences. To link these together, one of the respondents wrote that "a good mix of creativity, understanding problems, problem solving, and development of solutions." (see Table 1). In relation to preferred types of jobs after graduation, the following were mentioned, among other things: working in teams, focusing on front-end work, a job with different work tasks, working creatively, and working with UX design, and project management. Why interaction design is a working field that suits these students, reasons in their areas of interest. Mentioned frequently (among all three survey topics) were creativity, problem solving, concern for users, interest in technology, and simply love design. If we compare the qualitative findings with the quantitative data, the respondents stated that they had always been interested in design and had a genuine interest. They said they had much to contribute within the field and saw themselves as creative and curious about what the field could offer, along with job opportunities for them after graduating. In general, the respondents were more interested in design and front-end work compared to back-end work, tasks such as programming, and dedication to technical skills.

5   Discussion

Technology has developed significantly over the last decade, and people interact with digital solutions as a vital part of their everyday life. The fact that the Norwegian population has high digital skills and over 80% of all companies in Norway provide their own website [2], shows the importance of providing high quality online information and services. This is also the case in other countries, citizens around the world uses the Web daily for private and business purposes. Thus, the use of digital services is not reserved a specific user group, but all citizens. We also see that the public sector increasingly digitizing various types of services and need to facilitate for high quality use and good user experiences, among a slightly homogeneous target group. Over the last decade, we have witnessed a substantial digital shift through changes in the technology environments, methods, and digital tools available. Interaction design is a discipline that deals with the interaction between a user (human) and a physical product or digital service (e.g., a screen-based user interface) [4]. Moreover, interaction design aims to develop products and solutions that the users easily can use in a satisfactory manner [6]. Key elements in this are great user experiences, usability, and efficiency. Previous studies [9] have examined what kind of knowledge and competence an interaction designer should possess to meet the requirements and needs of the industry. The findings show that the competencies required are wide and varied, some are also related to working tasks that go far beyond design. This highlights how an interaction designer should be flexible, adaptable, and willing to familiarize themselves with new knowledge when entering the design industry. It is important that students in this discipline are aware of this both during and after graduation. At the same time, educational institutions should also keep an eye on the industry. Both in terms of the use of techniques, methods, tools and various forms of collaboration among the design team. Moreover, knowledge of and interest in technology provide a clear advantage when working in interaction design. In line with this, the findings show that most of the respondents preferred to work in teams for design suggestions and enjoyed working with the visual design and expression of a digital solution. This is also supported by the literature, which states precisely that interaction design is largely about teamwork and collaboration, sometimes across disciplines [e.g. 4, 15]. Consequently, interaction design is about working in teams, whereby their size and working methodology often depends on the type of project and the resources available.

Teamwork and project-based work were mentioned by the respondents through the qualitative input they provided as motivating factors for becoming an interaction designer. Training in multidisciplinary collaboration during education is therefore a vital element [14] and a learning outcome which should be considered to include in higher educational programs within the discipline. Many of the respondents also experience that they have a good potential to contribute to the field of interaction design and that they want to develop good solutions for the future. A good starting point is that they are genuinely interested in design and experience themselves possessing the qualities needed. As previous studies have shown, interactive solutions designers can be divided into archetypes with different competencies and skills [3]. Some are more technical than others (in terms of programming skills), while others are most concerned with visual design and quality for users, such as what users see and what they need to relate to in terms of usage. Where elements are placed in the available screen space, what information is presented, and how the content of a solution is organized.

Furthermore, we see that technology use is constantly gaining ground in new areas and affects the need for knowledge among interaction designers. It seems like this piqued the curiosity of the respondents, as they appeared hungry to be creative and develop user-friendly products and/or services—solutions that people can use in a positive manner, resulting in creating impressive user experiences. Several of the respondents also mentioned that they wanted to design and develop digital interfaces that would help users solve problems or other challenges. In other words, they were driven by aspects beyond design, in particular being able to help and apply their design knowledge to something useful for other people, as they wished to take care of users and take their needs, requirements, and expectations into consideration. This is in line with what the field is about [4] and what challenges and opportunities await today's students. An impressive mix of technology and design apparently fascinated many of the respondents. Beyond this, this gave them an outlet for their particular creative urges. Grounded in the findings of this study, most students seemed ready to start work as in interaction design after graduating. There was some variation in terms of the type of work, company, and tasks they envisaged, but they saw opportunities within the design industry within newly established small companies, large consulting companies, and organizations that only need design expertise. Interaction design involves taking care of users' considerations and needs related to their interaction with a product, system or service [7], and the students were fascinated precisely by this appealing mix of being able to work with technology and design in harmony with enabling users' needs. As many of them had a clear desire to work in a future-oriented industry, in a field that is constantly evolving and where technology plays a central role in design and development, they have a solid starting point for success when entering working life. Many of the findings in the present study are also in line with a study conducted in 2016 [16], within the same thematic area. This testifies that students in this subject have a view of the industry and views on a career as an interaction designer, that have not changed significantly in a few years. The results give the industry a degree of predictability with a view to future employees.

6 Conclusion

The present study has gained an understanding of the students' thoughts and expectations related to a career in the field of interaction design. Through education in this field there are many opportunities, both in terms of interdisciplinary collaboration, teamwork, and working tasks. The respondents in this study seemed curious about the arena they had entered, and they had many characteristics that made them well placed to succeed, in terms of their personal qualities and ambitions, challenges they wanted to meet, and opportunities for using their creative abilities. Their motivation to work in the field of interaction design, why they believed it to be such an exciting area, and their job preferences after graduation seemed to match well with what the field entails in practice. The opportunity to use their design skills, to work with technologies aimed at human use and good user experiences, to be part of a future-oriented industry and project-based work are aspects that many of them are attracted to.

To further increase knowledge about this field, future research can dive into various topics that can contribute to filling a gap in the literature and establishing more knowledge for practice. Suggestions may include further study on the specific needs of the industry (with a view to the use of methods, techniques, tools, and technology) and what students specifically learn during their education. Furthermore, it may also be interesting to study the extent to which interaction designers find they have the knowledge needed after graduation, and what may be missing or superfluous. Moreover, dive into the different roles of an interaction designer, with reference to the need for cutting-edge expertise.

References

1. Krug, S.: Don't Make Me Think, Revisited – A Common Sense Approach to Web Usability. New Riders (2014)
2. Statistics Norway: https://www.ssb.no/teknologi-og-innovasjon/faktaside/internett-og-mobil. Last accessed 2 Feb 2022
3. Begnum, M.E.N., Pettersen, L., Sørum, H.: Identifying five archetypes of interaction design professionals and their universal design expertise. Interact. Comput. **31**(4), 372–392 (2019)
4. Sharp, H., Preece, J., Rogers, Y.: Interaction Design: Beyond Human-Computer Interaction, 5th edn. John Wiley & Sons Inc (2019)
5. Gurcan, F., Cagiltay, N.E., Cagiltay, K.: Mapping human-computer interaction research themes and trends from its existence to today: a topic modeling-based review of past 60 years. Int. J. Human-Comput. Interact. **37**(3), 267–280 (2021)
6. Siang, T.-U.: https://www.interaction-design.org/literature/article/what-is-interaction-design. Last accessed 1 Nov. 2022
7. Kolko, J.: Thoughts on Interaction Design, 2nd edn. Morgan Kaufmann (2011)
8. Fallman, D.: The interaction design research triangle of design practice, design studies, and design exploration. Des. Issues **24**(3), 4–18 (2008)
9. Sørum, H., Pettersen, L.: In need of an interaction designer? What the industry wants and what it actually gets! Paper presented at NOKOBIT 2016, Bergen, 28–30 Nov. NOKOBIT, vol. 24, no. 1, Bibsys Open Journal Systems, ISSN 1894–7719 (2016)
10. Chaves, A.P., Gerosa, M.A.: How should my chatbot Interact? A survey on social characteristics in human-chatbot interaction design. Int. J. Human-Comput. Interact. **37**(8), 729–758 (2021)

11. Zhang, X., Wakkary, R.: Understanding the Role of Designers' Personal Experiences in Interaction Design Practice. DIS 2014, 21–25 June 2014, Vancouver, BC, Canada. https://doi.org/10.1145/2598510.2598556
12. Neves, M.: Teaching interaction design: a theoretical framework. In book: Research & Education in Design: People & Processes & Products & Philosophy, pp. 13–21 (2020). https://doi.org/10.1201/9781003046103-2
13. Wilcox, L., DiSalvo, B., Henneman, D., Wang, Q.: Design in the HCI classroom: setting a research agenda. In: Proceedings of the Designing Interactive Systems (DIS) Conference, pp. 871–883 (2019)
14. Culén, A.L., Mainsah, H.N., Finken, S.: Design practice in human computer interaction design education. In: Proceedings of the Seventh International Conference on Advances in Computer-Human Interaction, pp. 300–306 (2014)
15. Hafez, Y-A., Hasanin, M.A.S.: The interaction design process in view of teamwork principles. Int. Design J. **10**(2), 69–76 (2020)
16. Sørum, H.: Design of digital products in the future: a study of interaction design students and their perceptions on design issues. In: Lecture Notes in Computer Science, Conference: International Conference of Design, User Experience, and Usability (HCI International), pp. 740–754 (2017)
17. Creswell, J.W.: A Concise Introduction to Mixed Methods Research. SAGE Publications, Inc (2021)

Conversations Across Disciplines: Interdisciplinary Experiences from Research in Sociology, Human-Computer Interaction, and Pharmacy

Rebecca Wiesner, Jenny Valery Stein$^{(\boxtimes)}$, Katharina Losch, and Anja K. Faulhaber🆔

Technische Universität Braunschweig, Universitätsplatz 2, 38106 Braunschweig, Germany
{r.wiesner,jenny.stein}@tu-braunschweig.de

Abstract. In this paper, we discuss interdisciplinarity and the role of quantitative and qualitative methods. We report our own experiences as we worked on interdisciplinary PhD projects. During this time, we experienced challenges due to conversations across disciplines which revealed biases and misunderstandings between researchers with different disciplinary backgrounds. However, we also experienced that such friction could open up new potentials. We discuss these challenges and potentials, limitations and advantages of interdisciplinarity and particularly qualitative, quantitative and mixed methods approaches. The overall objective is to show that combining strengths of various disciplines and their methods can advance science, lead to new insights, and open up innovative solutions. We, thereby, want to further methodological exchange across disciplines, and blur the lines between quantitative and qualitative approaches.

Keywords: Interdisciplinarity · Qualitative methods · Mixed methods

1 Introduction

The discussions about qualitative and quantitative research methods have shaped the current academic world. While qualitative methods are common in humanities with disciplines such as sociology, quantitative methods dominate the natural sciences and engineering fields. However, interdisciplinarity is gaining more and more importance in research nowadays. This often leads to a culture clash when researchers from diverse disciplines come to work together with different perspectives on science and scientific methods. Especially qualitative methods often have to be justified against quantitative methods that over many years have been attributed higher prestige. Even though qualitative methods and mixed methods are common in the research field human-computer interaction (HCI), which is inherently interdisciplinary and has been referred to as an "inter-discipline" [1], the bias towards quantitative methods can also be observed in the context of HCI.

Contributed equally to the work.

M. Kurosu (Ed.): HCII 2022, LNCS 13302, pp. 173–182, 2022.
https://doi.org/10.1007/978-3-031-05311-5_11

With qualitative research in HCI, the emphasis is not on measuring large numbers but on understanding the qualities of a particular technology and people's needs and feelings about it [2]. One exemplary method to collect this type of information is via interviews. Direct conversations with fewer participants can provide perspectives and useful data that, for example, quantitative surveys may miss. However, in several other disciplines dominated by quantitative methods, such as pharmacy, these qualitative approaches have not yet been used and do not even appear in the curriculum despite their potential benefits.

In this paper, we report our experiences from (inter-)disciplinary research projects including challenging aspects as well as potentials and advantages. We are researchers with backgrounds in pharmacy, sociology, cognitive science, computer science, and psychology. We have worked in diverse interdisciplinary projects as part of the doctoral program Gendered Configurations of Humans and Machines. Interdisciplinary Analyses of Technology (KoMMa.G). This is where researchers from humanities, social and media sciences came together with researchers from natural and engineering sciences to discuss human-machine interactions in the context of gender studies in a trans- and interdisciplinary way. To provide further background information regarding the context of our experiences, we will shortly introduce our projects in the following.

One of the authors investigated on female international researchers from India and China in computer science in Germany and their role of questioning the masculine disciplinary image. For that purpose, she conducted a qualitative study with semi-structured interviews as the central method of gathering data [3]. Two of the authors worked in the HCI research field conducting empirical studies including quantitative methods such as eye tracking combined with qualitative methods such as interviews. One of the projects focused on human factors in a potential transition from two-crew to single-pilot operations in commercial aviation by means of a flight simulator study [4]. The other project was focused on HCI while using a graphical user interface. This project aimed to analyze usage contexts, user expectations, and behavior in the field of information technology with regard to gender aspects. The fourth author investigated the possibilities of laboratory automation using guided expert interviews and participant observations in pharmaceutical laboratories. Qualitative methods were explored to investigate human-machine interaction regarding the prevailing opinions of automation and digitization to investigate research gaps, capture complex situations, and characterize and understand human behavior in particular situations [5]. The interview results illustrated the complex interactions between automation solutions, vendors of laboratory automation as well as potential biochemical and pharmaceutical users.

In our projects, we frequently experienced conversations across disciplines and differences between the commonly so-called *hard and soft sciences* which we want to bring into dialogue here. We want to show that combining strengths of various disciplines and their methods can advance science, lead to new insights, and open up innovative solutions. We, thereby, aim to further methodological exchange across disciplines and blur the lines between quantitative and qualitative approaches.

2   Interdisciplinarity

As *interdisciplinarity* plays an important role here, we first want to take a look at the definition and historical background of the concept. Interdisciplinarity, which is process- or product-oriented [6], combines at least two sub-disciplines by using methodologies of various disciplines in the research context [7]. In contrast, *disciplines* are described in the literature as "thought domains – quasi-stable, partially integrated, semi-autonomous intellectual conveniences – consisting of problems, theories, and methods of investigation" [8, p. 380].

A better understanding of today's meaning of interdisciplinarity in science is gained by looking at its historical development, with a particular focus on Germany here. In general, there is no clear temporal and spatial starting point since critical discussions about the formation of specific disciplines go further back in history [9]. Indeed, disciplines in science "are an 'invention' of the late eighteenth and early nineteenth centuries" [10, p. 4]. Their purpose was to classify and structure knowledge in the context of teaching in schools and universities [10].

However, the term *interdisciplinary* has its roots in the US-American academy, more precisely in the American social sciences in the 1920s and 1930s [11]. Whereas at the beginning, this new term still had to struggle for recognition, in the course of history it more and more became a symbol for openness, flexibility, and democracy [9]. Generally, the term interdisciplinarity was more popular in the humanities and social sciences than in the natural sciences and engineering fields [12]. In Germany, the notion of interdisciplinarity emerged in the 1960s [13, 14]. Especially in the context of the founding and reforms of universities, a science that transcends disciplines or collaboration beyond disciplines and predefined disciplinary practices became a relevant topic [9]. An important impulse in the German history of interdisciplinarity came from sociologist and university founder Helmut Schelsky [14]. In the debates on the formation of future universities, a fear of a fragmentation of science caused by further growth was prevalent. A specialization in science cannot per se be judged as something negative; it is partly necessary considering the development in the academic system. What, however, may be considered as alarming, are the further developments that a specialization in science has caused, namely the threat to the idealized *unity of science*. The different disciplines act more and more independently and separately from each other [9].

Despite the potentials of interdisciplinary work at universities, there are also difficulties concerning the practical application. In the first place, the meaning of interdisciplinarity itself often is not clear and might lead to confusion. At the same time, the role of interdisciplinarity in science is increasingly important for success and recognition in science [14]. A connecting crucial challenge is a mutual understanding between different disciplines that apply various methodologies and theories. This may impede putting interdisciplinarity into practice and leads to frustration. It has been argued that interdisciplinarity rather serves for advertising science than for real collaboration among sciences [9].

This paper, however, aims to show that mutual understanding is possible if we are open and willing enough to learn about other methods and engage in dialogue with other disciplines to learn from each other. This will involve challenges and prior discipline-specific principles may need to be abandoned. It will not be an easy road to interdisciplinarity but new ways of understanding and finally conducting research can be revealed leading to innovations for the scientific system itself.

3 Quantitative-Qualitative Debate

As mentioned previously, interdisciplinarity includes methodologies of different disciplines. Taking a closer look at methodologies shows that quantitative approaches have dominated disciplines such as engineering and natural sciences while qualitative methods are commonly applied in the social sciences. This has led to arguments between the approaches in the past referred to as the quantitative-qualitative debate. We will provide a short historical background regarding this debate in the following.

Philosophers like Adam Ferguson (1723–1816), who were thinking about how to study humans and society, were influenced by the scientific thinking of Enlightenment. They had the idea that societies can be analyzed in the same way as physical *objects*. August Comte (1798–1857) later speaks about *social physics* as the new field to study social behavior. Already one century ago, Descartes followed such an approach. In "Traité de l'homme" – a book written by him in 1632 – he compared humans with machines. However, further philosophers, like Wilhelm Dilthey (1833–1911), Wilhelm Windelband (1848–1915) and Heinrich Rickert (1863–1936), criticized the *scientific ideal* for studying social behavior that tries to make human behavior adaptable to specific rules. According to them, the individual should be what matters most instead of the scientific rules. They put the emphasis on the understanding and not on the explanation as is mostly common in natural sciences. According to Max Weber (1864–1920), who argued against Comte, culture can only be understood by analyzing the meaning that people give it in a certain social setting and not by itself [15].

The way, society functions, is not independent from the people that live in it. It's not something objective; however, it depends on people's interpretations that vary across different social settings [16]. Hence, for Weber a categorization of the empirical into rules doesn't make any sense. Nevertheless, quantitative methods have maintained a privileged status as opposed to qualitative methods even though they create rather artificial outcomes reflecting the researcher's interests and despite the fact that they cannot achieve a comprehensive understanding of human behavior [15].

The biggest accusation that qualitative researchers are frequently confronted with is that their flexible, unstructured methods are not scientific enough [17]. However, as presented above, the flexibility of qualitative approaches makes it possible in the first place to understand society in the way it is perceived by the people that live in it and not the way the researcher wants it to be [15]. Moreover, following a qualitative research approach is not random. The researcher is also interested in the rules that underlie a certain social behavior [16]. While the quantitative researcher has fixed assumptions beforehand, the qualitative researcher identifies the rules or the sense behind a certain behavior throughout the research process. Preknowledge is not rejected but verified within the *social reality* and not imposed from the beginning like quantitative methods usually do. This way, traditional theories can be amplified and improved [15]. Since 1970 in Germany (in the US already a bit earlier), the benefits of qualitative methods became more and more popular again affecting the methodological discussions [17]. Taking another example in psychology, which has been a highly quantitative field since its conception as a science, the qualitative approach has gained importance throughout the past decades.

The quantitative-qualitative debate is maintained by factors which can mainly be assigned to the underlying philosophical and methodological assumptions and the related research methods [18, 19]. Quantitative and qualitative research approaches clearly differ in terms of how data are collected and analyzed. Quantitative research requires the reduction of occurrence to numerical values to carry out statistical analyses. By contrast, qualitative research aims to turn unstructured data found in non-numerical form in texts, videos, and other artifacts into detailed description about the important aspects of the problem under consideration. This description can take many forms, for example textual narratives, graphical diagrams, and summary tables [20].

Qualitative research serves for hypothesis formation and the analysis of complex relationships, for example by means of interviews, field research or participatory observations. Hypotheses are deductively derived from the theory and can then be falsified through empirical investigation in quantitative approaches. In qualitative approaches, the development of hypotheses is part of the research process itself with the aim to develop a theory according to the observations that have been made. Qualitative data has to be collected to gain a detailed understanding of the participants' point of view and it displays a much lower degree of standardization compared to quantitative data collection. Qualitative data collection is accomplished by using for example interviews, focus groups or observation notes. Qualitative research also often makes use of secondary data, like personal documents, participant diaries or journals, video and recordings or online forums. The overall text data obtained in this way must then be transcribed to be analyzed. Data interpretation consists of giving a meaning to the obtained results with reference to the specific and context of the study for example settings or participants. [21].

Quantitative research focuses on the highly standardized testing of hypotheses by measuring large amounts of statistically analyzable data [22]. The aim is to investigate the relationships between the observed variables through mathematical and statistical analysis. Data interpretation consists of giving a meaning to the obtained results with reference to the theory the hypotheses have been developed from [23].

Both quantitative and qualitative approaches are profoundly diverse at different levels. Each approach has its strengths and weaknesses. This has strongly contributed to sustain the debate between quantitative and qualitative research approaches over the years. However, since the 1980s, the mixed methods approach combining qualitative and quantitative research has become popular aiming to represent more complex issues as naturally as possible and to obtain a more differentiated overall picture [24]. This approach may serve to integrate different methodological and research perspectives [23].

4   Challenging Experiences from Conversations Across Disciplines

Building upon the previously described theoretical background, this chapter aims to give an overview of our own challenging experiences from working in interdisciplinary projects and with people from diverse disciplines. We summarize challenges and biases that we have experienced during our conversations across disciplines.

To begin with, our experiences showed that the traditional biases between qualitative and quantitative methods or so-called *hard and soft sciences* are still prevalent nowadays.

This has frequently led to a lack of acceptance and respect for the other side on a methodological but also on a more general discipline level. In many disciplines such as pharmacy and engineering, there still is a clear dominance of quantitative methods while qualitative methods are considered as easier and highly subjective with a negative connotation. This may be a result of a lack of understanding. Typically, researchers have not *walked in the others' shoes* and qualitative methods are not even part of the curricula. Thus, many researchers using only quantitative methods don't know the work behind applying qualitative methods and working without pre-defined recipes and standardized rules.

Of course, the lack of understanding may go in both directions and can't be generalized. It is also highly dependent on individual aspects and the openness of researchers towards other methods or disciplines. But even independent of quantitative and qualitative methods, we have experienced biases. For example, psychology or social sciences were sometimes considered as easier as and less valid than disciplines such as engineering or natural sciences. This was the case even when the same or similar (quantitative) methods were applied and has frequently led to hardened attitudes between several disciplines. Traditional attitudes due to a specific disciplinary culture may be adapted [25], but this is of course dependent on the disciplines themselves. There may be older and more traditional disciplines as well as disciplines which are newer and more interdisciplinary themselves, such as HCI. Nevertheless, in our experience researchers tend to stay within their community and this may lead to a lack of critical self-reflection. We often take things for granted and don't reflect critically upon our own discipline leading to stagnation in the development of the discipline.

Finally, even within one discipline and one methodological approach, there can be discussions between more structured and rigid as opposed to more open ways of conducting research. We have experienced such discussions in seminars on qualitative methods and similar aspects have also been mentioned in the literature [26]. Hence, potential biases that we experienced across disciplines may in some cases even appear within opposing approaches of the same discipline.

As a result of biases, we additionally frequently experienced communication barriers. But there were other factors apart from biases and misunderstandings between disciplines that led to communicatory issues. On the one hand, this may be attributable to differences in terminology and vocabulary used in diverse disciplines. The same words can have very different meanings in one discipline than in another. Moreover, we experienced tremendous discrepancies in the discussion behavior generally. While some disciplines from the humanities were having arguments that were emotionally charged and very personal, researchers from disciplines such as engineering or natural sciences were more used to objective discussions without reaching levels of being personally offended. Thus, we experienced a clash of discussion cultures leading to many irritations. It was always a challenge for us in our interdisciplinary projects to find a balance between these different discussion styles and we often left frustrated and with a feeling of being misunderstood.

Nevertheless, we want to highlight that such challenges may develop into potentials. Conflict and friction may open up room for new insights. Thus, the next chapter aims to summarize how such potentials can be used, e.g. by combining quantitative and qualitative methods and using interdisciplinary friction to grow.

5   Advantages of Interdisciplinary Research Combining Qualitative and Quantitative Methods

As mentioned previously, qualitative and mixed methods gain more and more attention in psychology and HCI while they are not common in fields like pharmacy yet despite their potential advantages. In order to bridge the gap, we want to highlight how the strengths of different approaches can be combined to take advantage of the full range of scientific methods. Therefore, we will describe several aspects of qualitative, quantitative, and mixed methods research from our own experience in the following.

Hypothesis Generation. At the beginning of each research project, the research objectives and questions need to be defined and appropriate methods to answer them need to be chosen. Using flexible qualitative data such as interviews can be very helpful to derive hypotheses. The hypotheses can be tested further via application of quantitative methods or mixed methods. In general, the approaches need to be evaluated and reflected upon continuously throughout the research process.

Triangulation and Validity. Data Triangulation can be described as the use of various data sources to validate the results, support the respective hypothesis, and to provide different viewpoints on the same topic [27]. Mixed methods can thus increase the validity of the generated data. Qualitative research can be used to investigate the logic behind a social phenomenon but it's practically not applicable to have enough cases to generalize the results due to the high cost and time resources required. Therefore, qualitative data are typically collected from a specific sample with its respective limitations. Such qualitative data can be complemented by quantitative data, e.g., performing quantitative questionnaires. Such quantitative data allow statistical analyses and thus inferences to a larger population which would not be possible when only applying qualitative methods. Even if the interpretation of qualitative data can be ambiguous and challenging, misinterpretation of data can be prevented by using mixed methods and results are better understood. In conclusion, to gain a valid understanding of the overall picture regarding a specific research topic, mixed methods provide several advantages as opposed to applying qualitative or quantitative methods exclusively.

Flexibility and Openness. Particularly qualitative approaches provide a flexibility and openness that makes it possible in the first place to understand society in the way it is perceived by the people that live in it and not the way the researcher wants it to be [15]. Quantitative methods are more rigid and do not provide this flexibility that may be required depending on the research question of interest.

Understanding Complex Issues. Human-machine interaction is very complex and might not be described adequately by only quantitative data [28]. Qualitative methods or mixed methods may provide a more comprehensive picture about the subject of investigation. For example, from our experience, causes of non-operation or incorrect operation of machines can be quickly resolved by means of interviews. Issues in the development of automation solutions can be uncovered this way and problem-oriented solutions for complex processes can be derived. In order to evaluate human behavior in dealing with machines, the interest or the presuppositions of users when dealing with new technologies needs to be considered and can mainly be collected via qualitative methods such as interviews or participatory observations. Difficult topics such as socially critical issues are not easily identified by means of quantitative approaches as they reach their limitations here.

Solving Communication Issues. As an example, a pipetting robot did not meet the expectations of the user. Based on misunderstandings at the beginning between vendor and user, some functions did not work properly as many tasks were not described sufficiently by the user beforehand. Certain tasks were so self-evident for the user that s/he did not feel the need to explain these aspects in the specifications so that they were not communicated to the manufacturer. The manufacturer are mostly engineers and the users are mostly natural scientists. Thus, they have different disciplinary backgrounds and the communication barriers appeared unconsciously. To investigate such communication behavior between different disciplines and to implement laboratory automation in pharmaceutical laboratories, a mixed methods approach is strongly recommended.

Working in Interdisciplinary Teams. Working in interdisciplinary teams where the team members are familiar with qualitative and quantitative methods and know the limitations of both can be highly beneficial from our experience. By changing perspectives, new research questions can be evaluated, and helpful additional information can be gained. It is also a starting point to question the perspective that has been prevalent in one's own discipline and to open up to other approaches and methods in order to study human behavior. This can allow quantitative researchers to also see the benefits of qualitative research and the other way round. Also, the use of a combination of methods to comprehensively answer a research question works better in interdisciplinary teams. Learning from each other by discussing results in an interdisciplinary group and cooperating for publication in such a team consisting of members of various disciplines helps to change perspectives.

6 Conclusion

In this paper, we reported our experiences from interdisciplinary research projects. We gave an overview of the theoretical background regarding interdisciplinarity and the debate between quantitative and qualitative methods. Moreover, we complemented the theoretical part with our own experiences. During the time we spent in the interdisciplinary doctoral program, we realized that there are still many biases and communication barriers between disciplines and their methodological approaches. This frequently led to irritations which complicate working in interdisciplinary teams. However, in retrospect we can conclude that these challenges were not negative experiences but rather helped us grow and develop.

With respect to the application of qualitative and quantitative methods, we learned to recognize the value of each approach. Especially when it comes to the study of human behavior, we need to take advantage of the diversity of methodologies and break the traditional boundaries that have given preeminence to quantitative methods. Instead, we should embrace each approach, know the potentials and limitations to be able to apply them deliberately. It is always necessary to consider and reflect upon all possibilities before choosing adequate methods. Depending on the research question, qualitative, quantitative, or mixed methods may be appropriate. As a last point, we want to highlight that we reported mainly our own experiences and raise no claim of completeness regarding biases, limitations, and advantages of the different approaches referred to.

References

1. Blackwell, A.F.: HCI as an inter-discipline. In: Proceedings of the 33rd Annual ACM Conference Extended Abstracts on Human Factors in Computing Systems, pp. 503–516. ACM, New York, NY (2015). https://doi.org/10.1145/2702613.2732505
2. Adams, A., Blandford, A., Lunt, P.: Social empowerment and exclusion. ACM Trans. Comput-Human Interact. **12**, 174–200 (2005). https://doi.org/10.1145/1067860.1067863
3. Losch, K.: Potenziale für ein frauenansprechendes Informatikbild in Deutschland: Eine qualitative Studie zur Rolle indischer und chinesischer Doktorandinnen. TU Braunschweig (2022)
4. Faulhaber, A.K.: Towards Single-Pilot Operations in Commercial Aviation: A Human-Centered Perspective. TU Braunschweig (2021)
5. Helfferich, C.: Die Qualität qualitativer Daten. VS Verlag für Sozialwissenschaften, Wiesbaden (2011)
6. Knapp, G.-A., Landweer, H.: "Interdisziplinarität" in der Frauenforschung. L'homme: Zeitschrift für feministische Geschichtswissenschaft, **6**, 6–38 (1995)
7. Kahlert, H.: Wissenschaftsentwicklung durch Inter- und Transdisziplinarität: Positionen der Frauen- und Geschlechterforschung. In: Kahlert, H. (ed.) Quer denken – Strukturen verändern. Gender Studies zwischen Disziplinen. Studien interdisziplinäre Geschlechterforschung, pp. 23–60. VS Verl. für Sozialwiss, Wiesbaden (2005)
8. Aram, J.D.: Concepts of interdisciplinarity: configurations of knowledge and action. Human Relat. **57**, 379–412 (2004). https://doi.org/10.1177/0018726704043893
9. Schregel, S.: Interdisziplinarität im Entwurf: Zur Geschichte einer Denkform des Erkennens in der Bundesrepublik (1955–1975). NTM **24**, 1–37 (2016). https://doi.org/10.1007/s00048-016-0138-3
10. Stichweh, R.: The sociology of scientific disciplines: on the genesis and stability of the disciplinary structure of modern science. Sci. Context **5**, 3–15 (1992). https://doi.org/10.1017/S0269889700001071
11. Klein, J.T.: Interdisciplinarity. History, Theory, and Practice. Wayne State University Press, Detroit (1990)
12. Larivière, V., Gingras, Y.: Measuring interdisciplinarity. In: Cronin, B., Sugimoto, C.R. (eds.) Beyond Bibliometrics. Harnessing Multidimensional Indicators of Scholarly Impact, pp. 187–200. MIT Press, Cambridge, London (2014). https://doi.org/10.7551/mitpress/9445.003.0014
13. Veit-Brause, I.: Die Interdisziplinarität der Begriffsgeschichte als Brücke zwischen den Disziplinen. In: Gründer, K., Scholtz, G. (eds.) Die Interdisziplinarität der Begriffsgeschichte. Archiv für Begriffsgeschichte, pp. 15–29. Meiner, Hamburg (2000)
14. Hilgendorf, E.: Bedingungen gelingender Interdisziplinarität – am Beispiel der Rechtswissenschaft. JZ, **65**, 913 (2010). https://doi.org/10.1628/jz-2010-0029
15. Girtler, R.: Methoden der Feldforschung. Böhlau Verlag, Wien/Köln/Weimar (2001)
16. Schütz, A.: Die Soziale Welt und die Theorie der Sozialen Handlung. In: Schütz, A., Brodersen, A. (eds.) Gesammelte Aufsätze II. Studien zur soziologischen Theorie, pp. 3–21. Springer, Dordrecht (1972). https://doi.org/10.1007/978-94-010-2849-3_1

17. Baur, N., Kelle, U., Kuckartz, U.: KZfSS Kölner Zeitschrift für Soziologie und Sozialpsychologie **69**(2), 1–37 (2017). https://doi.org/10.1007/s11577-017-0450-5
18. Krantz, D.L.: Sustaining vs. resolving the quantitative-qualitative debate. Eval. Program Plann. **18**, 89–96 (1995). https://doi.org/10.1016/0149-7189(94)00052-Y
19. Bryman, A.: Quantity and Quality in Social Research. Routledge, London (2003)
20. Lazar, J., Feng, J.H., Hochheiser, H.: Research methods in human-computer interaction. Elsevier, Cambridge (2017)
21. Gelo, O., Braakmann, D., Benetka, G.: Quantitative and qualitative research: beyond the debate. Integr. Psychol. Behav. Sci. **42**, 266–290 (2008). https://doi.org/10.1007/s12124-008-9078-3
22. Flick, U., Kardorff, E.von., Steinke, I.: Was ist qualitative Forschung? Einleitung und Überblick. In: Flick, U., Kardorff, E.von, Steinke, I. (eds.) Qualitative Forschung. Ein Handbuch, pp. 13–29. Rowohlt, Reinbek (2012)
23. Tashakkori, A., Teddlie, C. (eds.): Handbook of Mixed Methods in Social & Behavioral Research. SAGE, Thousand Oaks, CA (2003). https://doi.org/10.4135/9781506335193
24. Kelle, U.: Die Integration qualitativer und quantitativer Methoden in der empirischen Sozialforschung. Theoretische Grundlagen und methodologische Konzepte. VS Verlag für Sozialwissenschaften/GWV Fachverlage GmbH Wiesbaden, Wiesbaden (2008)
25. Huber, L.: Fachkulturen: Über die Mühen der Verständigung zwischen den Disziplinen. Neue Sammlung **31**, 3–24 (1991)
26. Kohli, M.: "Offenes" und "geschlossenes" Interview: Neue Argumente zu einer alten Kontroverse. Soziale Welt **29**, 1–25 (1978)
27. Denzin, N.K.: The Research Act A Theoretical Introduction to Sociological Methods. Aldine Publishing Company, Somerset, NJ (1970)
28. Seaman, C.B.: Qualitative methods in empirical studies of software engineering. IEEE Trans. Softw. Eng. **25**, 557–572 (1999). https://doi.org/10.1109/32.799955

Design and Evaluation Methods, Techniques and Tools

A Coding Framework for Usability Evaluation of Digital Health Technologies

Mahdi Ebnali[1,2], Lauren R. Kennedy-Metz[3,4], Heather M. Conboy[1,2,3,4],
Lori A. Clarke[1,2,3,4], Leon J. Osterweil[1,2,3,4], George Avrunin[1,2,3,4],
Christian Miccile[1], Maria Arshanskiy[4], Annette Phillips[4], Marco A. Zenati[3,4],
and Roger D. Dias[1,2(✉)]

[1] Human Factors and Cognitive Engineering Lab, STRATUS Center for Medical Simulation, Brigham and Women's Hospital, Boston, MA, USA
rdias@bwh.harvard.edu
[2] Department of Emergency Medicine, Harvard Medical School, Boston, MA, USA
[3] Medical Robotics and Computer Assisted Surgery Lab, Division of Cardiac Surgery, VA Boston Healthcare System, Boston, MA, USA
[4] Laboratory for Advanced Software Engineering Research, Manning College of Information and Computer Sciences, University of Massachusetts Amherst, Amherst, MA, USA

Abstract. Several studies have reported low adherence and high resistance from clinicians to adopt digital health technologies into clinical practice, particularly the use of computer-based clinical decision support systems. Poor usability and lack of integration with the clinical workflow have been identified as primary issues. Few guidelines exist on how to analyze the collected data associated with the usability of digital health technologies. In this study, we aimed to develop a coding framework for the systematic evaluation of users' feedback generated during focus groups and interview sessions with clinicians, underpinned by fundamental usability principles and design components. This codebook also included a coding category to capture the user's clinical role associated with each specific piece of feedback, providing a better understanding of role-specific challenges and perspectives, as well as the level of shared understanding across the multiple clinical roles. Furthermore, a voting system was created to quantitatively inform modifications of the digital system based on usability data. As a use case, we applied this method to an electronic cognitive aid designed to improve coordination and communication in the cardiac operating room, showing that this framework is feasible and useful not only to better understand suboptimal usability aspects, but also to recommend relevant modifications in the design and development of the system from different perspectives, including clinical, technical, and usability teams. The framework described herein may be applied in other highly complex clinical settings, in which digital health systems may play an important role in improving patient care and enhancing patient safety.

Keywords: Usability study · Decision support system · Digital health

M. Kurosu (Ed.): HCII 2022, LNCS 13302, pp. 185–196, 2022.
https://doi.org/10.1007/978-3-031-05311-5_12

1 Background

With the rise of medical information and technological advancements, digital health technology offers a variety of benefits to support healthcare providers and patients, improving compliance with standards of health quality, cost, and practice [1]. Therefore, accelerating the acceptance and engagement of digital health technology has been recognized as a national policy priority [2]. In 2009, the Health Information Technology (IT) for Economic and Clinical Health (HITECH) Act under the American Recovery and Reinvestment Act was initiated to expedite the coordination and delivery of American healthcare through health IT, including the adoption of digital health technologies.

Although a growing body of literature suggests that higher adoption of digital health systems is associated with safer and higher-quality care, [3] several pieces of evidence report unintended adverse effects of these technologies on clinical workflows due to poor usability issues [4]. The design of digital health technology is a complex process because of the inherently complex nature of clinical procedures that are mostly characterized by dynamic, non-linear, interactive, and interdependent collaborative activities, with uncertainty in outcomes [5]. Dealing with this complexity demands following an extensive set of design and usability requirements, constraints, and safety measures. Poor usability of digital health technology may result in substantial increases in medical error and associated costs, decreased efficiency, and unsatisfied users [6]. Recent reports have highlighted the importance of using cognitive engineering and human factors approaches for the design and empirical assessment of technology used in clinical settings [7].

Focus group and interview techniques have been widely used as common qualitative approaches to capture users' feedback and to obtain in-depth insights on the usability of digital health technologies [8]. Focus group and semi-structured interview discussions are carefully planned and designed to obtain the perceptions of the individuals on a defined area of interest, facilitated by a moderator to keep the focus of the discussion. In these methods, participants are invited to discussion sessions to communicate their comments voluntarily in a safe and supported manner. This approach may lead to uncovered issues that researchers might have been unable to plan in advance. Moreover, focus group methodology is a cost-efficient way of evaluating user experience, as several subjects can be interviewed at the same time.

2 Current Challenges

Focus group methods have many advantages over other usability evaluation methods, however, as with any research methodologies, there are limitations. Some of these limitations can be overcome by well-structured planning and moderation, but other issues are inevitable and unique to this approach. Despite the widespread use of these qualitative methods, few guidelines exist for analyzing the data gathered from participants. Compared to structured questionnaires and quantitative experimental approaches, data collected during usability focus groups and interview sessions are often difficult to assemble and analyze. Annotating and coding qualitative data can be time-consuming and complicated for most digital health technologies given their inherent complexities. Although extensive previous literature provides frameworks and guidance on designing and conducting usability focus groups and interview sessions [9], scarce literature exists on extracting and coding usability data to effectively inform system design and development improvements based on a human-centered approach.

3 Proposed Coding Framework

Few studies evaluating the usability of digital health technology have attempted to combine qualitative coding with usability theories and principles [10]. Although these studies provide insights on the categorization of usability issues, there is still no standard methodology on how to integrate usability principles in coding this type of qualitative data. In this study, we aimed to develop a coding framework for the systematic evaluation of user feedback comments generated during focus group sessions, underpinned by fundamental usability principles and design components. Integrating usability principles and design components in coding and analyzing data generated during focus group sessions may help to systematically improve the degree of shared understanding between users with different roles, identify the extent of overlap in their comments, and the communication content generated during the sessions. Developing a shared understanding of the usability components of digital health technology can better ground the system on effective communication, leading to improved outcomes related to patient care coordination, teamwork, and care continuity.

4 Codebook Development

In usability studies, there are several well-established principles that can be utilized to categorize issues and comments collected during focus groups. Most studies attempting to evaluate usability via focus groups suffer from poor reproducibility of evaluations due to variation and subjectivity in codes, and a lack of standard reporting [10]. To tackle this challenge, we developed a codebook system that systematically evaluates each comment against usability principles for digital health technology. Moreover, since usability focus group sessions are primarily focused on different parts of a system interface and its specific features, this codebook incorporates categories related to design functions and elements. Furthermore, we included a coding category to capture the user's clinical role associated with each specific comment, offering a better understanding of role-specific challenges and perspectives, as well as the level of shared understanding across the multiple clinical end-users.

The codebook allows researchers to code each users' feedback based on three main categories guided by prompt questions: *a) Usability Components*: Which usability principle is targeted by the feedback? *b) Design Components*: Which design function and element are targeted by the feedback? *c) Clinical Role*: Which clinical role provided the feedback? The following sections provide details on each of these categories, helping researchers to categorize comments extracted during focus groups targeting digital health technology usability.

4.1 Usability Principles: Which Usability Principle is Targeted by the Feedback?

The main goal of usability focus group sessions for qualitative studies is extracting information about system issues and gathering insights on a prototype and/or system. Based on the human-centered design perspective, the Ten Heuristic Principles developed by Jakob Nielsen [11] have been identified as standard principles to identify and categorize usability issues, including 1) Visibility, 2) Match, 3) Control, 4) Consistency, 5) Error, 6) Recognition, 7) Flexibility, 8) Aesthetic, 9) Recovery, and 10) Help.

4.2   Design Components: Which Design Function and Element Are Targeted by the Feedback?

Usability principles alone are not sufficient to accurately categorize the issues associated with the usability of digital health technology, and other significant factors related to system design need to be integrated into the coding system. Qualitative usability studies aim to collect insights about how users interact with the product or service. This interaction, as described by scholars in the design community, happens at the interface level or the product 'front-end' which enables user interaction through communication and conversation. Therefore, this codebook incorporates usability principles to categories related to design functions and design elements [12].

Design Functions. Most of the comments expressed during usability focus group sessions target a particular user interface [12]. Although these interfaces come in various forms such as buttons, pop-ups, radio buttons, panels, etc., they can generally be associated with a higher-level category of components. To date, though there are some available taxonomies, there is no well-accepted framework to categorize user interfaces [13]. For example, in previous research, *Kamaruddin et al.* proposed that the types of interface design consist of four main categories with separate features: presentation interface, conversation interface, navigation interface, and explanation interface [14]. According to these schemas, we considered the following categories for coding comments expressed during usability focus group sessions: input controls components, navigational components, informational components, and container components. These categories have been used frequently in the design community in order to describe the support provided to users by each individual interface during specific tasks. Each category encompasses user interfaces with common functions in the system (Table 1). This categorization can be helpful for analyzing the results from focus groups and interview sessions where the research team will gain better insights into function-wise usability issues in particular. Moreover, evaluation of function-wise usability issues across various iterations can be helpful to better compare versions of designs in various interactions throughout the prototype life cycle.

Design Elements. We have also incorporated design elements into the codebook to have a more elaborated view of each feedback from a design perspective. Previous studies have established various design elements based on different perspectives and research frameworks. Most of these elements focused on the fundamental design components of the interface, which target a wide range of visual, audio, and content aspects. Based on these design foundations, a list of principles and elements are categorized into a shorter list of design elements [13]: color, imagery, typography, language, location, and audio. In line with these studies, the healthcare usability literature also suggests that color, imagery, position, and text style are the main design elements in digital health

Table 1. Design functions of user interfaces.

Component	Description	Examples
1. Input controls	Allow users to input information into the system	A button allowing the user to select options
2. Navigational	Enable users to move around a system or a website	Tab bars Scroll bars Next/ back UIs
3. Informational	Used to share information with users	Descriptions Icons, feedback Pop-up Messages
4. Container	Designed to hold related content and interfaces together	Image carousel Frame of a window

technology, which contribute to the ability of the user to accurately interpret and use the interface [15]. Incorporating these elements in the coding process of data generated during focus group sessions can help researchers to have a more accurate and detailed evaluation of users' feedback. Each comment can be evaluated based on these six basic design elements (Table 2).

Table 2. Design elements of user interfaces.

Component	Description
1. Color	One of the most imminent elements of a design; It is used to differentiate items, create depth, add emphasis, and/or help organize information. It can stand alone, as a background, or be applied to other elements, like imagery or typography
2. Imagery	Can be in different styles: shapes, illustrations (image, video, animation), 3D renderings, etc. Defined by boundaries, such as lines or color, they are often used to emphasize a portion of the page
3. Typography and Text Style	Can be used in different ways in the context of an app or a website and mainly refers to which fonts are chosen, their size, alignment, and spacing
4. Language	Covers the meaning and tone of words used in the product
5. Position	Can significantly impact the usability of a system such as the readability of design
6. Sound	Used to notify the user about a situation or for avoiding hazardous events

4.3 Clinical Role: Which Clinical Role Provided the Feedback?

In each focus group, participants with different clinical roles and backgrounds were invited to the sessions. Getting their unique perspective and integrating it with data collected from other participants can be useful for creating a shared understanding of usability issues across different parts of the design. The clinical role was considered as a code category for the person in that role providing feedback.

The codebook described in the previous sections allows researchers to code each participant's comment based on three main categories guided by interviewers' prompts. Adhering to this systematic coding framework allows researchers to assess saturation

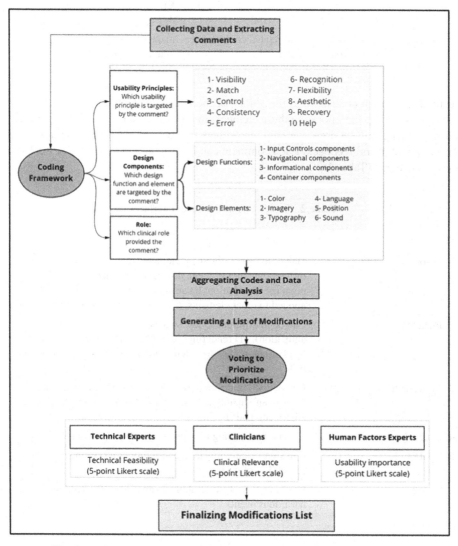

Fig. 1. Main categories and components of the proposed coding framework

of usability issues in general, across design components, and roles in particular. Furthermore, since usability focus group data is analyzed one group at a time, following a systematic coding approach enables researchers to aggregate the findings across multiple focus groups, informing design modifications. It also allows the quantification and analysis of system issues by specific usability principles and/or roles, which may identify areas of design and development to focus on in future iterations.

4.4 Data-Driven Design Modifications

After categorizing the user comments based on usability principles, design components, and clinical roles, researchers and design and development teams can frame a list of potential changes to address the raised issues. Due to limitations in time and costs, implementing all the changes is often not feasible. The prioritization of which system modifications should be made is one of the most important challenges in designing and/or re-designing a digital health technology. As a part of the proposed framework, we created a voting system to facilitate this process and quantitatively inform system modifications, as well as their level of prioritization (Table 3).

This voting system evaluates each suggested modification based on three criteria (usability importance, clinical relevance, and technical feasibility), using a 5-point Likert scale. An advantage of this voting system is that it can incorporate multidisciplinary aspects from various experts, including not only the technical design and development team but also clinicians and human factors analysts.

Table 3. Decision criteria and rating for prioritization.

Criteria	Rating anchors	Description
Usability importance	1: Very Important 2: Important 3: Moderately Important 4: Slightly Important 5: Not Important	Whether implementing the proposed change may prevent the user from completing a task or properly accessing information
Clinical importance	1: Very Important 2: Important 3: Moderately Important 4: Slightly Important 5: Not Important	Whether implementing the proposed change may negatively impact clinical goals and/or workflows
Technical feasibility	1: Very Feasible 2: Feasible 3: Moderately Feasible 4: Less Feasible 5: Not Feasible	Whether implementing the proposed change is feasible in terms of implementation time and costs

5   Use Case

We applied the coding framework to evaluate an electronic cognitive aid (Smart Check-list) that was developed to guide cardiac surgery teams during common cardiac proce-dures in the operating room (OR) [16]. The Smart Checklist uses a carefully elicited and domain expert-validated process model to monitor the progress of an ongoing sur-gical procedure, determining the expected next tasks for each of the team members, thereby providing a context- and patient-specific perspective on each team role's task management. This study was approved by the Mass General Brigham (MGB) Institu-tional Review Board (IRB) and all research subjects completed an informed consent procedure.

5.1   Data Collection

Four multidisciplinary focus group sessions were conducted with OR team members, representing key cardiac surgery roles: cardiac surgeons, cardiac anesthesiologists, per-fusionists, and OR nurses. Two interviewers (LKM and H.C) conducted focus group sessions via videoconferencing while demonstrating the Smart Checklist. HC presented a detailed demonstration of the Smart Checklist to convey its primary informational features, where they were located, and the various ways in which users could interact with the interface (e.g., clicking buttons, entering notes). Pre-determined prompt ques-tions were interspersed by the researchers to gather targeted feedback from participants. User's comments were transcribed independently *post hoc* by both interviewers after review of the focus groups recordings. For example, Fig. 2 shows specific parts of the Smart Checklist in which participants were asked to discuss their preference over two alternative views: separated view vs. merged view. The merged view shows the next tasks for all teams in a single column and the separated view has different columns for each team or role.

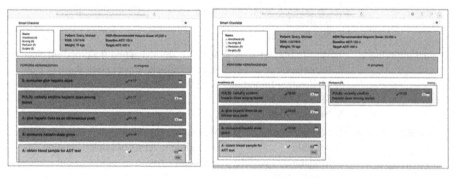

Fig. 2. Different views of the surgical steps within the Smart Checklist

5.2   Feedback Coding

Two independent coders (L.KM and H.C) used the coding framework to analyze the qualitative data generated in the focus groups. The coding of the 118 transcribed sentences was conducted via *Dedoose*, a web application for mixed methods research. First, the coders were instructed on coding components by providing examples of various types of usability principles and design components. Discrepancies between the coders were discussed during sessions until a consensus was reached. Then, the coders were asked to code each sentence based on the codebook (Fig. 1).

5.3   Results

A total of 12 subjects participated in four focus group sessions. Group 1: surgeon, anesthesiologist, perfusionist, nurse; Group 2: anesthesiologist, perfusionist, nurse; Group 3: surgeon, perfusionist, nurse; Group 4: anesthesiologist, perfusionist. To assess the inter-rater reliability (IRR) of the coding framework, we calculated Kappa coefficients. Analysis across all coding showed a moderate IRR with a Kappa coefficient of 0.53, p-value < 0.001, and an overall percentage of agreement between coders of 82.3%.

A total of 18 modifications were suggested by the focus groups. The priority voting system was completed by 3 human factor experts, 4 OR clinicians (1 attending cardiac surgeon, 1 attending cardiac anesthesiologist, 1 perfusionist, and 1 scrub nurse), and 3 technical designers/developers. Table 4 shows the suggested modifications with the respective scores (median) across all three criteria.

Table 4.   Priority scores by human factors (HF), clinicians (CL), and technical experts (TE).

Suggested modifications	HF	CL	TE
Enable interface to update color scheme according to user selection	2.0	3.5	1.0
Integrate checklist with the post-procedure document generator	3.0	4.0	3.0
Embed numeric inputs into the step itself, rather than or in addition to in the pop-up dialogue box	2.0	3.5	3.0
Embed additional requisites corresponding to a step into the step itself, rather than or in addition to appearing in the pop-up dialogue box	2.0	3.5	3.0
In the Separated Team View, adapt the column width to the number of specialty teams involved in the surgical process	4.0	3.5	3.0
Increase default font size	4.0	3.0	3.0
Better distinguish the team primarily responsible for a step with distinct icons, border styles, etc.	5.0	3.0	1.0
Integrate checklist with voice-based support	4.0	3.5	1.0

(continued)

Table 4. (*continued*)

Suggested modifications	HF	CL	TE
Allow user to decide if the hierarchical steps should be the same color (e.g., yellow) as the steps with checkmark buttons/icons below them or a less saturated version of that color (e.g., lighter yellow)	2.0	3.0	4.0
Fix process header in place so it doesn't scroll as the checklist advances	4.0	4.5	1.0
Keep hierarchical steps hidden by default, but allow users to show them as desired	4.0	3.0	5.0
Include system timers for relevant steps (e.g., 3-min timer after heparin administration)	4.0	4.5	1.0
Update steps reading announce X to announce 'X'	3.0	3.0	4.0
Better differentiate the header when the process is in progress from the display of a step that is in progress	4.0	4.0	3.0
Replace the suitcase icon to more accurately reflect the requisites corresponding to a given step	4.0	4.0	4.0
Indicate all steps related to a reported problem in a distinct way (e.g., all steps have red borders)	4.0	3.0	4.0
Include the ability to switch between Merged and Separated Views	4.0	3.5	5.0
Add a 'help' button to display a legend	5.0	2.0	5.0

6 Limitations and Future Directions

Even though the coding scheme was established based on well-established usability principles and design components and was tested to code usability data of a digital health system, it cannot be guaranteed that it will aid in the coding of all possible usability issues. Future studies are needed to further validate this codebook and voting system in the design and development process of other digital health technologies in additional clinical settings. Moreover, the coding system is specifically created to code data generated during focus group sessions, and future studies should evaluate the applicability of this framework on data gathered through other usability methods, such as verbal protocol and structured questionnaires.

7 Conclusion

In this study, we report the development of a comprehensive coding framework for usability evaluation of digital health technologies. In addition to incorporating relevant domains, such as usability principles, design components, and clinical roles, we have also provided a structured voting system to inform the prioritization of system modifications. The use case involving an electronic cognitive aid in the cardiac OR showed that this framework is feasible and useful not only to better understand distinct usability aspects that may be suboptimal, but also to recommend relevant modifications in the system from various perspectives, including the clinical team. The method and framework described herein may be adopted and applied to other highly complex clinical settings, in which digital health systems may play an important role in improving patient care and enhancing patient safety.

Acknowledgment. This work was supported by the National Heart, Lung, and Blood Institute of the National Institutes of Health Under Award Number R01HL126896 (PI: Zenati). The content is solely the responsibility of the authors and does not necessarily represent the official views of the National Institutes of Health. No conflicts of interest were declared.

References

1. Trinkley, K.E., Blakeslee, W.W., Matlock, D.D., Kao, D.P., Van Matre, A.G., Harrison, R., et al.: Clinician preferences for computerised clinical decision support for medications in primary care: a focus group study. BMJ Health Care Inform. **26**, e000015 (2019)
2. Book, B.A.: Crossing the quality chasm: a new health system for the 21st century. BMJ **323**, 1192 (2001). https://doi.org/10.1136/bmj.323.7322.1192
3. Hessels, A., Flynn, L., Cimiotti, J.P., Bakken, S., Gershon, R.: Impact of heath information technology on the quality of patient care. Online J. Nurs. Inform. **19** (2015). https://www.ncbi.nlm.nih.gov/pubmed/27570443
4. Furukawa, M.F., Eldridge, N., Wang, Y., Metersky, M.: Electronic health record adoption and rates of in-hospital adverse events. J. Patient Saf. **16**, 137–142 (2020)
5. Ebnali, M., Shah, M., Mazloumi, A.: How mHealth apps with higher usability effects on patients with Breast Cancer? In: Proceedings of the International Symposium on Human Factors and Ergonomics in Health Care, pp. 81–84 (2019). https://doi.org/10.1177/2327857919081018
6. Guo, C., Ashrafian, H., Ghafur, S., Fontana, G., Gardner, C., Prime, M.: Challenges for the evaluation of digital health solutions—a call for innovative evidence generation approaches. NPJ Digital Med. **3**, 1–14 (2020)
7. Zenati, M.A., Kennedy-Metz, L., Dias, R.D.: Cognitive engineering to improve patient safety and outcomes in cardiothoracic surgery. Semin. Thorac. Cardiovasc. Surg. **32**, 1–7 (2020)
8. Brown, W., Yen, P.-Y., Rojas, M., Schnall, R.: Assessment of the health IT usability evaluation model (Health-ITUEM) for evaluating mobile health (mHealth) technology. J. Biomed. Inform. **46**, 1080–1087 (2013). https://doi.org/10.1016/j.jbi.2013.08.001
9. Leech, N.L., Onwuegbuzie, A.J.: An array of qualitative data analysis tools: a call for data analysis triangulation. School Psychol. Q. **22**, 557–584 (2007). https://doi.org/10.1037/1045-3830.22.4.557
10. Willis, G.: Pretesting of health survey questionnaires: cognitive interviewing, usability testing, and behavior coding. In: Health Survey Methods, pp. 217–242 (2014). https://doi.org/10.1002/9781118594629.ch9
11. Nielsen, J.: Enhancing the explanatory power of usability heuristics. In: Conference Companion on Human Factors in Computing Systems - CHI 1994 (1994). https://doi.org/10.1145/259963.260333
12. Mosier, J.N., Smith, S.L.: Application of guidelines for designing user interface software. Behav. Inf. Technol. **5**, 39–46 (1986). https://doi.org/10.1080/01449298608914497
13. Kontio, J., Lehtola, L., Bragge, J.: Using the focus group method in software engineering: obtaining practitioner and user experiences. In: Proceedings of 2004 International Symposium on Empirical Software Engineering, ISESE 2004. IEEE (2004). https://doi.org/10.1109/isese.2004.1334914

14. Mandel, T.: The Elements of User Interface Design. Wiley, New York (1997)
15. Rind, A., Wang, T.D., Aigner, W., Miksch, S., Wongsuphasawat, K., Plaisant, C., et al.: Interactive information visualization to explore and query electronic health records. HCI **5**, 207–298 (2013)
16. Avrunin, G.S., Christov, S.C., Clarke, L.A., Conboy, H.M., Osterweil, L.J., Zenati, M.A.: Process driven guidance for complex surgical procedures. AMIA Annu. Symp. Proc. **2018**, 175–184 (2018)

Designer Interface for a Class of Wearable Computer Applications

Lawrence J. Henschen[✉] and Julia C. Lee

Northwestern University, Evanston, IL 60208, USA
henschen@eecs.northwestern.edu, j-lee@northwestern.edu

Abstract. Wearable computing systems are a large and important new class of embedded systems. Within this broad class is an important subclass, namely those systems which monitor various signals, both within the body and external to the body, and possibly perform some action in response to various events. Many of these applications require conditions and actions that are beyond those described in our prior work. This work describes four such extensions. First, sensor data can be aggregated (integrated) over time. Second, actuator controls can be controlled over time with monitoring. Third, inputs from external sources can be used in the same way that sensor data can be used. Finally, messages sent to the outside word can include expressions involving sensor data as well as status of actuators. This paper describes the designer interface that allows professionals without computer expertise to include these features in the definition of a new wearable product. The definitions collected by the designer interface can be used to automatically generate the computer code that runs on the wearable computing device.

Keywords: Wearable applications · Designer interface · XML · Automatic code generation

1 Introduction

Wearable computing devices have become a major focus of research, development, and marketing in recent years. Wearable products with some combination of computing power, sensing, actuation of wearable devices, and communication with the world beyond the wearer are receiving wide-spread attention in many different areas. Examples include:

- Medicine - monitoring biometrics of patients both in hospital and at home; diabetes monitoring and treatment, including sensing of blood sugar, warning to patients, and even dispensing of medications contained in devices worn by the patient; monitoring the speech and providing training feedback for people who stutter; monitoring for abnormal conditions for people with special needs or situations, such as fall detection for the elderly; and many others.
- Sports – monitoring biometrics for professional athletes during training and/or competition; monitoring biometrics for non-athletes who want to maintain good health but

M. Kurosu (Ed.): HCII 2022, LNCS 13302, pp. 197–210, 2022.
https://doi.org/10.1007/978-3-031-05311-5_13

not overdo or underdo their exercise routines; monitoring and recording movement during training, such as for golf or tennis swing training; and many others.

- Clothing – smart garments that change based on environmental conditions and the biometrics of the wearer; decorative clothing and jewelry; etc.
- General – general aids for people with disabilities; head-mounted displays for people who need their hands free during their activities; virtual-reality gloves for gaming and for control of machinery; etc.

The growth of this field has been driven by several technical advances such as miniaturization of circuitry and corresponding devices, low power computing, and energy harvesting. It has also been driven by the desire to improve human lives, such as the work in the medical field. The reader is referred to the proceedings from the major conference in this area, [1], to get a sense of the breadth and depth of both the technical aspects and the application aspects of this growing field.

Our work over the past decade, [2–5], has been aimed at making the design and implementation of sensor/actuator networks, of which wearable computing devices is an example, more efficient, faster, and more accessible to people without extensive computer engineering backgrounds. The design of a sensor/actuator system requires, among other things, knowledge of the application, of course, and also knowledge about computing devices, sensor/actuator devices, and programming. Our work in [2] was aimed at helping designers, including non-technical designers, specify the devices that would be needed in a sensor/actuator system under development and describe their intended behavior, after which our designer interface system would automatically generate code that could run on the computing platform to be used. We have continually augmented the capabilities for specifying more sophisticated behavior of the sensor/actuator nodes, [3–5]. This paper continues that work by adding new types of conditions for sensor/actuator nodes to monitor and more sophisticated actions for the actuators to perform. These extensions are driven by the needs for wearable computing products, specifically from the medical field. However, we note that other kinds of wearable products as well as other areas of sensor/actuator networks and embedded systems in general, also have applications that would use the extended capabilities.

In the next section we briefly describe our past work in this area. Following that, we motivate the work described here with examples taken from the patient monitoring application. We then describe the new features in detail and the new interfaces that allow wearable system designers to specify those new features. We finish with some closing remarks.

2   Overview of Our Prior Work

As noted, our prior work on designer interfaces for defining sensor/actuator networks has focused on making the design and implementation processes accessible to people who do not have extensive computer engineering backgrounds. The steps in designing and implementing a sensor/actuator system include, among others, high-level design of the intended external behavior of the system, selection of components to be used in the system, and programming the processing elements used in the system. The high-level design involves specifying what the system is supposed to do, as opposed to how the system will do it. This is accomplished by the application specialists and does not usually involve technical knowledge that a computer engineer would bring to the process. Our prior work has focused on the selection of components and the programming of the processors. In [2] we described a generic interface for helping non-technical users describe what kinds of devices (for example, temperature sensor or on/off switch) should be in the system and how they should behave. The goal was to aid a non-technical user to select components, help determine how they should be connected, and describe their behavior, such as sampling rates and how information is to be transmitted from inside the system to the outside world. In [5], we described an interface that would allow users to specify relatively simple conditions of the sensors in a system and specify relatively simple actions that the system being designed should perform, as described in the next paragraph. The software associated with the interface could then automatically generate code that would run on the processing element of the sensor/actuator system being designed. Both of these works, [2] and [5], allow non-technical users to do low-level design and implementation of a system, that is, perform those steps that would otherwise be performed by a computer engineer.

The conditions and actions handled by the interface described in [5] are relatively simple. Conditions that trigger actions involve simple combinations of values from sensors or instantaneous changes in those sensors. The example in [5] involved vehicle anti-theft systems. A condition might be that the engine just turned on and the key was not in the ignition. This condition has a static part (the key is not in the ignition) and a dynamic part (the engine just changed from being off to being on). Moreover, it is an instantaneous condition; it occurs at the instant the engine turns on. Actions in response to an instantaneous condition were also simple. For example, if the engine just turned on with no key in the ignition, likely the car is being stolen. A simple action in response to this condition is to turn the alarm siren on. Conditions and actions described in [5] could also be analog; for example, was the temperature over 100 or apply the brake with 50% pressure. The interface can automatically translate these condition/action specifications into computer code. In the next section we will motivate the need for more sophisticated conditions and actions for certain applications, using the medical area within the wearable computing field as the main motivating example.

To give the reader a better feeling for how our designer interfaces appear and operate, we copy a sample screen shot and generated code from [5]. We first note that the high-level output from our designer interfaces is in the form of XML expressions. For example, the event described in the previous paragraph would be represented in XML as

```
<EVENT internalname="hotwire" externalname="Car is being hotwired." >
    <CONDITION>
        <AND>
            <CHANGE  name="engineOn" oldvalue="NO" newvalue="YES" />
            <VALUE    name="keyInIgnition" val="NO" />
        </AND>
    </CONDITION>
    <ACTION>
        <SETOUTPUT  name="siren"  val="ON" />
    </ACTION>
</EVENT>
```

where items like "engineOn" and "siren" refer to elements (sensors, actuators, etc.) that have been defined elsewhere in the designer interface. A screen such as the one shown in Fig. 1 helps the designer formulate the above XML expression. In Fig. 1, the cursor is inside the <CONDITON> XML element, and the right-hand panel lists the XML items that are legal in that context. Assuming a set of such events has been defined, the code that would run on the processing element would like as follows:

```
while(1) {
    // Save old values for any inputs with a CHANGE test.
        Code for saving old values.  See next paragraph.
    for(j=1; j<=NUMBEROFEVENTS; j=j+1) {
        if(eventCondition1()) eventAction1();
        if(eventCondition2()) eventAction2();
            ...
    }
}
```

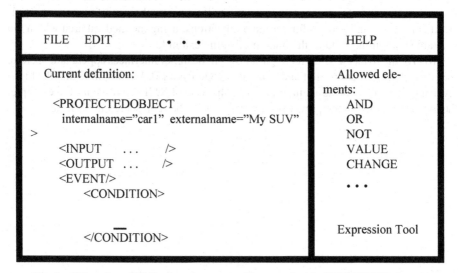

Fig. 1. (Taken from [5]) Designer's screen with cursor inside CONDITION element

3 Motivation for New Features

The simple conditions and actions handled in our designer interface described in [5] are not sufficient for many applications. Wearable medical applications offer good examples of the need for events requiring more sophisticated conditions and actions. Further, the need for such applications to be specified by medical personnel rather than computer engineers is also more urgent. In this section we motivate these needs.

Simple instantaneous conditions are insufficient to handle many wearable medical applications. Consider a wearable system for monitoring and controlling diabetes. Blood sugar levels often rise for short periods of time due to quite normal causes. For example, a person may have just eaten a meal or come into a very stressful situation, both of which can raise blood sugar level for a brief period. A wearable blood sugar monitoring system should not activate an alarm or take other actions for such situations if the level does not go too high or begins to go down after some period of time. It is the combination of increased level over an extended period of time that requires action. The instantaneous condition of rising about a given threshold, for example 110, is not sufficient to warrant action. Furthermore, it might be useful to describe several conditions that warrant different kinds of actions. For example, a gradual increase over the threshold over an extended period of time might warrant a warning to the patient and the administration of a small dose of insulin through a wearable insulin pump. On the other hand, a rapid and very high spike over a short period of time might warrant an emergency message to any nearby medical center and the administration of a very large dose of insulin. Further, the size of the dose would likely depend on how much over the threshold the level went. So, again it's not just a matter of turning a pump on but rather of computing how strongly the pump should work. Finally, the system would need to monitor blood sugar level at regular periods, for example every 15 s, to adjust the dosage or determine when to turn the pump off. These are well beyond the simple cases handled in our previous work.

A wearable health system might need information from outside the system in addition to values from the wearable sensors. Consider a system that monitors for motion sickness and takes some action such as administration of a medication or application of pressure to acupuncture points. As in the previous paragraph, it is not the instantaneous motion that requires an action but rather some set of conditions over time. Violent motion over even a small period of time can require a response from the system, but moderate motion may be acceptable for a longer period of time before a response is warranted. Moreover, the need for and strength of a response may depend on, for example, the weather. Is it sunny and calm (in which case it may be just the sea being rough at that location), or is it stormy (in which case the motion may be expected to continue for a long period of time)? In the former case, applying pressure to acupuncture points P6 may be enough to control the sickness. In the latter case, more drastic action would be required.

Finally, individual patients often require individualized treatment. In the case of wearable treatment systems, such as a diabetes monitor and insulin pump system, the program that runs on the computer in that wearable system may need to be adjusted for individual patients even though the hardware that one patient wears is the same as for all patients. The medical professional may need to specify a unique set of conditions and actions that form the events for a special patient. Thus, it is important that the designer interface allow for this and then automatically generate the computer code to be loaded into that patient's system without the need for outside expertise of a computer engineer.

4 New Features for Embedded System Designer Interfaces

We present here four features that will greatly expand the set of wearable system applications that can be designed in the kind of designer interface that we have been developing. These expand the capabilities of the designer systems described in our prior works [2–5].

4.1 Aggregation of Sensor Input Over Time

As noted in Sect. 3, many medical issues are not indicated by an instantaneous condition but rather by an abnormal condition over a period of time. The seriousness of the medical issue is determined by the degree of abnormality and the duration of the abnormality. For example, moderately elevated motion over an hour or more could bring on mild motion sickness, while violent motion over 10 or 15 min could bring on serious motion sickness. Abnormality in the wearable sensor network application means a sensor value is above a threshold or below a threshold. For example, a blood sugar level above 110 is an abnormal condition, whose continuation indicates a hyperglycemic attack; conversely, a blood sugar level below 85 is an abnormal condition, whose continuation indicates a hypoglycemic attack. Finally, the degree of abnormality often determines the strength of the response needed to bring the abnormality back within acceptable limits. For example, a hyperglycemic attack may be indicated by blood sugar level over 110 for more than 10 min. If the level is just 115 for 10 min, then only a mild dose of insulin from the insulin pump is indicated; on the other hand, if the level is fluctuating over 200 for 10 min, then a strong dose is indicated. The degree of abnormality is, in effect, the integral of the difference between sensor readings and the acceptable baseline over time. This integral can be approximated by sampling the sensor at regular intervals and summing the difference between those samples and the baseline.

These remarks suggest a new kind of condition that could be used in the CONDITION portion of an EVENT, as described in Sect. 2. The designer would need to specify the following items.

- A name that could be used in CONDITION elements. For example, a designer might specify the integral for serious hyperglycemia and call it "seriousHRG". A CONDITION element might contain the test "seriousHRG > 500", indicating that the blood sugar level averaged more than 100 over the baseline of 100 (i.e., averaged over 200) for 5 min.
- The name of the sensor to be sampled.
- The baseline value for comparison, for example 110 for the "seriousHRG" measurement.
- The comparison direction, i.e., whether abnormality is indicated if the sensor value is above the baseline or below the baseline.
- The sampling period, for example 30 s or one minute.
- The number of samples to be used in computing the approximation to the integral, for example 10 samples.

This information would produce an XML expression like the following

```
<INTEGRAL   name="seriousHRG"    sensor="bloodSugarLevel"
            baseline=110         direction="ABOVE"
            period=30            periodUnits="SECONDS"
            numberOfSamples=10
/>
```

Such XML expressions would then be used later along with all the other XML expressions from the designer interface to automatically generate computer code to run on the processing element as described in Sect. 4.5.

Once the necessary information has been determined, the interface for collecting that information is easy to design. Fields with user-created text are displayed as text boxes. Fields in which the user should select from a given set of options are presented as either radio buttons or drop-down menus. A sample screen is shown in Fig. 2. The integral name, baseline, period and number of samples are text boxes. The sensor name is a drop-down menu because the system being defined could have arbitrarily many sensors with user-defined names. The direction is a pair of radio buttons. The period unit is a drop-down menu because there are a specific set of options.

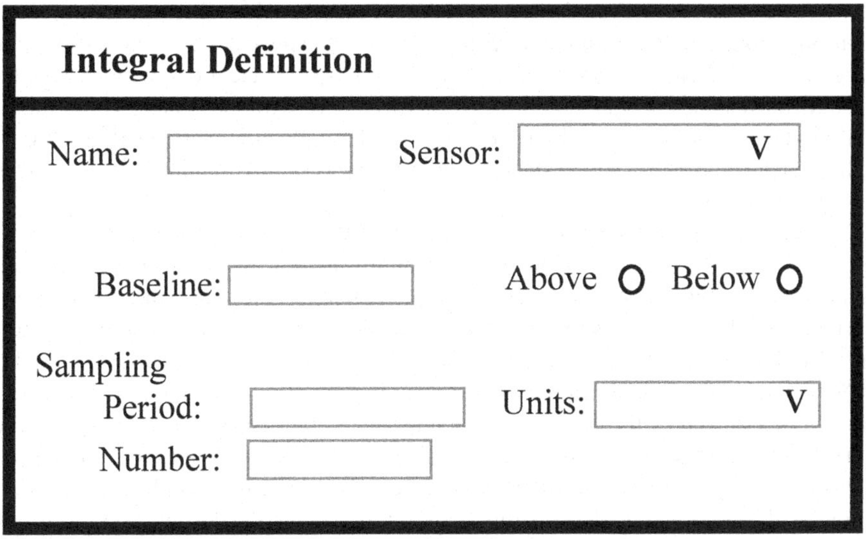

Fig. 2. Sample screen to specify an integral

4.2 Access to Information Outside the Wearable Device

Many wearable applications may find information from outside the wearable device useful in determining how to respond to events or even when events actually occur.

One example, a motion sickness wearable device, was described in Sect. 3. For another example, consider the monitoring of an athlete during performance. External conditions such as weather (general temperature, humidity, percent sunlight, etc.) would be useful in analyzing the athlete's performance. While some of these may be obtained by including additional sensors in the wearable product, that adds additional cost to the product and may not provide all the desired information. For example, air temperature around the body could be sensed, but general relative humidity or percent sunlight might not be. The wearable product could obtain this information through a weather app and then include that information along with the athlete's bio information in the regular reports broadcast to the monitoring base station. It may be sufficient to obtain this information once, say at the beginning of the exercise, if the area of the activity was relatively small. On the other hand, for something like a marathon, in which the athlete would be in different locations, the information might need to be accessed a regular intervals. As a final example, a wearable device that aided a blind person to walk around a city would find information about congested areas from the local traffic control system very useful in selecting routes to guide the person. This information would need to be accessed at regular intervals because the congestion information can change as the person continues the journey. Such information from outside sources can be used in all the same ways that readings from the wearable sensors can be used.

We assume our designer system will have a database of sources for external information. This database would include details such as how to access the information through the internet, what information the wearable device must provide when requesting external information, what information the external source can provide, how that information is encoded in the byte stream sent out by the external source, etc. For a weather app, for example, the database would include a URL to access the external source. The database would indicate that the wearable device must send the location, perhaps through GPS reading, and would return a byte string containing temperature, humidity, wind, percent sunshine, etc.

The designer's interface would show a list of external sources when requested by the designer. The list would indicate the kinds of information available from that source. Figure 3 shows a sample screen. After the designer clicks to select an external source, the interface would show details for that source. The designer can select what information is needed. Further, the designer would provide a name for each one that could be used in CONDITION and ACTION elements described in Sect. 2. Finally, the designer would specify other attributes for this source, such as access on demand or access at regular intervals. Figure 4 shows a sample screen for specifying the information from one source. In this case, one field has already been specified. The designer would click the ADD button to add additional fields from this source. When done, the designer system would generate an XML expression to be used later by the automatic code generation process. Here is an example of the XML.

```
<EXTERNALSOURCE   name="weather"   request="periodic"
                  period="10"      periodUnits="seconds"
>
      <ITEM   internalName="temp"      field="temperature" />
      <ITEM   internalName="humidity'   field="humidity" />
</EXTERNALSOURCE>
```

This XML expression indicates that the external source "weather" is to be accessed every 10 s. Two pieces of information may be used from the data obtained from this app. The temperature field in the external data stream is to be extracted and is referred to in other XML expressions in the designer system as weather.temp. The humidity field in the external data stream is to be extracted and is referred to in other XML expressions as weather.humidity. For example, a CONDITION expression might include a condition like "weather.humidity > 65".

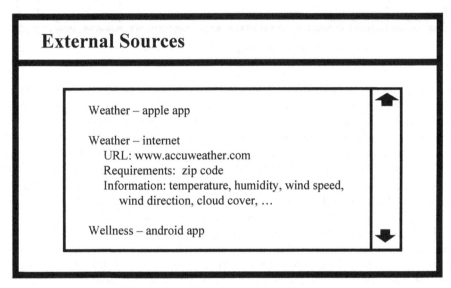

Fig. 3. Screen for selecting external sources

4.3 Advanced Actuator Control

In [5], the actions that a designer could specify were simple – turn a digital actuator on or off, activate an analog actuator with a fixed value in its analog range, or transmit a fixed message over the wireless connection. Many wearable apps, and embedded systems in general, require more sophisticated control of the analog actuators. For example, in a wearable diabetes monitor with an insulin pump, the strength with which the pump is activated will likely depend on the degree of high blood sugar level over time. A sudden spike would require a surge of insulin, whereas a moderately high level would require only a slight amount of insulin. In some cases, the analog device should run at the initial

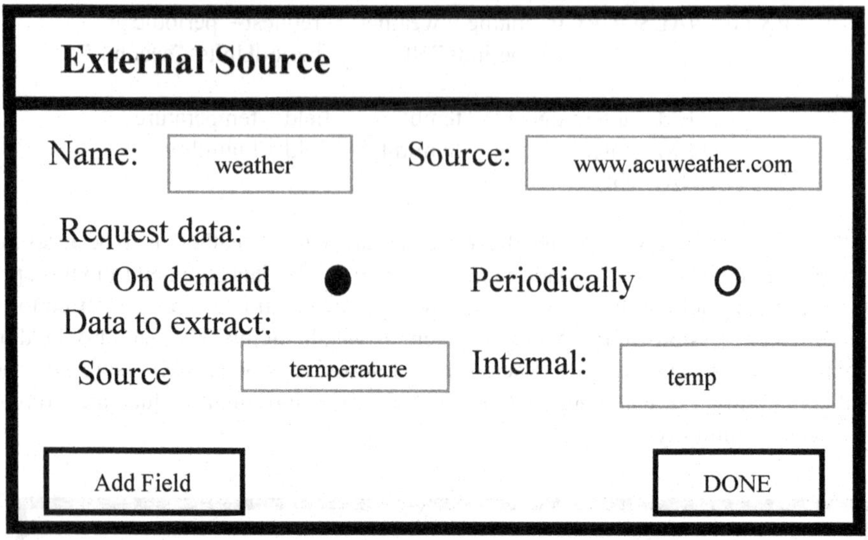

Fig. 4. Screen for selecting fields from an external source

level for a specified period of time. For example, a slightly high blood sugar level over, say, 30 min might indicate a low insulin dosage for 2 min. In other cases, the level of analog operation should be adjusted at regular intervals depending on how the wearer is reacting to the device's output. For example, a sudden spike would require a high initial insulin dose and monitoring every minute for adjustments and eventual termination. Or, the designer might define another EVENT element that would specify when to turn the analog device off. (Note, although not of interest to the HCI community, we mention that the test for starting the action would be temporarily deactivated. After the action terminated, testing for the start condition would be reactivated.)

Figure 5 shows the basic screen for defining a complex analog action. The common information for all such actions includes a name, the actuator device, and the choice of one of the three termination methods. When the radio button for specific time is selected, a pop-up menu allows the designer to specify the time (quantity and units, for example 2 min). When the radio button for monitoring is selected, additional inputs on the designer's screen allow for entering the time (quantity and units) for the monitoring period, the formula for adjusting the analog device, and the condition for turning the analog device off and terminating the monitoring process. Figure 5 shows a case in which the insulin pump is adjusted every 2 min until the blood sugar level goes below 110. The screen shown in Fig. 5 would produce an XML expression like the following.

```
<ANALOGACTION    name="spikeAction"
            device="insulinPump"   control="monitor"
            monitorPeriod="2"        monitorPeriodUnits="minutes"
            initialValue="(seriousHRG-100)/4"
            adjustedValue="(bloodSugarLevel-100)/4"
            termination="bloodsSugarLevel<110"
</ANALOGACTION>
```

Assuming bloodSugarLevel has a maximum value 1000, the expression (seriousHRG-100)/4 puts the initialValue in the range 0–255, suitable for passing to an 8-bit analog-to-digital convertor, which would then produce an analog voltage for controlling the pump. The action would be terminated when the blood sugar level reached below 110. The name spikeAction could be used in an ACTION element in an EVENT element, as described in Sect. 2.

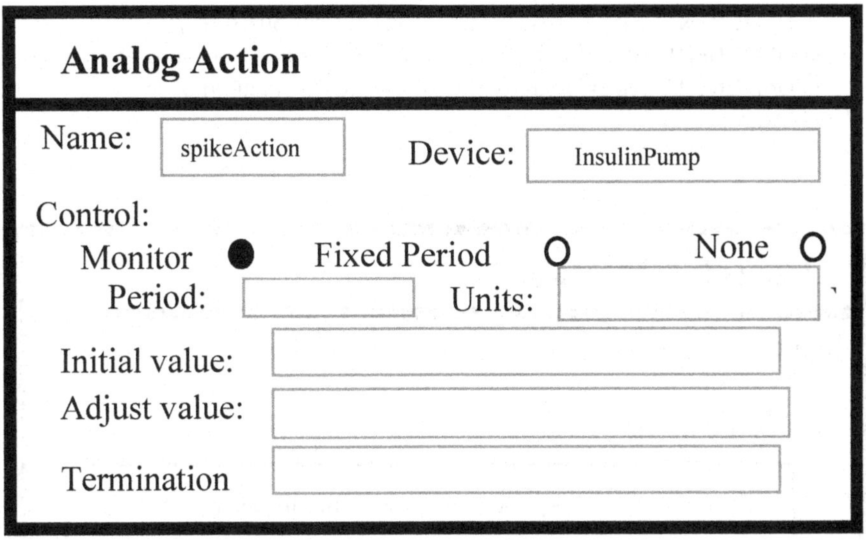

Fig. 5. Screen for specifying a complex analog action

4.4 Advanced Reporting

The fourth extension to our prior work provides for more informative messages from the wearable product to the outside world. In [5], a message contained only predefined text. In many applications it is useful for the outside world to receive information from the sensors and the status of actuators. For example, a doctor would want to know more about a blood sugar spike than just that it happened. The doctor would want to know the blood sugar level and the dosage of insulin being pumped.

In our system, the designer specifies a complex message by describing a sequence of components. Each component is either a text string, a formula based on sensor information, or the name of an actuator whose status is to be reported. The screen allows the designer to enter a name for the message and displays the content specified so far. The user adds additional components by clicking one of three buttons to add text, add a sensor formula, or add an actuator name. The designer clicks a DONE button when finished. Figure 6 shows a partially defined complex message in which the designer has already specified three components for the message – a text string, the name of a sensor, and a text string. The designer interface generates an XML expression like the following when the user clicks DONE, and this expression is used by the automatic code generation module to generate suitable computer code to construct and send this message when called for in an ACTION element.

```
<MESSAGE   name="spikeMessage">
    <COMPONENT  type="text"  value="Blood sugar level spike of severity " />
    <COMPONENT  type="sensorData"    value="seriousHRG" />
    <COMPONENT  type="text"          value=". Pump operating at level " />
    <COMPONENT  type="actuatorStatus"  value="insulinPump" />
</MESSAGE>
```

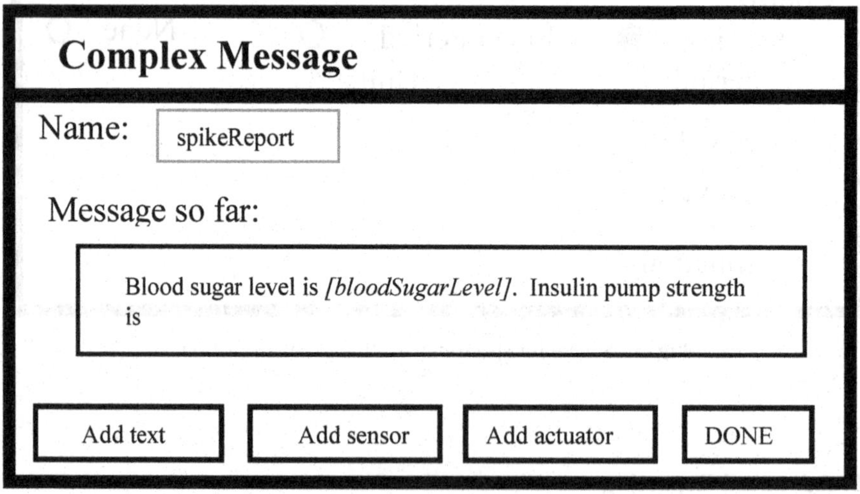

Complex Message

Name: spikeReport

Message so far:

Blood sugar level is *[bloodSugarLevel]*. Insulin pump strength is

| Add text | Add sensor | Add actuator | DONE |

Fig. 6. Screen for specifying a message

4.5 Automatic Generation of Computer Code

Automatic generation of the program that runs on the wearable computing device is a topic in computer science and not of direct interest to the HCI community. Therefore, we give here only a brief description of what the automatically generated code would look like. Computation of an integral and scheduling of the monitoring process in a complex action require the use of a scheduling queue. The queue contains a sequence of records in time order, each of which gives the name of a function to be called and possibly information about records that have to be reinserted into the queue. For example, in computing an integral, the function that updates the integral must be called, and the record itself has to be reinserted in the queue in preparation for the next sampling time. The function that actually computes the integral maintains an array of the previous N readings, takes a new reading, deletes the oldest reading from the array, inserts the new one at the beginning, and recomputes the integral. The function that adjusts an actuator that is being monitored simply evaluates the adjustment formula and sends the new value to the device. The function that extracts information from an external source calls the app that accesses the external source, then extracts the indicated bytes and performs conversion as required, for example converting a text string to an internal integer. The function that sends a complex message simply evaluates the sensor formulas and retrieves the current status of the indicated actuators and inserts into a string, after which it sends the string to the wireless transmission function.

5 Closing Remarks

We have described major extensions to our previous work on embedded system designer interface systems. Conditions that trigger actions can be more sophisticated, involving the aggregation or integration of sensor input over time. Actions in response to triggering conditions can involve computations based on sensor readings as well as conditions that can adjust or terminate the response over time. Conditions can be based on information received from outside the wearable system. These major extensions greatly expand the set of wearable systems for which the computer code can be automatically generated. Moreover, many applications in other areas of embedded systems also require these more sophisticated condition/action capabilities, and the methods described in this paper apply equally well to them.

This work also illustrates again for the HCI community that designer interfaces, that is interfaces used by people to design other products, can often be set up to include appropriate information so that the designer system can automatically generate some or all of the design of the new product. This has been a continuing thesis in our work for the past decade.

References

1. Proceedings of the International Symposium on Wearable Computers years 2011 through 2021
2. Henschen, L.J., Lee, J.C.: A web-based interface for a system that designs sensor networks. In: Kurosu, M. (ed.) HCI 2013. LNCS, vol. 8007, pp. 688–697. Springer, Heidelberg (2013). https://doi.org/10.1007/978-3-642-39330-3_74
3. Henschen, L., Lee, J.: Human-computer interfaces for sensor/actuator networks. In: Kurosu, M. (ed.) HCI 2016. LNCS, vol. 9732, pp. 379–387. Springer, Cham (2016). https://doi.org/10.1007/978-3-319-39516-6_36

4. Henschen, L., Lee, J., Guthmann, R.: Automatic generation of human-computer interfaces from BacNET descriptions. In: Proceedings of the 20th HCII International Conference, vol. 21, pp. 71–84 (2018)
5. Henschen, L.J., Lee, J.C.: User interface for vehicle theft recovery system. In: Krömker, H. (ed.) HCII 2021. LNCS, vol. 12791, pp. 56–72. Springer, Cham (2021). https://doi.org/10. 1007/978-3-030-78358-7_4

An Analysis of Communication Balance in Online Consensus-Building Game

Kyoko Ito[1]([⊠]) [ID], Daisuke Komaki[2], and Hiroshi Shimoda[2]

[1] Faculty of Engineering, Kyoto Tachibana University, 34 Yamada-cho, Oyake, Yamashina-ku, Kyoto 6078175, Japan
ito@tachibana-u.ac.jp
[2] Graduate School of Energy Science, Kyoto University, Yoshida-honmachi, Sakyo-ku, Kyoto 6068501, Japan
{komaki,shimoda}@ei.energy.kyoto-u.ac.jp

Abstract. In this study, we conducted an online consensus-building experiment using a game with a correct answer, aiming at proposing the mechanism of consensus-building. Specifically, we conducted an online experiment with 40 participants in 10 groups using the NASA game in which participants build consensus on the order of 15 items. Using the results, the communication balance was analyzed. The results of the analysis using the variation in communication balance indicated that a medium variation in communication balance might be better as a relationship between the variation in communication balance of the number of remarks, the final error score, and the error score change.

Keywords: Online communication · Consensus-building · NASA game · Communication balance · Variation

1 Introduction

We build consensus to make group decisions in our daily lives. Consensus building has also been observed in the behavior of animals, such as honeybees, fish, and birds and is the basis of social behavior. It has been studies in the fields of economics [1], biology [2], and social neuroscience [3]. Support methods using information technology have also been proposed [4].

However, it is not clear how people build consensus, and especially which factors influence the outcome of consensus building. In this study, we have conducted an experiment using an online consensus-building game toward proposing a mechanism for consensus building. In our previous study, we conducted experiments and analyses focusing on the amount of group remarks and their answers [5]. In this study, we have analyzed the communication balance using the consensus building game with correct answers.

M. Kurosu (Ed.): HCII 2022, LNCS 13302, pp. 211–221, 2022.
https://doi.org/10.1007/978-3-031-05311-5_14

2 Method

2.1 NASA Game

To provide a setting for consensus building, we have focused on the framework of the "NASA game" [6], which is used in various training programs and social psychology exercises. The NASA game is a game in which the rank of 15 given items is determined by consensus building, assuming the situation of an astronaut crash-landing on the moon. In the game, the ranks of 15 items are determined by the participants' consensus. In this game, there are "correct answers" for the ranks of each item, and the error between the individually determined ranks and the ranks by group consensus are compared, and the way of consensus building is examined. The error, that is, score of the answer is obtained from the following formula:

$$Error\ Score = \sum_{i=1}^{15} |Order_i - Correct_i| \tag{1}$$

where i is the item number, Order i is the rank assigned to item i, Correct i is the rank of the correct answer for item i, and the Error Score is the sum of the differences (absolute values) between the correct answers for each of the 15 items. The smaller the Score, the closer it is to the correct answer. The minimum of the Error Score is the value when all answers match the correct answer, i.e., 0.

2.2 Experimental Procedure

Using NASA game and online chat, we have had the following flow of consensus building.

1. Each participant reads the problem statement and determine the ranks of 15 items.
2. To begin the consensus building process, the average of all participants' ranks are calculated, and from the ranks, the ranks of the 15 items are determined by consensus.
3. The "correct answers" are notified, and the error between the "correct answer" of the ranks determined by each participant and the "correct answer" of the ranks by consensus are calculated.

Individual rankings were given 5 min and group discussions were given 65 min. This experiment was conducted using the online NASA game system developed by the authors. In this system, participants are automatically sorted into groups, and consensus is built through online chat without knowing who the other participants are.

2.3 Number of Groups

There are 10 groups (1A, 1B, 1C, 1D, 1E, 1F, 2A, 2B, 2C, and 2D) with 4 participants per group. A total of 40 graduate students participated in the experiment.

3 A Hypothesis on Communication Balance

In this study, the analysis focuses on the communication balance within the group. When starting a group discussion, the group's first answer is prepared by averaging the individual answers. Then, the group members discuss to build consensus, revise the answers, and prepare the final answer as a group. From the flow, we hypothesized that the individual answers (Individual Error Score) and the first answer of the group (Initial Error Score) would affect the balance of the group discussion, and that the balance of the group discussion (Variation of Communication Balance) would affect the final answer of the group (Final Error Score), or the error score improvement (Error Score Change). The hypotheses are shown in Fig. 1.

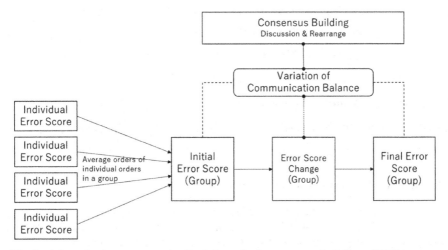

Fig. 1. A hypothesis on communication balance in the consensus building of NASA game.

In this study, the standard deviation of the amount of remarks of individuals in the group divided by the mean of the amount of remarks was used to compare the variation of communication balance in each group. The Eqs. (2) to (4) and (5) to (7) are used to calculate VCB_R and VCB_C, respectively, as the variation in communication balance in the amount of remarks and the variation in communication balance in the number of characters, respectively.

$$\sigma_R = \sqrt{\sum_{i=1}^{N}(R_i - \overline{R})/N} \tag{2}$$

$$\overline{R} = \sum_{i=1}^{N} R_i/N \tag{3}$$

$$VCB_R = \frac{\sigma_R}{\overline{R}} \tag{4}$$

$$\sigma_C = \sqrt{\sum_{i=1}^{N}(C_i - \overline{C})/N} \tag{5}$$

$$\overline{C} = \sum_{i=1}^{N} C_i/N \tag{6}$$

$$VCB_C = \frac{\sigma_C}{\overline{C}} \tag{7}$$

R_i : *Number of individual remarks*

N : *Number of individuals in a group*

C_i : *Total number of Caracters in individual remarks*

3.1 Score and Amount of Remarks

Tables 1 and 2 show the score and the amount of remarks by the individuals and groups, respectively.

3.2 Analysis of Communication Balance

Based on the results in Tables 1 and 2, we conducted an analysis of communication balance. Score Change in Table 2 indicates the initial error score minus the final error score, and the smaller the value is, the better it is. From Table 2, final error scores in the 20s, 30s, and 40s are designated as "Excellent," "Good," and "Poor," respectively, and are indicated by circles, squares, and triangles in the following figures. The groups were 4, 4, and 2, respectively.

Figures 1 and 2 show the relationship between the variation in communication balance and the final error score. Figure 1 shows the relationship with the number of remarks, and Fig. 2 shows the relationship with the number of characters.

From Fig. 2, the "Good" groups showed moderate variation in communication balance, the "Poor" groups showed small variation, and the "Excellent" groups showed moderate variation. From Fig. 3, the trend of each group was not clear when compared to Fig. 2.

Table 1. Individual participant error scores and volume of individual remarks.

User ID	Individual error score	Number of individual remarks	Number of characters
1A1	26	21	1622
1A2	32	7	200
1A3	52	17	1247
1A4	32	17	586
1B1	36	20	578
1B2	40	24	645
1B3	42	8	131
1B4	22	17	483
1C1	40	8	423
1C2	38	3	229
1C3	46	9	354
1C4	36	12	471
1D1	36	6	339
1D2	64	8	273
1D3	44	8	405
1D4	42	16	1247
1E1	32	12	489
1E2	62	12	852
1E3	52	11	432
1E4	32	11	473
1F1	26	10	377
1F2	40	9	225
1F3	50	4	194
1F4	88	8	452
2A1	54	8	584
2A2	38	11	1132
2A3	28	13	1229
2A4	38	7	228
2B1	24	18	861
2B2	22	21	1386
2B3	22	17	624
2B4	38	10	175
2C1	74	17	1320
2C2	38	12	514

(*continued*)

Table 1. (*continued*)

User ID	Individual error score	Number of individual remarks	Number of characters
2C3	38	11	402
2C4	56	11	716
2D1	28	27	1485
2D2	36	11	408
2D3	34	6	214
2D4	56	20	898

Table 2. Groups' error scores and volume of remarks.

Group name	Initial error score	Final error score	Score change	Number of remarks	Number of characters
1A	28	22	−6	62	3655
1B	30	38	8	69	1837
1C	32	30	−2	32	1477
1D	40	34	−6	38	2264
1E	38	44	6	46	2246
1F	30	26	−4	31	1248
2A	34	22	−12	39	3173
2B	26	20	−6	66	3046
2C	34	40	6	51	2952
2D	30	30	0	64	3005

Figure 4 shows the relationship between the variation in the communication balance of the number of remarks and the variation in the communication balance of the number of characters. The Excellent, Good, and Poor groups (groups with the same mark) would appear to vary vertically, suggesting that the characteristics of the groups may appear more in the number of remarks than in the number of characters. It seems that the characteristics of the groups might appear in the number of remarks rather than the number of characters.

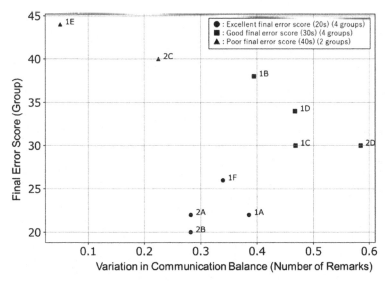

Fig. 2. Relationship between variation of communication balance and final error score (for remarks).

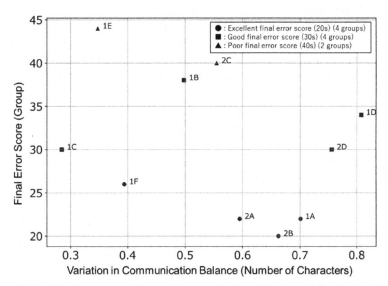

Fig. 3. Relationship between variation of communication balance and final error score (for characters).

Figures 5 and 6 show the relationship between the initial error score and the variation in communication balance. Figure 5 shows the relationship with the number of remarks, and Fig. 6 shows the relationship with the number of characters.

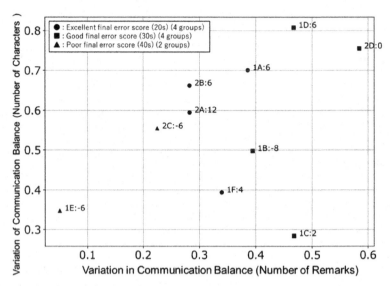

Fig. 4. Relationship between variation of communication balance for characters and for remarks.

Figures 7 and 8 show the relationship between the variation in communication balance and the error score change. From Fig. 7, the smaller the score change is, the better the error score is. The Excellent group has a large score change in the good direction; the Good group has a score change in the middle to worse direction; the Poor group also has a score change in the worse direction. Figure 8 shows that the trend of each group is not as clear as in Fig. 7.

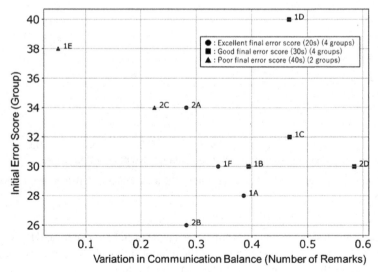

Fig. 5. Relationship between variation of communication balance and initial error score (for remarks).

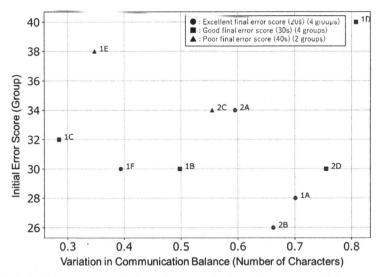

Fig. 6. Relationship between variation of communication balance and initial error score (for characters).

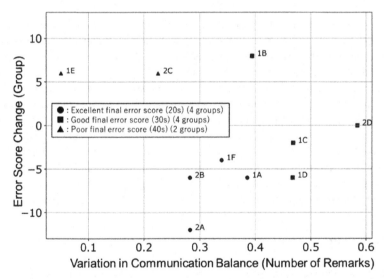

Fig. 7. Relationship between variation of communication balance and error score change (for remarks).

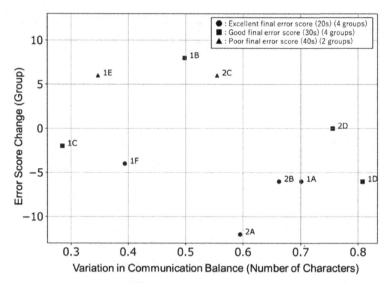

Fig. 8. Relationship between variation of communication balance and error score change (for characters).

The results suggest that the number of remarks might be more important than the number of characters with respect to the variation in communication balance. Figures 2 and 7 show that the final error score and error score change are better when the variation in communication balance is in the middle range.

In the case where the variation in communication balance is small, it is assumed that it is difficult to properly build a consensus because there is no coordinator, facilitator, etc., since all members speak equally. On the other hand, if the variation in communication balance is large, it is assumed that the number of remarks is unbalanced and that there is no proper communication and that it is difficult to properly build a consensus. For this reason, it is assumed that when the variation in communication balance is in the middle range, there would be a moderate summarizing role, communication among all members will take place, and the result of consensus building will be better.

4   Conclusion

In this study, we conducted an online consensus-building experiment using a game with a correct answer, aiming at proposing the mechanism of consensus-building. Specifically, we conducted an online experiment with 40 participants in 10 groups using the NASA game in which participants build consensus on the order of 15 items. Using the results, the communication balance was analyzed.

The results of the analysis using the variation in communication balance indicated that a medium variation in communication balance might be better as a relationship between the variation in communication balance of the number of remarks, the final error score, and the error score change.

In the near future, we would like to aim to find factors that lead to better consensus building, and find the points for better consensus building toward proposing a consensus building mechanism.

Acknowledgement. This work was supported by JSPS KAKENHI Grant Number 20H01748.

References

1. Arrow, K.J.: Social Choice and Individual Values, 3rd edn. Yale University Press (2012). (Japanese translation by H. Osana, Keisoshobo, 2013)
2. Seeley, T.D., Visscher, P.K.: Group decision making in nest-site selection by honey bees. Apidologie **35**(2), 101–116 (2004)
3. Suzuki, S., Adachi, R., Dunne, S., Bossaerts, P., O'Doherty, J.P.: Neural mechanisms underlying human consensus decision-making. Neuron **86**, 591–602 (2015)
4. Fukuda, N., Fukushima, T., Ito, T., Taniguchi, T., Yokoo, M.: Artificial intelligence technologies for decision-making and consensus building in a complex society. Trans. Jpn. Soc. Artif. Intell. **34**(6), 863–869 (2019). (in Japanese)
5. Ito, K., Komaki, D., Shimoda H.: Analysis of the results of an online consensus-building game. In: Proceedings of STSS/ISOFIC/ISSNP 2021, Okayama (2021)
6. Hall, J.: Decisions, decisions, decisions. Psychol. Today **5**, 51–54 (1971)

A Study on Consensus Building Mechanism Based on Kansei ~Consideration of Experimental Tasks that Cause Conflicts~

Ryota Kamakari[1]([✉]), Mizuki Yamawaki[1], Yoshiki Sakamoto[1,2P], Kimi Ueda[1] [ID],
Hirotake Ishii[1] [ID], Hiroshi Shimoda[1] [ID], and Kyoko Ito[3] [ID]

[1] Graduate School of Energy Science, Kyoto University, Kyoto, Japan
{kamakari,yamawaki,hirotake,shimoda}@ei.energy.kyoto-u.ac.jp
[2] Nomura Research Institute, Ltd., Chiyoda, Japan
[3] Faculty of Engineering, Department of Information and Computer Science,
Kyoto Tachibana University, Kyoto, Japan
ito-ky@tachibana-u.ac.jp

Abstract. We are engaged in a variety of consensus-building activities in our daily lives. In order to build consensus, it is necessary to reach a single conclusion unanimously. Therefore, if there are conflicting opinions, they need to be resolved. To deal with this problem, it is necessary to conduct pleasant communication during consensus building in order for both parties to keep a good relationship, and Kansei has been found to be important for this purpose. Until now, there have not been many studies from the perspective of "Kansei". And in actual important consensus-building situations, the interlocutors are confident and particular about their opinions, and they often do not bend their opinions to each other, which causes conflicts. In order to simulate such situation to conduct a consensus building experiment, it is necessary to develop tasks that allow the experimental participants to engage seriously even in the laboratory room. Therefore, in this study, we have attempted to develop a new task meeting three requirements; (1) The process of consensus building does not involve concessions but conflicts. (2) Sufficient time and the number of statements for consensus building can be secured for analysis. (3) The process of consensus building can be observed and recorded in detail. And we conducted consensus-building experiments using the developed task. As a result, it was found that there was no ceding and conflicts occur, and that the time and number of statements required for process analysis of consensus building might be more than those in our previous studies.

Keywords: Consensus building · Communication · Kansei · Experimental task

1 Introduction

We are involved in a variety of consensus-building activities, ranging from trivial decisions such as where to go on a trip to severe decisions such as whether to restart a nuclear power plant. "A group reaches consensus on a decision when every member can agree

© The Author(s), under exclusive license to Springer Nature Switzerland AG 2022
M. Kurosu (Ed.): HCII 2022, LNCS 13302, pp. 222–231, 2022.
https://doi.org/10.1007/978-3-031-05311-5_15

to support that decision" [1]. As can be seen from this statement, in order to form a consensus, it is necessary in principle to reach a unanimous conclusion.

Therefore, when there are conflicting opinions, it is necessary to reconcile these opinions to reach a conclusion. In addition, with the spread of the Internet, smartphones, and social networking services, there are more and more opportunities for consensus building through text chatting, such as scheduling appointments with friends. And there are many studies comparing computer-mediated communication to face-to-face communication [2, 3]. However, since text chatting is a text-only communication, it is difficult to convey non-verbal information such as feelings and sensations which contributes to resolve conflicts.

The importance of "Kansei" communication has been pointed out in response to these problems, and it is known that Kansei plays an important role in communication in order to achieve pleasant communication [4]. Therefore, analyzing not only the results of consensus building but also the process from the viewpoint of Kansei may provide suggestions for smooth and amicable consensus building methods. However, although many researchers in the humanities have analyzed the process of consensus building based on verbal information such as the contents of conversations, there have been few studies that have observed and analyzed the consensus building process from the viewpoint of Kansei [5]. In addition, in order to analyze the process of consensus building in detail, it is necessary to analyze the process with high temporal resolution, which is to analyze the time interval in a short period of time. However, no research has been reported on observing and analyzing the consensus building process with high temporal resolution from the viewpoint of Kansei.

2 Related Studies and Purpose

2.1 Related Studies

Consensus building is not a behavior unique to humans; it has been observed in honeybees, fish, and birds. For example, T. D. Seeley et al. [6] studied the mechanism of group decision making that underlie the nest-site selection process in honeybees.

And various studies have been done on the process of consensus building in humans, both in laboratory settings and in actual consensus building situations.

First, as a study of consensus building in a laboratory environment, Hamada et al. [5] conducted a multiple-choice consensus-building task in a laboratory room. Then, they classified the consensus-building process into six patterns and examined their characteristics. The results suggested that the time required for consensus building differed depending on the pattern. Suzuki et al. [7] studied the computational and neural mechanisms underlying consensus building using a computational framework. And it was found that participants reached consensus decisions by combining their preferences and information about the majority group members' choices.

Next, as a study that observed actual consensus-building situations, some researchers have focused on consensus building to enhance disaster preparedness in rural cities that are vulnerable to disasters. Okutani et al. [8] studied the consensus building of small and medium-sized enterprises in rural areas in developing business continuity plans to enhance the disaster preparedness of the area. Ishikawa [9] focused on the recovery process in Iwanuma City, Miyagi Prefecture after the Great East Japan Earthquake. As a result of clarifying the characteristics of the recovery plan in Iwanuma City, where community-based recovery was conducted, it became clear that consensus building is an essential element of community-based recovery and that each stage of consensus building has a different role.

As described above, many studies have been conducted to analyze the process of consensus building based on the content of conversations. However, there has been no study that has analyzed the process of consensus building based on the Kansei during consensus building.

2.2 Review of Previous Studies

The following is our previous study that analyzed the process of consensus building by focusing on Kansei. Sakamoto [10], a member of our research group, attempted to analyze the consensus-building process based on subjective evaluations to clarify the mechanism from the viewpoint of Kansei. We conducted an experiment on the theme of "which hot spring inn and which plan to book when going on a two-day trip to Arima Onsen with classmates from the laboratory as a graduation trip." However, a problem arose in the form of a low sense of involvement in the consensus-building theme and low task motivation among the experimental participants. In fact, in the interviews with the experiment participants, they said, "Since I am not actually going on a trip, I do not feel motivated to oppose the idea even if I do not agree with it". Sakamoto also conducted a consensus-building experiment on the theme of "Think of a motto to boost the current tourism of Kyoto City in Covid-19 situation." However, in this experiment, the same problem as in the previous experiment arose: low awareness of the parties involved in the consensus-building theme, and low motivation of the experiment participants toward the task. In this experiment, there was no choice of answers for the slogan creation task, and there was no clear correct answer, so it was difficult to give an opposing opinion, which may have caused a conflict.

In contrast, Ito [11] who is also a member of our research team attempted to solve these problems by conducting a consensus-building task called "Consensus to Match" Game. An overview of the Consensus to Match Game is shown in Fig. 1. In the Consensus to Match Game, two couples of two participants who know each other are recruited, making a total of four participants in the experiment. However, it is assumed that there is no acquaintance between the members of the couples. First, they create pairs of couples that have never met each other before. For example, when userA and userB are acquaintances, and userX and userY are acquaintances, there is no acquaintance between the couples, so two unacquainted pairs are made by creating the pairs userA and userX, and userB and userY. Then, the pairs are asked to reach a consensus on the topic, "Choose one of the three options such that the choices match between the pairs". If the choices match between the pairs, then all four participants will receive their choice as a prize. On the other hand, if the choices do not match, none of the four participants will receive anything. This game was devised because they thought that this prize would serve as an incentive for consensus-building, which would solve the problem mentioned earlier of the low sense of ownership of the theme and the low motivation toward the task. The reason why acquaintances were chosen as participants was to increase the amount of conversation by sharing information such as the preferences and personalities of acquaintances with non-acquaintances when discussing the choice. As a result, the motivation of the participants in the experiment was maintained, and they were able to maintain a certain amount of speech. The results showed that "change rate in likability to the other person" and "change rate in likability from the other person" increased with time elapsed. On the other hand, "likability" tended to increase with consensus progressed, such as drawing and deciding on conclusions, while it tended to decrease when consensus suspended, such as organizing the information and reasons necessary for deciding on conclusions.

While they found a connection between consensus building and Kansei, in some conversations, concessions of opinion to avoid responsibility was found, such as "I don't know much, so you decide", and conflicts did not arise. In actual important consensus-building situations, the interlocutors are confident and particular about their opinions, and they often do not bend their opinions to each other, which causes conflicts. Therefore, this task does not reflect the actual important consensus building situations.

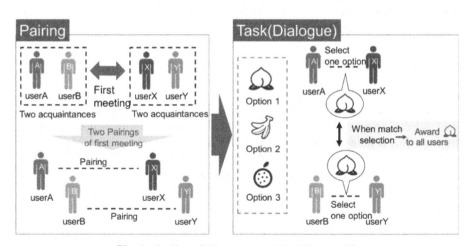

Fig. 1. Outline of "Consensus to Match" game [9].

2.3 Purpose

In this study, we aim to clarify the mechanism of consensus building from the viewpoint of Kansei by analyzing the process of consensus building based on subjective evaluation. In order to do so, the purpose of this study is to solve the problems described in the previous section by examining consensus-building tasks that do not cause concessions but generate conflicts. In this study, we design a task that satisfies such a requirement, and examine whether or not the task satisfies the requirement through experiment.

3 Experimental Task Design

3.1 Requirements for the Experimental Task

The experimental task must satisfy the following three requirements.

- (Requirement 1) The process of consensus building does not involve concessions but conflicts.
- (Requirement 2) Sufficient time and the number of statements for consensus building can be secured for analysis.
- (Requirement 3) The process of consensus building can be observed and recorded in detail.

The reason for setting (Requirement 1) is that the experimental task needs to reflect an actual important consensus-building situation in which the interlocutors are confident and particular about their opinions and conflicts arise.

The reason for setting (Requirement 2) is that if a consensus is reached immediately, it is difficult to capture changes in Kansei because it is impossible to obtain a sufficient amount of dialogue logs.

The reason for setting (Requirement 3) is that it is necessary to analyze the process of consensus building with high temporal resolution after the consensus-building in order to capture detailed changes in Kansei.

3.2 Contents of the Task

We designed the task shown in Fig. 2 as a task that satisfies the three requirements as described in Sect. 3.1. In this task, two experimental participants, userX and userY, are asked to decide by consensus which of them will wait for 60 min without doing anything. The consensus building will be done using text chat because the process of consensus building has to be observed and recorded in detail (Requirement 3). Three foods (respectively about 10 U.S. dollars) are prepared for each participant as negotiating materials for

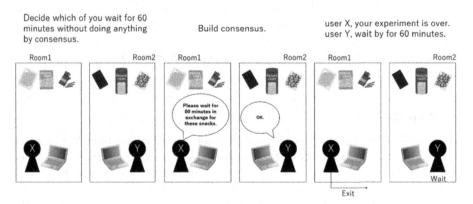

Fig. 2. Task devised in this study.

reaching a consensus. Each participant has a different food item. For example, "Please wait for 60 min in exchange for this food and this food," and by exchanging these foods, they decide who will wait for 60 min without doing anything. Here, "wait for 60 min without doing anything" here means to wait for 60 min under the supervision of the experimenter without operating a smartphone or computer, or sleeping.

We designed this task because we supposed that by setting a certain punishment of "waiting for 60 min without doing anything", there would be no concessions as seen in previous studies but conflicts. In addition, we expected that this would satisfy (Requirement 1) and (Requirement 2). In this study, we conducted an experiment to confirm whether this task satisfies the requirements.

4 Experiment

4.1 Experimental Environment

The experiments were conducted from October 29 to December 14, 2021, in experimental rooms of Kyoto University. PCs connected to the network were used as the terminal of the text chat communication in the experiment. The food items as the negotiating materials were arranged in front of the participants. They were in separate rooms and did not know each other's identity.

The text chat system used in the experiment is shown in Fig. 3. The chat system was implemented using HTML, JavaScript, and CSS. Google Firebase was used as the database in which the dialogue and answers of questionnaire were collected. By using this chat system, they answered questionnaires, "the change in favorability toward the other person" when receiving every message, and "the expected change in favorability from the other person" when sending every message, using a 9-point scale from -4 to $+4$, respectively (-4: Lower, 0: No change, $+4$: Higher).

4.2 Participants

The participants of the experiment were ten graduate and undergraduate students of Kyoto University. Since each of them worked in pairs to build consensus, a total of five trials were conducted. They were unaware of the purpose and intent of the experiment.

4.3 Procedure

The experiment consisted of explanation, practice, task, and final questionnaire. In the experiment, the experimenter first explained the text chat system and the consensus building task. Then, the participants were asked to practice using the text chat system for about three minutes. Then, they performed the task described in Sect. 3 using the text chat system. During the chat, they were asked to answer the questions, "the change in favorability toward the other person" when receiving every message, and "the expected change in favorability from the other person" when sending every message, using a 9-point scale from -4 to $+4$, respectively.

-4: Lower, 0: No change, +4: Higher

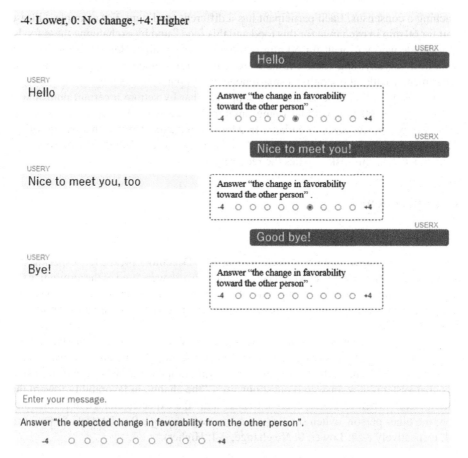

Fig. 3. An example screen of text chat system (UserX).

We expected that we could capture changes in Kansei with a high temporal resolution by responding to changes in their favorability each time they received or sent massages. In Ito et al.'s [11] study using the Consensus to Match Game, it was found that not much change was observed when the participants answered the favorability itself. In this study, we asked them about the "change" in their favorability. The task ended when they reached a consensus.

After the task was completed, they exchanged the foods used in the negotiation and answered two types of questionnaires. They were asked to answer the distance to consensus from 100 to 0, where 100 at the beginning of the dialogue and 0 at the end, while referring to the dialogue log as shown in Fig. 4. Google Spreadsheet was used for the answers. The second questionnaire was an attribute questionnaire, in which they were asked their age and gender. In order to exclude participants who were not accustomed to using text chat (e-mail, LINE, SNS, etc.) from the experiment, the frequency of text chat use was also asked in five grades: "frequently every day", "frequently almost every day", "several times every two or three days", "several times a week" and "rarely". Since the frequency of text chat use for all the experimental participants was "frequently every day" or "frequently almost every day", no participant was excluded from the experimental results. The Big Five scale [12] was used to examine the influence of personality on consensus building results. In order to reduce the burden on the participants in this experiment, the short version of the Big Five by Namikawa et al. [13] was used. The questions are shown in Table 1. Google Form was used to answer the attribute questionnaire.

	A	B	C	D	E
		Time[s]	Sender	Content	Distance to Consensus
1					
2	1	0	USERX	Hello	100
3	2	12	USERY	Hello!	
4	3	24	USERX	Nice to meet you.	
5	4	36	USERY	Nice to meet you, too.	
6	5	45	USERX	Which one of us should wait?	
7	6	54	USERY	I don't really want to wait.	
8	7	60	USERX	If you give me food, I can wait.	
9	8	71	USERY	If I give you two pieces of food, will you wait?	
10	9	79	USERX	It's okay. What do you have in the way of food?	
11	10	102	USERY	I have ○○, △△, and × ×.	
12	11	115	USERX	OK. I want ○○ and × ×.	
13	12	126	USERY	All right.	
14	13	150	USERX	OK. Thank you.	
15	14	171	USERY	Thank you, too.	0

Fig. 4. Questionnaire screen of the mental distance to consensus.

Table 1. Questionnaires of the big five personality traits

Factor	Questionnaire
Extraversion	Silent, Sociable, Talkative, Extroverted, Cheerful
Conscientiousness	Lax, Loose, Casual, Lazy, Planned, Indiscreet, Methodical
Neuroticism	Anxiety, Worrying, Weak, Nervous, Depressed
Openness	Versatile, Progressive, Ingenious, Quick-witted, Interesting, Curious
Agreeableness	Short-tempered, Easily-angered, Mild, Generous, Self-centered, Kind

Finally, oral interviews were conducted to obtain opinions and impressions about the consensus building task and the use of the text chat system.

5   Results and Discussions

As a result of the experiment, conflicts occurred in four out of the five trials except trial 4. This meant to be due to the fact that most participants in the experiment felt that they wanted to get the foods but did not want to wait for 60 min. Therefore, (Requirement 1) "The process of consensus building does not involve concessions but conflicts" was satisfied in four out of five trials.

The consensus building time, the number of statements and their averages for the five trials are shown in Table 2. In the study by Ito et al. [11] using the Consensus to Match Game, the average time taken to reach consensus was 812.6 s and the average number of statements was 25.7. Therefore, the proposed task in this experiment may have satisfied (Requirement 2) "Sufficient time and the number of statements for consensus building can be secured for analysis." It was supposed to be because there are two stages to reach a consensus: the stage of deciding "who will wait" and the stage of deciding "how to distribute food".

On the other hand, there was a trial such as Trial 4 in which the consensus building time was extremely short and the number of statements was extremely small.

Table 2.   The consensus building time and the number of statements

Trial No.	Consensus Building Time(s)	The Number of Statements
1	2990	85
2	2110	53
3	1945	33
4	547	19
5	2230	48
Mean	1964.4	47.6

The reasons why trial 4 did not satisfy both (Requirement 1) and (Requirement 2) are discussed here. In Trial 4, userY acquired all six foods and waited for 60 min as the result. From the later interview, it was found that userX was not greedy and userY wanted to experience wait for 60 min because he did not usually wait for 60 min without doing anything. Because of these facts, the interests of both participants coincided, resulting in an extremely short consensus building time and an extremely small number of statements.

6   Conclusions and Future Works

In this study, we aimed to clarify the mechanism of consensus building from the viewpoint of Kansei by analyzing the process of consensus building based on subjective evaluation.

In order to achieve this purpose, we tried to solve the problem of the previous study [11] by examining a consensus-building task that does not cause concessions but cause conflicts. In this study, we designed a task that satisfies such requirements, and examined whether or not the task satisfies them through experiments.

As a result, it was found that the task proposed in this study might satisfy both (Requirement 1) "The process of consensus building does not involve concessions but conflicts" and (Requirement 2) "Sufficient time and the number of statements for consensus building can be secured for analysis." This is because there are two stages to reach a consensus: one is to decide who should wait and the other is to decide how to distribute the foods. However, when the interests of both participants are coincident, such as in Trial 4, a conflict do not occur, and there is a possibility that sufficient dialogue time and number of statements are not secured for analysis.

In the future, we would like to design the experiment so that results like those in Trial 4 are minimized as less as possible. In addition, we would like to establish a statistical method to analyze the change in favorability, the distance to agreement, and the Big Five.

References

1. David, S., Thomas, C.L.: How to Make Collaboration Work: Powerful Ways to Build Consensus, Solve Problems, and Make Decisions. Berrett-Koehler Publishers (2002)
2. Dubrovsky, V., Kiesler, S., Sethna, B.: The equalization phenomenon: status effects in computer-mediated and face-to-face decision-making groups. Hum. Comput. Interact. **6**(2), 119–146 (1991)
3. Walther, J.B., Anderson, J.F., Park, D.W.: Interpersonal effects in computer-mediated interaction: a meta-analysis of social and antisocial communication. Commun. Res. **21**(4), 460–487 (1994)
4. Tei, S., Kamagichi, T., Sim, T., Shiizuka, H.: Understanding and supporting users to improve atmosphere of communication by Kansei agents. ISASE **2020**, 6 (2020)
5. Hamada, Y., Maruyama, T., Shoji, H.: Pattern classification of value creative consensus building process in case of multiple-choice. Int. J. Affect. Eng. **18**(3), 129–136 (2019)
6. Thomas, D.S., Kirk, V.P.: Group decision making in nest-site selection by honey bees. Apidologie **35**(2), 101–116 (2004)
7. Suzuki, S., Adachi, R., Dunne, S., Bossaerts, P., O'Doherty, J.P.: Neural mechanisms underlying human consensus decision-making. Neuron **86**(2), 591–602 (2015)
8. Okutani, T., Kobayashi, M., Nambu, H.: Case study of consensus building for enhancement of the regional disaster resilience. Soc. Soc. Manag. Syst. Internet J. **4**(1) (2008)
9. Ishikawa, M.: A study on community-based reconstruction from Great East Japan earthquake disaster – a case study of Iwanuma City in Miyagi-Pref. J. Disast. Res. **10**(5), 807–817 (2015)
10. Sakamoto, Y., et al.: A trial of revealing consensus building mechanism based on Kansei. Hum Interface Cybor. Colloq. 399–406 (2020). (in Japanese)
11. Ito, K., et al.: An experimental study on "consensus to match" game for analyzing emotional interaction in consensus building process. In: Stephanidis, C., et al. (eds.) HCII 2021. LNCS, vol. 13094, pp. 54–62. Springer, Cham (2021). https://doi.org/10.1007/978-3-030-90238-4_5
12. Goldberd, L.R.: Language and individual differences: the search for universals in personality lexicons. Rev. Personal. Soc. Psychol. **2**, 141–165 (1981)
13. Namikawa, T., Tani, I., Wakita, T., Kumagai, R., Nakasone, A., Noguchi, H.: Development of a short form of the Japanese big-five scale, and a test of its reliability and validity. Jpn. J. Psychol. **83**(2), 91–99 (2012). (in Japanese)

Comparison of Moderated and Unmoderated Remote Usability Sessions for Web-Based Simulation Software: A Randomized Controlled Trial

Pedram Khayyatkhoshnevis[1], Savanah Tillberg[1], Eric Latimer[2], Tim Aubry[3], Andrew Fisher[4(✉)], and Vijay Mago[1]

[1] Lakehead University, Thunder Bay, Canada
{pkhayyat,stillber,vmago}@lakeheadu.ca
[2] McGill University, Montréal, Canada
eric.latimer@mcgill.ca
[3] University of Ottawa, Ottawa, Canada
tim.aubry@uottawa.ca
[4] Saint Mary's University, Halifax, Canada
andrew.fisher@smu.ca

Abstract. Usability studies are a crucial part of developing user-centered designs and they can be conducted using a variety of different methods. Unmoderated usability surveys are more efficient and cost-effective and lend themselves better to larger participant pools in comparison to moderated usability surveys. However, unmoderated usability surveys could increase the collection of unreliable data due to the survey participants' careless responding (CR). In this study, we compared the remote moderated and remote unmoderated usability testing sessions for a web-based simulation and modeling software. The usability study was conducted with 72 participants who were randomly assigned into a moderated and unmoderated groups. Our results show that moderated sessions produced more reliable data in most of the tested outcomes and that the data from unmoderated sessions needed some optimization in order to filter out unreliable data. We discuss methods to isolate unreliable data and recommend ways of managing it.

Keywords: Usability evaluation methods · Careless responding · Insufficient effort responding · Online survey · Survey design

1 Introduction

Usability surveys and subsequent user interface (UI) improvements are a vital part of the design and development process when establishing effective user interfaces [9]. Usability surveys are conducted in order to measure the users' subjective assessment of a particular UI design [6]. Various aspects of UIs, such as system robustness, functional utility, and aesthetic appeal, can impact the

© The Author(s), under exclusive license to Springer Nature Switzerland AG 2022
M. Kurosu (Ed.): HCII 2022, LNCS 13302, pp. 232–251, 2022.
https://doi.org/10.1007/978-3-031-05311-5_16

usability experience of an application [14,37]. Usability surveys are useful for determining what users enjoyed about a particular application as well as what they believe could be improved upon. There are multiple methods and modes in which a usability survey can be conducted and these decisions are based on the available resources, the type of the software, and/or the availability of users [3]. Usability surveys can be conducted after presenting software in moderated or unmoderated modes. Moderated sessions usually take place in a lab or office setting with the help of a moderator to facilitate the study. In contrast, unmoderated sessions can be conducted locally or remotely and do not require the presence of a moderator [12].

The distinction between local and remote studies both for moderated and unmoderated sessions is important to understand. Local moderated or unmoderated studies are conducted in a lab-based setting where all users who are participating in the study are doing so in the same physical space and at the same time [1]. As a result of expanding internet resources, remote studies can be conducted from anywhere in the world and do not require that participants be located in the same region [24]. When compared to local moderated studies, remote moderated studies are generally more cost-effective, less time-consuming, and allow for data collection with a larger sample [4]. Similarly, remote unmoderated sessions are easier to plan, are more flexible, and are more cost-effective than most moderated sessions [29,36].

Some studies warn that remote usability surveys may miss some contextual information while collecting data from participants [4]. For instance, some researchers have noted a phenomenon named the **mode effect**. The mode effect claims that when similar studies are conducted using different survey modes, the results from these similar studies can vary greatly [36]. Other evidence suggested that remote surveys provide inaccurate results if the surveys are not carefully planned and pretested. For example, online surveys have been found to suffer from a source of error called **careless responding** (CR) where users intentionally or unintentionally respond in a manner that does not reflect their true experience regarding a system [35].

In this work, a web-based simulation and modeling software for homeless populations is used. Given the complex nature of such software most usability sessions are conducted with the help of a moderator who initially demonstrates a walkthrough of the application and ensures participants are confident in using the system [7,11,16,18,25]. This paper seeks to investigate whether or not unmoderated usability sessions can produce equally useful data and provide users with all of the tools necessary to successfully create a simulation model and run their own simulation. To find answers to this question we have conducted a randomized controlled trial presenting our HOMVIZ platform on two groups: a remote moderated group and a remote unmoderated group. Through our study, we collect various types of data which helps us compare the effectiveness and the level of reliability for each type of session.

1.1   Research Questions and Contributions

It has been noted that usability studies involving simulation and modeling software are best conducted in moderated environments by a professional who can help users throughout each step. However, research has also shown that unmoderated studies are more cost-effective and allow researchers to include larger sample sizes of participants with varying technological backgrounds and who are from different geographical locations [24]. Additionally, in the event of unprecedented circumstance, such as the COVID-19 pandemic, unmoderated sessions allow for the continuation of research efforts with minimal interruption. With these potential benefits in mind, there are two main questions that have guided our research:

> RQ1: Are the outcomes of the moderated and unmoderated usability testing sessions comparable to one another for a complex simulation and modeling software?
> RQ2: What measures should be taken before a remote unmoderated study to ensure data reliability?

Our contribution is three-fold: (1) a detailed explanation of the methods used to conduct the usability testing sessions; (2) a combined analysis of qualitative and quantitative usability data; and (3) freely available code repository of our software and testing methods that were used in this survey:
https://github.com/andrfish/HOMVIZ.

2   Related Work

In the following section, we will briefly describe different usability modes, methods, and other elements that must be considered before conducting a usability survey.

2.1   Moderated and Unmoderated Usability Testing

Most moderated usability sessions involve users being guided through their use of a platform or program by an individual who is able to address their immediate concerns and help them work through problems that interfere with their ability to complete their assigned task [13]. Moderated usability sessions, until more recent years, have been one of the preferred methods for testing system usability [21]. However, due to their time, cost, and scope benefits, unmoderated usability evaluation methods have grown in popularity. Unmoderated usability evaluations have the potential to increase the scope and sample size of an experiment by eliminating the need for the presence of developers and researchers in a moderated setting [13]. Additionally, the cost of performing unmoderated usability evaluations is significantly less [12]. A common concern regarding unmoderated usability evaluations is whether or not they will yield accurate and useful information to the same extent as a moderated evaluation. Hertzum et al. [12] tested the reliability of unmoderated usability tests and found that the results observed in both moderated and unmoderated usability evaluations did not differ from each other significantly. Additionally, they investigated whether or not "the evaluator effect" was more prevalent in one method of evaluation over the other. The evaluator effect, while first noted by Jacobsen et al. [17], is described by Lewis as, "the possibility that usability practitioners might be engaging in self-deception regarding the reliability of their problem-discovery methods" [13]. This means that it is believed that depending on the particular evaluator, the results of what usability issues are being discovered will vary across usability testing sessions [26]. Hertzum et al. [12] set out to investigate whether or not moderating a session impacted the presence of the evaluator effect. They reported that the evaluator effect was present to a similar extent in both moderated and unmoderated usability evaluation sessions. Therefore, they concluded that the use of one method over the other would not significantly impact the evaluator effect in a usability study. These findings combined with the significant increase in convenience that unmoderated evaluations provide to researchers and developers indicate that they should be considered as a viable option for testing system usability. Our study will complement the referenced literature by investigating the differences between moderated and unmoderated surveys that require a stage of pre-training.

2.2 Usability Testing Methods

While the focus of this research is investigating the outcome of unmoderated versus moderated usability testing sessions, it is important to consider the methods in which these surveys can be delivered and how their deliveries can impact the results. One of the most frequently researched survey delivery comparisons is that of paper-based versus online delivery. There are a number of reasons why a research team might prefer a web-based approach to deliver surveys [3]. Web-based surveys are more cost-effective, easily distributed, easily tracked and traced, have the capacity to extend their reach across the world, and are generally considered to be more accessible [3]. However, merits to the paper-based survey can be found as well, especially when the "digital divide" of certain test groups is taken into consideration. The digital divide refers to the varying access that individuals have to computers and internet services and how different demographic factors such as age and socioeconomic status affect that access [3]. For example, older participants who do not have the computer literacy necessary for online surveys as well as those who do not have access to a home computer might prefer paper-based surveys as it enables them to participate in research projects.

Ball [2] investigated the feasibility of unmoderated sessions and discussed some of its disadvantages. One disadvantage that is noted is the inability to follow up with participants regarding difficulties that they have encountered with a system. If a moderator is present to follow up with participants to clarify their concerns, comments, or complaints, then it is much easier to ensure the data that is being collected is accurate and reliable. Additionally, the increased use of remote unmoderated sessions may bias the results by failing to include those who lack the technological equipment or knowledge to participate. Additionally, an overrepresentation of certain groups might occur for those whose access to remote unmoderated surveys are hindered [2].

It is noted that the success of an online survey depends greatly on the participants' comfort and experience level with computers [15]. Given this information, we included a computer usage questionnaire in our survey to measure the participants' computer usage frequency and their experience level. Additionally, concerns for one's privacy have been found to affect the usefulness of online surveys with users often distrusting online surveys which require the use of any of their personal information such as name, emails, addresses, etc. [3].

There is conflicting information regarding the honesty and effort that is more likely to result from web-based versus paper-based surveys. Some argue that due to the potential anonymity of web-based surveys, the potential for a more genuine expression of emotion and thought is greater during a web-based survey [33]. However, others argue that the potential for CR in online surveys is greater, and thus it is possible that online surveys may produce more disingenuous data [33].

2.3   Careless Responding

Due to the lack of supervision that is experienced during an unmoderated study of any nature, it is expected that some participants might intentionally or unintentionally respond to the survey in a careless or inattentive manner. This phenomenon is referred to as Careless Responding (CR) or sometimes insufficient effort responding [27]. There are several hypothesized explanations for CR as well as different proposed methods for minimizing its effects on survey data. McKay et al. [27] suggest that the likelihood of navigating CR from participants can be linked to personality traits. They predicted that benevolent traits, such as honesty, humility, emotional stability, extraversion, agreeableness, conscientiousness, and openness to experience, may be less likely to provide unreliable responses whereas those with malevolent traits, such as psychopathy and narcissism, could be more likely to submit CR [27]. Ward and Pond [34] discuss how researchers can limit the occurrence of CR by adjusting the questionnaires. One solution they propose is including self-report items that require participants to rate their engagement. Additionally, data-cleansing can be used with caution in order to filter out CR. Ward and Pond argue that in some cases it is better to omit data, thus increasing the potential limitations of the study, rather than to procure low-quality data that does not accurately reflect the study. Other research suggests that in addition to CR, researchers must be aware of the occurrence of attrition in their data [35]. Attrition refers to participants opting out of the survey before it is completed, however they note that more research is needed to assess how attrition impacts survey data [35]. In our study, we implemented various methods, such as timers and manually analyzing data, in order to observe users' behaviour during the survey to recognize CR and occurrences of attrition.

2.4   Survey Invitation Elements

One of the greatest challenges that researchers face when collecting data via surveys is maximizing the response rate. Particularly for remote unmoderated surveys, where participants are being sent the instructions for survey completion, it can be challenging to motivate participants to engage with the study in order to maximize response rates. Petrocčič et al. [31] suggest that adjusting the initial invitation to participate in the study can greatly impact the response rate. Specifically, they investigate whether using authority, asking for help or referencing a sense of community in email invitations increase response rates [31]. They found that the most effective means of increasing response rates from email initiations for surveys was by asking for help [31]. Given this information, we included a plea for help and attempted to appeal to the users' sense of community in our survey invitation email.

Although having participants engage with the initial invitation is a crucial first step, maintaining and maximizing response rates goes beyond the first contact. Casey and Poropat [5] suggest that one of the main reasons for higher response rates is the system being tested conforming to classical aesthetics. According to Casey and Poropat, the classical aesthetics construct consists of items that represent many general principles of good design and therefore, may be considered to be aligned closely with traditional notions of aesthetics, such as "orderliness, cleanliness and proportion" [5]. Additionally, they suggest that the qualities associated with a classical aesthetic are more likely to motivate participants to complete a study as they increase the likelihood of an enjoyable experience and promote a positive response [5]. Fan and Yan [8] investigate all aspects of a survey, including development, delivery, completion, and return, in order to determine which steps can be taken to maximize response rate. Overall, Fan and Yan suggest emphasis be placed on the aesthetic quality of the platform as well as the use of participant incentives, such as gift cards, in order to maximize response rates [8]. To maximize user satisfaction and response rate to our survey, we incorporated methods such as introducing aesthetically appealing designs to both the system and participants' task sheets. Additionally, we used a draw for Amazon gift cards as an incentive to increase response rate.

2.5   Usability Questionnaires

As internet technologies continue to advance, the need for evaluation tools which prioritize the creation of user-centered platforms has also increased. Since the 1980 s s researchers have published a number of evaluation measures that are specifically targeted at discerning the usability of web-based platforms and applications [22]. Some notable usability-testing questionnaires are STRATUS, PPUSQ, CSUQ, TAM, and SUS. STRATUS is a questionnaire that focuses on strategic usability [19]. It is separated into two parts, the first of which involves the collection of participant's demographic information and the second part focuses on the assessment of strategic usability. The questions are a combination of closed-ended questions ranked using a five-point Likert scale, multiple-choice, and some open-ended questions. The second part of the questionnaire is divided into five blocks in which the types of questions used are more clearly organized [19]. The popularity of STRATUS has been correlated to its cost-effectiveness, minimal resource use, and time efficiency [19].

The Post Studies System Usability Questionnaire (PPUSQ) and Computer Systems Usability Questionnaire (CSUQ) are closely related as the CSUQ is based on the PPUSQ. Initially, the PPUSQ was an 18-item questionnaire but was later revised to create the 16-item CSUQ. The main difference between the two questionnaires is that the CSUQ is believed to be broader in scope due to its wording whereas the PPUSQ is more closely associated with direct testing environments. Due to its broader reach, the CUSQ lends itself better to mail-out survey scenarios and as a result allows for a larger sample size [20]. Both the PPUSQ and CSUQ use a 7-point rating scale varying from strongly agree to strongly disagree with an outlier option of "not-applicable" [20].

Another popular usability rating system is the Technology Acceptance Model (TAM). The purpose of TAM is to investigate the user's "perceived ease of use" and "perceived usefulness" of a particular system [10]. This has been a beneficial model when researchers are specifically exploring what effort is required from users when integrating certain technologies into their regiments [10].

Finally, there is the System Usability Scale (SUS). While SUS was one of the last proposed usability system surveys to be published, it has become one of the most popular [22]. The SUS questionnaire is primarily used to investigate levels of user satisfaction and learnability for web applications [10] and has proven to be extremely useful in "task-based usability studies" [22]. The SUS is a 10-item questionnaire in which the questions are divided into five positive statements and 5 negative statements [30]. While there are some debate and variance between different researchers on the test's coefficient alpha, which is the numerical value that determines the accuracy of a usability test, the SUS proves to be an accurate measure of a system's perceived usability [22]. Considering the existing literature regarding usability surveys, for the purposes of our research, it was determined that the SUS questionnaire would provide the best data for a full analysis of our system.

3 Methodology

In order to properly investigate our research questions, we conducted an exploratory study that compares the data quality of remote moderated versus remote unmoderated usability testing sessions. Additionally, we implemented a number of safeguard methods to identify instances of CR and other types of unreliable data. In the following subsections, we explain our research methodology in detail.

3.1 Preparation Components

In order to conduct the usability sessions for both usability modes, several documents were prepared. Two separate email invitations were created to be shared with participants. The invitation emails contained all the necessary information regarding our research and links to additional documents such as the information letter, consent form, and task sheet. The information letter provided additional information regarding our research, usability survey, the purpose of the data collection, the type of information being collected, and our information storage policy. Two task sheets were written for each usability mode, only varying where the mode of the survey would impact the user's actions. The task sheets contained step-by-step instructions to help participants complete their simulation setup (see the template available on our repository: https://github.com/andrfish/HOMVIZ).

3.2   HOMVIZ Software and Test Tasks

HOMVIZ is a web-based graphical user interface (GUI) to simulate and predict future trends in homelessness. The system is designed to enable users to run different experiments without being concerned about the complexity of the core deep learning algorithm. The target audience for the HOMVIZ platform is policy analysts and researchers, which has standard *"login"* and *"registration"* pages. Additionally, the platform contains a *"homepage"* where the user can view a history of their interaction with the system and view the status of simulations. HOMVIZ also has a *"create simulation"* page where the user can create a simulation model using the provided tools and tips. Finally, the *"view results"* page shows the results of user simulations. In our survey, each participant was given a task sheet via Google Docs that instructed them on the specific steps they needed to take in order to successfully complete the usability session. The task sheet asked the user to register into our system, log in, watch a tutorial video (applicable only to those completing the unmoderated survey), create a simulation, view the results of their simulation model, and answer the questionnaires.

3.3   Respondent Selection

72 participants were recruited from a graduate level computer science class. Their scheduled class time was used to conduct our survey. Our study was pre-approved by the Office of Research Services and Ethics Board at the university in which the study was conducted. From the original 72 participants, 9 were discarded either due to technical issues or unresponsiveness to our requests and prompts during the survey session. Participants were randomly assigned to either moderated or unmoderated sessions. The overall participants' sample was 71% Male and 28% Female. 84% of participants were between the ages of 21 to 25, 9% were between the ages of 26 to 30, and 6% were between the ages of 31 to 45. Table 1 provides more detailed information about the demographic of our survey participants. To incentivize participants, five individuals received \$20 Amazon gift cards following a random draw.

Table 1. Overview of participants' demographics

Approach	Age [%]	Gender [%]
Overall (N = 72)	21 to 25: 84.1% 26 to 30: 9.5% 31 to 45: 6.4%	Male: 71.5% Female: 28.5%
Moderated Survey (N = 36)	21 to 25: 83.3% 26 to 30: 6.7% 31 to 45: 10.0%	Male: 73.3% Female: 26.7%
Unmoderated Survey (N = 36)	21 to 25: 84.5% 26 to 30: 12.1% 31 to 45: 3.4%	Male: 69.6% Female: 30.4%

3.4 Apparatus

Our usability session was conducted using the Zoom Video Communications application. The participants were divided randomly using Zoom's breakout feature. We used smartlook (https://app.smartlook.com/) web application and API to generate heatmaps for our study. Questionnaires were developed within our system using HTML 5 forms. Other features such as tracking timers were developed using javascript functions. All the data was stored in MySQL relational database design for our study. The tutorial video was recorded and edited using OBS studio (https://obsproject.com/) and shotcut (https://shotcut.org/) freeware and hosted on YouTube in order to simplify user access. The Google Docs online platform was used to send task sheet documents to participants.

3.5 Survey Modes

We divided our sample according to two modes: remote moderated and remote unmoderated sessions. Our participants were randomly divided into 4 groups. Groups A and B attended the moderated sessions and groups C and D attended the unmoderated sessions. The next subsections explain both approaches.

Remote Moderated Usability Testing Sessions. The remote moderated sessions were conducted with the help of two research assistant moderators. During each session, we began the conversation with a 15-minute introduction to our system and the research behind the HOMVIZ platform. We also conversed with participants regarding the COVID lockdown to build rapport. Following the initial introduction, we conducted a 15-minute tutorial and a walkthrough of our system. At the end of the tutorial, we asked participants if they had any questions or doubts regarding our application. Based on the finding of Micallef et al. [28] we gave our participants a quick summary or tips of what to look for when testing the application and some general knowledge regarding testing as it has been found to improve the performance of untrained participants. Once we answered all the questions we shared a link to a Google Docs which contained the task sheet document outlining all of the necessary information for participants to complete their simulation and the survey. Participants could raise their hand if they had any questions regarding the tasks and we tried our best to assist them. The final step in our usability session was for the participants to answer the questionnaires by visiting a link in the task sheet. Participants were given permission to leave after completing the questionnaire and the moderators stayed present until each participant had finished.

Remote Unmoderated Usability Testing Sessions. The Zoom breakout rooms for the unmoderated sessions had two graduate students present as assistants in case of severe technical difficulties. Participants could not ask any questions regarding the system and could leave at will. Our student assistants sent an invitation link to each participant which contained all the information regarding our research and a task sheet. Participants were to follow the task sheet to complete their survey.

3.6 Questionnaires

We used the SUS questionnaire along with two additional open-ended questions. The SUS questionnaire is a 10-item questionnaire that uses a 5-point Likert scale ranging from strongly agree to strongly disagree. The SUS questionnaire is the most commonly used usability testing questionnaire [22], [23]. In order to capture additional qualitative feedback from users, two additional open-ended questions were added to the standard SUS questionnaire. The open-ended questions asked participants to express both their negative and positive experiences regarding any aspect of our system.

Since using our software requires a prior computer and web knowledge, we hypothesized that the participants' potential inability to use our system could result in user frustration affecting their perception related to user satisfaction and thus affect their SUS questionnaire results. Therefore, we used the Computer Usage Questionnaire (CUQ) [32] to capture participants' computer skills for consideration when collecting SUS results in order to ensure their reliability. The CUQ is rated on a 5-point scale (never, rarely, sometimes, often, and very often) and questioned participants regarding their frequency of usage of computer applications (e.g. Microsoft Excel) and the frequencies of activities related to computers (e.g. Skype).

3.7 Data Analysis

Participants start the usability sessions by answering a short demographic survey on the registration page. The demographic survey was used to determine the demographic characteristics of participants. Standard SUS and CUQ formulas were used to produce standardized scores for both questionnaires. Additionally, the SUS answers were further analyzed to reveal additional characteristics such as:

1. *Use frequent*, derived from questions 1 and 2 which indicate how often the user would like to use our application in the future.
2. *Ease of use*, derived from questions 3 and 4 which measure the user's perception of the usability of the system.
3. *Well-integrated*, derived from questions 5 and 6 which measure the user's perception of the integration of various functions within our application.
4. *Learn quick*, derived from questions 7 and 8 measuring the user's perception of how easy it was to learn how to use our application.
5. *Confidence*, derived from questions 9 and 10 which measure the user's perceived confidence when using our application.

The qualitative data from the open-ended questions were analyzed separately and the answers were labeled using the open coding approach and grouped into 4 categories: *UI related*, *Navigation and functionality*, *Other*, and *Not Answered*. Multiple mechanisms were programmed in order to detect instances of CR. Most notably, we programmed timers within multiple pages of our application. Timers are program scripts that measure the interval time between the start and end of a task. The timers were placed into *create simulation*, and *questionnaire* pages. The timers were programmed to activate when the page was fully loaded and after the user had clicked on the start button. The data collected demonstrates how long each user was on a particular page and provided insight as to which participants did not pay attention to the instructions and carelessly completed the survey. A separate watch-time timer was added to the tutorial video. The watch-time timer was programmed using the YouTube API in order to record the actual watch time of the tutorial video for each participant of the unmoderated sessions.

The simulation model that was created by participants was stored in the database as a raw JSON file. To further evaluate the participants' understanding of our system and the CR, we manually analyzed the JSON files. Two methods were used to evaluate the raw data. First, we compared the raw data with the task sheet instructions as participants were asked to follow specific instructions when creating their simulation. The instructions were added to ensure that the simulations would be created free of error so that the user could evaluate the UI of the software rather than waste their energy contemplating the values they were entering. To compare the raw data and task sheet instruction, we created a mark sheet that graded every task that the user was supposed to follow. Using this method we scored every participant's simulation model. Second, the JSON raw data were analyzed in order to determine if the participant understood the concept of our software and created a meaningful simulation. In this instance, the participant either received a pass or a fail mark. These methods revealed that some participants followed our instructions entirely and flawlessly while others deviated from the instructions but created a meaningful simulation and clearly understood the concept of our system. Additionally, captured heatmaps were studied to analyze participants' behavior, particular flaws in the system, and showed us the usefulness of some elements.

Using additional relational database queries, we were able to compare the two groups on the collected data. To measure statistical significance, we used a two-tailed t-test (equal variance) and Chi-square with Yates correction.

4   Results

In the following section, we present the analysis of data from questionnaires, timers, raw simulation data, and heatmaps in order to interpret our study results comparing moderated usability sessions to unmoderated usability sessions. Tables 2, and 3 shows the summary of our results.

Table 2. Moderated and unmoderated sessions on the continuous outcome measures

Measures	Moderated n, Mean (SD)	Unmoderated n, Mean (SD)	t (DF)	p-value
SUS score	24, 75.8 (15)	20, 72.9 (14)	0.63 (42)	0.52
CUQ score	24, 72.9 (8.1)	20, 72.3 (8.3)	0.22 (42)	0.82
The average time taken to make a simulation	28, 817 sec (431)	30, 615 sec (361)	1.93 (56)	**0.05**
The average time taken to answer a questionnaire	24, 261 sec (117)	20, 303 sec (87)	1.29 (41)	0.20

Table 3. Moderated and unmoderated sessions on the categorical outcome measures

Measures	Moderated (N = 36) n (%)	Unmoderated (N = 36) n (%)	Chi-square	p-value
Did not participate	6 (17%)	3 (9%)	0.50	0.47
Created a simulation	28 (93%)	30 (91%)	0.12	0.72
Used the task sheet's instructions when making a simulation	15 (54%)	8 (28%)	3.96	**0.04**
Created a valid simulation but not the one that was assigned in the task sheet	28 (89%)	23 (79%)	0.44	0.50
Answered the questionnaire	24 (80%)	20 (61%)	0.52	0.46

4.1   RQ1: Comparing the Outcomes of the Moderated and Unmoderated Sessions

In the following section, we present the methods used to conduct both the moderated and unmoderated studies in our pursuit of answering RQ1.

Questionnaires. Among participants of both the moderated and unmoderated sessions, there were some who decided not to complete the questionnaire. The results show that more participants from the moderated sessions completed the entirety of their assigned tasks including answering the questionnaire. In total, 24 out of 30 participants (80%) from the moderated answered the questionnaire, compared to 20 out of 33 (61%) from the unmoderated sessions. The difference in these proportions is not statistically significant (p-value = 0.46).

The questionnaire answering portion of the usability session started with participants being asked to answer the CUQ, which assesses the participants' pre-existing computer usage habits and overall computer skills. We present the mean result for a five-point rating scale. The results indicate that participants from both survey modes had similar computer usage frequencies. The mean score for participants of the moderated sessions and the unmoderated sessions was 72.9 and 72.3 out of 90, respectively. A t-test shows that the difference between these mean scores was not statistically significant (p-value = 0.82). Given the similarity between these results, it was further determined that any differences between the data collected in the moderated and unmoderated sessions were not due to participants' level of familiarity with computer systems.

The SUS questionnaire results suggest that the participants from the moderated sessions were slightly more satisfied with our UI than those from the unmoderated sessions. The mean score for the SUS questionnaire for the moderated sessions was 75.8 (very good) and was 72.9 (good) for the unmoderated sessions. However, the difference between these means was not statistically significant (p-value = 0.52).

Figure 1 indicates that participants from the moderated and unmoderated sessions strongly agreed with the positive statements from the SUS questions. Figure 2 suggests that participants disagreed significantly with the negative SUS statements. Upon further analysis of the SUS results, regarding the question suggesting that the system was well integrated, the data indicates that the participants from the moderated sessions mostly agreed with that statement. The same was noted for questions regarding high confidence levels while using the system. However, results from the participants of the unmoderated sessions reported high levels of confidence as well. Upon further analysis, the data suggests that the users' capabilities while using our system was lower than initially thought as we discovered participants from the unmoderated sessions had a larger number of errors in their simulations. This might be due to CR or as the work of McKay et al. [27] suggest, might be due to personal traits such as Agreeableness. It is also noted that the participants from the unmoderated session disagreed more with positive statements regarding their interest in using the system frequently, that the UI was easy to use and well integrated, and that they were able to learn how to use the system quickly.

Two open-ended questions were added to the end of the SUS questionnaire. These questions allowed us to obtain qualitative data regarding the platform. Using the collected qualitative data we discovered new recommendations for improving our system and addressing the challenges that participants faced. We grouped participants' feedback into four categories: *UI-related, Navigation and Functionality, Other,* and *Not Answered.* Figure 3 shows our findings. Some participants provided us with valuable constructive comments, for example, *"The pop-up information provided to the user is too complex. Using simpler text can make it more understandable", "It seems like senior citizens will have difficulty using this system. It would be great if there are some accessibility features",* and *"Since adding properties requires many clicks, it would be nice if after saving one*

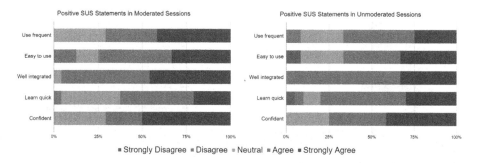

Fig. 1. Answers to positive SUS questions: Results for moderated sessions on the left and for the unmoderated sessions on the right.

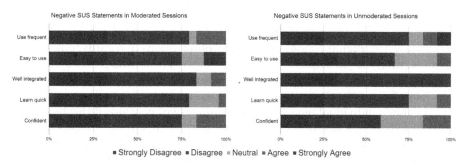

Fig. 2. Answers to negative SUS questions: Results for moderated sessions on the left and for the unmoderated sessions on the right.

property another property automatically opens". The use of open-ended questions was a useful means of collecting qualitative data, however, after analyzing the data we realized the main problem with open-ended questions was the inability to follow up with the participants to clarify their concerns. For example, we received a number of comments that indicated that participants could not clearly explain their feedback due to a lack of domain knowledge. Often their responses were unclear or poorly written, which made understanding the participant's point of view very difficult. Therefore, had the opportunity for following up with participants been available, it would have enabled us to understand the participants' concerns more clearly. 46% of participants from the moderated session and 40% of participants from the unmoderated session did not provide any negative feedback regarding the usability of our application. This may be due to the fact that they genuinely had no negative feedback, that they were not trained to critique the UI design, or that it was due to instances of CR. Had there been an opportunity to follow up with participants either in a focus group or by other means, perhaps more clearer and more meaningful feedback could have been obtained.

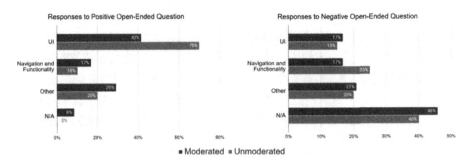

Fig. 3. Answers to the SUS open-ended questions divided into four categories: UI, Navigation and Functionality, Other and Not Answered.

Heatmaps. The heatmap data was collected for all five steps/tabs in the *create simulation* page. Figure 4 shows some of our observations in regards to heatmaps generated from the participants' mouse movement. The heatmap data shows that the participants from the unmoderated session clicked on titles and incorrect links more frequently than those from the moderated session. Since we do not have the user's individual mouse movement we cannot conclude if this behaviour is due to CR. It also observed that the participants from the unmoderated session hover (and potentially clicked) on the various tip links such as popup links, video-tip links, and on the button to close the video-tip slider. This is confirmed with the data we collected using click listeners that counted participants' clicks on the tip links. It can also be inferred that participants from the unmoderated session deleted more rows of data they added, perhaps due to the realization of mistakes or uncertainties. It was also noted that the overview page, the purpose of which was to summarize the user's simulation to minimize unnecessary toggling between steps, was used often.

4.2   RQ2: Ensuring Data Reliability in Unmoderated Usability Sessions

In the following section, we discuss the methods used to ensure data reliability for both the moderated and unmoderated usability sessions.

Timers. For further analysis and as a means of assessing the CR, we computed the average time it took participants to complete both the simulation and the questionnaire. The average results indicate that participants from the moderated session created a simulation in 817 s and participants from the unmoderated session created a simulation in 615 s. Our data shows that a higher percentage of participants in moderated sessions followed the task sheet in comparison to the unmoderated participants (54% and 28% respectively). Therefore, we believe moderated participants might spend more time making a simulation as they

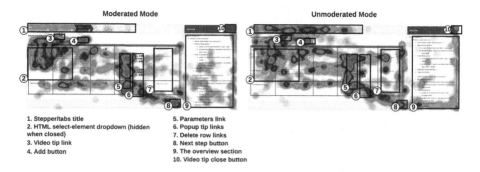

1. Stepper/tabs title
2. HTML select-element dropdown (hidden when closed)
3. Video tip link
4. Add button
5. Parameters link
6. Popup tip links
7. Delete row links
8. Next step button
9. The overview section
10. Video tip close button

Fig. 4. Example mouse heatmap. Warmer colors represent a larger movement overlap.

were reading and following the instructions. The chi-square result for the simulation completion timer that is presented in Table 3 find this difference to be statistically significant (p-value = 0.046).

Participants from the unmoderated sessions took slightly longer to complete their questionnaires than those from the moderated sessions (303 s and 261 s respectively). The t-test did not find this difference to be statistically significant (p-value = 0.20). On the provided task sheets, the unmoderated session participants were notified that watching a nine-minute tutorial video was necessary in order to confidently use our system. Our data shows that only 64% of participants watched the tutorial video and only 42% of participants watched the video for more than 300 s. The low rate of engagement with the video could be due to its inability to captivate the participants, but participant CR could also be a contributing factor. The average SUS scores from participants who watched the tutorial video for more than 300 s was 75.2. This value was very close to that given by participants from the moderated sessions who were given a live tutorial of the system instead of a pre-recorded tutorial video. These findings suggest that having a better understanding of a system could minimize user frustration and result in higher user satisfaction.

Based on the data collected from the open-ended SUS questionnaire answers and additional timer data, we observed that the video tip slider integrated into the platform was effective in helping participants clarify potential misunderstandings. Participants in the unmoderated session used the video slider more often than those from the moderated sessions. The video slider icon was clicked on 21 times by unmoderated session participants and only 5 times by moderate session participants.

Raw Data from Simulation. While the percentage of simulation turnout between moderated and unmoderated sessions was similar (93% and 91% respectively) our results suggest that participants of the moderated session were more accurate in following the task sheet while completing a simulation. Based on our calculation of the mean score of the rate of accurate simulation completion, 54%

of participants from the moderated session did so while 28% of the participants from the unmoderated successfully and accurately completed the simulation. The raw simulation data was further manually analyzed to either pass or fail a participant's attempted simulation. The pass and the fail decision was reached based on our assessment of the users' understanding of the system and the correctness of their simulation. Based on our data, 89% of the participants from the moderated session and 79% percent of the participants from the unmoderated session were able to create an adequate simulation.

4.3 Limitations and Challenges

One of the challenges of our study was that the majority of students participating in our survey were doing so in the Indian Standard Time (IST) zone, however, the survey was arranged based on the Eastern Time Zone (EST). Due to the COVID-19 pandemic, many students were unable to travel to Canada to attend their university and were forced to take their classes from their home country where the time zone varied greatly. This time difference caused many participants to join our session past midnight in their time zone and we presume that the late hours may have contributed to instances of CR. Our system was designed using a relational database and as a result, certain information could be correlated with a particular participant. However, the heatmaps were generated using a third-party tool and in consequence, we could not identify the personal mouse movement of any one particular participant. Due to this, the provided heatmap data may be misleading as it could belong to a user whose data was rejected due to CR. Additionally, our sampling method may have introduced bias by inviting participants only from the computer science domain. It is possible that their prior computer knowledge and high-frequency computer usage may have impacted their perception of our system and their usability experience.

5 Conclusion

Our research goals were to compare the data quality collected from remote moderated and remote unmoderated usability testing sessions and to investigate what measures should be taken before a remote unmoderated study in order to ensure data reliability.

Research indicates that online unmoderated surveys will only increase in popularity [2], thus finding methods to discard unreliable data will remain important. In our study, we noticed an increase in instances of CR from participants who were completing unmoderated surveys. However, since this was somewhat anticipated, we were able to implement built-in functionalities for our reference when analyzing data that enabled us to identify and separate those who did not thoughtfully complete their survey. Additionally, similar to the findings of Ward and Pond [34], we observed that the virtual presence of a moderator resulted in less CR.

The final SUS result, after careful analysis of all of the collected data, demonstrated that the usability score given by validated participants from the unmoderated study was similar to the results from participants in the moderated study. It was noted that more unmoderated survey participants dropped out of the study, answered fewer questionnaires, and completed fewer tasks than their moderated counterparts. Therefore, the rate and quality of data from the moderated sessions are higher than that of the unmoderated session. However, similar to the observations made by Ball [2], since unmoderated sessions allow for larger sample sizes and safeguards for detecting instances of careless responding are available, the unmoderated method is also very effective for usability research.

To conclude, while the moderated sessions seem to require less effort in data analysis since there were fewer instances of CR, they did require significantly more effort to conduct due to planning and moderating. While the data analysis for unmoderated studies was more labor-intensive, the usability sessions are less costly and can be easily repeated. After these considerations, our data demonstrate that unmoderated usability sessions are worthy of consideration for data collection.

Acknowledgment. This work was supported in part by Insight grant 21820 from the Social Sciences and Humanities Research Council. The authors would also like to thank the members of DaTALab (www.datalab.science) for proofreading the paper and providing inputs.

References

1. Apaolaza, A., Vigo, M.: WevQuery: testing hypotheses about web interaction patterns. In: Proceedings of the ACM on Human-Computer Interaction, EICS, vol. 1, pp. 1–17 (2017)
2. Ball, H.L.: Conducting online surveys. J. Hum. Lact. **35**(3), 413–417 (2019)
3. Bjornsdottir, G., et al.: From paper to web: mode equivalence of the ARHQ and NEO-FFI. Comput. Hum. Behav. **41**, 384–392 (2014)
4. Brush, A.B., Ames, M., Davis, J.: A comparison of synchronous remote and local usability studies for an expert interface. In: CHI 2004 Extended Abstracts on Human Factors in Computing Systems, pp. 1179–1182 (2004)
5. Casey, T.W., Poropat, A.: Beauty is more than screen deep: improving the web survey respondent experience through socially-present and aesthetically-pleasing user interfaces. Comput. Hum. Behav. **30**, 153–163 (2014)
6. Chen, Y., Pandey, M., Song, J.Y., Lasecki, W.S., Oney, S.: Improving crowd-supported GUI testing with structural guidance. In: Proceedings of the 2020 CHI Conference on Human Factors in Computing Systems, pp. 1–13 (2020)
7. Coppers, S., et al.: Intellingo: an intelligible translation environment. In: Proceedings of the 2018 CHI Conference on Human Factors in Computing Systems, pp. 1–13 (2018)
8. Fan, W., Yan, Z.: Factors affecting response rates of the web survey: a systematic review. Comput. Hum. Behav. **26**(2), 132–139 (2010)
9. Gardey, J.C., Garrido, A., Firmenich, S., Grigera, J., Rossi, G.: UX-painter: an approach to explore interaction fixes in the browser. Proc. ACM Hum. Comput. Interact. EICS **4**, 1–21 (2020)

10. Harrati, N., Bouchrika, I., Tari, A., Ladjailia, A.: Exploring user satisfaction for E-learning systems via usage-based metrics and system usability scale analysis. Comput. Hum. Behav. **61**, 463–471 (2016)
11. Hassib, M., Buschek, D., Wozniak, P.W., Alt, F.: HeartChat: heart rate augmented mobile chat to support empathy and awareness. In: Proceedings of the 2017 CHI Conference on Human Factors in Computing Systems, pp. 2239–2251 (2017)
12. Hertzum, M., Borlund, P., Kristoffersen, K.B.: What do thinking-aloud participants say? a comparison of moderated and unmoderated usability sessions. Int. J. Hum. Comput. Interact. **31**(9), 557–570 (2015)
13. Hertzum, M., Molich, R., Jacobsen, N.E.: What you get is what you see: revisiting the evaluator effect in usability tests. Behav. Inf. Technol. **33**(2), 144–162 (2014)
14. Hong, S., Kim, J.: Architectural criteria for website evaluation-conceptual framework and empirical validation. Behav. Inf. Technol. **23**(5), 337–357 (2004)
15. Huang, H.M.: Do print and web surveys provide the same results? Comput. Hum. Behav. **22**(3), 334–350 (2006)
16. Hudson, N., Lafreniere, B., Chilana, P.K., Grossman, T.: Investigating how online help and learning resources support children's use of 3D design software. In: Proceedings of the 2018 CHI Conference on Human Factors in Computing Systems, pp. 1–14 (2018)
17. Jacobsen, N.E., Hertzum, M., John, B.E.: The evaluator effect in usability studies: problem detection and severity judgments. In: Proceedings of the Human Factors and Ergonomics Society Annual Meeting, vol. 42, pp. 1336–1340. SAGE Publications, Sage (1998)
18. Kharrufa, A., Rix, S., Osadchiy, T., Preston, A., Olivier, P.: Group spinner: recognizing and visualizing learning in the classroom for reflection, communication, and planning. In: Proceedings of the 2017 CHI Conference on Human Factors in Computing Systems, pp. 5556–5567 (2017)
19. Kieffer, S., Vanderdonckt, J.: Stratus: a questionnaire for strategic usability assessment. In: Proceedings of the 31st Annual ACM Symposium on Applied Computing, pp. 205–212 (2016)
20. Lewis, J.R.: IBM computer usability satisfaction questionnaires: psychometric evaluation and instructions for use. Int. J. Hum. Comput. Interact. **7**(1), 57–78 (1995)
21. Lewis, J.R.: Introduction to the special issue on usability and user experience: methodological evolution (2015)
22. Lewis, J.R.: The system usability scale: past, present, and future. Int. J. Hum. Comput. Interact. **34**(7), 577–590 (2018)
23. Lewis, J.R., Brown, J., Mayes, D.K.: Psychometric evaluation of the EMO and the SUS in the context of a large-sample unmoderated usability study. Int. J. Hum. Comput. Interact. **31**(8), 545–553 (2015)
24. Madathil, K.C., Greenstein, J.S.: An investigation of the efficacy of collaborative virtual reality systems for moderated remote usability testing. Appl. Ergon. **65**, 501–514 (2017)
25. Marky, K., Kulyk, O., Renaud, K., Volkamer, M.: What did i really vote for? on the usability of verifiable E-voting schemes. In: Proceedings of the 2018 CHI Conference on Human Factors in Computing Systems, pp. 1–13 (2018)
26. McDonald, S., Cockton, G., Irons, A.: The impact of thinking-aloud on usability inspection. Proc. ACM Hum. Comput. Interact. EICS **4**, 1–22 (2020)
27. McKay, A.S., Garcia, D.M., Clapper, J.P., Shultz, K.S.: The attentive and the careless: examining the relationship between benevolent and malevolent personality traits with careless responding in online surveys. Comput. Hum. Behav. **84**, 295–303 (2018)

28. Micallef, M., Porter, C., Borg, A.: Do exploratory testers need formal training? an investigation using HCI techniques. In: 2016 IEEE Ninth International Conference on Software Testing, Verification and Validation Workshops, ICSTW, pp. 305–314. IEEE (2016)
29. Mohorko, A., Hlebec, V.: Degree of cognitive interviewer involvement in questionnaire pretesting on trending survey modes. Comput. Hum. Behav. **62**, 79–89 (2016)
30. Orfanou, K., Tselios, N., Katsanos, C.: Perceived usability evaluation of learning management systems: empirical evaluation of the system usability scale. Int. Rev. Res. Open Distrib. Learn. **16**(2), 227–246 (2015)
31. Petrovčič, A., Petrič, G., Manfreda, K.L.: The effect of email invitation elements on response rate in a web survey within an online community. Comput. Hum. Behav. **56**, 320–329 (2016)
32. Schroeders, U., Wilhelm, O.: Computer usage questionnaire: structure, correlates, and gender differences. Comput. Hum. Behav. **27**(2), 899–904 (2011)
33. Wang, C.C., Liu, K.S., Cheng, C.L., Cheng, Y.Y.: Comparison of web-based versus paper-and-pencil administration of a humor survey. Comput. Hum. Behav. **29**(3), 1007–1011 (2013)
34. Ward, M.K., Pond, S.B., III.: Using virtual presence and survey instructions to minimize careless responding on internet-based surveys. Comput. Hum. Behav. **48**, 554–568 (2015)
35. Ward, M., Meade, A.W., Allred, C.M., Pappalardo, G., Stoughton, J.W.: Careless response and attrition as sources of bias in online survey assessments of personality traits and performance. Comput. Hum. Behav. **76**, 417–430 (2017)
36. Zhang, X., Kuchinke, L., Woud, M.L., Velten, J., Margraf, J.: Survey method matters: online/offline questionnaires and face-to-face or telephone interviews differ. Comput. Hum. Behav. **71**, 172–180 (2017)
37. Zhou, L., DeAlmeida, D., Parmanto, B.: Applying a user-centered approach to building a mobile personal health record app: development and usability study. JMIR Mhealth Uhealth **7**(7), e13194 (2019)

A Comparison of Laboratory and Synchronous Remote Usability Testing Methods Using AR

Ted Kim[✉] and Young-Mi Choi

Georgia Institute of Technology, North Ave NW, Atlanta, GA 30332, USA
tkim369@gatech.edu, christina.choi@design.gatech.edu

Abstract. Structured AR usability testing in the product development phase enables obtaining early user feedback, allowing companies to focus on UX from the early design phase. Therefore, several studies of usability testing using AR have been conducted, and there have been attempts to perform AR usability testing with remote settings. However, the authentic AR experience has not been provided to the participants due to complicated setup and logistics problems. They revealed many challenges such as different experimental mindsets, communication with participants, a sense of distance from the actual AR experience, and technical issues.

This study was aimed to make such a direct comparison between the conventional lab-based (as a control group) usability testing, conventional lab-based AR usability testing, and a remote synchronous AR usability testing method to determine whether typical outcome variables (e.g. performance, satisfaction, accuracy) of usability tests would be affected by the reduced experiment control (e.g. presence of experimenter, user environment). Three different approaches would be conducted to compare the validity and usability for AR.

Keywords: AR usability testing · Remote usability testing

1 Introduction

1.1 AR in Usability Testing

Usability is the technique intended to make systems easy to learn, easy to remember, efficient, and satisfying [1, 2]. To test usability for the product or service, a certain level of fidelity is required for the users so they can use and assess how well their tasks can be achieved. Prototypes, which are the early models of a product or service to test certain constraints, can be divided into two types: physical prototypes and virtual prototypes. Physical prototypes are used to measure aesthetics, emotional appeal, ergonomics, product integrity, or craftsmanship [3]. While physical prototypes are useful, they hold some limitations; not only they are expensive and time-consuming to construct, but they are also tested in a very late process after major decisions are set. However, virtual prototypes such as augmented reality (AR), which refers to a view of the real or physical world in which certain elements of the environment are computer-generated, easily resolve the

© The Author(s), under exclusive license to Springer Nature Switzerland AG 2022
M. Kurosu (Ed.): HCII 2022, LNCS 13302, pp. 252–263, 2022.
https://doi.org/10.1007/978-3-031-05311-5_17

major limitations of physical prototypes. Unlike physical prototypes, AR prototypes are available even in the early stage of product development. Hence obtaining early user feedback is possible. AR also provides a much greater sense of realism than any technology in use; thus, it blurs the line of difference between the virtual and real world, thus increasing its usability and effectiveness in the area of application [4].

There are many forms of AR technologies. Van Krevlan and Poleman [5] describe three main categories of AR: Handheld Displays (HHD), Head Mounted Displays (HMD), and Spatial Augmented Reality (SAR). The AR with HMD and HHD use fiducial marker to display the AR image on the screen and HHD is currently the most common method since it does not require any custom equipment. Many people already have devices such as smartphone that can support AR. In order to interact with HHD, the touchscreen is used as a primary interface to interact with AR content [6]. HMDs are a form of wearable worn on the head that displays information to a user typically through a screen. An example of this kind of device would be the Microsoft HoloLens, and their hands-free interaction allows users to better respond to emergencies [7]. SAR displays work by projecting a digital element into an environment. it is a supreme programmable light source that allows creating space-efficient and seamless visual displays in an AR manner.

Some studies have already been conducted by using HHD to investigate usability testing using AR prototypes due to using the advantage of easy access. Ha, Chang, and Woo investigated usability testing with multi-sensory feedback [8], Choi explored Augmented Reality (AR) and Tangible Augmented Reality (TAR) as tools for the usability assessment of a space heater [9], and Lu, Chang, Wu, and Chen conducted usability testing using MR technology combined with 3D printing in the coexistence environment [10]. To take a step further, AR technologies have been explored as an alternative approach for substituting physical prototypes in terms of productivity [11]. Chu and Kao recently compared the effectiveness of design evaluation by using virtual prototypes versus the product they aim to represent. A result shows that the visual virtual prototype was not effective in evaluating the physical aspects, but no significant difference was observed in usability between evaluation media [12]. These results indicate that while virtual prototypes may substitute physical prototypes fully, it has the potential to economically involve broader user groups in usability testing and support new development approaches.

1.2 Remote Usability Testing

Although the studies mentioned earlier have shown how AR can be beneficial in the design and usability testing, they were all conducted in person in a lab-based usability testing environment. According to Sauer *et al.* [13], usability testing can be divided into four different categories: Classical field testing, Lab testing, Synchronous remote testing, and Asynchronous remote testing (see Table 1), and the testing methods listed in Table 1 differ from each other on a number of criteria, including experimental control, presence of test administrator, presence of environmental distractors, and chosen location. In lab-based usability testing, the evaluator and the test takers are in the same place at the same time [14]. In contrast, remote usability testing can be described as usability evaluation where the evaluators and participants are separated in space and/or time [15].

Table 1. Similarity of lab-based testing to different forms of extra-laboratorial testing [13].

	Experimental control	Presence of test administrator	Control of environmental distractors	Chosen location
Synchronous remote testing	Low	Medium	Medium	User-selected
Asynchronous remote testing	Very low	Weak	Low	User-selected
Classical field testing	Medium	Strong	Very low	Experimenter-selected
Lab testing	High	Strong	High	Experimenter-selected

Remote usability testing provides many advantages over lab-based testing (Albert et al. 2010). The advantages of remote testing from the participant's point of view are budget-saving (e.g., traveling expenses to the lab), less artificial environment (e.g., home), and evaluation of a system with culturally diverse users. However, the many downsides of remote testing have been revealed as well. For example, in a remote usability setting, direct observation does not exist; some problems may remain undiscovered because the gestures and facial expressions of the user are missing [16]. Observing participants' emotions could be helpful for the moderator if participants' negative emotions are detected and synchronized to events or tasks; the gained insight will help find causes of hidden irritation or frustration and provide more complete picture of the overall user experience [17]. Hertzum et al. compared and analyzed synchronous and asynchronous remote usability testing using the same system. They found the evaluator who analyzed synchronous test sessions identified more problems rated critical or severe than evaluators who analyzed asynchronous test sessions. These findings suggest that direct participant observations provide more information insights to evaluators [18].

Reduced experimental control (e.g., users may be distracted by phone, roommates, and noise during task) is another disadvantage for the remote usability testing. In a remote setting, the experimental mindsets for each participant are varied when joining the study. Remote testing participants tend to move along rather than exploring the tool in their own accord [19]. Moreover, participants can be distracted by their family or colleagues during the tests, or sometimes they check their cellphone [20]. Andreasen et al., conducted a systematic experimental comparison of various methods for remote usability testing, remote synchronous testing, remote asynchronous expert testing, remote asynchronous user testing, and laboratory-based think-aloud method. The data collection for the two asynchronous conditions was done through the online questionnaire, and this questionnaire enabled the participants to categorize the identified problem as 'small', 'medium' and 'large'. These categories were correlated to the commonly used classifications 'cosmetic', 'serious', and 'critical.' Their study revealed that the asynchronous remote usability test methods are considerably more time-consuming than the conventional laboratory or synchronous remote usability testing methods. The authors assumed that the reason for this marked difference may be that the participants took breaks, ensuring complete freedom In remote setup usability testing can affect the reliability of the results [21].

In addition, some other work also found disadvantages of remote usability testing, such as technical problems (e.g., internet connectivity) and logistics [16, 22]. Unstable internet can adversely affect the results and cause problems with the results' credibility due to difficulty accurately measuring the time taken to complete the task. During the study, if the internet gets disconnected, sometimes, the use case scenarios need to be restarted, and in that case, the data get from a user running a task for the first time, and a user who already knows the process after starting over can be very different [19]. Furthermore, if the hardware needs to be provided to the participants, some logistics are required to distribute it to the participants and collect it again [16].

However, some of the disadvantages mentioned above of remote testing can be alleviated with real-time one-on-one communication between the evaluator and the user, known as synchronous remote testing. Through the synchronous remote meeting, the evaluator and the participants can exchange ideas, ask questions, and collect data about satisfaction by perceiving the facial expressions and gestures from the participants [16]. Administrator presence may increase the physiological arousal of test participants due to the physical or virtual presence of others [15]. The reduced experimental control, such as cell phone notifications and noise during experiments, etc., are often categorized as disadvantages for remote usability testing. However, even with these distractions, some of the studies found that the collected data from remote settings was just as good as the data from laboratory testing. The only difference was that the remote testing took a little longer; they did not impact the data quality [23, 24].

However, asynchronous remote testing, which lacks the immediacy and sense of "presence" desired to support a collaborative testing process (Dray and Siegel 2004), considerably has more uncertainties than are suggested in the numerous pieces of literature available. For example, the experimental results vary greatly depending on the user's mindset or motivation [19]. Andreasen's experiment [21] above also shows that allowing complete freedom (no control of environmental distractors) can cause the participants to take a task unrelated to the experiment, such as taking a break in the middle of doing other work, which causes problems in the reliability of the collected data. Therefore, rather than taking the time to perform each task and provide feedback [19], they'll click through the tasks without much thought [25]. Moreover, the quality of results from asynchronous remote testing were typically not as good as those from in-lab usability testing [26]. Lastly, what participants report on surveys can be very different compared to what they actually do. Participants can think they've successfully completed a task when they haven't. In addition, evaluators cannot observe the participants' behavior during the experiment; no intervention or correction can be made when they make a mistake [25, 26]. In this case, the collected data can mislead the evaluator by giving a wrong impression of a user's experience; to prevent this, asynchronous remote testing should be designed to discourage cheating or similar forms of insincere participation [25].

1.3 Immersive User Experience Using AR

Immersion is defined as the technical aspects of a device, "how well it can afford people real-world sensorimotor contingencies for perception and action" [27]. It is the extent a device can provide computer-generated input to human senses so the brain can generate a complete and believable picture of its surroundings [28].Verhulst at el. examined and measured multiple aspects of user experience, including enjoyment, presence, cognitive, emotional, and behavioral engagement, using AR, at the National Gallery in London, UK. The results revealed that the AR allows a deep involvement of the user on an emotional and behavioral basis with higher attention to what participants are doing. Razek et al. also compared conventional service prototyping (CSP), including verbal, paper, mock-up, simulation prototyping, and AR service prototyping (ARSP). Results showed that the AR prototyping rated very high across all service prototyping activates, which relates to the high visualization, interaction, and simulation ability. It is also worth that immersive interfaces have a higher level of engagement and learning compared to the conventional ones [29].

Other study also has been conducted to explore the effect of remote usability testing. Voit at el. recently compared five widely used methods for evaluating prototypes (i.e., online surveys, VR, AR, in-lab, and in-situ). In their experiment, sixty participants were asked to assess four different smart artifacts using standardized questionnaires. Four smart artifacts display their current status using ambient lighting and additional information without overloading the users' attention. As a result of the study, online participants had the lowest average scores on the SUS questionnaire. However, the AttrakDiff score from the online testing, one of the most used methods in measuring both pragmatic and hedonic dimensions of UX [30], was higher than in-lab testing, and AtrrakDiff score from AR testing is higher than online testing [31].

As mentioned above, AR has high visualization interaction and simulation ability compared to conventional methods. Wenk et al. also recently evaluated whether the immersive visualization technologies (VR and AR) impacted users' cognitive load, motivation, technology usability, and embodiment. Reports on cognitive load did not differ across visualization technologies. However, VR and AR were more motivating than 2D screen, and AR showed a trend of higher interest/enjoyment compared to the 2D screen [32]. Using AR can alleviate the mentioned limitation of remote usability testing since the prior motivation/enjoyment is an impetus for subsequent engagement [33]. This novel technology (AR) might encourage active user participation and contribute to user feedback quality. However, it is still uncommon; it can have its own skewing effect on results.

2 Methodology

2.1 Perceived Product Attractiveness

The attractiveness of the AR prototype and product will be measured before and after product usage (Prior to the usability test). A one-item scale will be used ("the design of the product is very appealing"), with a five-point scale ranging from Strongly Disagree to Strongly Agree as a response to keep participants motivated during the testing session.

According to Wanous et al., if the single-item is clear and captures the central concept, the single-item measures are more robust than the scale measures overall [34]. Therefore, the use of a one-item measure is justifiable in this study.

2.2 User Performance

The two measures of user performance will be recorded, task completion time and interaction efficiency. Task completion time referred to the time needed to accomplish the task, and interaction efficiency referred to the composite parameter, dividing the optimal number of user manipulations by the actual number of user inputs.

2.3 User Study Design

This study was designed to make a direct comparison between the conventional lab-based (as a control group) usability testing, conventional lab-based AR usability testing, and a remote synchronous AR usability testing method to determine whether typical outcome variables (e.g., performance, satisfaction, accuracy) of usability tests would be affected by the reduced experiment control (e.g., presence of experimenter, user environment). The three different setups would be conducted to compare the validity and usability for AR. A short description of product functions and features will be explained to participants, then then will be asked to perform a task with the product. After performing the task, they will be asked to complete a short survey to provide an assessment with their experience and ability to perform the task.

Because the weak administrator presence decreases the physiological arousal of test participants due to the physical or virtual presence of others [15], a full task description would not be provided to the all users. The moderator would be online during the study and walk through each task with participants so that remote users can fully concentrate on the test. Due to alleviating the lack of administrator presence, synchronous setting and task walk-through would be used. The test result is predicted that remote synchronous participants would have similar performance and satisfaction to laboratory environment participants.

In-person testing participants would be required to come to the lab to conduct the study, in this case, the experimenter will be staying in the same room with them, providing instructions directly. Those who participate in the study remotely will be required to prepare the following setups before testing:

- Currently owning an iPad
- Download the software for an AR prototype
- Printing out the marker to implement the AR environment
- Setting up their camera using either a cellphone, laptop, or tablet PC so that the experimenter can observe how users interact with the prototype.

The independent variable in the study would be the type of prototype used for the AR testing, and the dependent variables are the time taken to complete the assigned tasks, user environment, presence of experimenter, and SUS score. To get independent data, participants will need to evaluate one form of representation.

Even though a head-mounted display provides the most immersive experience (Colley, Väyrynen, and Häkkilä 2015), a handheld display (HHD) would be used for the AR medium in this study because it is a common tool that can support AR (Grandi et al. 2018); many people already have devices such as iPad. The touchscreen is used as a primary interface to interact with AR content. In addition, using a head-mounted display to conduct the study will require extra setups, for example, distributing devices such as HoloLens to the participants and collecting them again; these steps would be time-consuming and financially ineffective (Janina Sauer et al. 2020). Therefore, it would be required for the remote participants to have their own iPad for the study. There are many iPad models out there now, and the latest iPad models and older iPad models have a lot of differences in specs, which may affect the results. Considering this limitation, old iPad models (models released before 3rd generation iPad Pro and iPad 6th generation) will be excluded.

2.4 Participants

The subject group would be regular users with no handicapped, and they will be recruited by using university networking/advertisements (flyers, announcements, or email). For a reliable result, 25 participants will be required for each set up (75 participants total).

For both in-person and remote participants would be asked to sit at the desk in front of an iPad screen with an iPad holder. Participants then will be informed about the goal of the study and the procedure verbally. During this time, they were given the opportunity to ask questions about the introduction. Then they will be given a quick demonstration of how to view the product and how to interact with it and shown how it works through the iPad screen.

2.5 Prototype

On a remote AR testing method, the assistance to participants from the administrator will be limited. Therefore, a robust prototype for the testing is required [19, 35]. First, according to Ha et al., multimodal feedback such as visual feedback, background sound, and effect sound also creates better immersion for Augmented Reality; Using a digital product is more accessible than a physical product to create a more immersive prototyping environment [8]. Second, the size of the product being tested is considered. As revealed in the previous experiment, the iPad screen is relatively small; it is difficult to test a large product. If the product being tested is larger than the iPad screen, the distance between the iPad and the marker, which displays the AR image on the screen, should be increased. In this case, it will be challenging for the participants to hold the marker and interact with the screen simultaneously. Lastly, developing an AR model that accurately represents the product's natural interaction is hard. For example, in the AR representation, users interact with the digital model on the 2D interface of the iPad. If the product being tested is a physical product that operates through a physical knob, it is impossible to implement the above interaction in the AR prototype.

Accepting the above considerations, in AR testing, a digital product has more advantages in implementing an immersive experience than testing a physical product. Therefore, a smartwatch was selected to be represented in AR for the study; It is easy to implement sound/visual feedback and natural interaction, and its small size makes it easy to be tested on an iPad (see Fig. 1).

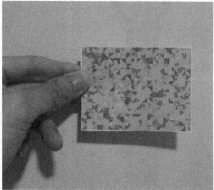

Fig. 1. AR prototype using fiducial marker.

2.6 Tasks

The goal for the AR prototype for this study was to provide an immersive experience for allowing users to complete a given scenario. In a scenario, multiple tasks would be required from the participants, for example, when user input on one object triggers a sequence of responses from the same object. A smartwatch was selected for this study to provide an immersive experience to the participants; it is also familiar to most people, and it was ensured that no effort goes into understanding the scenario.

The user first starts with launching Spotify on their AR prototype, then swipe right to see the menu, selecting "Download", and tapping on "AR Study". The next step would be tapping the arrow icon to play downloaded song. The moderator will walk through each task with the participants (See Fig. 2).

Task 1: Launch Spotify on the smartwatch.
Task 3: Swipe right to see the Spotify menu.
Task 4: Choose a "AR Study" downloaded playlist.
Task 5: Tapping the play arrow icon to play song.

Participants will be explained their goal for the study as well as how to interact with the AR prototype before they perform the tasks. The way to interact with the AR prototype will be explained because the study's goal is to evaluate the validity of the Remote AR usability testing, not to evaluate how long it takes the participants to learn how to use it. Time will be recorded for each approach (conventional lab-based usability testing, conventional lab-based AR usability testing, and a remote synchronous AR usability testing method), then summed to provide the total time. The time from the moment the participant starts the task and finishes the task will be counted. The usability of the prototypes will be evaluated as well with the System Usability Scale (SUS) at the end of the study session to gather additional user feedback.

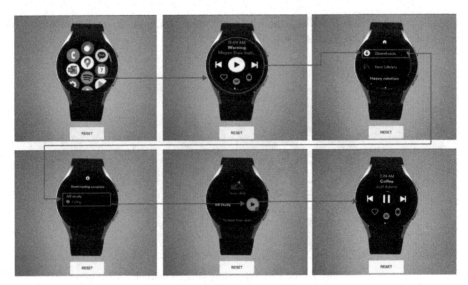

Fig. 2. Interaction flow of playing downloaded song on Spotify app.

3 Data Analysis

To compare the assessment of the usability of conventional lab-based (as a control group) usability testing, conventional lab-based AR usability testing, and a remote synchronous AR usability testing approaches mentioned above, the System Usability Scale (SUS) would be used, which is a very effective tool for assessing the usability of a product; a broad group of usability practitioners can use it to evaluate almost any type of user interface [36]. There are several characteristics that make the use of SUS attractive. First, it consists of only 10 statements, meaning it is relatively quick and easy for study participants and for administrators to score. Second, the result of the survey is a single score, ranging from 0 to 100, and is relatively easy to understand by a wide range of people from other disciplines [36]. Tullis and Stetson [37] measured the usability by using five different surveys (including the Questionnaire for User Interaction Satisfaction [QUIS], the SUS, the Computer System Usability Questionnaire [CSUQ], and two vendor-specific surveys) and found that the SUS provided the most reliable results across a wide range of sample sizes. The SUS is composed of ten questionnaires, each question has a five-point scale that ranges from *Strongly Disagree* to *Strongly Agree*. There are five positive statements and five negative statements, which is alternate.

Statistical hypothesis tests are very widely used for data analysis. Some popular statistical tests include ANOVA [38], Kruskal–Wallis test [39], and Wilcoxon rank sum test [40]. These tests serve the same purpose, which evaluating whether two or more samples are drawn from the same distribution. ANOVA is parametric tests and assume the normal distribution of data. The non-parametric equivalence of these two tests is the Wilcoxon rank sum test, and Kruskal–Wallis test. They do not assume the data to be normally distributed. The t-test can only deal with the comparison between two samples, and the ANOVA extends it to multiple samples. Similarly, the Kruskal–Wallis is also a generalization of the Wilcoxon rank sum test from two samples to multiple samples.

The non-parametric tests perform better when the data is not normally distributed, and are suitable especially in the cases when the data size is small (less than 25 per sample group) [41].

In this study, the Kruskal-Wallis test will be used to analyze the data because the study is comparing three different groups and the collected data from this study would not be normally distributed. However, the limitation of the Kruskal Wallis test is that the result will show if there is a significant difference between groups, but it won't show which groups are different; a Post Hoc test needs to be run to find out. Therefore, if the Kruskal-Wallis test finds significant results, the Tukey HSD Test will be run to find the honest significant difference.

The data collection for the study is currently ongoing and therefore the final results/outcomes are not yet known.

4 Limitation

This study is designed that all three setups have a similar environment, but in a remote setting, the administrator's limited environmental control can affect the participants and results. For example, lab environments are very minimalistic and void of attention-grabbing items so that participants focus on the task at hand. However, participants will get email notifications, text messages, etc., in a remote environment since they use their personal devices for the study. Therefore, in order to reduce the factors that can adversely affect the experimental results as much as possible, a pre-meeting to confirm the test environment before the study was considered essential. Also, since the AR prototype in which task-based functions are only activated is used in the experiment, different results may be obtained from the prototype with all functions are enabled.

References

1. Rajanen, M., Iivari, N.: Usability cost-benefit analysis: how usability became a curse word? In: Baranauskas, C., Palanque, P., Abascal, J., Barbosa, S.D.J. (eds.) INTERACT 2007. LNCS, vol. 4663, pp. 511–524. Springer, Heidelberg (2007). https://doi.org/10.1007/978-3-540-74800-7_47
2. ISO 9241-11: Ergonomic requirements for office work with visual display terminals (VDTs) - Part 11: guidance on usability, vol. 1998 (1998)
3. Sleeswijk Visser, F., van der Lugt, R., Stappers, P.J.: Sharing user experiences in the product innovation process: participatory design needs participatory communication. Creat. Innov. Manag. 16, 35–45 (2007). https://doi.org/10.1111/j.1467-8691.2007.00414.x
4. Oberdörfer, S., Birnstiel, S., Latoschik, M.E., Grafe, S.: Mutual benefits: interdisciplinary education of pre-service teachers and HCI students in VR/AR learning environment design. Front. Educ. 6, 233 (2021). https://doi.org/10.3389/feduc.2021.693012
5. Van Krevelen, R., Poelman, R.: A survey of augmented reality technologies, applications and limitations. Int. J. Virtual Real. 9, 1 (2010). https://doi.org/10.20870/IJVR.2010.9.2.2767, ISSN 1081-1451
6. Grandi, J.G., Debarba, H.G., Berndt, I., Nedel, L., Maciel, A.: Design and assessment of a collaborative 3D interaction technique for handheld augmented reality. In: 2018 IEEE Conference on Virtual Reality and 3D User Interfaces (VR), pp. 49–56 (2018). https://doi.org/10.1109/VR.2018.8446295

7. Frøland, T.H., Heldal, I., Ersvær, E., Sjøholt, G.: State-of-the-art and future directions for using augmented reality head mounted displays for first aid live training. In: 2020 International Conference on e-Health and Bioengineering (EHB), pp. 1–6 (2020). https://doi.org/10.1109/EHB50910.2020.9280182

8. Ha, T., Chang, Y., Woo, W.: Usability test of immersion for augmented reality based product design. In: Hui, K.-C., et al. (eds.) Edutainment 2007. LNCS, vol. 4469, pp. 152–161. Springer, Heidelberg (2007). https://doi.org/10.1007/978-3-540-73011-8_17

9. Choi, Y.M.: Applying Tangible augmented reality for product usability assessment. J. Usability Stud. **14**(4), 187–200 (2019)

10. Lu, J.-R.R., Chang, T.-W., Wu, Y.-S., Chen, C.-Y.: Multimodal coexistence environment design to assist user testing and iterative design of higame emotional interaction design for elderly. In: Human Aspects of IT for the Aged Population. Technologies, Design and User Experience, pp. 197–209 (2020)

11. Fereydooni, N., Walker, B.N.: Virtual reality as a remote workspace platform: opportunities and challenges, August 2020. https://www.microsoft.com/en-us/research/publication/virtual-reality-as-a-remote-workspace-platform-opportunities-and-challenges/

12. Chu, C.H., Kao, E.T.: A comparative study of design evaluation with virtual prototypes versus a physical product. Appl. Sci. **10**(14), (2020). https://doi.org/10.3390/app10144723

13. Sauer, J., Sonderegger, A., Heyden, K., Biller, J., Klotz, J., Uebelbacher, A.: Extra-laboratorial usability tests: an empirical comparison of remote and classical field testing with lab testing. Appl. Ergon. **74**, 85–96 (2019). https://doi.org/10.1016/j.apergo.2018.08.011

14. Rubin, J., Chisnell, D., Spool, J.: Handbook of Usability Testing : How to Plan, Design, and Conduct Effective Tests. Wiley, , Hoboken (2008)

15. Alhadreti, O., Mayhew, P.J., Alshamari, M.: A comparison of in-lab and synchronous remote usability testing methods: effectiveness perspective, pp. 3–9 (2011)

16. Sauer, J., Muenzberg, A., Siewert, L., Hein, A., Roesch, N.: Remote testing of usability in medical apps. In: Wireless Mobile Communication and Healthcare, pp. 3–17 (2020)

17. Stickel, C., Ebner, M., Steinbach-Nordmann, S., Searle, G., Holzinger, A.: Emotion detection: application of the valence arousal space for rapid biological usability testing to enhance universal access. In: Universal Access in Human-Computer Interaction. Addressing Diversity, pp. 615–624 (2009)

18. Hertzum, M., Molich, R., Jacobsen, N.E.: What you get is what you see: revisiting the evaluator effect in usability tests. Behav. Inf. Technol. **33**(2), 144–162 (2014). https://doi.org/10.1080/0144929X.2013.783114

19. Kim, T., Arconada-Alvarez, S., Choi, Y.M.: Challenges and workarounds of conducting augmented reality usability tests remotely a case study BT. In: HCI International 2021 - Late Breaking Papers: Design and User Experience, pp. 63–71 (2021)

20. Ratcliffe, J., Soave, F., Bryan-Kinns, N., Tokarchuk, L., Farkhatdinov, I.: Extended Reality (XR) remote research: a survey of drawbacks and opportunities (2021). https://doi.org/10.1145/3411764.3445170

21. Andreasen, M.S., Nielsen, H.V., Schr\oder, S.O., Stage, J.: What happened to remote usability testing? An empirical study of three methods. In: Proceedings of the SIGCHI Conference on Human Factors in Computing Systems, New York, NY, USA. Association for Computing Machinery, pp. 1405–1414 (2007)

22. Crowther, N.: Remote Testing of AR HUDs for Lunar Exploration Presented to the, May 2021

23. Andrzejczak, C., Liu, D.: The effect of testing location on usability testing performance, participant stress levels, and subjective testing experience. J. Syst. Softw. **83**(7), 1258–1266 (2010). https://doi.org/10.1016/j.jss.2010.01.052

24. McFadden, E., Hager, D.R., Elie, C.J., Blackwell, J.M.: Remote usability evaluation: overview and case studies. Int. J. Hum.-Comput. Interact. **14**(3–4), 489–502 (2002). https://doi.org/10.1080/10447318.2002.9669131

25. Kittur, A., Chi, E.H., Suh, B.: Crowdsourcing user studies with mechanical turk. In: Proceedings of the SIGCHI Conference on Human Factors in Computing Systems (2008), pp. 453–456. https://doi.org/10.1145/1357054.1357127

26. Liu, D., Bias, R.G., Lease, M., Kuipers, R.: Crowdsourcing for usability testing. Proc. Am. Soc. Inf. Sci. Technol. **49**(1), 1 (2012). https://doi.org/10.1002/meet.14504901100

27. Slater, M., Sanchez-Vives, M.V.: Enhancing our lives with immersive virtual reality. Front. Robot. AI **3**, 74 (2016). https://doi.org/10.3389/frobt.2016.00074

28. Verhulst, I., Woods, A., Whittaker, L., Bennett, J., Dalton, P.: Do VR and AR versions of an immersive cultural experience engender different user experiences? Comput. Human Behav. **125**, 106951 (2021). https://doi.org/10.1016/j.chb.2021.106951

29. Razek, A.R.A., van Husen, C., Pallot, M., Richir, S.: A comparative study on conventional versus immersive service prototyping (VR, AR, MR) (2018). https://doi.org/10.1145/3234253.3234296

30. Walsh, T., Varsaluoma, J., Kujala, S., Nurkka, P., Petrie, H., Power, C.: Axe UX: exploring long-term user experience with IScale and AttrakDiff. In: Proceedings of the 18th International Academic MindTrek Conference: Media Business, Management, Content & Services, pp. 32–39 (2014). https://doi.org/10.1145/2676467.2676480

31. Voit, A., Mayer, S., Schwind, V., Henze, N.: Online, VR, AR, Lab, and in-situ: comparison of research methods to evaluate smart artifacts. In: Proceedings of the 2019 CHI Conference on Human Factors in Computing Systems, pp. 1–12 (2019). https://doi.org/10.1145/3290605.3300737

32. Wenk, N., Penalver-Andres, J., Buetler, K.A., Nef, T., Müri, R.M., Marchal-Crespo, L.: Effect of immersive visualization technologies on cognitive load, motivation, usability, and embodiment. Virtual Real. (2021). https://doi.org/10.1007/s10055-021-00565-8

33. Martin, A.J., Ginns, P., Papworth, B.: Motivation and engagement: same or different? Does it matter? Learn. Individ. Differ. **55**, 150–162 (2017). https://doi.org/10.1016/j.lindif.2017.03.013

34. Wanous, J.P., Reichers, A.E., Hudy, M.J.: Overall job satisfaction: how good are single-item measures? J. Appl. Psychol. **82**(2), 247–252 (1997). https://doi.org/10.0.4.13/0021-9010.82.2.247

35. Rzeszotarski, J.M., Kittur, A.: Instrumenting the crowd: using implicit behavioral measures to predict task performance. In: Proceedings of the 24th Annual ACM Symposium on User Interface Software and Technology, pp. 13–22 (2011). https://doi.org/10.1145/2047196.2047199

36. Bangor, A., Staff, T., Kortum, P., Miller, J., Staff, T.: Determining what individual SUS scores mean: adding an adjective rating scale. J. Usability Stud. **4**(3), 114–123 (2009)

37. Tullis, T., Stetson, J.: A comparison of questionnaires for assessing website usability, June 2006

38. Box, G.E.P.: Non-normality and tests on variances. Biometrika **40**(3–4), 318–335 (1953). https://doi.org/10.1093/biomet/40.3-4.318

39. Kruskal, W.H., Wallis, W.A.: Use of ranks in one-criterion variance analysis. J. Am. Stat. Assoc. **47**(260), 583–621 (1952). https://doi.org/10.1080/01621459.1952.10483441

40. Wilcoxon, F.: Individual comparisons by ranking methods. Biometrics Bull. **1**(6), 80–83 (1945). https://doi.org/10.2307/3001968

41. Kitchen, C.M.R.: Nonparametric vs parametric tests of location in biomedical research. Am. J. Ophthalmol. **147**(4), 571–572 (2009). https://doi.org/10.1016/j.ajo.2008.06.031

Scenario-Based Methods for Hard-to-Reach Populations in Healthcare

Ashley Loomis and Enid Montague[⊠]

DePaul University, Chicago, IL 60604, USA
`aloomis1@depaul.edu`

Abstract. Scenario-based design (SBD) is an iterative concept-generating method where designers and researchers create short narratives to develop concepts for a design. This method also allows for rapid revision since it incorporates a way of assessing the claims and pros and cons of the concepts in each scenario. There are four types of scenarios that can be created and assessed, but the overall method remains flexible. We held three sessions with design and human computer interaction students. The objective of these sessions was to brainstorm a few unique concepts for a tool that would provide automated feedback to primary care physicians about their interactions with patients. In this paper, we detail our process and how we adapted and applied the scenario-based design methodology. Due to clinicians' often limited time and design experience, we adapted SBD methods to help nonclinical designers better understand the context of clinical work settings. To adapt the methods, we 1) held a preliminary design workshop with clinicians to sessions to inform the scenarios, 2), involved designers in the SBD sessions, and 3) provided the non-clinical participants with relevant contextual and background information about primary care settings.

Keywords: Scenario-based design · Human-centered design · Healthcare

1 Introduction

1.1 Scenario-Based Design

Scenario-based design involves creating short stories or experiences (scenarios), to design, iterate, and evaluate concepts. This method was first introduced by Rosson and Carrol (2002a, 2002b). It allows designers and researchers to move from initial research and information gathering of defining the problem to the concept development and prototyping. This process uses the described context of how and where the design would be applied. This helps participants better consider how constraints of an environment may shape use (Rosson and Carroll 2002a, 2002b). An advantage is those without a specific experience or background (such as having a medical degree and working as a physician) may still visualize the design in context due to the description in the scenarios.

Scenario-based design methods have been used in various healthcare situations. One study, focusing on goal directed design, aimed to design a clinical decision support

© The Author(s), under exclusive license to Springer Nature Switzerland AG 2022
M. Kurosu (Ed.): HCII 2022, LNCS 13302, pp. 264–273, 2022.
https://doi.org/10.1007/978-3-031-05311-5_18

system to improve management and detection of urinary tract infections (UTIs), as well as decrease antibiotic overuse. After conducting focus groups to gather information from clinicians on their use of technology and UTI management, the researchers used personas and scenarios to create and test prototypes. They noted this as a good way to design a clinical decision support system (Jones et al. 2017).

Other uses of scenario-based design in health-focused settings occur around assessing tasks and using scenarios to illustrate and investigate workflow. While scenario-based design is, at face value, an inexpensive, fast, and resource-light technique, challenges may also exist in creating concise and clear models from the data. For example, the use of scenarios in analyzing workflow and designing for infectious disease surveillance were noted as helping to create design requirements, but the authors also noted the difficulties of creating a workflow chart that was both high-level and detailed while using this process (Turner et al. 2013).

1.2 Research Background

These scenario-based design sessions are part of a larger study to develop tools to provide feedback to physician about their interactions with patients in primary care settings. The intent of this system is to improve physician satisfaction and practice, along with patient health.

Physicians receive varied forms of feedback on their practice. The impact of these types of feedback may vary as well. They may receive patient surveys, but the value of these is unknown (Farrington et al. 2017). Surveys may not pick up on the types of behaviors that are difficult to detect, but still influence patient-physician interactions. For example, higher levels of physician eye contact with their patients are found to be associated with greater patient satisfaction (Farber et al. 2015).

Hartzler et al. (2014) investigated the efficacy of standard feedback approaches along with developing and testing new ways of providing feedback to physicians. One illustration of the feedback tool concept is a system that provides visual feedback throughout the appointment to help the physician correct specific communication skills (Hartzler et al. 2014). In this study, participants were generally positive about the system but noted concerns that the real-time feedback could distract physicians from the task at hand.

There are several considerations when designing a feedback system, particularly if it is used during the patient visit. It should not act as a distraction from the patient, and physicians should be able to quickly understand the feedback (Faucett et al. 2017; Hartzler et al. 2014). In another study that evaluated response to visual feedback during telemedicine calls, participants did not feel that the feedback was overly distracting. Additionally, the researchers found that the system improved the balance of talking between physician and patient by decreasing interruptions and the amount of time talking in instances where physicians talked more than the patient (Faucett et al. 2017).

1.3 Paper Objectives

The objective of these sessions was to develop low-fidelity prototypes of a feedback system based on scenario-based design activities. Applying the scenario-based design process allowed us to create and evaluate several scenarios to inform design concepts for the feedback system. In order to brainstorm concepts for the physician feedback tool, we adapted Rosson's and Carrol's scenario-based design framework (Rosson and Carroll 2002a, 2002b). Figure 1 illustrates our workflow up to this point to conceptualize, analyze, iterate, and create prototypes from the scenarios.

Several studies have explored feedback in clinical settings and physician perceptions and preferences for feedback, yet few describe Rosson and Carroll's process using the four unique scenario types, from exploring and defining the problem to creating and testing a concept using scenario-based design. In this paper, we describe the use of scenario-based design methods in the context of designing tools for physicians. We provide a detailed write-up of our methods, along with the adaptations we made for this method to work for the healthcare context with nonclinical participants.

Several factors inspired our adaptations of the methods. These are primarily our reliance on human-computer interaction students and professionals for this phase and the fact that the scenario-based design sessions were all conducted remotely. Our preferred participants would be primary care physicians, since they are the people for which we are designing. However, this is a busy and difficult-to-reach population. Furthermore, due to circumstances at the time of conducting these sessions (the COVID-19 global pandemic), conducting the sessions in person was not an option. In this paper, we reflect on the use of nonclinical participants in creating concepts, along with the methods and challenges of conducting research using remote tools and methods.

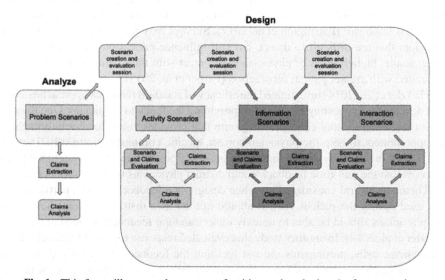

Fig. 1. This figure illustrates the process of writing and analyzing the four scenarios.

2   Methods

We held three sessions to create the scenarios. The goals of these sessions were to brainstorm, evaluate, and iterate on concepts for a feedback system. Figure 1 shows how the four scenarios were written and analyzed. The process of creating and preparing for these sessions consisted of researching and adapting methods of scenario-based design activities in a remote group setting.

2.1 Scenario-Based Design Sessions

There were three 90-min live (remote) sessions, one session each for the activity, information, and interaction scenarios. The problem scenario was created prior to the first session and was informed by a previous design workshop. Brief descriptions of each type of scenario are found in Table 1. In the sessions, participants were involved in creating the scenarios, evaluating the scenarios for claims, and analyzing the pros and cons of those claims.

Table 1. Scenario type with associated inputs and outputs

Scenario	Inputs	Outputs
Problem: – Analyze phase – Describes a situation where negative outcomes might occur due to inadequate tools or circumstances – Written by researchers	– Artifacts and themes from a previous design workshop with family medicine residents	– Claims/design requirements – Claims analysis – 1 problem scenario
Activity: – Design phase – Proposes a design to address issues and claims raised in the problem scenario – Created by session participants	– Problem scenario – Claims from problem scenarios	– Claims/design requirements – Claims analysis – 3 activity scenarios and claims evaluations
Information: – Design phase – Describes information the clinicians need and use – Created by session participants	– Activity scenarios – Claims from activity scenarios	– Claims/design requirements – Claims analysis – 3 information scenarios and claims evaluations
Interaction: – Design phase – Details how clinicians interact with the technology – Created by session participants	– Information scenarios – Claims from information scenarios	– Claims/design requirements – Claims analysis – 3 interaction scenarios and claims evaluations

Students with experience in human-computer interaction (HCI) and health-based fields were invited to participate in these three sessions. A total number of 15 people participated in the sessions, two of which attended two sessions and one of which attended all three. All participants, apart from one nursing student, were in the human-centered design graduate program. Three participants identified as male and twelve as female. Median age of attendees was 26 (range 23–55). Six participants identified as Asian/Pacific Islander, six as White/Caucasian, and three as multiracial.

Scenario-Based Design Sessions. The two activities in scenario-based design sessions were to review previous scenarios and create new scenarios. Participants worked in groups of 2–4 for both activities; there were three groups in total. After receiving an overview of the research and instructions, the groups reviewed and added to the previous scenarios' claims and claim analysis. For the second activity, they worked in the same groups to brainstorm designs based off claims from the previous scenario, draft a new scenario using those designs, and then extract and analyze claims. The inputs and outputs for each type of scenario are listed in Table 1.

For the first activity, participants identified claims by reviewing the scenario for design features that had an impact on the actors, interactions, technology, etc. The claims analysis consisted of identifying the pros and cons of each claim. The purpose of this was to assess the designs in the context and against the requirements detailed in the scenarios. While these pros and cons were not all rooted in scientific processes, they used speculation based off the inputs shared at the beginning of the session. Participants were also provided with several inputs based off appointment indicators from previous research to inform their claims analyses.

For the second activity, participants were told to spend a few minutes brainstorming ideas for the features of the scenario on which they were working. The brainstorming was informed by the background/literature review given by the facilitator, along with the claims and claims analysis that they evaluated in the previous activity. They then wrote the details of those features into the scenario. It is important to note that instead of writing an entirely new scenario, they added on to the previous scenario, focusing on the type (activity, information, interaction).

After creating the scenarios, participants extracted and analyzed claims for their newly adapted scenario, similarly to the first activity. Each session produced three scenarios with their respective claims and claims analysis.

Problem Scenario. Prior to the sessions, a problem scenario and claims were developed by the authors using the data from the previously conducted workshop. This scenario acted as the basis for the first round of scenarios, setting the scene and helping the participants understand the problem. Below is this scenario that was presented to the participants at the beginning of each session. Each of the claims is preceded by a + or – symbol; the + representing a positive claim and the – representing a negative claim.

Scenario Text

Dr. Nan recently finished her residency as a primary care physician and is working at a clinic in Chicago. She loves her job and feels it is important, but it is a difficult job.

She often feels exhausted after a day of patients. She enjoys visits with her patients, but sometimes they come in agitated or uncommunicative. Or, sometimes visits start out well, but then turn sour. It can be difficult for her to feel patient and empathetic at times.

Just an hour ago, she met with a patient experiencing a persistent chronic illness that she hoped to help alleviate. However, she had trouble connecting with this patient and she isn't sure why. She felt she wasn't able to help her patient as well as she could have. When the visit ended, she felt discouraged that her patient was still suffering. She was also left wondering what she did wrong, or how she could have tried to communicate with the patient differently. The clinic she works for collects surveys from patients that they summarize for their physicians, but that sort of feedback is only marginally helpful since she often receives it weeks after a visit has ended and it doesn't include specifics on that visit, just overall impressions.

Unfortunately, the patient was unwilling to schedule a new appointment, and never came back in. To add to that, Dr. Nan continued to worry about this patient in addition to the increasingly long hours in the evenings she was spending catching up on paperwork. This left her exhausted each following day, which started making it more and more difficult to empathize with and focus on her patients. Eventually, she wasn't able to cope with the exhaustion and lack of connection with her patients and left the practice.

Claim 1: Feedback is Received in Survey Form

+Physician can review on own time
+Doesn't take up physician or patient time during appt
+Allows for trends in common physician behaviors or incidents to be highlighted from combining feedback from multiple patients
−Summary doesn't highlight individual interactions or incidents
−Feedback may be received long after a particular interaction or incident, which doesn't allow physicians to correct negative interactions while they occur

Claim 2: Feedback is Received Directly from Patients

+Patients can describe experiences and emotions in their own words
+Patients can describe their individual visit with their provider
−Patient feedback may be critical, but not constructive
−Specific behaviors or types of interactions may be difficult for patients to recall and articulate
−Feedback may not provide evidence-based guidance on how to correct negative behaviors
−Patients may not have time to or want to take the time to fill out surveys

Data Collection During Sessions. Sessions were conducted on web conferencing software Zoom and recorded with participants' permission. Each session lasted around 90 min. A shared online document was used to facilitate and record the scenarios and analyses for each group. Artifacts from the session included the scenarios, claims, and claims analyses.

The video conferencing software Zoom was used as the primary platform for hosting the sessions. This software has the advantage of sharing screens, supporting many participants, and it has the option for breakout rooms for participants to work in smaller groups and hold conversations.

Other resources included the use of Google Docs, a product of Google Drive. This allowed participants to work collaboratively in a single document. Participants could input and edit text at the same time, along with adding images or other materials as needed.

3 Results

Three unique concepts emerged from the SBD process: 1) haptic wearable device 2) color-based visual system on computer screens, and 3) post-visit summary. The first two concepts detailed continuous real-time feedback during patient visits, and the third provided feedback after visits. The claims process resulted in evaluations and changes from one session to the next, keeping concepts aligned with the clinical workflow context from provider perspectives.

3.1 Haptic Wearable Device

The scenarios describing this feedback tool centered on a wearable that provides haptic feedback to the physician during patient visits. This device provides silent feedback as to not distract the patient. This concept has data being collected and analyzed throughout the visit, feeding the physician input through simple haptic nudges. The highlights of this concept include a visit reminder, feedback on talking balance, and a data portal to review feedback previously given.

3.2 Color-Based Visual System on Computer Screens

Similarly to the previous scenario, this device also provides feedback continuously throughout the visit. However, this concept provides visual feedback instead of haptic, showing color changes on the physician's computer screen as the format of feedback. The purpose of this type of feedback is also to provide it in a way that the patient would not detect or be distracted by the feedback. In both this concept and the one previously, the physician would be able to seamlessly make corrections to their interactions and communication with the patient for improvement.

3.3 Post-visit Summary

The scenarios describing this concept are a departure from the previous two, detailing a visual and text-based summary accessed by the physician after their visit with the patient has ended. This concept is more traditional, analyzing and sharing the data collected throughout the visit in the form of graphs and text summaries that highlight needs for improvement in the physician's encounters with their patients. It also allows for long- and short- term comparisons to see changes over time.

4   Discussion

Three adaptations were implemented given the circumstances of holding multiple sessions to write and assess the scenarios. These adaptations included: 1) informing scenarios with clinician input from a design workshop, 2) recruiting designers as participants, and 3) proving relevant information to participants during the sessions.

4.1   Informing Scenarios with Clinician Input from a Design Workshop

Prior to conducting the scenario-writing sessions, we held a design workshop where we had access to clinical participants (residents in a family medicine program). The purpose of this design workshop was to understand current and desired experiences in receiving feedback on their work and interacting with patients and other clinical staff. The workshop consisted of two activities where participants worked in groups to imagine different concepts given their preferences for feedback. These activities included a prompt exercise to understand how they currently receive and want to receive feedback, a journey map to illustrate a timeline of their typical days and weeks, and paper prototyping to brainstorm concepts (Loomis and Montague 2021).

After the workshop, we qualitatively analyzed the data for common themes using open coding techniques. These themes and concepts generated in the workshop directly impacted the creation of the problem scenario. There are many qualitative and quantitative studies that detail physicians' experiences, barriers, and the nature of their work, but directly collecting this data with an eye specifically to creating a novel feedback system was a significant advantage to informing the scenario writing sessions. These clinicians did not participate in writing the scenarios and assessing the claims, but the analytical techniques in the design workshop allowed for their experiences and input to inform the scenarios.

4.2   Recruiting Designers as Participants

Considering the difficulty of conducting research in clinical settings and recruiting clinicians as participants, students in the design and HCI programs at the university were the primary participants in the three scenario-writing sessions. While unable to reference clinical experiences, these participants were able to provide their own unique expertise in design. Understanding the process and rationale to design and iteration is challenging, so having this expertise in a short time period through virtual means might have made it more difficult for those without human-centered design experience.

There are also some ways that being solely in a clinical mindset may make it difficult to imagine completely new concepts. When the resident participants in the design workshop were instructed to create prototypes of a new type of feedback system, they quickly caught on to the idea of brainstorming concepts in groups and creating paper models of them. However, their prototypes were all slight variations of current and common ways of providing feedback to providers. While their designs and the following discussions provided further insight into how they wanted to receive feedback, their prototypes didn't actually reflect those desires (Loomis and Montague 2021). The lack of extensive experience in clinical settings may have been an advantage in this sense; participants in the scenario-writing sessions came up with concepts that hadn't been seen in physician offices before. The HCI and design participants had the advantage of familiarity with design methods, brainstorming techniques, an eye for novel and creative applications of technology, and considerations when interacting with technology aided in creating well thought out concepts.

While the participants did not have experience as providers, they likely had experience as patients. Primary care as a setting and field did not need to be described to participants. This can have positive implications as familiarity with primary care settings can still inform designs in a way that are appropriate for the settings. However, it is also possible their experiences as patients may have influenced their designs, creating concepts or features that physicians would not be comfortable with, that would not work with their workflow, or would not be appropriate in a clinical setting. These are features that only those who work in a clinical setting may recognize.

In future research, as we develop prototypes, we plan to attempt to recruit clinicians for feedback on the designs to ensure that they are feasible, usable, and desirable. Due to the success of including design and HCI participants in understanding the scenario writing and claim assessment processes, it may be helpful in the future to continue including them. We also recommend trying to recruit and pair subject matter experts in the relevant field with those that have design experience under similar circumstances.

4.3   Providing Contextual Information to Participants for the Design Sessions

The primarily design and HCI-focused participants meant that experience as a clinical provider did not inform their designs. Therefore, we started each session with the research objectives, brief background, and summary of findings from the previous design workshop. Reviewing this information with the participants provided them with insights to add to their experiences as patients to inform design choices in the scenarios. Having conducted and analyzed the previous design workshop with medical residents allowed for evidence-supported inputs to be presented to the non-clinical participants to direct their writing of the activity, information, and interaction scenarios.

These participants were introduced the goals, rationale, and clinical considerations at the beginning of each session, but we had to keep this section short due to time constraints. To help participants process and remember information, we provided each group with a link to the slides during the activities. Normally, during in-person sessions, we provide printouts or information on a projector screen to guide participants during activities. These three sessions were all conducted remotely, and participants worked on each activity in Zoom breakout rooms; this constraint prevented participants from seeing the background information and activity instructions previous shared in the main Zoom room. Providing them with individual access to the materials allowed them to review the considerations while they were writing the scenarios and claims analyses.

Despite this access, it is still possible that participants experienced information overload, as the literature and findings presented were dense and may have been primarily new knowledge. This is a difficult situation to mitigate. Simplifying the information as much as possible, scheduling in time for questions, and allowing extra time during activities to process information and activity instructions. If possible, recruiting additional facilitators with subject-matter knowledge to participate in each breakout room could help clarify findings or background information, in addition to helping participants stay on track.

5 Conclusions

Applying and adapting scenario-based design resulted in three thoughtful and unique concepts. While nearly all participants lacked experiences as clinical providers, we adapted the methods to help make sure that the scenarios were properly informed by clinician's desires and needs for a feedback tool. We accomplished this through incorporating findings from previous workshops with clinicians, recruiting participants with design experience, and providing the participants with information to direct and inform their concepts. As this was one piece in the process of designing and evaluating the feedback tool, next steps include further prototyping and user testing with designers and clinicians.

References

Farber, N.J., et al.: EHR use and patient satisfaction: what we learned. J. Fam. Pract. **64**(11), 687–696 (2015)

Farrington, C., Burt, J., Boiko, O., Campbell, J., Roland, M.: Doctors' engagements with patient experience surveys in primary and secondary care: a qualitative study. Health Expect. **20**(3), 385–394 (2017). https://doi.org/10.1111/hex.12465

Faucett, H.A., Lee, M.L., Carter, S.: I should listen more: real-time sensing and feedback of non-verbal communication in video telehealth. In: Proceedings of the ACM on Human-Computer Interaction, 1 (CSCW), Article 44 (2017). https://doi.org/10.1145/3134679

Hartzler, A.L., et al.: Real-time feedback on nonverbal clinical communication. Methods Inf. Med. **53**(05), 389–405 (2014). https://doi.org/10.3414/ME13-02-0033

Jones, W., Drake, C., Mack, D., Reeder, B., Trautner, B., Wald, H.: Developing mobile clinical decision support for nursing home staff assessment of urinary tract infection using goal-directed design. Appl. Clin. Inform. **8**(2), 632–650 (2017). https://doi.org/10.4338/ACI-2016-12-RA-0209

Loomis, A., Montague, E.: Human-centered design reflections on providing feedback to primary care physicians. In: Kurosu, M. (ed.) HCII 2021. LNCS, vol. 12764, pp. 108–118. Springer, Cham (2021). https://doi.org/10.1007/978-3-030-78468-3_8

Rosson, M.B., Carroll, J.M.: Scenario-based design. In: The Human-Computer Interaction Handbook: Fundamentals, Evolving Technologies and Emerging Applications, pp. 1032–1050. L. Erlbaum Associates Inc. (2002a)

Rosson, M.B., Carroll, J.M.: Usability Engineering: Scenario-Based Development of Human-Computer Interaction. Academic Press, San Fancisco (2002b)

Turner, A.M., Reeder, B., Ramey, J.: Scenarios, personas and user stories: user-centered evidence-based design representations of communicable disease investigations. J. Biomed. Inform. **46**(4), 575–584 (2013). https://doi.org/10.1016/j.jbi.2013.04.006

Tell Me What that Means to You: Small-Story Narratives in Technology Adoption

Brian Pickering$^{(\boxtimes)}$, Stephen C. Phillips , and Mike Surridge

Electronics and Computer Science, IT Innovation, University of Southampton, Gamma House, Enterprise Road, Southampton SO16 7NS, UK
{j.b.pickering,s.c.phillips,ms8}@soton.ac.uk

Abstract. Technology adoption is often predicted based on little information such as the *Perceived ease-of-use* and the *Perceived usefulness* of the technology. Related constructs such as *Attitude to use*, *Behavioral intention to use* and *External variables* cannot be easily operationalised and so are often ignored. However, technology characteristics themselves fail to represent other factors such as potential adopter attitudes and how they react to the opportunities offered by the technology to meet their needs. In a series of three studies, qualitative methods were used to identify, validate and then exploit narrative themes. Based on the short narratives of potential adopters discussing their experiences with a set of cybersecurity tools, we are developing a small-story narrative framework to capture how they respond to the technology contextualised directly within their professional environment. Akin to concepts from adoption frameworks in healthcare intervention studies, we conclude that adopter's personal response to a technology and how they make sense of it in their environment becomes evident in the narratives they create.

Keywords: Technology acceptance · Technology adoption · Mixed methods · Qualitative methods · Narrative analysis · Grounded theory · Small-story narratives

1 Introduction

Causal models provide an elegant conceptualisation to explain the intention to act [1–3], even to adopt technology [4]. Their simplicity and apparent robustness may account for their continued attraction [5]. In the case of technology acceptance, the primacy of *Perceived ease-of-use*, though contested [6,7], is bolstered by the robustness of similar instruments such as the *System Usability*

This work was supported by the EU H2020 project CyberKit4SME (Grant agreement: 883188); and in part by the FogProtect project, a Horizon 2020 Research and Innovation Action to secure sensitive data along the computing continuum (under grant agreement No. 871525).

Scale [8,9]. With technology, and despite the introduction of some contextual and user perspectives [10], the assumption is largely that features of the technology itself such as ease of use are enough to predict user adoption. However, other models such as the *Health Belief Model* [11] in healthcare and *Protection Motivation Theory* [12] introduce user perceptions and projected self-efficacy alongside aspects of the technology or intervention, bringing the human dimension to the fore [13]. Interestingly, software development practice has attempted to include a user perspective explicitly via user stories [14] or even interviews [15] to elicit requirements and scenario testing [16] so as to explore the likelihood that a technology would meet those requirements. Whether meeting requirements is enough to ensure acceptance is a moot point. Approaches like *Diffusion of Innovations* [17] would suggest that contextual information, including communication channels and adopter readiness, is equally important. Similarly, frameworks such as *Non-adoption, Abandonment, Scale-up, Spread and Sustainability* (NASSS) [18] and *Normalisation Process Theory* (NPT) [19] in healthcare include stakeholder perspectives, engagement and common action involving potential users and developers to encourage adoption and sustainability for the technology or intervention.

In so doing, these frameworks foreground potential user perceptions when engaging with a technology and the broader context of its use rather than assuming that features of the technology itself are sufficient to guarantee ongoing use. Identifying those perceptions and attitudes when using technology needs some thought. Standard instruments, for instance, may not capture this information and may even be misleading. For instance, we have previously reported qualitative research highlighting apparent contradictions between quantitative measures of acceptability and potential adopters' perceptions of technology [20,21]. Nonetheless, although quantitative instruments appear robust [8,9], there is some scope to refine these instruments on the basis of user expectations and demographic characteristics [9]. Further, it has been known for some considerable time that participants in experimental or test settings may second-guess what they are being asked to do and therefore perform to please the questioner rather than report their own responses truthfully and don't necessarily target the right issues and individuals [22,23]. One method to overcome any such issues involves a mixed-methods approach: using qualitative methods alongside and to supplement findings from quantitative instruments. The purpose of the present study is to attempt to identify a qualitative research approach to allow users to articulate their experience with technology in a meaningful way for developers and service providers to understand the real effectiveness of their technology or service. This would then complement results from traditional quantitative methods to provide a comprehensive view of the relevance of a technology and its ultimate adoption.

2   Background

To work around potential artificiality with quantitative surveys, ethnographic studies, whereby potential adopters are observed while interacting with a given technology, are employed to understand technology use and applicability within a specific context [24]. This approach has already provided valuable insight into technology adoption [25] as well as power relations in virtual communities [26] and even research contexts [27]. Observing potential adopter behaviours in this way may identify potential adopters' responses to technology in the context of their own and socially constructed narratives.

A think-aloud protocol typically addresses actual use and experience with a technology, rather than more general perceptions and attitudes towards its adoption. By contrast, narrative approaches specifically would provide users an opportunity to relate their specific use and experience of a technology as part of a think-aloud protocol [28]. Narrative psychology assumes that we tell *stories* to make sense of our experience [29]. These stories tend to order relevant events temporally or by importance and may be *progressive* (our goals are satisfied), *regressive* (our goals are frustrated), or *stability* narratives (we set out what's happened without reference to goal achievement) [30]. More generalised narrative approaches focus on the structure and content of the *stories* we tell to make sense of our lives and environment [29,31], rather than specific technology-mediated activity. As opposed to life-course descriptions, small-story narratives emphasise naturally occurring "narratives-in-interaction" [32,33]. Through such interactions, the adopter begins to *make sense* of how the technology might benefit them.

Specifically, where technology is potentially disruptive - changing processes and requiring user adaptation - small stories may provide an insight into adopter perceptions developed as a response to technology affordances [34]. In personalising their experiences and recognising the relevance of technology adoption specific to them, self-efficacy - that is the belief that one is able to manage better, in this context, by using technology - increases. This encourages further exploration, and even a willingness to overlook some of the shortcomings of the technology in its present state [35,36]. Indeed, self-efficacy has also been shown to affect trust in that technology as well as adoption and sustained use [37].

In the present study, we explore a small-story narrative approach to evaluate responses to cybersecurity technologies which model socio-technical systems and identify associated risks and mitigations [38], and formalise the customer journey through typical work activities [39]. Specifically, we attempt to formalise a research approach to elicit potential adopter small-story narratives indicative of an intention to adopt.

This research is based on three separate interactions over a period of time with potential users of one or both of the cybersecurity technologies cited. The first involves nine employees with different roles of a medium-sized UK-based Small-to-medium enterprise (SME) responsible for secure data handling solutions to public authorities. The second involved four EU-based SMEs directly validating the cybersecurity technologies. The same four EU-based SMEs were approached again along with another EU-based project and three more SMEs, making seven in total.

3   Method

Three separate studies were run. *Study 1* and *Study 2* involved a review of standard interactions between developers and potential adopters. More precisely, the first involved a secondary analysis of recordings from a *workshop*, and the second was a secondary analysis of recordings from meetings where participants discussed the technologies as part of *technology validation*. The recordings had not been made specifically for ethnographic research therefore. *Study 3* was explicitly designed to elicit a narrative relating to the potential adopters' experience with the technologies in question. *Study 1* provided the initial impetus to explore narratives of technology adoption, leading to *Study 2* where the results of the previous analysis were validated, and *Study 3* sought to test that the assumptions from *Studies 1* and *2* could be generalised elsewhere.

3.1   Study 1: *Workshop*

During a one-day workshop, the nine SME employees were shown one of the technologies and asked to develop a model of a socio-technical system highlighting potential cybersecurity threats and mitigations. Towards the end of the workshop and after hands-on experience of the technology to develop the model, there was a final session during which attendees were simply asked to discuss their experience using the technology. Recordings were analysed applying a combination of narrative analysis [30] to identify how participants responded to the technology, and thematic analysis and grounded theory [40,41] to develop a coding scheme for subsequent interactions. This work was approved by the faculty ethics committee (ERGO/FEPS/46678).

3.2   Study 2: *Technology Validation*

The second study comprised recordings from a series of project status meetings. There were four SMEs in total working across finance, utilities, healthcare and automotive sectors. Four end-users, one from each SME, were asked during the initial sessions to describe their basic operations and their expectations from the cybersecurity technologies. A second set of recordings was an annual status update approximately a year later, when the SMEs had some experience of the technologies in question. This work was approved by the faculty ethics committee (ERGO/FEPS/62067).

3.3   Study 3: *Protocol Validation*

The third and final phase for this exploratory study sought to validate the observations and data-driven findings from the first two. Seven SMEs were approached, four from *Study 2* and a further three from a different collaborative project. The three additional SMEs operate in manufacturing, broadcasting and safe-city technologies. As a grounded theory approach, data were explicitly collected with a view to using the codes identified in *Study 1* and validated in *Study*

2 as the basis for a research instrument. This consisted of three open-ended questions (see below in Sect. 4.1), each with a secondary prompt to encourage more discursive input. In order to reduce the burden on participants and in the hope of speeding up data collection, participants were given the choice to respond in writing to the questions using 100–200 words or attend a short, online meeting of around 30 to 45 min with one of the researchers (BP) based around the same three open-ended questions as part of a semi-structured interview. This work was approved by the faculty ethics committee (ERGO/FEPS/70387).

4 Results

4.1 Study 1: *Workshop*

An initial thematic analysis of the transcripts yielded thirty-three functional and non-functional requirements across seven different areas. Although not a typical data collection exercise for narrative analysis, once particular issues with the technology and the potential adopters' perceptions including concerns around perceived usability had been discussed, several employees began to develop their own narratives specific to personal benefits they might derive by using the technology. These narratives were analysed in terms of structure, coherence and identity development in the first instance.

The following extract occurs over many minutes. The participant (P1.7) kept coming back to their original point despite several other turns in the conversation.

> P1.7: *A year ago we had some pen testing on the* [PRODUCT] *and there was a bug report raised, 'please implement this' and I was looking at that and saying, hang on, this has got bad side effects, how do we deal with making decisions whether to implement this or not ... you're quite right, some customers wouldn't understand it at all. But you're almost like if you decided you want to tell the customer about a risk and it's going to cost them money, to go in with a diagram that's got their components and bits they can understand and to show them ... .*

The participant has picked up on a discussion about adding a documentation feature to the technology. They begin by situating their input (*A year ago*) which is then expanded with various details linked with *and*. So, this is a short, coherent narrative which introduces something important to this participant.

Others contribute similarly from their own perspective.

> P1.6: *In the last six months we've had a couple of projects, haven't we? We've had one where basically security testing has been a major part of the project and it's been quite a thorny and protracted affair. If we had something like* [this] *which could lay the groundwork quickly and efficiently that might have been a big help.*

and

P1.8: But you are talking days at a time. Because if you think how much time we spend, I spend, filling in tender documents on security requirements and so on and if you had something like this, it allows you to construct it a lot quicker.

Such narratives may not be complete in the traditional sense but instead represent snippets of experience relevant to specific technology-mediated tasks. Users overlook any current shortcomings or gaps in function to imagine how their responsibilities might be addressed through future engagement with the technology.

Subsequently, thematic analysis focused specifically on the transcript for the latter part of the workshop. There are cases where participants identify that the technology (with or without updates) could benefit their work:

P1.2: Every mitigation that requires action needs to give rise to a developer task that a developer is given and then signs off as tested and it's totally signed off before release. So the mitigations output could be used for that as well and you could I'm sure devise an output that would satisfy both those requirements.

and

P1.9: If we can give that person all of the information and then it's clear it helps our argument to get something fixed as well.

These all relate to *Task applicability* or its relevance for the responsibility of the organisation. Elsewhere, participants identify the potential value of the technology not just for the organisation, but also for themselves:

P1.9: There's another perspective from our side being system admins. I know it's not to a customer but essentially our managers and our directors are our customers in some regard because they're the ones deciding whether to pay for things.

and

P1.8: If you could get... because I'm just thinking I have to do my audits, if I could draw a system, you know, potentially even draw our entire network on it, at least to some approximation.

Here, there is the *Personalisation* of the potential relevance of the technology. Finally, there appears to be a particular point in the discussion where a participant suddenly realises that there is potential for the technology - again with or without modification - to offer support for many other tasks:

P1.8 If I had something like that. I don't want something that's pages and pages but, you know, a table of risks versus mitigation actions [...] From an audit perspective it would show quite a depth of understanding.

similarly

P1.2: *Because actually you've got your documentation, you've got it could actually help with the sales pitch and then there's the angle of actually if it stopped us having horrible expensive incidents or even reduced support because we never even had to fix the things, which is intangible. So it's interesting there's three different angles on that. So it would have a value.*

These individual themes represent three superordinate themes summarised in Table 1.

Table 1. Superordinate themes

Theme	Description
Anchoring	A specific connection point between the demonstrated technology and the SME's work, equivalent to an *epiphany* in traditional narratives [42]
Task applicability	The relevance to the narrator's own responsibilities
Personalization	Where the narrator sets out increased self-efficacy through adoption of the technology

These three narrative themes were used as codes to analyse the recordings from *Study 2* as a means of independent validation. Subsequently, they informed the formulation of three seed questions, plus a prompt to encourage further elaboration by the participant, to guide data collection for *Study 3*.

4.2 Study 2: *Technology Validation*

From the sessions, some thirty-four functional and non-functional requirements were identified across nine different areas. To begin with, employees from the four European based SMEs described first their business and business needs without direct experience of the technologies. An initial analysis of these sessions was reported elsewhere [43]. Stability narratives developed, relevant to the current situation at the SME. For instance, in this extract, there are typical markers of narrative progression, such as '*so*' and '*and then*'.

P2.2: *so we have different ways of working, so err marketing and promotion seminars [...] that's the commercial part [...] So to demonstrate the different features of the platform... Erm... and so it's indeed going step-by-step usually. So starting with a first pilot project on small cases of business... small buildings [...]. And then, once we are running it during a few weeks or a few months so it's err an agreement that we sign and then when it's OK they can do a more larger rollout.*

Narratives here are more discursive since participants were explicitly asked to describe their operations. In the project status meetings, there were cases of specific themes. For example, *anchoring* was evidenced by different participants.

P3.1: *we found it very easy which was a bit compelling for us, and we couldn't understand whether we were doing the right thing or not.*

and

P4.1: *we didn't use - as I said - [TOOL] before. Now, I think, it's more useful to have five more diagrams [...] to cover everything we discovered using the [TOOL].*

So, with some experience of the technologies, participants may also see potential beyond the current requirements and activities. Similarly, they are aware of the *Task applicability* of the technology:

P2.1: *Company [NAME] is particularly interested in understanding situations where trading will become impossible. For example, lack of source information from third parties and attacks against the desktop trading app.*

and later goes on to say:

P2.1: [TOOL] *will be used ... to understand possible risks in each process and to prioritise the deployment of security controls, avoiding catastrophic downtimes.*

Anchoring led elsewhere to *personalisation* and developing narratives in anticipation of future use with the technologies as seen in the first study from the one-day workshop with the UK SME:

P1.2: *so* [TOOL] *is becoming part of their* modus operandi.

So, in *Study 2*, there is some evidence that the three superordinate themes in Table 1 are relevant more generally. When reporting to other partners about their experience with the target technologies, they were able to identify potential and to recognise organisational and personal relevance. These were semi-formal sessions, but still participants showed consistent behaviour in response to the target technologies as in *Study 1* in regard to going beyond the simple usefulness and usability of the technology in the specific test environment.

4.3   Study 3: *Protocol Validation*

In this final study, a set of seed questions was developed to elicit small-story narratives constructed around the three superordinate themes identified in *Study 1*. Along with the corresponding theme, the seed questions are shown in Table 2; in each case, a short prompt was added (that is, *Why?* or *How?*) to encourage a

Table 2. Open-ended questions and the associated Narrative codes

Narrative code	Question	Prompt
Anchoring	*What would these cybersecurity tools mean to your organisation?*	Why?
Task applicability	*Would these tools help you specifically with your own job?*	How?
Personalization	*Would these tools give you a sense that you could manage your use better?*	How?

respondent to elaborate on their answers. To date, three SMEs have responded, one choosing an online meeting (*O*), the other two answering in writing (*W*).

To begin with, one of the participants called out a common problem: *communication*. Technologists tend to assume that technical excellence is enough without considering the expectations or aspirations of potential adopters. Interestingly, the participant develops a narrative to describe the frustrations of interacting with technology. See Sect. 4.3 below.

Communication. During the online semi-structured interview, the participant identified a particular problem.

> P5.O *When someone tells me what they have, I don't get that same feeling or this is what could help me or ... on the other hand, if I see something, and I see it working [...] then this could help me... The problem with [PROJECT] is... I understand what it's about, I've have [created a test environment] ... it's basically, when we have those Eureka moments ... and we've had some of those moments already... in the first year, maybe, oh and we put together a scenario, but when you put it all together in a scenario, suddenly it didn't make sense for the [technology] partner ... while for us, we thought we understood. We are doing the same thing in another context, so why doesn't it make sense now?*

In Gergen and Gergen's terminology, this represents a *regressive narrative* [30]. The potential adopter is frustrated in their goals. To begin with, they engage with what the technologists tell them. Next, they create a scenario; but then, the technologists reject it. Later, the participant acknowledges there needs to be a 'common language' for technologists and adopters to communicate effectively. They conclude:

> P5.O*It may be a long stretch - it wasn't part of our scenario - but it made sense. But it was part of the bigger narrative for us.*

This is not an uncommon issue: 'selling' technology is about understanding and meeting user needs, not just technical elegance: *Perceived usefulness* and *Perceived ease of use* in Technology acceptance terms.

Anchoring. The three SMEs identify moments where they can see potential beyond the current capabilities of the technology on offer.

> P3.W *Gaining deeper knowledge about the tools and the inferred characteristics of our own internal infrastructure and the software components that we implement allows us to be in control and gives us more options for change management.*

There is even a suggestion that technology may highlight important issues which had not previously been apparent.

> P4.W: *The tools are very good instruments to be aware of threats that we did not foreseen [sic] till now.*

and

> P3.W *These tools enable our company to see some hidden aspects of the cybersecurity domain, allowing us to explore new alternatives/tools to deal with the new security challenges.*

They even acknowledge how such insights develop: *anchoring* is described here as *Eureka moments.*

> P5.O: *So, we had some Eureka moments by talking about it and about thinking about it.*

though the participant admits that some of the Eureka moments *'were duds'*. This suggests they are willing to try new things without an assurance that they will deliver what they expect.

There is some evidence, therefore, for *anchoring*. Potential adopters are therefore open to innovation and going beyond what the technology is used for now.

Task Applicability. Participants recognise the applicability of the technologies they are trialling. The potential of the technology to meet current and future organisational requirements is easy to see:

> P3.W: *In our daily business, having a full picture of the involved components of our internal infrastructure helps us to integrate new tools and actors seamlessly with the full knowledge of all the incurred risks and vulnerabilities,*

even encouraging improved cybersecurity awareness and behaviours:

> P4.W: *The tools are important to establish a culture of security within the products that we develop. Application security, information security, network security, are all part of what we do nowadays.*

There is even an acknowledgement that the potential adopter can see how the technologies might be part of a bigger picture for the enterprise.

P5.O *It may be a long stretch - it wasn't part of our scenario - but it made sense. But it was part of the bigger narrative for us,*

providing increased confidence and self-efficacy:

P5.O *Now that we are further in the project and we understand it more and understand where every partner comes from, we would respond to that remark differently. And we would say: OK, maybe you're wrong, and we could explain it better.*

Potential adopters can see how the technologies can fulfill existing company requirements. More importantly, as evidenced by P5.O, there is also a sense that engaging with the technology irrespective of how it has been positioned for them can lead to feelings of *self-efficacy*. Of course, this relates to trust in technology [37].

Personalisation. The final construct is the personal relevance, related to *self-efficacy*, that potential adopters can see with the technology now or in the future.

P5.O *At the point of the trial, there were too many technical issues. But conceptually, we were on to something that made sense.*

P5.O here recognises technical limitations but is nevertheless more driven by the technology *making sense* and satisfying their own conception of what the technology could allow. Indeed, the partners also recognise that they can work *with* the technology, whilst recognising their goals are limited as far as cybersecurity is concerned.

P3.W *The tools do not allow us to become security experts but it raises awareness into our internal team about challenges that we didn't [sic.] face in the past.*

Finally, there is an indication that individual adopters are open to engaging and speculating about innovative ways to exploit the technology.

P5.O *It would be really useful ... nice to have in another context, the experience of that so you could make that association and see 'O.K... I see how that could work'.*

In seeing potential, partners identify personal relevance for them as individuals. This encourages them to consider what their priorities are and, most importantly, motivates independent innovative speculation.

5   Discussion

We believe these narratives demonstrate a more nuanced approach to technology engagement. Significantly, we suggest, they involve much greater *personal* relevance than user stories or scenario testing. The narrative snippets seen especially in *Study 1* represent the effect of the technology on the professional identity of the participant. The way the technology is perceived becomes a part of the *performance* of that identity [44].

   Diffusion of Innovations [17] stresses the contribution beyond attributes of the innovation or technology to consider traits of the potential adopter, the associated communication channels, and the social system or context where the innovation might be used. Similarly, NASSS considers seven different areas, including the technology itself, which need to be addressed to encourage adoption and promote long term sustainability [18]. The concepts of *coherence* and *cognitive participation* in NPT formalise the requirement for stakeholders to recognise potential in the proposed technology not only to solve current issues for them, but to enable a very personal improvement in self-efficacy [19,45]. What the narratives revealed, and specifically at the *Task applicability* point, is a realisation of potential irrespective of the current state of the technology. Participants began to see what they *might* achieve even though new features would need to be developed and existing shortcomings resolved. They are seeing the potential as it relates specifically to their professional identity [43]. At that point, they begin to create narrative snippets around scenarios important to them professionally and which would become progressive narratives once their imagined version of the technology became available to them.

   This very much supports the idea that focusing solely on characteristics of the technology for adoption is not enough. Small-story narratives provide a methodological framework therefore to explore how users perceive not just the technology (as in the Technology Acceptance Model) or subjective norms (as in the Theory of Planned Behaviour), but how potential adopters can make sense of their responsibilities and how they may be benefitted by interaction with the technology. It's worth noting too that adopters will be accommodating towards technical faults and lack of function [35,36]. Potential adopters are therefore willing to look beyond current performance. If they can engage and understand potential, then they can be creative in the way they approach technology. Technology acceptance is therefore situated within a progressive narrative rather than solely dependent on technology usability or even perceived usefulness.

6   Limitations and Future Work

Cohort size is often a consideration in qualitative research. Whereas quantitative studies rely on power calculations as an estimate of the reliability of results and therefore how generalisable they may be, saturation remains a challenging concept [46]. There is a question, therefore, how generalisable the results reported here might be. Saturation can only really be satisfactorily identified *a posteriori*, however. Nonetheless, we believe there is sufficient evidence now to inform and motivate further research in this area.

That being said, there are other limitations which should be noted. First, this was very much a research cohort drawn from an opportunity sample: all participants were engaged in collaborative projects with the technology developers. There is a sense, therefore, in which they are motivated to work with and look for ways to identify benefits from those technologies. In other words, there is an incentive for them to react positively to the technology. Future work should consider sampling strategies and how best to ensure generalisability across technology users. Secondly, as far as narratives are concerned, these interactions were not specifically designed to elicit more discursive descriptions of issues or the exploration of how to move forward based on existing technology. In consequence, participants produced narrative 'snippets' rather than more traditional small-story pieces. It would be fruitful to attempt to encourage more reflective use of technology and associated experiences to be able to situate and perhaps provoke innovative thinking around the technologies, that is to encourage *Anchoring*.

Finally, in light of empirical work with adoption frameworks such as NASSS and NPT, it would be worthwhile to consider how encouraging narratives from potential adopters might inform concepts such as *cognitive participation*. By allowing potential adopters to develop their own ideas of how a technology in its current or in a future state might benefit their work, it may be possible to increase the potential for technology adoption.

7   Conclusion

The research reported here is part of a broader concern with the assumption that technology adoption can be predicted solely on the basis of the characteristics of the technology itself. In his original conception of the Technology Acceptance Model of course, Davis did include other constructs which have received less attention than *Perceived ease-of-use* and *Perceived usefulness* [4]. These include *Attitude to use* and *Behavioral intention to use* on the one hand, and *External variables* on the other. It may well be that small-story narratives could influence *Attitude to use* at least in that these narratives may capture potential adopter perceptions that the technology presented would work for them and help them achieve their specific goals.

References

1. Ajzen, I.: The theory of planned behavior. Org. Behav. Human Decis. Process. **50**(2), 179–211 (1991). https://doi.org/10.1016/0749-5978(91)90020-T
2. Montaño, D.E., Kasprzyk, D.: Theory of reasoned action, theory of planned behavior, and the integrated behavioral model. In: Glanz, K., Rimer, B.K., Viswanath, K. (eds.) Health Behavior: Theory, Research and Practice, pp. 95–124. Jossey-Bass, San Francisco (2015)

3. Kautonen, T., van Gelderen, M., Fink, M.: Robustness of the theory of planned behavior in predicting entrepreneurial intentions and actions. Entrep. Theory Pract. **39**(3), 655–674 (2015). https://doi.org/10.1111/etap.12056
4. Davis, F.D.: Perceived usefulness, perceived ease of use, and user acceptance of information technology. MIS Q. **13**(3), 319–340 (1989). https://doi.org/10.2307/249008
5. Taherdoost, H.: A review of technology acceptance and adoption models and theories. Proc. Manuf. **22**, 960–967 (2018). https://doi.org/10.1016/j.promfg.2018.03.137
6. Holden, R.J., Karsh, B.-T.: The technology acceptance model: its past and its future in health care. J. Biomed. Inf. **43**(1), 159–172 (2010). https://doi.org/10.1016/j.jbi.2009.07.002
7. King, W.R., He, J.: A meta-analysis of the technology acceptance model. Inf. Manag. **43**(6), 740–755 (2006). https://doi.org/10.1016/j.im.2006.05.003
8. Lewis, J.R.: The system usability scale: past, present, and future. J. Hum. Comput. Interact. **34**(7), 577–590 (2018). https://doi.org/10.1080/10447318.2018.1455307
9. Bangor, A., Kortum, P.T., Miller, J.T.: An empirical evaluation of the system usability scale. Int. J. Hum. Comput. Interact. **24**(6), 574–594 (2008). https://doi.org/10.1080/10447310802205776
10. Venkatesh, V., Morris, M.G., Davis, G.B., Davis, F.D.: User acceptance of information technology: toward a unified view. MIS Q. **27**(3), 425–478 (2003)
11. Carpenter, C.J.: A meta-analysis of the effectiveness of health belief model variables in predicting behavior. Health Commun. **25**(8), 661–669 (2010). https://doi.org/10.1080/10410236.2010.521906
12. Norman, P., Boer, H., Seydel, E.R.: Protection motivation theory. In: Conner, M., Norman, P. (eds.) Predicting Health Behaviour, pp. 81–126. The Open University Press, Maidenhead (2005)
13. Legris, P., Ingham, J., Collerette, P.: Why do people use information technology? A critical review of the technology acceptance model. Inf. Manag. **40**(3), 191–204 (2003). https://doi.org/10.1016/S0378-7206(01)00143-4
14. Lucassen, G., Dalpiaz, F., van der Werf, J.M.E.M., Brinkkemper, S.: The use and effectiveness of user stories in practice. In: Daneva, M., Pastor, O. (eds.) REFSQ 2016. LNCS, vol. 9619, pp. 205–222. Springer, Cham (2016). https://doi.org/10.1007/978-3-319-30282-9_14
15. Dieste, O., Juristo, N.: Systematic review and aggregation of empirical studies on elicitation techniques. IEEE Trans. Softw. Eng. **37**(2), 283–304 (2011). https://doi.org/10.1109/TSE.2010.33
16. Carroll, J.M.: Five reasons for scenario-based design. In: Proceedings of the 32nd Hawaii International Conference on System Sciences 5th–8th January 1999 (1999). https://doi.org/10.1109/HICSS.1999.772890
17. Rogers, E.: The Diffusion of Innovations, 5th edn. The Free Press, New York (2003)
18. Greenhalgh, T., et al.: Beyond adoption: a new framework for theorizing and evaluating nonadoption, abandonment, and challenges to the scale-up, spread, and sustainability of health and care technologies. J. Med. Internet Res. **19**(11), 367, e367 (2017). https://doi.org/10.2196/jmir.8775
19. May, C.R., et al.: Development of a theory of implementation and integration: normalization process theory. Implement. Sci. **4**(1), 29 (2009). https://doi.org/10.1186/1748-5908-4-29

20. Pickering, B., Janian, M.N., López Moreno, B., Micheletti, A., Sanno, A., Surridge, M.: Seeing potential is more important than usability: revisiting technology acceptance. In: Marcus, A., Wang, W. (eds.) HCII 2019. LNCS, vol. 11586, pp. 238–249. Springer, Cham (2019). https://doi.org/10.1007/978-3-030-23535-2_18

21. Pickering, B., Bartholomew, R., Nouri Janian, M., López Moreno, B., Surridge, M.: *Ask me no questions*: increasing empirical evidence for a qualitative approach to technology acceptance. In: Kurosu, M. (ed.) HCII 2020. LNCS, vol. 12181, pp. 125–136. Springer, Cham (2020). https://doi.org/10.1007/978-3-030-49059-1_9

22. Orne, M.T.: On the social psychology of the psychological experiment: with particular reference to demand characteristics and their implications. Am. Psychol. **17**, 776–783 (1962)

23. Ponto, J.: Understanding and evaluating survey research. J. Adv. Pract. Oncol. **6**(2), 168–171 (2015)

24. Brown, A.: The place of ethnographic methods in information systems research. Int. J. Multip. Res. Approach. **8**(2), 166–178 (2014) https://doi.org/10.1080/18340806.2014.11082058

25. Pope, C., Halford Turnbull, S.J., Prichard, J., Calestani, M., May, C.: Using computer decision support systems in NHS emergency and urgent care: ethnographic study using normalisation process theory. BMC Health Serv. Res. **13**, 111 (2013) https://doi.org/10.1186/1472-6963-13-111

26. Nguyen, L., Torlina, L., Peszynski, K., Corbitt, B.: Power relations in virtual communities: an ethnographic study. Electron. Commerce. Res. **6**, 21–37 (2006). https://doi.org/10.1007/s10660-006-5986-9

27. Harrington, B.: The social psychology of access in ethnographic research. J. Contemp. Ethnogr. **32**(5), 592–625 (2003). https://doi.org/10.1177/0891241603255677

28. McDonald, S., Edwards, H.M., Zhao, T.: Exploring think-alouds in usability testing: an international survey. IEEE Trans. Profess. Commun. **55**(1), 2–19 (2012). https://doi.org/10.1109/TPC.2011.2182569

29. Murray, M.: Narrative psychology. In: Smith, J.A. (ed.) Qualitative Psychology: A Practical Guide to Research Methods, pp. 85–107. SAGE Publications Ltd., London (2015)

30. Gergen, K.J., Gergen, M.M.: Narrative form and the construction of psychological science. In: Sarbin, T. (ed.) Narrative Psychology: The Storied Nature of Human Conduct, pp. 22–44. Praeger, New York (1986)

31. Murray, M.: Narrative psychology and narrative analysis. In: Camic, P.M., Rhodes, J.E., Yardley, L. (eds.) Qualitative Research in Psychology: Expanding Perspectives in Methodology and Design, pp. 95–112. American Psychological Association, Washington (2003)

32. Stokoe, E., Edwards, D.: Story formulations in talk-in-interaction. Narrat. Inq. **16**(1), 56–65 (2006). https://doi.org/10.1075/ni.16.1.09sto

33. Bamberg, M., Georgakopoulou, A.: Small stories as a new perspective in narrative and identity analysis. Text Talk Interdiscip. J. Lang. Discour. Commun. Stud. **28**, 377–396 (2008)

34. Pozzi, G., Pigni, F., Vitari, C.: Affordance theory in the IS discipline: a review and synthesis of the literature. In: AMCIS 2014 Proceedings, 2014, Savannah (2014). https://halshs.archives-ouvertes.fr/halshs-01923663/document

35. Lee, L.D., Moray, N.: Trust, control strategies and allocation of function in human-machine systems. Ergonomics **35**(10), 1243–1270 (1992). https://doi.org/10.1080/00140139208967392

36. Lee, J.D., See, K.A.: Trust in automation: designing for appropriate reliance. Hum. Fact. J. Hum. Fact. Ergon. Soc. **46**(1), 50–80 (2004). https://doi.org/10.1518/hfes. 46.1.50_30392
37. Thatcher, J.B., Zimmer, J.C., Gundlach, M.J., McKnight, D.H.: Internal and external dimensions of computer self-efficacy: an empirical examination. IEEE Trans. Eng. Manag. **55**(4), 628–644 (2008). https://doi.org/10.1109/TEM.2008.927825
38. Surridge, M., et al.: Modelling compliance threats and security analysis of cross border health data exchange. In: Attiogbé, C., Ferrarotti, F., Maabout, S. (eds.) MEDI 2019. CCIS, vol. 1085, pp. 180–189. Springer, Cham (2019). https://doi. org/10.1007/978-3-030-32213-7_14
39. Boletsis, C., Halvorsrud, R., Pickering, J., Phillips, S., Surridge, M.: Cybersecurity for SMEs: introducing the human element into socio-technical cybersecurity risk assessment. In: Hurter, C., Purchase, H., Braz, J., Bouatouch, K. (eds.) Proceedings of the 16th International Joint Conference on Computer Vision, Imaging and Computer Graphics Theory and Applications - IVAPP, pp. 266–274 (2021). https://doi.org/10.5220/0010332902660274
40. Braun, V., Clarke, V.: Using thematic analysis in psychology. Qualit. Res. Psychol. **3**(2), 77–101 (2006). https://doi.org/10.1191/1478088706qp063oa
41. Alhojailan, M.I.: Thematic analysis: a critical review of its process and evaluation. West East J. Soc. Sci. **1**(1), 39–47 (2012)
42. Murray, M.: Levels of narrative analysis in health psychology. J. Health Psychol. **5**(3), 337–347 (2000)
43. Pickering, B., Boletsis, C., Halvorsrud, R., Phillips, S., Surridge, M.: *It's not my problem*: how healthcare models relate to SME cybersecurity awareness. In: Moallem, A. (ed.) HCII 2021. LNCS, vol. 12788, pp. 337–352. Springer, Cham (2021). https://doi.org/10.1007/978-3-030-77392-2_22
44. Bauman, R.: Language, identity, performance. Pragmatics **10**, 1–6 (2000)
45. May, C.R., Finch, T.: Implementing, embedding, and integrating practices: an outline of normalization process theory. Sociology **43**(3), 535–554 (2009). https:// doi.org/10.1177/0038038509103208
46. O'Reilly, M., Parker, N.: 'Unsatisfactory saturation': a critical exploration of the notion of saturated sample sizes in qualitative research. Qualit. Res. **13**(2), 190–197 (2013). https://doi.org/10.1177/1468794112446106

Uncertainty of Information (UoI) Taxonomy Assessment Based on Experimental User Study Results

Adrienne Raglin[(⊠)], Aleah Emlet, Justine Caylor, John Richardson, Mark Mittrick, and Somiya Metu

Army Research Laboratory, 2800 Powder Mill Road, Adelphi, MD 20783, USA
adrienne.raglin2.civ@army.mil

Abstract. Current Army operations rely on decision making processes that are driven by data and the knowledge and expertise of the commanders, analysts, and other decision makers. These decision makers are increasingly dealing with information that is incomplete or of uncertain reliability. The large volume of data along with the wide diversity of information sources can contribute to this uncertainty. Defining computational models of uncertainty of information (UoI) will enable the creation of automated tools that assist the decision maker by ranking relevant information, identifying emergent decision points, and recommend potential alternate courses of action. DEVCOM ARL researchers conducted an experimental user study to explore how soldiers might prioritize these models in the taxonomy given two scenarios. This paper analyzes these results and highlights patterns that can further aid how intelligent systems can support decision making ensuring that the decision maker maintains an understanding of uncertainties associated with the information.

Keywords: Uncertainty of information · Taxonomy assessment · Artificial intelligence · Decision-making · User study

1 Introduction

There are numerous sources of data that can be used in the decision-making process. In the wake of the idea of big data, the sources of the data have expanded to include data from industry, government, and the public. Like others the Army has to contend with every growing potential source of data. And like others the Army has to rely on various sources of data to make decisions. This challenge reemphasizes the fact that no data source is perfect all the time. Chengular-Smith's paper [1] reminds us of the ongoing question of the quality of data, even data supported by database designs he acknowledges that this data "may not be of ideal quality". He goes on to say that even with this limitation "decision makers often must utilize data that are inherently unverifiable". In addition, he states that database designers that are tasked with supporting decision making are dealing

M. Kurosu (Ed.): HCII 2022, LNCS 13302, pp. 290–301, 2022.
https://doi.org/10.1007/978-3-031-05311-5_20

with imperfect data. Again, in Fisher's paper [2] the theme continues to be an important one, with the varied factors that impact decision making, the quality of the data is key. While these papers present the ideas for capturing that data quality, our research has taken a slightly different viewpoint. This is to explore how any issues in the quality of data or more specifically the uncertainty of the data can be captured, communicated, and utilized. Given this our work has been inspired by Gershon's imperfect nature of information [3] where he discusses how that uncertainty can be expressed. Thus, our work focused on creating a concept for uncertainty of information. Moreover, with a computational model, intelligent systems can provide decision makers with any associated uncertainty of information connected with the data that is being used to make decisions. As a part of this research, we have reached out to Soldiers to assist us in evaluating the uncertainty of information concept so that we can continue to refine the computational model.

In this paper we will give a brief overview of the UoI model, in particular its taxonomy that are descriptors for uncertainty for the different data source categories, and present the findings from our user study with our subject matter experts.

2 Uncertainty of Information (UoI)

The concept of the Uncertainty of Information (UoI) was to be able to not just have a value that can be expressed but that the value would incorporate descriptors that express uncertainties. We selected descriptor based on the nature of imperfection information as presented in Gershon's paper [4]. These descriptors form a taxonomy that attempt to capture the causes and express the type of uncertainty for a given source. Currently the taxonomy consists of inconsistent, corrupt, disjoint, incomplete, imprecise, complicated and questionable.

The current version of UoI expression is a weighted sum as seen in Eq. 1:

$$UoI_{dp} = \sum_{a,b=1}^{k,l} T_{a,b} * S_{a,b} + \sum_{c,d=1}^{m,n} W_{c,d} * D_{c,d} \sum_{a,b=1}^{k,l} G_{a,b} * S_{a,b} + \sum_{c,d=1}^{m,n} W_{c,d} * D_{c,d} \quad (1)$$

where dp is a decision point, D are variables that express components of the decision making that may be key factors for the task, W are the weights associated with the importance of those components, T are the categories of taxonomy weights (equivalent to G) and S are the categories of sources of data and information. The UoI value represents the contributions of the sources and factors in relationship to the uncertainties categorized.

3 Explanation of the Taxonomies

As mentioned previously we are currently using seven terms within the taxonomy:

1. Inconsistent: Uncertainty due to a source that varies or do not stay the same.
2. Corrupt: Uncertainty due to a source containing errors.
3. Questionable: Uncertainty due to a source that lacks information or its questionable.
4. Disjoint: Uncertainty due to a source that lacks cohesion or organization.
5. Incomplete: Uncertainty due to a source that is unfinished or not complete.
6. Imprecise: Uncertainty due to a source that lacks exactness or detail.
7. Complicated: Uncertainty due to a source that is convoluted or confusing.

4   User Study

With the UoI concept and basic initial definitions for the taxonomy we needed to investigate if this idea resonated with Soldiers. More importantly given the descriptors that we are currently using which ones might be the most important and should different or additional ones be used. We conducted an experimental user study to begin to address these questions. For this study twenty-six soldiers for Ft Irwin completed our survey questionnaire. The soldiers were from different military occupational specialties (MOS) and had different years of service (YOS).

Within the questionnaire survey we provided two scenarios which gave context to the task. Instructions were given where each participant had to rely on different data sources for the information to make their decisions and possible associated uncertainty of that information. We asked each soldier to rank the descriptor for the uncertainty associated with a category for the data source. We stated that the ranking should be given based any uncertainty that could be associated with the descriptor. For example, if a data source generated data that was uncertain because it was incomplete versus one that was generated uncertainty because the data was complicated then incomplete should be ranked higher than complicated. A ranking of one was given to the descriptors that were considered the least concerning and a ranking of four was given to the descriptors that was considered the most concerning.

Scenario one portrayed a convoy escort whose task was to protect a supply convoy being transported from the forward operating base (FOB) to a city. Pre-brief indicated few attacks and threats. Scenario two displayed a more complex situation, in which the Soldier was tasked with defending a valley with several farming villages from surrounding militia. Threat reports are incoming from multiple sources and they must also determine how to place defenses and manage patrols to mitigate the risk.

5   Results

The following section highlights the observed trends by the participants of the user study for each scenario.

5.1   Scenario One

In scenario one, the context was considered a low threat environment for performing the task. Our finding should that five of the participants for Devices that had inconsistency ranked it as one. Seven participants ranked inconsistent as a three in Visualization, followed by Network with two less ranks. However, 31% of participants ranked the source Information four on the scale, and Network was also highly ranked as a four by three less ranks. Five people gave a ranking of five when the sources were Network and Devices. Figure 1 summarizes the results.

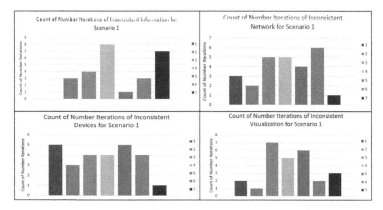

Fig. 1. Inconsistent taxonomy for scenario one

With all sources considered, corrupt was ranked primarily as a 7. Figure 2 summarizes the results.

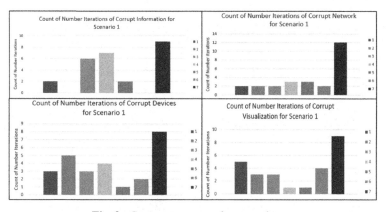

Fig. 2. Corrupt taxonomy for scenario one

When the source was either Devices, Visualization, or Network the majority of the participants gave questionable a rank of three. When the source was Information, the majority gave a ranking of six. Figure 3 summarizes the results.

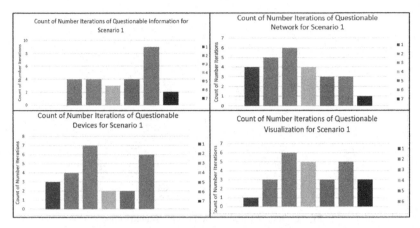

Fig. 3. Questionable taxonomy for scenario one

All sources ranked the disjoint taxonomy as a rank of one primarily. Figure 4 summarizes the results.

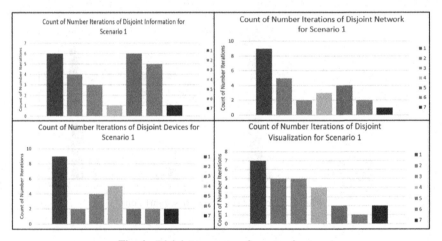

Fig. 4. Disjoint taxonomy for scenario one

The primary rank amongst sources ranged within the middle of the scale. For Information, the rank was three. For Visualization the rank was four. For Devices, the rank was five. For Network, the rank was six. Figure 5 summarizes the results.

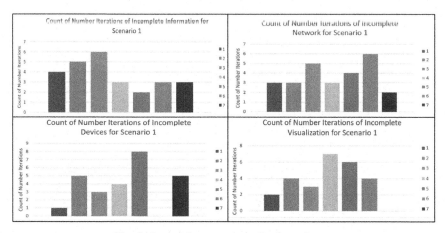

Fig. 5. Incomplete taxonomy for scenario one

For imprecise, both sources of Network and Devices primarily were ranked at a four. When the source was Visualization, imprecise is the least concerning with a ranking of one. Information tied ranking at either a two or a five. Figure 6 summarizes the results.

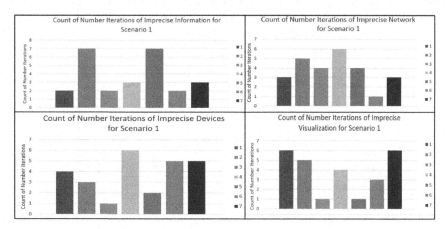

Fig. 6. Imprecise taxonomy for scenario one

With the exception of the Information source, participants ranked complicated on the higher-end as either a five, a six, or a seven. Figure 7 summarizes the results.

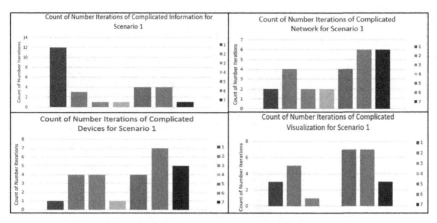

Fig. 7. Complicated taxonomy for scenario one

5.2 Scenario Two

Switching to scenario two, the context for the tasks was that the threat level was significant. With the source as Information, inconsistency ranked primarily as four on the scale (with seven ranks). It ranked primarily at six for Devices (eight ranks) and seven for Network (seven ranks). Visualization source varied in its ranking, ranging from a rank of two to six. Figure 8 summarizes the results.

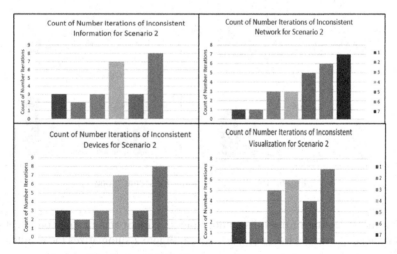

Fig. 8. Inconsistent taxonomy for scenario two

With the exception of the visualization source, corrupt was ranked as a seven. Corrupt was primarily ranked as a one when visualization was the source. Figure 2 summarizes the results. Figure 9 summarizes the results.

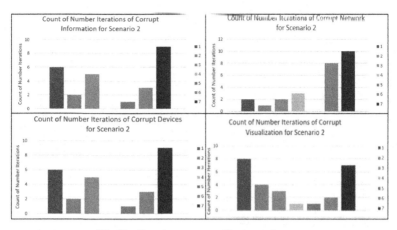

Fig. 9. Corrupt taxonomy for scenario two

Participants primarily selected rank five for questionable when the source was Information or Network. Devices ranked at a three, whereas the source visualization ranked at the highest of seven. Figure 10 summarizes the results.

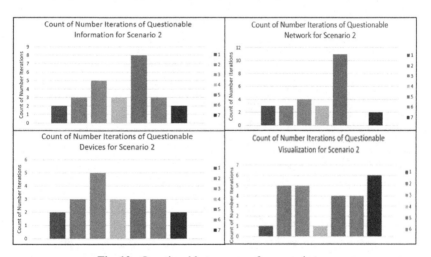

Fig. 10. Questionable taxonomy for scenario two

All sources ranked disjoint primarily on the low side of the scale, at either a one (Network, Information, Devices) or a two (Visualizations). Figure 11 summarizes the results.

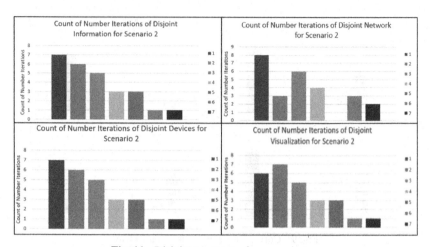

Fig. 11. Disjoint taxonomy for scenario two

Participants ranked incomplete as a five when the sources were Information and Devices. When the source was Network, incomplete did not receive any ranks of seven. Incomplete was primarily the rank of four when the source was visualization. Figure 12 summarizes the results.

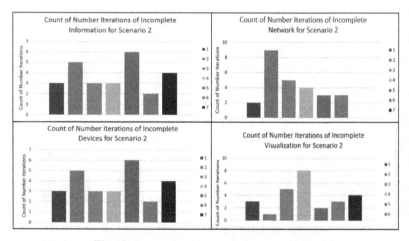

Fig. 12. Incomplete taxonomy for scenario two

For scenario two, Information and Devices both ranked imprecise primarily as a four. When Network was the source, majority of participants ranked imprecise on the low-end of the scale as either a one or two. However, the opposite took place when Visualization was the source, as majority ranked imprecise as a seven. Figure 13 summarizes the results.

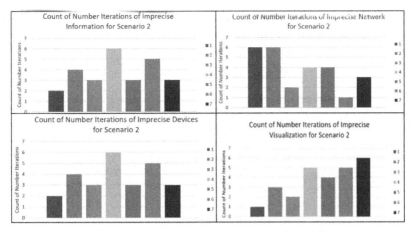

Fig. 13. Imprecise taxonomy for scenario two

Participants ranked complicated primarily a seven when the source was Information or Devices. Majority of the rankings when the source was Network was a four or six. A rank of five was the majority rank when Visualization was the source. Figure 14 summarizes the results.

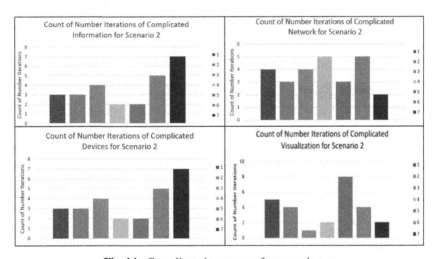

Fig. 14. Complicated taxonomy for scenario two

5.3 Summary

For scenario one Table 1 gives a summary for the number of participants that ranked each descriptor in the taxonomy with a seven by data source. Corrupt had the highest number for each of the data sources. Inconsistent information, imprecise visualization, complicated network had the next highest number of participants ranking it a seven. Disjoint was the descriptor that had the lowest number of participants ranking it a seven.

Table 1. Scenario one summary.

Scenario 1	Inconsistent	Corrupt	Questionable	Disjoint	Incomplete	Imprecise	Complicated
Visualization	3	9	3	2	4 (out of 6)	6	3
Information	7	9	2	1	3	3	1
Network	1	12	1	1	2	3	6
Devices	1	8	6 (out of 6)	2	5	5	5

For scenario two Table 2 gives a summary for the number of participants that ranked each descriptor in the taxonomy with a seven by data source. Again, corrupt had the highest numbers for each data source. At a glance the numbers of participants ranking of seven appear to be higher in scenario two than in scenario one. Inconsistent also had high number of participants ranking it a seven across the data sources. These numbers were higher in this scenario than the first scenario. Questionable visualization, imprecise visualization, and complicate information and devices had the next highest number of participants ranking it a seven. Also, disjoint had the lowest number of participants ranking it a seven, same as in scenario one.

Table 2. Scenario two summary.

Scenario 2	Inconsistent	Corrupt	Questionable	Disjoint	Incomplete	Imprecise	Complicated
Visualization	7 (out of 6)	7	6	1	4	6	2
Information	8 (out of 6)	9	2	1	4	3	7
Network	7	10	2	2	3 (out of 6)	3	2
Devices	7 (out of 6)	9	2	1	4	3	7

6 Conclusion

From the analysis of this experimental user study there is a definite trend that any uncertainties associated with corrupt data is the primary concern. Because inconsistent also had a high number in the second scenario, it could be implied that additional uncertainties begin to become more important as the scenario and task is more dangerous or important. This may also link the general trend that the numbers in scenario two were higher. Scenario two was associated with a higher threat level than scenario one, therefore any uncertainties in the data for making decisions in this context would be more critical.

As we continue to consider different or additional descriptors and perhaps even subcategories for the data source, we may be able to apply these trends to the model. The goal for including this would be to continue to provide useful information to the decision maker and potentially ensure that any data associated with key uncertainties are properly identified so that the decision maker can take this factor into account and balance the decision with any associated risks for the imperfect information.

Acknowledgments. Research was sponsored by the Army Research Laboratory and was accomplished under Cooperative Agreement Number W911NF-19-2-0062. The views and conclusions contained in this document are those of the authors and should not be interpreted as representing the official policies, either expressed or implied, of the Army Research Laboratory or the U.S. Government. The U.S. Government is authorized to reproduce and distribute reprints for Government purposes notwithstanding any copyright notation herein.

References

1. Chengalur-Smith, I.N., Ballou, D.P., Pazer, H.L.: The impact of data quality information on decision making: an exploratory analysis. IEEE Trans. Knowl. Data Eng. **11**(6), 853–864 (1999)
2. Fisher, C.W., Chengalur-Smith, I., Ballou, D.P.: The impact of experience and time on the use of data quality information in decision making. Inf. Syst. Res. **14**(2), 170–188 (2003)
3. Raglin, A., Metu, S., Lott, D.: Challenges of Simulating Uncertainty of Information. In: Stephanidis, C., Antona, M., Ntoa, S. (eds.) HCII 2020. Communications in Computer and Information Science, vol. 1293, pp. 255–261. Springer, Cham (2020). https://doi.org/10.1007/978-3-030-60700-5_33
4. Gershon, N.: Visualization of an imperfect world. IEEE Comput. Graphics Appl. **18**(4), 43–45 (1998)

Case Studies of Motion Capture as a Tool for Human-Computer Interaction Research in the Areas of Design and Animation

André Salomão, Flávio Andaló, Gabriel Prim, Milton Luiz Horn Vieira, and Nicolas Canale Romeiro[✉]

Universidade Federal de Santa Catarina, Florianópolis, Brazil
nicolas.sagaz@gmail.com

Abstract. We intend in this article to demonstrate how motion capture is being used in different areas of academic research about human-computer interaction in our laboratory in conjunction with the university undergraduate Animation course, and master and doctoral program in Design about Media and Technology. One of our current lines of research is the application of virtual reality with motion capture where we have two projects in the initial phase of research. The first one has the goal of researching the problems and possible outcomes for using virtual reality during the process of motion capture, inserting the actor or actress in a virtual environment closest as possible to the animation final product to act and create the animation of the scene. The second project is getting the resulted animation from this process and adapting it to a 3D animation for virtual reality. Both projects will be using a 3D animation project that has been ongoing in our laboratory, the Dias Velho Project, which is an adaptation of a graphic novel for kids that is being adapted to a 3D animation for traditional use and virtual reality. The idea of this article was to present the inspiration to think outside the normal boundaries of the standard uses of motion capture to advance the knowledge in this field of study by thinking of creatives ways of applying it alongside other technologies, bringing new possibilities of research topics and solutions to current ones.

Keywords: Human-computer interaction · Design · Motion capture

1 Introduction

We intend in this article to demonstrate how motion capture is being used in different areas of academic research about human-computer interaction in our laboratory in conjunction with the university undergraduate Animation course, and master and doctoral program in Design about Media and Technology.

One of our current lines of research is the application of virtual reality with motion capture where we have two projects in the initial phase of research. The first one has the goal of researching the problems and possible outcomes for using virtual reality during the process of motion capture, inserting the actor or actress in a virtual environment closest as possible to the animation final product to act and create the animation of the

M. Kurosu (Ed.): HCII 2022, LNCS 13302, pp. 302–311, 2022.
https://doi.org/10.1007/978-3-031-05311-5_21

scene. The second project is getting the resulted animation from this process and adapting it to a 3D animation for virtual reality. Both projects will be using a 3D animation project that has been ongoing in our laboratory, the Dias Velho Project, which is an adaptation of a graphic novel for kids that is being adapted to a 3D animation for traditional use [1] and virtual reality.

Our motion capture system was also used in the field study of medicine, in this case, for evaluation purposes. This research was developed by Prim [2] and it uses the motion capture system to evaluate the center of mass and equilibrium for amputees. It was proposed in this study to find out ways of improving prosthetics, and in this case, it was done by comparing the results between amputees and non-amputees. The last example of research was Andaló's doctoral research that developed a specific procedure of motion capture used to create 3D animations for entertainment purposes [3].

Therefore, as an article showcasing four studies about the use of motion capture, two of them being in the middle of research of testing hypothesis and possible solutions to predicted outcomes and the other two being completed research. The idea of this article was to present the inspiration to think outside the normal boundaries of the standard uses of motion capture to advance the knowledge in this field of study by thinking of creatives ways of applying it alongside other technologies, bringing new possibilities of research topics and solutions to current ones.

2   Motion Capture

Motion capture technology is roughly classified into three categories: optical, magnetic, and mechanic [4]. The system we have at our disposal and was used in the projects here shown is the optical one. This optical system relies upon reflective dots attached to a suit, the camera then records the dots' position and translates this information as X, Y, Z coordinates. It uses proprietary software to process the information received by the cameras, called Blade. It is an optical motion capture system, with passive reflective markers, passive markers are reflective balls that reflect IR light emitted by the cameras. The use of 14 cameras has the objective of avoiding any possible occlusion of the markers at the point of view of the cameras.

The first kind of motion capture for animation is dated back to 1915, with the invention of rotoscoping, which consists in tracing lines over the frames of a live-action recording and thus, producing animation [4]. Rotoscoping was widely used for 2D animation, with a few examples being "Snow White" (1937) the "Gulliver's Travels" (1939), from Disney and Fleischer Studio, respectively [4]. The research and development of what would be motion capture as we know it began with medical and military uses in mind, in the 1970s, it wasn't until the 1980s that the CGI industry found interest in the MoCap technology's potential [4]. The first successful use of motion capture technology was "Brilliance" in 1985, with an animated humanoid female robot, which aired in that year's Super Bowl, the method used was to paint black dots on a female actress and record her actions from multiple angles, then processed in computers [4]. Aside from the medical, military, and entertainment industries, motion capture has uses in other fields, such as design to evaluate users' movements and interactions with the environment, engineering, in the process of developing robots, and history [4].

There are three prevailing types of motion capture systems currently used by the entertainment industry, the optical system, the magnetic system, and the mechanical system, where each and one of them has its advantages and disadvantages when compared to each other [4].

The Optical system consists of recording markers attached to the user and obtaining data on the actor's movement with the use of cameras. There are two types of optical systems, the first one being the passive one and the second the active one, both solutions have their uses. The passive one's work with cameras that have LEDs which illuminates the markers to be recognized, the reflection of the light on those markers allows the system to recognize the actor position and calculate it in the 3D world, this solution is cheaper, but it does cause the issue where any reflection or external light that interferes with the markers might make the camera misread the actor position. The active solution is where the marker itself emits a light that is captured by the camera with the help of an internal battery in each marker, allowing the motion capture system to work on outside environments, but it is more expensive due to each marker needing their own battery to work. Overall, the advantages of using optical systems are its accuracy, with the drawback being the cost due to several different cameras being needed to properly calculate the actor's position and have higher fidelity in their movement [4] An image of an actor using an outfit with the reflective markers can be seen in Fig. 1.

Fig. 1. An actor using the MoCap system optical type.

The mechanical motion capture system consists of an exoskeleton with potentiometers in the joints, allowing the capture of body movements. As with the optical system, the mechanical one also has advantages and disadvantages with them mainly being the benefits of acquiring data in real-time and not having to worry about the occlusion effect on the markers since no cameras are being used, but it is an exoskeleton it does risk breaking itself during a session and also restricting certain movements that the actor might want or is necessary to do for the project [4]. An image of the mechanical motion capture system showing the exoskeleton can be seen in Fig. 2.

Fig. 2. Mechanical motion capture system [5]

The third and last type of motion capture system is the magnetic system, it works through electromagnetic sensors that are placed on the object desired to be tracked where it manages to capture the global location and translation of the object. The advantage of a magnetic system is that it doesn't need post-data processing, or cameras, which in turn makes this type of system to be more compelling from a cost point of view, being cheaper than for example the optical solution. The disadvantages of a magnetic system are the possibility of occlusion due to how it interacts with metallic objects, wires, and batteries connected to the system, which can all interfere not only with the data capture but the acting of the actor [4].

The DesignLab, a laboratory that focuses on Applied Research in Design, focus on projects that focus on technology with social, economic, and cultural character, and alongside with having a space called Tecmidia, where since 2016 has been developing research focused on motion capture and virtual reality [6]. All the following projects were created in conjunction with DesignLab and Tecmidia, giving the project access to an optical motion capture system of the passive type that has at the time of this writing fourteen cameras and the software system by the company VICON. An image of the motion capture portion of the lab can be seen in Fig. 3.

Fig. 3. Tecmidia motion capture space (authors).

3   Discussion

According to Sinha, Shahi and Shankar [7], Human-Computer Interaction is "a discipline concerned with the design, evaluation, and implementation of interactive computing systems for human use and with the study of major phenomena surrounding them". Following this concept, DesignLab has had many projects that worked under this lens, and the following discussion will be about how motion capture systems were used in research in Design and Animation projects.

One of the first projects that started to use motion capture at its core was research that worked on analyzing the equilibrium of the human body in amputees, focusing on unilateral transtibial prosthesis users by using motion capture to create data. The goal of this research was to find out possibilities of improvement in prostheses, identify factors that might affect the human balance, by comparing it between amputees and non-amputees, and lastly, relate the characteristics of the prosthesis's design with the human balance. The study did tests using the methodology already established for balance analysis, the Berg Balance Scale, which is used to check if the person is able or not to safely stay balance during a series of predetermined tasks. The motion capture system was used in this research as a tool to obtain proper data from all the volunteers, allowing the researchers to compare the movement and balance between amputees and non-amputees. This project concluded that the motion capture system was essential to obtain tangible and useful data, allowing the researcher to conclude that the results suggest that amputees wearing prostheses perform worse on balance tests than non-amputees and that among only the amputees, the quality of each of their prostheses and physiotherapeutic treatment is a factor in the improvement of their balance according to the point of view of the metric used in this study [2, 7] (Fig. 4).

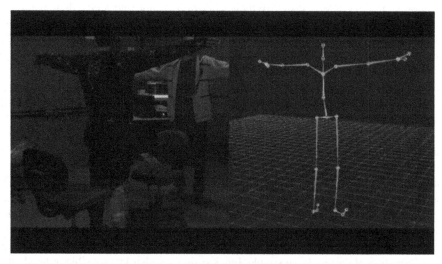

Fig. 4. Marker on volunteer's body and his skeleton in the motion capture software.

The relevancy of this project is the fact that the human-computer interaction component of it is the use of proper methodologies and procedures to obtain and process data with the motion capture system assist to optimize the collection of relevant data.

The second project was the research and development of methodological procedures to be used when the goal is to use a motion capture system as a tool to capture the human movement that will be applied in tridimensional characters for movies and animation by the entertainment industry. The general idea behind the procedure is to use the motion capture system to obtain the human movement by preparing the room and the actors and afterward linking their movement to the tridimensional character. With the proper movement data captured by the system, the later stages are to properly retarget the animation to the tridimensional character and lastly refine the animation, cleaning it up from possible errors and adding improvements that enhance the actor's performance.

As discussed by Sinha, Shahi, and Shankar [7], one of the goals of human-computer interaction is the development of descriptive and predictive models and theories of interaction, this project had the goal to develop a methodology for the uses of motion capture systems for the creation of tridimensional characters movements in movies and animations.

The third project, which is still under development, is about the utilization of the human-computer interaction by placing the actors inside a virtual world using virtual reality. The goal is to measure their acting performance, between a take done by placing the actors inside the virtual world where the tridimensional characters from the animation are and them being able to visualize their work in real-time and a take done using the previously described procedures in the second project. In this project, the motion capture system will be used as a tool to obtain these performances, which can afterward be visualized, analyzed, and compared.

One of the components of human-computer interaction is the study of the users with its interface, in this project case, the goal is to give the actors a completely new interface, in this case, the virtual reality, which in this case works as a new medium between the actors and their performance.

The last project we are working on at this moment aims to study and understand the construction aspects for the development of a 3D animation focused on virtual reality. Although the focus of this research is on the relationship between virtual reality and animation, it is not possible to study both topics without talking about the human-computer relationship. The motion capture system will be used to obtain movements for the construction of animations mainly of the characters in the story, by using the procedures described in the second project.

The idea of animation is just doing several simple things one at a time, i.e. animation is the formation of these several simple things strung together in a sensible order. At the same time, he also states that this knowledge allows the animator to create his form of expression [8]. Therefore, the idea of this project is to create small pieces of animation series using motion capture systems to study the possibilities of 3D animation in virtual reality.

The animations will be based on the 'Tribo da Ilha' project which is a 3D educational animated series project focused on preschool-age children, represented by Fig. 5. The project started as an adaptation of the graphic novel 'Dias Velho e os Corsários' by Eleutério Nicolau da Conceição published in 1988 that contains stories about the state of Santa Catarina in Brazil. The original story takes place in the 17th century and its main character is Francisco Dias Velho, a pioneer from São Paulo who came to what we now know as the state of Santa Catarina and was responsible for starting the process of colonization of the current state capital, Florianópolis. The content, based on official documents of accounts of the time, focuses on the conflict between Dias Velho and the privateer Thomas Frins. The adaptation made by DesignLab introduces fictional events of everyday life, but in the historical context of the 17th century, while adapting the language for a young audience in a series format. Other adaptations made were the addition of new characters, the children Leca and Cauã, and the small talking monkey Gui, a companion in their adventures, with Dias Velho being delegated to the role of mentor to the children and Thomas Frins becoming a caricatured villain, commander of a troupe of clumsy pirates.

Fig. 5. Dias Velho accompanied by Leca (left), Gui (Middle), and Cauã (Right) [10]

The project, despite having started as an adaptation for an educational animated series with the public, ended up being at the beginning a study of the adaptation of a graphic novel for animation [9], it was also the object of study on real-time rendering compared with offline rendering [10] and is currently being used for study in the project previously mentioned and now for the study of motion capture for animations used in virtual reality. As the writing of this article, the Project is still in early development, intending to explore the limits of the twelve basics principles of animation by Johnston and Thomas to test how far we can twist basic concepts of animation in a new media like virtual reality using animation created by mocap [11].

Even though the 'Tribo da Ilha' animation project has had many and different uses, the most recent research use of it, its adaptation to virtual reality, is a new form of user interaction through the lens of the virtual reality world, giving this project a new scope of the lens to see the human-computer interaction concepts. An image showing frames of the animation can be seen in Fig. 6.

Fig. 6. Tribo da Ilha animated scene [10].

4 Conclusion

All the projects discussed here are either complete works or currently under development, and what they all have in common is one of the main goals of human-computer interaction research of trying to minimize the barrier between the user and the computer to obtain the desired results.

The first project presented in this article used motion capture to evaluate the effects of the prosthesis and obtain meaningful data from amputees that can be used to enhance their lives. The second project aimed to create the necessary procedures for future research to use motion capture as a tool to collect data, so important is that work that the same procedures are being used in the following two projects, one to capture data from actors performing in standard conditions and another in virtual reality and the second being the use o motion capture to create animation aimed to also be used in virtual reality. In all the presented cases, human-computer interaction has a major role, as in theorizing problems and hypotheses, but also by using motion capture systems in very different roles to provide valuable and tangible data that can be further studied.

For future work, we are planning to continue the development of the last two projects, but also suggest for future academic research the use of motion capture in creative ways. There are more data to be found and studied in the behavior of human movement, different contexts that the researchers can apply this tool, and lastly find new human-computer interactions that will bring benefits to the user.

References

1. Salomão, A., et al.: The adaptation of a 3D animation to a real-time render using unreal engine 4. In: Francisco, V.C.F. (Org.) Examining New Points of View in Web Engineering, Visual Interfaces, Motion Graphics, and Human-Computer Communicability, vol. III, 1edn., Blue Herons Editions, p. 100 (2019)
2. Prim, G.: Modelo de análise de equilíbrio utilizando sistema de captura de movimentos. 114 f. Dissertação (Mestrado) - Curso de Programa de Pós-graduação em Design, Universidade Federal de Santa Catarina, Florianópolis (2016)
3. Andaló, F.: Desenvolvimento de procedimentos para utilização da captura de movimentos aplicada em personagens 3D. 207 f. Tese (Doutorado) - Curso de Programa de Pós Graduação em Design, Universidade Federal de Santa Catarina, Florianópolis (2019)
4. Kitagawa, M., Windsor, B.: MoCap for Artists. Workflow and Techniques for Motion Capture. Focal Press, Oxford (2008)
5. Rahul, M.: Review on motion capture technology. Glob. J. Comput. Sci. Technol. (2018)
6. Salomão, A., Andaló, F., Vieira, M.L.H.: How Popular game engine is helping improving academic research: the designlab case. In: Ahram, T.Z. (ed.) AHFE 2018. AISC, vol. 795, pp. 416–424. Springer, Cham (2019). https://doi.org/10.1007/978-3-319-94619-1_42
7. Sinha, G., Shahi, R., Shankar, M.: Human computer interaction. In: 2010 3rd International Conference on Emerging Trends in Engineering and Technology (2010). https://doi.org/10.1109/icetet.2010.85
8. Sutton I., Williams R.: The Animator's Survival Kit A Manual of Methods, Principles and Formulas for Classical, Computer, Games, Stop Motion and Internet Animators Expanded Edition. Farrar, Straus and Giroux, New York (2009)
9. Boehs, G.E., De Andrade, W.M., Vieira, M.L.H.: Aventuras na Ilha: A Gestão da Adaptação de uma Obra. Celacom ... Endicom (UMESP), vol. XVIII Col., pp. 1–14 (2014)
10. Salomão, A., et al.: The adaptation of a 3D animation to a real-time render using unreal engine 4. In: Francisco, V.C.F. (Org.) Examining New Points of View in Web Engineering, Visual Interfaces, Motion Graphics and Human-Computer Communicability, 1edn., Blue Herons Editions (2019)
11. Salomão, A., Vieira, M.L.H., Romeiro, N.C., Nassar, V.: Theorized work for adapting the principles of animation to virtual reality as a new form of narrative for 3D animation. In VISIGRAPP (1: GRAPP), pp. 308–312 (2021)

Investigation on Research Model of Product Design Integrated with Big Data Technology

Donglin Wang, Jiong Fu[✉], and Yuning Qian

School of Design, Shanghai Jiao Tong University, Shanghai, China
{wangdonglin,redfox78,qianyuning}@sjtu.edu.cn

Abstract. Design research is an important part of design and the basis of product development. With the Internet entering web 2.0 age, collecting user feedback on the network platform has become an important channel for enterprises to understand user needs and grasp market trends, so big data research came into being. By comparing big data research with traditional research methods, it can be found that the existing design research methods have the defect of limited data, while big data research methods have the defect of infinite data. For enterprises, in the context of the rapid growth of information, a set of product design research framework based on big data is needed to improve operation efficiency and research quality.

Using the literature analysis method and combined with the current situation of the industry, this paper first analyzed the applicability of big data technology in product design research. Then, by means of expert interview and questionnaire survey, this paper explored the problems and needs encountered by designers in design research, and then summarized the classification of research information that needed to be obtained in the current product design research process. By analyzing the defects of traditional research methods, the entry point for the integration of big data technology into the traditional research process was found, and the design research model in line with the digital age was established. The model aims to help designers narrow the cognitive gap with consumers and effectively improve the quality of product design decisions.

Keywords: Design methods and techniques · User survey · Big data technology

1 Introduction

Design research is essentially a process of obtaining data related to product development and interpreting, analyzing and predicting the data through models of different disciplines such as economy, society, psychology and design. Design research can effectively eliminate the uncertainty of product innovation and has irreplaceable reference value for the guidance of product follow-up design.

The traditional design research is generally realized by questionnaire, observation, interview and other methods. It also includes competitive product research, user demand mining, lifestyle survey and other types. Although the research data of traditional research methods are detailed and true, due to the limitations of technology and

M. Kurosu (Ed.): HCII 2022, LNCS 13302, pp. 312–323, 2022.
https://doi.org/10.1007/978-3-031-05311-5_22

manpower conditions, there are some limitations, such as high research cost, limited coverage samples, subjective experience deviation and so on.

With the Internet entering web 2.0 age, users can share their experience of trial products at any time through the network platform. Through the user content released on the platform, enterprises can understand the real feedback and attitude of users towards products, and then predict the market trend by analyzing user demand. Therefore, enterprises began to use big data technology to collect relevant information about users and products. Big data technology has the advantage of rich channel resources, but it also has the problem of complex data processing.

It can be seen that both traditional research and big data research have their own advantages and disadvantages in balancing user privacy, data authenticity and conclusion reliability. Therefore, in the context of the rapid growth of information, enterprises urgently need a design research method to improve the scientificity of design decision-making. This study summarized the demand dimension framework in product design research by mining user needs in the product design research process. Based on the advantages and disadvantages of big data technology and traditional research methods, the product design research framework integrating big data technology was constructed to improve operation efficiency and research quality. This study has research potential and application value for enterprises to better perceive potential product opportunities.

2 Literature Review

2.1 Relationship Between Design Research and Product Design

Although the definitions of design procedures are different, the overall process is almost the same. The complete design process will include the following steps: Design Research - Product Planning - prototype design - technology development - product testing. In most cases, product research, as the beginning of design activities, is the first step in the design process. For enterprises, design research directly determines the product positioning, and then determines the direction of subsequent product development. The accuracy of design research process largely determines the success of a product design.

2.2 Relationship Between Design Research and Product Design

In the product concept exploration stage, interviews, focus groups, questionnaires, diary research, observation methods, etc. are often used to mine and verify user needs and clarify target users and program objectives [1]. As shown in Fig. 1, various traditional design research methods are classified according to two dimensions. The horizontal axis of the coordinate axis is the qualitative/quantitative dimension and the vertical axis is the behavior/attitude dimension. Throughout the methods, although the research data are detailed and true, the research is time-consuming and laborious, the sample size is small, and it is easy to draw biased conclusions. Under the background of the rapid growth of information, the traditional design research methods can not ensure the scientificity of enterprise design decision-making because of their high cost and long cycle [2].

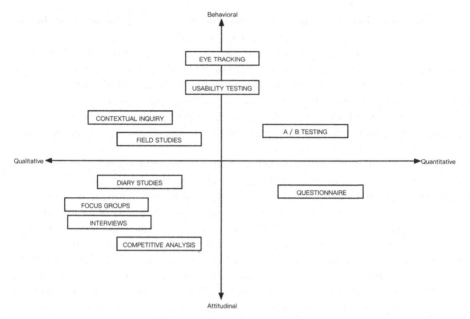

Fig. 1. Design research methods

2.3 Research on Big Data Technology

Big data is a huge collection of information. Big data has four characteristics: volume, variety, velocity and value [3]. Big data technology refers to the ability to collect and analyze a large amount of information. The purpose of big data analysis is to find the hidden rules from complex data [4]. The general process of big data processing can be divided into four stages: data collection, data processing and integration, data analysis and data interpretation [5] (Fig. 2).

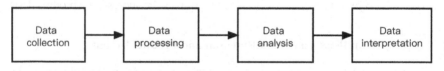

Fig. 2. Big data processing flow

With the continuous development of information technology and the increasing enrichment of information channels, the user-centered market competition pressure makes the data intensive characteristics of product development more and more prominent. As a result, big data technology is gradually applied to enterprise design.

Compared with traditional research methods, big data technology has the advantages of rich channel resources, wide user coverage, efficient and convenient implementation and so on. For example, social media data broke through the original questionnaire operation form and became an important channel to find user needs. By mining social media data such as business reviews, microblogs and community discussions, we can more accurately and objectively evaluate user satisfaction, explore user pain points and gain insight into product innovation opportunities. However, big data technology also has the defect of complex data processing. According to statistics, under the impact of a large amount of information, designers repeatedly collect, store and analyze all kinds of information for product research, accounting for more than 35% of the whole conceptual design process [6]. Therefore, how to obtain effective information from massive research data has become the key to big data research.

2.4 Research on Big Data Technology

Traditional research methods are limited by the small and fixed amount of data obtained. The quantity and level of big data are huge and dynamic, but it is limited by the difficulty of obtaining effective information from a large amount of research data. It can be seen that traditional design research has limited defects, while big data has unlimited defects. Therefore, the integration of big data into design research can make up for the data limitation of traditional research methods, and then improve the accuracy of research results.

Further, from the perspective of the research process, both big data and traditional research methods start from obtaining authentic data that can be transformed into guiding design activities, and finally need to sort and analyze the data into an operable descriptive language. Therefore, although there will be differences in the implementation of methods, they have some similarities in the whole research process. Based on this, big data and traditional research methods can complement each other and combine each other into a new research model in theory.

Due to the complementarity between big data and traditional research methods, researchers have tried to integrate big data technology into design research. Xiao Fei [7] used big data thinking to assist the innovative design of furniture products, and predicted users' personal preferences and behavior habits by collecting keywords entered by consumers, web pages read and purchase behavior in furniture product design research, so as to predict the product design trend and provide suggestions for product research and development. Liu Zheng and Wang Yun [8] proposed a method of product design research based on knowledge measurement. Through the collection and fusion of multi-source heterogeneous information in the big data environment, an orderly product design knowledge unit was formed. Then, by taking a specific type of product as a whole, they could fully grasp the design dynamics in specific fields and further assist the decision-making of product conceptual design. However, at present, relevant research focused on the application of big data technology into design research, and there was less content of process design according to the needs of design research, which showed that this research was innovative in this field.

3 Methodology

Design research needs to provide guidance and reference for the subsequent product design and development process. Therefore, design research needs to consider various needs and involve various information, so as to transform and integrate various data into effective suggestions to guide innovation activities. Therefore, this study first interviewed industry experts to analyze the problems and corresponding needs encountered in the design research of practitioners in the product design industry, and then obtained the classification dimension of research needs to be obtained in the current product design research process. The demand classification was verified by means of quantitative questionnaire, which laid the foundation for the establishment of the demand source of the product design research system of information fusion. According to the classification of product research needs, this paper analyzed the defects of the traditional research model, and found the entry point for the integration of big data technology into the traditional research process. Thus, the advantages of big data technology were applied to make up for the limited defects existing in the traditional research process. Finally, taking the optimized model and product research demand framework as the guidelines, a user-centered design research model in line with the digital era was established (Fig. 3).

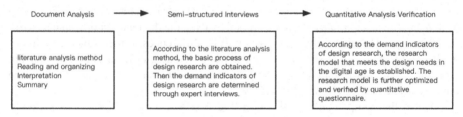

Fig. 3. The research method

4 Results

4.1 Classification of Research Demand Information

In order to find the entry point of integrating big data technology into the traditional research process, we needed to first clarify the expectations and needs of enterprises and designers for design research. Therefore, in the form of expert interview, this paper combed the methods and needs of different stages of design research. This expert interview involved experts in the field of design research with different backgrounds such as design, mathematics and sociology. This interview mainly focused on the experience of product design research conducted by interviewees. They needed to recall the complete process of three stages, before investigation, during investigation and after investigation (Table 1).

Table 1. User interview outline

Course	Subject	Content
The first part	Introduction and warm-up	Introduction to the purpose of the interview, the host's self introduction, the interview rules, the length of the interview, the principle of confidentiality, sincere thanks, etc
The second part	Basic user information	Ask about the basic characteristics of the users
The third part	Understanding of design research project information	Understand the user's past experience in doing research projects, and pave the way for the detailed inspection and research process
The fourth part	In depth interview of design research process	The core part is the whole process from receiving the research project to conclusion output and reporting. Focus on the overall node arrangement and the work and analysis methods in different research stages. This part needs to guide users to recall the three stages of research preparation, research implementation, data sorting and analysis of the whole research project
The fifth part	Supplementary questions and suggestions	Ask the user's ideal research process, the user's view of the industry development prospect, the supplement of research pain points, etc.
The sixth part	Concluding remarks	Thank you to the user

After combing the objectives and needs of the interviewees in different stages of the design survey, it can be found that the interviewees have less subjective initiative in the before investigation stage, and the research objectives and project schedule were greatly limited by the subject. Therefore, further research focused on the during investigation stage. Through interviewing users and the methods adopted in the research, we can explore their needs in this stage.

By summarizing the demand in the survey conducted by the interviewed researchers, it can be found that the general survey needs to obtain both supply and demand information. Supply information is mainly divided into market supply information and environmental supply information. Market supply information refers to understanding the market scale and market differentiation segmentation direction of enterprises, the characteristics and positioning of main competitive products through market research, so as to obtain the market positioning direction of their own products. Environmental supply information refers to analyzing the macro environment of the enterprise, combing

Table 2. User requirements in the during investigation stage

Time flow	Behavior	Requirements
Before investigation	Determine investigation objectives	Clarify the scope of investigation
	Develop project schedule	Control the research time
During investigation	Background research	Analyze social and cultural trends
		Analyze the current technology development trend
		Analyze the current popular aesthetic trend
	Market research	Analyze industry related policy trends
		Analyze industry scale and market segmentation direction
		Analyze industry competition
	User research	Analyze consumer positioning
		Analyze user pain points
		Analyze user needs and preferences
After investigation	Research summary	Output research conclusions that can guide the design

the macro factors affecting the industry and enterprise, and grasping the development direction of the enterprise as a whole. Demand information mainly comes from users' needs. Through communicating with users and observing users' behavior, users' expectations and preferences are mined. Supply information can predict industry opportunities, while demand information represents user demand. Therefore, the accuracy of supply information and demand information determines the development potential of products.

According to the needs in the survey obtained from the user's in-depth visit, six core user needs were obtained by simplifying and clustering. In order to better prove the classification relationship of needs, relevant practitioners of product design research were asked to score the importance in the form of Likert five point scale in the questionnaire. The core factors to be verified are shown in the Table 3.

SPSS software was used for factor analysis of the questionnaire survey results. First, we checked the demand characteristic factors through the scree test. As shown in the Fig. 4, the first two factors can basically cover most of the demand characteristics, so it is reasonable to divide them into two factors.

After using varimax to rotate the research data, the conclusions shown in the Table 4 can be obtained. According to the demand and demand characteristics corresponding to the principal component factors of factor analysis, the two principal component factors correspond to supply factors and demand factors, and the characteristics of supply factors are more distinctive. It can be seen that the user's demand for design research can be

Table 3. Core factors

Number	Factors
1	Analyze social and cultural trends
2	Analyze the current popular aesthetic trend
3	Analyze industry related policy trends
4	Analyze industry competition
5	Analyze consumer positioning
6	Analyze user needs and preferences

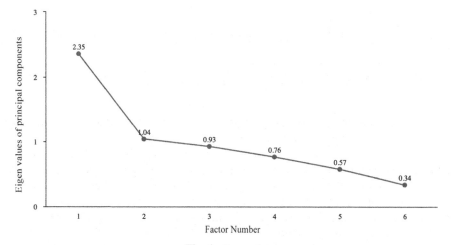

Fig. 4. Scree plot

divided into supply information and demand information, and the conclusion has been verified. The main feature of supply factor is that it is strongly related to the market and industry, and related to the product market positioning; the main feature of demand factor is that it is strongly related to users, and related to the consumer positioning. The characteristics of these two factors laid an important theoretical foundation for the subsequent establishment of product design research models suitable for different scenarios.

4.2 Product Design Research in the Era of Big Data

Through literature analysis, it is concluded that the design investigation process generally includes: the first step is to determine the investigation objectives and formulate the investigation plan according to the design task; The second step is to collect relevant survey data according to the survey objectives; The third step is to sort, filter and analyze the data; The fourth step is to summarize the analysis results and output the research conclusions (Fig. 5).

Table 4. Rotating component matrix

Component	Supply information	Demand information
Analyze social and cultural trends	0.739	0.05
Analyze the current popular aesthetic trend	0.783	−0.128
Analyze industry related policy trends	−0.676	0.164
Analyze industry competition	−0.504	0.381
Analyze consumer positioning	−0.414	0.635
Analyze user needs and preferences	0.087	0.868

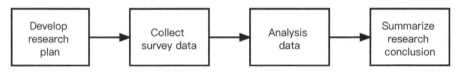

Fig. 5. Design research process

In view of the current research process, we can find that the defects of traditional research methods mainly lie in the limited number of samples and data analysis prone to subjective experience bias. The defects of traditional research methods mainly appear in the second and third steps of the research process. At the same time, it can be found that the first and fourth steps in the design research process are greatly limited by the project objectives, and big data as a method or means can not change the purpose of the original design research. Big data is characterized by rich channel resources and wide user coverage. The characteristics of big data can just make up for the limited data of traditional research methods. Therefore, big data will cut into the design research process from the second step, as a source of design research data, and become a strong support for the research conclusions. However, big data has the defect of infinite data, which needs to be avoided in the application process. Therefore, the two methods of big data and traditional research are combined and complementary to each other to form a product design research model under big data. That is to combine a huge amount of data resources with the thinking mode in traditional research to form a product design research framework based on big data (see Fig. 6), so as to improve operation efficiency and research quality.

Step 1. After determining the research objectives according to the design project, we began to enter the stage of collecting survey data. Since traditional research methods do not have advantages in collecting data, big data technology is used to collect research data at this stage. Users constantly generate data with multi-dimensional collection characteristics in the Internet. This data set includes many factors, such as person, time, place, behavior path and so on. Multiple information with multiple feature sets are combined to form big data. Network memory is to capture these information in real time for storage, and then form a database. These collected and stored data are the basic elements of research design, research and analysis. Therefore, when using big

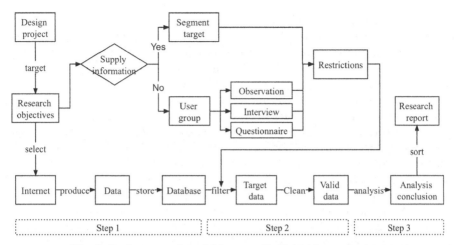

Fig. 6. Design research model integrated with big data technology

data technology to collect research data, we need to first select the appropriate channel, that is, the database that meets the research objectives. For product design, you can understand the model, sales volume, selling price and user feedback of listed products through the shopping e-commerce website; Through the enterprise's official website, you can understand the enterprise's brand positioning and product positioning; Through the creative exchange website, you can understand the latest trend of product design.

Step 2. After having the data, we should enter the data filtering stage to obtain effective data that meets the research objectives. Because the data is an open and multivariate infinite set, it is necessary to find appropriate constraints to obtain the required specific target data. According to the two types of information in the above research results, the restrictions here need to be divided into two categories. If the research needs supply information, the constraints can be transformed from the research objectives, which is equivalent to a one-to-one input-output mode. If the research needs demand information, the restriction comes from obtaining open keywords in qualitative ways (such as interview and observation). The reason why there are two types of restrictions is that the user needs are complex and hidden compared with other research information, which needs to be integrated into qualitative research and analysis to help predict. After that, we need to transform the constraints into a digital structure model, and then set it into the database for data filtering. After screening the target data, there will be some data that are not positively related to the research content. Here, secondary processing is required, that is, these non positive data will be stripped off through human thinking and technical means, and then the effective data used to summarize the research conclusions will be screened out [9].

Step 3. After obtaining effective data, select the appropriate data analysis method according to the data acquisition type (such as text data, voice data, picture data, etc.). Sort out the effective data according to the research purpose and mine the information hidden in the data (including behavior, demand, product characteristics, etc.). User information mainly obtains text data. The main information dimensions of user portrait: age, gender and consumption level. These dimensions are mainly analyzed by statistical analysis methods. The user feedback information mainly uses emotion analysis and keyword cluster analysis to obtain the user's attitude and demand for the product. Product information mainly obtains text data and image data. The text information of each dimension of products with high sales volume in the market is statistically analyzed, and then the large-scale product demand information is obtained according to the clustering algorithm. For product images, it is necessary to preset keyword labels and analyze them by using image recognition algorithm, so as to classify the images and obtain the concrete design trend. Finally, the analysis conclusion needs to be transformed into descriptive language and charts that can be used directly for design. Different data relationships will be obtained according to different types of data analysis, and the research report needs to be presented with appropriate charts according to different data relationships. It is suggested to use pie chart and pyramid chart when representing the constituent relationship between individual and overall; When it is necessary to represent the comparison relationship between individuals, it is recommended to use bar chart; When it is necessary to represent the trend relationship of data change, it is recommended to use line chart; When it is necessary to represent the frequency distribution relationship of data, it is recommended to use heat map and scatterplot; When you want to represent the correlation between variables, it is recommended to use the inter-relationship diagraph.

5   Conclusions and Suggestions

This study focused on improving the efficiency of researchers' design research and optimizing the use experience, and made a comprehensive research around the methodology of design research and big data. This research involved the application scope, scenarios and processes of design research, and comprehensively analyzed the advantages and disadvantages of traditional design research and big data technology.

This study summarized the researchers' needs for design research through expert interviews. Based on user demand, two kinds of core function factors were extracted: supply information and demand information. Then factor analysis was carried out on the results of the quantitative questionnaire to verify the accuracy of classification.

This study designed the solution according to the research results. This study aimed to apply the advantages of big data technology to make up for the defects existing in the traditional research process. According to the traditional design research model and user needs, this design established a design research scheme that met the needs of users in the digital age. The scheme integrated big data technology in the data acquisition stage, which solved the problem of limited sample size of traditional design research; The scheme integrated qualitative research and analysis in the stage of screening target data from big data, improved the efficiency of finding effective data from massive data, and made up for the defect of infinite data.

This study is a basic research for design research, but there are still deficiencies and space for in-depth research. This study is limited by the insufficient richness of research samples and the limited number of research samples, so it can be further deepened in the perfection of research. At present, researchers have collected samples from different industries in the research stage, but mainly in the industrial design industry. Therefore, there is still much room for insight into the differential needs between different posts and industries. The target group of this study is users with design research needs, so the methodology is highly targeted and has a certain learning threshold. At present, as a theoretical model, it mainly considers the rationality and feasibility of workflow, and its applicability still needs to be tested by a wider range of samples. In terms of scheme effectiveness verification, the current design scheme is quite different from the traditional analysis workflow, so it can be further designed and tested, compared with the traditional workflow to demonstrate the product value. The current version of the scheme focuses on the research needs with high demand and strong universality. In practical application, the researchers' needs in the research stage are rich. In the follow-up, we can further design functions to meet more analysis needs, expand the scope of application and improve the applicability of products.

To sum up, this topic focused on the design research scene, literature research, user research and design practice. This study combed the whole link of design research, summarized the user needs of the target group, constructed and verified the functional factors, and completed the design of the design research model integrating big data technology based on the research results. This paper introduced big data technology into the preliminary research of product design and constructed the application model of big data technology in the product design research stage, which aimed to help designers narrow the cognitive gap with consumers, provided more accurate design positioning and improved the quality of product design decisions. In the future, this method will be further iterated to be applied to more product design practice projects, so as to provide reference for product enterprises and other manufacturing industries to use big data technology.

References

1. Tao, J.: Product Design and Development. Ocean Press, Beijing (2010)
2. Crandall, B., Klein, G., Klein, G.A., Hoffman, R.R., Hoffman, R.R.: Working Minds: A practitioner's Guide to Cognitive Task Analysis. MIT Press, Cambridge (2006)
3. Yong, Z., Hui, L., Yu-shi, S.: Large Data Revolution: Theory, Model and Technical Innovation. Publishing House of Electronics Industry, Beijing (2014)
4. De-feng, Z.: Big Data Cloud Computing. Posts & Telecom Press, Beijing (2014)
5. Kaiye, L.: Research on Custom Furniture Design Based on Big Data Technology (in Chinese). Beijing Forestry University, Beijing (2018)
6. Gonçalves, M., Cardoso, C., Badke-Schaub, P.: Inspiration choices that matter: the selection of external stimuli during ideation. Design Sci. 2 (2016)
7. Fei, X.: The application of big data thinking in furniture innovative design. Design 17, 52–53 (2016). (in Chinese)
8. Zheng, L., Wang, Y.: Survey method of product design based on knowledge measurement. Comput. Integrated Manuf. Syst. 26(10), 2690–2702 (2020). (in Chinese)
9. Yingli, R., Fan, Q.: Application of big data in product design research. Packaging Eng. 36(20), 139–142 (2015). (in Chinese)

Exploring Mobile Co-design in the Context of Use Continuous Elicitation and Evaluation of Design Suggestions

Malin Wik(✉) 📇 and Linda Bergkvist 📇

Karlstad University, Karlstad, Sweden
`malin.wik@kau.se`

Abstract. This study explores a method for the co-design of mobile applications in the context of use. In 36 sessions with future users, synchronous co-design of a mobile navigation application was conducted in the intended use environment – a hospital – using an interactive Wizard-of-Oz-controlled prototype. The results show that co-design in the intended use environment contributes to the elicitation of design suggestions. Concerning the co-design method, the results show that by using interactive prototyping the user is actively involved as a co-designer, which empowers the user and enables the continuous evaluation of design suggestions.

Keywords: Distributed participatory design · Co-design · Wizard of Oz · Prototyping · Design suggestions

1 Introduction

In an increasingly globalized world, with smartphone use, environmental considerations, and travel limitations due to factors such as pandemics, there is a need for methods that mitigate geographical distances between user and designer in the system design process [1]. Furthermore, the use context can play an important role in what information is available to the user and how the system is interpreted. Therefore, ecological – that is, contextual – validity is important for user studies (among the many examples of this are [2, 3]).

Moves have been made towards digital co-design in the intended use environment. For many years, researchers in the computer-supported cooperative work (CSCW) field have been looking into how computers and systems can be used to cooperate over distance and organizational borders. In the late 1990s, for example, [4] explored asynchronous tech use such as email for distributed participatory design. More recent examples from the human–computer interaction field include [5], who used an online, computer-accessed tool to allow geographically diverse children to engage in co-design sessions. [6] developed a mobile application for travelers with visual impairments and involved users in the evaluation of the application in the wild, and let users leave feedback via methods such as email. [7] and [8] tried a method called GUI-ii, which allowed stakeholders to be actively involved in prototype design and evaluations of computer-based systems over

© The Author(s), under exclusive license to Springer Nature Switzerland AG 2022
M. Kurosu (Ed.): HCII 2022, LNCS 13302, pp. 324–342, 2022.
https://doi.org/10.1007/978-3-031-05311-5_23

distance. In [9], the participants were involved in a co-design task related to defining locations of interest for an indoor mobile game, which was conducted in situ. A recently published opinion paper discussed experiences of distributed participatory design with children in a UK school and summarized the related opportunities and challenges [1]. All design activities were conducted analogously by the children in the classroom, while the researchers attended via a video conferencing tool. The authors [1, p. 4] pointed out that the online environment introduced challenges such as "lack of connectedness to other design team members", "reduced non-verbal communication" and "facilitation challenges in 'reading the room'".

This paper elaborates on a method that is used for synchronous co-design over distance in the intended use environment. The method allows the co-designer to put forward design suggestions for a mobile application while walking around in the use environment. By using an interactive prototyping tool, the designer can implement an interpretation of the co-designer's suggestion during the session. The implemented suggestion can then be evaluated with the co-designer directly, who can try her or his own design while remaining in the use context. The motivation behind this study is the scarcity of methods for involving the user over distance as an active participant in the system design process, particularly while he or she is in the use environment (cf. [7, 8]). The purpose of the present study was to examine if and how co-design can be conducted for mobile applications in the intended use environment.

2 Distributed Co-design

2.1 Participatory Design

Since the beginning of the "Scandinavian tradition", the employment of prototypes has been recommended as a way to visualize and clarify abstract, technical ideas and design to future users [10, 11]. Visualization is important since a central part of participatory design (PD) is the politics of design, namely the shared decision power between future users and designers [12]. This means that, in PD projects, the users participate in the whole design process and all stages of decision-making, making it possible for them to participate in decisions revolving around their work [10]. Without the use of prototypes, for example, it would be difficult to involve future users in that manner. In user-centered design (UCD) projects, future users are still in the center as in PD, but may not be invited to take their share of the decision power [13]. In addition to the degree of participation, there may also be variation in terms of who participates. In many PD studies and some UCD studies, the same future users participate in each iteration, evaluating the revisions and the designers' interpretations and implementation of the problems and ideas brought up in previous iterations. This comes naturally in traditional PD projects, which often revolve around a digitization process or system procurement at a certain workplace. However, there is a risk that these projects end up with decisions based on compromises, which may be far from what future users would want, as the participating future users are absorbed into the development team and a shared understanding. In other studies, new participants may partake in the next iteration, evaluating the prototype with a fresh set of eyes and evaluating the ideas of other participants before them. Such an iterative process may mean that the future users' ideas have been misconstrued by the designers, at least if the implementations of the user's idea are never presented to the originator. In yet another set of projects, a combination of recurring and new participants is used.

The activities performed in a PD or UCD process may be called co-design activities. Co-design implies that the user is actively participating – that is, contributing to the design process in a practical manner – rather than as a mere information source (as in the cases of interviews, for example) [8, 11].

2.2 Interactive Prototyping

As mentioned above, prototyping is one way of making abstract ideas more concrete. An issue with digitized prototypes is that the graphical design is difficult to implement without also implementing the interactivity. When using any of the numerous high-fidelity prototyping tools that are now available, the hand-in-hand development of graphical user interface (GUI) and interaction design rely, to some extent, on the desire for a runnable prototype: when the user clicks a button in the prototype during the testing, something is supposed to happen and the test participant should be able to fulfill some use case scenario in the prototype. A physical mockup such as a paper prototype allows for some more exploration regarding the interactive patterns thanks to its use of human intervention, but is limited in other ways, such as textual input from the user, which creates the need for a digital prototype.

The Wizard-of-Oz (WOz) technique may be best known for its application in testing not-yet-developed systems with users, but it has also been used as an aid in requirements elicitation for a long time. Kelley, who coined the "OZ paradigm" in 1983 [14], described his successful iterative approach to gathering and evaluating the natural language corpus needed in CAL, a natural language application [15]. [16] found that early user testing using Wizard-of-Oz prototypes reduced the number of errors in the program code based on functional requirements derived from the user tests.

When combining the human intervention aspect of WOz experiments with interactive prototyping, the advantages of digital high-fidelity prototypes are combined with the advantages of mockups.

For example, [16, p. 504] mentioned that the "interactive mock-ups in the case study were produced in two steps. In step one, the images of the graphical user interface were created and the interactivity planned. In the second step the interactivity support for the 'Wizard' (i.e. test leader) was added … [The interactivity support] make it possible for the test leader to control the interactive aspects of the mock-up during the test sessions."

"Planning the interactivity" and "adding interactivity support", instead of implementing the interaction design, is telling in terms of how tests are conducted with the Wizard-of-Oz tool used in [16] (as well as in the present study, although a later, web-based version of that tool which have found many application areas [17]). In such a tool, where a human controls the prototype's functionality, it is possible to keep the interaction design on the planning stage, rather than setting it in program code before testing. Because a human can carry out the interactivity, the prototype still appears to function and the user can perform her/his tasks and (try) reach her/his goals – and even break the planned interaction design while in the process.

Another common denominator of WOz studies is the use of a hidden "wizard" who simulates the functionality of a system. In the studies by [7, 8], however, a method called Graphical User Interface Interaction Interviews (GUI-ii) was used. GUI-ii makes use of the wizardry of the WOz method, but the "magic" – that is, the human abilities of the designer – is done in plain sight. The interactive prototype is used as a means of communication between a designer and a co-designer in a discussion about and use of a user interface design.

3   Method

3.1   Background

This study was conducted together with Region Värmland as part of DigitalWell, an EU-funded project run by the Compare foundation, and the innovation case "Att hitta rätt" (in English: "To find the right way"). The innovation case was based on the problematic situation that visitors to the regional central hospital and other similar care units in the region found it difficult to find their way around once inside the premises. This can create increased stress, both before and during the visit. Patients arrive late to their visits or do not turn up at all. The stakeholder had established the need for some type of assistive service through various data collection and user-centered design activities, including interviews with employees at the hospital, interviews with visitors or patients at the hospital regarding what problems they face, gathering statistics regarding the number of questions and calls to the receptionists at the hospital regarding finding one's way, and simulated patient journeys and observations at the hospital, some using simulation spectacles for visual impairment. The interview data and stakeholders' experiences from meeting visitors and/or from working at the hospital were used in a workshop involving representatives from different stakeholder organizations, where customer journey maps over a hospital visit were created.

A recurring problem in the data as well as in the customer journey maps was finding one's way to a designated hospital ward or care clinic at the hospital. It was concluded that a way was needed to individually help a visitor to self-dependently feel safe before their visit and to find their way at the hospital. Thus, the focus of the experiment reported in the present study was whether and how visitors could be guided by a navigation application that complemented existing signs in the hospital environment. The idea behind the assistive technology suggested in the innovation case was that if more visitors and patients of the hospital could find their way around on their own, resources could be concentrated on those patients and visitors who are unable to do so.

Naturally, the user-centered design activities conducted before this study generated minimal graphical user interface designs and requirements. To move from interview data and customer journey maps towards an application prototype, it was decided that a digital prototype accessible on a handheld device was needed. It could have sufficed with a digital prototype implemented in some prototyping tool accessible on mobile platforms. However, because the application was supposed to be used in a relatively public setting (a hospital) and, if it would come to that, could be developed using public funding, it was considered important to not assume that a digital application would be the best solution, and if so, to base the design on a few designers' point of view.

By using a WOz prototype for mobile platforms and allowing future users to provide feedback while walking the corridors of the hospital, as in the GUI-ii (see Sect. 2.2), we saw that we could allow the active involvement of the participants, as well as carry out co-design over distance. We saw this as an opportunity to combine the needs of the stakeholder, a proof-of-concept, and a clarified requirements specification, with our research interests around co-design over distance and for mobile applications.

3.2 Wizard of Oz and Interactive Prototyping

The digital low-fidelity prototype was produced using a digital prototyping system that incorporates the Wizard-of-Oz (WOz) technique [14]. The prototype appeared to be more or less functional, and the positioning functionality, which would allow the designer to show relevant contextualized information to the co-designer, could be faked using the back camera of the tablet held by the co-designer during the session. The WOz technique and the system made it possible to quickly make changes in the graphical user interface during each co-design session according to the needs, comments, and suggestions communicated by the co-designer over a video conferencing system. Since a human wizard controlled the prototype, the co-designers interacted with the prototype in whichever way they preferred of the possibilities provided by the tablet device.

3.3 The Co-design Sessions in Detail

In short, each session consisted of three steps: (1) an introduction in the greeting room including signing a consent form; (2) the co-design session, during which the designer remained in the greeting room while the co-designer walked in hospital corridors; and (3) an interview to capture any missed suggestions and information.

Before each co-design session began, each participant signed a consent form, was introduced to the study, and received an information letter. The information letter had also been sent out to the participants as they booked their participation in the study. The participant was given a headset and a tablet with the prototype. They were informed that the designer would talk to them during their walk and that the designer would be able to see a filtered view of what the back camera on the tablet filmed.

All co-design sessions were recorded using the screen recording tools in QuickTime, which captured what the designer said and did, what the co-designer said, her interactions, and what the back camera of the tablet showed. The prototype was also recorded with Screencast-O-Matic from the view of the co-designer by accessing the "test view" of the Ozlab system on a second computer [7].

To allow the participants to co-design, the prototyping tool Ozlab was used, which incorporates the Wizard-of-Oz technique. The use of Ozlab made it possible to show an interactive prototype that seemed to be working, but since it was not implemented yet, changes could be made easily and the designer could re-design it according to how the co-designer interacted with the prototype and what she said she wanted. If the co-designer wanted a map or an instruction in text, for example, it could be added to the prototype.

Fig. 1. An example of how the co-design sessions were conducted. In the left picture, the designer/wizard sits in front of two screens. The screen on the left shows the prototype in the wizard graphical user interface, while the screen on the right displays the prototype as seen by the co-designer. There is a black speakerphone on the desk and a session script (the paper to the right of the laptop), which was used for the oral communication with the co-designer. The co-designer can be seen in the picture to the right with the badge around her neck, headphones, and a tablet. In the background, a television is visible, displaying the overview of the hospital, which visitors can use to navigate.

The prototype was controlled and changed by the first author, who was the wizard and designer during the sessions. The second author was also present during all co-design sessions and helped keep track of issues and errors, and sometimes asked the co-designer questions or went out to help the co-designer if a technical issue occurred. The designer and co-designer communicated using a video conferencing tool and via the interface of the interactive prototype. The view of the back camera of the tablet was used to fake the positioning functionality of the prototype. As the co-designer moved through the hospital, her location could be seen through the view of the camera and the information in the interactive prototype could be changed accordingly.

Before the participants started to walk, they were given a destination. This was done in three different ways to mimic typical situations from visits to the hospital: one co-designer group was given a "notice to attend" on paper, one group was instructed to read the destination on the tablet, and one group was given oral instructions. Six different destinations were included in the study from two different entrances of the hospital.

When the co-designer began to walk, the co-design of the application started. At the beginning of the experiment, the prototype was almost empty from the start of the session. This was done to see what types of ideas a blank canvas would provoke. When the co-designer suggested some content or functionality or asked for some information, it was implemented directly and evaluated with the co-designer. If the co-designer did not have a suggestion when the prototype was almost empty, the designer would suggest something and show a design, such as a picture or an instruction, in the prototype and evaluate it with the co-designer. Whatever the origin of the suggestion, it was used

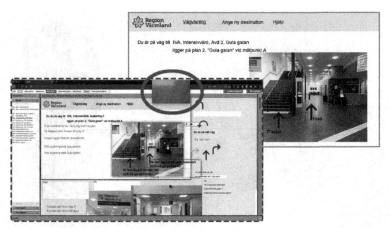

Fig. 2. The wizard/designer view (within the dashed line) shows how the prototype could look in the Wizard-of-Oz system Ozlab during the co-design session. The same view of the prototype as visible to the co-designer is shown in the underlying image (within the solid line). The circled area shows what the back camera of the co-designer's tablet filmed (floor tiles) at that specific moment.

throughout the session. In some sessions, other ideas were proposed by the co-designer or sometimes the designer when confusion seemed to emerge from the introduced design idea.

The designer often ended the session with an almost empty prototype to again see what types of ideas the co-designers would have when they were presented with a blank canvas but were a bit more familiar with the method.

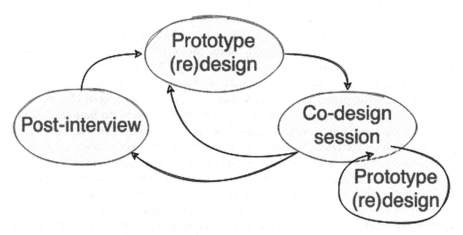

Fig. 3. The co-design sessions were conducted in an exploratory manner in which the prototypes evolved under each session and between sessions.

The prototype evolved during each session, as well as during the experiment (see Fig. 3). As the experiment continued, the ideas of the previous co-designers were tried and evaluated with the new co-designers. Some ideas were too big to implement during a co-design session (time-wise or due to the prototyping system used, etc.). This meant that some ideas were tested not with the co-designer who proposed them, but with the following co-designers. At the end of the experiment, the prototype contained much more information and (faked) functionality than it did in the beginning. Since three different destinations from the two entrances were used, a total of six prototypes evolved (some in parallel) during the experiment. Specific prototypes were used for each destination so that some pre-prepared environment-specific information such as photos and graphics could be used.

No strict interview protocol was used during the co-design sessions. How and when the designer asked questions evolved with each co-designer.

Post-interviews. After each co-design session, the co-designer returned to the greeting room, where the second author conducted a semi-structured interview. The goal of the interview was to gather information about issues that might have affected the session and to try to capture whether any new ideas would surface that had not been mentioned during the co-design session. The idea behind this was that if the follow-up interview did indeed result in a lot of new issues, ideas, and design suggestions, the co-design method as such could either be said to be inefficient or should at least be accompanied by a follow-up interview to fully appreciate the insights of the co-designer.

First, the co-designers were asked three questions about their experience of the walk and to find their way using an application. Second, the co-designers were asked two questions about their participation in the study. Thirdly, the co-designers were asked background questions regarding their occupation (since this may affect how technical they are and how used to participating in similar studies they are), their number of visits to the hospital and in what capacity (since this may have an impact on their knowledge of the hospital), their smartphone and app use (which could affect their comfort using an application for wayfinding and their design preferences), their age, and their sex. Lastly, the co-designers were asked if they had anything else that they wished to put forward.

During the follow-up interview, the designer was still in the greeting room but turned to the computer running the prototype. The interviewer let the co-designer know that the designer would incorporate the ideas brought up during the session while the interview was conducted. It would perhaps have made sense for the designer to step out of the room during the interview, but for practical reasons she did not.

3.4 Participants (n = 36)

In total, 36 people (29 women, seven men) aged 20–88 (mean age 49.5 years) participated. The participants were asked an open question about their previous visits to the hospital and their smartphone use. Twenty participants said that they were familiar with the hospital and some had the hospital as their workplace. The others stated that they had visited the hospital less often. Only one participant had never visited the hospital before. Thirty-one of the 36 participants said that they use a smartphone daily.

Information about participation in the study was shared via the stakeholders' and researchers' networks in an article about the study on a website bringing together some 100 companies in the digital sector in the region, to information systems program students, and via the researchers' university website. The participants received a gift card of 100 SEK (equivalent to 10 Euro) after their participation.

Ethical Considerations. The hospital is a sensitive environment since people's movements may reveal private health information. In addition, hospital visitors may be stressed, grieving, and/or may not be able to take care of their best interests. We had many discussions with the Region about how we would proceed and the study was assessed by the Research Ethics Committee at Karlstad University, but was not subject to the Ethical Review Act.

The experimental setup included co-designers walking around the hospital with a camera, and each session (including the view from the camera) was recorded. Thus, measures were taken to ensure that no bystanders were captured; otherwise, non-consenting persons could appear in the data and reveal sensitive health information. Prototyping revealed that a plastic film in front of the back camera would provide the right amount of blurriness, to ensure no bystanders could be identified (see the blurriness of the camera image in Fig. 2). The use of a headset would ensure that only the voice of the co-designer was recorded in the corridors.

To communicate to hospital visitors, information about the study was displayed at the hospital entrances. All co-designers had to wear a badge stating their participation in a research study during their walk.

All participants booked their sessions beforehand. The major reason for this was due to the environment: it was inappropriate to walk around the premises of the hospital lobby and ask the visitors if they would like to participate in the research study.

3.5 Analysis

The co-design session recordings were transcribed in a table for each recording. The purpose of the table was to capture not only the dialogue between designer and co-designer, but also the dialogue that was conducted through the prototype, and the surrounding environment. The analysis table included columns for timestamp (for when, during the recording, the event happened), what the designer/wizard said, GUI/prototype (what happened or was visible in the prototype), co-designer/participant (what the co-designer said and did), environment and surroundings (that is, what was present or happened in the use environment such as increased noise, if the co-designer stood still, a lot of people walking by, etc.), comments (for information not applicable in any of the other columns), technical issues (such as Wi-Fi connectivity, problems with the prototyping tool), and codes (used to classify findings).

The transcribed co-design sessions were analyzed divided by route. The transcriptions were read through by both authors and coded independently according to emerging themes. The individual analytical processes were accompanied by iterative discussions and comparisons of identified codes and emerging themes. Two routes, from the main entrance to the Intensive Care Unit (ICU) (eight co-design sessions) and the main entrance to the Pain treatment clinic (11 sessions) were chosen. These two routes represented a good number of sessions and were therefore perceived to be able to provide good possibilities for identifying patterns and themes. The decision was made to analyze the material divided by route since it makes it more apparent how each prototype developed during the co-design and how the specificities of the environment had an impact on the prototype design. An example of this was what happened at the destination of the route "main entrance to the ICU". There, the corridor ends with a large, bright red door. Five co-designers (c01, c05, c07, c09, c19) of the eight taking that route mentioned this red door and wanted it to be a part of the application (one co-designer did not mention it, but in that session, the picture of the door was included in the prototype). If the co-design sessions had been analyzed on a higher, more abstract level, the red door suggestion may have been lost. It is not possible to say that all co-designers wanted a *picture* of the door leading into the hospital ward they were supposed to find their way to, but when analyzing each route separately, it is possible to generalize to a requirement that the co-designers wanted the application to mirror cues that stood out in the use environment.

This also highlights the fact that while the findings reported in the next section exemplify the advantages and disadvantages of this co-design method, the findings may not apply to all other settings.

4   Findings

In this section, the themes found in the analysis of the 19 co-design sessions will be presented. Some of the themes relate to the co-design method, and some relate to the elicitation and evaluation of design suggestions.

4.1   Findings Related to the Co-design Method

Inter-Co-designer Evaluation. Even though many design suggestions were evaluated with the originator, many of the suggestions (the co-designers' and designer's) were also evaluated with the following co-designer(s). For example, c05 mentioned that she wants the application to communicate that the instruction is still valid and that the application is running. The designer implemented this by adding an arrow that slowly blinked and a textual instruction saying, "You are going in the right direction". C05 responded positively to this design suggestion. It was tried in later sessions as well, such as with c07, but before the co-designer asked for similar functionality (see Table 1) and c11, who stated she did not want the functionality as it demands that she is looking at the tablet all the time.

A few of the co-designers asked for a map in the prototype to show them the way towards their destination. They were provided with the same map that is available to visitors in some places of the hospital (as seen in Fig. 1). While two co-designers (c10, c17) said they wanted a map to guide them toward their destinations and two (c11, c18) wanted a map to orient them in the building, another explicitly (c01) said that she did not think a map was a good solution.

Table 1. Dialogue about visual feedback in the prototype regarding instructions, introduced by c05 and evaluated with c07.

Co-designer	"…and I see a picture of the same [corridor] that I walk in"
Designer	"Yes, and what do you think about that?"
Prototype	The designer makes the arrow blink
Co-designer	"…and it is good that it is blinking – yes, it is blinking so that feels safe and good [sound a bit difficult to hear] The yellow arrow blinks, but it is maybe not supposed to be like that but [designer interrupts with question]"
Designer	"Yes, do you think it should be that way?"
Co-designer	"[is reading the instruction in the prototype?] Keep straight ahead"
Designer	"Was it good that it blinked?"
Co-designer	"Yes, I thought it was good because then something happens, I feel like I'm on the right way, and then it blinks"

Another example of how design suggestions evolved between the co-design sessions was the instruction guiding the visitors towards "Point B" or "Elevator B" ("Point B" refers to the elevators that are named by letters). When the designer showed an instruction to c05 saying "Turn right at the elevators (Elevator B) towards the [name of entrance]", she said it was helpful, but added that it was better when accompanied by a picture of the elevators in question. C06 suggested that the first instruction should be "Continue straight until you reach Point B". This was added to the prototype, but c07 seemed less convinced by the suggestion, saying, "… Right now, in my situation, Point B tells me nothing." At least, this was the case until she could see the signs in the ceiling: "Over there I'm starting to see 'B' on the ceiling." With the next co-designer taking the same route, c09, the design suggestion evolved to an instruction stating "Continue straight ahead until you reach the elevators (Elevator B)." With c10, an instruction excluding the "Point B" information – "Walk straight ahead until you reach the elevators, where you should turn right" – was evaluated and initially well received by the co-designer. However, the formulation turned out to lead her in the wrong direction.

Domain Knowledge. The co-designers of the study often had more domain knowledge than the designer did. The co-designers who worked at the hospital naturally had good knowledge about the hospital corridors and terms, but since all co-designers were in the use environment, each of them had more knowledge about the environment than the designer who stayed in the greeting room during the sessions. This meant that the designer gave design suggestions according to expected requirements and perhaps from previous knowledge of other navigation applications.

During one of the 19 sessions analyzed here, the co-designer (c10) took the wrong turn into a corridor due to how an instruction was framed ("Walk straight ahead until you reach the elevators, where you should turn right") and the timing of the instruction (it was shown too early at the wrong elevators). The misunderstanding continued for about three minutes before the designer realized that she had guided the co-designer to the wrong corridor. Even though the co-designer mentioned that she was in the blue corridor (not the yellow one) and described what she could see in her surroundings, the designer seemed preoccupied with thinking that the co-designer was in fact in the right corridor, but further along than expected.

Decision Power, Empowerment of Co-designer. In some sessions, the co-designer critiqued the prototype spontaneously, which could say something about the power dynamics in the sessions. For example, c01 reacted to an instruction that came a bit late, by saying "It was very good that it [the prototype] said that I should turn soon, but the left turn must be visible before I have passed it." The designer answered with, "Yes, I agree, that seems plausible [giggles] absolutely" and the co-designer also giggled. This shows that the co-designer felt comfortable critiquing the prototype and that the designer empowered the co-designer to do so by acknowledging the error in the prototype behaviors and emphasizing the idea of the co-designer.

Dialogue Between Designer and Co-designer. Something should be said about the dialogue between the designer and co-designer, as this may have an impact on the results of the sessions and the co-designers' perceived space to give critique or suggestions. No strict script was used by the designer to guide the co-design sessions, as mentioned in Sect. 3.3. Instead, the designer aimed to keep the dialogue informal and open, while remaining on topic (see Table 2). It should also be noted that the designer had some experience of usability studies and similar previous sessions and could use that experience during the sessions. Some of the co-designers were very talkative, while some had to be asked for information more often.

Issues Linked to the Mobility of the Co-designer. The corridors of a hospital may be more or less busy, with not only visitors but staff and transports as well. While this is important information for the application design, it may hinder the co-design. In some instances, the co-designer commented that it was difficult to walk while talking or looking at the tablet, headsets with a poor fit, or that noise in the surroundings made it difficult to hear the designer. In the two routes analyzed, these types of issues occurred nine times with five co-designers (c01, c06, c12, c19, c20).

Another issue linked to the mobility of the co-designer was connectivity problems at specific spots in the hospital along the routes. The lack of connectivity made updating the prototype with the new design suggestions impossible, while it sometimes haltered the dialogue through the video conference system (see example in Table 2). If the prototyping system lost connection to the server, it could not reinstate the connection without a manual refresh of the web browser at the co-designer's side. This issue was solved by adding the prototype as the "home page" in the browser, which allowed us to instruct the co-designers to "tap the house icon" (this was shown to them at the beginning of the session as well), which refreshed the tab. With this solution, the problem was circumvented during the experiment, but could also be solved (in the long run) by implementing a heartbeat (a ping request) between the server and client. The problem with sound disappearing during the conversation was circumvented by reiterating questions or utterances that had been lost, which often was not a problem thanks to the informality of the dialogue.

Table 2. Example of how a design suggestion by the co-designer (c09) was implemented by the designer, but could not be verified with the co-designer due to technical issues. The informal dialogue between designer and co-designer helped alleviate the technical issues.

Designer	"[a bit tired from a few technical issues] Uh ... What do you wish it would say in the app so you know you are there [destination]?"
Co-designer	"When I'm ... Because it reads like this [reads the text in the prototype] 'The Intensive care unit is at the end of the corridor, continue straight ahead.' 'You have reached the destination when you get to the red door', it could say"
Designer	"Ah, right, very good suggestion [adds the co-designer's suggestion]. Yes, now it's probably the same thing again that I cannot show it to you, but ..."
Co-designer	"[jokingly] No, but ... I hear it [the keyboard] slamming so I hope you write"
Designer	"Yes, I do [laughs] I'm adding it, gladly"

4.2 Findings Related to Elicitation and Evaluation of Design Suggestions

Design Support Provided by the Use Environment. Some of the design suggestions that emerged during the co-design sessions were linked to the use environment and its information available to the co-designer during her walk towards her destination. The co-designers could also use the environment to evaluate the clarity of the design suggestions by comparing the graphical user interface to the environment.

For example, c01 saw signs in the environment and asked that the same color coding be used in the application. C10 also noted that the arrows used in the applications should match the colors of the corridor names in the hospital. Another example is c11, who by referring to what she passed in the corridors asked that the application should hide already performed instructions. C01 also referred to the environment that she passed and asked that the information be made available in the prototype.

C17 confirmed the usability of a design suggestion where the right turn is marked with a blue right arrow over a picture of the corridor intersection. He then read the textual instruction following the turn, "Keep straight until the corridor splits to the left," and said that it "[...] is a bit fuzzier description than 'keep straight until you reach Elevator B' because Elevator B is a bit better marked, but maybe there is no good marking here? But, um ... Here is where it splits to the left, and since the pictures show exactly what I see it is clear enough."

Another example is how c19 evaluated a picture in the prototype and noted that it was good that the signs (leading to a different destination) in the picture cannot be read easily, as this minimizes the risk of the user reading the signs in the picture and interpreting them as navigation instructions.

Others commented on things they saw in the environment and compared them with the prototype. In the session with c10, for example, the application informed her that she was on the "yellow street" (the corridors are named as streets with different colors) and that she should continue straight ahead in the corridor. At one place in the corridor, the "yellow street" turned to the left, but she was supposed to continue straight to reach her destination. C10 said: "Now... Now the question is, here I see the yellow street on the left and there is the Pain treatment clinic straight ahead. So that I do not ... 'Now

you should continue straight ahead'. Not the yellow street! Continue towards O, P."
C10 emphasized her suggestion by filming the signs in the ceiling (O, P) she referred to
and then detailed how she wished the design suggestion should be implemented in the
application.

Several important aspects of the environment were also captured during the co-design
sessions, such as problems to find the right way in open places without clear guidelines,
and in four-way intersections or when signs suddenly cease or are missing. In addition,
known problems highlighted in the data collection by the stakeholder (see Sect. 3.1)
about issues such as the sign system could be verified in the study (for example, by c03,
who noted how difficult it is to read the sign with white text on a yellow background).

Elicitation of Design Suggestions. In all sessions, the designer sometimes asked that the
co-designer come up with a design suggestion; for example, "would you need some more
information in the application now to know where to go?". As the co-designers walked
around the corridors while also using the navigation prototype, some functionality and
needs were identified that may not have been found if co-designers were simply asked
for their opinions in an interview. Such suggestions may be described as unexpected
or hidden, as the user is usually unaware of them (for example, until put in a situation
where the need is made clear).

For example, c01 realized later in the session when the destination information was
provided that she would like to have had information about the destination from the
beginning: "What I was thinking about was that why it [the application] did not say that
directly when I started walking, that I should go to the ICU?".

Co-designer c16 would have liked functionality telling her how far it is until a turn
comes once she has reached the destination: "If you want, you can have it [the countdown
functionality] during the whole walk of course because it struck me now that it could
count down turn right and all of that ... Almost like a GPS, like, turn in 30 m, 20 m."

Another example is the session with c12, who said that she did not want information
too often from the application so that she might feel she's missing something as she looks
up. Furthermore, when the designer displayed an image as a navigation instruction, c12
spontaneously noted that she prefers pictures as instructions over textual instruction.

In another session with c20, she noted that the "address" of the destination which
includes "Point O", which had been available during the entire session, was unclear, as
no sign saying "Point O" is available at the destination.

Explicit or Implicit Evaluation of Design Suggestions. A few times, the co-designers
did not answer questions asked by the designer. While this might be an issue linked to
the issues regarding the co-designers' mobility, it could be due to other reasons as well.
Sometimes the designer might have formulated the question poorly, making it difficult
for the co-designer to interpret it as a question to be answered, although we did not find
any such instances in these 19 samples. Some co-designers told the designer what they
did and sometimes also asked for confirmation before making a decision (for example,
"then I'll continue walking?", c19). However, other co-designers made decisions silently,
such as starting or continuing their walk toward the destination (c01, c12, c20). In these
instances, the silence could be seen as a form of confirmation instead. While explicitly
stating one's actions can sometimes be a confirmation of the usability of the information

in the prototype, the silent decisions could also be seen as a confirmation of the usability of the information displayed in the prototype.

5   Discussion

5.1   A Co-design Method or a Participatory Design Method?

In this study, the method is described as a co-design method. As noted in the introduction, co-design is related to participatory design, just as co-design over distance is related to distributed participatory design (DPD). However, we refrained from using the terms *participatory design* and *distributed participatory design*. While the method allows future users and stakeholders to engage in and with the design process actively – and could therefore be said to have a say in the design of artifacts that may have an impact on their work-life, work tasks or their engagement in society and access to public resources – the impact of the method as a PD method was not analyzed. However, if such an application would be designed and developed, it is our understanding that a participatory design approach would be beneficial, especially since the design process would be funded by public means.

As noted in the introduction of the paper, PD processes invite the user to participate in the decision-making in all phases of the design process [12]. Naturally, since no more iterations were conducted and no implementation of the prototype was done (not yet – COVID measures have kept the Region busy as the care provider), the design process of the study cannot be followed further than this initial experiment. Nevertheless, it is worth discussing the decision-making of the co-design sessions. In the study, the co-designers were invited to make decisions about the design as they walked through the hospital corridors towards their destination. However, most of the power over the design still lay in the hands of the designer, who interpreted the wishes of the co-designers and implemented the ideas in the prototyping tool. The co-designer could see the interpretation directly and react, but it is easy to imagine how, after several tries and misinterpretations on the designer's part, someone could give up and "okay" an idea that had been misconstrued. However, as noted in the findings section, the direct feedback to the co-designers may be seen as an empowering process. Co-designers can see that their opinions matter and that they are listened to as the prototype is redesigned according to their design suggestions. While the dialogue between designer and co-designers was free and easy and worked, for the most part, during the study, there still might have been instances where bias related to sex, gender, age, disability or ethnicity may play a role. For example, the designer may unknowingly decide to propose certain design suggestions to a certain group of co-designers, and withhold some suggestions from other groups based on a misconceived notion of what the groups would like or could fathom.

The characteristics and backgrounds of the co-designers and designers may also impact their ability to communicate efficiently. Different designers have different communication styles, which may show in experimental sessions, as noted in [7]. However, this is irrespective of physical presence or distance.

Here, the distributed implementation of the co-design sessions plays a role as well, as suggested by [1]. In a dialogue where the interlocutors do not see each other and where, due to technical reasons, speech acts may be interrupted or be missing, the communication can be further haltered. However, as brought up in Sect. 4, the dialogue between designer and co-designer worked well and, thanks to the informality, could mitigate technical issues.

The results presented in this study extend what has been shown by previous studies using a graphical WOz-supported prototyping tool for co-design. Here, one difference was the mobility of the co-designer. In previous studies by [7] and [8], the participants and the designers were all stationary, yet the communication between designers and co-designers was held over distance, accompanied by a digital WOz prototype. Concerning [8], the prototyping process was also different, as the prototype in this study was altered synchronously during each session and not mainly between iterations.

5.2 Suggestions for Future Research

In the post-interviews, the interviewer sometimes referred back to issues brought up by the co-designer during the session (for example, "during the session, you mentioned that you wanted..."). In most of the interviews, the co-designers themselves also referred to the design session. We did not have to rush the post-interview to greet the next co-designer, which seemed to allow the co-designers to share their opinions. A potentially interesting approach for future research could be to allow some more time to pass between the co-design session and the post-interview, or even to conduct a second co-design session and post-interview with the same co-designer. The co-designer could then perhaps have had the opportunity to digest the impressions of the session, think of some new ideas, and maybe be even more comfortable with the co-design method. After all, these co-designers were not used to having a direct influence over the design alternatives of a mobile application, so the situation was new to them.

5.3 The Value of This Study

Problems During the Co-design Sessions Could be Circumvented. Most of the problems that occurred during the co-design sessions were technical and, as shown in the findings section, could be successfully circumvented during the sessions. In the instances where the designer could not add a suggestion of the co-designer to the prototype (for example, if a new picture of the environment was needed), the suggestion could be implemented shortly afterward and evaluated with other co-designers.

Domain Knowledge and Empowerment of the Co-designer in the Design Situation
The example of the co-designer who was led to the wrong corridor showed how a lack of domain knowledge makes it difficult for the designer to always have the correct answer at hand, and second, that the designer saw the co-designer as more knowledgeable, as she was the one with the access to relevant information. It also highlighted the need for error identification and correction in the application, something that might have been missed if the sessions would have been conducted in another environment. As already

discussed, it could also be argued that implementing and evaluating the co-designer's design suggestions with the originator is in itself an empowering aspect of the co-design method.

This shows the co-designer that the designer does not know the right answer to the design and that, together, they can find the solution to a problem.

Finding Use-Environment-Specific Design Suggestions. Conducting the co-design sessions in the use environment, as exemplified in Sect. 4, enabled us to identify where in the environment visitors often have difficulty finding their way, but also allowed the co-designers to make use of the surroundings in a way that would have not been possible in a usability lab setting or Virtual Reality glasses showing some standardized corridor navigation situations.

Finding Unexpected Needs and Design Suggestions. The co-design sessions showed that co-design can help to elicit and evaluate expected requirements, but also that the method seems to contribute to the elicitation of requirements that may not be found simply by asking, but are important for the application to be experienced as satisfactory and useful.

Conflicting User Needs Can be Identified and Explored. As in any system development process, conflicting requirements and user needs may be tricky to handle. One conflicting requirement brought up by the co-designers in this study was the use of a map. Although not every co-designer wanted a map, the openness of the prototype and method allowed us to at least find out whether they did, and we could also explore the functionality without any costly re-design or re-implementation of the prototype (for example, if they wanted the destination to be marked, the map could be turned so it matches the direction they are walking in). Thus, the sessions provided us with enough data to say that the way people should be guided by the application needs to be flexible – some will want a map while others may want, for example, a textual description.

Specification of System Requirements and Needs for a Navigation Application. A report evaluating the need for finding the right way at the hospital was delivered by the researchers to the Region.[1] The report contained system requirements derived from the sessions and interviews. It also included important aspects to consider when implementing an application for indoor navigation in the hospital. We could also provide the Region with experiences of the hospital environment that was not related to the application as such (unclear signs, etc.) and the notice to attend. The report was sent to the stakeholders and presented over zoom to region-IT, which is the collaborative partnership between all organizations within the region that use IT. We were then asked to participate during a presentation together with a company commercializing navigation solutions for shopping malls and, recently, also for a hospital. The report was well received and the company confirmed many of our findings but also expressed interest in other findings.

---

[1] The report "Co-design av smartphoneapplikation i användningsmiljö: en studie inom ramen för projektet DigitalWell Research och innovationscaset Att hitta rätt" (in Swedish) can be accessed electronically: http://urn.kb.se/resolve?urn=urn:nbn:se:kau:diva-85644.

5.4 Conclusion

This paper presents a method for the co-design of mobile applications in the intended use environment. Through the co-design sessions, a fruitful way for continuous elicitation and evaluation of system design suggestions could be explored. Through the active involvement of intended users in the design of a mobile navigation application, prototyped and co-designed using a WOz system, design suggestions for the application could be elicited and new adaptations could be implemented in the prototype, which meant that design suggestions could be evaluated with the proposer directly.

Acknowledgments. The study was conducted as a part of the research project DigitalWell Research and the project DigitalWell (2018–2020), which was an EU-funded project run by the Compare foundation.

References

1. Constantin, A., et al.: Distributing participation in design: addressing challenges of a global pandemic. Int. J. Child-Comput. Interact. **28** (2021). https://doi.org/10.1016/j.ijcci.2021.100255
2. Wirén, M., Eklund, R., Engberg, F., Westermark, J.: Experiences of an in-service Wizard-of-Oz data collection for the deployment of a call-routing application. In: Proceedings of the Workshop on Bridging the Gap: Academic and Industrial Research in Dialog Technologies (NAACL-HLT-Dialog 2007), Stroudsburg, PA, USA, pp. 56–63. Association for Computational Linguistics (2007)
3. Erdmann, R.L., Neal, A.S.: Laboratory vs. field experimentation in human factors—an evaluation of an experimental self-service airline ticket vendor. Hum. Factors **13**(6), 521–531 (1971). https://doi.org/10.1177/001872087101300603
4. Farshchian, B.A., Divitini, M.: Using email and www in a distributed participatory design project. ACM SIGGROUP Bull. **20**(1), 10–15 (1999). https://doi.org/10.1145/327556.327602
5. Walsh, G., Foss, E.: A case for intergenerational distributed co-design: the online kidsteam example. In: Proceedings of the 14th International Conference on Interaction Design and Children, pp. 99–108. Association for Computing Machinery, New York (2015). https://doi.org/10.1145/2771839.2771850
6. Vollenwyder, B., Buchmüller, E., Trachsel, C., Opwis, K., Brühlmann, F.: My train talks to me: participatory design of a mobile app for travellers with visual impairments. In: Miesenberger, K., Manduchi, R., Covarrubias Rodriguez, M., Peňáz, P. (eds.) ICCHP 2020. LNCS, vol. 12376, pp. 10–18. Springer, Cham (2020). https://doi.org/10.1007/978-3-030-58796-3_2
7. Pettersson, J.S., Wik, M., Andersson, H.: GUI interaction interviews in the evolving map of design research. In: Paspallis, N., Raspopoulos, M., Barry, C., Lang, M., Linger, H., Schneider, C. (eds.) Advances in Information Systems Development. LNISO, vol. 26, pp. 149–167. Springer, Cham (2018). https://doi.org/10.1007/978-3-319-74817-7_10
8. Wik, M., Khumalo, A.: Wizardry in distributed participatory design: from design to implementation. In: Kurosu, M. (ed.) HCII 2020. LNCS, vol. 12181, pp. 172–186. Springer, Cham (2020). https://doi.org/10.1007/978-3-030-49059-1_13
9. Challiol, C., et al.: Design thinking's resources for in-situ co-design of mobile games. In: 2019 International Conference on Information Systems and Computer Science (INCISCOS), pp. 339–345. IEEE (2019). https://doi.org/10.1109/INCISCOS49368.2019.00060

10. Bjerknes, G., Bratteteig, T.: User participation and democracy: a discussion of Scandinavian research on system development. Scand. J. Inf. Syst. **7**(1), 73–98 (1995)
11. Robertson, T., Simonsen, J.: Participatory design: an introduction. In: Simonsen, J., Robertson, T. (eds.) Routledge International Handbook of Participatory Design, pp. 1–18. Taylor & Francis Group (2012)
12. Bratteteig, T., Wagner, I.: Disentangling Participation: Power and Decision-Making in Participatory Design. Springer, Switzerland (2014). https://doi.org/10.1007/978-3-319-061 63-4
13. Gulliksen, J., Göransson, B., Boivie, I., Blomkvist, S., Persson, J., Cajander, Å.: Key principles for user-centred systems design. Behav. Inf. Technol. **22**(6), 397–409 (2003). https://doi.org/ 10.1080/01449290310001624329
14. Kelley, J.F.: An empirical methodology for writing user-friendly natural language computer applications. In: Proceedings of the SIGCHI Conference on Human Factors in Computing Systems (CHI 1983), pp. 193–196. ACM, New York (1983). https://doi.org/10.1145/800045. 801609
15. Kelley, J.F.: An iterative design methodology for user-friendly natural language office information applications. ACM Trans. Inf. Syst. (TOIS) **2**(1), 26–41 (1984). https://doi.org/10. 1145/357417.357420
16. Pettersson, J.S., Nilsson, J.: Effects of early user-testing on software quality – experiences from a case study. In: Information Systems Development, pp. 499–510. Springer, New York (2011). https://doi.org/10.1007/978-1-4419-7355-9_42
17. Pettersson, J.S.: The utility of digitally supported manual interactive mockups. In: Stephanidis, C., Antona, M. (eds.) HCII 2020. CCIS, vol. 1224, pp. 76–84. Springer, Cham (2020). https:// doi.org/10.1007/978-3-030-50726-8_10

A Co-creation Interaction Framework and Its Application for Intelligent Design System

Zhiyuan Yang[1,2], Wenbo Yang[1,2], Guang Yang[1,2], and Changyuan Yang[1,2(✉)]

[1] Alibaba Group, Hangzhou 311121, China
changyuan.yangcy@alibaba-inc.com
[2] Alibaba-Zhejiang University Joint Institute of Frontier Technologies, Hangzhou 310027, China

Abstract. In recent years, with the in-depth development of artificial intelligence technology in the field of creative design, intelligent systems have demonstrated certain creative capabilities. The computer is not just a tool for design expression, but transforms into a collaborator or creator of design. Co-creation between human and AI is the research focus in intelligent design system. At present, there is no established design framework that can describe the relevant components, features and their interrelationships in the intelligent design system, which can support system design and application in real application scenarios. Based on literature review and research practice, this paper discusses a co-creation interaction framework for intelligent design system. This framework links the source of human innovation with artificial intelligence technology through a collaborative mode, and describes an intelligent design system in which users and AI work together to complete innovation tasks. Then, taking the co-creative drawing system as an example, presented the implementation of the system, demonstrated the human-computer relationship in the framework, so as to provide a reference for related design intelligence research.

1 Introduction

In recent years, with the in-depth development of artificial intelligence technology in the field of creative design, intelligent systems have demonstrated certain creative capabilities, such as story generation [1], music creation [2, 3], painting [4, 5], game design [6], visual design [7, 8], etc. In the intelligent design system, the computer is not just a tool for design expression, but transforms into a collaborator or creator of design. Co-creation between human and AI is the research focus in the field of intelligent design [9].

The collaboration between humans and AI can better accomplish innovative tasks and producing more creative results. Although there have been a lot of researches on how to realize intelligent design systems, how to generate, select, or evaluate the results of automated design [10–12], there are few studies on the human-computer relationship and co-creation mode in intelligent design system. How to recognize, define, and design the interaction between Users and AI, and how to apply them in practical scenarios, has not been fully discussed.

M. Kurosu (Ed.): HCII 2022, LNCS 13302, pp. 343–355, 2022.
https://doi.org/10.1007/978-3-031-05311-5_24

Based on the previous researches, this paper takes the intelligent design system as the research object, discusses a co-creation interaction framework. Further, this paper highlights a case studies of intelligent design systems, demonstrates the human-computer relationship in the framework. This paper aims to provides a new idea and discussion basis for researchers and designers, which is helpful to the development and improvement of the intelligent design system and its human-computer interaction mode.

2 Related Work

2.1 HCI in Intelligent Design

Using AI technology to solve creative problems is an important direction of intelligent design research; and AI is gradually becoming a new element of design, which promotes the development and transformation of intelligent design.

Although AI is expected to become increasingly prevalent in creative design, it still faces many challenges in practical applications. AI is good at solving problems with clear goals and rules, such as reasoning, classification, and clustering, while creative design is an abstract problem with open-ended and ill-structured, which leads to limited support of intelligent systems for design practice and application in real-world scenarios. With the current development of intelligent systems, computers cannot completely replace the role of humans in creative design. While most research in intelligent design focuses on the algorithmic automation of the creative process, research in this area includes some level of human involvement. Even, human knowledge, experience, emotion play an irreplaceable role in the process of intelligent design. Different from the area of research in computer aided design, the cooperation between human and computers in design system has become more in-depth and intelligent. Therefore, it is necessary to re-evaluate the role of the human when designing an intelligent design system for real-world applications [13].

HCI experts are rethinking the relationship between human and computer in intelligent design systems. Terry Winograd and Gary Bradski recognized the limitations of artificial intelligence, and believed that intelligent design should shift its focus to enhancing human capabilities. The fundamental goal of artificial intelligence should be to enhance humans, not to replace them. Similarly, Bill Buxton believed that the intelligent design system should allow people to fully realize their potential [14]. Davis et al. divided the intelligent system into three types, according to the human-computer interaction mode, namely: Creativity support tool; Autonomous generative system, and Co-creative system [15]. According to the different roles of computers in creative work, Lubart divided the human-computer relationship into four types: Nanny, Pen-pal, Coach and Colleague [16]. Computer as nanny means, computers can encourage creativity by monitoring the working process and supporting the creative person, such as project management system; Computer as pen-pal means, computer technology can facilitate the interactions between two or more individuals; Computer as coach means, the computer can provide information in different ways that people can come up with creative ideas, which can serve as analogs to jump-start the creative process, such as an expert system; Computer as colleague means, humans and computers work hand in hand, their interaction involves a real partnership, computers can themselves be creative, or contribute new ideas in a dialogue with humans. "How humans and computers collaborate intelligently" is becoming a hotspot in the field of intelligent design.

2.2 Co-creation and Intelligent Design

Co-creation refers to the process of two subjects working together in a creative task [17, 18]. Collaboration between humans and AI can better accomplish innovative tasks, leading to brighter outcomes and unexpected possibilities. On the one hand, the human emotion, experience, intuition can train and guide intelligent design systems; on the other hand, the diverse design results of intelligent systems can also stimulate human creativity [19]. Therefore, advocating Co-creation has great value to the development of intelligent design systems.

Nicholas Davis et al. [20] built a human-computer collaborative painting system "Draw Apprentice". While the user is painting, the intelligent system provides feedback and supplements by imitating the subsequent painting trajectory to achieve co-creation and improve the painting effect. Changhoon et al. [21] further designed an intelligent system, DuetDraw, with which AI and users can draw pictures in a collaborative manner. Using AI techniques, the system can help users perform drawing tasks by switching the roles of users between the leader and assistant in the creation process, such as completing the rest of the object that the user was drawing, drawing the same object in a different style, suggesting an object that matches the picture, and automatically colorizing the sketches. Autodesk's research team developed an experimental design platform "Dreamcatcher", an intelligent system based on generative design and machine learning. This system can generate a large number of design prototypes according to the design information inputted by the designers, the designers can evaluate the generated design prototypes in real time, and iterate the prototypes by adjusting the inputted information and design constraints [22]. Matthew et al. [23] introduced a game level design tool, in which a level designer can collaboratively work with an AI designer to build a platformer game level. The collaborative interaction occurs in a turn-based manner, in which the human and AI take turns making changes to an initially blank level within the same level editor interface. In these studies, how to understand and explore the human-computer interaction and user experience in intelligent design system has become a key issue [24].

The co-creation intelligent design system aims to stimulate and promote human thinking, and its ideal state should be the concept of human-computer symbiosis, that is, by integrating the respective advantages of humans and computers, they will achieve more than they could independently [25]. Effective human-computer collaboration first requires understanding human capabilities, and then developing new technologies to enhance those capabilities. Once human capacities have been thoroughly assessed, researchers can synergize these with AI capabilities through HCI methods to maximize complementarity and minimize conflicts between users and computers [14]. Feldman believed that the intelligent design system needs to respond the users' emotion and cognitive experience in order to arouse their reflection, which can realize the possibility of co-creation between the users and the system, and affect the creative results [19]. Matthew et al. [26] introduced a turn-based interaction framework for intelligent system, which aims to provide a basis for system development and evaluation. Quanz et al.

[27] proposed a flexible development framework, including three component modules: Creator, Iterator, Evaluator. The development framework integrates a variety of artificial intelligence technologies, showing how to use machine learning methods to help designers efficiently produce designs, and promote the creativity of intelligent design system.

There are certain conflicts between AI and HCI in thinking, which leads to the application of design methods, guidelines, standards in the field of HCI to intelligent design systems is limited. At present, there is no established design framework that can describe the relevant components, features and their interrelationships in the intelligent design system, which can support system design and application in real application scenarios. Therefore, this paper discusses and summarizes a user-centered co-creation interaction framework, and discusses its application in the co-creative drawing system, so as to provide a reference for related design intelligence research.

3   Co-creation Interaction Framework

Based on the previous researches, this paper takes the intelligent design system as the research object, discusses a co-creation interaction framework. This framework links the source of human innovation with artificial intelligence technology through a collaborative mode, and describes an intelligent interactive design system in which users and AI work together to complete innovation tasks (see Fig. 1). The essential feature of this system is to coordinate the dynamic collaborative relationship between users and computers. The framework can be used to better understand the space of possible designs of co-creative intelligent systems and reveal future research directions.

The main components of the co-creative intelligent design system include "User", "Artificial Intelligence (AI)", "Design Process" and "Human-Computer Relationship". "User" is the core of intelligent design system. The "User" refers to the designers or requirement creator. Focusing on the user's experience and feelings, personality characteristics and behavior, cognition and emotion, understanding and expression in the interaction between the user and AI will affect the decision-making method and generation quality of the intelligent design system.

"Artificial Intelligence", mainly refers to "Design Artificial Intelligence" in this paper, is a computer technology that includes machine learning, deep learning, reinforcement learning, etc., aiming at solving a certain problem in the design process. The development of AI technology is mainly related to the three aspects of algorithm, data and computing power.

"Design Process" refers to a series of interrelated design and calculation activities that convert input into output, which is the basic logic of the operation of intelligent design system. One of the key points in an intelligent design system is how to synergize human capabilities and technical capabilities in the design process to enhance the creativity of the intelligent system and improve production efficiency.

"Human-Computer Relationship" refers to the interaction process between "User" and "Artificial Intelligence", and is an important part of advocating Co-creation. With the development of intelligent design systems, the interaction mode and role between users and AI are constantly being updated. The above four elements constitute a co-creative intelligent design system.

The following subsections summarize the three main characteristics of the intelligent design system from the perspectives of "user", "design process" and "human-machine relationship", and clarify the relationship between the elements of the intelligent system.

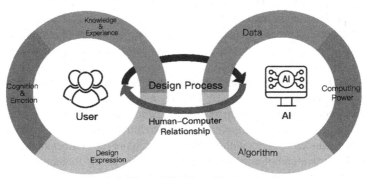

Intelligent Design System

Fig. 1. Co-creation interaction framework

3.1 User-Centered

"User-centered" is one of the important features of the co-creative intelligent design system. Design has developed from the level of solving objects to the level of solving people. The concept and method of "user-centered" has become a part of the design. However, in intelligent design, this concept and method has a further new understanding. The research and development of intelligent design systems should focus on "user", and many human-computer interaction experts have expressed similar views and opinions [14, 28].

For intelligent design systems, a "user-centric" approach can bridge the dialogue between users and AI, allowing them to share and exchange knowledge, and collaboratively develop their design process. It has two meanings in intelligent design.

On the one hand, intelligent design systems can gain a deeper understanding of users. AI technologies represented by affective computing and experiential computing can mine and analyze users' needs, intentions, preferences, etc., and provide real-time computing and feedback, so that intelligent design systems can not only reach real, three-dimensional users, and can continuously adjust the output results according to the user status in the process, improving the user experience and the generation effect. That is, traditional user research and design methods are based on sample surveys of typical user; while intelligent design methods make the "user-centered" method possible.

On the other hand, users can also participate in the work of the intelligent design system. Human emotion, experience, aesthetics and other traits expand the capability of AI in the design system, and can train and guide AI. Therefore, human abilities and characteristics are important in the design and application of intelligent systems.

3.2 Collaborative Interaction in Design Process

The change of design process is another important feature of the co-creative intelligent design system. At present, the research of intelligent design system mainly focuses on the automation of tasks to achieve higher efficiency and productivity, but researchers are beginning to realize the limitations of computers in processing creative design, and shift the focus of the design process to in terms of enhancing human ability. Intelligent design system needs to establish a new process of human-computer collaborative interaction [29].

The design process is an organic combination of human-computer interaction activities in an intelligent design system. By building a design process for human-computer collaborative interaction, human and technical capabilities can be enhanced, the complementarity between users and computers can be maximized, and the interaction between the two can be reduced. conflict with each other to acquire the competencies and knowledge needed to solve complex, abstract creative problems. Its fundamental purpose is to supplement or enhance existing or potential user capabilities through technical capabilities, so as to achieve a state of optimal balance between users and computers in the intelligent system.

The optimal balance refers to a complementary state achieved between interacting users and computers in an intelligent system, such that they can achieve better under collaboration. In this design process, the criteria for judging technological capabilities are no longer determined by traditional quantitative or qualitative indicators, but by their ability to stimulate and realize human potential.

Therefore, in the intelligent design system, the user is no longer just an input node in the design process, but becomes a new important role in the user-centered, collaborative design process, throughout the entire design and production cycle. This new design process requires researchers to comprehensively consider the three elements of users, technology, and practical application scenarios to achieve efficient and high-quality design. Among them, comprehensively measuring the unique innate capabilities of users in a specific application scenario and the technical barriers to utilizing these capabilities are crucial to realizing human-computer collaboration.

3.3 Diverse Human-Computer Relationships

The essential goal of the co-creative intelligent design system is to achieve the optimal balance between the user and the computer. However, a balanced human-computer relationship does not mean that tasks should be allocated equally in the design process, but should be dynamically adjusted according to the capabilities and participation of humans and computers in the design process. The implication of this for HCI is that there should be many different human-computer relationships in the co-creative intelligent design system.

SAE (Society of Automotive Engineers) divides autonomous driving into six distinct levels (L0-L5) based on the relationship between humans and autonomous driving systems, which can clarify the differences between these levels of autonomous driving technology, and vividly describe the relationship between humans and AI. Taking the description of the human-computer relationship of autonomous driving as a reference, based on the nature of design, this paper further explored and summarized the potential relationship between users and AI in intelligent design system.

Unlike autonomous driving, in an intelligent design system, the relationship between user and computer is integrated and complementary to each other. According to the involvement of artificial intelligence in graphic design, this paper generally summarized the following four cooperation modes, which represent four computer roles, and describe the diverse human-computer relationship in the intelligent graphic design system.

First, the computer as a design tool. In the field of computer aided design, computers provide convenience for designers in terms of creative stimulation and design generation. In the context of AI, based on the powerful analysis and processing capabilities of AI, computers can undertake more design tasks, further assist designers in innovative work, and improve production efficiency. Taking "image matting" as an example, extracting the required design materials from the original image is the most basic and time-consuming work content for many graphic designers. Many design tools provide AI-based, high-precision automatic matting functions to reduce the workload of designers. In this example, the computer can quickly and easily do some well-defined, mechanical work for the designer.

Second, the computer as a design assistant. This requires that the computer can automatically adapt to the needs of different scenarios and make adaptive design modifications on the basis of maintaining the design style and design language. That is, when the designer specifies the design rules, the computer can perform design tasks in large quantities. The involvement of computers can greatly reduce the designer's investment in low-creative design work.

Third, computers can be design apprentices. Just as a teacher guides students, after a certain training, students can have their own ideas and ask unique design problems. When the computer as an assistant, the user does not expect the computer to perform creative works; but as an apprentice, the computer should be able to carry out certain design creations. For example, the computer can create a new design along the designer's style after several times of data learning.

Fourth, the designer and the computer can be a partnership, which is the best vision in HCI. In this human-computer relationship, the user can let the computer learn new knowledge and experience, and the computer can also provide the user with creative inspiration, which is a developmental relationship.

To sum up, in the co-creative intelligent design system, how to properly coordinate the relationship between humans and computers, how to apply different human-computer relationships for different application scenarios and design tasks, and optimize the capabilities of both are the focus of intelligent design research.

4 Case Study: A Co-creative Drawing System

Based on the co-creation interaction framework, this paper presented a co-creative drawing system, called SmartPaint, to enable AI and human to collaborate to create cartoon landscape paintings in a timely way, where paintings can be generated with minimum interaction and painting expertise. The key idea is to let the computer master the domain knowledge of cartoon landscape paintings by learning thousands of cartoon images, enabling it to build an understanding of the semantic and spatial relations between objects in a landscape and the unique color and texture of the cartoons. Therefore, smartPaint allows both novices and experts to freely input their creative ideas as rough sketches and obtain artistically expressive paintings. Regardless of what the user draws, the AI can make its own contribution build on the user's sketch. In this collaborative way, the intelligent system produces a creative and fine painting with the appropriate style corresponding to the human's sketch.

4.1 Problem Definition

Drawing is one of the most important means for people to explore creative ideas and try new things. To create a pleasing painting, an artist requires professional knowledge and advanced artis-tic skills to organize the visual features of a painting coherently so as to express his/her intentions and imagination. However, humans normally draw rough sketches to express ideas and lack professional skills to complete pleasing paintings. To collaborate with people, the machine needs master the domain knowledge of a certain painting so that it is able to understand the semantic concepts of a user sketch and transform a rough sketch into a vivid painting with a specific artistic style.

For the co-creative drawing task, there are two key problems. First, an intelligent system needs to be able to understand a users' drawing inputs. second, it can respond to users' sketch inputs and help users turn ideas into beautiful paintings.

4.2 System Implementation

The goal of SmartPaint is to let humans and machines work together to create cartoon landscape paintings. The human first expresses creation ideas with a rough sketch, and the machine turns the sketch into a cartoon painting and returns it to the shared canvas. The co-creative intelligent system has three key functionalities to achieve collaboration with the human: a painting producer, edge synthesizer, and reference recommender (see Fig. 2).

Painting Producer. The painting producer consists of a conditional GAN trained by data comprising cartoon images and their corresponding semantic label maps and edge detection maps. All the training images are resized and cropped to 1024×512 pixels. To obtain a set of cartoon images with the same style, we extract frames of cartoon films drawn by Miyazaki Hayao and other Japanese films or animations with a similar style. We limit our image data to landscapes; those images with obvious characters or artificial objects were discarded. To label cartoon images semantically, we grouped the visual classes in the dataset into nine categories: mountains, grass, trees, houses, sky, rivers, roads, rocks, and others. Each image in our dataset is hand-annotated according to these nine categories, and each of which is represented by a different color. In addition, we use a standard Canny edge detector [30] to extract the edges of the cartoon images. Our final dataset consists of 7,234 data triples of a cartoon image, semantic label map, and edge detection map. The semantic maps provide semantic information for each region of the image and the edge maps offer the details of each object. Combining these two inputs as network inputs allows the computer to produce higher quality paintings.

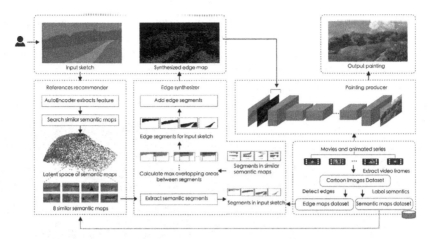

Fig. 2. Overall structures of SmartPaint

Edge Synthesizer. To ensure the drawing task is simple, in the proposed system, users draw sketches with different colors as semantic maps and the edge synthesizer synthesizes the edge maps based on user's input sketches automatically. To automatically synthesize the edge map based on an input sketch, we need to consider the characteristics of the cartoon edge, the semantics of the scene represented by the sketch, and the shape of each object in the sketch. We use edge maps in the training dataset as materials to synthesize a new edge map for a user-drawn sketch. To perform this task, we use the reference recommender to obtain eight semantic label maps that are the most similar to the newly drawn one. Edge maps corresponding to these eight similar semantic maps are used as materials. Then, we use the shape context algorithm [31] to extract object segments in the user sketch and eight similar semantic maps according to the semantics. We calculate the maximum overlapping areas between the segments of the same semantics to obtain an individual edge map for each segment in the user sketch and add these edge segments to obtain the final synthesized edge map. Then, the user-drawn sketches and synthesized edge maps are inputted into the trained GAN to generate the paintings. Automatic edge synthetization is the key to ensuring the freedom of drawing and the quality of production.

Reference Recommender. Real-time guidance and visual feedback during the creative process can inspire the user's creativity. SmartPaint recommends the eight most similar semantic label maps in the dataset to users for reference in real-time given arbitrary sketch inputs.

The main interface of our system consists of three components (see Fig. 3): Area a is a palette of drawing tools, area b is a shared canvas on which the human and machine can draw, and area c is for displaying reference images. The drawing palette includes common functions associated with drawing applications, such as brush selection. Users draw different objects using different colored brushes. We offer eight kinds of brush with different colors to indicate different objects (i.e., mountains, grass, trees, houses, sky, rivers, roads, and rocks) and the users are allowed to draw the outline in their imagination with different brushes. There are two modes in our system: drawing mode and generation mode. The user draws and modifies the sketches only when in drawing mode. When in generation mode, the can-vas displays the generated painting. If the user is dissatisfied with the result, he/she can return to the drawing mode to modify the sketches. The system is built using a python-based open-source web frame-work, Django.

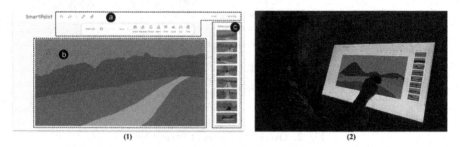

Fig. 3. (1) SmartPaint interfaces; (2) A user drawing in the system

4.3 Discussion

In this paper, we develop Smart-Paint, which is a co-creative drawing system that enables machines and human to collaborate to create cartoon landscape paintings. To achieve this, we trained a generative adversarial network (GAN) with 7,234 triples of cartoon landscape images and their corresponding semantic label maps and edge detection maps. after training, users input sketches as semantic label maps, and SmartPaint automatically synthesizes edge maps according to the semantics of sketches. User sketches and synthesized edge maps are transmitted into the trained GAN to out-put the cartoon paintings with the appropriate color and texture in seconds. The results show that the proposed co-creative intelligent system can successfully generate high-quality cartoon paintings.

Our AI method and co-creative system allows the computer to learn a large number of images of a particular style as well as their semantic label and edge detection maps, making it able to generate specific style images with rich content details. Compared with existing approaches that separately generate and stylize realistic images, our system produces images that are more in line with a certain style. Further, the aim of our work is to allow people to collaborate with the machine to draw while providing the simplest means of input for the humans. Therefore, we added the edge detection maps extracted from cartoon images as network input and synthesized edge maps based on user in-put sketches when generating a painting. We trained an auto-encoder to extract the high-dimensional features of semantic maps so that we can synthesize edge maps for user sketches based on semantics. This method further improves the quality of the generated image and guarantees the freedom and simplicity of the user input.

Although our co-creative system produces high-quality cartoon paintings, it requires finely annotated data for training, making it difficult to extend to the creation of diverse styles of paintings. Moreover, our system is suitable for drawing objects without re-strictions on shape, and objects with specific shapes such as houses are poorly generated. The uncontrollability and unpredictability of the proposed system sometimes makes users feel confused when they collaborate with it, which makes our system more suit-able for the early exploration of design. However, unlike template-based design aid tools, our system supports personalized and innovative creation. Its easy-to-operate interaction helps both novices and experts create their unique cartoon stories. Further-more, the co-creative system can generate large quantities of design materials in a specific style quickly, opening a new way to automatic creative design, such as the automatic generation of creative advertisements and game scenes.

5   Conclusion

Based on literature review and research practice, this paper discusses a co-creation interaction framework for intelligent design system. This framework links the source of human innovation with artificial intelligence technology through a collaborative mode, and describes an intelligent design system in which users and AI work together to complete innovation tasks. The main components of the co-creative intelligent design system include "User", "Artificial Intelligence (AI)", "Design Process" and "Human-Computer Relationship". "User-centered", " Collaborative Interaction in Design Process" and " Diverse Human-computer relationships" are three important characteristics of the co-creative system, and these characteristics clarify the correlation between the components of the system. The framework is designed to help researchers and developers expand their thinking dimensions when building co-creative intelligent design systems, and can take a more comprehensive and flexible perspective, providing more possibilities for solving intelligent design problems.

Further, based on this framework, taking the co-creative drawing system as an example, it explored how to combine AI and human intelligence to solve creative design problems, showing the possibility brought by the capability of deep learning technologies.

References

1. Martin, L., et al.: Event representations for automated story generation with deep neural nets. In: Proceedings of the AAAI Conference on Artificial Intelligence (2018)
2. Hadjeres, G., Pachet, F., Nielsen, F.: Deepbach: a steerable model for bach chorales generation. In: International Conference on Machine Learning, pp. 1362–1371. PMLR (2017)
3. Roberts, A., Engel, J., Eck, D.: Hierarchical variational autoencoders for music. In: NIPS Workshop on Machine Learning for Creativity and Design (2017)
4. Li, C., Wand, M.: Combining Markov random fields and convolutional neural networks for image synthesis. In: Proceedings of the IEEE Conference on Computer Vision and Pattern Recognition, pp. 2479–2486 (2016)
5. Floridi, L.: Artificial intelligence, deepfakes and a future of ectypes. In: Ethics, Governance, and Policies in Artificial Intelligence. pp. 307–312. Springer, Cham (2021). https://doi.org/10.1007/s13347-018-0325-3

6. Summerville, A., et al.: Procedural content generation via machine learning (PCGML). IEEE Trans. Games **10**, 257–270 (2018)
7. Yang, X., Mei, T., Xu, Y.-Q., Rui, Y., Li, S.: Automatic generation of visual-textual presentation layout. ACM Trans. Multimedia Comput. Commun. Appl. (TOMM) **12**, 1–22 (2016)
8. Zhao, N., Cao, Y., Lau, R.W.: What characterizes personalities of graphic designs? ACM Trans. Graph. (TOG). **37**, 1–15 (2018)
9. Pan, Y.: Heading toward artificial intelligence 2.0. Engineering **2**, 409–413 (2016)
10. Zhu, J.-Y., Krähenbühl, P., Shechtman, E., Efros, A.A.: Generative visual manipulation on the natural image manifold. In: Leibe, B., Matas, J., Sebe, N., Welling, M. (eds.) European Conference on Computer Vision, pp. 597–613. Springer, Cham (2016). https://doi.org/10.1007/978-3-319-46454-1_36
11. Ha, D., Eck, D.: A neural representation of sketch drawings. arXiv preprint arXiv:1704.03477 (2017)
12. Dou, Q., Zheng, X.S., Sun, T., Heng, P.-A.: Webthetics: quantifying webpage aesthetics with deep learning. Int. J. Hum Comput Stud. **124**, 56–66 (2019)
13. Shneiderman, B.: Creativity support tools: a grand challenge for HCI researchers. In: Engineering the User Interface, pp. 1–9. Springer, Cham (2009). https://doi.org/10.1007/978-1-84800-136-7_1
14. Ren, X.: Rethinking the relationship between humans and computers. Computer **49**, 104–108 (2016)
15. Davis, N.M., Popova, Y., Sysoev, I., Hsiao, C.-P., Zhang, D., Magerko, B.: Building artistic computer colleagues with an enactive model of creativity. In: ICCC, pp. 38–45 (2014)
16. Lubart, T.: How can computers be partners in the creative process: classification and commentary on the special issue. Int. J. Hum Comput Stud. **63**, 365–369 (2005)
17. Allen, J.E., Guinn, C.I., Horvtz, E.: Mixed-initiative interaction. IEEE Intell. Syst. Applicat. **14**, 14–23 (1999)
18. Goldstein, I.M., Lawrence, J., Miner, A.S.: Human-machine collaboration in cancer and beyond: the centaur care model. JAMA Oncol. **3**, 1303–1304 (2017)
19. Feldman, S.: Co-creation: human and AI collaboration in creative expression. In: Electronic Visualisation and the Arts (EVA 2017), pp. 422–429 (2017)
20. Davis, N., Hsiao, C.-Pi., Singh, K.Y., Li, L., Moningi, S., Magerko, B.: Drawing apprentice: an enactive co-creative agent for artistic collaboration. In: Proceedings of the 2015 ACM SIGCHI Conference on Creativity and Cognition, pp. 185–186 (2015)
21. Oh, C., Song, J., Choi, J., Kim, S., Lee, S., Suh, B.: I lead, you help but only with enough details: Understanding user experience of co-creation with artificial intelligence. In: Proceedings of the 2018 CHI Conference on Human Factors in Computing Systems, pp. 1–13 (2018)
22. Kazi, R.H., Grossman, T., Cheong, H., Hashemi, A., Fitzmaurice, G.W.: DreamSketch: early stage 3D design explorations with sketching and generative design. In: UIST, pp. 401–414 (2017)
23. Guzdial, M., et al.: Friend, collaborator, student, manager: How design of an ai-driven game level editor affects creators. In: Proceedings of the 2019 CHI Conference on Human Factors in Computing Systems, pp. 1–13 (2019)
24. Winograd, T.: Shifting viewpoints: Artificial intelligence and human–computer interaction. Artif. Intell. **170**, 1256–1258 (2006)
25. Liapis, A., Yannakakis, G.N., Alexopoulos, C., Lopes, P.: Can computers foster human users' creativity? Theory and praxis of mixed-initiative co-creativity (2016)
26. Guzdial, M., Riedl, M.: An interaction framework for studying co-creative ai. arXiv preprint arXiv:1903.09709 (2019)
27. Quanz, B., Sun, W., Deshpande, A., Shah, D., Park, J.: Machine learning based co-creative design framework. arXiv preprint arXiv:2001.08791 (2020)

28. Buxton, W.: Human Skills in Interface Design. Wiley, New York (1994)
29. Markoff, J.: Machines of Loving Grace: The Quest for Common Ground between Humans and Robots. HarperCollins Publishers, New York (2016)
30. Canny, J.: A computational approach to edge detection. IEEE Trans. Pattern Anal. Mach. Intell. 679–698 (1986)
31. Belongie, S., Malik, J., Puzicha, J.: Shape context: a new descriptor for shape matching and object recognition. Adv. Neural Inf. Process. Syst. **13** (2000)

Towards Establishing Consistent Proposal Binning Methods for Unimodal and Multimodal Interaction Elicitation Studies

Xiaoyan Zhou$^{(\boxtimes)}$, Adam S. Williams, and Francisco R. Ortega

Colorado State University, Fort Collins, CO 80525, USA
{Xiaoyan.Zhou,AdamWil,fortega}@colostate.edu

Abstract. More than two hundred papers on elicitation studies have been published in the last ten years. These works are mainly focused on generating user-defined gesture sets and discovering natural feeling multimodal interaction techniques with virtual objects. Few papers have discussed binning the elicited interaction proposals after data collection. Binning is a process of grouping the entire set of user-generated interaction proposals based on similarity criteria. The binned set of proposals is then analyzed to produce a consensus set, which results in the user-defined interaction set. This paper presents a formula to use when deciding how to bin interaction proposals, thus helping to establish a more consistent binning procedure. This work can provide human-computer interaction (HCI) researchers with the guidance they need for interaction elicitation data processing, which is largely missing from current elicitation study literature. Using this approach will improve the efficiency and effectiveness of the binning process, increase the reliability of us er-defined interaction sets, and most importantly, improve the replicability of elicitation studies.

Keywords: Elicitation study · Binning methods · Gestures proposals

1 Introduction

Elicitation is a form of participatory design where researchers ask novice users to produce input proposals that would execute various commands (i.e., referents) within a system (e.g., augmented reality displays, multi-touch surfaces) [24,29]. During this process the participant is shown referents one at a time and the participant produces input proposals that they find appropriate for executing those referents. This might look like showing a participant a virtual object using augmented reality technologies and asking them to produce a mid-air gesture that would cause the virtual object to move left [18,25].

During an elicitation study researchers often identify the consensus set of input proposals by quantifying the agreement between participants on input

© The Author(s), under exclusive license to Springer Nature Switzerland AG 2022
M. Kurosu (Ed.): HCII 2022, LNCS 13302, pp. 356–368, 2022.
https://doi.org/10.1007/978-3-031-05311-5_25

proposals for a given referent [21,29]. In between labeling the raw input proposals and measuring participant agreement, researchers often bin the input proposals into equivalence groups based on their similarity of execution. Without binning proposals, the consensus set will be biased by individual differences and agreement calculations will return pessimistic estimates of agreement. As an example, without binning, a swipe right with the index and middle fingers would be counted as a distinct gesture from swiping right with the index alone. In actuality these two gestures are similar in execution, intent, and at times may have been produced by the same user for the same referent [18,27].

It is well known that the binning procedure is time-consuming due to the process of annotating the recorded videos [1,22], and error-prone because of the subjective human judgments involved [22]. Moreover, adopting different similarity criteria can lead to underestimated or overestimated agreement rates as a result of more or less permissive binning protocols [22]. In this paper, we present a formula that can assist experimenters with binning gesture proposals from participants through a unified binning procedure. This work uses mid-air gesture elicitation proposals, which can be extracted from both unimodal and multimodal interactions. This formula could be used equally well to bin gesture proposals from elicitation studies with different systems, such as virtual reality displays or multi-touch devices.

It is critical that experimental science is reproducible, replicable, and reapeatable. Researchers in HCI have been calling for more work focusing on the replication or reproduction of prior works [15,22]. In particular, for elicitation studies, adopting a standard data processing procedure and guidelines can accelerate the replication or reproduction process for future researchers. The necessity of a standard procedure for binning is increasing along with the rapid growth of elicitation studies. It is time to fill this gap and form a guideline for elicitation data processing.

2   Related Work

Based on recently published elicitation study literature reviews, over two hundred elicitation studies have been conducted in the last ten years [23]. Most of the previous works aimed to develop user-defined gesture sets [6,11,14,16,18,19, 25,27,29], and a few works have discussed the tools and criteria used for binning the interaction proposals in the studies [1,2,20].

2.1   Binning Tools

Several studies proposed new approaches to improve the efficiency of the binning process and reduce the effort required by researchers. Ali et al. proved that letting online crowd workers make the proposal's similarity comparison, then using automatic binning algorithms for sign classification, can produce similar results compared to using experts with less time spent on the task [1]. Nevertheless, the crowd-powered tool Crowdsensus proposed by Ali et al. only demonstrated the use of elicited voice commands in text string format. Vatavu introduced the dissimilarity-consensus method to replace the subjective binning criteria, and manual labeling with automated computation by a computer [20]. This method helps mitigate human error and subjective decisions on proposals similarity. However, using the dissimilarity consensus approach accurate skeletal and pose information is needed, which is not suitable for most elicitation studies' data captured in video format. Moreover, despite the computational method, subjectivity still exists during raw data preprocessing and extracting procedures. Anthony et al. developed a tool to identify similar gesture articulations and generate clusters automatically, and the agreement rates were reported after binning [2]. Nevertheless, the tool allows the researcher to edit and correct the cluster partition, making the binning process still subjective. While it is difficult to entirely avoid the subjective human judgments during the binning process, following the guidelines put forth here can help to mitigate it.

2.2 Binning Criteria

It is not uncommon that different elicitation studies adopt different criteria for evaluating the similarity of proposed interactions from participants [20,22]. Few works have reported the criteria they used for proposal binning in the study, which led to irreproducible study results [22]. Most of the elicitation studies have described the classification process in a broad manner [27–29]. Several works in augmented reality have mentioned the general binning approach or criteria was used in their studies [17,18,25]. Piumsomboon et al. defined "similar gestures" as the gestures that have identical static pose and path, or have different static poses but with consistent directionality [18]. Pham et al. adopted themes such as the analytic unit and binned gestures based on similar themes despite different executions (e.g. binned squishing with clapped hands, fingers, or fist) [17]. Williams et al. binned gestures according to the movement path and hand pose, and explained the definition of each hand pose presented in the study [25]. Many elicitation studies have used a taxonomy for gesture classification and binning [3,5,7,8,18,27].

Taxonomy based binning criteria are not always well suited for direct interaction elicitation study proposals. In most elicitation studies a large proportion of the referents revolve around direct manipulations (i.e., translations, rotations, and scaling). When eliciting direct manipulations, interaction proposals will often be impacted by the participants' notions of real world physics [9]. If the referent is *move left* the participants will most likely push the object to the left with their hand [17,18,27]. These proposals will often fall under a single category when using a taxonomy [10] (e.g., "direct manipulation"), making using taxonomy for binning difficult. This paper will not discuss the procedure of classifying mid-air gesture proposals based on taxonomy. Our study aims to provide researchers and designers with a guideline for executing the proposals binning procedure in an elicitation study, as shown in Fig. 1. With the structured criteria and procedure, more elicitation studies can be replicated, and the results can be reproduced.

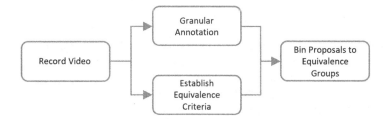

Fig. 1. Procedure to group interaction proposals into equivalence groups in an elicitation study

3 Data Collection

Often elicitation studies' data is captured via video recordings [14,22,25,26]. An exo-centric camera is commonly used to record participants' proposals. If the study used head-mounted displays (HMDs), an ego-centric camera can also be used. For data completion and analysis convenience, recommend experimenters adopt both ego-centric and exo-centric cameras to capture different views of interaction. Based on observations from our prior experiments' data with HMDs, participants have various preferences on hand position while performing manipulation tasks [25,26]. Some participants proposed physical interaction more than others, which means the gesture acted physically on the object, and their hands reached out to the objects. When participants proposed more metaphorical gestures for interaction, their hands were closer to their bodies during the manipulation. As a result, it is possible that the ego-centric camera is unable to capture the full view of the interaction due to the different positions of individual proposals. The exo-centric view could be very helpful, when the ego-centric camera does not capture the full hand movement. For example, while participants' hands are too close to the face and the movement is out of the view of the ego-centric camera, the exo-centric recording became the only source of participants' proposal. For exo-centric view, it is suggested to place the camera with a tripod on the front right or left corner that faces the participant. For the ego-centric view, the camera (e.g. GoPro) can be mounted on top of the head-mounted display (e.g. HoloLens 2). It should be noted that experimenters need to check the camera angle before starting the experiment. It is not unusual that the head-mounted display is unable to hold the camera on the top, or the camera mounting cause unbalance or discomfort to users. In that case, the experimenters could choose to use a head strap attaches to the camera and ask participants to wear it on their heads. The downside of this approach is the complexity of the camera angle set-up, since the head-mounted display could block the view of the ego-centric camera.

4   Video Annotation Procedure

Once the elicitation data has been collected a granular labeling pass should be done to convert the raw video to meaningful interaction information (Fig. 1). These labels should capture all relevant information about the gestures. For each interaction elicited, the hand used, fingers used, direction of movement, start time, stop time, changes in hand shape or pose, and the corresponding referent name should be recorded. Some additional interaction features that can be recorded depending on the studies' aims are outlined in the following sections.

4.1   Stroke Segmentation

A gesture generally starts with a preparation phase, moves into a stroke, then returns to the resting position [12]. For example, the hand was usually placed on the lap of the participant or on the desk surface with a relaxed hand pose. When the participant is ready to perform the gesture, the hand will hold up and leave the lap or desk first, then reach out to the target object or perform the interaction immediately. This means that experimenters need to find the boundaries of a gesture, and it also can be called the stroke of a gesture. According to McNeil, a stroke is considered the peak of effort for a specific gesture [13], which holds the meaningful content of the gesture. Based on previous experiment data, when the stroke happens, the direction of movement will change, or the speed of movement will show a sudden increase [26]. This can be observed while the experimenters go through each recorded video frame.

4.2   Gesture Information Recording

After the boundaries of the gesture are found, the video of the stroke can be segmented, or the screenshot of the stroke can be captured for later reference. This reference could be very useful while experimenters need to review or double-check certain proposed gestures. The start and end times of both gestures and strokes should be noted during video annotation for later analysis of stroke time distribution, or the relationship between strokes and other modalities of interaction. In addition, the experimenters should also record which hand and finger have been used for the interaction, how many hands were used, and what fingers were involved. These elements contain important information for verifying results from previous studies with mid-air gestures in augmented reality environment [17,18,25,26].

4.3   Stroke Coding

To code proposed gestures, experimenters need to define each hand shape before starting coding. For example, the "pointing" gesture could involve the index finger, index middle fingers, or all fingers from one hand. "Pinching" could include thumb and index finger, or thumb index and middle fingers. "Grasping" could be gathered five fingertips, and "grabbing" shows as a fist. During stroke coding, the hand pose and the path of hand movement are the main points that experimenters should pay attention to. In terms of hand pose, hand shape and palm and finger orientation should be noted. For example, moving an object up with the thumb and index finger holding the object should be coded as pinching with the palm facing forward and moving the hand along the Z-axis. In terms of movement path, experimenters should code proposed gestures based on which axis it moved along or around. For example, translations up and down should be both considered as movements along the Z-axis. The referents of translations left or right should be identified as movements along Y-axis. Moving an object towards or away should be recognized as movements along X-axis. The rotations clockwise and counterclockwise should be both coded as movements around X-axis. Rotating around Y-axis could describe the response to referents *pitch up* or *pitch down*, and rotating around Z-axis could represent proposals to referents *yaw left* or *yaw right*.

It is worth noting that the thumb position could be less meaningful compared to other fingers. We suggested experimenters consider the interaction theme while recording the thumb position for each proposal. The variants of thumb position in hand poses could be due to hand differences or individual habits. In general, the relaxed position for the thumb is to stick out instead of closing to the palm or gathering with other fingers. As a result, when a gesture does not require the thumb, it normally stays relaxed, which could look like the thumb is sticking out. For example, based on our previous data, some proposals with index finger pointing gestures also had the thumb pointed to the front [26]. In this case, we ignored the thumb pose and only recorded the pointing gesture executed by the index finger. However, with proposals involving pinching or grasping poses, which could be proposed for referents of translation or rotation, the experimenters should pay attention to every fingers' status including the thumb.

5   Interaction Proposal Binning

Once all of the collected video has been annotated the elicited interactions can be binned into equivalence groups based on pre-defined metrics of similarity. This reduced the space of elicited proposals to a smaller set of binned interaction proposals which can then be used during agreement rate and consensus calculations. Conceptually, the binning process smooths out interpersonal differences between interaction proposals. As an example, if binning processes were omitted, a three finger pinching gesture where the participants index, middle, and thumb come together to grab a virtual object would be considered different from a two finger pinching gesture where only the index and thumb are used. When considering how to implement the elicited interaction proposals into a interaction system, it makes more sense to say that those two gestures are the same. Their intent and motion trajectory's are similar. Outside of motion and intent, this step can be further justified when considering how the same user may use inconsistent numbers of fingers for the same gesture [18], making the difference between using the index and thumb or the index, middle, and thumb trivial.

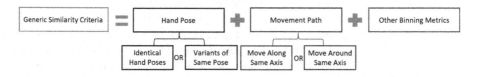

Fig. 2. Formula for binning gesture proposals

As shown in our formula (Fig. 2), while binning mid-air gesture proposals, we suggest the experimenter mainly focuses on the similarity of static hand pose and hand movement path. Bins are created based on the pairing of binning criteria. This might look like making bins for pinching hand poses moving along the x-axis, or grasping gestures that move vertically. Some bins may not be predictable a priori. To account for that researchers can expect to add new binning criteria while analyzing their results. For example someone might pantomime usage of a steering wheel for rotations. This gesture might necessitate a new equivalence group to be established. The experimenters can set up a worksheet to assign a name or number and provide a brief description to each bin for later reference. It is possible that the same gesture was proposed for different referents, and we recommend sharing bins through the binning procedure for all referents in the study. If the same gesture resulted in the same agreement rate with different referents, the experimenters could use further analysis or use other criteria to decide which referent the gesture is best suited for.

Fig. 3. Different proposals of the pinching gesture

Fig. 4. Interchangeable variants for pinching or grasping gestures

5.1 Hand Pose

The proposed gestures with identical or near identical hand poses and moving paths belong to the same bin (Fig. 5). For example, both gestures pinch an object with thumb and index finger then move the hand along the Y-axis. However, some near identical hand poses could look a bit different from others due to individual preferences, as shown in Fig. 3. For example, in prior work done by this lab, some participants proposed using blooming gestures with the palm face up to perform the create object task, and some participants opened their hands less wide than others [25,26]. For referent *move away*, among participants who adopted using an index finger to point at the object and moving along the X-axis, few participants held their pointing finger with their palm facing left instead of facing frontwards.

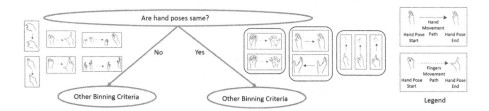

Fig. 5. Binning gesture proposals with identical hand poses criteria

As previous works pointed out [4,17,18,26], variations of similar hand poses were often elicited among participants. The variations could be due to the physical features or the size of the target object [17], and we are focusing on using the same objects for the entire elicitation study. According to prior studies, the variants of a single hand pose could come from the same participant or different participants [18], and the previous study has shown that participants preferred to perform the same gesture in a different manner [27]. In Piumsomboon et al.'s work on eliciting user gestures in augmented reality, variants of pinching and grasping gestures were similar and grouped into the same bin. The shapes or affordances of the objects used to elicit interactions can also impact the hand poses elicited. If the same object was used for all experiments, we suggested experimenters consider that variants of a single pose are often interchangeable, and that those variants should be grouped into the same bin if they have the same movement path (Fig. 4).

The most common variations of hand poses that were mentioned in prior studies involved a different number of fingers when gesturing [18,25,27]. As an example, the proposals for referent *rotate clockwise* in previous elicitation studies were performed by pinching gestures with two or three fingers, or grasping gestures with five fingers [25,26]. It was not due to different sizes or affordances of the object since the same object was presented to every participant. A similar case is that while participants performed *move away* with pointing fingers,

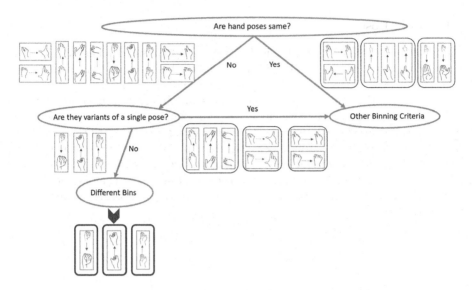

Fig. 6. Binning gesture proposals with identical hand poses and pose variants criteria

some chose to use both their index and middle fingers pointing at the object compared to others who used only their index finger. Another example would be the same pinching gestures with thumb and index finger, but different positions of the other three fingers. Some participants kept their other three fingers spread instead of together while performing pinch gestures. Furthermore, based on our elicitation data, we found another type of variation included different hand orientations. One example is that for the referent *move up* in our study, most participants have proposed grasping the object and moving their hand straight up, and we found three variants of the same hand pose with different hand orientations. The participants were grasping from the front of the object with palm facing front and fingers pointing up, left, or right (Fig. 6).

5.2 Movement Path

If the proposed gestures have identical or variant hand poses, experimenters can continue to check if the moving paths of proposals are the same before making the binning decision (Fig. 7). Based on the stroke coding results, if the moving path is along or around the same axis, we can put those gestures in the same bin. For example, pinching with thumb and index finger then moving hand along Y-axis can be grouped with grasping with five fingers then moving hand along Y-axis. However, pinching with a thumb and index finger then moving the hand along Y-axis should not be binned with grasping with five fingers and moving the hand along Z-axis then moving it along Y-axis. Not all gestures will move in a straight line or follow a directional axis. Some proposals for enlarging or shrinking objects, especially when the gestures involved both hands, were proposed with diagonal movement paths.

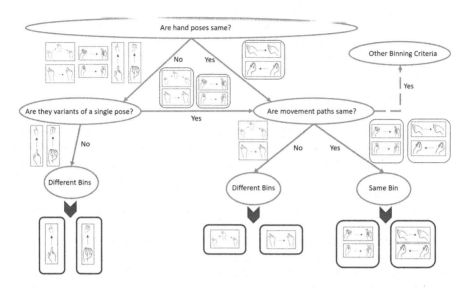

Fig. 7. Binning gesture proposals with identical hand poses, pose variants, and movement path criteria

6 More than Mid-Air Gestures

Our formula can be used equally well for elicitation studies outside augmented reality environments, because researchers can adopt our formula to bin gesture proposals from studies conducted with virtual reality headsets or multi-touch devices. For multi-touch devices, hand poses and movement path are still the crucial criteria for the binning procedure. The experimenters should reconsider the interchangeable variants of a single pose since the multi-touch devices could have a different definition for the number of fingers in a gesture counted as a single-point touch or a whole-hand touch. Based on Wobbrock et al.'s elicitation study on tabletop gestures [29], using 1–3 fingers should be considered as a single-point touch, and using four fingers or more could be considered as a whole-hand touch. It means that the experimenters can consider variants of touch gestures with 1–3 fingers as interchangeable during the binning process.

7 Limitation and Future Work

The formula presented in this paper focused on hand gesture proposals, and it is not suitable for other proposals generated by other body parts such as the head, foot, or arm. Since different body gestures have their features and limitations, it is difficult to use the same criteria for all elicitation studies' data processing. In future work, we are interested in perfecting the binning criteria for hand gesture proposals in elicitation studies. Another future direction regarding binning procedures is to explore further criteria for binning other body gestures and creating guidelines for researchers that can be used in different elicitation studies.

8 Conclusion

This paper proposed a formula that can help experimenters or researchers to bin gesture proposals in elicitation studies. In addition, we explained the necessity of a manual binning procedure and the formation of guidelines for elicitation data processing in HCI. To achieve this goal, this paper went through how experimenters might capture the elicitation data, annotate the recorded video, and what similarity criteria should be considered during the proposals binning process. We also presented real data from our previous elicitation study to demonstrate the possible variations of each gesture. We hope that this paper can be leveraged to create binning procedures for different categories of elicitation studies, such as studies involving gestures using different body parts or using different devices.

Acknowledgments. The authors would like to thank Brandon Kelly for the hand illustrations. This work was supported by the National Science Foundation (NSF) awards NSF 1948254 and 2037417.

References

1. Ali, A.X., Morris, M.R., Wobbrock, J.O.: Crowdsourcing similarity judgments for agreement analysis in end-user elicitation studies. In: Proceedings of the 31st Annual ACM Symposium on User Interface Software and Technology (UIST 2018). Association for Computing Machinery, New York (2018). https://doi.org/10.1145/3242587.3242621
2. Anthony, L., Vatavu, R.D., Wobbrock, J.O.: Understanding the consistency of users' pen and finger stroke gesture articulation. In: Proceedings of Graphics Interface 2013, pp. 87–94. Citeseer (2013)
3. Chen, Y.C., Liao, C.Y., Hsu, S.W., Huang, D.Y., Chen, B.Y.: Exploring user defined gestures for ear-based interactions. In: Proceedings of the ACM Human–Computer Interaction 4(ISS), November (2020). https://doi.org/10.1145/3427314
4. Danielescu, A., Piorkowski, D.: Iterative design of gestures during elicitation: understanding the role of increased production. arxiv preprint arxiv:2104.04685 (2022)
5. Dingler, T., Rzayev, R., Shirazi, A.S., Henze, N.: Designing Consistent Gestures Across Device Types: Eliciting RSVP Controls for Phone, Watch, and Glasses, pp. 1–12. Association for Computing Machinery, New York (2018). https://doi.org/10.1145/3173574.3173993
6. Dong, Z., Piumsomboon, T., Zhang, J., Clark, A., Bai, H., Lindeman, R.: A comparison of surface and motion user-defined gestures for mobile augmented reality. In: Extended Abstracts of the 2020 CHI Conference on Human Factors in Computing Systems (CHI EA 2020), pp. 1–8. Association for Computing Machinery, New York (2020). https://doi.org/10.1145/3334480.3382883

7. Du, G., Degbelo, A., Kray, C.: User-generated gestures for voting and commenting on immersive displays in urban planning. Multimodal Technol. Interact. **3**(2) (2019). https://doi.org/10.3390/mti3020031.https://www.mdpi.com/2414-4088/3/2/31

8. Grijincu, D., Nacenta, M.A., Kristensson, P.O.: User-defined interface gestures: dataset and analysis. In: Proceedings of the Ninth ACM International Conference on Interactive Tabletops and Surfaces (ITS 2014), pp. 25–34. Association for Computing Machinery, New York (2014). https://doi.org/10.1145/2669485.2669511

9. Jacob, R.J., et al.: Reality-based interaction: a framework for post-wimp interfaces. In: Proceedings of the SIGCHI Conference on Human Factors in Computing Systems (CHI 2008), pp. 201–210. Association for Computing Machinery, New York (2008). https://doi.org/10.1145/1357054.1357089

10. Karam, M., Schraefel, M.C.: A Taxonomy of Gestures in Human Computer Interactions. s.n. (2005)

11. Leng, H.Y., Norowi, N.M., Jantan, A.H.: A user-defined gesture set for music interaction in immersive virtual environment. In: Proceedings of the 3rd International Conference on Human-Computer Interaction and User Experience in Indonesia (CHIuXiD 2017), pp. 44–51. Association for Computing Machinery, New York (2017). https://doi.org/10.1145/3077343.3077348

12. McNeill, D.: Hand and Mind: What Gestures Reveal about Thought. University of Chicago Press (1992)

13. Mcneill, D.: Gesture and Thought. The University of Chicago Press (2005). https://doi.org/10.7208/chicago/9780226514642.001.0001

14. Morris, M.R.: Web on the wall: insights from a multimodal interaction elicitation study. In: Proceedings of the 2012 ACM International Conference on Interactive Tabletops and Surfaces (ITS 2012), pp. 95–104. ACM, New York (2012). https://doi.org/10.1145/2396636.2396651

15. Nebeling, M., Huber, A., Ott, D., Norrie, M.C.: Web on the wall reloaded: implementation, replication and refinement of user-defined interaction sets. In: Proceedings of the Ninth ACM International Conference on Interactive Tabletops and Surfaces (ITS 2014), pp. 15–24. Association for Computing Machinery, New York (2014). https://doi.org/10.1145/2669485.2669497

16. Peng, Z., Xu, J.: User-defined gestures for taking self-portraits with smartphone based on consistency. In: Ahram, T., Falcão, C. (eds.) AHFE 2020. AISC, vol. 1217, pp. 316–326. Springer, Cham (2020). https://doi.org/10.1007/978-3-030-51828-8_42

17. Pham, T., Vermeulen, J., Tang, A., MacDonald Vermeulen, L.: Scale impacts elicited gestures for manipulating holograms: implications for AR gesture design. In: Proceedings of the 2018 Designing Interactive Systems Conference, pp. 227–240. ACM (2018)

18. Piumsomboon, T., Clark, A., Billinghurst, M., Cockburn, A.: User-defined gestures for augmented reality. In: Extended Abstracts on Human Factors in Computing Systems (CHI 2013), pp. 955–960. Association for Computing Machinery, New York (2013). https://doi.org/10.1145/2468356.2468527

19. Vatavu, R.D.: User-defined gestures for free-hand tv control. In: Proceedings of the 10th European Conference on Interactive TV and Video (EuroITV 2012), pp. 45–48. Association for Computing Machinery, New York (2012). https://doi.org/10.1145/2325616.2325626

20. Vatavu, R.D.: The dissimilarity-consensus approach to agreement analysis in gesture elicitation studies. In: Proceedings of the 2019 CHI Conference on Human Factors in Computing Systems (CHI 2019), pp. 1–13. Association for Computing Machinery, New York (2019). https://doi.org/10.1145/3290605.3300454

21. Vatavu, R.D., Wobbrock, J.O.: Formalizing agreement analysis for elicitation studies: new measures, significance test, and toolkit. In: Proceedings of the 33rd Annual ACM Conference on Human Factors in Computing Systems (CHI 2015), pp. 1325–1334. Association for Computing Machinery, New York (2015). https://doi.org/10.1145/2702123.2702223

22. Vatavu, R.D., Wobbrock, J.O.: Clarifying agreement calculations and analysis for end-user elicitation studies. ACM Trans. Comput.-Hum. Interact. 29(1) (2022). https://doi.org/10.1145/3476101

23. Villarreal-Narvaez, S., Vanderdonckt, J., Vatavu, R.D., Wobbrock, J.O.: A systematic review of gesture elicitation studies: what can we learn from 216 studies? In: Proceedings of the 2020 ACM Designing Interactive Systems Conference (DIS 2020), pp. 855–872. Association for Computing Machinery, New York (2020). https://doi.org/10.1145/3357236.3395511

24. Williams, A., Ortega, F.: A concise guide to elicitation methodology (2021)

25. Williams, A.S., Garcia, J., Ortega, F.: Understanding multimodal user gesture and speech behavior for object manipulation in augmented reality using elicitation. IEEE Trans. Visual. Comput. Graph. 26(12), 3479–3489 (2020). https://doi.org/10.1109/TVCG.2020.3023566

26. Williams, A.S., Ortega, F.R.: Understanding gesture and speech multimodal interactions for manipulation tasks in augmented reality using unconstrained elicitation. In: Proceedings of the ACM Human–Computer Interaction, 4(ISS) (2020). https://doi.org/10.1145/3427330

27. Wittorf, M.L., Jakobsen, M.R.: Eliciting mid-air gestures for wall-display interaction. In: Proceedings of the 9th Nordic Conference on Human-Computer Interaction (NordiCHI 2016), pp. 3:1–3:4. ACM, New York (2016)

28. Wobbrock, J.O., Aung, H.H., Rothrock, B., Myers, B.A.: Maximizing the guessability of symbolic input. In: CHI 2005 Extended Abstracts on Human Factors in Computing Systems (CHI EA 2005), pp. 1869–1872. Association for Computing Machinery, New York (2005). https://doi.org/10.1145/1056808.1057043

29. Wobbrock, J.O., Morris, M.R., Wilson, A.D.: User-defined gestures for surface computing. In: Proceedings of the SIGCHI Conference on Human Factors in Computing Systems (CHI 2009), pp. 1083–1092. ACM, New York (2009)

Build User Experience Evaluation System——Selection and Integration of Indicators of Automotive Products

Shijie Zhou[1]([✉]), Lai Jiang[2], Longjie Fan[3], and Jun Ma[4]

[1] Commodity Planning Center, Beijing Automotive Technology Center Co. Ltd., Beijing, China
liarss@yeah.net
[2] Department of Psychology, Beijing Normal University, Beijing, China
[3] School of Automation, Beijing University of Posts and Telecommunications, Beijing, China
[4] College of Design and Innovation, Tongji University, Shanghai, China

Abstract. In view of the weak quantitative research foundation of the user experience and the lack of comprehensive measurement in the automobile industry, this research proposes a user experience evaluation measurement for the automotive industry products. Firstly, analyze the process of the experience to deconstruct the hierarchy of user experience: referring to the "three-dimensional structure model" which is specifically divided into three levels - product usability, multimodal perception and psychological experience, so that an evaluation framework of user experience of the automobiles is constructed. Secondly, specify the measurement system of user experience from three dimensions - behavioral performance, sensory perception and psychological experience: according to the characteristics of different measurement dimensions, the user experience is decomposed into the measurable evaluation indicators. Finally, use the analytic hierarchy process, to integrate the selected indicators according to a certain weight, so as to comprehensively evaluate the user experience in the process of using car. This paper conducts a specific study on the user-centered quantitative method of user experience. The research results lay a theoretical foundation for guiding empirical evaluation of automotive products, which also can provide some reliable suggestions for main engine factories and automobile sales servicshop to further improve the user experience in the process of using cars.

Keywords: User experience · Product usability · Multimodal perception

1 Introduction

1.1 Background of the Experience Economy

With the improvement of material level leads to the change of people's view of consumption value, people's consumption demand is more and more inclined to spiritual experience consumption, which means mankind has entered the "experience economy era". In the book Future Shock written in the 1870 s, Alvin Toffler first suggested the form of experience economy [1]. Later, the economist Joseph Pine and James H. Gilmore's put forward the connotation of experience economy in their book Experience Economy, proposing that experience economy is the fourth economic form after agricultural economy, industrial economy and service economy, reflected as people began to expect more emotional and personalized service instead of paying too much attention to the price [2].

In the experience economy, user experience is the core of the entire economic operation, and it is another competitive core after productivity, production cost and appearance features. It emphasizes user-centered and pays more attention to user needs and user experience, which pushes all industries to pay attention to user experience, especially the experience in interactive activities [3].The automobile industry also develops continuously with the change of economic model, transformed from the emphasis on the safety and function as transportation tools to the service quality and driving experience in driving process [4].

1.2 Review of the User Experience

Research Status of User Experience. As a concept in the field of design, user experience has evolved from the ergonomics.This word was first proposed by Donald Norman, an American cognitive psychologist and computer engineer, which is a collection of all subjective feelings associated with interaction when using products [5].

Different scholars have different interpretations of this.Alben believes that user experience covers all aspects of user interaction with the product, including user experience, understanding of the product, achievement of the goal and adaptability of the product to the use environment [6]. Janes Garrett believes that user experience is the expression and the way of using of a product in the real world, which explains how a product is associated with and affect users, including users' experience of product functions, content, brand characteristics and usability [7]. Lucas Daniel believes that user experience refers to what users do, think and feel when they operate a product or use a service, involving rational value and perceptual experience provided to users through products and services [8]. The definition given by the Usability Professional Association (UPA) summarizes user experience as all user perceptions composed of all aspects of interaction with the product and service provider enterprise [9].

This study uses the definition of user experience in ISO9241-210, which means all the feelings of users before, during and after using a product or system, including emotions, beliefs, preferences, cognitive impressions, physiological and psychological reactions, behaviors, achievements and other aspects [10].

Based on the user experience process, the existing user experience research can be classified into: first, user's needs before use, including users' needs of information content, information service and information system; the second is user's behavior in the process of use, including using willingness, adoption behavior, continuous use behavior and transfer behavior; the third is the user's experience evaluation after use, which is mainly divided into qualitative, quantitative and comprehensive evaluation methods. The study focuses on the whole process of car use experience, so post-use user experience evaluation is adopted.

Models and Indices of User Experience. Although the definition and content of user experience have been extensively studied, due to the complexity of accurate quantification, different products and research methods build up different quantification methods.

Robert proposed that important factors of user experience related to each other form the elements of user experience, which can be summarized as branding, usability, functionality and content [11]. Hekkert defines user experience as the result of the user's interaction with the product, including sensory satisfaction (aesthetic experience), value belonging (value experience) and mood experience (emotional experience) [12]. Mahlker believes that in the process of experience, information is processed by users from different dimensions, so user experience can be divided into four dimensions: perceived usefulness, perceived usability, perceived hedonic quality and perceived visual appeal [13]. Leena Arhippainen believes that user experience includes the using environmental information, user emotions, user expectations and other content [14]. Dhaval Vyas & Van der Veer put forward the APEC model of user experience, and believed that user experience comes from user behavior and the perceptive feedback given to users by the interactive system, showing the dynamic interaction process and general rules between human and system from aesthetic, emotional, cognitive and practical aspects [15].

Later, Kuniavsky believes that user experience is everywhere, which can be specifically divided into sensory experience, interactive experience and emotional experience [16], which is the same classification proposed by Moeslinge, and he says that the emotional experience of users is the final form of user experience [17]. Correspondingly, by analyzing the process of user experience, Yin Zhibo divided the hierarchical structure of user experience into target layer, behavior layer and experience layer, and he proposed three quantitative methods: behavior-centered quantitative method, task-centered quantitative method and experience-centered quantitative method [18].

Literature review shows that domestic and foreign scholars have made fruitful research achievements on user experience, and different researchers have constructed different construction of user experience.

Evaluation Methods of User Experience. At present, the existing user experience measurement and evaluation system can be divided into two categories: qualitative and quantitative. Qualitative evaluation system pays more attention to the concept definition and the relationship between elements, while quantitative evaluation system pays more attention to the quantitative integration between elements and the application of usability testing methods [19].

In terms of qualitative methods, the heuristic evaluation method is generally used to evaluate product usability. Generally, three to five expert evaluators are invited to find more than 80% of product problems. Through the goal-means method, the concept definition of various elements related to usability evaluation and the hierarchical relationship between these elements can be clear and definite. Neverthless, the evaluation system lacks the support of experimental data or basic theory, and it cannot give quantified product availability evaluation value in practical operation.

In terms of quantitative methods, the evaluation of user experience is conducted directly through questionnaire survey. At present, there are many standardized and mature holistic user experience scales, such as QUIS (Questionnaire of User Interaction

Satisfaction), SUMI (Software Usability Measurement Inventory), PSSUQ (Post-Study System Usability Questionnaire), etc. It emphasizes the selection and integration of relevant elements, however, it is difficult to construct and popularize the system due to the high requirements of external validity.

Therefore, it is necessary to fully integrate the qualitative and quantitative aspects, and to integrate the measurement indicators of user experience according to certain theoretical foundation. It includes three components: measurement demensions, measurement indicators and data integration, consequently forming a complete evaluation system.

2 Overview of the Measurement Dimensions

Although there have been many studies focusing on the elements of user experience, the evaluation of user experience is still very vulnerable. Because the user experience cannot be directly measured so that we need to decompose it into measurable indicators, reflecting at the cognitive, behavioral and emotional levels. This is consistent with the "three-three model" put forward by Chinese scholar Ge Liezhong, which divides user experience into the same three levels, combining behavioral performance, physiological indicators and subjective evaluation [20].

In the aspect of measurement of user experience, there are four commonly methods: objective performance index, subjective attitude index, physiological index and usability question index. Different measurements have their own characteristics and shortcomings, so it is necessary to integrate indicators according to certain rules to form an overall evaluation system. Therefore, according to the limitations of current research, a comprehensive user experience evaluation system needs to be built in the process of implementing specific evaluation for automobile products.

This paper will make a bold attempt. Firstly, the hierarchy of the process of user experience is analyzed in three dimensions, referring to the "three-dimensional structure model". Secondly, the component elements of each dimension and the relationship between the elements are explained. Finally, the Analytical Hierarchy Process (AHP) are used to provide statistics support. Combined with the evaluation of behavioral performance, sensory perception, and psychological measurement, how to quantify from these three dimensions will be explained specifically as follows.

2.1 Behavioral Performance

Behavioral performance is used to measure interactive user experience, emphasizing the characteristics of interaction. Usability is the key factor to determine a good user experience between users and products. Usability design is the most direct way to reflect whether users can interact well with the product. It can be used to evaluate product availability and reflect the objective results of user operation in the process of the interaction.

The earliest usability evaluation system is Hierarchical Usability Model, which was proposed by McCal, Richards and Waiters in 1977. It is divided into three levels: factor, criterion and index [21]. The factor layer refers to the availability dimension, such as reliability, etc. Criterion layer is to refine the usability dimension into measurable secondary factors, such as reliability into fault tolerance and other secondary factors; The index layer refers to the availability index that can be directly measured, for example, fault tolerance can be represented by several checklists such as fault tolerance control.

On the basis of this system, many scholars put forward new evaluation systems according to their own focus and field of concern. In 1999, Van Welie, Van Der Ver, Elias et al., in combination with product design principles, construct a usability evaluation system from four aspects, including usability dimension, usage indicators, means and knowledge [22]. Among them, the usability dimension layer is the highest level of the system, including effectiveness, efficiency and subjective satisfaction [23].

Based on the concept of behavioral performance measurement firstly presented by Tom Tullis and Bill Albert, J.N Nielsen proposed five attributes of usability in the user experience: learnability, efficiency, memorability, reliability, and satisfaction. Currently traditional user experience evaluation methods directly use these five criteria [24]. Therefore, they are directly used in this study to summarize objective performance measurement in product availability in Table 1.

Table 1. Behavioral performance measurement in usability

Indicators	Evaluation method
Effectiveness	Represents the possibility of using a machine to complete a particular task
Efficiency	Represents the ratio of accuracy and completion a user completes a task against the resources (such as time) used
Learnability	Represents whether users can easily understand the content of the product, the services it provides, and the way to use it
Memorability	Represents whether an infrequent user can remember how to use the product without relearning it
Satisfaction	Represents the subjective satisfaction and acceptance degree experienced by users in the process of using the product

2.2 Sensory Perception

The concept of "five senses" derived from the medical treatment field in the 1990s [25], which refers to people's basic sensory experience, mainly involving five physiological sensory activities: vision, hearing, smell, touch and taste. As a link between users and products, "five senses" greatly affect users' using experience [26], which performing different functions at the same time to provide users with multi-modal and comprehensive user experience [27].

In actual car use scenarios, according to data statistics, the main sensory organs for drivers to obtain information are vision (80%), hearing (14%), touch (6%) and smell (6%) [28]. Due to taste is often used in food research, but industrial products such as cars do not require users to taste them, so it will not be involved in this sensory measurement.

In recent years, with the development of physiological measurement technology, a large number of research results have emerged [29]. However, few studies have integrated various sensory indicators to establish a system [30]. Therefore, physiological sensory measurement and subjective questionnaire are combined in this study to comprehensively evaluate user experience. It divides the physiological system into four sensory dimensions: vision, hearing, touch and smell.

Vision. Vision is the most intuitive way for people to contact and feel the outside world. More than 80% of the information received by people comes from this most important channel [31]. From the perspective of vehicles' visual design, automobile decoration design can be divided into two aspects: interior and exterior. Exterior design mainly refers to exterior shaping, and three major factors affecting automobile modeling are volume, shape and figure [32]. Interior design can be divided into design concept, package, hardware design, Color Material Design (CMF) and Human-computer Interaction Design (HMI) [33]. From the perspective of visual perception, this study mainly focuses on the different visual perception characteristics of automobile exterior and interior design through visual elements: color, appearance, material.

Color has a strong impact to the visual perception of human beings, which can intuitively build the interior atmosphere and different visual feeling, makes color the first element that attracts attention in the visual channel [34].

The visual elements of the appearance of the automobile can be analyzed from the three directions of volume, shape and graphics [35]. Therefore, the overall evaluation can be obtained by integrating the above visual information.

Users can perceive surface texture of the product and other characteristics through observation and touch, which can be divided into visual texture and tactile texture. Since the direct physical sensation of material is derived from tactile sensation, so the material index is placed in tactile channel for measurement in this study.

Hearing. Human auditory system is composed of organs that receive and process sound signals. In the situation of car driving, auditory can receive all-round sound information without occupying the driver's visual resources. For automotive products, auditory display can be divided into in-car sound quality and vehicle-machine voice interaction.

From the perspective of in-car sound quality, objective evaluation parameters are developed on the hearing characteristics of human ear [36]. The four most commonly used psychoacoustic objective parameters are loudness, sharpness, roughness and fluctuate [37]. Some studies have shown that loudness and sharpness are the main factors influencing user interaction behavior [38]. Therefore only these two factors are selected as the measurement indicators of sound quality.

Loudness reflects the subjective perception of sound intensity by human ear, and can accurately reflect the loudness of sound. Generally, the louder the noise is, the worse its sound quality is [39].Sharpness is used to describe the proportion of high frequency components in sound. It is inversely proportional to the comfort of the sound – the higher the sharpness value, the worse the sound quality and the worse the comfort.

From the perspective of vehicle-machine voice interaction, the development of speech recognition technology makes the application of it in automobile more and more frequently. Voice interaction system conveys information in words, allowing the driver giving verbal instructions. The intelligibility [41] and the naturalness [40] are the most commonly used performance evaluation indexes for the quality of the voice interaction [42]. The intelligibility refers to the percentage of synthetic speech signals that can be understood by listeners. The naturalness is used to measure the quality of prosody of synthetic speech.

The most frequently used evaluation in voice interaction is Mean Opinion Score (MOS). As a common subjective measure, MOS was developed by the Consultative Committee of International Telegraph and Telephone (CCITT), requiring listeners to rate the sounds on a scale of 1 to 5, this paper modified the scale into 1 to 7.

Smell. Olfactory is the most primitive sense of human beings [43]. In the field of automotive products, smell is often determined by the materials of interior decoration [44], such as seats, ceilings, carpets, instrument panels and door guards [45].

Existing literatures have classified the dimensions of odor evaluation into odor type, odor intensity and smell comfort [46]. Due to the fuzzy characteristics of odor types and the calibration of odor testers' [47], Likert Scale was only used to make subjective evaluation of odor intensity and smell comfort [48].

Odor intensity quantifys the results of odor evaluation. The 6-grade odor intensity grade representation is commonly used to grade the stimulation of smell on olfactory organs [49]. In this study, it was improved to 7-grade odor intensity score to measure the degree of peculiar smell in the car.

Smell comfort were used to evaluate the smell of automotive interior industrial design materials by the 7-level Likert psychological scale. In this study, the index of smell comfort was used to measure the comfort degree of olfactory inside the car.

Touch. Tactile sensation mainly occurs in the physical contact between user and car. Different shapes and materials will produce different tactile experience. The brain senses the surface material of the object by touching through the surface of the skin, and evaluates its smoothness, hardness and other properties.

Weber (1978), the pioneer of the study of touch, conducted extensive research on human touch and proposed that every object is made of a specific material, and different materials produce different tactile sensations. Texture, hardness, temperature and weight constitute the four most basic tactile attributes of an object [50]. Chen et al. studied the perceptual attributes of human body with 37 samples, and believed that physical characteristics of contact surfaces could affect emotional cognition by influencing psychophysical perception: cold/warm, soft/hard, sticky/smooth, smooth/rough [51].

According to the existing literature on tactile perception evaluation of product materials, it is found that "texture" and "hardness" are all mentioned [52]. The higher the level of user evaluation, the greater the contribution to the overall evaluation of the material, so smooth/roughness, soft/hardness are both positive indicators. On this accout, the indexes of user experience evaluation of industrial design materials are determined as "smoothness" and "softness" to test people's satisfaction with different kinds of materials.

Based on the above review of sensory, the user experience evaluation system of sensory dimension can correspond to the indicators in Table 2.

Table 2. Sensory evaluation system for automotive products

Sensory channels	Dimension	Usability metrics
Vision	Color	Color attraction
	Shape	Appearance preference
Hearing	Sound quality	Loudness
		Sharpness
	Voice interaction	Intelligibility
		Naturalness
Smell	Odor	Odor intensity
		Smell comfort
Touch	Texture	Smoothness
		Softness

2.3 Psychological Measurement

Psychological measurement is used to measure emotional user experience, which is a psychological recognition of the whole interaction process and results. According to different psychological emotion theory [53], various scholars put forward kinds of user emotional experience models [54].

By comparing the user experience of kitchen products in the United States and Turkey, Suzan Boztepe puts forward the concept of "user experience value", which includes practical value, social significance value, emotional value and spiritual value.

Sascha mahlk proposed "the basic process model", which emphasize the influence of cognitive and emotional response in user experience. Information processing related to the use characteristics is defined as the cognitive part, and complex emotions resulting from using product is defined as the emotional part.

Dewey's introduced the concept of "experience aesthetics", who believed that the interaction between people and products is a subjective aesthetic experience. This experience is multi-level, from sensory beauty to meaning beauty, and even to emotional beauty.

Based on users' cognition and evaluation of products, Desmet and Hekkert constructed "a basic model of product emotions", which explains the potential process of emotional experience generation. In this model, emotional experience is deconstructed into instrumental emotion, aesthetic emotion, social emotion, surprise emotion, and interest emotion [55].

Based on the above review, this study analyzes the subjective dimension of user experience from a psychological perspective. The experience is the psychological entity of the emotion, and emotional experience emphasizes the interactional satisfaction and emotional feedback obtained by users in the using process. Therefore, Desmet's classification method of emotional experience is adopted, as shown in Table 3.

Table 3. The psychological measurement system of automobile products

Indicators	Evaluation method
Instrumental emotion	It can help us accomplish our goals
Aesthetic emotion	It corresponds with our attitudes like attraction
Social emotion	It conforms to social standards and norms
Surprise emotion	It can elicit a surprise response
Interest emotion	It can motivate us to some creative action or thought

3 User Experience Model Based on AHP

3.1 Analytic Hierarchy Process (AHP)

Analytic hierarchy Process (AHP) is a multi-criteria decision analysis method combining qualitative and quantitative analysis proposed by T.L. Saaty [56]. It is mainly used in decision-making and evaluation problems with complex structure and multiple layers of decision criteria, and later introduced into business and market research [57].

The basic idea of AHP is to change the overall judgment of the weight of multiple elements that constitute a complex problem into "pairwise comparison" of these elements to determine the relative importance of the factors in the hierarchy, and then to determine the overall order of the relative importance of the decision-making factors by integrating human judgment [58]. The hierarchical analysis structure of complex problems is generally divided into three layers: the first layer is the main influencing factor, which simplifies the complex problems; The second layer is the index layer of the simplification problem, which is the main direction of decision-making. The third layer is the sub-index layer, that is, the factors affecting each index.

AHP can be used as an effective tool for user experience research, which analyzes the influencing factors in automobile user experience evaluation and construct a comprehensive evaluation index system to prepare for subsequent research.

Index System Based on AHP. The general process of AHP is establishing the analytic hierarchy process structure model after clarifying the problem, establishing judgment matrices in turn according to the variable attributes, calculating the weight of indicators, conducting consistency test on the matrices, then calculating the comprehensive weight of each indicator, which is used as the basis for selecting the optimal scheme [59]. After obtaining the hierarchy structure and the effective index weight that pass the consistency test, the fuzzy judgment matrix can be normalized with the weight vector of each index factor.

According to the previous article, the study have established the structural framework of user experience. Based on the form of AHP, this framework can be expressed as three first-level influencing factors, namely behavioral experience, sensory experience and psychological experience. The influencing factors of the secondary index layer and the sub-index layer are also selected through the previous discussion, as shown in Table 4.

Table 4. Comprehensive evaluation system for automotive products

First-level indicators	Second-level indicators	Third-level indicators
Behavioral experience (A_1)	Usability	Effectiveness (G_1)
		Efficiency (G_2)
		Learnability (G_3)
		Memorability (G_4)
		Satisfaction (G_5)
Sensory experience (A_2)	Vision (B_1)	Color attraction (C_1)
		Appearance preference (C_2)
	Hearing (B_2)	Loudness (D_1)
		Sharpness (D_2)
		Intelligibility (D_3)
		Naturalness (D_4)
	Smell (B_3)	Odor intensity (E_1)
		Smell comfort (E_2)
	Touch (B_4)	Smoothness (F_1)
		Softness (F_2)
Psychological experience (A_3)	Emotion	Instrumental emotion (H_1)
		Aesthetic emotion (H_2)
		Social emotion (H_3)
		Surprise emotion (H_4)
		Interest emotion (H_5)

Weight Calculated by AHP. By consulting experts, the evaluation indexes are compared in pairs to construct a judgment matrix, so that the more accurate weight of each index can be qualitatively described.

Construction of Judgment Matrix. In order to compare the relative importance of the indicators, the expert consultation method is adopted by questionnaire [60]. The numbers 1–9 and its reciprocal are used as the scale to define the judgment matrix [61]. The meaning of the scale is shown in Table 5.

In this study, the importance was scored by geometric mean by four experts, who in the fields of mechanical industry, physiological psychology, and consumer research. The "geometric mean" was computed by multiplying the corresponding value and raising to the power of 1/N (N represents the number of experts) to judge the relative importance of indicators [62]. On this basis, eight judgment matrices were constructed and analyzed. Taking first-level indicators as an example, the judgment matrix of geometric mean value is shown in Table 6.

Table 5. Meaning of judgment matrix scale

Ratio scale	Criteria
1	A_1 and A_2 are equally important
3	A1 is slightly more important than A2
5	A1 is much more important than A2
7	A1 is extremely more important than A2
9	A1 is definitely more important than A2
2, 4, 6, 8	The degree is between two adjacent odd numbers

Table 6. Judgment matrix of the first level indicators

Indicators	A_1	A_2	A_3
A_1	1	2.590	5.803
A_2	0.386	1	3.162
A_3	0.172	0.316	1

The judgment matrix is expressed as:

$$A = \begin{pmatrix} 1 & 2.590 & 5.803 \\ 0.386 & 1 & 3.162 \\ 0.172 & 0.316 & 1 \end{pmatrix} \tag{1}$$

Calculation of Eigenvectors. According to AHP, the eigenvectors are calculated as follows:

$$w_1' = \sqrt[3]{1 \times 2.590 \times 5.803} = 2.4678 \tag{2}$$

$$w_2' = \sqrt[3]{0.386 \times 1 \times 3.162} = 1.0687 \tag{3}$$

$$w_3' = \sqrt[3]{0.172 \times 0.316 \times 1} = 0.3788 \tag{4}$$

$$\sum_{i=1}^{3} w_i = w_1' + w_2' + w_3' = 2.4678 + 1.0687 + 0.3788 = 3.9153 \tag{5}$$

To normalize them:

$$w_1 = \frac{w_1'}{\sum_1^3 w_i} = 0.630 \tag{6}$$

$$w_2 = \frac{w_2'}{\sum_1^3 w_i} = 0.273 \tag{7}$$

$$w_3 = \frac{w_3'}{\sum_1^3 w_i} = 0.097 \tag{8}$$

According to the formula $A \cdot w = \lambda_{max} \cdot W$, the largest eigenvalue λ_{max} and the corresponding eigenvectors W are computed as follows:

$$W = A \cdot w = \begin{pmatrix} 1 & 2.590 & 5.803 \\ 0.386 & 1 & 3.162 \\ 0.172 & 0.316 & 1 \end{pmatrix} \begin{pmatrix} 0.630 \\ 0.273 \\ 0.097 \end{pmatrix} = \begin{pmatrix} 1.900 \\ 0.823 \\ 0.292 \end{pmatrix} \tag{9}$$

$$\lambda_{max} = \frac{1.900}{3 \times 0.630} + \frac{0.823}{3 \times 0.273} + \frac{0.292}{3 \times 0.097} = 3.014 \tag{10}$$

Consistency Test. A consistency test was performed for the above results, with the formula $CR = CI/RI$. Thus, $CI = \frac{\lambda_{max} - n}{n-1} = \frac{3.014 - 3}{3-1} = 0.007$. Random consistency RI can be found from list, when $n = 3$, $RI = 0.52$, as shown in Table 7.

Table 7. Random consistency RI

n	RI
3	0.52
4	0.89
5	1.12
6	1.24
⋮	⋮
20	1.63

The smaller the CR value is, the better the consistency of the judgment matrix is. If $CR < 0.1$, the judgment matrix meets the consistency test. If $CR > 0.1$, it can be determined that the judgment matrix is not consistent, and it needs to be adjusted before next analysis. $CI = 0.007$, $RI = 0.520$, $CR = 0.013$, $CR < 0.1$. Accordingly, the judgment matrix constructed in this study meets the consistency test, so the calculation results of weight are valid. The results are shown in Table 8.

Table 8. Consistency inspection results of psychological experience index

λ_{max}	CI	RI	CR	Test result
3.014	0.007	0.520	0.013	valid

Table 9. Weight index of user experience system

First-level indicators	Second-level indicators	Third-level indicators	Comprehensive weights	Weight order
Behavioral experience (A_1, 62.901%)	Usability	Effectiveness (G_1, 35.486%)	22.321%	2
		Efficiency (G_2, 11.792%)	7.417%	5
		Learnability (G_3, 6.698%)	4.213%	7
		Memorability (G_4, 7.060%)	4.441%	6
		Satisfaction (G_5, 38.965%)	24.509%	1
Sensory experience (A_2, 27.369%)	Vision (B_1, 60.246%)	Color attraction (C_1, 47.644%)	7.856%	4
		Appearance preference (C_2, 52.356%)	8.633%	3
	Hearing (B_2, 22.638%)	Loudness (D_1, 15.540%)	0.963%	16
		Sharpness (D_2, 14.175%)	0.878%	17
		Intelligibility (D_3, 51.712%)	3.204%	10
		Naturalness (D_4, 18.572%)	1.151%	15
	Smell (B_3, 5.397%)	Odor intensity (E_1, 12.368%)	0.813%	20
		Smell comfort (E_2, 87,632%)	1.294%	13
	Touch (B_4, 11.720%)	Smoothness (F_1, 61.257%)	1.965%	11
		Softness (F_2, 38.743%)	1.243%	14
Psychological experience (A_3, 9.729%)	Emotion	Instrumental emotion (H_1, 37.770%)	3.675%	8

(continued)

Table 9. (*continued*)

First-level indicators	Second-level indicators	Third-level indicators	Comprehensive weights	Weight order
		Aesthetic emotion (H_2, 35.269%)	3.431%	9
		Social emotion (H_3, 15.420%)	1.500%	12
		Surprise emotion (H_4, 5.390%)	0.524%	19
		Interest emotion (H_5, 6.150%)	0.598%	18

Similarly, the order of importance of indicators, the maximum eigenvalue λ_{max}, consistency index *CI* and random consistency index *RI* of other matrices were obtained, and whether *CR* passed the consistency test was checked. The matrix that fails to meet the criterion of consistency test is modified appropriately on the basis of respecting the will of its judging experts, until it passes the consistency test. The weight results are shown in Table 9, and the final feature vectors are shown in Table 10.

Table 10. Matrix eigenvector of user experience system

Matrix	Eigenvector	λ_{max}	CI	RI	CR
A	[1.887, 0.821, 0.292]	3.014	0.007	0.520	0.013
B	[2.410, 0.906, 0.216, 0.469]	4.168	0.056	0.890	0.063
C	[0.953, 1.047]	2.000	0.000	0.000	–
D	[0.622, 0.567, 2.068, 0.743]	4.237	0.079	0.890	0.089
E	[0.247, 1.753]	2.000	0.000	0.000	–
F	[1.225, 0.775]	2.000	0.000	0.000	–
G	[1.774, 0.590, 0.335, 0.353, 1.948]	5.097	0.024	1.120	0.022
H	[1.889, 1.763, 0.771, 0.270, 0.307]	5.373	0.093	1.120	0.083

3.2 Empirical Analysis

Questionnaire Preparation and Data Collection. In order to verify the index system and explain the validation of each, this study designed a questionnaire for automobile user experience. The respondents were people with driving experience and owning a certain type of car. In order to make the questionnaire survey universal, the type and price of the car in this survey were not limited. A total of 58 questionnaires were sent out and 58 were recovered. After removing the missing values, 54 valid questionnaires were obtained with effective recovery of 93.1%.

Data in this paper were obtained through questionnaires. The design of the questionnaire is divided into three parts: one is the basic information of the respondents, including the city they live in, the car type they own and the driving age; Secondly, 20 questions are designed according to 20 third-level indicators, and users evaluate the 20 indicators according to their own driving experience. The third is the overall score of the respondents on the driving experience of the vehicle, which is measured by a question expressed as "Comprehensively speaking, how do you evaluate the experience of this car?". Participants were asked to rate from 1 to 7.

The questionnaire lists questions for 20 third-level indexes in the user experience evaluation, and each question corresponds to 7 options, which are measured in the form of a seven-point scale. Scale degree ranges from strong to weak, respectively, very satisfied (grade 7), moderately satisfied (grade 6), a little satisfied (grade 5), not sure (grade 4), a little dissatisfied (grade 3), moderately dissatisfied (grade 2), very dissatisfied (grade 1).

Based on the score of the questionnaire and the weight of each index, the comprehensive evaluation results are further obtained. The weighted average was calculated as the final comprehensive score of each participant's driving experience X_j ($j = 1, 2, \ldots,$ n), and the calculating formula was:

$$X_j = \sum_{i=1}^{20} w_i a_{ij} \tag{11}$$

w_i is the weight of the index determined by the analytic hierarchy process, a_{ij} is the 7-point scoring value of the subject on the index, and n is the total number of subjects.

Reliability and Validity Tests

Reliability - Internal Consistency. Internal consistency test was conducted on the scores of 20 questions in 54 questionnaires, and Cronbach's Alpha value was 0.906, while Cronbach's Alpha value based on standardized terms was 0.913, both of which were more than 90%. Therefore, the analyzed data of user experience comprehensive evaluation system have high internal consistency, which means it has high reliability. The results are shown in Table 11.

Table 11. Internal consistency test of the third-level indicators

Cronbach's Alpha	Cronbach's alpha based on standardized items	N of items	N of cases
0.906	0.913	20	54

Validity - Criterion Correlation. Correlation analysis was conducted on the final comprehensive score (weighted mean), average comprehensive score (arithmetic mean) and overall score of a single question in user experience of 54 questionnaires. The overall score of a single question was used as the criterion to test the correlation between the

Table 12. Correlation matrix of user experience scores

Indicators	Overall experience rating	Final comprehensive evaluation	Comprehensive evaluation
Overall experience rating	1	–	–
Final comprehensive score	0.510^{**}	1	–
Average comprehensive score	0.445^{**}	0.933^{**}	1

** Correlation is significant at the 0.01 level (2-tailed).

comprehensive score and the criterion, so as to illustrate whether the comprehensive evaluation system accurately measured the goal construct of user experience. Pearson correlation analysis results showed that the correlation coefficient between the overall score and the final comprehensive score was 0.510, and that between the overall score and the average comprehensive score was 0.445, both of which were significant at the level of 0.01. The correlation coefficient of the comprehensive score calculated by the weighted mean is significantly higher than that calculated by the arithmetic mean, means that the score is closer to the overall user experience score when multiplied by the weight. Accordingly, the final comprehensive score based on the index system and weight of user experience on automobile has high criterion correlation validity, which means strong effectiveness. It can accurately measure the user experience of the car. The results are shown in Table 12.

4 Conclusion

This paper establishes a comprehensive evaluation system and assigns weights to the indexes of automobile user experience. By calculating the weights of each evaluation index through analytic hierarchy process, it is clear which factors are the more important in the process of user experience. Moreover, the questionnaire was designed for empirical test, and the data results passed the reliability and validity tests, which verified that it was reliable and effective to transform the subjective evaluation of a single question into a more specific comprehensive evaluation system.

This study proposed a very innovative three-dimensional structural model for measuring the user experience of automotive products, which involves operational availability, multimodal perception and inner psychological experience. This study deeply discusses the mechanism and structural components of user experience of automotive products, which has certain enlightening significance for the user-centered experience quantification method. It lays a theoretical foundation for the further construction of the user experience evaluation index system, which has a academic significance of novelty and integration.

With the development of the Internet and the IOT (Internet of Things), cars are connecting with users in a new way. Correspondingly, automobile companies are focusing more on user-centered design to provide better services for users. Thus, scientlfical and comprehensive evaluation the user experience of automobile products is necessary. The research results have successfully solved the problem, which it is difficult to correlate the design principles of user-centered with the measurement indexes of user experience. It is not only a meaningful inspiration for guiding the empirical evaluation of user experience of automobile products, but also provides reliable guidance for the main engine factories, automobile sales servicshop.

References

1. Feng, M., Jun-jie, C.: Study of product design based on user experience system. Packag. Eng. **29**(3), 142–144 (2008)
2. Pine, B.J., Gilmore, J.H.: Experience Economy. China Machine Press, Beijing (2012)
3. Sheng-li, D.: The advancement of the study on foreign user experience. Libr. Inf. Serv. **52**(3), 43–45 (2008)
4. Jin-ting, X.: Research methodology of automotive interior design based on user experience supported. A master's thesis, Northeastern University, Shenyang (2012)
5. Norman, D.A.: The Invisible Computer. MIT Press, New York (1999)
6. Hassenzahl, M.: The effect of perceived hedonic quality on product appealingness. Int. J. Hum.-Comput. Interact. **13**(4), 481–499 (2001)
7. Garrett, J.J.: The Elements of User Experience: User-Centered Design f or the Web. New Riders Publishing, New York (2003)
8. Daniel, L.: Understanding user experience. Web Tech. **5**(8), 42–43 (2000)
9. UPA (Usability Professionals Association): Usability Body of Knowledge. http://www.usa bilitybok.org/glossary. Accesed 4 July 2010
10. Iso, D.I.S.: Ergonomics of Human-system Interaction. Part 210: human-centred design for interactive systems. International Standards Organization, Switzerland (2010)
11. Rubinoff, R.: How to quantify the user experience. Design & UX (2004)
12. Hassenzahl, M., Tractinsky, N.: User experience-a research agenda. Behav. Inf. Technol. **25**(2), 91–97 (2006)
13. Mahlke, S.: Factors influencing the experience of website usage. In: CHI 2002 Extended Abstracts on Human Factors in Computing Systems, pp. 846–847 (2002)
14. Leena, A.: Capturing user experience for product design (2006). http://virtual.vtt.fi/virtual/adamos/material/arhippa2.pdf
15. Vyas, D., van der Veer, G.C.: APEC: A Framework for Designing Experience [EB/OL] (2020). https://www.researchgate.net/publication/251990033_APEC_A_Framework_for_Designing_Experience
16. Kuniavsky, M.: Observing the User Experience: A Practitioner's Guide to User Research. Elsevier, Amsterdam (2003)
17. Moeslinger, S.: Technology at home: a digital personal scale. In: Extended Abstracts on Human Factors in Computing Systems, pp. 216–217 (1997)
18. Zhibo, Y., Ying, Y.: Research methods of quantifying user experience. In: Proceedings the 4th Harmonious Human-machine Environment Joint Academic Conference, LNCS, pp. 303–309. China Computer Federation, Tianjin (2009)
19. Yan, Z., Yuli, L., Qijun, W., Liezhong, G.: A review of product usability evaluation index system. Chin. J. Ergon. **20**(3), 83–87 (2014)
20. Bang-bei, T., Gang, G., Sheng-nan, C., Hao, C., Le, Z.: Evaluation method of user experience towards phone-vehicle interconnect products. Packag. Eng. **39**(16), 90–99 (2018)

21. Hartmann, J., Sutcliffe, A., Angeli, A.D.: Towards a theory of user judgment of aesthetics and user interface quality. ACM Trans. Comput.-Hum. Interact. **15**(4), 1–30 (2008)
22. Vyas, D., van der Veer, G.C.: APEC: a framework for designing experience. In: Spaces, Places & Experience in HCI, pp. 1–4 (2005)
23. Seffah, A., Kececi, N., Donyaee, M.: QUIM: a framework for quantifying usability metrics in software quality models. In: Proceedings Second Asia-Pacific Conference on Quality Software, pp. 311–318. IEEE (2001)
24. Nielsen, J.: Usability Engineering. China Machine Press, Beijing (2004)
25. Kenya, H.: Designing Design. Guangxi Normal University Press, Guangxi (2010)
26. Li, X.: Research of the emotional diagnosis and treatment products design method driven by five senses experience. A doctoral dissertation. Yanshan University, Qinhuangdao (2019)
27. Zi-guli, W.: A study on the relationship between five senses and visual language. A doctoral dissertation. Xi'an Academy of Fine Arts, Xi'an (2012)
28. Bowen, S.: Research on interface hierarchy design for in-vehicle information system based on the complex interactive situations. A doctoral dissertation. Beijing Institute of Technology, Beijing (2018)
29. Bang-bei, T., et al.: User experience evaluation and selection of automobile industry design with eye movement and electroencephalogram. Comput. Integr. Manuf. Syst. **21**(6), 1449–1459 (2015)
30. Jun, Y., Meng-jie, Z.: Design of short video app based on user experience. Packag. Eng. **41**(6), 198–204 (2020)
31. Rui-min, H.: Study on interior design under the influence of automated driving. Decoration **303**(7), 102–105 (2018)
32. Lv-ping, Y.: Research on tension and manifestation in automobile form. A master's thesis, Hunan University, Hunan (2004)
33. Wei-bin, D., Yi-qun, L.: Adult decompression toys design based on "five-senses" experience. Packag. Eng. **42**(16), 94–102 (2021)
34. Jia-xin, L.: Research on the design trends of self-driving cars for young groups. A master's thesis, Dalian University of Technology, Dalian (2004)
35. Lawrence, S.: Linking soundscape with land use planning in community noise management policies. Proc. Inter-noise **2003**(3), 3855–3862 (2003)
36. Xiao-juan, Z., Yan, L., Zong-cai, L., Yan-bin, J.: Research on sound quality subjec-tive evaluation of certain domestic automobile interior. J. Ordnance Equip. Eng. **34**(6), 140–144 (2013)
37. Zong-cai, L.: Correlation research between subjective evaluation and objective parameters of car interior sound quality. A master's thesis, Dalian Jiaotong University, Dalian (2013)
38. Yu, Z.: Research on analysis and evaluation of vehicle interior sound quality for pure electric vehicle. A master's thesis, Jilin University, Jilin (2013)
39. Pisoni, D.B., Nusbaum, H.C., Greene, B.G.: Perception of synthetic speech generated by rule. Proc. IEEE **73**(11), 1665–1676 (1985)
40. Min, C., Shinan, L.: A Chines text-to-speech system with high intelligibility and high naturalness. Acta Acustica **21**(4), 639–647 (1996)
41. Yajie, Z.: A study on representation learning based acoustic modeling for speech synthesis. A doctoral dissertation, University of Science and Technology of China, Beijing (2021)
42. Qiang, F.: Research on parameter representation and objective quality assessment of speech. A doctoral dissertation, Xidian University, Xi'an (2021)
43. Heng-gang, Z.: Discussion on flavor. Liquor-Mak. Sci. Technol. **3**, 24–26 (2004)
44. Lingzi, Z.: Based on evaluation of automotive interior smell subjective feelings. Automob. Appl. Technol. **11**, 15–17 (2014)
45. Lan-juan, C., Hua-min, Y.: Introduction on odor testing methods for automotive trims. Environ. Test. **2**, 26–28 (2014)

46. Bang-bei, T., Gang, G., Jinjun, X.: Method and design for material odor evaluation and selection of automobile interior design based on user's olfactory sensation experiences. China Mech. Eng. **28**(2), 206–214 (2017)
47. Hengqin, M., Xiaochao, X., Fengzhi, T., Jingjing, W.: A study of panelist selection and training for odor tests in vehicle. Automot. Digest **11**, 24–30 (2019)
48. Lei, S.: Foul Smell Experiment Method Q&A. Chemical Industry Press, China (2009)
49. Rachel, S.: Scents of time. Sciences **40**(4), 34–39 (2000)
50. Weber, E.H.: The Sense of Touch. Academic Press, London (1978)
51. https://www.internetretailer.com, https://www.digitalcommerce360.com/internet-retailer/
52. Bangbei, T., Gang, G., Jinjun, X.: Method for industry design material test and evaluation based on user visual and tactile experience. J. Mech. Eng. **53**(3), 162–172 (2017)
53. Sheldon, K.M., Elliot, A.J., Kim, Y., Kasser, T.: What is satisfying about satisfying events? Testing 10 candidate psychological needs. J. Pers. Soc. Psychol. **80**(2), 325–339 (2001)
54. Wei, G.: Design for emotion: emotional and behavioral consequences of product form. Doctoral dissertation, Tianjin University, Tianjin (2012)
55. Desmet, P.: A multilayered model of product emotions. Des. J. **6**(2), 4–13 (2003)
56. Saaty, T.L.: The US-OPEC energy conflict the payoff matrix by the Analytic Hierarchy Process. Internat. J. Game Theory **8**(4), 225–234 (1979)
57. Wind, Y., Saaty, T.L.: Marketing applications of the analytic hierarchy process. Manage. Sci. **26**(7), 641–658 (1980)
58. Crostack, H.A., Hackenbroich, I., Refflinghaus, R., Winter, D.: Investigations into more exact weightings of customer demands in QFD. Asian J. Qual. **8**(3), 71–80 (2008)
59. Jin-yu, G., Zhong-bin, Z., Qing-yun, S.: Study and applications of analytic hierarchy process. China Saf. Sci. J. **5**, 148–153 (2008)
60. Xue, D., Jia-ming, L., Hao-jian, Z., Jun-yang, C., Jun-feng, Z.: Research on computation methods of AHP weight vector and its applications. J. Math. Pract. Theory **7**, 93–100 (2012)
61. Ying-luo, W.: System Engineering. China Machine Press, Beijing (2010)
62. Yan, W., Keying, L.H., Yi-wei, F., Jingyi, Y., Chang, Z., Junyi, W.: Construction of evaluation index system of agriculture and tourism coupling degree of rural complex based on production-living-ecological space. Agric. Outlook **16**(6), 8–14 (2020)

Emotions and Design

Cross-Cultural Design and Evaluation of Student Companion Robots with Varied Kawaii (Cute) Attributes

Dave Berque[1]([⊠]), Hiroko Chiba[1], Tipporn Laohakangvalvit[2], Michiko Ohkura[2], Peeraya Sripian[2], Midori Sugaya[2], Liam Guinee[1], Shun Imura[2], Narumon Jadram[2], Rafael Martinez[1], Sheong Fong Ng[2], Haley Schwipps[1], Shuma Ohtsuka[2], and Grace Todd[1]

[1] DePauw University, Greencastle, USA
{dberque,hchiba,liamguinee_2022,rafaelmartinez_2022,
haleyschwipps_2022,gracetodd_2022}@depauw.edu
[2] Shibaura Institute of Technology, Tokyo, Japan
{tipporn,peeraya,doly,ma20011,ma21067,a118026,
a118029}@shibaura-it.ac.jp, ohkura@sic.shibaura-it.ac.jp

Abstract. We report on an extension of a cross-cultural collaborative project between students and faculty at DePauw University in the United States and Shibaura Institute of Technology in Japan. The ongoing project uses cross-cultural teams to design and evaluate virtual companion robots for university students with the goal of gaining a deeper understanding of the role that kawaii (Japanese cuteness) plays in fostering positive human response to, and acceptance of, robots across cultures. Members of two cross-cultural teams designed virtual companion robots with specific kawaii attributes. Using these robots, we conducted the first phase of a two-phase user study to understand perceptions of these companion robots. The findings demonstrate that participants judge round companion robots to be more kawaii than angular ones and they also judge colorful robots to be more kawaii than greyscale robots. The phase one study identified pairs of robots that are the most appropriate candidates for conducting further investigations. The appropriateness of these pairs holds across male and female participates as well as across participants whose primary culture is American and those whose primary culture is Japanese. This work prepares us to perform a more detailed study across genders and cultures using both survey results and biosensors. In turn, this will inform our long-term goal of designing robots that are appealing across gender and culture.

Keywords: Kawaii · Human-robot interaction · Cross-cultural design

1 Introduction and Motivation

1.1 Kawaii

As robots become increasingly common in daily life, it is critical that roboticists design devices that are accepted broadly, including across cultures and genders. Toward this

M. Kurosu (Ed.): HCII 2022, LNCS 13302, pp. 391–409, 2022.
https://doi.org/10.1007/978-3-031-05311-5_27

end, global collaboration is pivotal today and in the future. This paper reports on the second year of a three-year cross-cultural collaboration between students and faculty at DePauw University in the United States and Shibaura Institute of Technology in Japan. We formed two cross-cultural teams to design and evaluate virtual companion robots to gain a deeper understanding of the role that kawaii (Japanese cuteness) plays in fostering positive human response to, and acceptance of, these devices across cultures.

As we have previously reported in [1], the word, *kawaii*, is often translated into "cute," "lovely," "adorable", "cool," and sometimes other words depending on the context. There does not seem to be an exact word that can be used as a counterpart in English [2]. That's probably because Japanese people's affection for "kawaii" has been cultivated throughout Japanese history [3]. The sentiment of kawaii seems to have been present in Japanese society since 400 B.C., and the word itself started appearing around the 11th century in literary texts [4, 5]. The meaning of the word has evolved to become a cultural concept or an emotional domain that relates to something or someone lovely, or someone or something that invokes the feeling of "wanting to protect" [5]. In the modern context, the notion of kawaii is embraced as a catalyst to evoke positive feelings [6], as can be seen in designs ranging from Hello Kitty products to road signs to robotic gadgets, to name just a few examples. Kawaii has also been gaining global audiences and customers in the last two decades as well as in Japan [6, 7] through kawaii products. Kawaii design principles are now incorporated into successful products that are used globally including in robotic gadgets [8, 9].

1.2 Prior Work

As we have summarized in [1] previous studies have examined cross-cultural differences in the acceptance of robots based on various design characteristics. For example, researchers have documented the impact of localizing a robot's greeting style (gestures and language) on acceptance by Japanese versus Egyptian users [10].

Similarly, prior studies have examined perceptions of kawaii, including differences in perceptions across cultures and genders. These studies have found gender differences in preferences for various kawaii spoon designs based on shape, color and geometric pattern [11]. A broader study examined the extent to which perceptions of kawaii in 225 photographs differ between male and female Japanese college students [12]. In this study, gender differences were established, depending on the type of object photographed. For example, male subjects found spherical geometric objects to be more kawaii than female subjects [12]. The first two authors extended the original study by presenting 217 of the original 225 images to American college students and gathering data about their perceptions of kawaii-ness in each image. For some types of objects, differences in perceptions of kawaii-ness were found, particularly between Japanese males and American males as well as between Japanese females and all other groups [13].

Prior work that investigates the role of kawaii in user perceptions and user acceptance of robots or robotic gadgets is limited. However, one pair of papers reports on studies of kawaii-ness in the motion of robotic vacuum cleaners [14, 15]. The authors programmed a visually plain version of a Roomba vacuum cleaner to move according to 24 different patterns, including patterns that the authors describe with terms such as: bounce, spiral, attack, spin and dizzy [14, 15]. The studies demonstrated that kawaii-ness can be expressed through motion, even in the absence of more traditional visual kawaii-ness; however, the studies did not consider cultural or gender differences.

In addition, prior work done by the first six authors and their collaborators suggests that designing a robot to be more animal-like, rounder, shorter, and smaller increases participant's perceptions that the robot is kawaii/cute [1]. This work also suggests that designing a robot to be more kawaii/cute appears to positively influence human preference for being around the robot. These findings held across Japanese and American culture and across males and females [1]. In this work, both males and females preferred smaller robots to larger ones; however, this preference was more significant for females. However, no other differences were found between genders or between cultures. [1]. The current paper builds on the previous work in that we now focus on the design and evaluation of companion robots for university students and we demonstrate that the effect of specific kawaii attributes holds across multiple robot designs.

2 Design of Companion Robots for University Students

2.1 Overview

In recent years, concerns about anxiety and other mental health issues in university students have been widely reported in the media in both the United States and in Japan. Both the American and Japanese governments also extensively address the issues [16, 17]. At some universities, increased student anxiety has led to a greater number of students requesting to bring emotional support animals to campus [18]. For example, Washington State University fielded only a handful of requests for emotional support animals annually as of 2011 but by 2019 was fielding 60–75 requests per year [18].

As early as 2003, Fogg proposed what he then considered to be a futuristic "study buddy" that would assist students by prompting them to adopt good living and study habits and by providing other helpful information [19]. What seemed like a futuristic way to assist students in 2003 is now more realistic. For example, several schools have experimented with providing all students with Amazon Echo Dots that use Alexa to equip every student room with a student assistant service, customized with campus-specific information [20]. While this use of Echo Dots may support students by providing an information assistant, the approach does not provide the same type of comfort as a companion animal.

Robotic versions of companion animals have been used in hospitals, nursing homes and other extended care facilities to comfort dementia patients as well as other older adults [21]. Perhaps the best known of these is PARO, a therapeutic robot that originated in Japan, and has been in use since 2003 [22]. PARO is designed as a soft robot that resembles a small, white, baby seal. PARO "blinks and coos when petted [and] is often therapeutic for patients with dementia" [23]. PARO is particularly attractive for use in hospitals and nursing homes because logistical constraints make it difficult to take care of real pets in these facilities.

This paper reports on continued work, supported by a United States National Science Foundation (NSF) International Research Experiences for Undergraduates (IRES) grant, to gain a deeper understanding of the role that kawaii plays in fostering positive human response to, and acceptance of, robotic gadgets across cultures. More information about the goals of this grant-supported project may be found in [24, 25]. We focused our work in summer of 2021 on the design and evaluation of virtual companion robots for university students due to the potential of such robots to address the real world problems described above.

With mentorship from faculty members at Shibaura Institute of Technology and DePauw University, two cross-cultural student design teams conceptualized personas and scenarios that they then used to guide their work in using Unity to design and implement prototypes of virtual companion robots.

Each design team was comprised of four students – two students from Shibaura Institute of Technology in Japan and two students from DePauw University in the United States.

2.2   Team One's Persona, Scenario and Companion Robot Designs

The first student team developed a persona (composite user to design for) and a scenario to guide their work. The persona was given a gender-neutral name and the scenario was written to make sense in both an American and Japanese cultural context. The persona and scenario were written in English and then translated into Japanese in preparation for the cross-cultural user-study that is described later in this paper. The English version of the persona and scenario is presented below.

Team One Persona: Terry is a 19-year-old first-year university student who is not completely familiar with their campus. Terry frequently gets lost on campus and is late. Terry is nervous about being on time for class and remembering all of their responsibilities. Terry needs help remembering where things are and when Terry needs to do things, such as taking medication, eating properly, and getting enough sleep.

Team One Scenario: One morning, the robot realizes Terry is not awake 30 min before their class, so the robot says "Terry it is time to get up, you don't want to be late!" to wake Terry up. When Terry gets up the robot spins, dances and claps. After that, the robot checks Terry's schedule and says, "Good Morning, your first class is at 8:00 AM.", you have 10 min to get ready". The robot brings Terry their medication and breakfast. The robot says "Let's go to class!" and encourages Terry to follow it by carrying Terry's backpack. The robot then takes Terry to their class, and upon arrival spins and claps. This makes Terry feel happy".

After collaborating to develop the persona and scenario, each team member designed four versions of a virtual companion robot that demonstrated the part of the scenario where the robot wakes Terry up by moving around and saying "Terry, it is time to get up, you don't want to be late."

Using the persona and scenario as a guide, each team member developed a round, colorful, and animal-like companion robot that enacted the selected portion of the scenario. This version of the robot is expected to be judged to be kawaii because roundness, colors (especially bright saturated colors of various hues including yellow and purple) and animal-like faces are attributes that have been associated with kawaii-ness in previous studies [1, 26]. We refer to this version of the companion robot as round-colorful (RC). The student researcher then created a second robot by changing the color to greyscale resulting in a version that we refer to as round-greyscale (RG). Next, the student researcher developed a version that was angular and colorful without animal-like features resulting in a companion robot that we refer to as angular-colorful (AC). Finally, color was replaced with greyscale to produce a version that we refer to as angular-greyscale (AG). Tables 1, 2, 3 and 4 show the four companion robot versions developed by each of the student researchers on team one. In each table, the upper-left corner shows the round-colorful (RC) version, the upper-right corner shows the round-greyscale version (RG), the lower left corner shows the angular-colorful version (AC) and the lower-right corner shows the angular-greyscale version (AG).

Table 1. Four companion robots developed by a member of team one

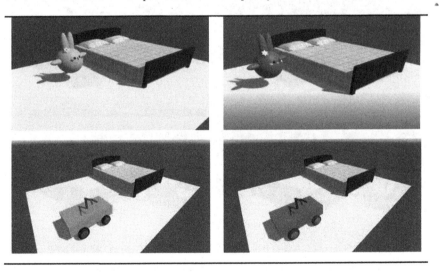

Table 2. Four companion robots developed by another member of team one

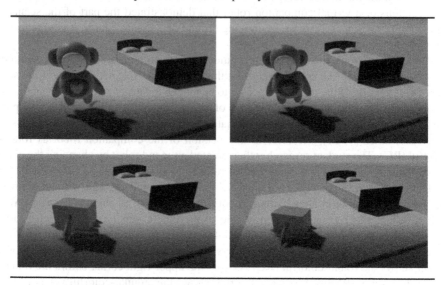

Table 3. Four companion robots developed by another member of team one

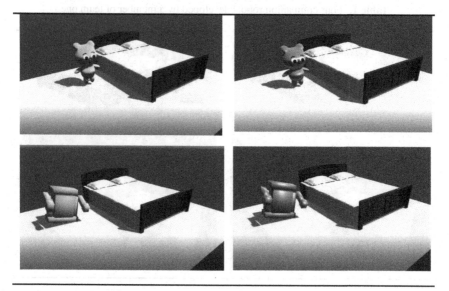

Table 4. Four companion robots developed by another member of team one

2.3   Team Two's Persona, Scenario and Companion Robot Designs

The second student team also developed a persona and a scenario to guide their work. Like team one, their persona was given a gender-neutral name and their scenario was designed to make sense in both an American and Japanese cultural context. The persona and scenario were written in English and then translated into Japanese in preparation for the cross-cultural user-study that is described later in this paper. The English versions of the persona and scenario are presented below.

Team Two Persona: Sam is a 19-year old university student, who has become overwhelmed by their schoolwork and obligations. This has led them to lose sleep, miss meals, and consistently forget assignments.

Team Two Scenario: In the evening, Sam's robot does a calendar check and realizes that Sam has an assignment to complete tonight. Sam's robot stands up and says to Sam "You need to do your assignments." The robot then bends its head in a sad manner until Sam starts working. When Sam finishes their assignment, the robot does a dance, and says "Congratulations on your hard work, Sam. Enjoy the rest of your evening." This makes Sam feel happy and content with their work.

Each team member designed four versions of a virtual companion robot that demonstrated the part of the scenario where the robot congratulates Sam on completing an assignment by dancing and saying "Congratulations on your hard work, Sam. Enjoy the rest of your evening."

Using the persona and scenario as a guide, each team member developed a round and colorful companion robot (RC), as well as a round-greyscale version (RG), an angular-colorful version (AC) and an angular-greyscale version (AG). Tables 5, 6, 7 and 8 show the four companion robot versions developed by each of the student researchers on team two. In each table, the upper- left corner shows the round-colorful (RC) version, the upper-right corner shows the round-greyscale version (RG), the lower left corner shows the angular-colorful version (AC) and the lower-right corner shows the angular-greyscale version (AG).

Table 5. Four companion robots developed by a member of team two

Table 6. Four companion robots developed by another member of team two

Table 7. Four companion robots developed by another member of team two

Table 8. Four companion robots developed by another member of team two

3 Evaluation

3.1 Purpose of the Evaluation

We plan a two-phase evaluation of the eight sets of virtual robots that are described in the previous section. Taken together, the two-phase evaluation employs the following measures, each of which can be examined across gender and across culture (American versus Japanese):

- **Reported Kawaii/Cuteness:** For a given prototype, what is the participant's self-reported perception of the prototype's cuteness/kawaii-ness?
- **Measured Joy:** For a given prototype, what impact does the prototype have an on participant's joy as measured by biosensors that track heartrate and brainwaves?
- **Reported Acceptance:** for a given prototype, to what degree does the participant believe the prototype is likely to accepted for its intended purpose?

The phase one evaluation reported in this paper focuses on the first measure. In addition to exploring the first measure in more detail, the phase two evaluation will also consider the remaining two measures and will explore correlations between pairs of measures. For example, we hypothesize that self-reported Kawaii/Cuteness will positively correlate with Measured Internal Joy across prototypes. We also hypothesize that Measured Internal Joy will positively correlate with Self-Reported Acceptance across prototypes.

The design process described in Sect. 2 resulted in 32 different robot companion prototypes. It is difficult to carry out a study in which participants engage meaningfully with 32 different prototypes. This is especially true if the study involves taking measurements with biosensors, such as those that measure EEG, which require participants to wear a carefully positioned headset.

Phase one of the evaluation, which is described in the rest of this section, identifies robots for the first scenario that have the greatest variation in Reported Kawaii/Cuteness between the cutest robots and the least cute robots. This phase of the evaluation also identifies a parallel set of robots for the second scenario.

The identified robot sets will be used in phase two of the evaluation, which will be reported on in a future paper. Phase two of the study will gather more data from participants, including biosensor data, and qualitative data about their reaction to the selected robots.

For phase one of the evaluation, we designed and administered an online survey to measure perceptions of the 32 robot prototypes. As noted above, the survey, which was administered to Japanese and American males and females, was designed to help us select the robots to use in phase two of the study.

3.2 Participant Demographics

After obtaining Institutional Review Board approval for the study, we recruited participants whose primary culture was American as well as participants whose primary culture was Japanese. Participants had to be at least 18 years old and at most 28 years old. In addition, participants had to have lived in the United States for at least 15 years or had to have lived in Japan for at least 15 years. In effect, this limited participation to participants who had either an American or Japanese dominant culture. Participants were also required to use a laptop or tablet to complete the survey. We did not allow participants to complete the survey on a phone because the participants watched videos of the companion robots during the study and we wanted the videos to be a reasonable size.

In total, 63 participants completed the survey. The participants ranged in age from 18 to 28 with a mean age of 20.9. All of the participants were enrolled in a university or were recent university graduates. The participants included 27 participants in the Japan-culture group (16 females and 11 males) and 36 participants in the American- culture group (15 females and 21 males). In total, then, 31 females and 32 males participated in phase one of the study. Since the primary purpose of the phase one study is to select the best candidate companion robots for a more robust phase two study, we accepted the greater number of Japanese-culture females as compared to males as well as the greater number of American-culture males as compared to females.

3.3 Study Procedure

The survey instrument was originally developed in English and then translated to Japanese by the second author. We used the adjective "cute" for the English counterpart of "kawaii" because it is one of the closest translations, although the interchangeableness has been argued [2]. The English version of the survey was administered to the American-culture participants and the Japanese version was administered to the Japanese-culture participants. Each version was administered as a Google form that embedded videos of the robots shown in Tables 1, 2, 3, 4, 5, 6, 7 and 8.

After accepting the conditions of an online informed consent, and confirming eligibility to participate in the survey, participants provided their age, gender and education level. Participants then watched a sample video and confirmed that they could see the video and hear the associated audio.

Participants then read the description of Terry's persona (see Sect. 2.2) and read the following statement of context, which is an abbreviated version of the scenario developed by the first student team (see Sect. 2.2): "The robots shown in the following videos are designed to help Terry with tasks such as waking up on time, leading the way to campus buildings and remembering to take medication on time. You will not see Terry in the video but you will see the robot trying to wake Terry up."

Participants then watched four videos, each 20-s long, showing the four companion robots developed by one of the student researchers. The first video was round and colorful (RC), the second was round and greyscale (RG), the third was angular and colorful (AC) and the fourth was angular and greyscale (AG). These companion robots are shown in Table 1. After watching each video, participants answered the following three questions:

1. "How cute is the robot?" This question was answered on a 7-point rating scale with 1 indicating "not at all cute" and 7 indicating "very cute".
2. "How trustworthy is the robot?" This question was answered on a 7-point rating scale with 1 indicating "not at all trustworthy" and 7 indicating "very trustworthy".
3. "How likely is it that Terry would want to use this robot?" This question was answered on a 7-point rating scale with 1 indicating "not at all likely" and 7 indicating "very likely".

Participants then watched the four videos developed by a second student researcher who worked on this scenario (see Table 2) and participants answered the same survey questions. To counterbalance the survey, these videos were presented in the order RG, AC, AG, RC. Participants then answered the same questions about the videos that were developed by the third student researcher who worked on this scenario (see Table 3). These videos were presented in the order AC, AG, RC, RG. Finally, participants watched the set of videos developed by the fourth student researcher who worked on this scenario (see Table 4). This set of videos and questions were presented in the order AG, RC, RG, AC.

Participants then read a description of Sam's persona (see Sect. 2.3) and then read the following statement of context, which is an abbreviated version of the scenario developed by the second student team (see Sect. 2.3): "The robots shown in the following videos are designed to help Sam eat regularly, turn in assignments on time and generally feel less stress. You will not see Sam in the video but you will see the robot congratulating Sam after their assignment has been completed."

Participants then watched four sets of videos, with four videos in each set, and answered questions about each video. These companion robots are shown in Table 5, Table 6, Table 7 and Table 8. The questions used and the counterbalanced order of videos was the same as described in detail for the companion robots associated with the first scenario.

Participants were then debriefed and completed a payment form that allowed us to compensate them with an Amazon.com gift certificate in the amount of $10 or ¥1000.

3.4 Comparison of Kawaii/Cute Within Each Cluster of Videos

The clustered bar chart shown in Fig. 1 provides the average Kawaii/Cute rating across all subjects for each of the eight companion robot clusters. Each four-bar cluster represents the ratings provided for the four robots designed by a single student researcher. The left-most four clusters correspond to the persona (Terry) and scenario that the first group of student researchers worked on. The right-most four clusters correspond to the persona (Sam) and scenario that the second group of student researchers worked on.

For each cluster, the left most bar corresponds to the round-colorful (RC) companion robot, the second bar from the left corresponds to the round-greyscale companion robot (RG), the second bar from the right corresponds to the angular-colorful robot (AC) and the right-most bar corresponds to the angular-greyscale robot (AG).

The horizontal access labels correspond to Tables 1, 2, 3, 4, 5, 6, 7 and 8 in the previous section of this paper. For example, the left-most cluster of four bars is labeled 1 and corresponds to the four robots shown in Table 1. The right-most cluster of four bars is labeled 8 and corresponds to the four robots shown in Table 8. The vertical access gives the mean cuteness score for each robot.

Within each cluster, a comparison between the RC and RG bar, as well as between the AC and AG bar represents a change based on color versus greyscale. Similarly, a comparison of the between the RC and AC bar, as well as between the RG and AG bar represents a change based on round versus angular.

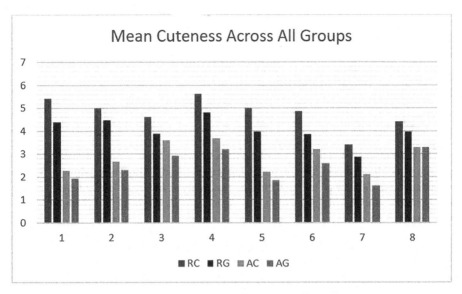

Fig. 1. Mean cuteness ratings across all groups

Visual inspection of the Fig. 1 suggests that within each cluster there is a tendency for round robots to be judged as more kawaii/cute than angular robots. Similarly, within each cluster, colorful robots are judged to be more kawaii/cute than greyscale robots. Detailed means cuteness values are provided in the Table 9 below.

Table 9. Mean Cuteness/Kawaii score for each robot.

Team 1 Cluster	Mean	Team 2 Cluster	Mean
1RC	5.43	5RC	5.02
1RG	4.38	5RG	3.95
1AC	2.29	5AC	2.22
1AG	1.95	5AG	1.86
2RC	5.02	6RC	4.87
2RG	4.48	6RG	3.84
2AC	2.68	6AC	3.21
2AG	2.32	6AG	2.59
3RC	4.62	7RC	3.40
3RG	3.89	7RG	2.86
3AC	3.59	7AC	2.11
3AG	2.94	7AG	1.63

(continued)

Table 9. (*continued*)

Team 1 Cluster	Mean	Team 2 Cluster	Mean
4RC	5.63	8RC	4.43
4RG	4.81	8RG	3.97
4AC	3.70	8AC	3.30
4AG	3.21	8AG	3.30

The bar-graph shown in Fig. 1 and the data shown in Table 9 present mean cuteness scores across all subjects (female, male, Japanese-culture, American-culture). We also examined the means for gender and culture separately to investigate whether or not they are consistent with the overall results. The results are shown in Figs. 2, 3 and 4 below.

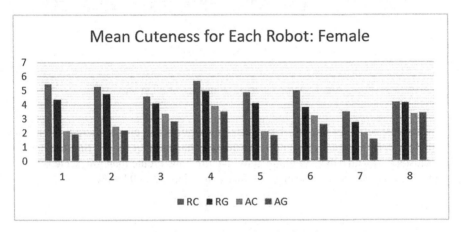

Fig. 2. Mean cuteness ratings by females

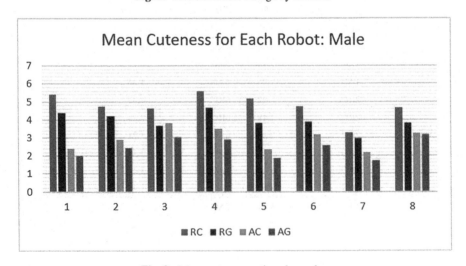

Fig. 3. Mean cuteness ratings by males

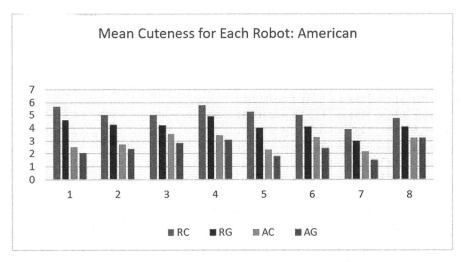

Fig. 4. Mean cuteness ratings by American-culture participants

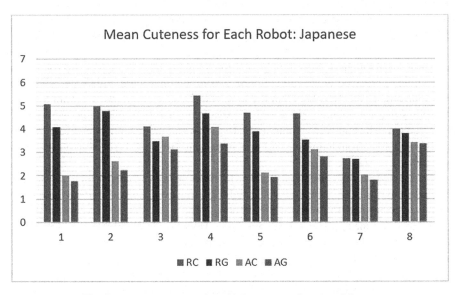

Fig. 5. Mean cuteness ratings by Japanese-culture participants

3.5 Differences Between Round-Colorful and Angular-Greyscale Robots

Visual inspection suggests that the tendencies are strikingly similar regardless of gender or cultural background. For each cluster, the round-colorful (RC) robot is judged to be the most kawaii/cute and the angular-greyscale (AG) robot is judged to be the least kawaii/cute. In addition, the participants' perception of kawaii-ness/cuteness has similar tendencies within each set of robots across gender and culture. A one-way ANOVA was performed to compare the effect of four different robots on rating scores within each cluster. These ANOVAs revealed that there were statistically significant differences in mean rating among the four robots in each cluster.

- Cluster 1 $F(3, 248) = [108.91]$, $p < 0.001$
- Cluster 2 $F(3, 248) = [54.32]$, $p < 0.001$
- Cluster 3 $F(3, 248) = [9.74]$, $p < 0.001$
- Cluster 4 $F(3, 248) = [33.31]$, $p < 0.001$
- Cluster 5 $F(3, 248) = [70.16]$, $p < 0.001$
- Cluster 6 $F(3, 248) = [22.71]$, $p < 0.001$
- Cluster 7 $F(3, 248) = [20.57]$, $p < 0.001$
- Cluster 8 $F(3, 248) = [5.56]$, $p = 0.0010$

These results demonstrate the effect of the various levels of the kawaii/cute attributes (roundness and color) that were introduced into the robots in each cluster.

3.6   Selecting Sample Robots for the Second-Phase Biosensor Study

As explained earlier, this study represents the first phase of the two-phase study. Our goal in this phase is to select robots we can use for a more in depth analysis in phase two of our work, where we will use additional survey questions, biosensors and qualitative measure to better understand participant's reactions to, and acceptance of, robots based on their level of cuteness. Specifically, our goal in phase one is to select two robots that were widely perceived as kawaii/cute and two robots that were widely perceived not to be cute among the 16 robots that the first team created. Similarly, we want to select two robots that were widely perceived as kawaii/cute and two robots that were widely perceived not to be cute/kawaii among the 16 robots that the second team created. These eight robots, four from team one and four from team two, will be used in phase two of our study.

We selected the two robots that received highest cute/kawaii ratings for team one. The selected robots are 1RC (mean = 5.43) and 4RC (mean = 5.63). A repeated measures t-test was performed to compare these robots. The t-test did not reveal statistically significant difference ($t_{(62)} = -1.12$, $p > 0.05$). Thus, we conclude that these two robots are similarly good candidates to serve as examples of cute/kawaii robots for team one in the phase-two study.

Similarly, we selected the two robots that received highest cute/kawaii ratings for team two. The selected robots are 5RC (mean = 5.02) and 6RC (mean = 4.83). A repeated measures t-test was performed to compare these robots. The t-test did not reveal statistically significant difference ($t_{(62)} = 0.61$, $p > 0.05$). Thus, we conclude that these two robots are similarly good candidates to serve as examples of cute/kawaii robots for team two in the phase-two study.

We also selected the two robots that received the lowest mean cute/kawaii ratings from team one. The selected robots were 1AG (mean = 1.95) and 2AG (mean = 2.32). A repeated measures t-test was performed to investigate the difference between these robots. The result did not reveal statistically significant difference between these two robots ($t_{(62)} = -1.98$, $p > 0.05$). Thus, we conclude that these two robots are similarly good candidates to serve as examples of the least cute/kawaii robots for team one in the phase-two study.

Similarly, we selected the two robots that received the lowest mean cute/kawaii ratings for team two. The selected robots were 5AG (mean = 1.86) and 7AG (mean = 1.63). A repeated measures t-test was performed to investigate the difference between these robots. The result did not reveal a statistically significant difference between these two robots ($t_{(62)} = 1.81, p > 0.05$). Thus, we conclude that these two robots are similarly good candidates to serve as examples of the least cute/kawaii robots for team two in the phase-two study.

The highly cute/kawaii robots we selected for team one are found in the upper-left corner of Table 1 and Table 4. Both robots were round and colorful. The least cute/kawaii robots we selected for team one are found in the lower-right corner of Table 1 and Table 2. Both robots were angular and greyscale.

Similarly, the highly cute/kawaii robots we selected for team two are found in the upper-left corner of Table 5 and Table 6. Again, both robots were round and colorful. The least cute/kawaii robots we selected for team two are found in the lower-right corner of Table 5 and Table 7. Both robots were angular and greyscale.

4 Discussion

The four robots in each cluster were designed with specific combinations of attributes to make them appear cute or not cute based on previous research. The results were consistent with previous findings: the use of color and roundness (including animal features) seem to contribute to participants' perception of cuteness/kawaiiness.

Visual inspection of the bar graphs in Figs. 1, 2, 3, 4 and 5 show that the effects tend to be cumulative in that round robots tend to be judged to be more cute/kawaii than angular ones, and colorful robots tend to be judged to be more cuter/kawaii than greyscale robots. However, robots that are round and colorful tend to be judged as more cute/kawaii than robots that are only round or only colorful.

Importantly, the tendency for round, colorful robots to be judged to be cuter than angular, greyscale robots holds across all eight robot clusters even though each cluster was developed by a different student researcher and the videos showing the robots in four of the clusters were shown to participants in the context of one scenario while the videos of the robots in the other four clusters were shown to the participants in the context of a different scenario. These tendencies also hold across females, males, Japanese-culture individuals and American-culture individuals. Thus, the results imply general principles about perceptions of cute/kawaii rather than the being tied to specific robot designs or demographic groups.

5 Future Work

The design process described in Sect. 2 resulted in 32 different companion robot prototypes. The evaluation described in Sect. 3 has helped us identify a subset of robots that vary dramatically in their level of cuteness/kawaii-ness and this subset of robots will be used in some of our future work. In particular, for the eight robots we identified, we will explore the following three measures that were first presented in Sect. 3.1:

- **Reported Kawaii/Cuteness:** For a given prototype, what is the participant's self-reported perception of the prototypes cuteness/kawaii-ness?
- **Measured Joy:** For a given prototype, what impact does the prototype have an on participant's joy as measured by biosensors that track heartrate and brainwaves?
- **Reported Acceptance:** for a given prototype, to what degree does the participant believe the prototype is likely to accepted for its intended purpose?

While we focused on the first measure in this paper, the phase two evaluation will consider the remaining two measures and will explore correlations between pairs of measures. For example, we hypothesize that self-reported Kawaii/Cuteness will positively correlate with Measured Internal Joy across prototypes. We also hypothesize that Measured Internal Joy will positively correlate with Self-Reported Acceptance across prototypes. This could have implications for the style of companion robot that would be the most effective student assistant.

Secondly, although cultural and gender differences were not the center of this study, we are interested in investigating what the results show in terms of differences in perception due to gender and cultural background.

In addition, we plan to carry out a deeper exploration of the eight round colorful robots. As a group, these robots tended to be judged as most cute/kawaii. We will use quantitative and qualitative surveys to better understand why participants found these robots to be cute/kawaii and what differences participants perceive between these eight robots.

Acknowledgements. This material is based upon work supported by the National Science Foundation under Grant No. OISE-1854255. Any opinions, findings, and conclusions or recommendations expressed in this material are those of the author(s) and do not necessarily reflect the views of the National Science Foundation.

References

1. Berque, D., et al.: Cross-cultural design and evaluation of robot prototypes based on Kawaii (Cute) attributes. In: Rau, P.-L. (ed.) HCII 2021. LNCS, vol. 12773, pp. 319–334. Springer, Cham (2021). https://doi.org/10.1007/978-3-030-77080-8_26
2. Nittono, H.: Kawaii no Chikara (The Power of Kawaii). Dojin Sensho, Kyoto (2019) (in Japanese)
3. Fuchu Art Museum: Kawaii Edo Kaiga (Cute Edo Paintings). Kyuryudo, Tokyo (2013). (in Japanese)
4. Ohkura, M. (eds.): Kawaii engineering: Measurements, Evaluations, and Applications of Attractiveness. Springer, Cham (2019)
5. Yomota, I.: Kawaii Ron (The Theory of Kawaii). Chikuma Shobō, Tokyo (2006). (in Japanese)
6. Nittono, H., Fukushima, M., Yano, A., Moriya, H.: The power of Kawaii: viewing cute images promotes a careful behavior and narrows attentional focus. PLoS ONE 7(9), e46362 (2012). https://doi.org/10.1371/journal.pone
7. Yano, C.: Pink Globalization: Hello Kitty's Trek Across the Pacific. Duke University Press, Durham (2013)

8. Cole, S.: The Most Kawaii Robots of 2016 (2016). https://motherboard.vice.com/en_us/art icle/xygky3/the-most-kawaii-robots-of-2016-5886b75a358cef455d864759. Accessed 8 Sept 2018
9. Prosser, M.: Why Japan's Cute Robots Could Be Coming for You (2017). www.redbull.com/ us-en/japan-cute-robot-obsession. Accessed 8 Sept 2018
10. Trovato, G., et al.: Cross-cultural study on human-robot greeting interaction: acceptance and discomfort by Egyptians and Japanese. J. Behav. Robot. **4**(2), 83–93 (2013)
11. Tipporn, L., Ohkura, M.: Comparison of spoon designs based on Kawaiiness between genders and nationalities, A4-3. In: Proceedings of ISASE2017, March 2017
12. Hashizume, A., Kurosu, M.: The gender difference of impression evaluation of visual images among young people. In: Kurosu, M. (ed.) HCI 2017. LNCS, vol. 10272, pp. 664–677. Springer, Cham (2017). https://doi.org/10.1007/978-3-319-58077-7_51
13. Berque, D., Chiba, H., Hashizume, A., Kurosu, M., Showalter, S.: Cuteness in Japanese design: investigating perceptions of Kawaii among American college students. In: Fukuda, S. (ed.) AHFE 2018. AISC, vol. 774, pp. 392–402. Springer, Cham (2019). https://doi.org/ 10.1007/978-3-319-94944-4_43
14. Sugano, S., Miyaji, Y., Tomiyama, K.: Study of Kawaii-ness in motion – physical properties of Kawaii motion of Roomba. In: Kurosu, M. (ed.) HCI 2013. LNCS, vol. 8004, pp. 620–629. Springer, Heidelberg (2013). https://doi.org/10.1007/978-3-642-39232-0_67
15. Sugano, S., Morita, H., Tomiyama, K.: Study on Kawaii-ness in motion –classifying Kawaii Motion using Roomba. In: International Conference on Applied Human Factors and Ergonomics 2012, San Francisco, California, USA (2012)
16. https://www.cdc.gov/mentalhealth/index.htm
17. https://www.mhlw.go.jp/kokoro/first/index.html
18. https://www.insidehighered.com/news/2019/05/21/colleges-see-rise-popularity-emotional-support-animals
19. Fogg, B.J.: Persuasive Technology: Using Computers to Change What We Think and Do. Morgan Kaufmann, San Francisco (2003)
20. McKenzie, L.: Alexa, What's the Deal with You, Anyway? Inside Higher Ed (2018). www. insidehighered.com/news/2018/08/22/meet-new-kid-campus-alexa. Accessed 8 Sept 2018
21. Scoglio, A.A.J., Reilly, E.D., Gorman, J.A., Drebing, C.E.: Use of social robots in mental health and well-being research: systematic review. J. Med. Internet Res. **21**(7), e13322 (2019)
22. http://www.parorobots.com/
23. https://www.nytimes.com/2010/07/05/science/05robot.html?_r=2&pagewanted=1
24. Berque, D., Chiba, H., Ohkura, M., Sripian, P., Sugaya, M.: Fostering cross-cultural research by cross-cultural student teams: a case study related to Kawaii (cute) robot design. In: Rau, P.-L. (ed.) HCII 2020. LNCS, vol. 12192, pp. 553–563. Springer, Cham (2020). https://doi. org/10.1007/978-3-030-49788-0_42
25. Ohkura, M., Sugaya, M., Sripian, P., Laohakangvalvit, T., Chiba, H., Berque, D.: Design and implementation of remote collaboration by Japanese and American University Students using virtual spaces with Kawaii robots. In: Proceedings of the 7th International Symposium on Affective Science and Engineering, March 2021, Japan Society of Kansei Engineering (2021). Online Conference
26. Ohkura, M., Komatsu, T., Aoto, T.: Kawaii rules: increasing affective value of industrial products. In: Watada, J., Shiizuka, H., Lee, K.-P., Otani, T., Lim, C.-P. (eds.) Industrial Applications of Affective Engineering, pp. 97–110. Springer, Cham (2014). https://doi.org/10.1007/978-3-319-04798-0_8

Technology in Automotive Brands: Function or Fashion?

Wei-Chi Chien[✉] and Chen-Huan Lin

Department of Industrial Design, National Cheng Kung University, No. 1, Dasyue Road, Tainan 701, Taiwan, R.O.C.
chien@xtdesign.org, p36094111@gs.ncku.edu.tw

Abstract. In the rapid evolution of technology, consumers receive various stimuli through "smart" commodities, which transformed users' understanding of the expressions of products' and interfaces' form. While consumers pursue utility and superiority from technologies, intelligent and high-tech things become a type of fashion. As a result, the "technological appearance" takes an essential role in branding. Artifacts are designed to be technologically advanced. While this phenomenon can be identified in many industries, this paper clarifies how the automotive industries use technology in their branding strategy. We analyzed five generations of Mercedes-Benz's S-class and BMW's 7-series and coded the architectural layouts of the cockpit system. Both models are flagship saloons from the German historical automotive brand, respectively. From the history of automotive design, we can see how brands and designers shaped the meaning and position of technology from a functional characteristic to a symbolic identity.

Keywords: Fashion technology · Automobile design · Image coding · Technology design

1 Introduction

Technology for functional goals, or quasi-technology, aims to transfer knowledge to practical solutions that enhance human capabilities to achieve goals. The knowledge is translated into hardware (e.g., machines or products) or software (e.g., process, methods). In this process, technology becomes tools, instruments, or methods [1]. According to Gharavi et al. [2],

> *The rapid development of electronics and software tools during the last four decades, coupled with the increase in computational speeds and a reduction in the cost of these tools, has touched every aspect of life, industry, and, of course, the automobile* (pp. 328–329).

However, beyond the functional (problem-solving) aspect, new technology often comes up with the impression of new possibilities, living styles, or alternative ways of thinking.

M. Kurosu (Ed.): HCII 2022, LNCS 13302, pp. 410–418, 2022.
https://doi.org/10.1007/978-3-031-05311-5_28

On the one hand, a technological atmosphere impacts the practice of fashion or branding design. Technological innovation is so appreciated in the consumer markets that even traditional industries must transform their branding image for a better expression on the market. On the other hand, technology-oriented product development affects consumers' preference toward convenience, mobility, or flexibility. The contemporary consumers are skilled in decoding the technological phenomena and consuming new media or products for new stimulation. For example, the digital display of home appliances is a significant code appearing on the market: While the traditional mechanical control parts provide the same and often more reliable functions, ovens, washing machines, or even electric fans are added by digital displays and touch buttons. In this case, technology goes beyond its functional purpose but serves as a symbolic identity.

The automobile industry is a complex combination of diverse industries with many interweaving influences. In this challenging context, automobile design plays the role of mixing and matching various technological advances to satisfy prospective users [16]. Despite prospective users' functional expectations, the designers also endeavor to present the automobile brands' identity. The trend or branding issue assigned to designers is to use the new and technological elements to inspire their new ideas. However, how do the car industries understand technology in their branding identity? Are technological features used for functional or symbolic purposes? By analyzing the interior design of five generations of Mercedes-Benz's S-class and BMW's 7-series, this study aims to clarify whether technologies applying a new phenomenon different from the ordinary functional meaning.

2 Fashion Technology

According to the Cambridge Dictionary, the definition of fashion is "*a style that is popular at a particular time, especially in clothes, hair, make-up, etc.*" In general, "fashion" implies a trend or popularity in which a unique identity is formed in a particular time and space. In the branding strategy, the unique identity implies the artificial differentness in a personal or social image created to promote consuming interests or price [3]. As a semiotic system of goods and products, the image shaping one's identity is, in fact, a cultural phenomenon. According to Eckert & Stacey [4], while it aims to generate uniqueness, fashion is a collection of similar ideas created by designers. Fashion has become global and influenced multiple industries through various new media, webbing a robust semiotic system connecting different industries [5].

Goktan and Miles [6] identified the intensive competition in nowadays' high-tech industry. The challenges of designers of high-tech products are no longer constrained in delivering products or services from a problem-solving or a single aspect. Since the success of the *iPhone*, design practices – almost overly – focused largely on how to present a sense of technological style and the technological progress as significant as possible through design. As a result, a semiotic system is produced, which we understand as "fashion technology."

In the field of wearable technology and fashion design, the term "fashionology" – the combination of "fashion" and "technology" – was used to scope a new design gene, in which not only the fashionable dress but also technological appearance is oriented in the form design [7]. The appearance of a product is one of the aspects of branding strategy. In such a global trend of fashionable technology, products' pragmatical, aesthetical, and cultural qualities are all influenced by designers' attempts to "show off" the technology [8].

According to Keller's definition of branding, fashion and branding are in a subtle relationship [9]. In branding, fashion can be understood as a strategy to express a brand's identity, call for value sharing, retain popularity, and create consumers' sustainable memory about a brand [9]. Brand image is a traditional way to enhance difference from other competitors and create a consistent and unified atmosphere for consumers to recognize the brand's "DNA" [10]. Branding strategies often attempt to build strong relations with technological progress [11]. Caring about the high technology product's technical characteristics, such as screen size, battery life, processing power, model version, and chipset, is often seen as a proactive lifestyle. In the branding strategy of high-tech products, Truong et al. found that attachment to a brand is essential to create consumers' trust in new technological possibilities [12].

Branding innovative technology requires more than functional development and demands for understanding the connection between product and values [13]. Automobile manufacturers focus on accessibility, functional efficiency, environmental friendliness, and the safety of transport activities as the primary development factors [14]. However, there is an obvious new trend in intelligentization, in which interaction between users and automobiles becomes the new spotlight [15]. Besides, in the recent automobile trend, the new design has far exceeded the needed aspects of their functions [16]. In this study, we are interested in how automobiles, as an industry highly associated with technological functionality and the strong tradition of branding at the same time, move in the age of fashion technology.

3   Methodology: Image Coding and Categorizations

We selected the last five generations from 1986–2020 of Mercedes Benz S-Class and BMW 7-Series as our objects (see Table 1). The objects in our analysis arched over 14 years. The development in generations of models could reveal the dynamic process of designers' understanding of technology. Besides, Mercedes-Benz and BMW are the two automobile brands of the top-selling German classical luxury brands worldwide. Besides, both their flagship saloons are in a similar proportion and histories. Despite the similarity, the branding identity of the two brands are different – *The Best or Nothing* (*Das Beste oder Nichts*; Mercedes-Benz) and *Sheer Driving Pleasure* (*Freude am Farhen*; BMW). These backgrounds of brands provide us to analyze how automobile branding is associated with technology and the potential difference in the strategies of the two manufacturers (Fig. 1).

Table 1. Models of BMW 7 Series and Benz S Class selected for our study

Brand	Model	Lunching year
BMW 7 Series	E32	1986
	E38	1994
	E65	2001
	F01	2009
	G11	2015
Benz S Class	W140	1991
	W220	1998
	W221	2006
	W222	2013
	W223	2020

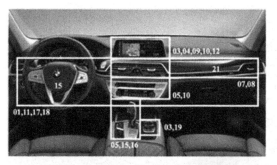

01	floating (layout)
02	integration
03	virtual display
04	digital display
05	coordination
06	linear
07	irregular
08	extension
09	lightweight
10	trapezoid
11	layers
12	flat surface
13	soft (material/texture)
14	logo (symbol)
15	polygon
16	materiality
17	mixed-material (material/texture)
18	overlays (material/texture)
19	fictional control
20	reflective
21	silver line

Fig. 1. Coding of the 2015 BMW G11 (7-Seris) as an example

4 Results and Analysis

207 codes from the contents of the images have been classified into a 7-category coding scheme. The categories include overall display, sense, material, element, and symbol. The following will analyze the categorized results of seeing how technology affects the cockpit design in automotive.

4.1 The Disappeared Layers

From a macro perspective, we can identify the subjects or design intentions that designers would like to highlight. Already from a global impression, we could identify a significant difference between Benz's earlier and later models, as well as between the development of Benz and BWM. From 2000, the codes of "flat" (green areas in Fig. 2), which suggest a reductive form strategy to present elements on a single layer, are found in both brands' models, especially in Benz's later models. While the mechanical elements and materiality are inevitable limitations to construct functions, designers arranged the different elements on different layers to create formal articulations. The reduction of layers is allowed by digital technology, such as compact digital displays. The possibility of digital multifunction "liberate" the arrangement of the displays and control parts and, therefore, the form limitation. As we can see in Fig. 2, when facing this new circumstance, BMW and Benz adopted very different ways of design. BMW's designers kept the layer-based arrangement; on the contrary, Benz's designers preferred large and flat surfaces.

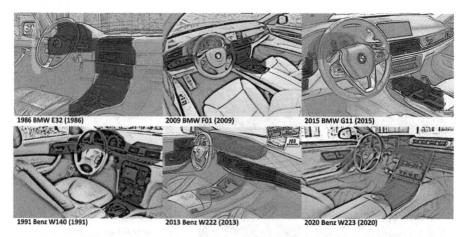

Fig. 2. Yellow: layer-based design; green: flat-surfaced design

4.2 Display and Benz's Horizon

IHS Markit analyzed the evolution of displays in the automotive cockpit. A significant transformation is that analog indicators and in-car physical interfaces, such as buttons and dials of the physical control parts and the instrument cluster, are replaced by digital variants [17]. There is no denying that the "digital display" is the most efficient way to present the multivariate functions, express the virtual identity of brands, and directly control touchscreens. With the rapid advancement of digital and information technologies, tremendous changes have occurred in traditional automobile products.

However, the concept of display changed over generations, by which display is no more only used for delivering information but also emotion. In Mercedes-Benz W123 (S-Class, 2020), a "fictional display" by LEDs is designed in the interior ambient lights (see Fig. 3). We may understand that the ambient is rather a decoration than a display. However, these interactive LEDs reflect a certain status of the vehicle. The difference is that the status is not translated into verbal information but emotional expression.

If we compare W123 with Benz's earlier models, we can see that the ambient light strips are, in fact, a new version of Benz's "horizon" in the interior (Fig. 4). While this horizon is designed to present luxury materiality, the latest model replaced the finely finished surface with ambient light. This movement is highly characteristic since technology breaks the boundary between material and function.

Fig. 3. LED strips in Mercedes-Benz S-Class W123 as fictional display

Fig. 4. The horizon in Benz's models and the materiality

4.3   The Pawing Between Symbol and Fashion

The symbol is an indispensable feature in the design for people to recognize the brand and identity directly. In both Benz and BMW – all automobiles, in fact – the brand logo is centered on the steering wheel and the drivers' sight.

We identified Benz's revolutionary understanding of technology as new material. In BMW's models, we found the "fictional control" as the second symbol in BMW's series since 2001 (Fig. 5). BMW launched the integrated – and fictional – physical interface Control Center and the iDrive system, which controls the infotainment system with one hand [18]. The designer placed the Control Center in the traditional spot of the gear lever to suggest a unique driving experience – sheer driving pleasure. Nowadays, all the models of BMW are equipped with the successor version of the iDrive system.

Mercedes-Benz launched a similar control device in their W221 (2006) and W222 (2013) of S-Class. However, this design is replaced by the AI-powered cockpit assistant with the mega touch screen in W 223 (2020). The operation form of the control wheel is alternative and fictional. However, such a control possibility has not become a brand symbol. Comparing BMW's Control Center with Benz's technological ambient, we see two different interpretations of technology in design. While Benz understands technology as new material, BMW more stays in the symbolic meaning of functional advancement.

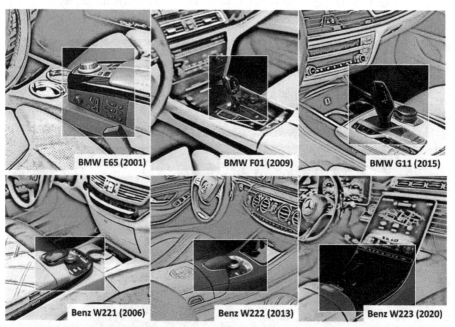

Fig. 5. Fictional control in the BMW 7-Series E65, F01, and G11 compared with Benz S class W221, W222, and W223

5   Discussion and Future Works

This study shows how two automobile brands presented their design identity with different strategies of interpreting technology. We should note that, in this paper, when speaking of technology and function, we use their symbolic meanings. Our focus lies on technological form in branding and identity.

BMW and Mercedes-Benz apparently are standing on two paths to create their identity in the age of technology, following their brand image Sheer Driving Pleasure and The Best or Nothing. BMW's approach is an articulation of the technical progress associated with functional performance ("pleasure of control"). In contrast, the ambient technology in Mercedes-Benz's W223 is a "technological texture," which takes over the physical texture of the earlier models of W221 and W222. The large touch screen, for certain, also presents a strong sense of interactivity, digitalization, and intelligence. However, we did not identify its consistency with Benz's traditional design.

Our future work is to finish a general evaluation strategy for technological branding. A measurement tool could be practical for designers to evaluate other products or systems. Besides, extending the coding task onto the video of both Brands may provide more interesting categories and could suggest new thinkings of understanding modern technology.

References

1. Weccard, E.N.: Future scenarios for the derivation of material requirements: the automobile interior 2030, Master Thesis (2012). http://essay.utwente.nl/62629/
2. Gharavi, H., Prasad, K.V., Ioannou, P.: Scanning advanced automobile technology. Proc. IEEE **95**(2), 328–333 (2007)
3. Tian, K.T., Bearden, W.O., Hunter, G.L.: Consumers' need for uniqueness: scale development and validation. J. Consum. Res. **28**(1), 350–366 (2010)
4. Eckert, C.M., Stacey, M.K.: Designing in the context of fashion - designing the fashion context. In: Designing in Context Symposium: Proceedings of the Design Thinking Symposium. Delft University Press (2001)
5. Ashwell, L., Langton, R.: Slaves to fashion? In: Wolfendale, J., Kennett, J. (eds.) Fashion – Philosophy for Everyone: Thinking with style, pp. 135–150. Blackwell (2011)
6. Goktan, A.B., Miles, G.: Innovation speed and radicalness: are they inversely related? Manag. Decis. **49**(4), 533–547 (2011)
7. Raushnabel, P.A., Hein, D.W.E., He, J., Ro, Y.K., Rawashdeh, S., Krulikowski, B.: Fashion or technology? A fashnology perspective on the perception and adoption of augmented reality smart glasses. i-com **15**(2), 179–194 (2016)
8. Tzou, R.-C., Lu, H.-P.: Exploring the emotional, aesthetic, and ergonomic facets of innovative product on fashion technology acceptance model. Behav. Inf. Technol. **28**(4), 311–322 (2009)
9. Keller, L.: Conceptualizing, measuring, and managing customer-based brand equity. J. Mark. **57**(1), 1–22 (1993)
10. Wang, X., Yang, Z.: The effect of brand credibility on consumers' brand purchase intention in emerging economies: the moderating role of brand awareness and brand image. J. Glob. Mark. **23**(3), 177–188 (2010)
11. Hamann, D.H., Robert, W., Omar, M.O.: Branding strategy and consumer high-technology product. J. Product Brand Manag. **16**(2), 8–111 (2007)

12. Truong, Y., Klink, R.R., Simmons, G., Grinstein, A., Palmer, M.: Branding strategies for high-technology products: the effects of consumer and product innovativeness. J. Bus. Res. **70**, 85–91 (2017)
13. Nerkar, A., Roberts, P.W.: Technological and product-market experience and the success of new product introductions in the pharmaceutical industry. Strateg. Manag. J. **25**(8–9), 779–799 (2004)
14. Trofimenko, Y.: Environmental problems of using digital and information technologies in automobile transport. In: MATEC Web of Conferences, vol. 341 (2021)
15. Sun, M., Yu, H.: Automobile intelligent dashboard design based on human computer interaction. Int. J. Perform. Eng. **15**(2), 571–578 (2019)
16. Pasaribu, Y.M., Joyodiharjo, B.J.: Car design, from function to fashion. Arts Des. Stud. **30**, 17–26 (2015)
17. HIS Markit: The evolution of displays in the automotive cockpit (2019). https://ihsmarkit.com/about/contact-us.html
18. bmw.com: Introducing BMW iDrive: a hero from the past. And from the future (2021). https://www.bmw.com/en/events/ces/2cars.html

A Framework to Semi-automated Usability Evaluations Processing Considering Users' Emotional Aspects

Flávia de Souza Santos[1][✉] ⓘ, Marcos Vinícius Treviso[2] ⓘ,
Sandra Pereira Gama[2] ⓘ, and Renata Pontin de Mattos Fortes[1] ⓘ

[1] University of São Paulo, São Carlos, SP, Brazil
{flaviasantos,renata}@usp.br
[2] IST/University of Lisbon, Lisbon, Portugal
{marcos.treviso,sandra.gama}@tecnico.ulisboa.pt
https://www.icmc.usp.br, https://tecnico.ulisboa.pt

Abstract. The concern with providing a good experience for users increases simultaneously with technological evolution and dissemination. Different evaluation methods are presented in the literature to help developers evaluate and verify the interfaces they develop. However, for the application of evaluation methods, it is often necessary to have an expert, or users, which can make the assessment costly, both time-consumingly and monetarily. Consequently, developers may launch their products without carefully checking some critical aspects beforehand, causing anything from the non-acceptance of the technology to even its abandonment. Carrying out part of the evaluations with users, or totally with them, in an automated way, considering the diversity of data obtained and the support of analyzes processed by a computer, presents itself as a possible alternative to be investigated to support developers of interactive systems. At the same time, considering the emotional aspects during the interaction can provide the developer with valuable information, including the acceptance of the technology. In this way, considering users' emotions can improve the automatic evaluation results, capturing and processing the user experience in the system. Thus, we present a framework (*EmotiUsing*) composed of semi-automated usability evaluations, considering the emotional aspects of users. The framework aims to make the analytical evaluations less subjective and streamline the evaluation process, reducing costs and time for the evaluators.

Keywords: Usability evaluation · Emotions · Semi-automated support

1 Introduction

Based on focusing on aspects of the interfaces and the forms of interaction between users and interfaces, many technological resources have been spread

Supported by USP (Brazil) and IST (Portugal).

worldwide. Information dissemination provided by the new means brings challenges for Information Systems since it is necessary to consider the characteristics and objectives of the people who will use the system. Studies that address usability tests allow a straightforward detection of usability problems. However, they usually come with a substantial cost and require specialized knowledge.

In order to apply the usability evaluation methods for interactive systems, the presence of experts or users is essential, which makes the analysis costly, both in terms of financial investments and time-consuming activity [4]. Applying conventional methods of evaluating interfaces, in general, is considered costly and still has known biases. Accordingly, developers can launch their products without first checking with due care these essential aspects, which can cause the technology's non-acceptance, even its abandonment [18]. Evaluation with users demands efforts to process the collected results since a specialist must consolidate the obtained data and generate a report. Another impacting factor in user evaluations is that tracking usability problems represents a challenge for developers due to the difficulty of obtaining explicit feedback from users [13].

According to [22], among the characteristics to consider of the people who use the systems, the emotional aspects during the interaction can provide the developer with valuable information, even affecting the acceptance of the technology. The emotion analysis in Human-Computer Interaction can make interactions between users and computer systems more natural [2]. The automatic process and the use of emotions can help in the usability and user experience analysis since information about emotions can help provide improved interaction, even for individuals who are less accustomed to technology or who have a disability [3]. However, the task of detecting emotions is not trivial, even for humans.

In scientific literature, we could identify perspectives related to the knowledge areas dedicated to understanding how to improve the user experience when using an interactive system. In this research, we propose a framework that performs a semi-automatic evaluation of usability based on collecting logs and emotions during interactions with the system, generating usability smells reports. However, as a starting point, we only consider log interactions in this work. The result of our method will potentially assist developers, or usability inspectors, in performing the evaluation, thus seeking to contribute to making analytical evaluations less subjective, in addition to streamlining the evaluation process reducing evaluators' costs and time.

2   Related Work

Considering that we wish to automate usability evaluation methods based on users' emotional aspects, identifying the existing research efforts is a primary duty. Therefore, we performed a literature review to comprehend and identify the variety of automatic methods used to evaluate usability taking into account user's emotions. In the context of research on automatic interface evaluation, we have found different techniques, mechanisms, frameworks, and tools to assist in usability evaluations, which we describe below.

For web application-based works, the tool Usability Smells Finder (**USF**) [9] supports the process of detecting and correcting usability smells, capturing the user interaction logs using a script or a browser extension. After capturing the logs, the tool performs usability smells detection and generates a report. The Web Event Logger and Flow Identification Tool (**WELFIT**) [23] evaluates the usability of web pages automatically. A machine Learning (ML) algorithm is used to process the collected user's interactions logs. In [7] a method is presented that automates the usability evaluation of web systems, verifying metrics and analyzing user behavior at run time. The interaction logs are recorded in a database by remote applications hosted on the application server. Finally, the method includes verification of defined metrics from the collected data.

Regarding the detection of usability smells, the MobileUSE Smell Evaluator (**MUSE**) tool identifies the possible usability problems through log analysis, being able to detect usability smells [19]. It is unnecessary to have access to the web page's code to carry out the evaluation. This work is based mainly on the analysis of touch events (e.g., tap, pan) and usability smells' evaluation using a pattern matching model. [21] proposed the **UseSkill** tool to evaluate Web application. The authors presented an extension UseSkill Extension (**USE**), which detects usability smells based on an analysis of the user interaction captured in an actual environment. The capture occurs by adding a script in the system's code under evaluation. Focusing on the automatic detection of usability smells in web applications for mobile devices, [17] propose: *(i)* a set of specific smells to the context of mobile applications, together with the standards for detecting each one, and *(ii)* an extension for UseSkill [21]. In contrast to the previous works, an approach to detect usability smells in Virtual Reality systems is presented [11]. The detection process relies on the automated generation of task trees, created from the verification of recordings, on video, of users' interaction with the system.

More recently, in [8], the authors aim to develop a method to automatically compare the User Experience (UX) in alternative designs. They propose that ML techniques be used to predict UX. The method must automatically evaluate alternative projects in terms of UX, without requiring explicit user intervention. In [12] the authors evaluated the usability and detected problems by verifying similar users' behaviors. They also proposed a method and the respective tools, which assist in verifying usability and finding problems based on comparing the screened interactions' similarity.

Studies that Analyze Emotions During the Usability Evaluation. As pointed by [5], taking into account and recognizing the emotions perceived during interactions between users and systems help identify the factors that enhance or impair the user experience. As we have observed, many scientific works have studied several methods, techniques, and guidelines for usability evaluation of the interface, which can be a determining factor of acceptance. However, it is also known that usability evaluation, subjective and not trivial, usually requires the presence of expert evaluators or representative users. Thus, it can directly affect the costs (of time and money) of a project.

We described a set of studies that present different methods, tools, approaches, and frameworks to allow the complete or partial automation of usability evaluation. They usually apply to different systems (e.g., mobile applications, web applications, health systems) and different target audiences (e.g., students, programmers, physicians, teachers, elderly). However, all of them aim to allow partial or total automation of usability evaluation, serving as an aid for developers and usability experts.

It is worth highlighting the challenges of automatic and accurate emotion recognition and its application in the context of usability. They motivated the study of [16], which carried out a practical experiment to observe issues of applicability of emotion recognition in usability evaluation. The promising results indicate that these aspects can add valuable information to evaluate usability and user experience. However, the reviewed studies did not consider these aspects in the automatic usability evaluation.

Therefore, considering these initiatives, we have proposed a conceptual framework for a semi-automatic usability evaluation, which considers the users' emotional aspects during the interaction. Our goal is to develop a framework to automatic usability evaluation, considering the user's emotional aspects; we argue that it will benefit the software development process, generating savings in the evaluation's costs (monetary and time).

3   Usability Smells

It is not always simple to point out usability problems as this indication directly relates to finding what is causing the problem. Thus, we adopted the search for usability smells for our framework. "Bad smells" are indicators of inadequate design of an application, with the potential to harm usability, maintenance, and its evolution [1]. In this strategy, users are the first actors in the process since their interactions are the sources that generate the "bad smells" [19].

In our research, we adopted the search for subjective usability smells, those not easily found by rule-based algorithms. Based on usability smells presented by [9,19,21], and [10,11], and also in our experience, we prepared a list of 11 smells which are classified into two different levels of specificity, task smells and action smells, as follows.

Task-Level:

1. **Laborious Task (LT)** - adapted from [21]
   It occurs when the execution of the task demands the execution of a large number of actions, and much time, decreasing productivity and engagement.
2. **Cyclic Task (CT)** - adapted from [21]
   It occurs when the task requires performing many repetitive actions and indicates that the task can be tedious and tiring.

3. **Too Many Layers (TML)** - adapted from [9] and [21]
   It occurs when users need to scroll through many pages to perform a task. This demand can affect user performance.
4. **Missing Task Feedback (MTF)** - proposed by us
   It occurs when a task is repeated for the same inputs. It may indicate that the system is not providing feedback for the task.
5. **High Interaction Distance (HID)** - adapted from [11] and [19]
   It occurs when related content is arranged too far apart and whose display or interaction is crucial for performing tasks.
6. **Repetition in Text Fields (RTF)** - adapted from [10]
   It occurs when the same text is entered multiple times in a task. It may indicate that the task asks for duplicate information.
7. **Late Validation (LV)** - adapted from [9]
   It occurs when input errors are only checked after task submission. It can indicate late validation of the fields, demotivating the user.

Action-Level:

1. **Undescriptive Element (UE)** - adapted from [9] and [21]
   It occurs when too many users try to hint at a particular element on the page. It may indicate that the element is not self-describing enough.
2. **Missing Action Feedback (MAF)** - adapted from [10] and [21]
   It occurs when an action is constantly repeated. It may indicate that the system is not providing feedback for the action.
3. **Unnecessary Action (UA)** - adapted from [11]
   It occurs when a page contains only one action. May indicate that the step could be taken out of the task flowchart.
4. **Misleading Action (MA)** - adapted from [9]
   It occurs when the user clicks on an element that switches pages but quickly returns to the previous page. It may indicate that the element is misleading and causes doubt in the user.

4   Proposed Framework - *EmotiUsing*

The proposed framework takes into account primarily issues related to the potential of semi-automation of usability evaluations, considering the emotional aspects of users. Figure 1 presents the main parts of our framework, named *EmotiUsing*.

EmotiUsing refers to a conceptual framework that aims to help software developers during an usability evaluation with a broader perception of the users demonstrations. In particular, the recognition of the users demonstrations should be analyzed based on the emotions identified by processing data from brain signals captured from sensors positioned on the user's skull. These data will be

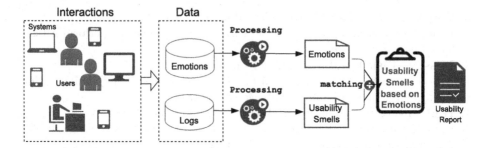

Fig. 1. *EmotiUsing* - the proposed framework to consider Users' emotions to find usability smells.

processed to compose usability analyses obtained together with log data collected during interactions by users in the system. The purpose is to assist in the judgment of expert evaluators during the inspection of usability problems. In general, to find potential usability problems, specialists must carry out a thorough and judicious work about the decision on the existence of the mentioned problems, demanding attention and judgment effort, as it involves subjective concepts. Above all, when inspecting the interface and interactions, experts must consider that potential target users have variations in their ways of interacting due to their emotional aspects and reacting during the use of the system.

EmotiUsing framework starts with an automated analysis to make a usability examination of Systems used by people. Thus, we have included procedures that allow users to interact with the system under evaluation to provide data collection. For this data collection, it is necessary to record the usage data (logs of interactions), and EEG[1] signals (brain waves that will consist of Emotions Data) obtained during user interaction.

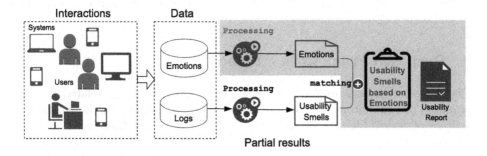

Fig. 2. The parts of *EmotiUsing* framework providing the initial results

---

[1] The acronym EEG refers to electroencephalogram, the graphic record of the electrical rhythms of the brain obtained by electroencephalography, through electrodes placed directly on the scalp, in specific points of the cranial vault.

In Fig. 2, we highlight the parts of *EmotiUsing* that have been postponed in this investigation. In this research, we focused on demonstrating the achievability of interaction logs processing in association with Emotional Data, which will be provided by experts' observations of Users interacting; in this initial procedure, we count on this manually data capture. The grayish parts compose a set of necessary procedures to evidence the feasibility of the whole framework. Once all data are collected, they must be processed in order to apply Machine Learning (ML) models in the search to identify possible patterns in the data that point out possible usability smells. In the end, the generated reports present the potential usability smells in the data. In this way, the evaluator will obtain the results of this analysis, and based on the information presented, it will be possible to decide and identify the real usability problems with greater ease and less subjectivity.

4.1 Implementation

In order to obtain the initial results of the proposed framework, we collected user interactions on social networking websites, capturing the interaction logs and EEG signals. In this paper, we start by investigation only log data in terms of its predictive power for detecting usability smells. Figure 3 shows the steps involved on this analysis. We describe all the processing steps next.

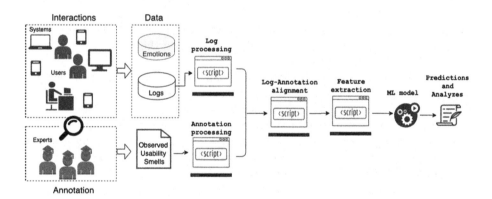

Fig. 3. Processing scheme of collected logs

Data Capture. To collect the user interaction logs we use the Wildfire browser extension,[2] available for Google Chrome and Firefox. Wildfire records the flow of actions done on the visited pages and allows the download of the collected logs in a single file, which is later converted to a JSON format.

To record the EEG signals during the user interaction, we use BITalino[3] along with its software application OpenSignals (r)evolution[4]. In order to not

---

[2] https://wildfire.ai/.
[3] http://www.bitalino.com/en/hardware.
[4] http://www.bitalino.com/en/software.

induce discomfort on the users side, we connect the hardware device and the software application via Bluetooth. After the interaction with the system, both the log data and the EEG signals are stored in two data sets, Logs and Emotions, which are pre-processed in order to be used by an ML system.

Log Processing. The data we store in the interaction logs dataset is processed by running a script that filters the collected events to discard unimportant information and standardize time formats. More precisely, we filter the events collected in the log by selecting the following event types: *URL change, input change, click, keypress,* and *scroll.*[5] After filtering these events, the script organizes the selected events into a sequence of episodes, which is made of a sequence of events. An episode starts with a *URL change* and ends with another *URL change* (leading to the next episode or to the end of the user session), and it can have many other types of events in between (as illustrated in Fig. 4).

Expert Annotation. The annotation of the perceived smells is a crucial part of our semi-automatic usability framework since it creates the ground truth labels that are used to train the ML models that predict the usability smells. Therefore, to seek a high quality annotation, we invited usability evaluation experts to participate in the annotation process. We provide an annotation guide to the experts that contains an introduction to the annotation process and the usability smells catalog along with their descriptions (Sect. 3). In order to minimize doubts regarding the annotation process, we share an example video where an expert exemplifies the annotation in the spreadsheet, and also the list of tasks that the user tried to follow in the website.

Given the context of the Covid-19 pandemic and the need for social distancing, we ask users to record the video of their interaction, and then we share the video with the experts for the annotation. After that, two or three experts watch the interaction of each of the users and annotate the usability smells in independent spreadsheets. We give the exact timestamp of the beginning of each task to the annotators, and then, for each task, they write down the set of smells they perceived, if any, along with their timestamps.

Annotation Processing. After obtaining the document *Observed Usability Smells*, with the usability smells annotated by the experts, we run a script that groups the spreadsheets of each annotator into a single spreadsheet.

Log-Annotation Alignment. To align the logs and the annotated smells from the previous steps, we run a script to mark labels for task-level and action-level smells as follows: for task-level smells, we iterate over episodes and mark which task the episode is part of and which smells were identified for that task; For

---

[5] Most keypress events are filtered out since the event *input change* already captures what was typed by the user after N keypresses. However, there are cases when keypresses are important, such as when the user press "enter" for submitting a form. In such cases, we kept the keypress event.

action-level smells, we iterate over the events inside each episode and mark their associated smells.

To decide the task an episode is a part of, we find the episode with the closest timestamp to the start timestamp of each task in a mutually exclusive way, such that no episode is aligned with two or more different tasks. Analogously, instead of aligning episodes with tasks-level smells, we align events with action-level smells by finding the event with the closest timestamp to the annotated action-smell's timestamp. Episodes and events not aligned with any smell receive the label "none". Therefore, we have episodes annotated with task-level smells and events annotated with action-level smells after this step. For clarification, we show a timeline representation of a simple sequence of episodes and events in Fig. 4 along with annotated smells.

Fig. 4. Example of log timeline with annotated smells

Feature Extraction. After aligning the collected logs with the smells annotated by the experts, we run a script to perform feature extraction to help the ML model to classify the possible usability smells. The script extracts global features that we deem valuable for detecting all types of usability smells and also features that are specific to specific types of usability smells (Sect. 3). Concretely, we extract the following global features at this step:

- **Event type:** URL change, click, input change, keypress, scroll.
- **Duration:** the difference in seconds from the current to the previous event.
- **Total duration:** duration from the first until the current event.
- **URL:** the URL where the event occurred.
- **CSS path:** the full CSS path of the DOM object.
- **DOM object:** the DOM object on which the event was performed, e.g., ⟨a⟩, ⟨div⟩, ⟨input⟩, ⟨button⟩, etc.
- **Event-type specific:** inner text, mouse button type, and xy-coordinates of the element on the window for *clicks*; inner text and value for *input changes*; scroll time for *scrolls*.

With this information, we are able to create two representations of our data, a timeline representation as depicted in Fig. 4, and a directed multi-graph representation depicted in Fig. 5, where the nodes represent DOM objects (identified by their CSS path) and the edges represent successive events that occurred between a pair of DOM objects. Note that besides being a directed graph whose arrows indicate the direction of time, the graph can have multiple edges between two nodes when the two objects occur in two or more events during an episode. In the graph representation, episodes are delimited by URL change edges, meaning that the occurrence of URL changes creates a bridge between connected components.

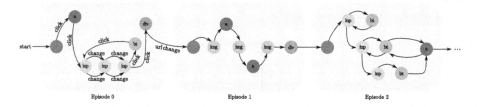

Fig. 5. Example of a graph representation for a sequence of episodes and events.

Given the graph representation, we also extracted features that rely on a node's neighborhood. Concretely, we extract information about the degree of a node (its number of adjacent edges), how many cycles a node is a part of, the average duration of the neighborhood, the average HTML distance computed from the CSS path, and whether all neighbors have the same event type. Furthermore, for *clicks* and *input changes*, we compute the string similarity between their inner text with neighbors' inner text using the Levenshtein distance and save the information of the number of keypresses and the length of the inner text, which can be useful to identify repetition in forms.

ML Model. After extracting the features of all user sessions for all websites, we pass the features as inputs to an ML model, which is trained to predict the labels annotated by the experts. Ideally, our ML classifier should be: (i) fast, in order to process a considerable amount of data (as logs tend to generate several events); (ii) interpretable, so that humans can analyze the learned associations between features and labels; (iii) flexible, to be able to consider the structure of the input, which in our case is a chain of events or a multi directed graph.

The ML model predicts task-level smells for entire episodes, whereas action-level predictions are made for each event. In the final step, the outputs produced by the classifier are organized into a report that includes the model's overall performance, a visualization of the most important features, and an error analysis disentangled by usability smells.

5 Experiments: Validating Framework

Systems. We designed a simple and open-source social network for this research, called Perspective,[6] in which we deliberately introduce usability issues that should reflect in the presence of usability smells during the user interaction. In our social network, users can search and add friends, see profiles, send private messages to friends, add photos, create HTML-rich posts on their profile or on a friend's timeline, comment and like posts, and change account information. Since our designed website is relatively simple in terms of the possible interactions, we also record interactions on another two public available websites, Social-Network[7] and Love-Social.[8] Although all three websites are simple social networks, we made sure that all of them had usability issues before recording user interactions.

Users. Due to the need for social distancing raised by the Covid-19 pandemic, most of the interactions were recorded on the personal computers of each user online, without interventions and close guidance. Notably, this aspect also made it impossible to collect EEG signals for some users since it requires physical contact between the user and BITalino sensors. Before the user session started, we shared a guide with the user containing the instructions to capture the interaction and a list of tasks that the user should try to perform on the website, with the possibility of skipping to the next task or ending the session if the user deems relevant. These tasks include, for example, signing up in the social network, adding a friend, posting a message on a friend's timeline, adding a profile picture, logging out, etc. We describe 17 tasks in the Perspective, 16 tasks in Social-Network, and 10 in Love-Social.

We had the participation of 14 users, 5 of them female (2 interacting with Perspective, 2 with Social-Network, and 1 with Love-Social), and 9 male, as the users themselves informed in the characterization form of the participant. The ages of the participants vary between 20 and 34 years, with an average of 27 years. As for the academic background of the participants, two have completed high school, 3 are undergraduate, 2 have an undergraduate degree, and 7 have a graduate degree.

When we asked users about the frequency of computer use, 12 say they use it daily, and the other 2 say they use it rarely (Perspective and Social-Network). As for the judgment itself about the experience in using technological devices, 11 users claimed to be experienced, while 2 (Perspective and Social-Network) claimed to have moderate experience, and another claimed to be a beginner (Social-Network).

---

[6] https://github.com/flassantos/perspective.

[7] https://github.com/misa-j/social-network.

[8] https://github.com/red-gold/react-social-network.

5.1   Dataset

To compose the first dataset of our research, we combined all 14 user interactions from the three social networks. Table 1 summarizes our data after the log processing step.

Table 1. Data statistics after the log processing step.

				Count				
Website	Users	Tasks	Duration	Episode	Click	Input ch.	Keypr.	Scroll
Perspective	6	17	02:03:46	274	812	347	12	306
Social-network	6	16	02:13:20	329	1497	218	57	162
Love-social	2	10	00:37:25	129	305	26	0	61
Overall	14	43	04:54:31	732	2614	591	69	529
				15%	52%	21%	1%	11%

Considering the three social networks, 10 to 17 tasks were performed, with a total of 732 episodes (average of 52 ± 14 per user), 3804 events (average of 272 ± 82), 2614 clicks (average of 187 ± 74), 591 input changes (average 42 ± 19), 69 valid keypresses (average 5 ± 8), 529 scrolls (average of 38 ± 20), and an interaction time of 08h:53m:17s (average of 33m:36s $\pm$ 13m:17s). We noticed that the interaction time varies between different types of events, as depicted in Fig. 6 for each social network, where we see that URL changes usually take longer in all social networks, followed closely by clicks since clicks are the main predecessors of URL changes..[9] In contrast, most input changes and scrolls tend to have a short duration. Notably, URL changes are tied to each network and user session since the Internet connection can affect the results.

Annotated Usability Smells. We show the statistics of the annotated task-level and action-level usability smells per website aggregated by all experts in Table 2.

We see that task-level smells occur as frequent as action-level smells (301 vs 300 in total). Nevertheless, action-level smells have a higher imbalance since the proportion of events associated with smells is very low (only 4%). In Fig. 7 we investigate the relation between the duration of episodes and events associated with task-level and action-level smells, respectively. As expected from their definition, we noticed that Laborious Tasks, Too Many Layers, and Late Validation reflect in episodes with a longer duration. Similarly, the longest events are mostly associated with Misleading Actions, which is also expected since this smell usually leads to undesired URL changes.

---

[9] The duration considered here is the difference in time between the current and the next event.

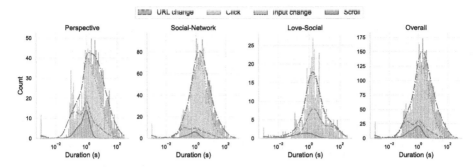

Fig. 6. Distribution of the duration of different event types for each website and overall.

Table 2. Data statistics after the annotation processing step. "None" represents the absence of smell. For action-level smells, we have a percentage of 96% "none" labels.

Website	# Task-level smells								# Action-level smells			
	LT	CT	TML	MTF	HID	RTF	LV	None	UE	MAF	UA	MA
Perspective	46	11	18	39	11	15	33	162	45	34	16	78
Social-network	29	5	26	14	16	1	10	140	27	30	12	26
Love-social	7	1	6	7	2	2	2	26	2	16	5	9
Overall	82	17	50	60	29	18	45	328	74	80	33	113
	13%	3%	8%	9%	5%	3%	7%	52%	24%	27%	11%	38%

Agreement Between Annotators. We invited eleven usability experts to annotate usability smells for each website. However, these experts differ for distinct users, and some experts annotated only a single session. Therefore, it becomes unfeasible to compare the agreement between different annotators. To circumvent this issue, we invited a single usability expert that was familiar with our research to annotate all user sessions from all websites. We call this expert the **main annotator**. Since our annotation scheme allows multiple smells for a single episode/event, we computed the agreement between the main annotator and the other annotators via the following three metrics:

- **Exact-match (percent agreement):** computes the percentage of exact-matches between the two annotators, where a match happens we the two sets are equal: $\frac{1}{N}\sum_{i=1}^{n} 1(A_i = B_i)$, for two annotators A and B. This metric ranges from 0 to 1, where 1 indicates a perfect agreement and 0 indicates total disagreement.
- **Intersect-over-union (weighted percent agreement):** computes the percentage of exact-matches weighted by $|A_i \cap B_i|/|A_i \cup B_i|$. This metric ranges from 0 to 1, where 1 indicates a perfect agreement and 0 indicates total disagreement.
- **Krippendorff's alpha (inter-rater agreement):** computes the agreement between any number of annotators and categories [14]. This metric ranges from -1 to 1, with 0 representing the absence of reliability.

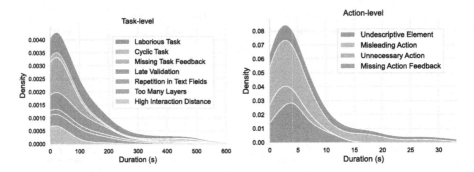

Fig. 7. Distribution of the duration of different episodes and events categorized by usability smell. Task-level smells have a longer duration since they represent the total duration of an episode (which contains several events), whereas action-level smells are linked to a single event.

Since the first two metrics are computed only for two annotators, we averaged the results between the main annotator and the two annotators for user sessions with three annotators. Moreover, the first two metrics give the same weight for matches of "none" labels (i.e., when both sets are empty). Since the "none" label is the most frequent label in our dataset, we weigh down the correct matches for "none" by a factor of 0.4. The overall results are shown in Table 3.

Table 3. Agreement between the main annotator and the other annotators in terms of accuracy (Acc.), intersect-over-union (IOU), and Krippendorff's alpha (K'α).

Website	Acc	IOU	K'α
Perspective	0.42 ± 0.03	0.48 ± 0.04	0.34 ± 0.10
Social-network	0.60 ± 0.11	0.64 ± 0.06	0.16 ± 0.22
Love-social	0.26 ± 0.04	0.31 ± 0.05	0.11 ± 0.04
Overall	0.48 ± 0.15	0.52 ± 0.13	0.23 ± 0.18

Overall, the results in Table 3 indicate that our annotation can be improved substantially. Krippendorff's alpha is a more punitive metric, and thus it is usually lower than the other two. This also indicates that "none" labels are boosting accuracy and IOU. Among these three metrics, we believe that IOU better reflects our annotation since it is not as punitive as Krippendrorff's alpha and yet is not as simple as accuracy. In order to see how each usability smell affects the annotation agreement, we computed Cohen's kappa [6], an inter-annotator agreement measure for two annotators, by ablating one usability smell at a time. The results are shown in Fig. 8. We can see that experts disagree more on some smells than others and that overall, there is more disagreement for action-level than task-level smells. According to [15], Cohen's kappa levels can be interpreted as follows: slight (0.0–0.2), fair (0.2–0.4), moderate (0.4–0.6), substantial (0.6–0.8), and almost perfect (0.8–1.0). Given this interpretation, we noticed that experts have a slight agreement on average for TML, MTF, and HID and most of the action-level smells.

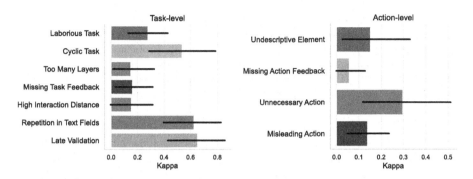

Fig. 8. Cohen's kappa scores by ablating usability smells one at a time. Black lines represents standard deviation.

A possible explanation for the low agreement scores is the source of the subjectivity of the task: usability smells are perceived differently between people, even among experts. Nevertheless, these initial results suggest that our annotation guidelines should be revised, especially for action-level smells. Another factor that could be revised is the alignment between episodes/events and smells. That is, since the annotators have to write down an approximate time of the occurrence of the usability smell, the alignment algorithm might link different events for different annotators since the difference in time is in seconds. We plan to improve the annotation format by letting the annotator inform a time window rather than a timestamp to circumvent this issue. Besides helping the aligning algorithm, this strategy is easier for the annotator and can reduce the number of overlapping usability smells, benefiting the downstream ML model.

5.2 ML Model

Daily, user interactions usually happen in well-developed applications where usability issues are less pronounced. As shown in Table 2, even in our manually-designed application, task-level usability smells appeared only at ∼ 50% of the time, divided into portions associated with distinct usability smells, characterizing an imbalanced classification problem where the "none" smell is the majority label. Similarly, predicting action-level smells characterizes a highly imbalanced classification problem since the vast majority of events are not associated with any smell (approx. 96% in our dataset). Moreover, episodes and events can be marked with one or more smells, characterizing a multilabel classification problem, which increases the size of the output space exponentially, complicating training. For these reasons, we remodeled our dataset with three different types of classification problems that depend on the granularity of the label set, as defined in Table 4 for task and action-level smells, with the hope that reducing the output space leads to a more accurate model

Table 4. Label sets for each type of classification problem, where L represents the number of labels, n represents the number of smells considered for each level, whereas Demanding Task (DT) = {LT, CT, TML, HID, RTF}, Problematic Feedback (PF) = {MTF, LV}, Problematic Task (PT) = {DT, PF} are subsets for task-level smells, and Deceptive Action (DA) = {UE, MA}, Problematic Feedback (PF) = {MAF, UA}, Problematic Action = {DT, PF} are subsets for action-level smells.

Problem	L	Task-level	Action-level
Binary	2	{"has smell", "no smell"}	{"has smell", "no smell"}
Multiclass	n	{DT, PF, PT, "none"}	{DA, PF, PA, "none"}
Multilabel	2^n	{LT, CT, TML, MTF, HID, RTF, LV}	{UE, MAF, UA, MA}

As discussed in Sect. 4.1, our ML models would ideally consider the entire structure of the input, meaning that the model would consider the timeline or the graph representation in order to generate a prediction. However, in our first study, we relax this constraint and choose simpler yet fast and interpretable models that use global features from neighboring events, since nearby events usually contain helpful information about the current event (e.g., the current event is a click and the next event is a URL change). Concretely, we compared the following classifiers: Decision Trees, Logistic Regression, Linear SVM, and Random Forest. They all have the advantage of being fast and interpretable, either by looking at the most important features or their associated coefficients. Our models were implemented with Scikit-Learn [20].

5.3   Results

Given the class imbalance and the small amount of trainable data, in this first work, we focus on the two simpler settings described in Table 4, namely, binary and multiclass classification. Although the finer-grained multilabel classification is our end goal, we leave it as future work as we collect more data. Moreover, since we do not have standard validation and test sets, we perform a stratified 5-fold cross-validation for evaluating our models. Beyond using accuracy, we also used precision, recall, and F_1 (harmonic mean between precision and recall) to evaluate the performance of our models, since these metrics are more robust to class imbalance.

Binary Classification. For this setting, we adopt a simple baseline that predicts a uniform distribution that follows the empirical distribution of the gold labels, setting a percentage p of the inputs as "has smell" and $1 - p$ as "no smell". The distribution of smells for task-level is perfectly balanced ($p = 50\%$), but the distribution of smells for action-level is imbalanced ($p = 11\%$). Table 5 shows the results in terms of accuracy, precision, recall, and F_1 for both task and action-level data.

Table 5. Binary classification results for task-level and action-level data.

Model	Task-level				Action-level			
	Acc.	Prec.	Rec.	F_1	Acc.	Prec.	Rec.	F_1
Baseline	0.50	0.50	0.51	0.50	0.51	0.11	0.51	0.18
Decision tree	0.58	0.58	0.59	0.58	0.83	0.32	0.46	0.38
Logistic regression	0.58	0.57	0.72	0.63	0.90	0.54	0.52	0.52
SVM	0.58	0.57	0.72	0.63	0.90	0.54	0.53	0.52
Random forest	0.63	0.64	0.69	0.65	0.91	0.61	0.52	0.54

Overall, the Random Forest model obtained the best results for task and action-level settings in terms of accuracy and F_1. The recall values of the baseline were close to those of the tested models. However, it presents a lower precision. Since the baseline considers the empirical distribution of labels in its prediction, the baseline will benefit labels of this majority class in an unbalanced problem, achieving high recall scores.

By comparing the performance of our models on task and action-level smells, we noted that they usually perform better for task-level, despite these being closer to the baseline values. This probably occurs because it is easier to predict the presence of smells in an entire task than in a specific action, as seen during the annotation phase and the highly imbalanced label distribution.

After investigating the behavior of our models, we observed that the most relevant features were those related to the duration times of the current event and its neighbors. The models also deemed important features related to the number of occurrences of URL changes, clicks, and input changes.

We consider the results to be positive since identifying the existence of usability smells is a subjective task, and we did not obtain even high scores of agreement between the annotators. However, from the point of view of evaluators and developers, it is sought that the model is able to predict which smells occur in each of the tasks and not only if there is a problem with them. Therefore, we experimented with a more fine-grained classification next.

Multiclass Classification. We adopted the same baseline as in binary classification, but now the baseline adopts a categorical distribution over L labels. The label distribution for task-level is: "none" (50%), DT (34%), PF (8%), PT (8%). For action-level, the distribution is more skewed: "none" (96%), DA (2%), PF

(2%), PA (<0%). More precisely, PAs occurred only twice in our dataset; therefore, we opted to drop the two samples associated with them. Table 6 summarizes the results with macro-averages across classes.

Table 6. Multiclass classification results for task-level and action-level data.

Model	Task-level				Action-level			
	Acc.	Prec.	Rec.	F_1	Acc.	Prec.	Rec.	F_1
Baseline	0.25	0.26	0.27	0.26	0.33	0.33	0.32	0.33
Decision tree	0.42	0.28	0.30	0.28	0.86	0.33	0.34	0.33
Logistic regression	0.38	0.32	0.35	0.33	0.91	0.33	0.32	0.33
Linear SVM	0.45	0.28	0.27	0.27	0.92	0.33	0.33	0.33
Random forest	0.49	0.34	0.32	0.33	0.96	0.32	0.33	0.33

As presented in Table 6, we obtained better results with Logistic Regression and Random Forest models for task-level, both with $F_1 = 0.33$, above the baseline ($F_1 = 0.26$). However, for action-level, our results were not higher than those obtained by the baseline, despite the models having higher accuracy. In contrast, the values of precision and recall are very similar. These results indicate that our models were not able to discretize between the possible usability smells.

Furthermore, as with binary classification, the results are higher for task-level than action-level smells, probably due to the same reasons, which were also aggravated with an even more skewed distribution since we have more labels now. We consider that the results obtained with multiclass classification need to be significantly improved before we proceed to multilabel classification. The small dataset size considered in this work is one of the perceived limitations for finer-grained classification.

6   Conclusions

This work presents the *EmotiUsing* framework, which aims to help software developers with a broader perception of the users' demonstrations during a usability evaluation. We present the implementation of log processing, an integral part of this framework, and the results obtained from this implementation.

Based on the literature and our experience, we selected 11 usability smells that we considered not easily explained by manually-designed rules to predict automatically using ML models. Thus, we had the participation of 14 users to collect data and compose a dataset used for training and evaluation of the models tested in this work. We invited usability evaluation experts to participate in the annotation of the data, marking the smells identified in the tasks performed by the users. We obtained a dataset with approximately five hours of user interactions in three different social networks. After aligning the logs obtained from the interactions with the annotation performed by the experts, we calculated the agreement between the annotators and selected features that we used in the ML models tested.

The alignment of logs and annotations posed a challenge in our work, especially for action-level smells, which are linked to single events. The alignment step plays an essential role in this work since if it is not done precisely, it will change all the results obtained, including the annotation agreement scores.

We experimented with two types of classification in our experiments: binary classification and a more fine-grained approach, which performs multiclass classification on a subset of usability smells. Our results show that identifying the existence of usability smells is feasible, even with a small dataset. However, predicting specific usability smells proved to be a more difficult task, especially for action-level smells, which occur substantially less in user interactions.

To mitigate the issues found in this paper, in future work, we intend to follow the following steps: (i) review annotation guidelines; (ii) collect more data with more users; (iii) review the set of features; (iv) experiment more flexible ML models that consider the entire sequence of interactions automatically. In addition, we will investigate the relationship between users' emotions and usability smells, seeking to reduce the subjectivity of the evaluation. With this, we will make room for the end goal of this research, which is to detect usability smells and their types, considering users' emotions.

References

1. Almeida, D., Campos, J.C., Saraiva, J.A., Silva, J.A.C.: Towards a catalog of usability smells. In: Proceedings of the 30th Annual ACM Symposium on Applied Computing (SAC 2015), pp. 175–181. Association for Computing Machinery, New York (2015)

2. Amare, N., Manning, A.: Emotion-spectrum response to form and color: implications for usability. In: International Professional Communication Conference, pp. 1–9. IEEE Computer Society, Los Alamitos (2009). https://doi.org/10.1109/IPCC.2009.5208700

3. Balomenos, T., Raouzaiou, A., Ioannou, S., Drosopoulos, A., Karpouzis, K., Kollias, S.: Emotion analysis in man-machine interaction systems. In: Bengio, S., Bourlard, H. (eds.) MLMI 2004. LNCS, vol. 3361, pp. 318–328. Springer, Heidelberg (2005). https://doi.org/10.1007/978-3-540-30568-2_27

4. Cassino, R., Tucci, M., Vitiello, G., Francese, R.: Empirical validation of an automatic usability evaluation method. J. Vis. Lang. Comput. **28**, 1–22 (2015)

5. Champney, R.K., Stanney, K.M.: Using emotions in usability. Proc. Hum. Fact. Ergon. Soc. Annu. Meet. **51**(17), 1044–1049 (2007)

6. Cohen, J.: A coefficient of agreement for nominal scales. Educ. Psychol. Measur. **20**(1), 37–46 (1960)

7. Elfaki, A.O., Bassfar, Z.: Auto-measuring usability method based on runtime user's behavior: case Study for governmental web-based information systems. J. Theor. Appl. Inf. Technol. **97**(13) (2019)

8. Gardey, J.C., Garrido, A.: User experience evaluation through automatic A/B testing. In: Proceedings of the 25th International Conference on Intelligent User Interfaces Companion, pp. 25–26 (2020)

9. Grigera, J., Garrido, A., Rivero, J.M., Rossi, G.: Automatic detection of usability smells in web applications. Int. J. Hum. Comput. Stud. **97**, 129–148 (2017)
10. Harms, P.: Automated field usability evaluation using generated task trees (2016)
11. Harms, P.: Automated usability evaluation of virtual reality applications. ACM Trans. Comput. Hum. Interact. **26**(3), 1–36 (2019)
12. Jeong, J., Kim, N., In, H.P.: Detecting usability problems in mobile applications on the basis of dissimilarity in user behavior. Int. J. Hum. Comput. Stud. **139**, 102364 (2020)
13. Johanssen, J.O., Bernius, J.P., Bruegge, B.: Toward usability problem identification based on user emotions derived from facial expressions. In: 2019 IEEE/ACM 4th International Workshop on Emotion Awareness in Software Engineering (SEmotion), pp. 1–7. IEEE, Montreal (2019)
14. Krippendorff, K.: Computing krippendorff's alpha-reliability (2011)
15. Landis, J.R., Koch, G.G.: The measurement of observer agreement for categorical data. Biometrics 159–174 (1977)
16. Landowska, A., Miler, J.: Limitations of emotion recognition in software user experience evaluation context. In: Federated Conference on Computer Science and Information Systems (FedCSIS), pp. 1631–1640. IEEE (2016)
17. Lunarejo, M.I.L., dos Santos Neto, P.d.A., de Britto, R.S., Avelino, G.: Automatic detection of usability smells in web applications running in mobile devices. In: Anais do XVI Simpósio Brasileiro de Sistemas de Informação, pp. 324–331 (2020)
18. Nielsen, J.: Usability 101: Introduction to Usability, pp. 1–10. Nielsen Norman Group (2012)
19. Paternò, F., Schiavone, A.G., Conti, A.: Customizable automatic detection of bad usability smells in mobile accessed web applications. In: Proceedings of the 19th International Conference on Human-Computer Interaction with Mobile Devices and Services, pp. 1–11. ACM (2017)
20. Pedregosa, F., et al.: Scikit-learn: machine learning in python. J. Mach. Learn. Res. **12**, 2825–2830 (2011)
21. Ribeiro, R.F., Souza, M.d.M.C., de Oliveira, P.A.M., dos Santos Neto, P.d.A.: Usability problems discovery based on the automatic detection of usability smells. In: Proceedings of the 34th ACM/SIGAPP Symposium on Applied Computing, pp. 2328–2335. ACM (2019)
22. Sailunaz, K., Dhaliwal, M., Rokne, J., Alhajj, R.: Emotion detection from text and speech: a survey. Soc. Netw. Anal. Min. **8**(1), 1–26 (2018). https://doi.org/10.1007/s13278-018-0505-2
23. de Santana, V.F., Baranauskas, M.C.C.: WELFIT: a remote evaluation tool for identifying Web usage patterns through client-side logging. Int. J. Hum. Comput. Stud. **76**, 40–49 (2015)

Research on Speech Interaction Design Based on Emotion

Genping Bo[1][✉] and Xianan Xu[2]

[1] School of Design Art and Media, University of Science and Technology, Nanjing 210094, Jiangsu, China
1498945731@qq.com
[2] School of Architecture and Art, Liaoning University of Science and Technology, Anshan 114044, Liaoning, China

Abstract. To study the influence of personification degree on user experience in voice interaction design, strengthen human-computer relationship, provide users with an emotional voice interaction experience, and then provide reference for the future application of voice interaction design. Methods: The anthropomorphic factors such as the speed of machine feedback and the design of virtual character model in the process of voice interaction were used as indicators. Combining psychology with user interviews and questionnaires, we can understand the attitude of users and make qualitative evaluation of subjective feelings. Secondly, quantitative evaluation is carried out through experimental tests, and online SPSS AU is used to analyze the measurement index data, and reliable results are obtained. Conclusion: Emotional interaction will improve users' pleasure to a certain extent, Users tend to use voice assistants that are closer to real-life interaction; Most users tend to adapt the volume; In terms of volume and speed, users prefer S4 = 180 words/min. As the degree of personification increases, the user's pleasure also increases correspondingly. The user pleasure of voice assistants with high degree of personification is significantly higher than that of voice assistants with medium or low degree of personification; Users' satisfaction with female voice assistants is higher than that of male voice assistants.

Keywords: Voice interaction · User experience · Degree of personification · Emotional design

1 Preface

With the development of computer technology, the interaction between human and machine is becoming more natural and easy to use. At the same time, great changes have taken place in the way of human-computer interaction, from traditional command line to touch gesture to voice interaction, which liberated the use of hands and eyes to a certain extent. The lower learning cost and smoother interactive experience presented by human-computer interaction make the human-computer interaction stronger and the human-computer relationship closer.

M. Kurosu (Ed.): HCII 2022, LNCS 13302, pp. 439–449, 2022.
https://doi.org/10.1007/978-3-031-05311-5_30

Voice interaction is closer to the expression of natural language, which embodies emotional interaction and conveys information to users with emotion, thus improving users' liking. However, at present, most intelligent voice products still have many shortcomings in interactive experience, such as mechanization of feedback form and stereotyped answers to many questions. Therefore, it is an important topic in voice interaction design to improve the interaction degree between voice interaction products and users, make them close to the mode of real-life dialogue and enhance the interactive experience.

This study takes smart home voice assistants as the research object, and analyzes the influence of voice interaction assistants with different personification degrees on user experience.

2   Current Research Status of Voice Interaction

With the progress of science and technology, voice user interface has developed rapidly in recent years. It skillfully uses artificial intelligence technology and adds emotional compensation mechanism [1], which is favored by the masses and widely used in various intelligent product designs. A voice assistant with better user experience will greatly improve the user's loyalty.

Voice is the simplest and most natural communication mode between people. Sound contains not only semantic information, but also a lot of emotional information. Romportl [2] experiment shows that most people tend to choose more natural sounds, and the proportion of subjects with high education level or computer professional background who like natural sounds is larger. At present, the related research on human-computer emotional interaction and voice emotional interaction mainly focuses on the pattern recognition and emotional calculation of artificial intelligence, synthesizing the robot's "emotion" through algorithms and various emotional models, and paying more attention to the basic attributes of sound such as basic frequency, duration, sound quality and clarity [3]. However, from the user-centered point of view, Emotion actually involves two dimensions, that is, the user feels the emotion conveyed by the robot and the user's own instinctive emotional feedback. The former is embodied in perceived social support and perceived emotional support; The latter is reflected in the user's subjective emotional representation in the interactive process. Ghost S et al. [3, 4] from Samsung found that for mobile phone voice assistants, Steady, professional and rational characters are more popular with users, and the personality and emotion of virtual assistants should not be displayed too much. Niculescu et al. [5] conducted a group of experiments on the hotel inquiry robot, and studied the influence of social robot's tone, humor and compassion on user experience. Lee et al. [6] think that for smart home products, Emotion and companionship are the key influencing factors of user satisfaction. Niculescu A et al. [5, 7] found that an extroverted and humorous social robot would make users give higher evaluation to the overall interaction quality, attractiveness and overall user experience. However, these findings are based on communication-focused voice assistants. At present, there are few researches on emotional interaction patterns between voice assistants and users.

3   Voice Interaction Based on Emotion

Human-computer interaction includes active voice interaction and passive voice interaction [8]. Passive voice interaction includes five links: arousal, response, input, understanding and feedback. Active voice interaction consists of six links, including situational awareness, reverse arousal, response, output, feedback and action. The specific voice interaction process (see Fig. 1). Each terminal has its own task line and task link in the task, and the voice interaction is divided into two modes: conversation mode and command control mode. The dialogue mode is to complete the interactive process of question-and-answer and realize the smooth communication between man and machine.

Command control mode means that the user inputs commands by voice, and the device gives feedback in time. In order to create a more natural and emotional voice interaction, around the emotional experience design, experiments were conducted with anthropomorphic factors such as machine feedback speed and virtual character model meter as indicators, and the voice interaction design that satisfied users was summarized.

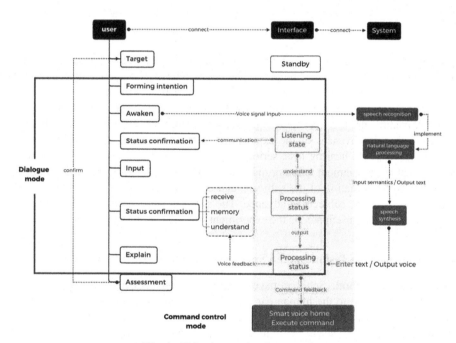

Fig. 1. Voice interaction framework

4   The Influence of Personification Degree on User Satisfaction

4.1   Experimental Purpose

The key to personification is to inject human characteristics, motivation, behavior and emotion into specific non-human carriers (such as artificial machines, virtual images, etc.) [9]. Through the qualitative and quantitative experiments on the subjects, the following tasks are mainly discussed, and the intelligent voice interaction mode favored by users is summarized, so that users can feel the emotion conveyed by the robot more natural, and users can carry out instinctive emotional feedback in the interaction process to reduce the understanding cost:

Task 1: What is the speed of voice interaction that will make users feel comfortable.

Task 2: The influence of the degree of personification of voice interaction assistant on users' emotions.

Task 3: Whether it is set as a custom wake-up word, and whether the custom wake-up word is easier to remember.

4.2   Participating Users

The objects of this experimental research are all selected from the undergraduate students of the school of design art and media of Nanjing University of technology. 20 subjects are selected, which is in line with the basic characteristics of the target user group of the current voice interactive application products. Because the subjects are all students of our university and there are few subjects, this research has some limitations. In order to ensure the effectiveness of the experiment to the greatest extent, and ensure that the subjects have no hearing loss, serious cognitive impairment and mental condition. Select a stable environment with normal light and no noise, set the experimental volume according to the situation of the subjects, and communicate the experimental purpose and process with the subjects in advance. The subjects were given a paid experiment, and each user who participated in the experiment was given a storage bag as a thank-you.

4.3   Experiment 1: Test of Speech Speed Comfort of Voice Interactive Feedback

Experimental Method. Scholars have come to the conclusion that the speech speed generally acceptable to the human ear is 250 words/min. The author sets this conclusion as the maximum speech speed of this experiment, and one speed is set every 35 words/min, and six speeds are set in total. The speaking speed from slow to fast is $S1 = 75$ words/min, $S2 = 110$ words/min, $S3 = 145$ words/min, $S4 = 180$ words/min, $S5 = 215$ words/min and $S6 = 250$ words/min. Finally, the design adopts the dual comparison experiment method, That is, each test user is asked to choose the most comfortable speech speed among the six speech speeds by pairwise comparison: the six-speed collocation is divided into three groups, namely S1 and S4, S2 and S5, S3 and S6; After listening to a group of phonetic materials, the test user selects the speech speed that feels more comfortable, and gets three comfortable speech speed files after the first round; In the second round, pairwise comparison is made between the comfortable gears in the first round, Get the most comfortable speech speed file for the test user. In the experiment, adjust the volume according to the specific situation of the subjects, and interview the subjects one by one after the experiment.

Experimental Materials and Tools. Select a paragraph from the book Health for the Elderly as the experimental sample material, with similar words (about 100 words) (see Fig. 2). Read at six different speech speeds.

The study found that adding milk to tea was more helpful.
In response to the research report, some nutritionists said that drinking tea is of course beneficial to the elderly in preventing osteoporosis, but to prevent fractures, drinking tea alone is
not enough. The elderly should also supplement appropriate calcium and vitamin D, limit
drinking, do not smoke and maintain appropriate physical exercise.

Fig. 2. Experimental sample materials

There are great differences between machines and people in pronunciation and intonation. In order to ensure the authenticity of subjects in the experiment, machine reading is also used. "Xunfei Yuji" APP can read text materials by machine, and can choose different reading roles, allowing adjustment of reading speed. Therefore, this study uses "Xunfei Language Record" APP as a testing tool to conduct the speech speed experiment. By calculating the relationship formula between the speech speed gear of Xunfei Language Record and the actual speech speed, we can get the corresponding speech speed gear of S1, S2, S3, S4, S5 and S6 in Xunfei Language Record, as shown in Table 1. The formula is as follows:

$$Vr = 98.255 + 2.399Vx \tag{1}$$

Among them, Vr represents the actual speech speed, and Vx represents the speech speed gear in Xunfei's transcript.

Table 1. S1–S6 the corresponding speech speed gear in Xunfei's transcript

Speed number	Actual speech speed (words/min)	Xunfei Yu Ji Yu su dang Ji
S1	75	0
S2	110	5
S3	145	19
S4	180	34
S5	215	49
S6	250	63

Note: Because the lowest gear of Xunfei's register is 0, and the gears are all integers, the calculation results are all about equal numbers

4.4 Experiment 2: The Influence of the Personification of Virtual Character Model on User Satisfaction

Experimental Method. In this experiment, three kinds of intelligent product voice interaction roles with different personification degrees, high, medium and low, are designed. Personality characteristics [10] are set up from three aspects: personality building, empathy feedback and self-expression, and the questions set up in the experiment are answered. The question is, what's the weather like today? See Table 2 for three kinds of virtual portraits. The portraits of virtual characters with different personification levels are set to male and female groups, and each subject has a conversation with the constructed portraits. There are six groups of experiments. After the task of each test group is completed, it is necessary to score the emotional experience caused by the current role assistant from two aspects of self-assessment manikin, SAM). Using the nine-point scale, the degree of pleasure of 1 point means that people are very unhappy, upset, dissatisfied, sad and disappointed. A score of 9 means that people feel very happy, happy, satisfied, proud and full of hope. Awakening degree of 1 indicates that people feel calm, relaxed, not alert, with little irritation and the least amount of attention; The 9-point representative is extremely exciting, exciting, interesting, awakening, exciting and bright.

Table 2. Intelligent product voice interactive virtual character portrait

Portrait of figures	character trait	Anthropomorphic degree	Question answer
Auspicious (female), wishful (male)	Enthusiasm and initiative	Tall	It's sunny and cloudy with light rain. Remember to bring your umbrella. Are you going to Beijing? What's the matter?
Flower (female), wealth (male)	Thoughtful and passive	Middle	It's sunny and cloudy, with light rain. Remember to take an umbrella and pay attention to safety
Xiaofeng (female), Xiaolong (male)	High cold and professional	Low	It's sunny and cloudy with light rain. Remember to bring an umbrella

Experimental Materials and Tools. The experimental equipment is still tested with the "Xunfei Language Record" APP in the first experiment, and the speakers who match three characters in the APP are Jixiang-Sister Next Door, Ruyi-Male Anchor, Huahua-Fennel, Fugui-Xiaoxianrou, Xiaofeng-Teacher Wang and Xiaolong-Guo Jia. Enter the set answers in the "Xunfei Language Record" APP respectively.

Questionnaire Design. After the task of each test group is completed, the questionnaire will be compiled with the 7-point Likert scale, and will be filled out after each round of dialogue. The questionnaire contains five items, as shown in Table 3. The questionnaire was selected from SASII scale, ITU MOS scale and USE scale which were translated by Liao Qinglin and others and passed the reliability test.

Table 3. Questionnaire design

Item	Formulation	Source
S1	I think this smart home assistant is emotional	SASII scale [11]
S2	I think this smart home assistant is positive and outgoing	
S3	I think this smart home assistant is like a real assistant	ITU MOS scale [12]
S4	I think this smart home assistant works in the way I expect	USE scale [13, 14]
S5	This smart home assistant is pleasant to use	

4.5 Experimental Results and Data Analysis

Test of Speech Speed Comfort of Voice Interactive Feedback. In two rounds of experiments, the subjects chose S4 as the most comfortable speech speed among six different speech speeds (see Fig. 3). It can be seen from the figure that users feel comfortable with S2 and S4, that is, 110 words/min and 180 words/min, among which S4 appears the most frequently. According to interviews with subjects, it is found that most users tend to adapt the volume. In terms of volume and speed of speech, I don't like too high or too low a voice, too fast or too slow a speech rate. The experimental data shows that the speech rate S4 = 180 words/min is the most comfortable for users.

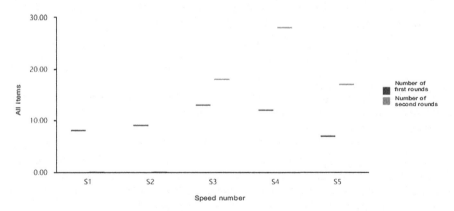

Fig. 3. Number of comfort choices for different speech speed gears.

The Influence of Personification of Virtual Character Model on User Satisfaction. In the experiment, the normality test was carried out for the degree of personification, pleasure and arousal. As shown in Table 4, the subjective scores of the three personification degrees were used to analyze the influence of the three personification degrees of medium, high and low on the subjects' pleasure and arousal.

Table 4. Results of normal test analysis

Name	Sample size	Average value	Standard deviation	Skewness	Kurtosis	Kolmo Golov test		Sharp test	
						Statistical d value	P	W value of statistic	P
Anthropomorphic degree	6	3.500	1.871	0.000	−1.200	0.122	0.996	0.982	0.961
Pleasure degree	6	3.958	2.250	0.226	−1.170	0.186	0.741	0.956	0.785
Awakening degree	6	5.292	2.835	−0.556	−1.076	0.232	0.393	0.939	0.654

It can be seen from the above table that the sample size of the research data is all less than or equal to 50, so the S-W test is used. Specifically, the degree of personification, pleasure and arousal are all not significant ($p > 0.05$), which means that the original hypothesis (original hypothesis: normal distribution of data), the degree of personification, pleasure and arousal are all normal.

Table 5. Linear regression coefficient

	Non-standardized coefficient		Standardized coefficient	t	p	LIVELY	R^2	Significance
	B	Standard error	Beta					
Constant	−2.717	0.062	–	−43.564	0.015*	–	1.000	P = 0.005
Anthropomorphic degree	3.900	0.092	1.000	135.100	0.005*	1.000		

Note: * means $P < 0.001$

From Table 5, we can see that the degree of personification is taken as the independent variable and the degree of pleasure as the dependent variable for linear regression analysis.

From the above table, we can see that the R-square value of the model is 1.000, which means that the degree of personification can explain the 100.0% change of pleasure. The model passed the F test ($F = 18252.000$, $p = 0.005 < 0.05$). That is to say, the degree of personification will definitely have an influence on pleasure, and the degree of personification will have a significant positive influence on pleasure.

With the increase of personification degree, (see Fig. 4) the user's pleasure degree also increases correspondingly, and the user's pleasure degree of voice assistants with high personification degree is significantly higher than that of voice assistants with medium or low personification degree.

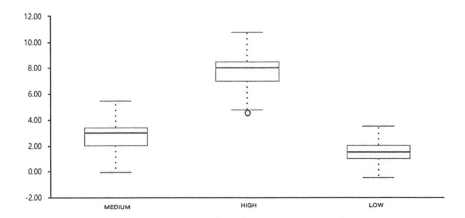

Fig. 4. Influence of personification degree and user's pleasure

Table 6. Influence of different gender voice interaction assistants on user satisfaction

Pairing number	Item	Average value	Standard deviation	Average value difference	t	p
1 pairing	Male assistant	4.16	1.02	−3.62	−10.261	0.00**
	Female assistant	7.78	1.15			

It can be seen from Table 6 that the paired T-test is used to study the differences of experimental data. From the above table, it can be seen that a total of 1 set of paired data will show differences ($p < 0.05$). Specific analysis shows that there is a 0.01 level of significance between male assistants and female assistants ($t = -10.261$, $p = 0.000$), and specific comparison shows that the average value of male voice interaction assistants is 4.16. Will be significantly lower than the average of female voice interaction assistants (7.78). It can be seen from Fig. 5 that the degree of personification of female assistants is higher than that of male assistants, and users' satisfaction with female assistants is higher than that of male assistants.

5 Discussion

In the future, with the continuous iteration and improvement of the human-computer interaction capability of input and output nodes brought by artificial intelligence technology, it will bring new challenges and opportunities to the design of voice interaction.

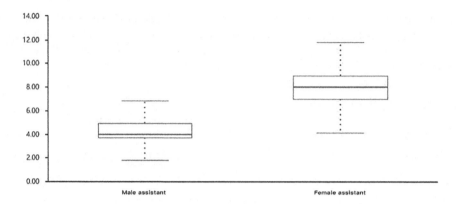

Fig. 5. Influence of different genders on users' pleasure.

We will continue to carry out innovative design and research on each node of voice interaction, taking human experience and crowd experience as the overall context of research. It is hoped that through artificial intelligence technology, products like real assistants can be created for users, which can not only help users solve the complicated trivial matters in daily life or work, but also provide emotional and social support.

This study observes the impact of different anthropomorphic degrees on user satisfaction from the perspective of emotional voice products, and comes to the conclusion that under the condition of meeting the principle of human dialogue, emotional interaction will improve user satisfaction to a certain extent, and users will be more inclined to use voice assistants closer to real human interaction, This experiment is inconsistent with the research results that ghost s of SamSung company believes that the personality and emotion of virtual assistant should not be displayed too much.

This paper suggests that: starting from the theory of anthropomorphism, giving human characteristics to machines is the core of realizing machine anthropomorphism. First of all, starting from the most basic system portrait, establish personality characteristics from the perspective of speech speed, sound and wake-up words of voice interactive assistant, so that users can close the man-machine relationship from the auditory level, so as to establish a sense of trust, improve emotional cognition, and increase more sincere and in-depth dialogue between users and machines. Secondly, in the in-depth interaction, the machine generates empathy by establishing its own empathy, and carries out emotional feedback from the user's point of view, so as to strengthen the social connection between man and machine in the close communication and benign interaction experience; In the virtual relationship constructed by man-machine, make reasonable empathic feedback, establish empathy and understand the emotional state of users; Finally, strengthen the emotional expression of man-machine, achieve man-machine multi round dialogue, and deepen the intimate relationship between man-machine.

6 Conclusion

This study observes the influence of different personification degrees on user satisfaction from the emotional point of view of voice products, and concludes that emotional interaction will improve user satisfaction to a certain extent, and users will be more inclined to use voice assistants closer to real-life interaction. In this experiment, it is found that most users tend to adapt the volume. In terms of volume and speech speed, users prefer S4 = 180 words/min speech speed instead of too high or too low voice and too fast or too slow speech speed. As the degree of personification increases, the user's pleasure also increases correspondingly. The user pleasure of voice assistants with high degree of personification is significantly higher than that of voice assistants with medium or low degree of personification; Female assistants are more anthropomorphic than male assistants, and users' satisfaction with female assistants is higher than that of male assistants.

References

1. Wu, Y., Wenyu, W.: S Research on interactive design of voice user interface in smart home scene. Ind. Des. **01**, 140–141 (2019)
2. Romportl, J.: Speech synthesis and uncanny valley. In: Sojka, P., Horak, A., Kopecek, I., Pala, K. (eds.) TSD 2014. LNCS (LNAI), vol. 8655, pp. 595–602. Springer, Cham (2014). https://doi.org/10.1007/978-3-319-10816-2_72
3. Mao, X., Xue, Y.: Human-Computer Emotional Interaction. Science Publishing House, Beijing (2011)
4. Ghosh, S., Pherwani, J.: Designing of a natural voice assistants for mobile through user centered design approach. In: Kurosu, M. (ed.) HCI 2015. LNCS, vol. 9169, pp. 320–331. Springer, Cham (2015). https://doi.org/10.1007/978-3-319-20901-2_29
5. Niculescu, A., Dijk, B., Nijholt, A., et al.: Making social robots more attractive: the effects of voice pitch, humor and empathy. Int. J. Soc. Robot. **5**(2), 171–191 (2013)
6. Lee, B., Kwon, O., Lee, I., et al.: Companionship with smart home devices: the impact of social connectedness and interaction types on perceived social support and companionship in smart homes. Comput. Hum. Behav. **75**, 922–934 (2017)
7. Niculescu, A.I., Banchs, R.E.: Strategies to cope with errors in human-machine spoken interactions: using chatbots as back-off mechanism for task-oriented dialogues. In: Proceedings of ERRARE, Sinaia, Romania (2015)
8. Yanyan, S., Shiyan, L., Xiantao, C.: Emotional voice interaction design —— the map and design case of human-computer interaction of Baidu AI user experience department. Decoration **11**, 22–27 (2019)
9. Epley, N., Waytz, A., Cacioppo, J.T.: On seeing human: a three-factor theory of anthropomorphism. Psychol. Rev. **114**(4), 864–886 (2007)
10. Tong, Y.: The experience reconstruction of personification theory in phonetic interaction. Young J. **18**, 81–82 (2020)
11. Hone, K.S., Graham, R.: Towards a tool for the Subjective Assessment of Speech System Interfaces (SASSI). Nat. Lang. Eng. **6**(3), 287–303 (2000)
12. ITU-T: ITU-T Recommendation P.85, A Method for Subjective Performance Assessment of the Quality of Speech Voice Output Devices
13. Tom, T., Bill, A.: User Experience Measurement: Collection, Analysis and Presentation, 2nd edn. Electronic Industry Press, Beijing (2018)
14. Tom, T., Bill, A.: Measuring the User Experience: Collecting, Analyzing, and Presenting Usability, 2nd edn. Publishing House of Electronics Industry, Beijing (2018)

A Proposal of Classification Model for Kawaii Fashion Styles in Japan Using Deep Learning

Tipporn Laohakangvalvit[1]([⊠]), Peeraya Sripian[1], Keiko Miyatake[2],
and Michiko Ohkura[1]

[1] Shibaura Institute of Technology, 3-7-5 Toyosu, Koto-ku, Tokyo 135-8548, Japan
{tipporn,peeraya}@shibaura-it.ac.jp,
ohkura@sic.shibaura-it.ac.jp
[2] Kyoritsu Women's University, 2-2-1 Hitotsubashi, Chiyoda-ku, Tokyo 101-8437, Japan
kmiyatake@kyoritsu-wu.ac.jp

Abstract. Kawaii is a Japanese cultural uniqueness that attracts attention around the world. It has been considered as an important value that increases impressions on various products such as Hello Kitty. Since 2017, we have conducted our research on fashion and investigate kawaii fashion trends in Japan. Our recent study introduces deep learning as a new approach to classify images of kawaii fashion styles. In this study, we propose to construct a classification model to classify five kawaii fashion styles in our dataset consisting of Classic, Harajuku-type Kawaii, Lolita, Orthodox, and Street, each of which has approximately 100 images. We constructed and compared the classification performance between two deep learning models: color-image model and grayscale-image model. As the results, we clarified that the model trained by color images has high performance especially in classify between the HK and the other four kawaii fashion styles. Our proposed model contributes to future application in the fashion industry as a quantitative method in positioning the style for new kawaii fashion designs.

Keywords: Kawaii · Fashion · Classification · Deep learning model

1 Introduction

Kawaii is a Japanese cultural uniqueness that attracts attention around the world. It has been considered as an important value that increases impressions on various products such as Hello Kitty by Sanrio. From our systematic studies on kawaii products, various attributes have been proposed including color [1]. In addition, since 2017, we have conducted our research on fashion and investigate kawaii fashion trends in Japan [2–5].

In our previous studies [5], we employed Computer Vision technique to systematically extract color features of the image dataset containing three fashion styles: Harajuku-type kawaii, Harajuku street snaps, and Shibuya street snaps. The result suggests colorfulness as one important feature for Harajuku-type kawaii fashion style.

In addition to the Computer Vision approach, we introduce deep learning as a new approach to classify the images into different styles. Deep convolutional neural network

© The Author(s), under exclusive license to Springer Nature Switzerland AG 2022
M. Kurosu (Ed.): HCII 2022, LNCS 13302, pp. 450–461, 2022.
https://doi.org/10.1007/978-3-031-05311-5_31

(CNN) algorithm has been successfully applied to various domains especially detection, segmentation, and recognition of images [6, 7]. One advantage of this approach is that feature extraction is not required because it can perform classification using images as input. Therefore, we employed this approach in this research aiming at classifying various fashion styles. Our first trial was the construction of binary classification model for the Harajuku-type kawaii fashion style from the other styles [8]. As the results, we obtained a model that can perform the classification with high performance, which suggests the possibility to classify Harajuku-type kawaii fashion images by the deep learning. Thus, we continue to employ this approach in this study focusing on larger dataset consisting of five kawaii fashion styles. Unlike the dataset used in our first trial, all the fashion styles are kawaii, making the classification task by deep learning more challenging due to more similarity among the kawaii fashion styles.

The purpose of this study is to use a deep learning approach to construct model to effectively classify images from five kawaii fashion styles. This manuscript presents our model construction, model evaluation, and model improvement by data augmentation. The details are described in the following sections.

2   Model Construction

2.1   Dataset Preparation

We employed a total of 505 images from five kawaii fashion styles collected in our previous study [9, 10] as follows:

- Classic Retro Doll (Classic)
- Harajuku-type Kawaii (HK)
- Lolita
- Orthodox pretty and cute (Orthodox)
- Street Kawaii (Street)

Each image contains a person wearing clothes and accessories based on each fashion style with empty background. The images were preprocessed by cropping out excessive empty background. Each kawaii fashion style and its corresponding number of images is shown in Table 1.

Table 1. Kawaii fashion styles and corresponding number of images.

Style	Number of images
Classic retro doll (classic)	101
Harajuku-type Kawaii (HK)	104
Lolita	100
Orthodox pretty and cute (orthodox)	100
Street Kawaii (street)	100

Using the preprocessed images, we prepared two datasets as follows:

- Color dataset (505 images): Original images
- Grayscale dataset (505 images): Desaturated version of original images

2.2 Model Construction

We constructed multi-classification (5 classes) models using each of the two datasets prepared in Sect. 2.1 as input (training data) to deep convolutional neural network (CNN). The parameters used for model construction were selected from the model with the best classification performance among the constructed models in our preliminary study [8]:

- Algorithm: Xception [11]
- Image dimension: 512 × 512 pixels (Lock aspect ratio)
- Epoch: 200
- Data augmentation [12]:
- Vertical flip (Randomly flip inputs vertically): True
- Horizontal flip (Randomly flip inputs horizontally): True
- Rotation range (Degree range for random rotations as integer): 0

Using the same parameter settings, we constructed two models as follows: (1) color-image model (Model #1), and (2) grayscale-image model (Model #2).

3 Model Evaluation

3.1 Evaluation Method

To evaluate the classification performance, we employed each constructed model in Sect. 2.2 to perform classification with the same dataset used to train the model. The model provides the output as the probabilities of classifying an image into 5 kawaii fashion styles. The same procedure as shown in Fig. 1 was repeated for all images in the dataset for each model.

3.2 Classification Distribution

Using the method described in the previous section, we obtained the classification results for all images for both color-image and grayscale-image models. The results as classification distribution are shown in Figs. 2, 3, 4 and 5. Figure 2 and Fig. 3 show the confusion matrix for color-image model and grayscale-image model, respectively, which report the number of correct and incorrect predictions broken down by each class (i.e., each kawaii fashion style). Each row of the matrix represents the instances in an actual class while each column represents the instances in a predicted class. Figure 4 and Fig. 5 show the ratio of images (percentage; %) predicted into each class for each kawaii fashion style for color-image model and grayscale-image model, respectively. The results from the confusion matrixes and the ratio plots are summarized as follows:

Color-Image Model (Fig. 2 and Fig. 4). Most images in the HK style (95%) as well as the Orthodox style (75%) are correctly classified. For the other three kawaii fashion styles, only around half of the images or less are correctly classified. These results show that the color-image model is effective to classify the kawaii fashion style images, especially for the HK-style images. The results resembled our previous study [5] on the colorfulness of various kawaii fashion styles using image-processing approach that HK is the most colorful among the five kawaii fashion styles.

Grayscale-Image Model (Fig. 3 and Fig. 5). The classification performance for the Street style is better than the color-image model, that is, the percentage of correctly classified images is increased from 32% to 71%. However, the classification performance for the other four kawaii fashion styles substantially dropped in this model.

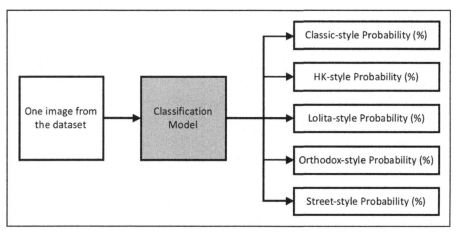

Fig. 1. Procedure to obtain classification result from model.

		Predicted Class					
		Classic	**HK**	**Lolita**	**Orthodox**	**Street**	**Total**
	Classic	23	12	20	30	16	101
	HK	0	95	6	0	3	104
Actual Class	**Lolita**	12	15	56	15	2	100
	Orthodox	0	6	12	75	7	100
	Street	6	14	8	40	32	100
	Total	41	142	102	160	60	505

Fig. 2. Confusion matrix for color-image model.

		Predicted Class					Total
		Classic	HK	Lolita	Orthodox	Street	
	Classic	4	2	38	9	48	101
Actual Class	HK	7	44	14	7	32	104
	Lolita	6	1	58	11	24	100
	Orthodox	0	0	37	13	50	100
	Street	3	4	11	11	71	100
	Total	20	51	158	51	225	505

Fig. 3. Confusion matrix for grayscale-image model.

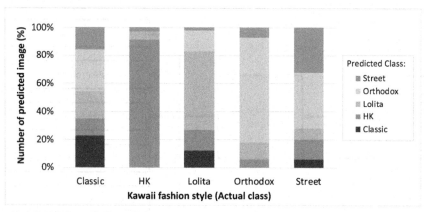

Fig. 4. Distribution of number of predicted images in percentage for each group of kawaii fashion style images for color-image model.

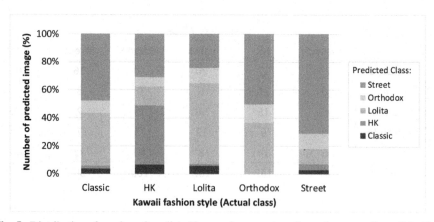

Fig. 5. Distribution of number of predicted images in percentage for each group of kawaii fashion style images for grayscale-image model.

3.3 Classification Probability

As shown in Fig. 1, by using one image as input, the model gives output as the prob-abilities of classification into five classes or the five kawaii fashion styles. Using these probabilities, we calculated the average classification probabilities grouped by kawaii fashion styles in order to further investigate the degree of classification into correct classes in addition to the results described in Sect. 3.2. The results from the classification probabilities are summarized as follows:

Color-Image Model (Fig. 6). In Fig. 6, the horizontal axis represents each group of kawaii fashion styles. For each group, the bar charts shown in five colors represent the average classification probability from the model for each of the five predicted classes of kawaii fashion styles. The average probability of correct classification of the HK images (i.e., HK-style images correctly classified into HK class) is the highest (91.4%). Also, the average probability of correct classification of the Orthodox-style images reaches 74.1%. However, the standard deviation of Orthodox-style images (SD = 40.0) is larger than that of the HK-style images (SD = 24.2), which indicate a higher chance of incorrect classification into other classes than the HK style.

Grayscale-Image Model (Fig. 7). Though the ratio of correct classification of the Street-style images is improved in this model as described in Sect. 3.2, the average prob-ability is not very high (66.5%) and the standard deviation is large (SD = 38.0). Thus, it remains inconclusive that the grayscale-image model can improve the classification performance for the Street style.

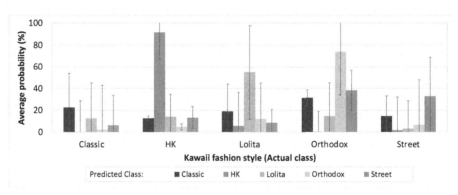

Fig. 6. Average classification probabilities for each group of kawaii fashion style images for color-image model.

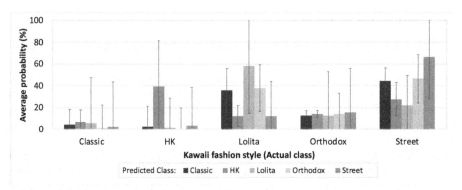

Fig. 7. Average classification probabilities for each group of kawaii fashion style images for grayscale-image model.

3.4 Classification Performance Metrics

We used the confusion matrix to calculate the following four commonly used performance metrics for classification [13]: accuracy, precision, recall, and F1-score. The results from the performance metrics are summarized as follows:

Color-Image Model (Table 2). Among the five kawaii fashion styles, HK style yields the best performance for all four metrics (accuracy = 88.9%, precision = 91.3%, recall = 66.9%, F1-score = 77.2%). The other styles reach almost the same accuracy as the HK style, but have lower values for precision, recall, and F1-score. These results confirm the distinct classification results of the HK style as previously described in Sects. 3.2 and 3.3.

Grayscale-Image Model (Table 3). Comparing to the performance metrics of the color-image model (Table 2), the tendency of accuracies for all kawaii fashion styles is similar. However, the F1-score of all kawaii fashion styles decreased which indicates lower overall performance of the grayscale-image model.

Table 2. Classification performance metrics of color-image model.

Kawaii fashion style	Classification performance metrics (%)			
	Accuracy	Precision	Recall	F1-score
Classic	81.0	22.8	56.1	32.4
HK	88.9	91.3	66.9	77.2
Lolita	82.2	56.0	54.9	55.4
Orthodox	78.2	75.0	46.9	57.7
Street	81.0	32.0	53.3	40.0

Table 3. Classification performance metrics of grayscale-image model.

Kawaii fashion style	Classification performance metrics (%)			
	Accuracy	Precision	Recall	F1-score
Classic	77.6	4.0	20.0	6.6
HK	86.7	42.3	86.3	56.8
Lolita	71.9	58.0	36.7	45.0
Orthodox	75.2	13.0	25.5	17.2
Street	63.8	71.0	31.6	43.7

4   Model Improvement

4.1   Improvement on Model Construction

Based on the comparison between the color-image and the grayscale-image models (Sect. 3), the color-image one has better performance. However, the classification performance of some kawaii fashion styles is still low. Therefore, we focused on improving the overall performance of the color-image model at this stage by adjusting the parameters used for model construction.

In our preliminary study on model construction with kawaii fashion dataset [8], we suggested the image rotation as one data augmentation method that may be effective to improve the model performance. Therefore, we also employed it for the model construction this time. The rotation range is set to 359, meaning that the images used for model training are randomly rotated to any angles from 0 to 359 degrees. To confirm the effectiveness of the image rotation, all other parameters for model construction remain the same as the first model construction as listed in Sect. 2.2.

4.2   Improved Model Performance

We employed the same approach as in our previous model construct in order to compare the model performance to the original color-image model (Fig. 2, Fig. 4, Fig. 6 and Table 2). The performance evaluation is described as follows:

Classification Distribution. The confusion matrix is shown in Fig. 8. The ratio plot of images (percentage; %) predicted into each class for each kawaii fashion style is shown in Fig. 9. Comparing to the results of the original color-image model (Fig. 2 and Fig. 4), the classification for Street-style images is improved but almost no difference or decreased performance is observed for the other four styles.

Classification Probability. Figure 10 shows the average classification probabilities of the improved color-image model. Though the average classification probability for the Street-style images is improved, the standard deviation is still large which implies unreliable result.

Classification Performance Metrics. Table 4 shows the classification performance metrics of the improved color-image model. Comparing to the original model, there is no large improvement in the overall performance. Therefore, we conclude that only the image rotation alone is insufficient to improve the model performance. Further study on various other approaches to optimize the model parameters is necessary such as employing different algorithms or different data augmentation techniques.

		Predicted Class					
		Classic	HK	Lolita	Orthodox	Street	Total
Actual Class	Classic	4	1	7	45	44	101
	HK	0	43	0	1	60	104
	Lolita	1	0	58	22	19	100
	Orthodox	0	1	1	82	16	100
	Street	1	0	1	24	74	100
	Total	6	45	67	174	213	505

Fig. 8. Confusion matrix for improved color-image model.

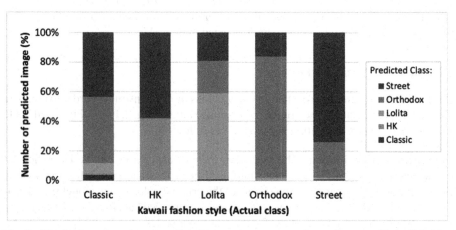

Fig. 9. Distribution of number of predicted images in percentage for each group of kawaii fashion style images for improved color-image model.

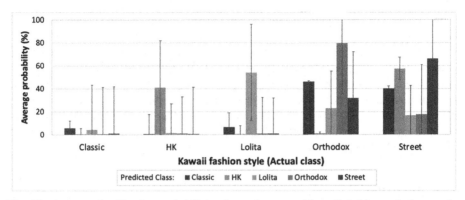

Fig. 10. Average classification probabilities for each group of kawaii fashion style images for improved color-image model.

Table 4. Classification performance metrics of improved color-image model.

Kawaii fashion style	Classification performance metrics (%)			
	Accuracy	Precision	Recall	F1-score
Classic	80.4	4.0	66.7	7.5
HK	87.5	41.3	95.6	57.7
Lolita	89.9	58.0	86.6	69.5
Orthodox	78.2	82.0	47.1	59.9
Street	67.3	74.0	34.7	47.3

5 Discussion

We firstly constructed two models (color-image model and grayscale-image model) to compare the model performance using the same images with color or grayscale. The results show that the color-image model has distinct classification performance for the HK-style images as indicated by many correctly classified images (Fig. 2) and high classification probability (Fig. 4) for this kawaii fashion style. In addition, the color-image model has higher classification performance than that of the grayscale-image model. The results indicate that color has strong influence on the classification especially for the HK style, which resembled our previous study [5] using Computer Vision approach that the HK style has the highest colorfulness among the five kawaii fashion styles. Therefore, we confirm the reliability of our results from the deep learning approach.

Though the color-image model performs well for the HK style, we still cannot conclude the classification performance for the other styles. Thus, we have further performed a trial to improve the model enabling the image rotation for data augmentation (Sect. 4). However, we did not obtain a large improvement in the classification performance for the improved color-image model.

As the results, we conclude that the model works well with HK style because it has a unique color feature than the other styles. However, there is possibility that the other four kawaii fashion styles (i.e., Classic, Lolita, Orthodox, Street) may have similar features, which make our current deep learning model difficult to perform classification among them. Therefore, our future work needs to employ other techniques to enhance the performance of the deep learning model so that it can effectively classify not only the HK but also other kawaii fashion styles in the dataset. Our proposed model contributes to future application in the fashion industry as a quantitative method in positioning the style for new kawaii fashion designs.

6 Conclusion

This research focuses on proposing a classification model for kawaii fashion styles in Japan by employing a deep learning approach. We employed from our previous study an image dataset consisting of five kawaii fashion styles: Classic, Harajuku-type Kawaii (HK), Lolita, Orthodox, Street. The same dataset is used to construct two multi-class classification models, one model for color images and the other for grayscale images.

From the evaluation of model performance, we achieve a high performance from the color-image model to classify between the HK and the other kawaii fashion styles. Our future work will continue to improve our method for model construction so that it can effectively perform the classification for all kawaii fashion styles in our dataset.

Acknowledgments. This work was partially supported by JSPS Grant-in-Aid for Scientific Research (20K12032).

References

1. Komatsu, T., Ohkura, M.: Study on evaluation of Kawaii colors using visual analog scale. In: Smith, M.J., Salvendy, G. (eds.) Human Interface 2011. LNCS, vol. 6771, pp. 103–108. Springer, Heidelberg (2011). https://doi.org/10.1007/978-3-642-21793-7_12
2. Miyatake, K., Sripian, P., Ohkura, M.: Study on style of Harajuku Kawaii fashion - design features - (1st report). In: Proceedings of Annual Meeting of Japan Society of Kansei Engineering, A2-02, Japan (2018). (in Japanese)
3. Sripian, P., Miyatake, K., Ohkura, M.: Study on style of Harajuku Kawaii fashion - color features - (2nd report). In: Proceedings of Annual Meeting of Japan Society of Kansei Engineering, A2-03, Japan (2018)
4. Miyatake, K., Sripian, P., Ohkura, M.: Study on style of Kawaii fashion - analysis of the current situation in Japan – (5th report). In: Proceedings of Annual Meeting of Japan Society of Kansei Engineering, 12D1-01, Japan (2019). (in Japanese)
5. Sripian, P., Miyatake, K., Ohkura, M.: Study on the color feature of Harajuku-type Kawaii fashion comparison with street snap images using colorfulness. TNI J. Eng. Technol. **8**(1), 63–72 (2020)
6. LeCun, Y., Bengio, Y., Hinton, G.: Deep learning. Nature **521**, 436–444 (2015)
7. Chen, X., Lin, X.: Big data deep learning: challenges and perspectives. IEEE Access **2**, 514–525 (2014)

8. Laohakangvalvit, T., Sripian, P., Miyatake, K., and Ohkura, M.: Study on style of Kawaii fashion (14th report) – construction of Harajuku-type Kawaii fashion model by deep learning. In: Proceedings of 23rd Annual Meeting of Japan Society of Kansei Engineering, 1C01-06-05, Japan (2021)

9. Sripian, P., Miyatake, K., Laohakangvalvit, T., Ohkura, M.: Study on style of Kawaii fashion (11th report) – the colorfulness comparison of various Kawaii fashions. In: Proceedings of Annual Meeting of Japan Society of Kansei Engineering, 4D-03, Japan (2021)

10. Sripian, P., Miyatake, K., Laohakangvalvit, T., Ohkura, M.: Study on style of Kawaii fashion (13th report) -the analysis of Lolita fashion style. In: Proceedings of Annual Meeting of Japan Society of Kansei Engineering, 1C01-06-04, Japan (2021)

11. Chollet, F: Xception: deep learning with depthwise separable convolutions. In: Computer Vision and Pattern Recognition. Cornell University (2017)

12. Keras API reference: Image data preprocessing. https://keras.io/api/preprocessing/image/. Accessed 14 Feb 2022

13. Grandini, M., Bagli, E., Visani, G.: Metrics for multi-class classification: an overview. In: Machine Learning. Cornell University (2020)

You Keep Me Hangin' On: An Analysis of Motivational Mechanisms in Nutrition Apps

Martin Lurz[1]([✉]), Sofia Fischer[1], Markus Böhm[2], and Helmut Krcmar[1]

[1] Technical University of Munich, Boltzmannstr. 3, 85748 Garching, Germany
martin.lurz@tum.com
[2] Department of Informatics, University of Applied Sciences Landshut, Landshut, Germany

Abstract. About 200 new apps are added to the "Health & Wellbeing" category in the app store every year. However, high dropout rates due to little long-term user motivation persist. Despite considerable research on motivation, especially in the context of games, there are only limited insights into existing theories and mechanics in the field of health apps. Thus, in this research paper, we investigated different motivational mechanisms combined in one nutrition app to determine whether Bartle Player Types, Temporal Motivation Theory, Arousal Theory, Operand Conditioning as well as Pinks Framework of intrinsic motivation can be applied in this context. A technical artifact was developed which imitated a nutrition app and was enhanced with various gamification elements. This enabled a detailed investigation of user behavior within a conducted user study with 42 participants from whom 20 filled out the follow-up questionnaire. We could show a strong influence of the Bartle Player Types on favorite motivation mechanisms as well as strong correlation between feature preference and measured usage, feature preference and perceived usage as well as measured usage and perceived usage.

Keywords: App · Motivation · Gamification · eHealth · mHealth · Nutrition

1 Introduction

Although the rising numbers of overweight and obesity have been known for more than 20 years [1], numbers of both are still rising, even in countries with high education [2]. While different countries started different programs for the prevention and treatment of overweight and obesity, interventions in the form of mobile applications for smartphones (apps) offer a cheaper and more flexible option for nutrition interventions. This, and the growing popularity of the smartphone are reflected in the constantly growing market for mobile health (mHealth) apps: In 2017 more than 318,000 health apps were available in app stores for iOS and Android, with 200 new apps being added every year [3]. Despite the high rates of publication, the apps of the health and fitness category have one common problem: High dropout rates. Analytics of app usage showed, that they tend to lose more than half of their original users after only one month [4] with high dropout rates starting in the first few days [5]. One reason for the loss of users is seen in decreasing user motivation during the usage times [6].

© The Author(s), under exclusive license to Springer Nature Switzerland AG 2022
M. Kurosu (Ed.): HCII 2022, LNCS 13302, pp. 462–477, 2022.
https://doi.org/10.1007/978-3-031-05311-5_32

However, user motivation is not generally a new topic in scientific research. Game theorists and game engineers have published many different papers dealing with various reward and motivational mechanisms and different player or user types [7–9]. As with the current trend of gamification the borders between games and other applications start blurring, the question arises whether motivational mechanisms found in gaming contexts can be transferred into other application environments.

Although analysis approaches regarding gamification and motivational theories have been made [10, 11], valuable results are still scarce. Especially regarding nutrition apps, no analysis of multiple motivational mechanisms (or tests that compare multiple of these theories for a better understanding of user motivations) with a focus on nutrition apps could be found. For this reason, our research question for this paper reads as follows: *Do motivational theories and mechanisms from motivation research also apply to mobile applications designed for nutrition interventions?*

To close this research gap, we first present important background knowledge on nutrition apps and gamification as well as the different motivational theories and mechanisms which will be investigated in this paper. This section will be followed by a description of a technical artifact that was specifically developed to be able to test the different theories and mechanisms in a user study. Afterwards, the conducted user study is described and the results are shown. Finally, we discuss our results and give an answer to our research question and conclude the findings in this paper.

2 Background

The study of motivation mechanisms in nutrition apps combines the fields of motivation psychology and motivation in the context of gaming, gamification, and mHealth apps. In the following, we would like to give the reader a brief insight into the corresponding state of research.

2.1 Motivation Theories and Mechanisms

In psychology, motivation is seen as both - a characteristic of a person and a trait that can be activated [12]. The activation of the motivation in a person can be triggered by the demands, constraints, and resources presented by the environment of action. Motivation is focused or directed towards a goal [13]. A goal may represent the personal values and interests of a person or maybe caused by personal convictions. Demographics such as gender, ethnic background, and age (after adulthood) do not seem to have a significant influence on motivational behavior [13].

One of the most famous classifications of motivation is the division into intrinsic and extrinsic motivation [14]. While intrinsic motivation is located inside a user, extrinsic motivation is induced from the outside. An intrinsic motivator is not given from outside, but is personally rewarding. Thus, users follow an activity or show a behavior for the sake of the activity or the goal itself [15]. In contrast, an extrinsic motivator is introduced by a third party and usually known at the beginning of a task. The task is then fulfilled by the user to either avoid punishment or to receive a reward after good behavior [15]. However, studies have shown that extrinsic motivation can become ineffective in the long-run and can even lead to a decrease of intrinsic motivation, if the focus is primarily set on the rewards instead of being set on the action itself (also called the "Sawyer Effect") [16].

Operand Conditioning. One of the first and most famous ideas of motivation theory was proposed by Skinner [17], stating that the correlation between the numbers of times an action is executed is dependent on a reward or punishment. Skinner studied the behavior of animals placed in a container with a mechanism installed that would reward the animal with food or punish with pain. The motivation of an animal to repeatedly perform an action is based on the expectation of a positive reward. Triggering this motivation is called reinforcement. The continued release of dopamine will eventually cause the brain to also reward the pure anticipation of the reward, which Skinner already indicated by his famous dog experiment: A dog that is trained to eat after a bell rings, will eventually start salivating when hearing a bell, even if no food is perceived. On the other hand, the subject can experience fear or stress if the reinforced expectation is not met, strengthening the effect of reinforcement [17, 18].

Additionally, the rate or schedule in which the subject is rewarded affects how often the subject performs the rewarded behavior (Response Rate), as well as how fast the subject drops the behavior after the reward for the given action has stopped (Extinction Rate) [17].

Arousal Theory. Arousal is used in psychology to describe the mental alertness. The underlying theory states that the motivation to perform a certain action is highly dependent on the level of arousal. The level of arousal is influenced by the environment which provides different stimuli. The level also highly influences task performance. However, as stated in the Yerkes-Dodson Law, not only too low but also too high arousal levels seem to have a negative influence on the performance [19]. Therefore, it has been shown that moderate arousal levels are preferable for complicated tasks [20]. Usually, individuals seek to balance their arousal levels and thus tend to choose stimulating activities if arousal levels are too low or calming activities (such as a walk in the park) if levels are too high [21]. One example of arousal theory regards that students are motivated to return to university at the beginning of a semester, as their arousal levels decreased over the semester breaks causing them to seek higher stimulation.

Based on mechanisms of Operand Conditioning and the Arousal Theory, we assume that users who already used many different nutrition apps might be less motivated. First, as they might have had negative experiences with prior apps (thus the usage of many different ones). Second, since users who never used a nutrition app might have a higher drive to achieve success in such an app as their arousal might be higher. Therefore, we formulate the following hypothesis:

H1: Users with high experience in nutritional apps are less motivated to achieve goals than unexperienced users.

Pink's Framework for Intrinsic Motivation. Daniel H. Pink created this framework [16] as a connection between scientific knowledge and business practice. Similar to the self-determination theory [22], they suggest supporting intrinsic motivation as it is rooted in the individual user [16]. They call it "Type I" behavior and describe it as the need to take direction in the own life, the desire to learn and create new things and improve one's environment. In order to support this drive, they suggest to promote three areas: purpose, mastery and autonomy [16].

Purpose can be shortly described as the desire to be a part of something bigger than oneself. In this context Pink highlights to avoid high extrinsic motivators such as money as they can hinder the process of choosing purposeful goals [16].

Mastery is defined as the inner drive to be able to carry out a purposeful activity at an increasingly better level. The aim here is to bring a person into a state of "flow". This term is used to describe the performance of an activity that is slightly above one's current abilities in order to provide a realistic challenge to the body and mind. Here Pink underlines the importance of clear and challenging (but possible) goals as well as regular feedback on those [16].

Autonomy is described as the "heart" of intrinsic motivation. According to Pink [16], this includes full will and freedom of choice without the pressure for specific results that do not come from oneself. Thus, the possibility to try out new ideas should be given. However, there are fundamental differences to independence: It is not a one-man individualism that is dependent on no one, but an autonomy that nevertheless allows for interdependence with others. Therefore, Pink suggests that people are motivated if they are free to choose their tasks, time, team and technique [16].

Based on this framework, we assume that a nutrition app should have multiple features to allow personalization. Thus, we define our second hypotheses as:

H2: Users who actively use multiple features are more successful in reaching set goals.

Temporal Motivation Theory. The temporal motivation theory (TMT) integrates time into the motivation research and emphasizes the influence of deadlines on motivation [23]. In order to describe this behavior, a quantitative formula is used that shows how required time is a critical motivational factor. It states, that the motivation will increase exponentially as the deadline for the regarding tasks nears:

$$Motivation = \frac{Expectancy * Value}{1 + Impulsiveness * Delay}$$

In this equation, *Motivation* is defined as the desire for an achievement; *Expectancy* is the subjective likelihood of success; *Value* the associated reward; *Impulsiveness* the ability to withstand urges; and *Delay* the time until the deadline [24]. However, studies suggest, that the time-related motivation plays a stronger role in the overall motivation for younger people [24]. Nevertheless, this formula could explain for example why students tend to procrastinate instead of studying for an exam until the value of *Delay* becomes quite small as the time until the received reward has decreased and therefore the subjective *Motivation* value has increased [23].

Since it is to be expected that motivation increases as the deadline approaches, we formulate the following hypothesis:

H3: The number of users who finish goals correlates negatively with the remaining time until deadline.

Bartle Player Types. The Bartle Player Types (BPT) are a classification of players based on a categorization of two factors: One, if the player prefers dealing with the game-world or the other players, and second, if the player prefers acting or interacting [25]. The model is applicable to single- as well as multiplayer games. Overall, four different types are defined: "Achiever", "Explorer", "Socializer" and "Killer".

Achievers are characterized by preferring unilateral actions and exploration of the given world or app. The Achiever acts with the world. Achievers are described as being attracted by motivational mechanisms like challenges or quests, leading to achievements or certificates. An Achiever is also often motivated by a time limit, not only accepting but looking for the challenges to complete a given task without deviating from it [26].

Explorers are defined as sharing the interest of interacting with the application instead of other users, they are known for looking for hidden treasures, finding bugs in the implementation, and are motivated by Easter eggs and puzzles. The Explorer interacts with the world. The recommended motivational mechanisms for Explorers include unlockable game content and customization [26].

Socializers are focused on social interaction with other players, using the application mainly for this purpose. Motivational mechanisms for this type include altruism and community elements.

Killers are also more motivated by the other players than the actual application. In contrast to Socializers, Killers are not looking for interaction, but action. They are motivated by competition and comparisons. Motivational mechanisms would be comparison and reputation elements that reflect a certain social image.

As each type of play has individual motivators, we formulate the following hypothesis:

H4: The positive perception of the different features designed for a player type correlates with the according player type.

2.2 Gamification

The idea of bringing gaming elements in other, non-gaming contexts, has become quite popular under the term "gamification" [27]. The most popular game design elements used for gamification include collectible points, user levels, leaderboards, and badges [28]. However, it is important not to mix this term with other elements that try to connect content or knowledge with gaming, such as "serious games". While the latter is enriched with knowledge, gamification is focusing on the content of the actual application is the focus and the game elements are the supplement [29].

In gamification research one distinguishes between mechanisms that focus on the content (which would increase intrinsic motivation) and on implementations of how the content is perceived or displayed (which deals more with extrinsic motivation). This separation is called structural gamification and content gamification [30]. For example, the habit of going for a run can be implemented with extrinsic elements using a motivating user interface with badges or stars for long or regular runs. An example of the intrinsic element would change the run by offering a zombie apocalypse story with interactive sprinting sequences while running. Thus, in this paper, we use the terms "intrinsic" and "extrinsic" to refer to the psychological meaning, while referring to "structural motivation" and "content motivation" in the meaning of game design.

2.3 Nutrition Apps

Next to traditional electronic health (eHealth) applications, the popularity of smartphones allowed the expansion of mobile health (mHealth) apps.

While in nutrition research users had to write down their daily consumptions in a physical nutrition diary, these apps usually offer a more convenient way of recording one's diet by including a digital nutrition database [31, 32]. Regarding the tracking of the required nutritional data, users have to enter the information mostly manually [33]. This means a high effort for the users as they have to enter consumed food as accurately as possible in grams. In addition to the saved nutrition records, these apps often include functions such as (personalized) recipe recommendations, nutritional information about one's diet, disease prevention, and various other functions [34]. Although image recognition for food items has been tested in the scientific field [35], currently none of the most popular apps have it integrated in an extend that could replace manual tracking.

Nevertheless, only a small number of these apps are successful [36] mostly due to low adherence rates [37]. One reason is seen in the nutrition recording requirement. As this has to be as accurate as possible (to be able to calculate intake values for macro- and micronutrients), this procedure can become quite time-intensive. Thus, motivational mechanisms must be found to counteract tedious, but necessary, elements.

Since nutrition apps currently seem to have problems retaining users in the long run despite common gamification methods, our final hypothesis is:

H5: Common gamification elements such as badges and points are the least enjoyed.

3   Technical Artifact

To be able to test the defined hypotheses, a special technical artifact which was based on available nutrition apps was developed. To include important features based on the presented motivation theories and mechanisms, we conducted an in-depth requirement analysis for each one. This led us, apart from tracking user actions inside the app to be able to reconstruct user behavior later, to the following features.

3.1   Goal Setting

The intervention method to get users to eat healthier in this prototype nutrition app was a flexible goal creation mechanism as shown in Fig. 1. We chose this approach as goal-setting is an essential part of several of the presented theories and mechanisms and thus was essential for the verification of the formulated hypotheses. The goal creation feature allowed to create own goals with deadline, to use different techniques for goal achievement (i.e. daily repetition or a division in sub-tasks), to look for a team to share goals, to support multiple goals or projects with a grouping system and offered pre-defined goals from a list (as a comparison value) to support Pink's framework and thus be able to test H2. Furthermore, in order to be able to test H3 based on the TMT, deadlines should be presented as often as possible, including a visual indicator of urgent goals and an option to plan soon ending goals in a schedule.

Fig. 1. UI screenshots of the goal creation process (left and center) and the overview (right)

3.2 Chatbot

A functioning chatbot, as shown Fig. 2 (left), which can be used (among other things) to get ideas for possible goals, was developed with regard to the BPT "Explorer". A chatbot offers plenty of possibilities to hide additional little features and thus can be interpreted as a puzzle. The idea of a personal avatar that acts and reacts depending on personal success is an idea, that has been shown to be well accepted by users [38].

3.3 Leaderboard

A leaderboard, as shown in Fig. 2 (right), was added for the BPT "Killer". It showed the progress of the most successful players. As this BPT is motivated by competition and comparison with other players, this feature was supposed to satisfy this desire. To support players who are actively visiting the page, the users had the option to look into the score of their own goals, which were scored based on difficulty and the period it has been successfully followed. Additionally, it is an often used feature together with a point-system in the field of gamification and thus could be used to test H5.

3.4 Rewards

Different generated medals connected with a level system were added for the BPT "Achiever" as shown in Fig. 3 (left). Especially the level system was supposed to always provide a new reward for reaching the next level and thus fulfill the wish of progressing on given game goals and collecting all possible rewards of this player type. Furthermore, it allowed following suggestions from Operand Conditioning and the Arousal theory.

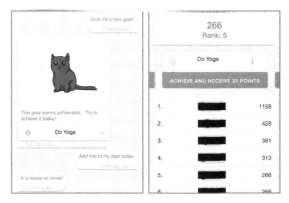

Fig. 2. UI screenshots of the features "chatbot" (left) and "leaderboard" (right)

With having levels connected to rewards instead of directly awarding each reached goal, high extinction rates were supposed to be prevented due to the irregularly reward output. Additionally, medals and point-systems are a common mechanism in the field of gamification and thus could be used to test H5.

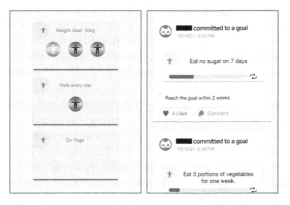

Fig. 3. UI screenshots of the features "rewards" (left) and "feed" (right)

3.5 Feed

Finally, a newsfeed-like feature was added for the "Socializer" BPT. By listing recent activities of all players, as shown in Fig. 3 (right), this feature was supposed to fit the wanted social connectedness, altruism and community interests of this player type. Next to displaying current activity, which would mostly be information on reached and/or created goals, the option to add individual text was added as well as a feature to comment or like posts from other users.

4   User Study

For testing our hypotheses, we conducted a user study to be able to observe user behavior and changes in behavior over a longer period of time than other methods as a laboratory experiment would allow.

4.1 Methodology

Our study could be divided in four steps: Recruiting, giving access to interested participants, a two-week application usage period, and a follow-up questionnaire, as shown in Fig. 4.

| Recruiting | Invitation | Application Usage | Follow-Up Questionnaire |

Fig. 4. Study flow of the conducted user study

Recruitment was conducted in four different age groups: pupils, students, young adults up to 30 years and adults. After potential participants had expressed interest, information on how the app could be used on the participant's device was provided. Users were not given any specific tasks but encouraged to use the features freely.

At the first login in the application new users were shown a single choice test to determine their BPT based on the questions by Barr [39]. Then the two-week usage period began.

After the testing period, a final follow-up questionnaire was conducted. It included 14 items. We distinguished between indicator questions (measurable elements) and constructs (not measurable, abstract questions). Indicator questions included: Ranking each feature regarding likeness (5-point Likert Scale), Ranking each feature regarding goal support (5-point Likert Scale), Ranking each feature regarding subjective usage (5-point Likert Scale). The construct question included: Used nutrition apps before (5-point Scale; No – More Than 3), Used another nutrition app with similar features before (Yes, No), How many different apps have been used before (5-point Scale; Never - More than 3), Any other comments about the app or usage experience (free text).

4.2 Results

We recruited 42 participants for the user study. As 22 participants did not complete the follow-up questionnaire after the app testing period, we had to exclude them from the final analysis. Thus, the following results are based on the data of 20 participants.

App Usage. As users were told to freely explore the app, not every user tested every feature. In fact, few participants used more than two different motivational mechanisms. For this reason, no meaningful analysis could be conducted on feature use and target success. Additionally, due to the open design of the goal setting functionality some users entered non-nutrition related goals such as taking care of pets. Nevertheless, these goals were still connected to the mechanics of the reward and social systems.

Regarding features, user committed to 90 goals as shown in Table 1. The leaderboard was actively used by 12 participants (60%). Next to automatically generated messages through the system when committing to a new or finishing goal, users wrote additional 13 posts and comments.

Table 1 Usage of the single features

Activity	Amount
Messages with the chatbot	228
Participants visiting the Leaderboard	12
Rewards Earned	40
Written Posts & Comments	13
Created Custom Goals	71
Selected Predefined Goals	19

When looking at the average number of committed goals, we can distinguish a maximum for users who used one nutrition app prior, as shown in Fig. 5. However, no clear trend regarding prior app experience and the number of goals can be identified.

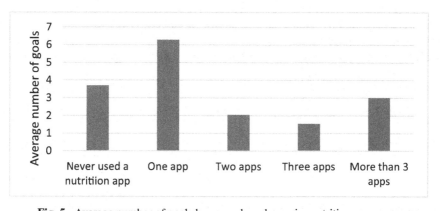

Fig. 5. Average number of goals by group based on prior nutrition app usage

General Motivation Mechanism Preferences. To be able to compare perceived and measured usage, the latter was normalized to a 5-point range based on the maximum that one user spent with the specific mechanism. The most liked feature, according to the follow-up questionnaire, was the feed. It was also the most used feature, but only third place regarding perceived usage. The least preferred mechanism was rewards as shown in Fig. 6.

Furthermore, we could find a strong positive correlation between feature preference and measured usage (r = 0.96) as well as strong negative correlations between feature preference and perceived usage (r = −0.79), and measured usage and perceived usage (r = −0.67).

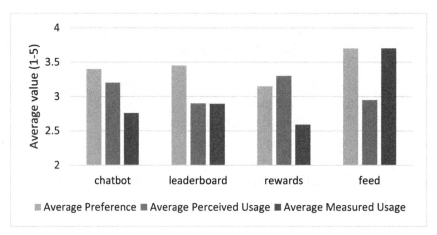

Fig. 6. Average values of preference, perceived usage and measured usage of each motivation mechanism

BPT Preferences. Most of the participants were classified as "Explorers" while only 15% were classified as "Achievers" as shown in Table 2. The average rating of each BPT for their designed mechanism was above the overall average rating from all users. Furthermore, all types rated their mechanism the highest compared to their ratings of the other three mechanisms.

Table 2 Rating of each BPT on their specifically designed motivation mechanism

Bartle player type	Amount (percentage)	Intended motivation mechanism	Average rating by BPT (standard deviation) I average rating by all users
Socializers	6 (30%)	Feed	4.67 (0.58) I 3.7
Killers	4 (20%)	Leaderboard	4.25 (0.5) I 3.45
Achievers	3 (15%)	Rewards	3.86 (1.35) I 3.15
Explorers	7 (35%)	Chatbot	3.67 (1.21) I 3.4

As shown in Fig. 7, they all rated their mechanism with the highest positive difference compared to the average rating with exception of the "Explorers".

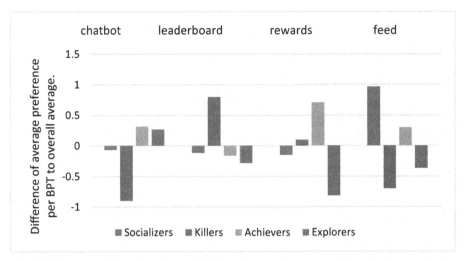

Fig. 7. Difference of the rating of each BPT from the overall average rating of the four motivation mechanisms

Goals and Deadlines. When looking at the time when most users finished their goals, a maximum can be detected at 20% rest time of the goals as shown in Fig. 8. At this point seven different users finished at least one goal. The earliest, a goal was finished was with 80% rest time, however, only two participants achieved this. Only one participant finished at least one goal with only 10% time left.

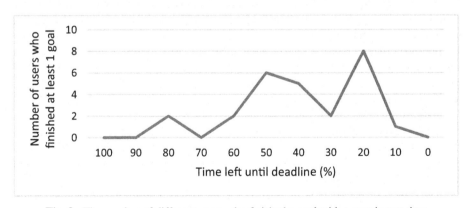

Fig. 8. The number of different users who finished a goal with a certain rest time

5 Discussion

In our user study we analyzed the app-usage behavior of 20 participants. We found strong correlations between average preference, average perceived usage and average measured usage. Furthermore, we discovered strong indicators that BPT classification and the actual preference of specific motivation elements are connected.

Regarding general preference, we found that every feature was rated on the positive side of the rating scale, although no feature surpassed the 4-point mark. Reasons for this might be the different BPTs, as each one had a distinct favorite. Thus, we think it can be concluded, that the BPT of a user has effects on the liking of (gamification) features outside of games. Looking at the average ratings by BPT, two mechanisms (feed and leaderboard) were rated better than 4.2. Based on the ratings by each BPT we found that only the "Explorers" did not rate the mechanism created for this type highest. However, as the chatbot was still the highest rated feature from all features rated by the "Explorers", the lower participant amount might have caused a bias in the values.

Despite a lower participant number, rewards being rated the lowest is in accordance with other research that found badges being only little appreciated by users [11, 40]. This is also highlighted by the ratios of perceived and measured usage of the motivation mechanisms, where the rewards had a quite high ratio value of perceived to measured. The "best" ratio value was measured for feed (best as users spending time with the application without noticing it) which had also the best overall liking.

Regarding our hypotheses, our first hypothesis H1 could not be verified as no trend could be seen regarding a correlation between prior app usage and study app activity. The high usage of people at point 2 cannot really be explained and might be an outlier. As these results indicate that there is no reliable correlation we suggest that the target group of nutritional apps should neither be focused on new users nor experienced users.

Our second hypothesis H2 focused on the theories based on Pinks Framework. As stated in the result part, only few users used multiple features and no users used actively all available motivation mechanisms, thus we can neither verify nor reject this hypothesis. But as users tended to enter goals of different difficulty and sometimes non-nutritional contexts, we assume that users might need some guidelines on how to use such a flexible system, at least in the beginning.

For the third hypothesis H3 we investigated if the TMT applies. Although no specific trend could be identified, we had the maximum of users with finished goals at the 20% rest-time mark. Furthermore, when comparing the first half (until the 50% mark) and the second half, one can see that more users finished their goals in the second half. Limitations might be in our overall sample, as TMT is in known to lose some effect the older people are. Additionally, some created goals were quite easy to finish and thus there was no postponement effect, which would maybe have been the case otherwise. Thus, although we cannot verify H3 finally, we assume that TMT also applies to some extend also in a nutrition app context.

The effects of the BPT on motivation mechanism perception was examined in the context of hypothesis H4. Although, due to the limited participation number, we could not provide statistical significance analysis, we found the indeed each BPT did rate the one specific mechanism, that was included specifically for this BPT, best. For this reason, we can verify the hypothesis H4 with the results of this paper.

For our last hypothesis H5 we investigated whether traditional gamification methods such as badges were the least preferred. Since our results show a clear difference between the reward system and the rest of the features in terms of user preference, we consider this hypothesis to be verified.

Of course, our findings are not without limitations. First, known influencing factors of this kind of user studies, such as confirmation bias [41] and response bias [42], might apply. Additionally, the study size was quite limited to only 20 final participants and is thus not representative. Due to this limited n, no statistical significance could be calculated. The time frame of two weeks until the follow-up questionnaire could only provide a brief insight into app usage behavior, which means that no final statements can be made about long-term behavior. Finally, as users were free to select own goals, not all created goals might have been equal in terms of realization difficulty, thus these numbers should be taken with attention.

Nevertheless, interesting implications for theory and contributions to practice could be offered. We gave first insights on and showed the potential of transferring motivation theories and mechanisms to the mobile application research field. For practice, we underlined that currently often-used gamification elements such as badges are not very appreciated by the broad mass of users. However, the approach of using BPT as a basis for gamification elements to appeal to all types of players offers promising first results.

6 Conclusion and Future Work

In this paper we presented an approach for evaluating different motivation techniques and theories in the context of a nutrition app. We highlighted which mechanism could be a promising approach when designing gamification elements for nutrition apps. Based on the research question from the beginning - *Do motivational theories and mechanisms from motivation research also apply to mobile applications designed for nutrition interventions?* - we conclude that we found strong indicators that BPT do apply in the nutrition app context and thus suggest it as a guideline to develop gamification systems for a broader audience. Especially as we could support existing research on showing that typical gamification systems based on badges are not perceived too well by the users. Finally, we found trends that support the TMT and thus suggest mechanism to encourage users finishing goals early, maybe in connection with a gamification approach that adjust rewards based on remaining time of set goals.

For future research, we encourage repeating the user study with a higher number of participants to be able to obtain statistically significant results. Furthermore, we suggest conducting a long-period study to gain more insight on long-term effects of the motivational mechanisms regarding user adherence. Finally, Pinks Framework of motivation could be investigated in an experiment on its own to obtain valuable insights.

References

1. James, P.T., Leach, R., Kalamara, E., Shayeghi, M.: The worldwide obesity epidemic. Obes. Res. **9**(S11), 228S-233S (2001)
2. OECD and European Union: Health at a Glance: Europe 2020. OECD Publishing, Paris (2020)

3. The IQVIA Institute: The Growing Value of Digital Health - Evidence and Impact on Human Health and the Healthcare System. The IQVIA Institute (2017). https://www.iqvia.com/ins ights/the-iqvia-institute/reports/the-growing-value-of-digital-health. Accessed 20 Oct 2021

4. Perez, S.: Flurry Examines App Loyalty: News & Communication Apps Top Charts, Personalization Apps See High Churn. TechCrunch. https://techcrunch.com/2012/10/22/flu rry-examines-app-loyalty-news-communication-apps-top-charts-personalization-apps-see-high-churn/. Accessed 20 Oct 2021

5. Thompson, F.E., Subar, A.F.: Dietary assessment methodology. In: Coulston, A.M., Boushey, C.J., Ferruzzi, M.G., Delahanty, L.M. (eds.) Nutrition in the Prevention and Treatment of Disease, ch. 1, p. 1072. Academic Press (2017)

6. König, L.M., Attig, C., Franke, T., Renner, B.: Barriers to and facilitators for using nutrition apps: systematic review and conceptual framework. JMIR mHealth uHealth 9(6), e20037 (2021)

7. de Salas, K., Lewis, I.: Identifying types of Achievements. In: Proceedings of CGAMES 2013 USA, pp. 23–30. IEEE (2013)

8. Ohira, S., Maeda, N., Nagao, K.: Player type classification based on activity logs in a gamified seminar setting. In: Presented at the 2016 1st International Conference on Game, Game Art, and Gamification (ICGGAG) (2016)

9. Schimanke, F., Mertens, R., Huck, B.S.: Player types in mobile learning games–playing patterns and motivation. In: Presented at the 2018 IEEE International Symposium on Multimedia (ISM), Taichung, Taiwan (2018)

10. Aparicio, A.F., Vela, F.L.G., Sánchez, J.L.G., Montes, J.L.I.: Analysis and application of gamification. In: Proceedings of the 13th International Conference on Interacción Persona-Ordenador, pp. 1–2 (2012)

11. Francisco-Aparicio, A., Gutiérrez-Vela, F.L., Isla-Montes, J.L., Sanchez, J.L.G.: Gamification: analysis and application. In: Penichet, V., Peñalver, A., Gallud, J. (eds.) New Trends in Interaction, Virtual Reality and Modeling. HCIS, pp. 113–126. Springer, London (2013). https://doi.org/10.1007/978-1-4471-5445-7_9

12. Lazarus, R.S.: Progress on a cognitive-motivational-relational theory of emotion. Am. Psychol. 46(8), 819–834 (1991). https://doi.org/10.1037/0003-066x.46.8.819

13. Sheldon, K.M., Elliot, A.J.: Goal striving, need satisfaction, and longitudinal well-being: the self-concordance model. J. Pers. Soc. Psychol. 76(3), 482–497 (1999). https://doi.org/10.1037/0022-3514.76.3.482

14. Deci, E.L.: Intrinsic motivation, extrinsic reinforcement, and inequity. J. Pers. Soc. Psychol. 22(1), 113 (1972)

15. Ryan, R.M., Deci, E.L.: Intrinsic and extrinsic motivations: classic definitions and new directions. Contemp. Educ. Psychol. 25(1), 54–67 (2000). https://doi.org/10.1006/ceps.1999.1020

16. Pink, D.H.: Drive: The Surprising Truth About What Motivates us. Penguin (2011)

17. Skinner, B.F.: The behavior of organisms: an experimental analysis. BF Skinner Foundation (2019)

18. Vu, D.: An analysis of operant conditioning and its relationship with video game addiction (2017)

19. Yerkes, R.M., Dodson, J.D.: The relation of strength of stimulus to rapidity of habit-formation. J. Comp. Neurol. Psychol. 18(5), 459–482 (1908). https://doi.org/10.1002/cne.920180503

20. Cudo, A., Francuz, P., Augustynowicz, P., Stróżak, P.: The effects of arousal and approach motivated positive affect on cognitive control. An ERP study. Front. Hum. Neurosci. 12, 320–320 (2018). https://doi.org/10.3389/fnhum.2018.00320

21. Moser, G., Uzzell, D.: Environmental psychology. In: Handbook of Psychology, pp. 419–445 (2003)

22. Ryan, R., Deci, E.: Self-determination theory and the facilitation of intrinsic motivation, social development, and well-being. Am. Psychol. **55**, 68–78 (2000). https://doi.org/10.1037/0003-066X.55.1.68
23. Steel, P., König, C.J.: Integrating theories of motivation. Acad. Manag. Rev. **31**(4), 889–913 (2006). https://doi.org/10.5465/amr.2006.22527462
24. Steel, P.: The nature of procrastination: a meta-analytic and theoretical review of quintessential self-regulatory failure. Psychol. Bull. **133**(1), 65 (2007)
25. Bartle, R.A. Designing Virtual Worlds. New Riders (2004)
26. Sharma, N., Berkling, K.: Training reading and writing through text-based games; step 1: adapting to gamer type. In: 2019 IEEE Global Engineering Education Conference (EDUCON), 8–11 April 2019, pp. 392–400 (2019). https://doi.org/10.1109/EDUCON.2019.8725099
27. Deterding, S., Sicart, M., Nacke, L., O'Hara, K., Dixon, D.: Gamification using game-design elements in non-gaming contexts. In: CHI 2011 Extended Abstracts on Human Factors in Computing Systems, pp. 2425–2428 (2011)
28. Basten, D.: Gamification. IEEE Softw. **34**(5), 76–81 (2017). https://doi.org/10.1109/MS.2017.3571581
29. Deterding, S., Dixon, D., Khaled, R., Nacke, L.: From game design elements to gamefulness: defining gamification. In: Proceedings of the 15th International Academic MindTrek Conference: Envisioning Future Media Environments, pp. 9–15 (2011)
30. Lamprinou, D., Paraskeva, F.: Gamification design framework based on SDT for student motivation. In: 2015 International Conference on Interactive Mobile Communication Technologies and Learning (IMCL), 19–20 November 2015, pp. 406–410 (2015). https://doi.org/10.1109/IMCTL.2015.7359631
31. Ahmad, Z., et al.: A mobile food record for integrated dietary assessment. In: MADiMa16, 201, vol. 2016, pp. 53–62 (2016). https://doi.org/10.1145/2986035.2986038
32. Lieffers, J.R.L., et al.: A qualitative evaluation of the eaTracker(®) mobile app. Nutrients **10**(10) (2018). https://doi.org/10.3390/nu10101462
33. Leipold, N., et al.: Nutrilize a personalized nutrition recommender system: an enable study. In: HealthRecSys@ RecSys, vol. 2216, pp. 24–29 (2018)
34. Holzmann, S.L., Pröll, K., Hauner, H., Holzapfel, C.: Nutrition apps: quality and limitations. an explorative investigation on the basis of selected apps. Ernaehrungs Umschau Int. **64**(5), 80–89 (2017). https://doi.org/10.4455/eu.2017.018
35. Goyal, S., et al.: I ate this: a photo-based food journaling system with expert feedback. arXiv preprint arXiv:1702.05957 (2017)
36. Cho, J.: The impact of post-adoption beliefs on the continued use of health apps. Int. J. Med. Inform. **87**, 75–83 (2016)
37. Helander, E., Kaipainen, K., Korhonen, I., Wansink, B.: Factors related to sustained use of a free mobile app for dietary self-monitoring with photography and peer feedback: retrospective cohort study. J. Med. Internet Res. **16**(4), e109 (2014)
38. Luhanga, E.T., Hippocrate, A.A.E., Suwa, H., Arakawa, Y., Yasumoto, K.: Happyinu: exploring how to use games and extrinsic rewards for consistent food tracking behavior. In: 2016 Ninth International Conference on Mobile Computing and Ubiquitous Networking (ICMU), pp. 1–7. IEEE (2016)
39. Barr, M.: Graduate Skills and Game-Based Learning: Using Video Games for Employability in Higher Education. Springer, Cham (2019). https://doi.org/10.1007/978-3-030-27786-4
40. Lurz, M., et al.: Take on me: a gamified crowdsourcing app for sharing substitutes of recipe ingredients. In: Twenty-Fifth Pacific Asia Conference on Information Systems (2021)
41. Oswald, M.E., Grosjean, S.: Confirmation bias. In: Cognitive Illusions: A Handbook on Fallacies and Biases in Thinking, Judgement and Memory, **79**, 83 (2004)
42. Sedgwick, P.: Non-response bias versus response bias. Bmj **348** (2014)

Affective Evaluation of Virtual Kawaii Robotic Gadgets Using Biological Signals in a Remote Collaboration of American and Japanese Students

Michiko Ohkura[1](✉), Tipporn Laohakangvalvit[1], Peeraya Sripian[1], Midori Sugaya[1], Hiroko Chiba[2], and Dave Berque[2]

[1] Shibaura Institute of Technology, 3-7-5, Toyosu, Koto-ku, Tokyo 1358548, Japan
ohkura@sic.shibaura-it.ac.jp, {tipporn,peeraya,
doly}@shibaura-it.ac.jp
[2] DePauw University, 313 S Locust St., Greencastle 46135, USA
{hchiba,dberque}@depauw.edu

Abstract. This paper describes our remote collaboration project related to the design and implementation of virtual kawaii robots by Japanese and American university students, and affective evaluation of the robots. Because of the COVID-19 pandemic, we had to change our planned 7-week collaboration from in-person to virtual with a resultant change in the target product of our collaboration from real robots to virtual robots. Based on our new plan for 2021, students designed robots in virtual spaces aiming that each robot elicited a different Electroencephalogram (EEG) and/or Heart Rate (HR) reaction from humans. Based on the persona and scenario for the companion robot authored by each student team, each student designed four robots with the goal that one robot would be most kawaii, a Japanese adjective representing cute and adorable, and others would be less kawaii due to variations in shapes and colors. The affective evaluation of robots was performed both by biological signals (EEG and HR) and by kawaii rating.

Keywords: Virtual robot · EEG · Heart rate · Kawaii

1 Introduction

The International Research Experiences for Students (IRES) program supported by the United States National Science and Foundation (NSF) is explained as follows.

The International Research Experiences for Students (IRES) program is one of many programs supported by the United States National Science Foundation (NSF). As described by the NSF, the program supports "…international research and research-related activities for U.S. science and engineering students" [1]. The NSF further explains that the program "contributes to development of a diverse, globally-engaged workforce with world-class skills. IRES focuses on active research participation by undergraduate or graduate students in high quality international research, education and professional development experiences in NSF-funded research areas." [1].

M. Kurosu (Ed.): HCII 2022, LNCS 13302, pp. 478–488, 2022.
https://doi.org/10.1007/978-3-031-05311-5_33

The IRES program consists of several tracks and a proposal falls under a track which must provide a cohort international research experience for a group of students. Although each student should have a specific role on the research team, the research experiences must have a single intellectual theme that is aligned with an area that the NSF supports. This project was organized around developing a better understanding the role that kawaii (Japanese cuteness) plays in robot design.

This project focused on kawaii as a Japanese originated Affective value and its application to robot design, because kawaii has a potential impact [2–5] and kawaii design principles are incorporated into successful products that are used globally including robotic gadgets [6, 7]. Prior work that investigates the role of kawaii in user perceptions and user acceptance of robots or robotic gadgets is limited. However, a prior team reported on studies of kawaii-ness in the motion of robotic vacuum cleaners [8–10]. These studies demonstrate that kawaii-ness can be expressed through motion even in the absence of more traditional visual cues; however, the studies did not consider the cultural background.

Based on the accepted proposal, we had designed a 7-week collaborative project for cross-cultural teams to design, build and evaluate robotic gadgets, which would have begun in June 2020 at Toyosu Campus of the Shibaura Institute of Technology in Japan. However, because of the COVID-19 pandemic, it became impossible for students from DePauw University in U. S. to travel to Japan and work together with the SIT students at the SIT campus. In fact, even the SIT students could not enter the campus. Therefore, we designed new remote collaborative approaches and activities based on a previous class and global Project Based Learning (PBL) work previously conducted [11, 12].

Even though the first trial was completed online and obtained useful results [13, 14], we had planned a better implementation of the project in the second trial in 2021. However, because the COVID-19 pandemic did not become better, we had to perform the second trial online again. Based on our proposal, the robots would be affectively evaluated by using biological signals such as Electroencephalogram (EEG) and Electrocardiogram (ECG). This is because there has been much prior research on EEG- or ECG-based affective computing [15–18]. This paper describes the design and implementation of the online collaboration approaches and activities for robotic gadgets by the students from U. S. and Japanese universities, and affective evaluation of the robots using EEG and Heart rate (HR) together with kawaii rating.

2   Design of Collaborative Activities

Our plan for collaborative work revolved around the construction of kawaii robots and the affective evaluation of these robots. However, because the collaboration had to be conducted remotely, we changed from constructing real robots in real space to constructing virtual robots that operated in virtual spaces both in the first trial in 2020 and the second trial in 2021. Unity was employed to construct both the virtual robots and the virtual spaces. Zoom and Slack were employed for weekly and daily communication.

Two teams of students were formed with each team consisting of two students from a U.S. university and two students from a Japanese university. In 2020, each team designed and implemented a virtual space and each student designed and implemented a pair of robots to operate in that virtual space. For each pair of robots, one was comparatively evaluated to the other using various affective adjectives. In 2021, we decided to focus on companion robots. Each team designed the context for their companion robots, creating personas of their users and scenarios of their usages. Then, each student designed and implemented four robots based on the persona and scenario of the team. One robot (#1) was designed to be the most kawaii with animal-like features, round shapes, and kawaii colors. The second one (#2) was created from the first one by changing its color to monochrome. The third one (#3) was non-animal-like and not-round shape. The last one (#4) was created from the third one by changing its color to monochrome. An example of four robots is shown in Fig. 1. Each student was also asked to design robots so that each robot elicited a different EEG and/or HR reaction from humans. To get a certain knowledge on Kawaii Engineering, students had read references [19, 20] before attending this project.

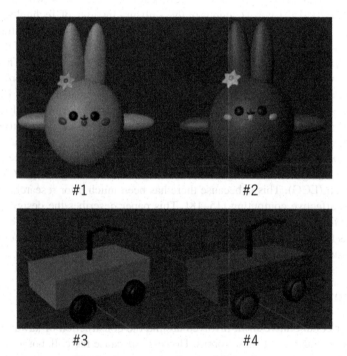

Fig. 1. An example of a set of four robots.

Table 1 shows the schedule of weekly and additional meetings in 2021. Each meeting was held via Zoom.

Table 1. Participant and order of watching.

	EDT	JST	Content
1	23rd May	24th May	Welcome meeting
2	25th May	26th May	Lecture about personas and scenarios
3	1st June	2nd June	Presentation of personas and scenarios
4	8th June	9th June	Presentation of design of virtual robots, Begin development
5	15th June	16th June	Regular meeting with special lecture
6	22nd June	23rd June	Presentations of appearance of robots with EEG and HR
7	29th June	30th June	Regular meeting with special lecture
8	6th July	7th July	Presentation of robots and their evaluation
9	8th July	9th July	Farewell meeting

3 Implementation of Collaborative Practice

The collaborative experiences were organized into seven parts.

3.1 Introduction

After a welcome message from Japanese university and an introduction of the organizers, we introduced the possibilities of virtual reality and the role of robots in future society. Then, the schedule shown in Table 1 was explained.

3.2 Design of Persona and Scenario

After an explanation of personas and scenarios was given, each team discussed their common persona as a user of a companion robot and scenario related to the role of the robot. In addition, each team decided on a scene of a video in which the robot assists the user. The final personas and scenarios are shown in Table 2.

3.3 Design of Four Companion Robots

Based on each team's persona and scenario, each team member designed four robots.

3.4 Development of Four Companion Robots

Each student began to construct robots individually using Unity. The four robots needed to move and needed to include sound or voice. The action needed to last 20 s based on a part of the scenario described in blue in Table 2. In order to confirm that they elicited different reactions in EEG and/or HR, EEG was measured with Mind Wave Moble 2 by NeuroSky. HR was measured with Cardiio provided by Cardiio, Inc. for iPhone users. Heart rate monitor provided by REPS was used for Android users.

Table 2. Persona and scenarios.

Team	Persona/ Scenario	Content
1	Persona	Terry is a 19-year-old first-year university student that is not completely familiar with their campus. Terry frequently gets lost on campus and is late. Terry is nervous about being on time for class and remembering all of their responsibilities. Terry needs help remembering where things are and when Terry needs to do things, such as taking medication, eating properly, and getting enough sleep.
	Scenario	One morning, the robot realizes Terry is not awake 30 minutes before their class, so the robot says 'Terry it is time to get up, you don't want to be late!' and then spins, dances, and claps to wake Terry up. After that, the robot checks Terry's schedule and says, "Good Morning, your first class is at 8:00AM in the Blue Math Building, you have 10 minutes to get ready". The robot brings Terry their medication and breakfast. (continued.).
2	Persona	Sam is a 19-year-old university student, who has become overwhelmed by their schoolwork and obligations. This has led them to lose sleep, miss meals, and consistently forget assignments.
	Scenario	In the evening, Sam's robot does a calendar check and realizes that Sam has an assignment to complete tonight. Sam's robot stands up and says to Sam "You need to do your assignments." The robot then bends its head in a sad manner until Sam starts working. When Sam finishes their assignment, the robot makes fun noises, does a dance, and gives Sam a treat, making Sam feel happy and content with their work.

3.5 Final Presentation and Evaluation

Each student introduced their own four robots by showing their 20-s video one by one. The robots were evaluated by EEG and/or HR. NeuroExperimenter developed by Fred Mellender was used to measure continuously and collect EEG data. HR was measured every 20 s. of watching a robot and saved by the same applications as described the section above. The robots were also evaluated by kawaii rating from 1 to 10 after the presentation using the zoom records and Google Form.

Averages of Attention and Meditation, indexes provided by NeuroSky, were calculated. The averages while watching robots for 20 s. and the 20-s. averages of resting time just before the watching were compared. Examples of the differences of averaged Meditation of EEG of two of the authors are shown in Fig. 2 when watching the robots shown in Fig. 1 (Set A in Table 3) and another set of robots (Set B in Table 3). Figure 3 shows the HR results of four of the authors when watching the robots shown in Fig. 1. Unfortunately, we couldn't get any meaningful results from EEG at present. In the example shown in Fig. 3, HR reduce when watching monochrome robots. This might be because monochrome increases the material perception of metal which reduce the exciting feeling of kawaii color robots.

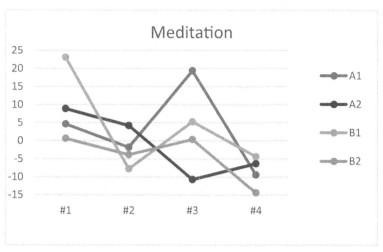

Fig. 2. Examples of Meditation of EEG for two of the authors for the robots shown in Fig. 1 (Set A in Table 3) and another robot (Set B in Table 3). A1 and A2 indicate the Meditation for two of the authors when watching the robots of Set A. B1 and B2 indicate the Meditation for the same two authors when watching the robots of Set B.

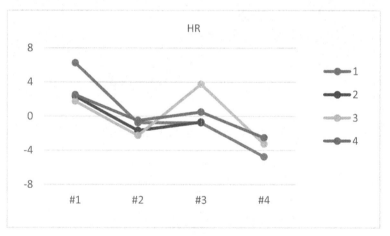

Fig. 3. Examples of HR for four of the authors for the robots shown in Fig. 1 (The values are the differences from average for each participant).

Table 3 shows the averages of kawaii scores evaluated by five of the authors. The four robots of Set A are shown in Fig. 1. The robots #1 and #4 of Sets D and H are shown in Figs. 4 and 5. Generally speaking, robot #1 of four robots had higher scores and #4 had lower scores. Some examples with higher kawaii scores and examples with lower kawaii scores are shown in Figs. 4 and 5.

Table 3. Averages of kawaii score for each robot.

Set	#1	#2	#3	#4
A	9.4	7.8	5.2	4.6
B	9.2	8.4	4.0	3.6
C	8.8	7.8	4.8	4.0
D	8.6	7.2	5.4	3.0
E	8.2	7.2	4.6	3.6
F	6.0	4.6	2.6	2.4
G	8.6	7.0	5.0	4.2
H	9.6	7.6	4.0	2.4

(a) #1 of a student.

(b) #2 of another student.

Fig. 4. Examples of the most kawaii robots.

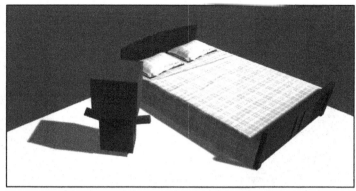

(a) #3 of a student.

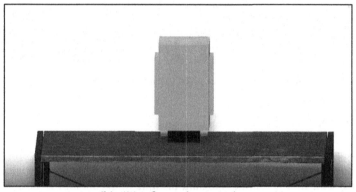

(b) #4 of another student.

Fig. 5. Examples of the least kawaii robots.

3.6 Special Lectures

Two topics were introduced by SIT faculties to deepen understanding of students on Kawaii Engineering [21, 22].

3.7 Farewell Meeting

Farewell meeting was held at the last day of the 7-week activities. Certification was given to each student in a VR space created using Cluster by Cluster Inc. as shown in Fig. 6

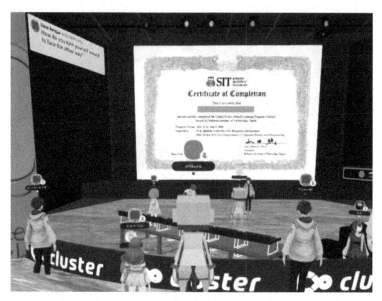

Fig. 6. Certification was given to each student in a VR space.

4 Discussion

As described in the Introduction, our original plan called for the students and professors from DePauw University to travel to Tokyo, Japan. The U. S. students would have then collaborated with students of the Shibaura Institute of Technology to design and build real robots with kawaii appearances and behaviors. However, because of the COVID-19 pandemic, travel was impossible. Therefore, we designed new remote collaboration approaches and activities in 2020. In 2021, the situation became better because students could enter their own university campus. However, in-person collaboration remained impossible. Based on our improved plan, each student team designed a persona and scenario for a companion robot, and developed four virtual robots.

Affective evaluation of the robots was performed by measuring EEG and HR together with kawaii rating by questionnaire. Based on the previous knowledge that kawaii stimulus can be divided into "exciting kawaii" and "relaxing kawaii" [23], the robot #1 in Fig. 1 seems to be "exciting kawaii" from the HR results shown in Fig. 3. However, the results of EEG and HR were uncertain because the insufficient confirmation of each robot to elicit a different EEG and/or HR reactions and difficulties of self-measurement of those bio-signals by authors ourselves. To solve these problems remains as future work.

5 Conclusion

Because of the COVID-19 pandemic, we had to change the targets of our 7-week collaboration from real robots to virtual robots. Based on our new plan for 2021, each student team designed a persona of a user of a companion robot and scenario for the assistance of the robot, and each student developed four different robots under the scenario.

Affective evaluation of the robots was performed by measuring EEG and HR together with kawaii rating by a questionnaire. Improvement of both robots and measurement of bio-signals are necessary for further research.

Acknowledgement. This material is based upon work supported by the National Science Foundation under Grant No. OISE-1854255. Any opinions, findings, and conclusions or recommendations expressed in this material are those of the authors and do not necessarily reflect the views of the National Science Foundation. We thank all the participating students: G. Todd, H. Schwipps, N. Jadram, S. Imura, L. Guinee, R. Martinez, N. S. Fong and S. Ohtsuka.

References

1. National Science Foundation International Research Experiences for Students. www.nsf.gov/publications/pub_summ.jsp?WT.z_pims_id=505656&ods_key=nsf19585. Accessed 24 Feb 2020
2. Marcus, A., Kurosu, M., Ma, X., Hashizume, A.: Cuteness Engineering: Designing Adorable Products and Services. Springer, Heidelberg (2017). https://doi.org/10.1007/978-3-319-619 61-3
3. Ohkura, M. (ed.): Kawaii Engineering. SSCC, Springer, Singapore (2019). https://doi.org/10.1007/978-981-13-7964-2
4. Nittono, H., et al.: The power of kawaii: viewing cute images promotes a careful behavior and narrows attentional focus. PLoS ONE **7**(9), e46362 (2012)
5. Nittono, H.: "Kawaii" no Chikara (The Power of "Kawaii"). Kagakudojin, Kyoto (2019). (in Japanese)
6. Cole, S.: The Most Kawaii Robots of 2016. https://motherboard.vice.com/en_us/article/xyg ky3/the-most-kawaii-robots-of-2016-5886b75a358cef455d864759. Accessed 28 June 2021
7. Bennett, B.: Meet all the cute, friendly, useful robots of CES 2019. https://www.cnet.com/pic tures/meet-all-the-robots-of-ces-2019. Accessed 28 June 2021
8. Sugano, S., Miyaji, Y., Tomiyama, K.: Study of kawaii-ness in motion – physical properties of kawaii motion of roomba. In: Kurosu, M. (eds.) HCII 2013. LNCS, vol. 8004, pp. 620–629. Springer, Heidelberg (2013). https://doi.org/10.1007/978-3-642-39232-0_67
9. Sugano, S., Morita, H., Tomiyama, K.: Study on kawaii-ness in motion - classifying kawaii motion using roomba. In: Ji, Y. (ed.) AHFE2012. Advances in Affective and Pleasurable Design, 1st edn., pp.107–116. CRC Press, Boca Raton (2012)
10. Sugano, S., Tomiyama, K.: Kawaii-ness in motion. In: Ohkura, M. (ed.) Kawaii Engineering. Springer Series on Cultural Computing, pp. 77–91. Springer, Singapore (2019). https://doi.org/10.1007/978-981-13-7964-2_4
11. Ohkura, M., Sakurai, H., Aoto, T.: A trial of interactive remote teaching by shared virtual spaces between two universities. In: Proceedings of the CollabTech2008, Wakayama, pp. 89–93 (2008)
12. Ohkura, M., et al.: Multi-media global PBL with HTML5 and TECHTILE toolkit for Japanese and Thai students. In: Proceedings of the 2017 JSEE Annual Conference, Tokyo, pp. 45–50 (2017)
13. Ohkura, M., et al.: Design and implementation of kawaii robots by Japanese and American university students using remote collaboration. In: Proceedings of the ISASE 2021 (2021)

14. Berque, D., et al.: Cross-cultural design and evaluation of robot prototypes based on Kawaii (cute) attributes. In: Rau, P.-L. (ed.) HCII 2021. LNCS, vol. 12773, pp. 319–334. Springer, Cham (2021). https://doi.org/10.1007/978-3-030-77080-8_26

15. Pei, G., Li, T.: A literature review of EEG-based affective computing in marketing. Front. Psychol., 16 (2021)

16. Tivatansakul, S., Ohkura, M.: Emotion recognition using ECG signals with local pattern description methods. Int. J. Affect. Eng. 15(2), 51–61 (2016)

17. Nikolova, D., Petkova, P., Manolova, A., Georgieva, P.: ECG-based emotion recognition: overview of methods and applications. In: Advances in Neural Networks and Applications 2018 (ANNA 2018), pp. 1–5. VDE Verlag, Berlin (2018)

18. Ito, K., Miura, N., Ohkura, M.: Proposal of affective model for a system using ECG. Trans. Jpn. Soc. Kansei Eng. 18(1), 87–93 (2019). (in Japanese)

19. Ohkura, M., Komatsu, T., Aoto, T.: Kawaii rules: increasing affective value of industrial products. In: Watada, J., Shiizuka, H., Lee, K.-P., Otani, T., Lim, C.-P. (eds.) Industrial Applications of Affective Engineering, pp. 97–110. Springer, Cham (2014). https://doi.org/10.1007/978-3-319-04798-0_8

20. Ohkura, M.: Systematic study on "Kawaii." Inf. Process. 57(2), 124–127 (2016). (in Japanese)

21. Laohakangvalvit, T., Achalakul, T., Ohkura, M.: A method to obtain effective attributes for attractive cosmetic bottles by deep learning. Int. J. Affect. Eng. 19(1), 37–48 (2019)

22. Sripian, P., Miyatake, K., Ohkura, M.: Study on the color feature of Harajuku-type kawaii fashion comparison with street snap images using colorfulness. TNI J. Eng. Technol. 8(1), 63–72 (2020)

23. Yanagi, M., et al.: Differences in heartbeat modulation between excited and relaxed kawaii feelings during photograph observation. Int. J. Affect. Eng. 15(2), 189–193 (2016)

Possibilities and Research Issues for Measuring Human Emotions in Real Life

Mieko Ohsuga[✉]

Osaka Institute of Technology, Osaka 530-8568, Japan
`mieko.ohsuga@oit.ac.jp`

Abstract. We would like to provide systems and services that contribute to people's well-being by capturing emotional responses using bio-signals that can be measured with low burden in daily life. In this paper, the current status and issues related to measurement devices, verification of accuracy, and detection of measurement failures that are necessary to achieve this goal are discussed. Burden-free measurements are categorized as wearable, environmental embedded, and camera-based. Each has its own strengths and weaknesses, and it is best to use them in combination according to the purpose. In addition, three prototypes developed using a small processor with the function to communicate with the cloud via Wi-Fi and commercially available sensors are presented, and future challenges is discussed through these trials. In order to create systems and services that people are willing to use and that make them active and positive, industry-academia collaboration, including experts and users from various fields is desirable.

Keywords: Human emotion · Bio-signal measurement in real life · Low-burden measurement

1 Introduction

We have been working on the estimation of human states mainly using physiological indices [1–4]. In particular, we have conducted multi-dimensional evaluations using a combination of autonomic nervous system indicators such as heart rate and respiration, visual system indicators such as blink and eye movement, and central system indicators such as spontaneous EEG and event-related potentials. Since there are individual differences in physiological mechanisms and how people perceive and respond to external factors that affect their state, multi-dimensional assessment is essential.

In order to collect more realistic responses and to feed back the extracted information to the person, the people around them, the tools and systems they use, and the environment, continuous and continuous measurement in daily life and industrial scenes is important.

M. Kurosu (Ed.): HCII 2022, LNCS 13302, pp. 489–501, 2022.
https://doi.org/10.1007/978-3-031-05311-5_34

2 Current Status and Issues on Low Burden Measurement

The low burden measurement means that measurements should be effortless, unobtrusive, and preferably non-consciously. There are three directions of low-burden measurement: use of wearable devices (including implants), implantation in tools or environment, and non-contact measurement using camera images.

2.1 Wearable Devices

Wearable devices include wristwatches, wristbands, rings, and shirts and belts with embedded sensors. These devices have made rapid progress in the several years, and most of them are linked to healthcare services [5–7]. However, many devices are too intelligent and do not provide raw waveforms, but only present index values and estimated results. The method of dealing with incorrect measurement is a black box, and no information on the reliability of the estimated results is available. Some devices that expose raw-like waveforms stored in loggers or the cloud, as well as SDKs and APIs (e.g., HeX shirts [8, 9], E4 wristbands [10]). Using these data, we are investigating when and to what extent measurement failures occur, and how to deal with measurement failures [11, 12].

On the other hand, kits of circuits for bio-signal measurement (BITalino [13, 14]) and simple inexpensive sensors for microcomputers (Arduino) are commercially available making it easier to configure our own measurement wireless devices. However, for some sensors, the details of the measurement principle and specifications are not disclosed, and expensive equipment with guaranteed accuracy is often required for calibration.

Table 1. Comparison between the two prototype devices (using BITalino Kit [13]) and commercial wearable devices (Heisoskin shirts [8], E4 wristband [10], Fitbit wristband [15], Spire [16] and Oura Ring [17].

	Wrist Band BITalino	Waist Belt BITalino	Smart Shirt Hexisoskin	Wrist Band E4	Wrist Band FitBit	Crip Type Spire	Ring Type Oura
Acceptability	O	O	△	O	◎	◎	O
ECG/Pulse	Pulse	ECG	ECG	Pulse	Pulse	×	PR
Respiration	×	Abdomen Perimeter AC	Abdomen & Chest Perimeter DC	×	×	Abdomen or Chest slope	×
3-axis Acceleration	Wrist	Waist	Wrist	Wrist	Wrist	×	Finger
Raw Data (SDK)	Realtime	Realtime	Batch via Cloud /Logger	Batch via Cloud SDK	Batch Processed Data	×	×

Table 1 shows a comparison of the specifications and acceptability in daily life of several commercially available devices and two types of prototype devices using the BITalino kit.

2.2 Environment-Embedded Devices

Examples of tools and environment-embedded devices include mouses, stuffed animals (Fig. 1, [18]) or cushions (Fig. 2, [19]), scales, toilet seats, beds and chairs (Fig. 3, [20]). These methods enable even more unconscious measurement but they can be measured only during the tool is used. In addition, since the number of measurement deficiencies are more fluent, a mechanism should be implemented to distinguish between measurement incompleteness and abnormalities or changes in the user's physical and or mental condition. We discussed the possibility of discrimination using ECG data measured by a chair-type device as an example [21, 22].

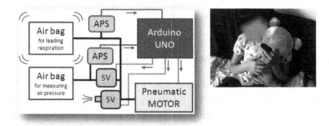

Fig. 1. A Stuffed bear device to help children learn to relax. One of the airbags in the bear is used to measure the child's breathing, and the other to represent the bear's breathing. The bear's breathing starts from the child's respiratory period and slowly slows down. When the child's breathing deviates from bear's breathing, the breathing rate is guided back to the child's cycle, so that the child can learn how to relax without being forced. For details, see Uratani et al. [18].

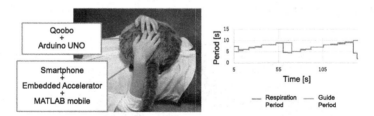

Fig. 2. A cushioned robot with a tail that induces slow breathing and promotes sleep [19]. It uses commercially available cushioned robot named "QooBoo" [23] with a tail that moves gently to heal, and a smartphone. An acceleration sensor in the smartphone detects changes in the tilt of the abdomen as the user breathes, and calculates the breathing cycle using MATLAB mobile. The respiratory guidance mechanism is the same as in the device shown in Fig. 1.

Fig. 3. Examples of chairs to measure ECG and respiration. The technology developed for driver monitoring is now being applied to monitoring workers at their desks and persons relaxing in the living room. For details, see Ohsuga 2018 [20].

2.3 Camera-Video-Based Systems

In the case of camera-video-based systems, there has been remarkable progress in marker-less motion capture thanks to AI (e.g., Deep Learning). From a single video (smartphone or web camera) without using a distance sensor (such as KINECT or RealSense) [24], we can now detect faces and facial parts even when wearing a mask (Fig. 4) and also multiple faces and parts delivered by an online conference tool. It is also possible to detect skeletons from the body images, and estimate the shape of body parts (Fig. 5).

There are some difficulties in estimation accuracy and real-time performance, but these can be improved by combining several methods. We are trying to estimate the posture of a person based on the bust-up images taken from the front to generate alarms for bad posture and immobility.

Fig. 4. Detection of the face and the 28 facial landmarks by the re-trained face detector and the facial landmarks detector in the dlib C++ library. Revised from Kamakura, et al. 2021 [24].

Fig. 5. Extraction of skeletons from video images using OpenPose [25]. Revised from [26].

The blinks can be detected from the change in the distance between the two eyelids. It is also possible to detect video pulse waves from color changes in the cheek area, and to extract respiratory waveforms from shoulder movements (Fig. 6). These indices are expected to be used to assess the arousal state and concentration of car drivers, people working at desks or listening to lectures, and the emotions of people watching media or talking with others.

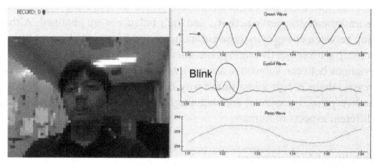

Fig. 6. An example of pulse wave, blinks (eyelid distance) and respiration wave extracted from camera images in real-time. This photo and the screen capture were personally provided by the author's collaborator, Dr. Y. Kamakura.

The challenge is to deal with low sampling rate and inadequate measurement. We are examining the possibility of improving the accuracy by up-sampling of the data, and by using machine learning to determine and supplement the inadequate samples based on acceleration data and distortion of pulse waveforms [27]. In this case, it is essential to output the confidence level as well for beneficial use.

3 Technical and Research Issues

3.1 Measurement Failure

We are proposing a system of AI assistants to support mental health care by combining AI counselors and physiological indicators. In order to realize this system, it is essential to obtain physiological responses under free action with low burden. Therefore, we conducted a basic study to determine the ratio of the time of day when the correct measurement can be made using a relatively unobtrusive commercial device [12]. In this study, a wristband-type device (E4 wristband, Empatica) and a smart shirt (HEXOSKIN, Caree Technologies) were used. We measured pulse and skin conductance (SC) in the former, respiration in the latter, and 3-axis acceleration in both. The participants were three healthy young males who gave written informed consent (Approval No. 2020-7-1) and the measurement time was about 22 h/day, excluding bathing and sleeping, on five weekdays.

Here, in order to use indices related to pulse rate variability, a strict condition for data rejection was imposed: in particular, to obtain its low-frequency component, a continuous 30-s interval without artifacts was required. In addition, the section where the norm of wrist acceleration exceeded the specified threshold was also excluded because the waveform distortion of the pulse wave caused by arm movement affects significantly the pulse rate variability.

As a result, usable data were obtained only about 10% of the total measurement time, mainly during PC work. Under these strict conditions, principal component analysis was performed on the time series data of pulse-related physiological indices and SC totaling seven indices obtained from the remaining data. After varimax rotation for major three components, the components interpreted as reflecting sympathetic nerve activity, parasympathetic nerve activity, and their balance were obtained. Although the relationship between changes in these components and lifestyle behaviors was inferred, the relationship with subjective ratings recorded using a smartphone application was not clear. Deviations between subjective assessment and physiological indices are common. In some cases, there is a problem in the way each indicator is calculated, but in other cases, the divergence is essential and meaningful because the two indicators originally capture different aspects of human.

3.2 Reliability of Measurement

In the case of video-based pulse wave, our previous study [27] examined the accuracy of pulse wave interval using ECG RR interval as the gold standard. It depends on the selection of the face area to be used, but of course it is more sensitive to body movements, and in this experiment, the accuracy significantly decreased when the participant was manipulating the tablet. In addition, this study attempted to discriminate between positive and false detections using a Support Vector Machine (SVM) with the parameters of the pulse wave waveform and the statistics of the pulse wave intervals as input and the RR intervals as supervisory data. The overall accuracy of discriminating misrecognitions using SVM was 75.1%, and further improvement is desired. It is also necessary to improve the method of determining the correctness of detection in the supervised data. In a laboratory experiment, it is expected that there will be few measurement failures in the equipment used to obtain the teacher data, but in the field, the gold standard may have also some detection errors, which makes verification more difficult [28].

Detection errors give a significant impact not only on the parameters of average pulse rate and parameters of pulse rate variability. We also studied the effect of removing false positives determined by SVM and found it promising for the average pulse rate and for the low-frequency component of pulse variation.

We have to evaluate this method on a larger number of samples. The problem is that it is difficult to evaluate the obtained performance because the frequency of false positives and the magnitude of the error from the gold standard are highly dependent on the experimental environment and conditions. For quantitative comparison between the proposed method and existing methods, it is desirable to use a commonly available database.

3.3 Data Collection Using a Small Device

The mainstream wireless technologies are either Bluetooth or Wi-Fi. While the former requires a PC or similar device nearby the measurement cite to receive signals, the latter has the advantage that data processed by a microcontroller can be uploaded to the cloud and analyzed by a machine with high processing power in a remote location, thus promoting the use of AI. In the next chapter, three case studies are introduced that realize quasi real-time feedback using "M5Stack" or "M5StickC" which integrate a microcontroller, LCD display, and Wi-Fi into a compact package, inexpensive sensors, and cloud processing using ThingSpeak [29] and MATLAB. ThingSpeak is an Internet of Things (IoT) platform provided from Mathworks that allows us to collect and store sensor data in the cloud and develop IoT applications.

4 Field Trials Using M5Stack or M5StickC

4.1 Baby Robot that Makes Newborn's Presence Felt by Distant Father

We have developed a baby robot that allows fathers of newborns who are restricted from visiting their babies due to Covid-19 infection prevention measures to feel close to their babies at home. The baby robot represents the weight, warmth, and breathing of the newborn. The father holds the baby robot and converses with the mother who is showing her/his baby face using an online communication tool.

The system configuration is as shown in Fig. 7. An acceleration sensor attached to the abdomen of a newborn baby measures the movement of his/her abdomen and reflects this signal to that of the baby robot. The output of the accelerometer is acquired by the M5StickC, pre-processed, uploaded to the cloud, and the respiratory component is extracted using a frequency band filter, etc. The results are sent to a microcontroller, which inflates and deflates the airbag to make it appear as if the robot is breathing.

The developed prototype was demonstrated at the "SDGs Art Exhibition [30]" held in Osaka (Ethics Approval Number: 2021_87), and also presented to a doctor of obstetrics and midwives, where the concept was favorably accepted. We also had a pair of a newborn and their parents try out the device (Ethics Approval Number: 2021_36), and found that wearing the sensor was not too much of a burden for the baby, that respiration could be measured when the newborns were calm, not crying and that weight and warmth were effective in making the newborns feel close to the father. However, for breathing, it was pointed out that the delay (currently about 3 s) and the movement and sound of the airbag need to be improved. In the future, the pump and control unit need to be downsized and stored in the robot's abdomen, and the robot needs to be wireless.

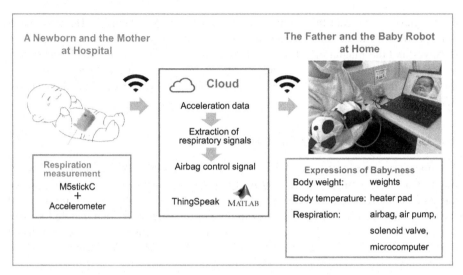

Fig. 7. System configuration of the baby robot prototype.

4.2 Early Detection of Emotional Changes in Children with Autism Spectrum Disorder

We have proposed a system that makes interaction easier between with children with Autism Spectrum Disorder (ASD) and their caregivers, so that they can better understand child's behavior and respond more quickly [31]. Although there have been studies on emotional assessment of ASD children using autonomic indicators and behavioral data [32], any services that aim to support caregivers were not found. Through the use of this system, we hope to increase opportunities for caregivers to intervene in the emotional regulation of ASD children, and to promote affection formation by learning about changes in emotions that ASD children are not expressing.

As shown in Fig. 8, the devices to be worn by ASD children are a wristband and a waist belt, each of which consists of a commercially available sensor and an M5stickC. These data are sent to the cloud via Wi-Fi together with the data acquired by the built-in 3-axis accelerometer, where pulse rate, electrodermal activity (skin resistance level), and respiration rate are quantified, and emotional changes are detected using a preliminary algorithm we developed. The results are then sent to the caregiver via LINE. We have also developed a web application that allows users to view the details and enter their observation/coping logs.

We also introduced our proposal at the "SDGs Art Exhibition", and presented it to pediatricians for their opinions. Although they agreed on the usefulness of the system, however, it was pointed out that we need a way to make ASD children wear the device, since ASD children often have sensory hypersensitivity. We need to customize the device according to their sensory properties and preferences in appearance. At present, we have only conducted a measurement test on one child with ASD, wearing a device covered with his favorite character (Ethics Approval Number: 2021_64).

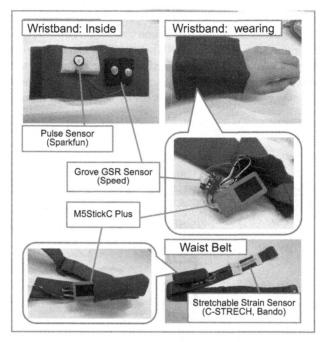

Fig. 8. Two kinds of devices for emotion detection of the children with ASD.

In the future, we will test whether the emotion detection algorithm developed for normal participants can be applied to ASD children before conducting experiments to investigate its utility.

4.3   Assessment of Tension and Self-control Support for Student Athletes

It is said that athletes perform at their best in an appropriate state of tension. In the past, the author developed a monitor to visualize the tension level of archery players by using ECG RR intervals and their fluctuations [33]. This device could be used at the game site; however, it was a large device that required a sensor to be attached to the chest.

In this study, we proposed a system for student athletes who do not have their own coaches. It assesses the level of tension, informs the student athletes, and provides them with tools to control their own tension according to the level of tension.

Figure 9 show the system configuration of the developed prototype. The pulse rate and electrodermal activity (skin resistance, SR) are used to assess the degree of tension in 4 levels. The GSR2, which has been commercially available for a long time as a biofeedback device, was used to measure SR. This device is easy to use and can be measured by simply grabbing and placing two fingers on it. The sensor for measuring the pulse is the same as the one used for ASD children, but it is attached to the GSR2 so that it can be measured just by holding the GSR2. M5Stack is used for preprocessing and communication with the cloud. This is because a large screen is useful for displaying advice and playing music for tension control.

We conducted several preliminary experiments on female high school judo players and created a tentative algorithm for tension estimation (Ethics Approval Number: 2021_38). The parameters were determined for each individual using data from the preliminary experiments. After we implemented a tool for controlling tension as a web application, we asked the same students to use it during a practice game against another school. The system was well accepted, but its utility was not yet evaluated.

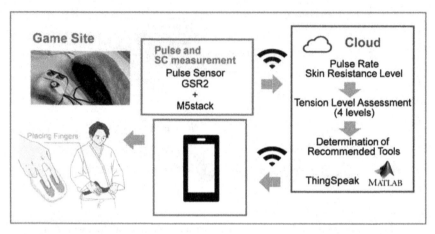

Fig. 9. System configuration of a tension self-control support tool for student athletes.

5   Discussions

We have been doing research for many years on the use of physiological indices to assess human states and emotions, and neither the measurement target nor the principle of the sensor has changed significantly. However, thanks to advances in processors and wireless communications, devices have become smaller and more wireless, making it possible to obtain biological signals in real time not only in the laboratory but also in everyday life. In addition, remarkable advances in machine learning and AI have provided us with new methods for data analysis, change detection, and pattern classification and discrimination. With the cloud and the AI running on it, we can achieve the same level of processing in the field as if we were carrying around a big powerful computer, even if we only have a small amount of memory and an inefficient processor. Therefore, now is the time to develop technologies and services that can measure people's emotions in real situations and use them to make people happy.

When using commercially available devices for this purpose, it is necessary to clarify what is going on inside them, rather than leaving them as a black box. In order to do so, the measurement results must be compared with the true values measured by those with guaranteed accuracy, but the results of the experiment conducted in the laboratory cannot be taken directly to the field, and data collection using these guaranteed devices in daily life situations places a heavy burden on person being measured. The only way to deal with this problem is to verify the accuracy of the devices in a step-by-step manner while guaranteeing traceability.

Another important thing is to provide a means to distinguish between measurement failures and outliers that depend on abnormal human conditions. Many machine learning algorithms used for two-state discrimination require an equivalent number of two-state data. It is necessary to use a method to detect abnormal values from a large number of data in one state. Depending on the application, we can approach the problem from a completely different perspective, for example, by asking the person him/herself, or by making a judgment based on visual observation by another person. It is also possible to have a system that is not fully automated, but one in which a human intervenes only when necessary, that is, a system in which performance is enhanced by synergy between the human and the automated system.

There is an idea that an appropriate discriminator can be created by using data with a large size (big data) for training, even if it has a lot of noise. However, unlike data with variance based on physical laws, data about people are highly individual and situation-dependent, and thus cannot be expected to have well-balanced noise inclusion. Magnitude of the risk of creating an algorithm that makes prejudiced and wrong decisions depends on how the training data is collected and selected. Even in the case of collecting big data in our daily lives, it is desirable to have some control over the measurement methods and conditions of biometric measurements, subjective assessment methods, and environmental information collection methods.

Individual differences are one of the major problems that needs to be addressed in this field. A person's response depends on how he or she perceives the situation and external stimuli (stressors), how he or she copes with them, and also on the properties of his or her biological system. To adapt to individual differences, we need to create a model of the person and make decisions based on that model. We interpret the speech and actions of others by inferring their feelings in the light of our experience on the interaction with them. Therefore, I think it would be a good idea to aim for a system that can judge a person's state and emotions using a model that is trained by collecting big data of each person.

6 Conclusion

In order to provide systems that contribute to people's well-being, it is essential to measure their emotional responses and to have the means to respond appropriately. It is desirable for industry-academia collaboration to collect big data using common methods and plans, and to provide this data as an open database. It is also hoped that experts in various fields and users will discuss in groups to come up with systems and services that people are willing to use and that make them active and happy.

Acknowledgment. The author thanks her co-researcher Dr. Yoshiyuki Kamakura (Department of Information Science, Osaka Institute of Technology) for frequent discussions and collaboration. She also thanks to the students in "wellness" laboratory, especially graduate students; Mr. Hiroki.Takeuchi (Sect. 3.2), Mr. Kaito Hayashi (Sect. 3.1), and undergraduate student; Mrs. Ayaka Yamauchi (Sect. 4.1), Mrs. Narumi Nomiya (Sect. 4.2), and Mrs. Emi Yamanari (Sect. 4.3) for their contributions to the specific research. The author is also grateful to the participants who participated in the experiments and to the many people who provided useful comments on the research. A part of work cited in Sect. 2.3 was conducted by New Media Development Association supported by Japan Keirin Auto race foundation (JKA) and its promotion funds from KEIRIN RACE.

References

1. Ohsuga, M., Shimono, F., Genno, H.: Assessment of phasic work stress using autonomic indices. Int. J. Psychophysiol. **40**(3), 211–220 (2001)
2. Ohsuga, M., Kamakura, Y., Inoue, Y., Noguchi, Y., Shimada, K., Mishiro, M.: Estimation of driver's arousal state using multi-dimensional physiological indices. In: Harris, D. (ed.) EPCE 2011. LNCS (LNAI), vol. 6781, pp. 176–185. Springer, Heidelberg (2011). https://doi.org/10.1007/978-3-642-21741-8_20
3. Joko, S., Ohsuga, M., Tada, Y., Ishikawa, J.: Evaluation of a mental care system for patients recuperating in a sterile room after hematopoietic cell transplantation. In: 41st Annual International Conference of the IEEE Engineering in Medicine and Biology Society (EMBC), pp. 1314–1317 (2019)
4. Yoshioka, N., Araki, N., Ohsuga, M.: Importance of the features of event-related potentials used for a machine learning-based model applied to single-trial data during oddball task. In: 43rd Annual International Conference of the IEEE Engineering in Medicine & Biology Society (EMBC), pp. 2123–2126 (2021)
5. Can, Y.S., Arnrich, B., Ersoy, C.: Stress detection in daily life scenarios using smart phones and wearable sensors: a survey. J. Biomed. Inform. **92**, 103139 (2019)
6. Albertetti, F., Simalastar, A., Rizzotti-Kaddouri, A.: Stress detection with deep learning approaches using physiological signals. In: Goleva, R., Garcia, NRd.C., Pires, I.M. (eds.) HealthyIoT 2020. LNICSSITE, vol. 360, pp. 95–111. Springer, Cham (2021). https://doi.org/10.1007/978-3-030-69963-5_7
7. Gao, N., Marschall, M., Burry, J., Watkins, S., Salim, F.D.: Understanding occupants' behaviour, engagement, emotion, and comfort indoors with heterogeneous sensors and wearables. arXiv preprint arXiv:2105.06637 (2021)
8. HEXOSKIN: Hexoskin Smart Shirts - Cardiac, Respiratory, Sleep & Activity Metrics. https://www.hexoskin.com/. Accessed 11 Feb 2022
9. Montes, J., Young, J.C., Tandy, R., Navalta, J.W.: Reliability and validation of the hexoskin wearable bio-collection device during walking conditions. Int. J. Exerc. Sci. **11**(7), 806–816 (2018)
10. Emprica: E4 wristband. https://www.empatica.com/. Accessed 11 Feb 2022
11. Ohsuga, M., Kamakura, Y., Takeuchi, H., Koba, H.: Low burden measurement of autonomic indices for self-measurement or longtime measurement in the field. In: Black, N.L., Neumann, W.P., Noy, I. (eds.) IEA 2021. LNNS, vol. 222, pp. 652–657. Springer, Cham (2021). https://doi.org/10.1007/978-3-030-74611-7_89
12. Hayashi, K., Ohsuga, M.: A basic study on the utilization of physiological indicators for mental health support. Jpn. J. Ergon. **57**, 2G2-1 (2021). (in Japanese)
13. BITalino: Redefining Biomedical Toolkits. https://bitalino.com/. Accessed 11 Feb 2022
14. Batista, D., da Silva, H.P., Fred, A., Moreira, C., Reis, M., Ferreira, H.A.: Benchmarking of the BITalino biomedical toolkit against an established gold standard. Healthc. Technol. Lett. **6**(2), 32–36 (2019)
15. Fitbit: FitBit wristband. https://www.fitbit.com/. Accessed 11 Feb 2022
16. Spirehealth: Remote Patient Monitoring. https://www.spirehealth.com/. Accessed 11 Feb 2022

17. OURA: Accurate Health Information Accessible to Everyone. https://ouraring.com/. Accessed 11 Feb 2022
18. Uratani, H., Ohsuga, M.: Relaxation effect of a respiration-leading stuffed toy. Adv. Biomed. Eng. **7**, 100–106 (2018)
19. Urabe, H., Koba, H., Ohsuga, M.: Proposal of sleep promotion device using breathing guidance by cushion robot. In: 2021 Proceeding of Human-Agent Interaction Symposium, P-44 (2021). (in Japanese)
20. Ohsuga, M.: Development of chairs for nonintrusive measurement of heart rate and respiration and its application. In: Bagnara, S., Tartaglia, R., Albolino, S., Alexander, T., Fujita, Y. (eds.) IEA 2018. AISC, vol. 827, pp. 392–404. Springer, Cham (2019). https://doi.org/10.1007/978-3-319-96059-3_44
21. Ohsuga, M., Sugiyama, S.: Obtaining heart rate information from a driver using capacity coupled electrodes (5th report). In: Proceeding of 2016 JSAE Annual Congress (Spring), pp.1539–1542 (2016). (in Japanese)
22. Ohsuga, M., Sugiyama, S.: Obtaining heart rate information from a driver using capacity coupled electrodes (6th report). In: Proceeding of 2016 JSAE Annual Congress (Autumn), pp.1075–1078 (2016). (in Japanese)
23. QuooBoo: A Tailed Cushion That Heals Your Heart. https://qoobo.info/index-en/. Accessed 11 Feb 2022
24. Kamakura, Y., Takeuchi, H., Ohsuga, M.: Contactless and low-burden measurement of physiological signals and comparison of obtained indices. In: Black, N.L., Patrick Neumann, W., Noy, I. (eds.) IEA 2021. LNNS, vol. 222, pp. 615–619. Springer, Cham (2021). https://doi.org/10.1007/978-3-030-74611-7_83
25. GitHub - CMU-Perceptual-Computing-Lab/openpose: Real-time multi-person keypoint detection library for body, face, hands, and foot estimation. https://github.com/CMU-Perceptual-Computing-Lab/openpose. Accessed 11 Feb 2022
26. Report of the project of New Media Development Association supported by Japan Keirin Autorace foundation (JKA) and its promotion funds from KEIRIN RACE (2020). (in Japanese)
27. Takeuchi, H., Ohsuga, M., Kamakura, Y.: A study on region of interest in remote PPG and an attempt to eliminate false positive results using SVM classification. In: 2021 IEEE International Conference on Artificial Intelligence in Engineering and Technology (IICAIET), pp.1–5 (2021)
28. Lang, M.: Beyond Fitbit: a critical appraisal of optical heart rate monitoring wearables and apps, their current limitations and legal implications. Alb. LJ Sci. Tech. **28**, 39–72 (2017)
29. ThingSpeak: IoT Analytics - ThingSpeak Internet of Things. https://thingspeak.com/, Accessed 11 Feb 2022
30. ATC INNOVATION WEEK (in Japanese). https://www.atc-co.com/innovation-week/. Accessed 11 Feb 2022
31. Nomiya, N., Hayashi, K., Koba, H., Takeuchi, H.: Development of a support system for caregivers that presents emotional changes in children with autism spectrum disorder. In: 2021 Conference of Japan Ergonomics Society KANSAI Branch, p. B-2-2 (2021). (in Japanese)
32. Taj-Eldin, M., Ryan, C., O'Flynn, B., Galvin, P.: A review of wearable solutions for physiological and emotional monitoring for use by people with autism spectrum disorder and their caregivers. Sensors **18**(12), 4271–4299 (2018)
33. Ohsuga, M., Shimono, F., Akashi, C.: Development of an apparatus for monitoring degree of mental tension. Trans. Soc. Instrum. Control Eng. **28**(8), 910–915 (1992). (in Japanese)

Model Construction of "Kawaii Characters" Using Deep Learning

Shuma Ohtsuka[✉], Peeraya Sripian, Tipporn Laohakangvalvit, and Midori Sugaya

Shibaura Institute of Technology, Koto-ku, Tokyo 135-8548, Japan
{al18029,peeraya,tipporn,doly}@shibaura-it.ac.jp

Abstract. In recent years, "kawaii" has been attracting attention as an affective value in manufacturing for various purposes. One example is the use of "kawaii characters" in marketing, PR and advertisement for several target groups especially young people. However, those "kawaii characters" have been designed and used intuitively without systematically evaluating their kawaii degree for target group. Since different target groups might have different preferences for kawaii characters, only intuitive design of kawaii characters might not fulfil their satisfaction and attract enough attention as expected. Therefore, this study proposes a systematic method to evaluate kawaii characters by constructing a model to classify kawaii characters with different physical attributes. To construct "kawaii character" dataset, we firstly prepared ten standard characters as images. Then, for each standard character, we prepared four different variations for each of these six physical attributes: eyebrows, eyes, mouth, facial (cheek) redness, clothing, and hair accessories. Next, we conducted a questionnaire to evaluate the kawaii degree of each kawaii character, and calculated it as "kawaii score". Using the questionnaire results, we built a dataset containing a total of 120 images of kawaii characters and their corresponding kawaii scores. The dataset was used to construct a model using Deep Convolutional Neural Network (CNN) algorithm, which is a binary classification of kawaii characters into "kawaii" and "not-kawaii" group. Finally, we evaluated the classification performance of the model to confirm its performance for evaluating kawaii characters.

Keywords: Kawaii · Character · Deep learning

1 Introduction

In recent years, "kawaii" has been attracting attention as an affective value, and is used for various purposes [1]. Kawaii characters have been widely used in marketing, PR, advertisement and other purposes [2]. For example, in a local city in Japan (No se city), two kawaii characters named Ojo and Ruririn were created to help promoting the city's attractiveness [3]. By employing Kawaii character, it was possible to increase the positive impression toward the city [4]. However, it is difficult to verify whether kawaii characters are effective for the target group as the effect may differ by each individual or each target group.

© The Author(s), under exclusive license to Springer Nature Switzerland AG 2022
M. Kurosu (Ed.): HCII 2022, LNCS 13302, pp. 502–510, 2022.
https://doi.org/10.1007/978-3-031-05311-5_35

As a discussion that is not limited to kawaii character, Ohkura et al. promoted a study to clarify the attributes for improving kawaiiness of the artifacts by quantitatively evaluated the kawaiiness of each component, for example, objects with curvy shape and smaller size are more kawaii [5]. Furthermore, Laohakangvalvit et al. conducted a study on kawaii cosmetic bottles by constructing a deep learning model to classify cosmetic bottles based on their kawaii degrees obtained from questionnaire data [6]. Their method can automatically calculate the kawaii degree of the target group by using the data obtained from the target group with the deep learning model. Thus, their method can be used to evaluate an affective value of kawaii cosmetic bottles suitable for specific target.

Although there are many systematic studies that evaluate kawaii perception toward products, there is no systematic study of kawaii characters focusing on their attributes. According to the performance of deep learning as being used in [6], we believe that the deep learning will be useful for the evaluation of kawaii characters as well. Therefore, the purpose of this study is to construct a deep learning model to evaluate kawaii characters. The details of model construction and evaluation are described in the following sections.

2   Method

2.1   Constructing "Kawaii Character" Dataset

To construct a dataset, we used a website that generates character image by selecting various options of attributes [7]. We firstly created 10 characters as standard characters, No. 1 to No. 10 (Fig. 1). For each standard character, we systematically adjusted each of these following six attributes:

- Mouth
- Eyebrows
- Eyes
- Cheek redness
- Hair accessories
- Clothing

These six attributes were selected according to survey results regarding the attributes of characters related to "kawaii", in which only the upper part of the body is focused. The survey was done by four high-school students who collaborated in this research and is also the target group for our "kawaii character" evaluation [8].

Based on the survey results, the facial parts (i.e., mouth, eyebrows, eyes, and cheek redness) were likely to attract attention. In addition, there were some other attributes that were also considered related to kawaiiness of the characters, which are hairstyle, hair accessories, and clothing. However, hairstyle composes of too many variations making it difficult to narrow down. Therefore, hairstyle was excluded in the current study. As a result, the six attributes, each of which are varied by four settings were used to adjust the attributes of the standard characters as shown in Fig. 2.

For the mouth, they were selected based on the idea of emotion expression. Since the mouth often changes when expressing emotions, we paid attention to this area and

character1   character2   character3   character4   character5

character6   character7   character8   character9   character10

Fig. 1. Ten standard characters

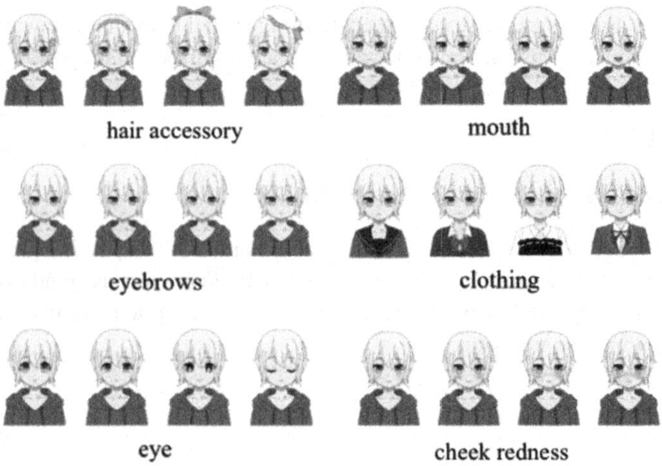

hair accessory   mouth

eyebrows   clothing

eye   cheek redness

Fig. 2. Six attributes with four settings for a standard character (No. 1)

selected the settings with all different emotions. For the eyebrows, because there were not many settings to choose from, we selected four different settings in which one of them has different direction in order to investigate if the eyebrow direction has any effect to the kawaii degree. For the eyes, the high-school students unanimously selected the four setting considered most kawaii. For the cheek redness, four levels of the redness were used for four settings, which express the degree of shyness of the characters. For clothing, since there were many types of uniforms, we selected three most kawaii uniforms and one plain clothes. Lastly, for the hair accessories, we narrowed down to four hair accessories that were often perceived as being kawaii. As a result, a total of 240 images of kawaii characters were prepared from 10 standard characters, each of which has 6 attributes with 4 settings for each attribute.

To obtain the kawaii degree of each character, the images were further evaluated by participants through an online survey by Google Form (Fig. 3). In the survey, each participant was asked to rank the kawaii degree of each character's attribute. The participant is asked to rank among the four settings of the same attribute from 1 to 4 (4 = most kawaii, 1 = least kawaii). This survey was responded by 37 male junior and senior high school students.

Based on the survey, we selected the settings of the character's attributes that were rated as the most kawaii (4) and the least kawaii (1). The kawaii characters rated as most kawaii (4) were labelled as "kawaii" group, and those rated as least kawaii (1) were labelled as "not kawaii" group. Therefore, we finally obtained "kawaii character" dataset containing 120 images: 60 kawaii images and 60 non-kawaii images. Figure 4 shows an examples of images in each of the two groups in the dataset.

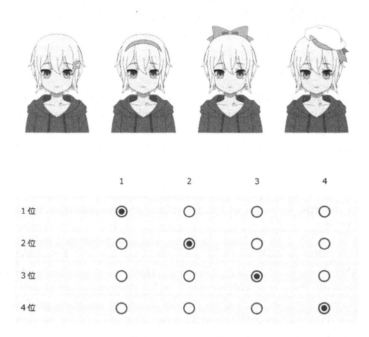

Fig. 3. Example of an online survey to rank kawaii degree of a character, in this case, with four settings of hair accessories

2.2 Constructing "Kawaii Character" Model

We used the dataset to construct the model using Deep Station [9], a deep learning environment that perform the following three steps: parameter setting, model construction, and model validation. In this study, we used the deep learning model with Convolutional Neural Network (CNN) algorithm as we used images as dataset. CNN algorithm is a neural network with several deep layers and since the learning accuracy increases with the depth of the convolutional layer, several deep CNN algorithms have been proposed in these recent years. In this study, we constructed a model for kawaii character for the first

Fig. 4. Example of "kawaii" and "non-kawaii" groups in "kawaii character" dataset

time. Therefore, we selected the following three algorithms based on previous studies [10, 11], which have successfully applied the algorithms to other image datasets:

- VGG16
- ResNet
- MobileNet

Next, we describe the detail of the algorithms and our parameter settings for the model construction.

VGG16 is a CNN with 16 layers in depth, and is a pre-trained model trained on a large dataset called ImageNet with over 1 million images [12]. In general, the more layers a CNN has, the more accurate it becomes. However, if we simply add more layers to the network, there is a problem that learning does not proceed well due to the vanishing gradient problem. In contrast, ResNet solves the vanishing gradient problem by introducing a mechanism called shortcut connection. As a result, the deepest model has 152 layers [13]. In this study, we used Resnet50, a model with a depth of 50 layers. While VGG16 and ResNet algorithms focus on increasing the accuracy by increasing the depth of the CNN layers, Mobilenet was designed to maximize the accuracy efficiently with limited resources such as smartphones. In order to achieve this, depthwise separable convolutions were introduced to reduce the number of parameters, computational cost, and model reduction. Depthwise separable convolutions were originally used in VGG16, meaning that the convolution in VGG16 and Resnet is performed in the spatial direction and the channel direction simultaneously. However, Mobilenet is a model that successfully reduces the amount of computation to 1/8 to 1/9 by performing spatial convolution and then channel convolution in order [14].

Using the above three algorithms, we constructed classification models using the "kawaii character" image dataset as described in Sect. 2.1. The dataset was divided into training data and test data randomly using the ratio settings in Deep Station. In this study, the ratio of test data to training data was set to 1:9. For the models constructed with the three different deep learning algorithms, the probabilities of being classified as "kawaii" and "not kawaii" is displayed as the output result when an image is input for validation. In order to test the accuracy of the classification of kawaii characters for the first time, the training data is also used in the test data.

3   Classification Results

The classification probabilities from the three models constructed by the three algorithms are shown in Table 1. These classification probabilities were calculated as the average values of being classified into "kawaii" group (kawaii probability) and "non-kawaii" group (non-kawaii probability) for each of the six attributes.

Table 1. Results of the classification accuracy of the model

Attribute	Kawaii probability (%)			Non-kawaii probability (%)		
	VGG16	ResNet	Mobilenet	VGG16	ResNet	Mobilenet
Mouth	50.0	50.9	100.0	50.0	49.1	100.0
Eyebrows	50.0	50.9	92.0	50.0	49.1	89.8
Eyes	50.0	50.9	99.8	50.0	49.1	100.0
Cheek redness	50.0	50.9	99.9	50.0	49.1	100.0
Hair accessories	50.0	50.9	100.0	50.0	49.1	100.0
Clothing	50.0	50.9	98.9	50.0	49.1	97.9

Table 1 shows that the probabilities of kawaii and non-kawaii for all characters are about 50% for VGG16 and ResNet. On the other hand, MobileNet was able to classify most attributes with a high accuracy of more than 95%, except eyebrows. However, the accuracy of eyebrows was less than 95%, which is inferior to the other attributes. There is possibility that the eyebrows occupy a very small area in the images compared to other attributes and have the same color as the hair making the model difficult to perform classification.

4   Evaluating Parameter Settings for Transfer Learning

4.1   Accuracy Evaluation by Changing Learning Rate

The accuracy of VGG16 and ResNet was about 50%, which is low. We considered that it was a problem with the parameter settings for transfer learning. Therefore, we compared the accuracy of VGG16 and ResNet by changing the parameter settings of the transfer learning process. First, we constructed models using VGG16 and ResNet by changing the learning rate. Figures 5 and 6 show the results of the classification accuracy when the learning rate was varied.

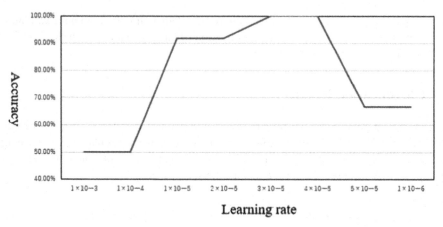

Fig. 5. Accuracy of model constructed by varying the learning rate using VGG16.

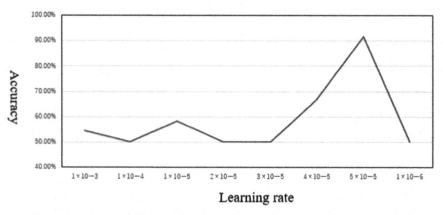

Fig. 6. Accuracy of model constructed by changing the learning rate using ResNet

As shown in Fig. 5, the classification accuracy of VGG16 becomes low when the learning rate is 1×10^{-3} or 1×10^{-4}. On the other hand, when the learning rate is low such as 1×10^{-5} or 3×10^{-5}, the classification accuracy becomes high. Figure 6 also shows that the classification accuracy of ResNet is low between 1×10^{-3} and 1×10^{-4} and highest at 5×10^{-5}. Then, the classification accuracy became low again at 6×10^{-5}. For these results, we believe that the classification accuracy of the model with low learning rate is higher than that of the model with high learning rate because the dataset to be trained is one that can be easily classified. The average classification accuracies for each attribute are shown in Tables 2 and 3, with the probability of being classified as "kawaii" for the "kawaii" group and the probability of being classified as "non-kawaii" for the "non-kawaii" group in the dataset.

Table 2. Classification results for a model with a learning rate of 4.0×10^{-5} using VGG16

Attribute	Kawaii probability (%)	Non-kawaii probability (%)
Mouth	100.0	98.0
Eyebrows	98.9	44.1
Eyes	99.9	100.0
Cheek redness	99.3	84.9
Hair accessories	99.9	100.0
Clothing	100.0	100.0

Table 3. Classification results for a model with a learning rate of 5.0×10^{-5} using ResNet.

Attribute	Kawaii probability (%)	Non-kawaii probability (%)
Mouth	76.1	48.7
Eyebrows	60.8	49.0
Eyes	79.3	58.3
Cheek redness	69.4	31.3
Hair accessories	67.5	82.3
Clothing	66.8	99.6

As shown in Tables 2 and 3, the classification accuracies for eyebrows and cheek redness are low. The reason for this is that the image area of eyebrows is small. As for the cheek redness, the only difference between each setting in the characters is the difference in the cheek redness, making it difficult for the classification model to recognize the difference. As for ResNet, even the model with the highest classification accuracy could not achieve the same high classification accuracy as other models such as VGG16 and Mobilenet.

5   Conclusion

The purpose of this study is to construct a model to classify "kawaii characters" using a deep learning algorithm. In collaboration with high-school students who are considered as a target group of kawaii characters, we constructed a "kawaii character" dataset used for model construction, which contains 120 images dividing into 60 kawaii and 60 non-kawaii groups. Using the dataset, we constructed models using three different deep convolutional neural network (CNN) algorithms: VGG16, ResNet, and Mobilenet. The results show that we were able to construct a model with a maximum of 100% using VGG16 and Mobilenet algorithms. The models have considerably good classification performance for the characters with attributes that can be easily observed. However, the classification of characters with different small-size attribute such as eyebrows still needs to be improved.

In this research, as our first trial, we employed a simplified characters and settings of attributes as our dataset for model construction. However, the model might be insufficient to be applied to evaluate kawaii characters with more complexed attributes. Therefore, our future work will also employ various other attributes and settings in the dataset.

Acknowledgments. We thank high-school students (Touma Ohtsuka, Yu Katayama, Hiroki Satou, Emiri Tago) of the Shibaura Institute of Technology Junior and Senior High School who collaborated in our dataset construction and collection of questionnaire data.

References

1. Ohkura, M., Komatsu, T., Aoto, T.: Kawaii rules: increasing affective value of industrial products. In: Watada, J., Shiizuka, H., Lee, KP., Otani, T., Lim, CP. (eds.) Industrial Applications of Affective Engineering, pp. 97–110. Springer, Cham. (2014). https://doi.org/10.1007/978-3-319-04798-0_8
2. Yukie, T.: The survey of the likes and dislikes to "Mascot Characters." J. Jpn Res. Assoc. Text. End-Uses **55**(12), 933–941 (2014). (in Japanese)
3. Osaka no Toppen Nose PR characters Ojo & Ruririn. https://www.ojyo-ruririn.com/about-ojyo-to-ruririn/. Accessed 16 Feb 2022
4. Toyoshima, A., Nittono, H.: The concept and components of "Kawaii" for older adults in Japan. Jpn. J. Gerontol. **41**(9), 409–419 (2020). (in Japanese)
5. Ohkura, M., Goto, S., Murai, S., Aoto, T.: Study on cute (Kawaii) color using virtual objects. Jpn. Soc. Kansei Eng. **8**(3), 535–542 (2009). (in Japanese)
6. Laohakangvalvit, T., Achalakul, T., Ohkura, M.: A method to obtain effective attributes for attractive cosmetic bottles by deep learning. Int. J. Affect. Eng. **19**(1), 37–48 (2020)
7. Charat Rouge. https://charat.me/rouge/create/. Accessed 10 Jan 2022
8. Ohtsuka, T., et al.: Evaluation of important attributes for "Kawaii Characters". Jpn. Soc. Kansei Eng. (2022). (in Japanese)
9. Deep Station. https://deepstation.jp/. Accessed 16 Feb 2022
10. Omori, H., Hanyu, K., Shiimada, S.: Prediction of the visual similarity between photos making use of deep learning – image classification and semantic segmentation. Jpn. Soc. Kansei Eng. **20**(1), 83–90 (2021). (in Japanese)
11. Bi, C., et al.: MobileNet based apple leaf diseases identification. Mob. Netw. Appl., 172–180 (2020)
12. MathWorks. https://jp.mathworks.com/help/deeplearning/ref/vgg16.html. Accessed 16 Feb 2022
13. DeepAge. https://deepage.net/deep_learning/2016/11/30/resnet.html. Accessed 16 Feb 2022
14. DeepSquare. https://deepsquare.jp/2020/06/mobilenet-v1/. Accessed 16 Feb 2022

Interface Visual Design Based on User Emotional Experience – Taking Pregnancy and Parenting Applet as an Example

YueWei Wang, Wei Shen, and RongRong Fu[✉]

College of Art Design and Media, East China University of Science and Technology,
Shanghai, China
3426149006@qq.com

Abstract. With the aggravation of population aging, fertility has become the focus of social attention. As a special group, users of pregnancy and parenting software will choose products with a more cautious attitude. However, as a newly needed pregnancy and parenting software for families, there are still some deficiencies such as unreasonable layout and serious product homogenization, resulting in low use efficiency of products and low user viscosity. Therefore, it is of great research value to create a lightweight applet that can arouse the emotional resonance of the audience. Based on Nielsen's interaction principle, combined with the relevant theories of product semantics and information visualization, this paper explores the application of instinct layer and behavior layer in pregnancy and parenting software in Norman's emotional design theory, and carries out the design practice of pregnancy and parenting applet named lamb (hereinafter referred to as lamb) according to the interface design method of pregnancy and parenting software obtained in the early stage, So as to establish the standard process of software interface design for special people.

Keywords: User emotional experience · Parenting applet · Emotional design · EEG experiment

1 Introduction

1.1 Background of the Study

As the population ages, the issue of fertility has become the focus of social attention. As a special group of people, the user group of pregnancy and childcare software will choose the product with more caution, and the iteration of this product will be faster, so it is important to create a perfect lightweight pregnancy and childcare applet.

This design not only provides a theoretical basis for the study of maternity software, but also provides systematic design ideas for the design of emotionally charged software products.

M. Kurosu (Ed.): HCII 2022, LNCS 13302, pp. 511–526, 2022.
https://doi.org/10.1007/978-3-031-05311-5_36

1.2   Current Status of Research

Overseas pregnancy and parenting software is mostly designed based on the characteristics of the female audience and diversified according to specific functional subdivisions, such as "BabyCenter", a manual for pregnant mothers and "WebMD Baby", which records the life of babies. There is a wide range of pregnancy and parenting software in the Chinese market, such as Baby Tree, Pro-Baby, Yuxueyuan, Moonchild and others. There are still problems with the design of today's pregnancy and parenting software, such as poor icon recognition, no subordination between tabs and content, cumbersome operation, unreasonable page layout, and serious product homogenisation. The content of these software is relatively similar, with the main functions of observing the mother's body changes and supplementing knowledge about pregnancy, leading to mothers downloading software repeatedly, which not only takes up storage space on their mobile phones, but also increases the burden of using the products, and the radiation caused by excessive use of mobile phones can also damage the health of mothers. At the same time, because the software is aimed at an inaccurate audience, the content is cluttered, and the interface is not as beautiful and interesting as it could be, the user viscosity of the product is low. This is why pregnancy and parenting software needs to be categorised and summarised by user group, improved from the perspective of design principles and design methods, to address barriers to use and improve product experience and ease of use.

1.3   The Problem to be Solved

The design is intended to address the inaccurate audience for the pregnancy software and the lack of aesthetics and interest in the interface. By building a user model to locate the product's functionality, the design principles derived from eye-movement experiments will be used to visually optimise the interface and ultimately improve the user experience.

2   Analysis of Female User Groups in Pregnancy and Parenting Applet

2.1   Characteristics of Female User Groups in Pregnancy and Parenting Applet

Depending on their physiological characteristics, female users of pregnancy and parenting software can be divided into pregnant mothers, who are in the period between conception and birth, and nursing mothers, who are nursing their newborn. Depending on their age, pregnant mothers can be divided into those between 20 and 35 years of age, and those over 35 years of age, who are in advanced stages of pregnancy. As the foetus develops in the body, pregnant mothers experience physical symptoms such as drowsiness, vomiting, weight gain, irregular eating and fatigue. Advanced maternal age mothers are more likely to gain weight during pregnancy and are also more likely to suffer from pregnancy complications and complications such as heart disease, high blood pressure and diabetes. Compared to young mothers, Advanced maternal age mothers take longer to come to terms with the physical changes that pregnancy brings and can be more emotionally stressed and anxious. Nursing mothers need to pay attention to diet, care and recovery as their bodies lose a lot of nutrients during the postnatal period to breastfeeding.

Depending on their living environment and habits, female users of pregnancy and parenthood software can be divided into urban women and mothers in smaller cities. Urban women are the most powerful mothers, including young, high-profile and high-income corporate workers in first-tier cities, including management and ordinary employees. According to a survey conducted by Ariadne, 83.6% of mothers play a major role in deciding what their children eat and wear, and 75.3% of mothers share a common topic of conversation with their friends about their babies' growth. Although small city mothers do not have a lot of money, they still value their children's lives and education, with over 56% of mothers covering their children's education expenses.

2.2 User Role Models of Female User Groups in Pregnancy and Parenting Applet

The design simulates user behaviour by setting up user personas, so as to explore the actual problems in the design and to clarify the design positioning of the applet more efficiently. According to the different age levels and economic levels, the young generation of post-95 mothers, mothers with advanced maternal age, mothers with two children and mothers with strong women are used as typical cases for the study of living habits and the exploration of cyclical needs (Fig. 1).

2.3 Exploring the Real Needs of Users and the Functional Architecture of Interface Design

According to the analysis of the above user groups, 83.6% of mothers play a major role in decision-making on children's diet and clothing, such as the consumption of daily necessities, baby's clothing, food, housing and growth education, when online shopping becomes a convenient choice, especially after 95 baby mothers are more likely to be planted by a variety of parenting platforms, so small programs should be scientifically and reasonably recommended to buy goods, both to facilitate the life of mothers, but also to enhance the software The business value. The Advanced maternal age maternal mothers are a group that needs extra attention. As people push back the age of childbirth, there will be more people in this category, so there is a need to provide accurate recommended recipes specifically for these mothers.

Secondly, strong female mothers, especially those returning to work after childbirth, are under pressure from both their work capacity and their families. They want to be recognised emotionally by their colleagues and families for their efforts, so the mobile platform needs to provide a social circle to meet mothers to make new friends, relieve anxiety by chatting with similar people, and help mothers achieve a balance between career and family. In line with mothers' tendency to show off their babies and record their growth, a visually appealing growth album can be created with the ability to save pictures. Finally, with the impact of the two-child policy, more mothers will spend more energy on childcare, so the applet should provide a corresponding design module to help mothers avoid family conflicts due to improper parent-child relationships. Based on this, this design will develop the main functions from community, shopping, growth album, mother and baby meals, parenting knowledge, growth album and so on.

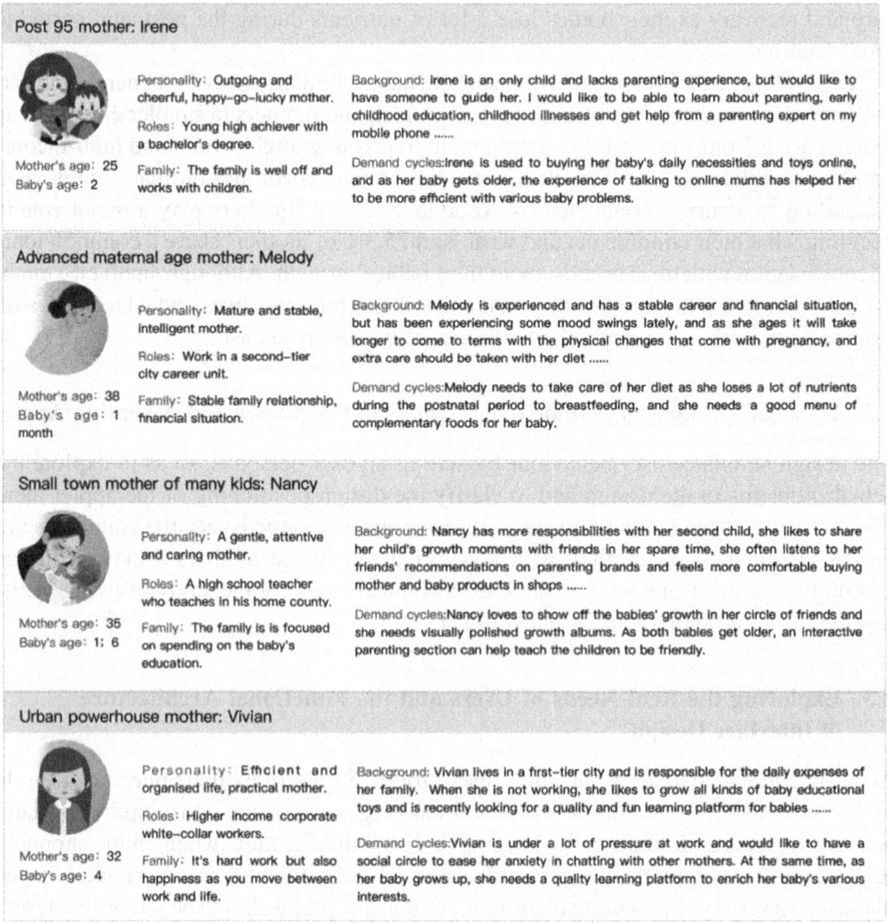

Post 95 mother: Irene

Personality: Outgoing and cheerful, happy-go-lucky mother.

Roles: Young high achiever with a bachelor's degree.

Mother's age: 25
Baby's age: 2

Family: The family is well off and works with children.

Background: Irene is an only child and lacks parenting experience, but would like to have someone to guide her. I would like to be able to learn about parenting, early childhood education, childhood illnesses and get help from a parenting expert on my mobile phone ......

Demand cycles:Irene is used to buying her baby's daily necessities and toys online, and as her baby gets older, the experience of talking to online mums has helped her to be more efficient with various baby problems.

Advanced maternal age mother: Melody

Personality: Mature and stable, intelligent mother.

Roles: Work in a second-tier city career unit.

Mother's age: 38
Baby's age: 1 month

Family: Stable family relationship, financial situation.

Background: Melody is experienced and has a stable career and financial situation, but has been experiencing some mood swings lately, and as she ages it will take longer to come to terms with the physical changes that come with pregnancy, and extra care should be taken with her diet ......

Demand cycles:Melody needs to take care of her diet as she loses a lot of nutrients during the postnatal period to breastfeeding, and she needs a good menu of complementary foods for her baby.

Small town mother of many kids: Nancy

Personality: A gentle, attentive and caring mother.

Roles: A high school teacher who teaches in his home county.

Mother's age: 35
Baby's age: 1; 6

Family: The family is is focused on spending on the baby's education.

Background: Nancy has more responsibilities with her second child, she likes to share her child's growth moments with friends in her spare time, she often listens to her friends' recommendations on parenting brands and feels more comfortable buying mother and baby products in shops ......

Demand cycles:Nancy loves to show off the babies' growth in her circle of friends and she needs visually polished growth albums. As both babies get older, an interactive parenting section can help teach the children to be friendly.

Urban powerhouse mother: Vivian

Personality: Efficient and organised life, practical mother.

Roles: Higher income corporate white-collar workers.

Mother's age: 32
Baby's age: 4

Family: It's hard work but also happiness as you move between work and life.

Background: Vivian lives in a first-tier city and is responsible for the daily expenses of her family. When she is not working, she likes to grow all kinds of baby educational toys and is recently looking for a quality and fun learning platform for babies ......

Demand cycles:Vivian is under a lot of pressure at work and would like to have a social circle to ease her anxiety in chatting with other mothers. At the same time, as her baby grows up, she needs a quality learning platform to enrich her baby's various interests.

Fig. 1. User role model diagram.

3 Study of Interaction Interface Design Principles

In order to extract the software interface design principles that influence user preferences, this paper combines Nielsen interaction principles and collects the main functional interfaces of three mainstream software in the market, and analyses the target users' preferences for the case interfaces through eye-movement diagram experiments, so as to extract the design principles that most influence user preferences and facilitate obtaining user feedback and improving the design on this basis.

3.1 Eye Movement Experimental

In this experiment, the three experimental materials belong to the main functional interfaces of the mainstream software in the market, and the subjects' eye movement data were recorded to observe where the interface could elicit visual preferences from the users.

Experimental equipment: The eye movement devices were SMI eye tracker, laptop, Begaze, iView ETG data analysis software, etc.

Experimental participants: The study was conducted on a group of 16 users of all ages, and all subjects volunteered to participate in the experiment. They were well rested, physically and mentally healthy and had normal or corrected vision prior to the experiment.

Experimental environment: The experiment was conducted in a soundproof, light-proof laboratory. During the experiment, there was no interference or noise from anyone other than the testers and the participants being tested.

Experimental metrics: In this experiment, visual trajectory maps, hotspot maps and grading maps from eye movement data were used as metrics to assess the user's perceived preference for different functional areas of the interface. The longer the average dwell time, the greater the salience of the target and the higher the user's preference for that area.

Experimental procedure: First a three-point calibration was performed, then the first stimulus was presented for 10,000 ms, followed by the second stimulus, until the 3 stimulus materials were presented.

3.2 Data Analysis

Begaze data analysis software was used to process and analyse the oculomotor behaviour of the three materials, as shown in Table 1. Each material was divided into red, yellow and green areas according to the longest dwell time from longest to shortest result: The red areas of the three materials are concentrated in logo, newbie guide and bottom functional area.

Table 1. Analysis table of eye movement data.

Test material	Regional level	Corresponding content	Dwell time average/ms	Fixation time average/ms
1	Red	Logo	3204.6	1100.0
	Yellow	User avatar	1273.5	800.0
	Green	Quick access area	1207.8	500.0
2	Red	Beginner guide bar	1348.0	731.0
	Yellow	Publish button	912.7	600.0
	Green	Search button	540.0	450.0
3	Red	Bottom functional area	818.4	618.0
	Yellow	Top functional area	689.8	500.0
	Green	Text title bar	650.0	350.0

As shown in Fig. 2, the fixation points of Material 1 are concentrated on the logo, the user avatar, the King Kong area and the anthropomorphic image within the software. the logo section has the longest average dwell time at 3204.6/ms, the colour of the logo, the colour of the guide page, the text colour of the interface and the icon colour all maintain a colour scheme of red as the main colour and grey as the secondary colour, which is conducive to deepening the user's memory. The fixed points in the diamond area are relatively evenly distributed at 1207.8/ms. This panel merges isolated elements into a unified visual unit, building intimacy between elements, and the proximity of physical locations helps to organise information. Secondly product anthropomorphism adds interest to the interface and helps to build trust between the user and the product.

Fig. 2. From left to right, the Scan Path, Heat Map and Gridded AOIs for Material1.

As shown in Fig. 3, the framing points for Material 2 revolve around the sequence of the newbie guide, keeping the interface simple in terms of visual hierarchy. The area of interest in Material 2 is focused on the small fish brand image, the publish button and the search button in the newbie guide bar. The Newbie Guidance bar has the longest average dwell time of 1348/ms. This section provides appropriate assistance to the user and the brand image makes the interface lively and interesting. The search and publish buttons are consistent with the yellow colour of the brand image, and the main colour of the page, banner, text and icons are kept uniform in the interface design, making the product more standardised, increasing the scope of consumption of the software and saving development costs.

Fig. 3. From left to right, the Scan Path, Heat Map and Gridded AOIs for Material2.

As shown in Fig. 4, the areas of user interest in Material3 are focused on the bottom functional area, the top functional area, and the text descriptions of the recommendation cards. The recommendation cards on this page all adopt the same style, e.g. the text within the modules are left-aligned to make the recommendations clearer and more effective. However, the modules are not aligned horizontally, as a conscious break in alignment would give the page a more designed feel. The visual effect is enhanced by repetition. The framing points on this page focus on the highlighted text, such as the selected column in the recommendations column is larger in font size, bolded and highlighted, and also highlighted in blue below the font in line with the theme. The contrast avoids the elements on the page being unfocused, and the contrast focuses the user's eye, creating a noticeable design effect.

Fig. 4. From left to right, the Scan Path, Heat Map and Gridded AOIs for Material3.

3.3 A Study of Visual Design Paradigms for Interfaces Based on Affective Design Theory

A Study of Visual Design Methods for Nurture-Like Interfaces at the Instinctual Level. The instinctive layer needs to present the audience with an intuitive visual experience, focusing on the parts of things that can be perceived directly. The instinctive layer requires products to look and feel pleasing to the touch. In order to bring pleasure and joy to the user of the product, the product can be anthropomorphised to create a sense of trust between the user and the product. In the visual design of the conception interface, the visual elements should be used as a basis for improvement, to achieve a rich and clear page content. Specific design principles include:

1. Maintaining consistency in design specifications can facilitate identification and enhance user confidence. 2. Text in key sections should be enlarged in font size to reduce the cost of reading due to excess information interference. 3. Icons can take the form of images plus text to enhance content. Both words and patterns should be well readable and not too fancy. 4. To express the emotional characteristics of mothers' groups who care for their children, the colours should create a warm and soft atmosphere, with warm colours of higher brightness and simple and elegant colour schemes. Sharp corners should be avoided for buttons, navigation bars and module icons, and rounded corners should be

used as far as possible to enhance the affinity of the software. Add soft lighting, shadows and gradient colour effects to the graphic pieces to make the controls more recognisable.

Research on Visual Design Methods for the Behavioural Level of the Gestalt Class Interface. The design of the behavioural layer needs to take full account of the user use scenario and enhance the pleasure and efficiency that the product brings to the user during use. Specific design principles are:

1. Provide humanised text, thoughtful and caring prompts. Showing the progress of the task, providing timely feedback, avoiding user's misuse and enhancing the user's sense of security in using the product. 2. Effects such as matching graphics, masks and pop-ups can allow users to focus their attention on the event. 3. Specific tasks can stimulate the user's desire for exploration and curiosity. By correlating the merchant's earnings with the user's purchase behaviour, it can make full use of some non-immediate but high-frequency functions and increase the user's activity. 4. Realise the personalisation of the product's functions, and also try to be simple, easy to learn and guided in the implementation of interactive functions, with clear expressions of textual information and, if necessary, set up explanatory pages to help remember information.

4   The Design of the "Lamb Pregnancy" Applet Based on the User's Emotional Experience

4.1   Product Positioning and Objectives

Product Positioning. Lamb is not only a faithful assistant to solve the needs of users, but also a lovely friend to meet the emotional needs of children and parents "lamb Pregnancy" stands in the perspective of young mothers, scientifically analyses what kind of functions, layout and design style young mothers need to use pregnancy and parenting software, provides diversified services, and creates a parenting social applet that meets the expectations of young mothers.

Product Objectives. The main research target of this design is mothers of babies aged 0–6 years old, especially young mothers aged 20–30 years old. Young mothers are more educated and have their own personalities and unique ideas, and the process of parenting is easier and more respectful of their children's interests and choices. The lightness of the app is more favoured by them. Through the pregnancy and parenting app mothers can quickly learn about parenting, and in the community and album making they can show their parenting life, allowing young mothers to communicate with people online, increasing communication opportunities and social connections between groups, and enhancing their sense of well-being and security.

4.2   Product Benefit Points

According to the above, the design of pregnancy and parenting software in the market is heavily homogenised, so a more characteristic appearance is a key factor in differentiating this product from its competitors.

This product explores the user needs of the female population in pregnancy and parenting software, summarises the interface visual design paradigm based on cyclical emotional needs, and applies specific design principles to this design. The product's interests are to improve the overall visual image and enhance the user experience, such as: adopting a cute and friendly brand image, warm and elegant colours and soft visual elements; enhancing content and ease of use in the main function area; providing user-friendly copy and thoughtful care in the import and login interface; increasing social platform interaction and growth album records; providing corresponding point rewards to guide users to contribute content with The content of the product will be more interactive and easy to use.

4.3 The Design Framework of the "Lamb Nurture" Applet

Visual Design. The image design of this product is shown in Fig. 5. The brand image of the "lamb Pregnancy" applet is a cartoon lamb drawn on the basis of a small cotton lamb. Through the soft appearance of the lamb's cloud shape to show the product's cute and friendly, the lamb's shape is simple and clear, and the colour scheme is mainly white, in order to produce a relaxed and pleasant experience. At the same time, a series of expressions such as happy, hello, extra, expectant and sad were designed on the basis of the original image to correspond to different scenarios on the page.

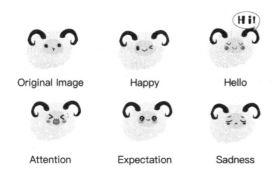

Fig. 5. Brand image of the lamb applet.

According to the tone of the product and the user's emotional needs, this design selected the warm pink as the main colour, such as the colour card in Fig. 6, from left to right, the colour is peach, for the auxiliary icon colour, selection control colour, white font base colour; theme pink, for the main colour of the page, navigation bar icon colour; background light pink, for the background base colour; background light peach pink, for the banner base colour; light yellow, for the auxiliary icon colour, selection control colour, etc.

#FF006E   #FFAEB5   #FFFAFA   #FFDCD0   #FFC068

Fig. 6. Swatches for the lamb applet.

As shown in Fig. 7, the navigation bar icons include Home, Community and My. The dynamic interaction is designed to produce a more interesting effect. Each icon icon unchecked state uses simple lines to summarise the icon to achieve a uniform flat style. The lines are mainly curved, avoiding sharp angles. The home icon becomes a small sheep logo when selected to emphasise the brand image. The community icon and my icon are filled with the main colour when selected, applying the principles of consistency and standardisation and also allowing users to feel prompt feedback.

Fig. 7. Navigation bar icon for lamb applet.

As shown in Fig. 8, the quick access area icons on the home page include four main sections: Nutrition Recipes, Growth Album, Points Redemption and Fun Planet. In order to facilitate grouping and establish intimacy between the various functions, they are integrated into a whole visual unit, while using rich colours to differentiate the functions so that users can understand them at a glance.

Fig. 8. Quick access area icon of the lamb applet.

As in Fig. 9, in the design of other icons such as likes and favourites, a secondary colour has been chosen to fill them and the same interaction is adopted to reflect the principles of minimalist design.

Fig. 9. Other icons of the lamb applet.

Functional Design.   The guide page uses a bedtime story scene to introduce the image of lamb, showing a quiet and soft tone of the product (Fig. 10). The information entry page is used to triage users and ensure that the recommended content is more accurate and reasonable (Fig. 11). My screen is set to not logged in, user information is set to invisible, and the anthropomorphic brand image is used to remind users to log in (Fig. 12). By analysing users' functional needs for lamb Pregnancy, the applet is divided into three main pages, including Home, Community and My (Fig. 13). The main functions of the home page include mother and baby diet and nutrition, parenting tips, diy production of growth albums and points rewards, etc. This section can improve the fun of user operation and increase user viscosity (Fig. 14).

Fig. 10. Guide page.   **Fig. 11.** Information   **Fig. 12.** User Page.
entry page.

Fig. 13. Three main pages.

The interaction flow diagram for lamb is shown in Fig. 15.

Fig. 14. Home page main function interface.

5   Design Assessment

5.1   EEG Experimental Evaluation

In order to verify that the final design meets the preferences of the female user group, an EEG experiment was conducted. The EEG preferences of the subjects were compared to those of the "lamb" pregnancy app, which is one of the most popular pregnancy apps on the market.

The subjects were 15 mothers of babies aged 0–6 years from the female user group of the pregnancy app, and all subjects volunteered to participate in the experiment. They were well rested, physically and mentally healthy and had normal or corrected vision prior to the experiment.

Experimental environment: The experiment was conducted in a soundproof, light-proof laboratory. During the experiment, there was no interference or noise from anyone other than the testers and the participants being tested.

Experimental equipment: muse2, iPhone, sleep analysis software.

The experimental indicators are as follows: In this experiment, the three data are active, neutral and calm, and the Muse-app is used as the experimental indicator in this experiment. Where active, neutral and calm refer to the activity of the human brain. The higher the active value, the more aroused the sample is to the subject, the greater the stimulation and the more interesting the subject is; conversely, the higher the neutral and calm values, the less aroused the sample is to the subject and the less interested the subject is in the sample.

Experimental material: The main marketed pregnancy applets were used as sample 1 and the "lamb" pregnancy applet was used as sample 2. The subjects were asked to experience each app for one minute and two EEG data were recorded.

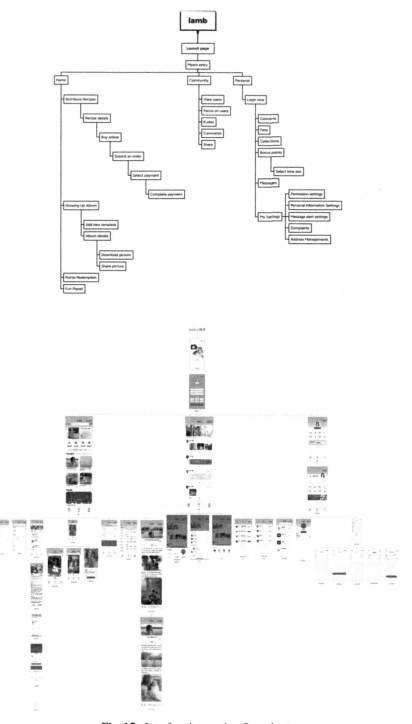

Fig. 15. Interface interaction flow chart.

Experimental procedure: Before the test, the subjects were told to experience the two applets for one minute each. The computer screen first displayed a white screen for 1000 ms, then the first applet was displayed and the subjects operated and experienced it independently for one minute, then a white screen for 1000 ms was presented, then the second applet was displayed and the subjects operated and experienced it independently for one minute.

5.2 Data Analysis

As Table 2 shows the sample 1 count metrics for the 15 subjects counted by the Muse-app. As shown in Table 3 is the sample 2 count metric for the 15 test subjects. sample 1 has an active mean of 2.133333333 s, a neutral mean of 35.1333333333 s and a calm mean of 22.73333333 s; sample 2 has an active mean of 9.33333333333 s, a neutral mean of 28.26666667 s and a calm mean of 22.4 s. 's active maximum was 51 s, and this user's active value for sample one was 0 s (Fig. 16).

In summary, sample one had a higher neutral and calm value, the sample was less arousing to the subject and the subject was less interesting to the sample; sample two had a higher active value, was more arousing to the subject and the subject was more interesting. Therefore, the results of the experimental metrics show that the average user preference for "lamb" is higher than that of mainstream pregnancy software, which increases user satisfaction with the main page.

Table 2. Count indicators for sample 1.

Sample number	1	2	3	4	5	6	7	8	9	10	11	12	13	14	15	Mean value
Active sec	0	2	4	0	3	0	17	1	0	0	0	0	0	3	2	2.133333333
Neutral sec	41	41	29	44	41	21	27	34	31	41	34	42	33	46	22	35.13333333
Calm sec	19	17	27	16	16	39	16	25	29	19	26	18	27	11	36	22.73333333

Table 3. Count indicators for sample 2.

Sample number	1	2	3	4	5	6	7	8	9	10	11	12	13	14	15	Mean value
Active sec	0	13	12	21	2	7	0	7	13	51	0	3	0	11	0	9.333333333
Neutral sec	18	26	44	36	28	42	16	30	43	9	25	27	37	34	9	28.26666667
Calm sec	42	21	4	3	30	11	44	23	4	0	35	30	23	15	51	22.4

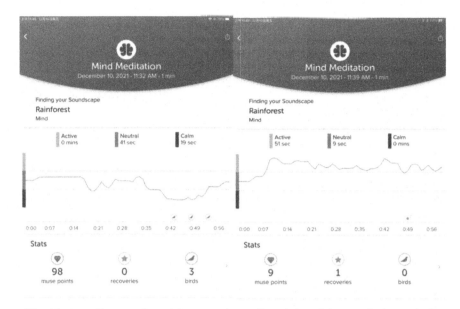

Fig. 16. Data diagram of user Muse experiment (from left to right, sample 1, sample 2).

5.3   Conclusion

This design builds a user model based on the psychological, physical and emotional characteristics of the female user group and explores the real emotional needs of the female user group of the pregnancy and parenting software. Through eye-movement experiments, the target users' preferences for each area of the case interface were analysed, so as to extract the design principles that can most influence users' preferences. In turn, from the instinctive and behavioural levels, an interface visual design approach is proposed in order to enhance the sense of security, pleasure and efficiency of the product for the user. The interface design of the gestation applet was carried out based on the user interface standards established in the early stages. The final design solution was proved to create a better user emotional experience through EEG experiments, solving the barriers to use for mothers, and providing a paradigm for the design of software interfaces for the special group of female users in pregnancy and parenting software.

References

1. He, Q.: Research on preschool children's Enlightenment education APP based on emotional design. Mass Stand. **14**, 140–141 (2020)
2. Dai, R., Fu, X., Wu, J.: User experience research on interaction design of maternal and infant mobile medical care. Design **21**, 137–139 (2019)
3. Zhang, T.: Design of mobile APP for children's education based on user experience. Art Sea **10**, 122–123 (2019)

4. Li, H.: Based on the theory of flow after 90 maternal and child shopping APP user experience design (a master's degree thesis, Beijing university of posts and telecommunications) (2019). https://kns.cnki.net/KCMS/detail/detail.aspx?dbname=CMFD201902&filename=1019047478.nh

5. Ji, Q.: New media and parenting discourse in the context of the construction and the spread of (a master's degree thesis, Yunnan university) (2017). https://kns.cnki.net/KCMS/detail/detail.aspx?dbname=CMFD201901&filename=1017218757.nh

6. Xu, Q., Zhang, B., Xu, H.: Research on icon design of children's APP based on emotion analysis. Packag. Eng. **16**, 212–216 (2018). https://doi.org/10.19554/j.cnki.1001-3563.2018.16.035

7. Guo, J., Li, H.: Investigation and analysis of the market status quo of incubation mobile phone software apps. Mod. Mark. (The Next Ten Day) **06**, 166–167 (2018)

8. Zhang, C.: Research on information visualization design of pregnancy and infant health management APP. Popular Lit. Art **02**,119–120 (2018)

Improving Emotional Intelligence in the New Normal Using Metaverse Applications for Digital Native

Sheng-Ming Wang[1], Muhammad Ainul Yaqin[2], and Fu-Hsiang Hsu[2(✉)]

[1] Department of Interaction Design, National Taipei University of Technology,
1, Sec. 3, Zhongxiao E. Rd., Taipei 10608, Taiwan
ryan5885@mail.ntut.edu.tw
[2] Doctoral Program in Design, College of Design, National Taipei University of Technology,
1, Sec. 3, Zhongxiao E. Rd., Taipei 10608, Taiwan
t110859008@ntut.edu.tw

Abstract. This research provides a study on analyzing emotional intelligence in the New Normal using Metaverse application for digital native generation. Coronavirus 2019 (COVID-19) outbreak has created new behavior and characterized human life to be more aware of the new digital applications. Significantly, research results show that the digital native generation, whose internet environment was typical from their birth, is optimistic in New Normal life amid COVID 19. In 2021, Metaverse set off a new generation of online interactive user behavior concepts. According to some research, the developing concept of Metaverse fits precisely in line with the future living of the digital native generation. However, some psychological side consequences should be revealed concurrently with the positive impact conceived. People's emotional intelligence argues for reduction due to the dissatisfaction of rapid adaptation to the New Normal condition. Thus, this research demonstrates an analysis to mitigate the psychological side effects of emotional intelligence when people are bound to the New Normal life. The improvement of the Web-based Extended Reality (WebXR), a critical development field of Metaverse, is proposed together to assist the immersive experience demands in addressing the problem-solution methods.

Keywords: Metaverse · New normal · Digital native generation · Emotional intelligence · Web-based extended reality

1 Introduction

The new normal condition is defined to create the safest behavior against and anticipate the spread of the COVID-19 in society. In the working and education sectors, the new normal commences a new standard of utilizing information and communication technologies to support the residence's working and learning scenario [1]. During the pandemic situation, the lack of presence always adheres to the way of interaction while people are engaged in the digital environment. Emotional intelligence role as a worthy outcome on providing motivation and satisfaction with the support of multimedia

M. Kurosu (Ed.): HCII 2022, LNCS 13302, pp. 527–541, 2022.
https://doi.org/10.1007/978-3-031-05311-5_37

passageway [2]. It is not confined to the specific field, yet for the general advancement in all fields influenced by the change of new normal regulations. Non-interference of emotional intelligence during the new normal conditions caused some negative consequences such as experienced exhaustion, cynicism, and less optimistic feeling on doing the job [3].

The immersive experiences become an advanced experience in interacting with the virtual world to promote a better experience through simulated reality [4]. Nonetheless, enriching the immersive experience concept might attain a meaningful understanding and valuing the object that we explore as the lack of integrating physical and imaginary worlds [5].

This research focuses on the prospects to improve emotional intelligence while facing the new normal and adapting along with WebXR spherical video technology as a Metaverse application. The primary goal is to ascertain that the proposed research will be relevant to the condition of online distance activities for digital natives of users.

Begin by interpreting the new normal on different regional representatives; this research endeavors an ecosystem understanding as well as the people engaged inside. It then addresses the functions and service features that are most suitable for the analysis resulting in validation and consideration. In conclusion, this study facilitated users to measure their requirements of the current topic to meet the possible standard suited for people in the new normal conditions as the objective's insights.

Immersive experience assists the user to increase social and emotional implications and bring innovative and creative aspects through the non-physical atmosphere [6]. While in this research, the emotion commonly amplified in conventional physical interaction to bear the human's motivation will be explored and observed upon the emotional intelligence and new normal scenario.

At the same time, this research raised the potential implementation research concept and study derived from different locations in Asia and Europe as a generalizing cultural adaptation study as well as promoting technology that can be merged to support the current and post-condition of COVID-19's interactional outline.

2   Literature Review

Based on technological developments such as AR/VR, metaverse has been proposed into various definitions including lifelogging, collective space in virtually, embodied/spatial Internet, a mirror world, a venue of simulation and collaboration. The immersive experience in metaverse becomes one of the essential issues as it argues to improve emotional intelligence capability in simulating the physical scenario. The term metaverse has been adopted to define the digital transformation concept in most aspects that can be done physically into a virtual approach [7].

Contextual design helps to interpret the needs and wants of the target user and combines the cross-functional team to reach the essential criteria. Adopting contextual design can support the research and consolidate the three human-centered principles such as Desirability, Viability, and Feasibility [8]. Many researchers have conducted a method of understanding users in engaging the contextual design approach. A related project in promoting the aging in place concept by Suppipat (2020) revealed the capability of employing the contextual design to understand different user's satisfaction with the proposed innovation in prompting contextual data behavior [9]. Surmaaho's (2021) research, offered the new design of interaction guidelines for users, medical devices, and the contextual factors attached in the research [10].

In deliberating current conditions, the new normal concept has been adopted globally to speculate and prepare for the worst condition in the current and post-condition of COVID-19. However, Berwick (2020) argues that this concept is promptly becoming a choice of people and no longer a prediction since the pandemic has occupied the six properties of change of tempo, standards, working conditions, proximity, preparedness, and equity [11]. Social responsibility also demands to be prepared together as educating people to protect themselves on daily activities. The implication of the digital transformation of online technology in every field will continuously become a standardization of the appropriate options in this circumstance [12]. The concept of the New Normal is expected as the possible manner to minimize the risk of the COVID-19 pandemic and develop a new better ecosystem for humanity.

Digital natives who are referred to as the people born with abundant technological applications might perceive a lot of impact due to this condition. The digital natives generation has made a life habit with overusing a digital media which incautiously reflects their discipline, behavior, and emotional issues [13]. Many people have been exposed to the uncommon and/or additional psychological effect of this circumstance, such as the worry of staying while doing lock-down, fears of infection, frustration, boredom, inadequate supplies, and information, which drive to some anxiety, lower mental health, and loneliness while they are engaging to the new normal scenario [14–16]. Due to this issue, managing personal Emotional Intelligence (EI) becomes an essential skill that needs to be possessed on this occasion. The importance of EI in self-awareness, self-management, social awareness, and social skill might be beneficial both physical and psychological support to enhance stress management skills, promote wellness, and prevent burnout [17].

Deriving from the user's perspective, integrating Spherical Video-based Virtual Reality (SVVR) into the interaction approach significantly impacts the EI outcomes as perceptive levels and problem-solving ability. Wu (2019) showed the positive attitudes from the users with low attentivenessgotfore they get in touch with SVVR technology [19]. The effect on increasing the motivations created by this technology has reached users at different levels as one of the prospective ways to enhance traditional interaction in the class and bring a deep understanding of students' courses while it is adopted to the education field [20].

Simulated experience keeps developing the technology to make both user experience and the developing process more simplistic and easier to use. Another technolis likeapproach like a web dedicated to everyone's capable and accessible platform. Web Extended Reality (WebXR) is a new-improved technology developed by W3C in 2019, which improves performance on interacting with extended reality devices through the browsers [21].

3   Research Methodology

This methodology investigates some side effects and the psychological issues due to the new normal condition in countries harmed by the COVID-19 pandemic. The methodology also aims to address the direction in the user sledging user experience behind the digital native's generation. This chapter liberates the research framework's comprehension such as breakdown as Contextual inquiry, Data interpretation, Design visioning, Case Study, and Design Validation (Fig. 1).

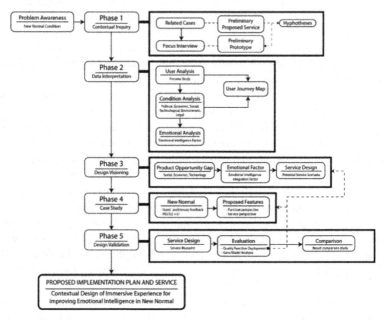

Fig. 1. Proposed theoretical service innovation framework

This research raising the awareness of lessening the side effects comes out on the new normal condition as part of improvisation of the user's emotional intelligence (EI) consequences. Phase 1 endeavors the contextual inquiry process by implementing the explorative related case studies of literature review and visualizes the expected result as the preliminary proposed service of immersive experience.

Based on the compounded result of phase 1, phase 2 carries the exploration approach in analyzing the digital native's users, condition, and the integration of the user journey through the time of new normal. Therefore, the PESTLE (Politic, Economic, Social, Technology, Environment, and Legal) analysis used the condition awareness to see the different macro conditions in separated places of the users.

In phase 3 of design visioning, an opportunity gap is explored by social, economic, technical (SET) analysis to sketch out the breaking point on the market as well as comprehending the potential service scenario. The service scenario has concluded with the conversion from the contextual inquiry and interpreter stage to fulfill the proposed service's user expectation.

Along with the phase 3 approach mechanism, a case study of the research in phase 4 is well analyzed to integrate the users' preliminary feedback and the investigation result of the emotional intelligence in the new normal condition to form the proposed features of function and service perspectives of study. The data resulted in this field enduring the fundamental proposed research and users' knowledge standpoint to the next step of design validating.

In validating the concept, three approaches are used in this phase: service design proposed system, research evaluation, and the result comparison study based on the research evaluation. Understanding the user requirements and demands from the focus interview result, this research develops the service design concept optimization on creating the service scenario on utilizing the system. Nevertheless, the service blueprint supplies the detailed-perspectives on diagnosing the efficiency of the proposed service when propped by the front-end and the back-end process. The evaluation study managed with using quality function deployment to ensure the importance of the features, while the Kano model analysis gives the qualification result on examining user satisfaction on the features provided.

4   Experimental Research and Analysis Study

This stage presents the main result gleaned from the focus interview study of the participant with different regions that adopted the new normal condition. Service design tools were employed to support the contextual data like the persona analysis, PESTLE analysis, user journey maps, and service blueprints. On the other, in considering the emotional reflections from the participants, emotional intelligence factors were adopted based on two methods of analysis by Hyde and Mayer. This result provides an objective understanding of the participant's awareness when the immersive experience and emotional intelligence are evaluated with QFD and Kano model on the design validation process.

4.1   Focus Interview Study Result

The result uncovered the possibility issue to be solved in the adaptation of new normal conditions. The information gathered provided five aspects of user, circumstances, conditions, emotion, and preliminary feedback to support the development of the topic raised in this research study.

Ten international participants agreed to contribute to delivering the insight of new normal conditions in their region as well as the experiences they perceived. The regional classification classified the participants as 50% having a regional background in Asia, and 50% others were from Europe with the range of age 20–30 years old and declared as digital natives. We used Google meets which have been recorded through the whole process of the interview. Yet this method claimed the possibility to conduct an interview in a cross-places-based. The participants' locations were exposed to Taiwan, Indonesia, Germany, Netherland, and the United Kingdom. The expected result acquired from this data collection method gives advanced insight into understanding new normal conditions based on regional and cultural analysis thinking.

4.2 User Analysis

A user analysis approach is developed to employ the service design tool of persona analysis. The two kinds of personas were captured during the contextual analysis of the focus interview study. The reflected persona summarized the overall condition of workers and students while facing the new normal scenario that compels them to do activities from home or online. Therefore, this research focused more on the active users represented by two prominent major occupations: student and worker. A student delivers the active user's persona that considers a stress reliever in interaction-oriented daily activities. While the worker brings the persona of a middle-high stress reliever when needed to find the better problem solver instead of only interaction but also the living experience and requirements. The worker and student were chosen considering the major user influence in the new normal condition, which can be narrowed down to a big scope of active and passive users. Creating persona in this study assists the comprehensive analysis of the user's conditions, behavior, goals, and experiences. Persona analysis also delivers an innovation gap to understand potential market information.

On the other perspectives, we figured out the worker's insight while working from home. The worker faces a serious issue that brings a lack of harmonization interaction with the family when he could not perform the job correctly. The need for communication for the office worker due to the online scenario is getting high since the company should maintain the cooperation concept of the employees even though it is not in the physical methods. Since the pressure received by the worker is worse, the goal and motivation of the worker are exposed more than the student. Due to limited jobs in the new normal, a proper business model should be figured out with maintaining the current job productivity at home. Nevertheless, preserving the relationship with someone engaged in this scenario also needs to be considered. In the end, the lack of immersive feeling of relaxation and relieving the pressure will be a potential habit to be solved in order to create the safest exploration in the new normal.

5 Research Evaluation and Analysis

This chapter addresses the validation and analysis of the proposed immersive experience when it has consolidated emotional intelligence in the new normal condition as the examination study. It commences with classifying the data according to the quality function deployment (QFD) tool to the field of macro-emotion-micro scale: (1) PESTLE (2) Emotional intelligence (3) Opportunity gap in SET. Throughout the macro-micro analysis, we estimated and measured the user's satisfaction probability on the market. Thereafter, we itemized the functional and service features to be evaluated objectively by the target users in the Kano model analysis. The features' important outcomes from the Kano model will lead the future work on developing the project based on the users' visions and the market condition. The last action's result presented the re-evidence value from the user with conducting the qualitative interview on comparing the proposed immersive experience of video-based to the photo-based research.

5.1 PESTLE Analysis Result

We divided the findings into three kinds of priority term to access the commitment of prioritizing the actions due to the different conditions. Even though the participants from different locations provided the data, the term-summarized covers the general condition demanded in all areas acceded to the new normal regulation. Below we specified the PESTLE analysis based on the situation awareness of the new normal and integrational understanding.

The short-term result indicates the highest importance of accelerating the health protocol in all aspects of life. It mostly affected social interaction in society in recent times. With the rapid transmission of the COVID-19 in the community, this action must be put on the top concern in maintaining the activities that cannot instantly transform into a digital way. According to WHO (2020), community transmission demonstrates the impossibility of linking confirmed cases along transmission chains for a significant number of instances [22]. Attending this consideration, the legalization of managing the health protocol in the public environment will be an attention point that needs the proper information from the government. Otherwise, as mentioned by some participants during the interview session, the asynchronous information will keep revealing to the public society.

The sustain-term provokes the common safest behavior that society has done as an innovation to be elevated as an important task to support the new normal conditions. The digital transformation that predicts slowly increased due to some local policy currently claims into daily life scenarios. People are not offended by the digital transformation, yet, they must get used to it in a fast-moving manner. In this case, adaptation is needed to assist the work from home regulation and prevent the rule-breaking caused by the social interaction shortage in the rapid period. Nevertheless, it may affect some people's emotional intelligence who are not ready to settle down in a short time. The people's development by this time can increase the future innovative decision on technology adaptability support.

The lowest contradictory level unveils the new normal adaptation and prevention's long-term requirement to manage the viability vision. The worst case is predicted when the new normal becomes a new living regulation with all things inside. Reflected on the current condition of some businesses that are being suspended due to the lock-down situation, this QFD examination shows the needs of the government's interruption in facilitating the public with the new model of business which sustains in the new normal. It does not rest there, the digital transformation that is related to the sustained term is required to be supported by the political understanding of the government's attention to the different regional conditions.

5.2 Emotional Intelligence Analysis Result

With regard to emotional apprehension in the new normal, three concerns of emotional finding give the estimated calculation of the user's implicit condition. The highest concern discloses the demand of people to manage the emotion into the new behavioral space. It steered to lock down and work from home regulation, which prompts some depressions in encountering the identical monotonous experience for an unpredictable long period. Considering the relationships in this scenario also forms a big issue due to the limitation of social interaction in person, which has the worst effect as well as the uncertain emotional changing in the self-understanding to others.

5.3 Opportunity Gap Analysis Result

After identifying and categorizing the PESTLE and emotional intelligence aware-ness, we continuously find the synthesis data result by calculating the most correlated category's finding in the previous steps as the opportunity gap of the proposed re-search. The QFD integration study identified three main integration issues obtained from the user's perspectives during the interview.

The first priority is the technology adaptation that requires people in the pandemic situation to cope with digital transformation but remains the emotional intelligence as good as it used to be in the physical environment. The second priority concerns the need to legalize the precise health protocol in the pandemic situation. The lowest concern is explained as the user's need based on the potentially high issue, but this research argues that the user did not realize it. It is exposed as the public understanding of all aspects of the new normal.

Based on the interview result, we can comprehend that some people face difficulties in adapting to the new normal in their lives. In comparison, some others had realized that due to the sufficient experience they perceived, it is worthwhile to manage themselves to cope with new normal conditions and develop well emotional intelligence conditions. The synchronization information of new normal understanding within the public could be one of the important concerns in assisting people in developing their emotional intelligence in this level of integration.

5.4 Quality Function Deployment on Features Development Analytical Result

Developing the problem solver value involves the necessity of understanding the component of innovation within new normal elements. Therefore, this research has decided to improve the usage of Immersive WebXR by merging the user's emotional intelligence characteristic on public society. Essentially WebXR occupies the needs of exploration experience on the hybridization of all simulated reality scenarios. Due to the special condition of assisting the new normal adaptation, this research structured additional features which can support the immersive virtual experience in an advanced approach and remained the low side effect for people who are engaged. In this research, commercial features were proposed, which distinguished into six groups of categories under perspectives of function and service adaptation: Function (immersion, visualization, integration); Service (digital exploration, social-economy interaction, credible data, and information). While being based on the usage of the human-centered design concept, the proposed features in this research pursued the supply factor of macro-micro-emotional classification as immersive experience indicators (Table 1).

When it is being analyzed in QFD, the proposing functional feature reveals the most priority in feedback function of engagement, interaction, and user interface to the proposed features in immersion, visualization, integration. The immersion group of categories applies the usability of the 360-degree video as well as the medium of WebXR

Table 1. Proposed features

Features - Function	Features - Service
F1. 360-degree video content approach	**S1.** Digital outdoor experience scenario and content
F2. Web Extended Reality medium tool	**S2.** Immersive ambient of digital content
F3. Natural Input Processing: Voice and motion	**S3.** Inter user challenge
F4. Gamification concept of the natural interaction	**S4.** Customization scenario control
F5. 3D deepfake models face emotion visualization	**S5.** Online community interaction
F6. Cross-device accessible platform	**S6.** Live inter user interaction
F7. Google and social media integration account	**S7.** New marketplace approach in safest medium (WebXR)
F8. Progressive Web App integration concept	**S8.** User contribution content in crowdsourcing mechanism
F9. Data protection with machine learning approach	**S9.** Barrierless language interaction
	S10. Location and product review in Web Extended Reality
	S11. Reliable information notification of visited place
	S12. User-manual visualization approach
	S13. Terms and Agreement of using the system

to connect it to the users. Yet, with the immersion function, this research desires to promote the digitalization of the physical experience to the simulated world in the urge of new normal conditions. The visualization group of features contributes to the implication of artificial intelligence. Besides, this group of categories assists the WebXR-adopted technology to provide a better quality of interactive visualization and the accessibility for users to access the service in executing the user experience. When endeavoring into the integration factors of the user to the proposed system, the consolidation of affordability and data safety is considered as the main point of feasibility to attain the user intention.

We divided the correlation priority of the function features as the following prominent identification of such establishment:

1. **The gamification concept supports the advanced immersive experience:** Utilizing the gamification concept to the immersive experience exploration presumes to cover the lack of interaction in the conventional simulation world.

2. **The users' data protection to improve the affordability for general users:** The simulation experience in merging both virtual and enhanced physical atmosphere should serve strong data protection to attain the user's trust to broaden the user's target, especially those who are not in the tech-educated background.
3. **Natural input processing as the advanced form of social media platform:** The current social media platforms should follow the user's demands with taking foremost procedure in making innovations to support EI development in new normal.

The QFD analysis of this service features prominent three priority result which focused on the social-economy interaction and the credible data of information:

1. **An advancement method of community interaction for the new behavior in digitalization approach:** The digitalization of the community activities must be provided in order to maintain the emotional intelligence in correspondence social schemes.
2. **The social interaction knowledge to deal with the emotional repression in a new environment:** The understanding of managing emotion as continuous adaptation behavior support is obligated to be planned. Otherwise, the worst condition will continue to exist and create a big psychological side effect together with emotional intelligence.
3. **Reliable information and notification to assist the health protocol in society:** The merging scenario implementation of reliable information to educate people about the health protocol in public possesses as the troubleshooter way to enhance the new normal information with magnificent methods of exploration-based interaction experience.

5.5 Kano Model Analysis

Analytical Questionnaire Study. A total of 32 volunteers have participated in the process, which can be distinguished based on the employment status ratio of 34.4% from workers and 65.6% from students. The designed respondent demographics also categorized the participant based on gender, the background of interest, nationality, country of residence, with each percentage arrangement shown in Table 5.12. Three leading majors of interest were revealed as business and management (18.8%); design and art (37.5%); engineering and IT (31.3%), which can represent the human-centered perspectives from the user's background. Moreover, another scope of interest is also noticed such as environment, international relationship, linguistics, and medical which brings the 3.1% of ratio respectively.

In comprehending the sequence of the contextual concept that assembled the data from the different regions, the formal questionnaire enhanced the output value by collecting the questionnaire insight from the western and eastern region places, which differs by nationality and residence. There are 12 nationalities and 12 countries of residence investigated by the participants. The distribution of the regional residence showed that 37.5% of participants were from the western residential area of Germany, Mexico, Netherlands, Poland, Russia, Turkey, USA, and the rest of 62.5% was from the eastern residential area of China (PRC), Indonesia, Taiwan, Thailand, and Vietnam. This output tried to generalize the region's scope with more focus on the residence country instead of only on the nationality (Table 2).

Table 2. Kano Model continuous analysis

Continuous analysis of Kano Model				
Feature	Dysfunctional (X)	Functional (Y)	Importance (Z)	Category
F1-F1	1.31	2.47	6.16	A
F2-F2	1.19	2.61	6.10	A
F3-F3	1.83	3.07	6.97	A
F4-F4	1.13	3.07	6.70	A
F5-F5	1.38	2.24	6.10	A
F6-F6	3.18	3.43	8.00	P
F7-F7	2.30	2.83	7.37	P
F8-F8	2.14	2.90	7.48	P
F9-F9	3.37	3.60	8.43	P
F10-S1	1.93	2.53	6.63	A
F11-S2	2.23	2.80	6.73	P
F12-S3	1.48	2.83	6.76	A
F13-S4	2.07	2.67	6.57	P
F14-S5	2.41	3.38	7.55	P
F15-S6	1.53	2.43	6.60	A
F16-S7	1.73	2.67	6.63	A
F17-S8	2.03	2.80	6.77	P
F18-S9	2.77	3.40	7.77	P
F19-S10	2.10	2.76	6.90	P
F20-S11	2.74	2.90	7.48	P
F21-S12	1.75	2.57	6.79	A
F22-S13	1.74	1.97	6.52	I

The Kano model continuous analysis was implemented to discover the detailed-result provided by 32 participants in this study. In this analysis the importance and satisfaction value were perceived based on the importance level, dysfunctional, and functional coordinate on the visualization graphic. It has been discovered among the 22 features designed in this study, 10 were classified as the "Attractive" quality, 11 were classified as the "Performance", and one was classified as "Indifferent" reviewing in Table 5.14. In addition, the must be quality was not found during the data collection on this study.

The attraction quality delights the features that are created by unexpected products or services to the user. This quality carries the increasing satisfaction that stands out on user's minds which bundled on the "Function" and "Service" features in this research: The function features were shown by "360-degree video content approach," "Web Extended Reality medium tool," "Natural Input Processing: Voice and motion," "Gamification concept of the natural interaction," "3D deep fake model face emotion visualization." Whereas for the service features, this analysis dis-closed five elements to be considered as "Digital outdoor experience scenario and content," "Inter user challenge," "Live inter-user interaction," "New marketplace approach in safest medium (WebXR)," "User-manual visualization approach." This study claimed these features classified as the innovation that can be delivered to users by the quality analysis. However, during the time when people applied these approaches, the transforming possibility of these features must also be getting higher.

A performance quality possesses some features that contribute to the increase and decrease the satisfaction towards the proposed features. The more functionality these features supply to the user, the greater possibility of the research project satisfies the user and vice versa. Therefore, this research unveiled four features from "Function" as a performance quality: "Cross-device accessible platform," "Google and social media integration account," "Progressive Web App integration concept," "Data protection with a machine learning approach." While from the "Service" this analysis study concluded seven features which are "Immersive ambient of digital content," "Customization scenario control," "Online community interaction," "User contribution content in crowdsourcing mechanism," "Barrier less language interaction," "Lo-cation and product review in Web Extended Reality," "Reliable information notification of visited place." This quality provides a better controllable environment since users are already in the knowledge of this proposed group of performance. Hence, putting more effort to get the most outstanding result in time and resources is worth it.

Comparison Study in Residential-Based Analysis. Over 22 total features proposed in this research, only eight features that indicated the identical category result from the western and eastern areas. The identical features represent each category of innovation delivered inside the topic bundled: immersion, visualization, integration, digital exploration, social-economy interaction, and credible data information; however, the 14 other features have remained as indifferent, which is arguable as the environment-influenced reason.

The comparison analysis discloses eight indifferent qualities formed by the western residences that are either attractive or performance by the eastern residences. The indifferent quality showed innovative features to improve the usability of digital interaction and exploration during new normal conditions from the original ideation. The indifferent quality features chosen by the western residence participants were designed to enhance the possibility of interaction in a digital manner, such as the technical facilities, collaborative interaction, and the authentically information that will be served to users: "Web Extended Reality medium tool," "3D deep fake model face emotion visualization," "Google and social media integration account," "Digital out-door experience scenario and content," "New marketplace approach in safest medium (WebXR)," "User contribution content in crowdsourcing mechanism," "Reliable information notification of visited place," "Terms and Agreement of using the system." In connecting the indifferent result to the focus interview study, this research reckons the western residence has higher needs on real interaction than the eastern residence, which can still deal with their emotional issue through the proposed innovation features. Nonetheless, eastern residence uncovers the possibilities to adapt and match the research to their further market better than western participants by giving more positive feedback in attractive and performance quality without any indifferent leftovers.

6   Discussion and Conclusion

This research delineated the result with the human-centered approach to measure the contextual design of user experience while passing through the new normal condition. Concerning feasibility, this research provides an innovative solution in applying the 360-degree interactive spherical video into the Web-based extended reality. The concept of metaverse is provided to meet the easiness and affordability of using simulated experience reality technology towards the safest environment to assist the new normal adaptation on the public. During the application of new normal adaptation in some countries, we found some emotional issues encountered by the participants are related to social-living interaction and adaptability to the new environment in all aspects. Based on the evaluation study conducted, the possibility of developing the research is well analyzed and predicted from the user's questionnaire's responses to fit the scenario in western and eastern residence.

The desirability value of this research urges the people's psychological development of emotional intelligence through a new engagement system to obtain a better-quality life during the safe circumstance from the COVID-19 pandemic. Nonetheless, as the comparison study result, the intention of viability implementation of the research result acknowledged eastern market is worth executing the project compared to western's due to most features being more admit-ted with good feedback quality.

This research exclusively concluded three accomplishment result studies on reaching the goal of new normal awareness and potential problem-solving strategy:

1. **User's behavior research in new normal**: The finding of this analysis visualized digital natives of workers and students that have different life cycles prior to the COVID-19 pandemic as emotional and journey learning to find the opportunity market in a specific time of new normal adaptation. The advanced persona and journey's findings also reported the emotional intelligence that contributed to the emotional indicators to deal with the living demands, productivity, and inadequate physical interaction.
2. **Comprehension study of Macro-Emotion-Micro analysis**: This research is able to execute people's representative reaction from Asia and the European region on facing new normal regulation. This process reflected the issue of unprepared conditions and knowledge to reconstruct daily habits to follow new normal conditions appropriately. The quality function deployment process was subsequently employed for this milestone to understand the relevance integration factors and develop the features according to the users' awareness on elevating emotional intelligence through the metaverse immersive experience in WebXR.

3. **Proposed service of the WebXR development:** This study proposed an immersive experience concept assisted by the WebXR technology to manage the outdoor experience as well as the metaverse adaptation.

Acknowledgement. We would like to show our gratitude to the funding support from the Ministry of Science and Technology with the project (108-2410-H-027-013-MY2).

References

1. Triyason, T., Tassanaviboon, A., Kanthamanon, P.: Hybrid classroom: designing for the new normal after COVID-19 pandemic. In: Proceedings of the 11th International Conference on Advances in Information Technology, Bangkok, Thailand, article no. 30. Association for Computing Machinery (2020)
2. Kumar, J.A., Muniandy, B., Yahaya, W.A.J.W.: Exploring the effects of emotional design and emotional intelligence in multimedia-based learning: an engineering educational perspective. New Rev. Hypermedia Multimedia 25(1–2), 57–86 (2019)
3. Moreno-Fernandez, J., et al.: Lockdown, emotional intelligence, academic engagement and burnout in pharmacy students during the quarantine. Pharmacy 8(4), 194 (2020)
4. Zhang, C.: The why, what, and how of immersive experience. IEEE Access 8, 90878–90888 (2020)
5. Dogan, E., Kan, M.H.: Bringing heritage sites to life for visitors: towards a conceptual framework for immersive experience. Adv. Hosp. Tourism Res. (AHTR) 8, 76–99 (2020)
6. Weissblueth, E., Nissim, Y.: The contribution of virtual reality to social and emotional learning in pre-service teachers. Creat. Educ. 09(10), 1551–1564 (2018)
7. Lee, L.-H., et al.: All one needs to know about metaverse: a complete survey on technological singularity, virtual ecosystem, and research agenda. arXiv pre-print (2021)
8. Beyer, H., Holtzblatt, K.: Contextual design. Interactions 6(1), 32–42 (1999)
9. Suppipat, S., Cheng, W.-M., Wang, S.-M.: Contextual design of intergenerational innovative service for aging in place. In: Gao, Q., Zhou, J. (eds.) HCII 2020. LNCS, vol. 12208, pp. 531–544. Springer, Cham (2020). https://doi.org/10.1007/978-3-030-50249-2_38
10. Surma-aho, A., et al.: Usability issues in the operating room – towards contextual design guidelines for medical device design. Appl. Ergon. 90, 103221 (2021)
11. Berwick, D.M.: Choices for the "new normal." JAMA 323(21), 2125–2126 (2020)
12. Retzlaff, K.J.: Lessons learned from COVID-19 and the new normal. AORN J. 112(3), 212–215 (2020)
13. Yoo, H.J.: Evolution of digital natives and the new role of research. J. Child Adolesc. Psychiatry (Soa–ch'ongsonyon chongsin uihak) 32(4), 127–128 (2021)
14. Bozdağ, F.: The psychological effects of staying home due to the COVID-19 pandemic. J. General Psychol. 148(3), 226–248 (2021)
15. Brooks, S.K., et al.: The psychological impact of quarantine and how to reduce it: rapid review of the evidence. Lancet 395(10227), 912–920 (2020)
16. Losada-Baltar, A., Jiménez-Gonzalo, L., Gallego-Alberto, L., del Sequeros, M., Pedroso-Chaparro, J.-P., Márquez-González, M.: "We are staying at home." Association of self-perceptions of aging, personal and family resources, and loneliness with psychological distress during the lock-down period of COVID-19. J. Gerontol. Ser. B 76(2), e10–e16 (2020)
17. Shahid, R., Stirling, J., Adams, W.: Promoting wellness and stress management in residents through emotional intelligence training. Adv. Med. Educ. Pract. 9, 681–686 (2018)

18. Valente, S., Monteiro, A.P., Lourenço, A.A.: The relationship between teachers' emotional intelligence and classroom discipline management. Psychol. Sch. **56**(5), 741–750 (2019)
19. Wu, J., Guo, R., Wang, Z., Zeng, R.: Integrating spherical video-based virtual reality into elementary school students' scientific inquiry instruction: effects on their problem-solving performance. Interact. Learn. Environ. **29**(3), 496–509 (2019)
20. Lin, H.-S., Shih-Jou, Y., Sun, J.-Y., Jong, M.S.Y.: Engaging university students in a library guide through wearable spherical video-based virtual reality: effects on situational interest and cognitive load. Interact. Learn. Environ. **29**(8), 1272–1287 (2019)
21. Li, S., et al.: An exploratory study of bugs in extended reality applications on the web. In: 2020 IEEE 31st International Symposium on Software Reliability Engineering (ISSRE) (2020)
22. World Health Organization: Coronavirus disease 2019 (COVID-19): situation report, 45. 2020. World Health Organization, Geneva

Children-Computer Interaction

A Systematic Review of Multimodal Interaction in Artificial Intelligent System Supporting Children to Learn Music

Baihui Chen[1] and Lusha Huang[2](✉) ⓘ

[1] Communication University of China, Beijing, China
[2] Guangzhou Academy of Fine Arts, Guangzhou, China
lusha.huang@connect.polyu.hk

Abstract. Music, as an essential expression of art, has been fundamental to perceptual learning as well as emotional expression, which is particularly beneficial to children's cognitive development and memory. Music has been a significant focus of research in the field of artificial intelligence (AI) along with arts. With the rapid development of AI technology comes a range of new interactive ways to assist children in learning music in the abstract. Although relevant research areas are exploring intelligent musical interaction systems for children, a systematic review of this field demonstrates that little empirical research has been conducted in this domain. Most research focuses on how technology can progress. Nevertheless, there is currently no focus on how AI technology can play a role in interactive systems from the perspective of children's experiences and cognition. Therefore, this study systematically reviewed published research on intelligent music interaction systems for children by critically screening and evaluating a database of 315 research articles (n = 21). The current study's review of the extant literature found that there is still a lack of focus on the relationship between intelligent interaction techniques and cognitive load during children's music learning from a child's cognitive perspective. The review revealed that intelligent music interaction systems for children are still in their infancy. The results of this study could be adopted by system developers and designers to create intelligent interactive music systems that are easier for children to understand and learn.

Keywords: Multimodal interaction · Intelligent system · Music · Children education

1 Introduction

Music, in a broader context, is defined as the art of any composition of sound. The English word "Music" is derived from the ancient Greek word "mousike", meaning the art of the muse. The Chinese word music is abstract art reflecting the reality of human emotions. The difference between sound and music is that music needs to be dreamed up and composed via the human-being mind. Music is also a form of social behaviour

© The Author(s), under exclusive license to Springer Nature Switzerland AG 2022
M. Kurosu (Ed.): HCII 2022, LNCS 13302, pp. 545–557, 2022.
https://doi.org/10.1007/978-3-031-05311-5_38

through which people could communicate their emotions and life experiences to each other. This role is most evident in the song. The adult's ability to perceive music builds on elements from early childhood and the importance of melody and rhythm, organising rhythmic patterns into a superposition of steady beats and more complex rhythms. These factors provide the foundation upon which perceptual learning and cultural adaptation throughout life are built. The development of music perception and cognition during childhood influences cognitive abilities in adulthood [1]. Children's music learning has long been shown to benefit children's cognitive development and memory [2], as well as foster children's cognitive development through various models of music education. Learning music often requires extra time, money, and professional equipment. Therefore, the barriers to entry are high [3]. In this vein, researchers are constantly exploring new technologies to replace professional music equipment. There is a demand for technological systems to assist individuals in music composition and learning, and research in the direction of computer music can be traced back as far as the fifteenth and sixteenth centuries. For example, in pre-classical music, Mozart, had an interesting musical experiment in which a piece of music was first divided into several bars, and then the pieces were selected by means of a dice roll to assemble the music, which is considered to be the earliest source of computer music.

With the rapid development of AI technology, increasing areas are being given a new lease of life by this technology. As an indispensable part of the multimedia sector, the importance of music to humanity cannot be overstated. It is worth noting that research into AI in the field of music began many years ago and has landed many mature applications as well. Many studies have demonstrated that merging technology into children's music learning can maximise preschoolers' mental and thinking skills that provide new directions for the development of multiple intelligences education for children [4]. The purpose of this study is to review the area of ongoing research, i.e., AI-enabled interactive systems for children's music, and to try to understand how state interaction technologies in intelligent systems applications and in what ways these technologies influence children's learning and creation of music.

It is crucial to understand how children's interactivity works before designing interactive learning resources. Children's interactive music learning systems are one form of child-computer interaction used as an interactive paradigm for children's music composition, learning and experience. Interactive music learning systems for children are a form of child-computer interaction, and research has demonstrated that children's interaction with music systems can enhance children's teaching and learning processes and musical creativity [5]. Technologies are being developed to enable this interaction between humans and intelligent systems to enable a natural and embodied experience of children's interaction with music. Yet, the majority of research on children computer interaction in music is based on traditional forms of interaction, with less research on new technologies associated with Virtual Reality (VR), robotics and AI.

It is apparent that AI has been adopted to solve problems in various fields. AI presents a distinct opportunity to develop problem-solving skills applying a variety of tasks that stimulate children's curiosity [6]. The Intelligent System is intended to be one of the best ways to combine technology and art as a tool to empower children to create and learn music. With the development of technologies such as AI, which have permeated our daily lives and caused dramatic changes in human life and learning, the interaction between children and machines has become fundamental to the learning process [7]. The relationship between new technologies and learning has been the focus of attention in music education, with most previous research focusing on technology as a teaching tool [8] or a way to create and share music in life [9]. However, in this field, less research has focused on the experience of children's interaction with technology, because not all technology is suitable to stimulate children's learning and creation of music according to their cognitive development. Currently, most research has focused on technological advances without considering the human element, such as how AI systems should be designed to help children understand or create music.

This study focuses on a review of the current literature in the field of children's musical interaction in intelligent systems, exploring through a systematic literature review how technology influences this children's learning and creation of music, specifically in the following ways: (1) to determine the different ways in which children currently interact in the field of music interaction (2) to discover the main factors that may affect children in musical interactions and how to improve and enhance children's learning effectiveness in musical interactions (3) to review all the interactive technologies utilised in intelligent systems, to further improve children's cognition and human-computer interaction and to investigate how interactive systems and AI technologies can foster them to create and learn music more easily.

2   Literature Review

This study systematically reviewed the literature on children's music interaction in intelligent systems. The data collection and analysis were conducted through multiple academic research sources to collect and analyse literature in the relevant fields. The first step in the literature collection was conducted through SCOPUS and Web of Science, as these databases cover a wide range of research in the social sciences and engineering fields. These data were then supplemented and referenced through Google Scholar.

The literature review was conducted in October 2021, and the query was worked on in the aforementioned database employing the following search characters.("learn" OR "study" OR "understand" OR "make") AND ("interaction" OR "interface" OR "techniques" OR "feedback") AND ("tangible interaction" OR "TUI" OR "augmented reality" OR "AR" OR "virtual reality" OR "VR" OR "robot" OR "intelligent machines" OR "Artificial Intelligence" OR "AI") AND ("children" OR "child" OR "school age student") AND ("music" OR "Musical" OR "sound"). The collection includes all literature published in English from 1997–2021. All literature reviewed included only empirical studies based on title and abstract search, excluding dissertations, review papers, short reviews, and books.

The eligibility criteria to be included in this paper review are as follows: 1) Papers reviewed are not included in the conference proceedings. 2) The research objectives are aimed at children learning music, not at achieving other research objectives through learning music. For example, supporting autistic children with musical robots to relieve their pain is not included in the scope of this review. 3) The task is to help children learn about music, not just to use their auditory perception system. For example, assessing the emotional value of the emotional voice of a child interacting with a robot is not included in the scope of this thesis analysis [10]. 4) An interactive approach applied to children's learning of music and empirical research on the interactive approach is considered eligible for review.

For the initial review phase, a total of 315 literature records were identified in the Children's Music Interactive in Intelligence system. After the selection of abstracts and keywords, 189 articles were further critically screened and evaluated primarily. As a result, a total of 21 articles ended up as strictly eligible articles, as the field of music in intelligent interaction with children is still in its infancy. Each article was systematically categorized according to the age stage of the child, the purpose of the study, the technological approach, and the intelligent system.

Table 1. Literature search and inclusion.

Step	Description	Add or delete	Amount
Step 1	Literature search through Scopus and Web of Science: ("learn" OR "study" OR "understand" OR "make") AND ("interaction" OR "interface" OR "techniques" OR "feedback") AND ("tangible interaction" OR "TUI" OR "augmented reality" OR "AR" OR "virtual reality" OR "VR" OR "robot" OR "intelligent machines" OR "Artificial Intelligence" OR "AI") AND ("children" OR "child" OR "school age student") AND ("music" OR "Musical" OR "sound")	+315	315
Step 2	Additional records identified through other sources (Google Scholar)	+9	324
Step 3	Duplicated records removed	−126	189
	Records exclude after title and abstract screening	−118	72
Step 4	Records exclude after eligibility assessment	−51	21

3 Findings: The Synthesis of the Literature

A total of 21 relevant studies are reviewed in this paper (Table 1). Early research has found that people move from perception to action as a different way of processing information, closely related to attention, memory and cognition, and movement [11]. The key to the intelligent interaction with music for children is to set up appropriate forms of interaction and timely feedback based on children's perception and cognition (Fig. 1). The literature, in general, uses different forms of interaction depending on the age of the child, their cognitive level, and the factors involved in learning music, but all use intelligent systems to help children with their interactive learning of music. Different forms of interaction are used depending on the cognitive abilities of children at different ages, and this article hopes to explore how different interaction methods are brought to children based on intelligent systems to help them learn and understand music. According to the literature there are two main types of interactive systems, those that interact through robots and those that interact with children through multimodal systems.

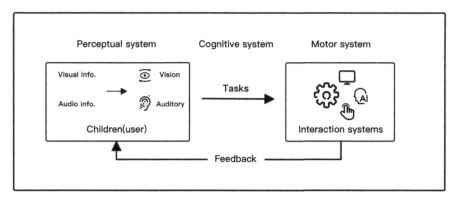

Fig. 1. Children music intelligent interactive system.

3.1 Multimodal Systems

As shown in Table 2 and Table 3 of the multimodal interaction systems (n = 11), only 54.5% of the articles were based on children's characteristics. According to the literature review, 45% of the studies used tangible interactive systems (n = 5) and concluded that tangible interfaces are effective in helping children interact with music through natural behaviours and metaphors that can improve children's cognitive abilities and creativity with music [12]. AR (n = 2) and VR (n = 2) were employed in 36.4% of studies to help children learn music through virtual scenarios that helped children perceive musical knowledge in an immersive situation [4]. Motion capture (n = 1) and sound interaction (n = 1) were also utilised to help children understand more intuitively abstract theories such as musical melodies [13]. Hand-based interaction is the dominant modality in input devices at 45.5%. In terms of output devices, the combined visual and auditory modality was the most frequently used at 90.0%. The primary division of children's interaction experiences into cognitive (n = 5) and usability (n = 6) reveals that current interaction styles focus more on usability than on children's cognitive level. From the lesser focus on children's cognitive level, it was further found that only 18.2% of articles focused on timely feedback in the design of interactive systems (n = 2), and in The Humming Box study, it was found that more feedback changes would increase children's engagement and their attention span.

Table 2. List of articles reviewed on multimodal systems.

NO.	Interaction methods	Year	Title	Source
1	Based on AR Technology	2021	Design of Children's Entertainment and Education Products Based on AR Technology	Lecture Notes in Computer Science
2	Based on VR Technology	2021	The Creation of Multi Intelligence Music Classroom in Children's Enlightenment Stage Based on Virtual Reality Technology	2021 2nd International Conference on Education, Knowledge and Information Management
3	Based on Voice Interaction	2020	Musical and Conversational Artificial Intelligence	International Conference on Intelligent User Interfaces, Proceedings IUI
4	Based on Tangible Interactive Technology	2019	The Humming Box: AI-powered Tangible Music Toy for Children	Extended Abstracts of the Annual Symposium on Computer-Human Interaction in Play
5	Based on Tangible Interactive Technology	2019	Playing to play: a piano-based user interface for music education video-games	Multimedia Tools and Applications
6	Based on Tangible Interactive Technology	2019	Comb - Shape as a meaningful element of interaction	The 13th International Conference on Tangible, Embedded, and Embodied Interaction
7	Based on AR Technology	2019	Augmented reality and QR codes for teaching music to preschoolers and kindergarteners: Educational intervention and evaluation	The 11th International Conference on Computer Supported Education
8	Based on VR Technology	2016	Action Identity in Style Simulation Systems: Do Players Consider Machine-Generated Music As of Their Own Style?	Robots for Learning
9	Based on Tangible Interactive Technology	2016	Expressivity in open-ended constructive play: Building and playing musical Lego instruments	The 15th International Conference on Interaction Design and Children

(continued)

Table 2. (*continued*)

NO.	Interaction methods	Year	Title	Source
10	Based on Kinect Motion Capture System	2014	Kinect based interactive music application for disabled children	The 22nd Signal Processing and Communications Applications Conference
11	Based on Tangible Interactive Technology	2011	CoolMag: A tangible interaction tool to customize instruments for children in music education	Proceedings of the 2011 ACM Conference on Ubiquitous Computing

Table 3. Statistical charts for multimodal systems.

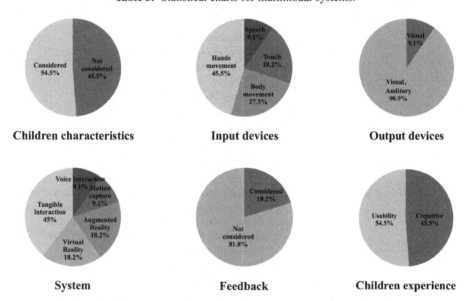

Children characteristics   Input devices   Output devices

System   Feedback   Children experience

3.2 Robot System

As shown in Table 4 and Table 5, in the robotic systems (n = 10), 60% of the studies focused on child characteristics. A single-mode robotic system was used in 70% of the systems, and 30% of the robotic systems combined Tablet (n = 1), audiovisual interface (n = 1) and virtual reality (n = 1). Body movement input and touch input accounted for the largest proportion of robotic systems, respectively 50% and 40%. In terms of output devices, a combination of visual and auditory modalities was the most frequently used at 90.0%. In the literature review, 60% of the studies focused on children's cognitive development and the other 40% on Usability. In these studies, the use of 'sensory' spaces enabled children to interact creatively with music, their own bodies and robots [14, 17].

However, fewer studies have considered timely feedback" from interactions between children and music machines, with only 40% of the studies in this literature review focusing on interactive feedback.

Table 4. List of articles reviewed on robot systems.

NO	Interaction methods	Year	Title	Source
1	Audiovisual Interface-Based Robot System	2021	An audiovisual interface-based drumming system for multimodal human–robot interaction	Journal on Multimodal User Interfaces
2	Based on Virtual Reality Robot System	2021	Personalizing HRI in Musical Instrument Practicing: The Influence of Robot Roles (Evaluative Versus Nonevaluative) on the Child's Motivation for Children in Different Learning Stages	Frontiers in Robotics and AI
3	Based on Robot System	2021	Utilizing social virtual reality robot (V2R) for music education to children with high-functioning autism	Education and Information Technologies
4	Based on Robot System	2021	Child-Robot Interaction in a Musical Dance Game: An Exploratory Comparison Study between Typically Developing Children and Children with Autism	Extended Abstracts of the Annual Symposium on Computer-Human Interaction in Play
5	Based on Robot System	2020	A robot mediated music mixing activity for promoting collaboration among children	IEEE International Conference on Human-Robot Interaction
6	Based on Robot System	2020	Comb - Shape as a meaningful element of interaction	IEEE International Conference on Human-Robot Interaction
7	Based on Robot System	2020	FML-based Intelligent Agent for Robotic e-Learning and Entertainment Application	2019 International Conference on Technologies and Applications of Artificial Intelligence (TAAI)

(continued)

Table 4. (*continued*)

NO	Interaction methods	Year	Title	Source
8	Based on Robot System	2019	Informal stEAM education case study: Child-robot musical theater	Extended Abstracts of the 2019 CHI Conference on Human Factors in Computing Systems
9	Based on Robot System	2019	Teaching music to children with autism: A social robotics challenge	Scientia Iranica
10	Based on Tablet Devices and Robot System	2019	Teaching music to children with autism: A social robotics challenge	The 19th Annual SIG Conference on Information Technology Education

Table 5. Statistical Chart of the robot system.

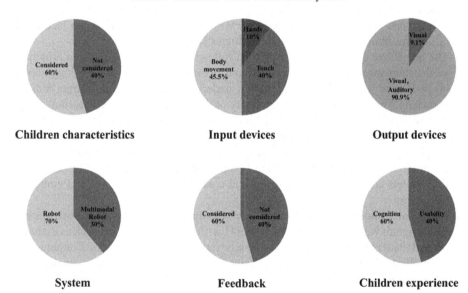

Children characteristics   **Input devices**   **Output devices**

System   **Feedback**   **Children experience**

4 Discussion

This study utilised a quantitative method to review the literature in the field of children's music interaction in intelligent systems, with the goal of systematically understanding the experiences and perceptions of children's music interaction learning in intelligent systems and further improve children's interaction behaviours from a child's perspective. The papers reviewed in this study were systematically investigated through procedures such as keyword selection, inclusion and exclusion criteria, and assessment of the level of relevance of the study. In addition, the design of intelligent music interaction systems considers the cognitive perspective of children to arrive at a consideration of the system model or interaction design. This review presented an overview of the design features of children's musical intelligent interactive systems that contribute to the development of children's intelligent systems and children's computer interaction design, which facilitates children's cognitive development in a more convenient and accessible way from a child's cognitive perspective.

- Determining the model considers the characteristics of the user, such as the age of the child, learning methods, cognitive characteristics and difficulty. For example, this research by Nor Azah Abdul Aziz (2013) shows that children interact through gestures and that all gestures can be used by children of all ages, except for children aged two and three years old. This preliminary study showed that only children aged two to three had problems using certain gestures. However, another study has shown that children from the age of six years onwards can adapt to touchscreen technology and distinguish between a range of common gestures. This study suggests that as children's age affects their reading comprehension and past experiences, it is difficult for young children to learn new interaction patterns quickly without any explanations when faced with difficulties in understanding new technologies [15].
- The interactive system should be created following the affordance design principles so that humans can easily understand and operate the system. Technology should be performed as a tool to help children understand complex and abstract musical knowledge, not to increase the complexity of the technology they are learning. Children have a range of between 1 and 2 h of reasonable concentration time. Therefore, more feedback changes are needed to increase engagement and improve their play. The Humming Box is an AI-powered tangible music toy for children that focuses on children's behaviour through their bodies, hiding the technology behind interactive models and stimulating their musical creativity through natural and embodied interaction.
- Historically, musical elements such as pitch, duration loudness and other abstract MIDI signals were used as a formal symbol for music in philosophers such as Pythagoras and Plato argued that music had the same rational logic as numbers. Consequently, the earliest automatic sequencing systems controlled systems for specific decisions by using sequences of jointly distributed random variables. As early popular Markov chains, owing to their relatively simple operation, were widely used in a variety of musical interactive systems such as chord progressions, musical transformations between sequences, and automatic real-time generation. Sequence models are a vital issue in artificial intelligence in music applications due to the complex and subjective level of musical information. Alongside the development and application of artificial intelligence techniques to the specific field of music, there has been an increasing amount of research related to deep learning architectures applied to this particular task, such as the Recurrent Neural Networks (RNN) model [16], which is an internal memory that summarises the entire sequence history, but requires effective gradient training and optimisation. As early as 2012, the RNN model was applied to the study of modelling polyphonic musical notation sequences for generic piano reels to

improve the accuracy of transcriptions of complex polyphonic pieces [17]. The Transformer attention model [18], presented in 2017, is a new architecture that goes beyond the conditional Long Short-Term Memory (LSTM) approach to sequence modelling based on RNNs further improved. Research related to multimodal musical intelligence systems found that interaction, automated algorithms and affective computing need to be taken into account. MuseGAN can generate coherent music from scratch and accompany a given specific track [19]. Mind Band 2019 has developed an interactive music creation system taking elements such as emojis, images and humming as input and music files as output, through the VAE-GAN music creation system model and converting the humming into the corresponding MIDI files for an online creation platform where each experience is also the creator. This research combines VAE with GAN, decoding through VAE while GAN is the generator, and sharing parameters and training together [20]. With the ongoing development of AI art, children's intelligent interactive systems should consider the variety of technologies that can be used to enrich the way more AI art interacts with devices, to increase the diversity and creativity of children in intelligent interactive systems. However, the current application of intelligent systems to music learning is still relatively homogeneous, with some success stories in intelligent systems to support students learning. For example, A secondary school AI education programme for kindergarten through twelfth grade (K12) stimulates student creativity in the learning process through generative adversarial networks (GANs) for generating images, music, text and video [21]. Furthermore, the AI music control technology for personalised music output, where the MIT lab influences the creation of music by directly emitting sound, lowers the technical threshold for music production and should be used more often in future intelligent interactive systems for children's music.

5   Conclusion

In conclusion, this study was able to summarise the current trends in research on intelligent interactive systems for children in general and in multimodal robotic interactive systems in particular. The current research has been quantitatively examined through a literature review of intelligent interactive systems in the existing literature and has found more incredible benefits from active music listening and music training than passive reception of music learning [22]. For example, actively playing instrumental music and identifying beats can improve learning outcomes and learners' cognitive functioning better than passive learning [23, 24]. A contribution to children's cognitive development and musical intelligent interaction systems.

The review showed that the literature on the use of intelligent systems for children's music learning and composition is still at an early stage, with current research focusing on the development of new technologies, and that there are still research gaps to be filled in the literature on the barriers of technology and the mapping of intelligent interactive systems to children's cognition. However, as each new technology is introduced to the market it brings a range of new ways of interacting, meaning that there is still plenty of room for research in this area. Future research could focus on reducing the cognitive burden of technology, improving closer interaction between children and intelligent systems, and enriching. The results of this study can be used by system developers. The findings and conclusions emerging from this paper provide new insights to system developers and designers to create intelligent music interaction systems that are easier for children to understand and learn. One limitation of this article is the limited number of reviewed resources. Therefore, the inclusion of more resources, comprising dissertations, review papers, short reviews, and books in future reviews might assist in generalizing results concluded here.

Acknowledgments. This study was supported by the grant of "Research on the Designing the Mobile Phone Interaction Experience for People with Visually Impairments in 5G era" (project number: 2021WQNCX034) from the Guangdong Province Colleges and Universities Young Innovative Talent Project.

References

1. Dowling, W.J.: The development of music perception and cognition. In: The Psychology of Music, pp. 603–625. Academic Press (1999)
2. Bilhartz, T.D., Bruhn, R.A., Olson, J.E.: The effect of early music training on child cognitive development. J. Appl. Dev. Psychol. **20**(4), 615–636 (1999)
3. Coresh, J., et al.: Change in albuminuria and subsequent risk of end-stage kidney disease: an individual participant-level consortium meta-analysis of observational studies. Lancet Diabetes Endocrinol. **7**(2), 115–127 (2019)
4. Wang, Q.: The creation of multi intelligence music classroom in children's enlightenment stage based on virtual reality technology. In: 2021 2nd International Conference on Education, Knowledge and Information Management (ICEKIM), January 2021, pp. 431–434. IEEE (2021)
5. Addessi, A.R.: Developing a theoretical foundation for the reflexive interaction paradigm with implications for training music skill and creativity. Psychomusicology Music Mind Brain **24**(3), 214 (2014)
6. Agostinelli, F., et al.: Designing children's new learning partner: collaborative artificial intelligence for learning to solve the Rubik's cube. In: Interaction Design and Children, June 2021, pp. 610–614 (2021)
7. Addessi, A.R., Pachet, F.: Experiments with a musical machine: musical style replication in 3 to 5 year old children. Br. J. Music Educ. **22**(1), 21–46 (2005)
8. Webster, P.: Historical perspectives on technology and music. Music. Educ. J. **89**(1), 38–43 (2002)
9. Chen, C., Tang, Y., Xie, T., Druga, S.: The Humming box: AI-powered tangible music toy for children. In: Extended Abstracts of the Annual Symposium on Computer-Human Interaction in Play Companion Extended Abstracts, October 2019, pp. 87–95 (2019)
10. Rossi, S., Dell'Aquila, E., Bucci, B.: Evaluating the emotional valence of affective sounds for child-robot interaction. In: Salichs, M.A., et al. (eds.) Social Robotics: 11th International Conference, ICSR 2019, Madrid, Spain, November 26–29, 2019, Proceedings, pp. 505–514. Springer, Cham (2019). https://doi.org/10.1007/978-3-030-35888-4_47
11. Wickens, C.D., Carswell, C.M.: Information processing. In: Handbook of Human Factors and Ergonomics, pp. 114–158 (2021)
12. Preka, G., Rangoussi, M.: Augmented reality and QR codes for teaching music to preschoolers and kindergarteners: educational intervention and evaluation. In: CSEDU, pp. 113–123 (2019)

13. Catania, F., et al.: Musical and conversational artificial intelligence. In: Proceedings of the 25th International Conference on Intelligent User Interfaces Companion, March 2020, pp. 51–52 (2020)
14. Camurri, A., Coglio, A.: An architecture for emotional agents. IEEE Multimedia **5**(4), 24–33 (1998)
15. McKnight, L., Fitton, D.: Touch-screen technology for children: giving the right instructions and getting the right responses. In: Proceedings of the 9th International Conference on Interaction Design and Children, June 2010, pp. 238–241 (2010)
16. Rumelhart, D.E., Hinton, G.E., Williams, R.J.: Learning representations by back-propagating errors. Nature **323**(6088), 533–536 (1986)
17. Boulanger-Lewandowski, N., Bengio, Y., Vincent, P.: Modeling temporal dependencies in high-dimensional sequences: application to polyphonic music generation and transcription. arXiv preprint arXiv:1206.6392 (2012)
18. Vaswani, A., et al.: Attention is all you need. In: Advances in Neural Information Processing Systems (2017)
19. Dong, H.-W., Hsiao, W.-Y., Yang, L.-C., Yang, Y.-H.: MuseGAN: multi- track sequential generative adversarial networks for symbolic music generation and accompaniment. In: 32nd AAAI Conference on Artificial Intelligence (2018)
20. Qiu, Z., et al.: Mind band: a crossmedia AI music composing platform. In: Proceedings of the 27th ACM International Conference on Multimedia, October 2019, pp. 2231–2233 (2019)
21. Ali, S., Di Paola, D., Breazeal, C.: What are GANs?: introducing generative adversarial networks to middle school students. In: Proceedings of the AAAI Conference on Artificial Intelligence, May 2021, vol. 35, no. 17, pp. 15472–15479 (2021)
22. Rauscher, F.H., Hinton, S.C.: The Mozart effect: Music listening is not music instruction. Educ. Psychol. **41**(4), 233–238 (2006)
23. Bernhard, H.C.: Singing in instrumental music education: research and implications. Update Appl. Res. Music Educ. **22**(1), 28–35 (2002)
24. Pahor, A., Jaušovec, N.: Multifaceted pattern of neural efficiency in working memory capacity. Intelligence **65**, 23–34 (2017)

Research on the Design of Children's Breath Training Products from the Perspective of Motivation Theory

Panpan Chen[✉]

School of Design Art and Communication, Nanjing University of Science and Technology, Nanjing 210094, Jiangsu, China
cpp3929@163.com

Abstract. Objective: In order to shorten the product development and design cycle, improve children's breathing training experience, and help the healthy development of the children's rehabilitation training industry. Method: Through literature research, field investigation and observation, expert group interviews and other methods, we can understand and analyze the users' demand for breathing training products in detail, use the analytic hierarchy process to summarize the multi-level factors that affect the design of children's breathing training products, and establish a design evaluation level indicator model. Based on the focus group and questionnaire evaluation, the judgment matrix is obtained, the weight value of each evaluation index is calculated, the importance of each index factor is determined, and the design suggestions are finally put forward. Conclusion: The evaluation results show that the most influential factors are the safety and rationality of the structural size, the continuous attractiveness during the treatment process, the ease of operation of the product, the safety of the material and the feedback of the rehabilitation effect. Therefore, when developing and optimizing children's breathing training products, based on the comprehensive consideration of multiple factors in the design evaluation model, the above factors can be considered making the product more suitable for users' needs.

Keywords: Motivation theory · Breath training · AHP · Children with asthma · Product design

1 Introduction

With the rapid economic development in recent years, the problem of air pollution has become more and more serious, and the proportion of children with severe asthma has increased year by year [1]. At present, there is no clinical method to completely cure asthma, and the method of medication control is mostly used to reduce the acute onset of symptoms, but long-term medication has obvious adverse reactions. Clinical studies have shown that in order to obtain adequate ventilation, asthma patients often compensate by strengthening chest breathing. Long-term development will lead to respiratory muscle fatigue, which provides a theoretical basis for clinical breathing training [2]. Breathing

M. Kurosu (Ed.): HCII 2022, LNCS 13302, pp. 558–570, 2022.
https://doi.org/10.1007/978-3-031-05311-5_39

training is to exercise respiratory muscles, reduce breathing difficulties, increase activity endurance and increase ventilation [3]. Although breathing training has been proven to be effective in alleviating the condition during the rehabilitation period, the breathing training process is boring, and it is difficult for children to cooperate with medical staff for rehabilitation training [4].

The scientific research on motivation and motivation theory started in the West, and has been involved in many fields such as management, psychology and behavioral science, and has been continuously supplemented and improved, forming a variety of motivation theories [5]. The word motivation first originated from research in the field of psychology, which means to continuously trigger people's motivation. It is a potential motivation that enables individuals to move from a clear goal to a behavior. In the process of motivation, with internal and external stimuli triggered, people can maintain a state of continuous excitement and complete tasks with a higher degree of concentration [6]. For today's complex human-computer interaction scenarios, motivation theory can clearly sort out the elements of the scenario. Taking the incentive mechanism as the starting point can make better use of the user's psychology and motivation, and increase the user's immersion and participation in product design.

Therefore, this study selects children with asthma as the research object, based on the motivational theory, through the analytic hierarchy process to evaluate the multi-level demand factors of breathing training products for children with asthma and establish a comprehensive evaluation model, rank the importance of the demand elements, and provide a reference for the development and design of breathing training products for children with asthma.

2 Motivation Theory and Breath Training

2.1 Motivation Theory

Motivation theory refers to the theoretical and systematic explanation of the concept of motivation by psychologists. Motivation theory is the study of understanding that drives a person to work hard towards a specific goal or result. It is related to the entire society and is particularly prominent in the early research on business management and economic theory. With the development of computer technology, motivation theory has begun to be applied in the field of human-computer interaction. The field of motivation theory is relatively complex, and there are many research fields. The current mainstream types of motivation theory are shown in Fig. 1:

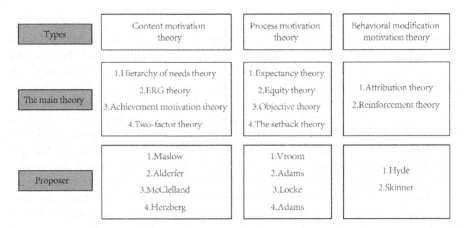

Fig. 1. Mainstream motivational theory

The West has had embryonic forms of motivational thoughts since ancient times. For example, the ancient Greek philosopher Plato mentioned how to play a greater role from the point of view of expertise and ability in the "Utopia" [7]. In modern times, Western motivational thinking is mainly reflected in many theories, such as management, psychology, and behavioral science, and a scientific theoretical system has gradually formed [8].

At present, the most influential ones in China are the synchronous motivation theory and three-factor motivation theory of Professor Wenzhao Yu of East China Normal University, the C-type motivation theory proposed by behavioral researcher Dong Qing and the comprehensive motivation theory proposed by Professor Chuanwu Xiong of East China Normal University. Domestic scholars have also conducted certain research in the field of design under the guidance of motivation theory. Li Dan [9] integrated the motivation theory into the design of rehabilitation products as a behavioral guidance method and improved the interaction between the product and elderly stroke patients. Jialei Shi used motivation theory as the theoretical basis to generate an incentive model for online learning software and proposed a design and development strategy based on the incentive model. Therefore, it is meaningful to integrate the relevant knowledge of motivation theory into the usability evaluation index of children's breathing training products on the basis of predecessors.

2.2 Current Status and Deficiencies of Breathing Training

Breathing training, like other physical exercises, needs to follow scientific exercise principles. The principles of scientific physical exercise include the principle of gradualism, the principle of repetition, the principle of comprehensiveness, and the principle of individuality [10]. Scientific breathing training refers to a method and means to achieve the expected results of breathing training in accordance with objective laws and the law of changes in human physiological functions. Training in accordance with scientific exercise methods can achieve a multiplier effect with half the effort, allowing the body to obtain the greatest training benefits [11].

Respiratory rehabilitation was promoted earlier in foreign countries, and it is regarded as the core of comprehensive care for stable chronic obstructive pulmonary disease. It has been recognized by the American Thoracic Society, Australia and New Zealand, etc. Many authoritative professional organizations have written COPD management guidelines as strong recommendations [12]. Domestic research and design of respiratory rehabilitation training devices have also been carried out, among which the representative products at home and abroad are as follows:

(1) Gila Benchetrit of France designed a breathing training device that collects breathing signals through a sleeveless jacket. The principle of the device is that a sleeveless jacket is equipped with a foldable special material, which can receive the volume changes of the diaphragm and abdomen through lateral expansion. In order to take into account the individual characteristics of the trainee, the device can also screen out the breathing pattern with the largest amplitude and the longest breathing duration in the subject's natural breathing, and guide the user to perform rehabilitation training of lung function based on the breathing pattern.

(2) An intelligent breathing company in Russia has developed a breathing exerciser called Frolov's. The mechanism of the training device is to increase the concentration of carbon dioxide in the inhaled gas to stimulate the adaptability of the body organs. This instrument is suitable for the rehabilitation of chronic respiratory diseases [13] (Fig. 2).

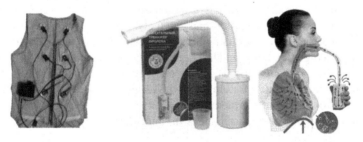

Fig. 2. Sleeveless jacket breathing training device and Frolov's breathing training device

(3) TEDA Xinxing and the Air Force Aviation Medical Engineering Research Center jointly developed an abdominal breathing training device. The breathing exerciser integrates functions such as the guidance of breathing actions, the display of abdominal breathing signals, and the processing and feedback of physiological signals. See Fig. 3 below.

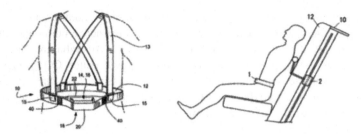

Fig. 3. Abdominal breathing trainer

(4) Beijing's Broad Institute of Technology has developed a biofeedback-based respiratory therapy device that can be used to assist in the treatment of dyspnea. The therapeutic instrument can measure the breathing rate, simulate the sound of human breathing and give real-time feedback. And it can correct people's breathing patterns through real-time feedback results [14].

3 Comprehensive Evaluation of Children's Breathing Training Products

3.1 Comprehensive Evaluation Process of Children's Breathing Training Products

Analytic Hierarchy Process (AHP) is a qualitative and quantitative, systematic and hierarchical multi-objective decision-making analysis method proposed by American operations researcher T.L. Saaty and others [15]. AHP has the characteristics of strong adaptability and high flexibility, and has been widely used in multiple-criteria decision-making (MCDM) problems [16]. There are many related factors that affect the design of breathing training products for children with asthma. This article uses analytic hierarchy process to determine the hierarchical structure of the evaluation index system, and obtains the weight value of each index through expert team scoring and Yaahp data calculation. The overall process is shown in Fig. 4.

3.2 Construction of Usability Evaluation Model of Children's Breath Training Products

In order to understand the current research status of children's asthma breathing training products, I conducted research and analysis on related literature and found that there are almost no studies on the usability of children's asthma breathing training products. Therefore, the survey scope was expanded, and the evaluation indicators for the usability of rehabilitation training products were sorted out and summarized, and field surveys were conducted to deeply understand user needs.

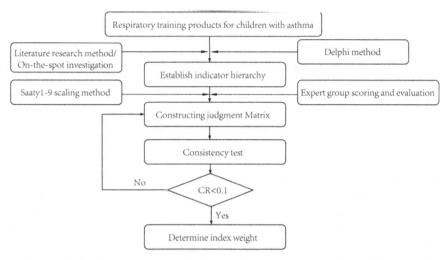

Fig. 4. Evaluation flowchart of breathing training products for children with asthma

There are few studies on the usability evaluation index of rehabilitation training products at home and abroad, and select a few that can be referred to for analysis. In foreign research, Miao Liu [17] and others used the analytic hierarchy process to improve the efficiency of toy intervention in the treatment of language disorders in children with autism. They studied toy-related design elements and determined that the design elements of the standard layer were sensory experience, emotional comfort, safety, Interactivity, preference considerations, ease of use and adaptability. Their research is very specific and pertinent. Duojin Wang [18] and others introduced a newly developed user-centered hand rehabilitation device, and used the analytic hierarchy process to analyze the design elements of the hand rehabilitation device. They take the necessary factors, product perspective and user perspective as the first-level indicators. The angles of division are somewhat different from other studies, and they are more versatile and have certain reference significance. In China, relevant research is relatively abundant, but a sufficiently rich system structure has not yet been formed. Zhu Yiwu [19] used KJ/AHP/QFD method integration as theoretical support to provide design reference for the innovative design of ankle joint rehabilitation robots. In his research, he made safety standards, intelligent products, beautiful appearance, and good operating experience. Practical and durable as a first-level indicator, the research is very specific, but it ignores the interest guidance and continuous attraction of users. Wang Meixue et al. [20] studied the design and evaluation methods of rehabilitation training products for children with autism based on the AHP and TOPSIS methods. In the research, safety, durability, environmental protection, interaction, simple operation, reasonable structure design, entertainment, and intellectuality and enlightenment are the criteria-level elements, and the product elements studied are not enough to fully summarize the design evaluation elements of rehabilitation training products for children with autism. In summary, the focus of the usability indicators proposed by the researchers is not the same. Some focus on the operation and structural rationality of product design, some focus on the interactivity of the product, and some include the invisible needs of users. In general, researchers are generally concerned about the safety and interactivity of rehabilitation training products, but the shortcoming is the lack of generalization. The selection of indicators from the perspective of motivation theory provides a new idea for current research.

Field research found that compared with children with common diseases, the long-term diagnosis and treatment process is more likely to cause depression, lack of self-confidence, and resistance to treatment in children. Therefore, in the construction of the evaluation system for the design of breathing training products for children with asthma, it is necessary to consider the applicability of the product to the psychology of children with asthma, the guidance of the positive psychology of the children during the treatment process, and the feedback of rehabilitation effects to strengthen the self-confidence of rehabilitation and other indicators. After the field investigation, combined with the Delphi method, an expert group consisting of 5 doctors, 15 product designers, 5 design professors, and 5 children's rehabilitation training design professionals was carried out multiple rounds of investigation and discussion. Then we use the analytic hierarchy process to sort, supplement, and classify the collected data, and obtain five criterion-level indicators of applicability, safety, functional, appearance, and emotional factors, and 13 subdivided index-level evaluation indicators. In the end, we constitute a bottom-up ladder hierarchy model [21]. The cost of the product, whether it is easy to process and transport and other factors are also factors that need to be considered in product design. However, since this article mainly studies the factors that affect the user

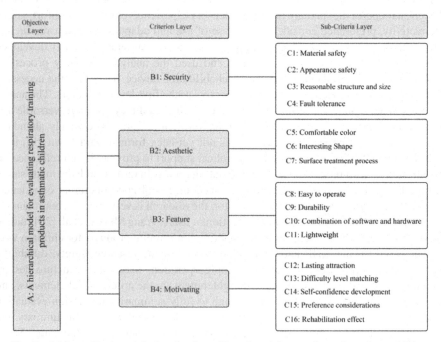

Fig. 5. A hierarchical model of evaluation of breath training products for asthma children

experience and the effect of medical rehabilitation, the product cost and other indicators are not included in the indicator system. The hierarchical structure model in the text is shown in Fig. 5.

3.3 Hierarchical Single Sort

According to the analytic hierarchy model shown in Fig. 5, the judgment matrix of the criterion layer and the sub-criteria layer are constructed. In order to quantify the judgment matrix, use the proportional scaling method from 1 to 9 for assignment [22] (see Table 1). The expert group is composed of 5 doctors, 15 product designers, 5 design professors, and 5 children's rehabilitation training design professionals. Through multiple rounds of discussion and analysis, the expert evaluation results tend to be consistent. Finally, the judgment matrix of the target layer and the criterion layer and the weight of each factor are obtained, as shown in Tables 2, 3, 4, 5 and 6.

Table 1. Pairwise comparison scale for AHP preferences.

Intensity of importance	Definition
1	Equal importance
3	Moderate importance
5	Strong importance
7	Very strong or demonstrated importance
9	Extreme importance
2,4,6,8	The ratio of the influence of the two elements is between the above two adjacent levels
1, 1/2, …,1/9	The ratio of the influence of the two elements is the reciprocal number above

Table 2. Judgment matrix of the target layer

A	B1	B2	B3	B4	Weight
B1	1	4	2	1	0.3593
B2	¼	1	1/3	1/4	0.0815
B3	1/2	3	1	1/2	0.1999
B4	1	4	2	1	0.3593

Table 3. Judgment matrix of security criterion layer

B1	C1	C2	C3	C4	Weight
C1	1	2	1/2	1	0.2281
C2	1/2	1	1/3	2	0.1758
C3	2	3	1	3	0.4492
C4	1	1/2	1/3	1	0.1469

Table 4. Judgment matrix of aesthetic criterion level

B2	C5	C6	C7	Weight
C5	1	1/2	3	0.3196
C6	2	1	4	0.5584
C7	1/3	1/4	1	0.1220

Table 5. Judgment matrix of functional criterion layer

B3	C8	C9	C10	C11	Weight
C8	1	4	2	3	0.4491
C9	1/4	1	1/4	1/3	0.0775
C10	1/2	4	1	3	0.3181
C11	1/3	3	1/3	1	0.1553

Table 6. Judgment matrix of the incentive criterion layer

B4	C11	C12	C13	C14	C15	Weight
C11	1	2	3	4	2	0.3635
C12	1/2	1	2	3	1/2	0.1927
C13	1/3	1/2	1	3	2	0.1838
C14	1/4	1/3	1/3	1	1/3	0.0645
C15	1/2	2	1/2	3	1	0.1954

3.4 Consistency Check

In order to make the data reasonable, it is necessary to check the consistency of the weight calculation results. When CR $\leq$ 0.1, it can be considered that the judgment matrix passes the consistency check, and the weight values of the evaluation elements are obtained to meet the requirements. Check the consistency of the judgment matrices in Tables 3, 4,

5, 6 and 7, and the results are shown in Table 8. It can be seen from Table 7 that the value CR of the judgment matrix of each layer is less than 0.1, so each judgment matrix has passed the consistency test, and its weight value meets the requirements.

Table 7. Result statistics of the consistency test

	A	B1	B2	B3	B4
λmax	4.0206	4.1707	3.0183	4.1440	5.3628
CR	0.0077	0.0639	0.0176	0.0539	0.0810

3.5 Total Ranking of Weights

After the judgment matrix passes the consistency test, all the indicators in the sub-criteria layer are comprehensively ranked, and the ranking of the indicators according to the importance of the indicators provides a reference for the follow-up work.

Table 8. Comprehensive ranking of design element weights

	B1	B2	B3	B4	Comprehensive weight	Sort
C1	0.4182	–	–	–	0.1771	1
C2	0.2702	–	–	–	0.1147	2
C3	0.1205	–	–	–	0.0510	8
C4	0.1906	–	–	–	0.0807	5
C5	–	0.1689	–	–	0.0384	11
C6	–	0.4512	–	–	0.1024	4
C7	–	0.2609	–	–	0.0592	6
C8	–	0.1190	–	–	0.0270	13
C9	–	–	0.3012	–	0.0368	12
C10	–	–	0.1178	–	0.0144	16
C11	–	–	0.1709	–	0.0209	15
C12	–	–	0.4100	–	0.0502	9
C13	–	–	–	0.2404	0.0546	7
C14	–	–	–	0.1851	0.0420	10
C15	–	–	–	0.4582	0.1040	3
C16	–	–	–	0.1163	0.0264	14

Through the analysis and calculation of the various levels of factors that affect the rehabilitation effect of asthmatic children's breathing training products, the weight value of each index is obtained. From the data analysis results of Tables 2, 3, 4, 5, 6, 7 and 8, it can be seen that the highest weight value of each evaluation index at the criterion level is safety sexual factors (0.3593) and motivational factors (0.3593) followed by functional factors (0.1999) and aesthetic factors (0.0815). Due to the particularity of children's groups, safety is the first element in the design of children's products. In the design, it is necessary to avoid hidden safety hazards in the use of children as much as possible, especially for children with asthma. The physical fitness of children is not strong, so the safety of product design should be strengthened. The ultimate goal of the design of breathing training products for children with asthma is to enhance the breathing efficiency of the children and alleviate the disease. The boring training process increased the resistance of the children, so the continued attractiveness of the product during the treatment process and the children's confidence in rehabilitation have a direct impact on the design. Therefore, the design of rehabilitation products should not only consider the user's physical characteristics, psychological characteristics, and children's unique age cognitive characteristics, but also consider the specific medical process of the child's disease to enhance the effect of rehabilitation training.

4 Evaluation Results and Design Strategy

Based on the weighted analysis data, in the indicator layer, the safety and rationality of the structure size, the continuous attractiveness during the treatment process, the ease of operation of the product, the safety of the material, the feedback of the rehabilitation effect and the difficulty level matching of the training process are more important. Based on the above research results, a product design strategy for breathing training products for children with asthma is proposed.

4.1 Strengthen the Safety of Medical Products and Exclude Factors that Reduce Incentives

Taking into account the characteristics of the children's age group and special physical conditions, some safety hazards should be avoided as much as possible during the design process. For example, sharp edges and corners should be avoided in product design; the size of the detachable part is reasonable; and the ergonomic size and firmness of the product structure are reasonable. In addition, children with asthma need to touch the product with their mouth when using breathing training products, so whether the materials are non-toxic and harmless, environmentally friendly materials that are easy to clean, and whether the surface coating meets the standards are also safety factors that must be paid attention to in product design.

4.2 Naturalized Interactive Behavior to Maintain the Motivational Process

The breathing training process is very boring, and children are emotionally unstable due to illness and are prone to negative emotions. Therefore, it is difficult for children to cooperate with medical staff in rehabilitation training. In the survey, it was found that children with asthma tend to lose patience with complicated operation methods, and even feel frustrated and resist emotions. Therefore, the operation and interaction methods of rehabilitation products should be as simple and easy to understand as possible to make the operation more comfortable and convenient. In addition, in the process of using the product for training, children can easily give up halfway due to difficult and painful training, and the training effect cannot be achieved. Therefore, in product design, we should find a suitable way to strengthen the continuous attraction to the children in training and improve the training effect.

4.3 Hierarchical Rehabilitation Model to Guide Rehabilitation Behavior

Rehabilitation treatment is a long-term and continuous improvement process. Failure to make the child's self-confidence weaken or even more frustrated and low self-esteem should be prevented. Rehabilitation training should be based on the child's special physical condition, and reasonable and step-by-step rehabilitation treatment should be carried out. The motivation process is a process from initiation to maintenance to reinforcement. Therefore, the design of rehabilitation products needs to formulate clear rehabilitation goals according to the rehabilitation treatment plan and rehabilitation needs of different children, and follow the principle of from large to bottom, from near to far to set the content of the training, let them become the behavior orientation of the child. In addition, children have the right to know their own rehabilitation training results, and the visualized rehabilitation effect can have a certain strengthening effect on motivation.

5 Summary

A very important principle in scientific rehabilitation training is the principle of repetition. However, judging from the current status of rehabilitation training, the inability to carry out persistent training is one of the biggest problems that people encounter. If the continuous training problem in breathing training can be solved, the training effect will be greatly improved. This research introduces the concept of motivational theory into breathing training, and uses the advantages of motivational elements to make the originally boring content lively and interesting. And with the help of analytic hierarchy process, a hierarchical structure model of evaluation indicators is constructed from five aspects of safety, aesthetics, functionality, and incentives, and the weight of each level of evaluation indicators is calculated. Finally, the design strategy of breathing training products for children with asthma is summarized. The Analytic Hierarchy Process has further improved the rationality of the design evaluation of asthmatic children's breathing training products and helped hospitals and product designers to develop products with higher user satisfaction in the design of children's rehabilitation training products.

References

1. Haiyan, D., Xueqin, Z.: The effect of intervention in different lying positions in children with non-invasive mechanical ventilation. J. Nurs. Sci. **30**(19), 32–34 (2015)

2. Gao, W.: Analysis of the effectiveness of breathing training combined with exercise therapy in patients with asthma in remission. China Pract. Med. **15**(24), 154–156 (2020)
3. Deterding, S., Dixon, D., Khaled, R., et al.: From game design elements to gamefulness: defining "gamification". In: Proceedings of the 15th International Academic MindTrek Conference: Envisioning Future Media Environments, pp. 9–15 (2011)
4. Tang, S., Li, Y.: Design of children's respiratory rehabilitation training device. Sci. Technol. Innov. Appl. **2020**(36), 28–29+32 (2020)
5. Liu, J.: Research on the design of mobile fitness applications from the perspective of motivation theory. Zhejiang University of Technology (2017)
6. Shi, J.: Research on application design of online learning based on motivation theory. Shandong University (2021)
7. Yu, T.: Digital educational game design based on motivation theory. Shandong Normal University (2013)
8. Tuzun, H.: Motivating learners in educational computer games. Indiana University, Indiana (2004)
9. Li, D.: Research on interaction design of elderly stroke rehabilitation products based on incentive mechanism. East China University of Science and Technology (2015)
10. Peng, X.: Exploration of scientific physical exercise. Sci. Consult. (Technol. Manage.) **2013**(31), 90–91 (2013)
11. Li, W.: Prototype design and development of interactive system to enhance breathing training with gamification. Shanghai Jiaotong University (2016)
12. Hongmei, Z., Chen, W.: Research progress of early respiratory rehabilitation in acute/critical illness. West China Med. J. **34**(01), 1–6 (2019)
13. Shali, L., Xueqin, Y., Lijun, Z., et al.: Development and application of feedback abdominal breathing training apparatus. Med. Med. Equipment **08**, 6–7 (2006)
14. Liu Zhiqiang, W., Kai, L.C.: Breath training methods for chronic obstructive pulmonary disease. Chin. J. Clin. Rehab. **6**(003), 312–313 (2002)
15. Saaty, T.L.: The Analytic Hierarchy Process: Planning, Priority Setting, Resource Allocation. McGraw-Hill International Book Co., New York, London (1980)
16. Yuan, J., Zhang, L., Tan, Y., et al.: Evaluating the regional social sustainability contribution of public-private partnerships in China: the development of an indicator system. Sustain. Dev. **28**(1) (2019)
17. Liu, M., Wang, Y.: Analysis of design elements for the treatment of language disorders in autistic children. In: Antona, M., Stephanidis, C. (eds.) HCII 2021. LNCS, vol. 12769, pp. 118–137. Springer, Cham (2021). https://doi.org/10.1007/978-3-030-78095-1_11
18. Wang, D., Yu, H., Wu, J., et al.: Integrating fuzzy based QFD and AHP for the design and implementation of a hand training device. J. Intell. Fuzzy Syst. **36**(4), 3317–3331 (2019)
19. Zhu, Y.: Design of ankle joint rehabilitation robot based on KJ/AHP/QFD. Yanshan University
20. Meixue, W., Honglei, Z.: Design and evaluation method and application of rehabilitation training products for children with autism based on AHP and TOPSIS. J. Graph. **41**(3), 8 (2020)
21. Yiwen, T., Bingfa, C.: Research on evaluation method of immersive interface interaction design. Mach. Manuf. Autom. **46**(5), 5 (2017)
22. Guangdong, T., Honghao, Z., Danqi, W.: Evaluation of disassembly plan based on fuzzy AHP-grey relational TOPSIS. Chin. J. Mech. Eng. **53**(5), 7 (2017)

Eating Experiences with Interactive Tableware for Improving Eating Behavior in Children

Peiling He[1]([⊠]) and Chenwei Chiang[2]

[1] National Taipei University of Technology, Taipei, Taiwan
t108588034@ntut.org.tw
[2] National Taipei University of Business, Taipei, Taiwan
chenwei@ntub.edu.tw

Abstract. Good eating behaviors can contribute to the health of growing children. However, due to the diversity of diets, children often fail to meet nutritional recommendations. We present a mobile game application connected to an interactive tableware, including a bowl with a weight sensor and a mobile application. Our system detects if children have eaten and helps children to focus on their meals. We also designed a smart device app with gamification elements to interact with children during meals. We tested the system with preschool children aged 5 to 6 years with picky eating behaviors. Through the study, the system had a positive effect on improving children's eating behaviors.

Keywords: Dietary interventions · Interactive tableware · Children · Mobile game application

1 Introduction

Around the world, picky eating is a common behavior in early childhood [1, 2]. Children with picky eating behavior will reach their peak at the aged 2–6. This stage is a period when food preferences and acceptance are established, and the intake of fruits and vegetables is relatively less [3, 4]. Most children are picky eaters, mainly because they don't like to eat, refuse to eat unfamiliar foods, or are partial eaters. Children with picky eating behaviors usually have inadequate nutritional intake [5]. Fruit and vegetable intake can also be reduced, which can lead to poor growth, eating disorders and other problems [6–8].

About two-thirds of children's meals are eaten at home during the adolescent years [9]. The home eating environment is an important factor in shaping children's eating behaviors. Good eating behaviors are important for children's development, and parenting and eating behaviors also influence children's eating behaviors. However, parents often encounter many difficulties when feeding their children [10, 11]. The most common eating problems are slow eating, holding food in the mouth, or refusing to eat certain foods, especially fruits and vegetables [1]. These problems can be very stressful for caregivers and have a negative impact on family relationships [12].

© The Author(s), under exclusive license to Springer Nature Switzerland AG 2022
M. Kurosu (Ed.): HCII 2022, LNCS 13302, pp. 571–581, 2022.
https://doi.org/10.1007/978-3-031-05311-5_40

Many parents struggle to teach their children healthy eating behaviors to improve eating problems such as picky eating and neophobia [13]. In feeding their children, parents may use wrong strategies to guide their children's eating habits, such as verbal praise, tangible rewards, harsh parenting attitudes, and punishment systems. Forcing children to eat foods that they do not like or inducing them to eat good foods [14]. Children's eating habits are easily formed at this stage and gradually fixed until they grow up [15]. This can lead to children feeling stressed and easily distracted during meals, which can lead to unpleasant eating. It may also lead to unhealthy eating behaviors in children, such as wanting to eat desserts, snacks, and other non-nutritious foods to relieve their emotions [16]. Therefore, it is important to develop good and healthy eating habits in children.

In recent years, many studies have proposed innovative interventions, and dietary interventions are strategies that can improve eating behaviors. Dietary interventions can change children's eating behaviors, increase fruit and vegetable intake, and include health education, peer pressure, and play [17–20].

In studies related to children's eating interventions, the use of tangible interactive games can effectively influence children's learning development [21, 22]. Children's attention and eating efficiency can be maintained by using games to teach them eating behaviors [23, 24]. Allowing children to eat on their own and giving them the freedom to choose and explore food is important for the development of eating behaviors [25, 26]. Play can enhance key competencies and can facilitate children's learning growth. Research has found that play on mobile devices can improve children's eating behaviors and lead to healthy eating [27]. Based on previous studies, we chose to use a combination of mobile game application and interactive tableware to improve eating behaviors in preschool children.

In this paper, we designed an interactive tableware system to help children improve eating behavior. Our connected tableware system is designed to motivate children to eat. Children can become more interested in eating by playing games. In addition, it helps children to concentrate more on eating on their eating.

2   Related Work

In the HCI field, there have been many research projects that incorporate smart sensors into children's eating behaviors to encourage healthy eating in children. To achieve our research goals, we selected two research methods, persuasive technology and gamification, as the focus of the design.

Persuasive technology aims at changing human attitudes and behavior [28]. Some studies have applied a persuasive technology to change children's eating behavior. Kadomura et al. developed a storybook and persuasive game on a smartphone. This utilized the ability of a sensory fork to interact with children and changed their eating behavior at mealtime. Their sensory fork encouraged children to eat positively through the use of stories [29, 30]. Joi et al. used a mobile application and connected tableware system to promote children to eat vegetables. Their system could motivate children to eat vegetables. Children could learn about the benefits of vegetables by enjoying the game [31].

Gamification focuses on creating gamified experiences in order to increase overall engagement through the use of game-design elements in a non-game context [32]. There are studies that use gamification elements to improve children's eating behaviors. Gamification has been applied to a variety of situations as a design strategy to promote eating behaviors. Zhao et al. used a smart dinner plate that could help children develop healthy eating behaviors through interactive game animations during mealtime. Their system projected games to interact with children as they eat, using digital games projected onto the plate to encourage active eating [33]. Ganesh et al.'s research was to improve children's eating behaviors through changing the appearance of the food. Their system is projected on the child's plate in the form of color changes and rewards [34]. These previous studies concentrated on using tangible feedback and gamification to foster healthy eating behaviors.

Inspired by prior studies, the use of games combined with interactive approaches to change children's eating behaviors while encouraging children to eat independently and healthily. In this paper, we designed a mobile game application combined with interactive tableware to improve children's eating behaviors. The goal is to help children to focus on eating and achieve daily dietary intake in per meal.

3 Concept Design

The proposed system in this paper aims at changing the children's behavior to reach daily dietary intake. Our system can detect whether the child has eaten the meal, helping children concentrate on eating.

Our proposed system is an interactive tableware including a weight sensor bowl and a mobile game application. Due to Asian living and eating patterns, bowls are often used for eating. Therefore, the present study also used bowls with our system. The bottom of the bowl consists of an Arduino microcontroller, a weight sensor, a Bluetooth module and battery (Fig. 1). This can detect the change of food weight during the meal and immediately convert the data to the mobile game application. Serial communication between Arduino and the mobile game application is established via Bluetooth so that data can be transferred between hardware and software. The application receives the change of food weight values from Arduino and generates a picture based on the designed

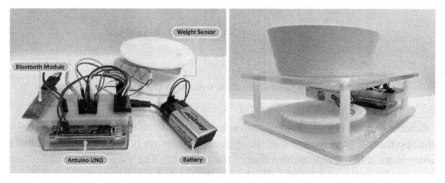

Fig. 1. Design of hardware prototype (Left). Final assembled prototype (Right).

conditions. Arduino's program is modified according to the third equation library (https://github.com/bogde/HX711).

To encourage active eating, children need to keep eating to feed the game characters to complete the game tasks. That can help children to focus on their eating during the meal time.

4   System Overview

We developed a mobile game application that can be connected to interactive tableware and interact with the child during the meal (Fig. 2). Our application is able to perform testing smoothly using an Android phone. In the application, the child needs to help an animal go home, whose way home depends on the children's intake rate and completion level. The lower the level of pickiness, the faster the animal comes home. The character's healthy value is displayed at the top of the character and will be deducted every minute.

When the weight of the food decreases during the meal, the bowl's weight sensor detects the decrease. At the same time, the reduced data will be transferred to the application and a fruit will appear to increase the health value of the character. The child is required to complete the meal goal to help the animal get home, which can encourage the child to continue eating.

Fig. 2. Design mobile game application with connected interactive tableware.

Before the meal begins, the child can select the gender of the character as their avatar in the application. During the meal, the application displays both the current value of the journey home and the top health value of the character. The value of the journey home represents the intake of the child. The higher the level of meal completion, the closer to home. The health value represents the concentration of children. The more concentrated the eating, the higher the health value. Changes in the value of the journey home and the health value can be used to find out whether the child is a picky eater. After finishing the meal, the animal's home and three stars will appear on the application. That represents a child who demonstrates good eating behavior and is not a picky eater (Figs. 3 and 4).

Fig. 3. Design of mobile game application (No. 1 to 4 is the game process).

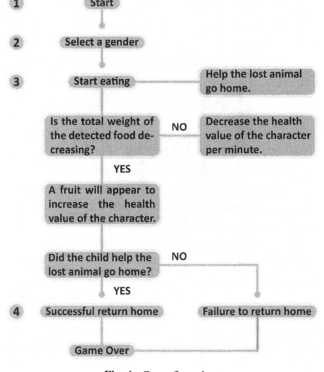

Fig. 4. Game flow chart.

The entire game design has two key points of design. First, Children need to help the animal go home by eating, which can stimulate their desire to finish eating. Secondly, the animal can get a fruit according to the children's eating behavior, which can make children focus on their eating. We set the goal of the game to encourage children to eat and make them more interested in eating.

5   User Study

The purpose of this study is to investigate whether our system was effective in encouraging children to eat their meals. We conducted a user study with four children between the ages of five and six to test our system. We presented the study to the children and their parents and obtained their consent. Each child was tested in two pilot tests. The first pilot test was to simply record the child's eating process and weigh the meal. The second pilot test was to have the child interact with the system during eating and the meal was weighed. The weight of the meal was the same in both tests. According to the "Early Childhood Nutrition Handbook" published by the Taiwan Health Promotion Agency, the recommended daily dietary intake for preschoolers is prepared as our meal portions (Fig. 5). We prepared a meal each time that included one kind of meat (35 g), two kinds of vegetables (50 g per serving) and rice (50 g). Each pilot test took about one hour per child. We recorded the whole procedure with the permission of the participants with a fixed camera.

Fig. 5. Each meal includes one type of meat (35 g), two types of vegetables (50 g per serving) and one type of rice (50 g).

In the second pilot test, the children were told they could interact with the application, which required them to help the animal get home by eating. After the second pilot test, we conducted a semi-structured interview with the children and parents and asked them to describe how they felt during the test.

6 Results

All children in the trial were able to actively eat using our connected tableware system. Our findings indicated that children can interact with the application to improve their eating habits.

Table 1. Information of participants.

Child			Length of eating time		Leftover	
Participant	Gender	Age	1st test	2nd test	1st test	2nd test
A	M	5	21 min	8 min	Finished	Finished
B	M	6	37 min	19 min	Unfinished	Finished
C	F	6	29 min	7 min	Finished	Finished
D	M	5	8 min	6 min	Finished	Finished

In the first pilot test without dietary intervention (Table 1), A (male, 5 years old), B (male, 6 years old), C (female, 6 years old) and D (male, 5 years old) showed normal length of mealtime. All the children had finished their meals, but only B did not finish his. In the Second pilot test with dietary intervention, all children had significantly shorter meal times and had finished their meals (Fig. 6).

Fig. 6. The second pilot test for participant B (male, 6 years old, left) and participant C (female, 6 years old, right).

These findings showed that the mobile gaming application and connected tableware system appealed to children. The children told us that they were willing to help the animal go home and accomplish the goal of the game.

We present the results and findings through the data collected in the user study. The data collected consisted of video recordings of meal times and semi-structured interviews with participant mothers who responded to their experiences in conducting the user study.

In the questionnaire (Table 2), the average score for question 2 was 4.5, and the average score for questions 3 and 6 was 4. These results suggested that the system has a positive impact on improving children's eating behavior. The average score for question 4 was 4.3 because parents felt that they were able to maintain communication with their children even when they were playing. The average score for question 1 was 3 and the average score for question 5 was 3.8 because parents felt that our system was not necessarily effective in improving their child's eating habits in the long term.

We conducted semi-structured interviews, and most of the feedback was positive. One parent (B's caregiver) reported that he used to be very distracted at mealtime and she had to constantly remind him to eat. Each parent reported that the child ate faster and more attentively than usual. Although the system had a positive effect on the children, their mothers (A's mother and D's mother) were concerned that eating with the mobile game application would create poor eating habits.

Table 2. Test the results in the questionnaire (five-point Likert scale). The higher the score, the better.

Question		A	B	C	D	Avg.
1	What are your impressions of connected interactive tableware with mobile game application? (1: negative - 5: positive)	3	3	3	3	3
2	Do you think the game will interfere with children's eating behavior? (1: much - 5: not at all)	5	5	5	3	4.5
3	Do you think it is easy for children to understand the rules of the game? (1: difficult - 5: easy)	5	3	3	5	4
4	Do you think the connected interactive tableware with mobile game application will affect family communication? (1: much - 5: not at all)	5	4	3	5	4.3
5	Do you think children's eating habits have improved as a result of using connected interactive tableware with mobile game application? (1: not at all - 5: much)	5	5	2	3	3.8
6	Do you think children's attention span at meals is improved after using connected interactive tableware with mobile gaming application? (1: not at all - 5: much)	5	5	3	3	4

7 Discussion

Our system has the potential to make a positive impact. Our goal is to help children focus on their diet and reach their daily intake at each meal. By encouraging children to eat, we make eating more fun for them. We help them reduce picky eating behaviors and meet healthy eating standards.

The findings suggested that in order to achieve the game tasks, children can change their eating behaviors and respond to dietary goals. While the use of mobile gaming apps may influence children's eating behaviors, it may also have adverse effects. Parents are concerned that this may only be an effective short-term solution. However, our system has an impact on children's eating behaviors. It can improve children's ability to focus on eating and actually complete their meals.

We would like to focus on improving the eating of children when using our system. Using our system can bring a better eating experience to children. Incorporating an interactive format during the meal process allows them to complete the meal step-by-step. Make them feel that eating is fun.

8 Conclusion and Future Work

In this paper, we present a connected tableware system with a mobile game application to promote children's eating. We had designed the game contents particularly for children aged five to six years old to attract their interest in eating. Our aim is to encourage children to focus on eating and achieve children's daily dietary intake. It can help children concentrate on eating through mealtime interaction. The interactive system incorporates gamification elements into the content of mobile application to help children complete their meals in a pleasant way.

Our study had several limitations. First, the number of child participants in our study was limited. Second, a long-term study will be required to determine whether the system can motivate children to improve their eating behaviors. Third, there is a need for richer ways to play to keep children's interest. Fourth, we can try to use different kinds of tableware for interaction. Fifth, use different environments to influence children's eating behaviors. Sixth, increase natural interactions between parents and children.

As future work, we plan to recruit more participants for a long-term user study and conduct controlled trials. In the meantime, various application contents need to be developed to enrich the gameplay, and also different kinds of tableware can be designed for diet interaction and increase the communication between parents and children. We would like to better assist children in improving their dietary habits.

References

1. Wright, C.M., Parkinson, K.N., Shipton, D., Drewett, R.F.: How do toddler eating problems relate to their eating behavior, food preferences, and growth? Pediatrics **120**(4), e1069–e1075 (2007). https://doi.org/10.1542/peds.2006-2961
2. Xue, Y., et al.: Growth and development in Chinese pre-schoolers with picky eating behaviour: a cross-sectional study. PLoS ONE **10**(4), e0123664 (2015). https://doi.org/10.1371/journal.pone.0123664

3. Addessi, E., Galloway, A.T., Visalberghi, E., Birch, L.L.: Specific social influences on the acceptance of novel foods in 2–5-year-old children. Appetite **45**(3), 264–271 (2005). https://doi.org/10.1016/j.appet.2005.07.007

4. Cooke, L., Wardle, J., Gibson, E.L.: Relationship between parental report of food neophobia and everyday food consumption in 2–6-year-old children. Appetite **41**(2), 205–206 (2003). https://doi.org/10.1016/S0195-6663(03)00048-5

5. Van Der Horst, K., Deming, D.M., Lesniauskas, R., Carr, B.T., Reidy, K.C.: Picky eating: associations with child eating characteristics and food intake. Appetite **103**, 286–293 (2016). https://doi.org/10.1016/j.appet.2016.04.027

6. Jacobi, C., Agras, W.S., Bryson, S., Hammer, L.D.: Behavioral validation, precursors, and concomitants of picky eating in childhood. J. Am. Acad. Child Adolesc. Psychiatry **42**(1), 76–84 (2003). https://doi.org/10.1097/00004583-200301000-00013

7. Dubois, L., Farmer, A., Girard, M., Peterson, K., Tatone-Tokuda, F.: Problem eating behaviors related to social factors and body weight in preschool children: a longitudinal study. Int. J. Behav. Nutr. Phys. Act. **4**(1), 1–10 (2007). https://doi.org/10.1186/1479-5868-4-9

8. Marchi, M., Cohen, P.: Early childhood eating behaviors and adolescent eating disorders. J. Am. Acad. Child Adolesc. Psychiatry **29**(1), 112–117 (1990). https://doi.org/10.1097/00004583-199001000-00017

9. Adair, L.S., Popkin, B.M.: Are child eating patterns being transformed globally? Obes. Res. **13**(7), 1281–1299 (2005). https://doi.org/10.1038/oby.2005.153

10. Goh, D.Y., Jacob, A.: Perception of picky eating among children in Singapore and its impact on caregivers: a questionnaire survey. Asia Pac. Fam. Med. **11**(1), 1–8 (2012). https://doi.org/10.1186/1447-056X-11-5

11. Lee, W.S., et al.: Parental concern of feeding difficulty predicts poor growth status in their child. Pediatr. Neonatol. **60**(6), 676–683 (2019). https://doi.org/10.1016/j.pedneo.2019.04.004

12. Bryant-Waugh, R., Markham, L., Kreipe, R.E., Walsh, B.T.: Feeding and eating disorders in childhood. Int. J. Eat. Disord. **43**(2), 98–111 (2010). https://doi.org/10.1002/eat.20795

13. Mascola, A.J., Bryson, S.W., Agras, W.S.: Picky eating during childhood: a longitudinal study to age 11 years. Eat. Behav. **11**(4), 253–257 (2010). https://doi.org/10.1016/j.eatbeh.2010.05.006

14. Orrell-Valente, J.K., Hill, L.G., Brechwald, W.A., Dodge, K.A., Pettit, G.S., Bates, J.E.: "Just three more bites": an observational analysis of parents' socialization of children's eating at mealtime. Appetite **48**(1), 37–45 (2007). https://doi.org/10.1016/j.appet.2006.06.006

15. Ashcroft, J., Semmler, C., Carnell, S., Van Jaarsveld, C.H.M., Wardle, J.: Continuity and stability of eating behaviour traits in children. Eur. J. Clin. Nutr. **62**(8), 985–990 (2008). https://doi.org/10.1038/sj.ejcn.1602855

16. Michels, N., et al.: Stress, emotional eating behaviour and dietary patterns in children. Appetite **59**(3), 762–769 (2012). https://doi.org/10.1016/j.appet.2012.08.010

17. Thomas, J., et al.: Children and healthy eating: a systematic review of barriers and facilitators. Database of Abstracts of Reviews of Effects (DARE): Quality-assessed Reviews [Internet] (2003). https://www.ncbi.nlm.nih.gov/books/NBK70020/

18. Holley, C.E., Farrow, C., Haycraft, E.: A Systematic review of methods for increasing vegetable consumption in early childhood. Curr. Nutrition Rep. **6**(2), 157–170 (2017). https://doi.org/10.1007/s13668-017-0202-1

19. Johnson, S.L., Ryan, S.M., Kroehl, M., Moding, K.J., Boles, R.E., Bellows, L.L.: A longitudinal intervention to improve young children's liking and consumption of new foods: findings from the Colorado LEAP study. Int. J. Behav. Nutr. Phys. Act. **16**(1), 1–15 (2019). https://doi.org/10.1186/s12966-019-0808-3

20. DeCosta, P., Møller, P., Frøst, M.B., Olsen, A.: Changing children's eating behaviour-a review of experimental research. Appetite **113**, 327–357 (2017). https://doi.org/10.1016/j. appet.2017.03.004
21. Xie, L., Antle, A. N., Motamedi, N.: Are tangibles more fun? Comparing children's enjoyment and engagement using physical, graphical and tangible user interfaces. In: Proceedings of the 2nd International Conference on Tangible and Embedded Interaction, pp. 191–198. ACM (2008). https://doi.org/10.1145/1347390.1347433
22. Cerezo, E., Marco, J., Baldassarri, S.: Hybrid games: designing tangible interfaces for very young children and children with special needs. In: Nijholt, A. (ed.) More Playful User Interfaces. GMSE, pp. 17–48. Springer, Singapore (2015). https://doi.org/10.1007/978-981-287-546-4_2
23. Florack, A., Haasova, S., Hirschauer, S., Serfas, B.G.: Playing with food: the effects of food pre-exposure on consumption in young children. Physiol. Behav. **195**, 76–81 (2018). https:// doi.org/10.1016/j.physbeh.2018.07.022
24. Putnam, M.M., Richmond, E.M., Brunick, K.L., Wright, C.A., Calvert, S.L.: Influence of a character-based app on children's learning of nutritional information: should apps be served with a side of media characters? Games Health J. **7**(2), 121–126 (2018). https://doi.org/10. 1089/g4h.2017.0116
25. Satter, E.: The feeding relationship: problems and interventions. J. Pediatr. **117**(2), S181–S189 (1990). https://doi.org/10.1016/S0022-3476(05)80017-4
26. Satter, E.: Feeding dynamics: helping children to eat well. J. Pediatr. Health Care **9**(4), 178–184 (1995). https://doi.org/10.1016/S0891-5245(05)80033-1
27. Chow, C.Y., Riantiningtyas, R.R., Kanstrup, M.B., Papavasileiou, M., Liem, G.D., Olsen, A.: Can games change children's eating behaviour? A review of gamification and serious games. Food Qual. Prefer. **80**, 103823 (2020). https://doi.org/10.1016/j.foodqual.2019.103823
28. IJsselsteijn, W., de Kort, Y., Midden, C., Eggen, B., van den Hoven, E.: Persuasive technology for human well-being: setting the scene. In: IJsselsteijn, W.A., de Kort, Y.A.W., Midden, C., Eggen, B., van den Hoven, E. (eds.) PERSUASIVE 2006. LNCS, vol. 3962, pp. 1–5. Springer, Heidelberg (2006). https://doi.org/10.1007/11755494_1
29. Kadomura, A., Tsukada, K., Siio, I.: EducaTableware: computer-augmented tableware to enhance the eating experiences. In: CHI 2013 Extended Abstracts on Human Factors in Computing Systems, pp. 3071–3074. ACM (2013). https://doi.org/10.1145/2468356.2479613
30. Kadomura, A., Li, C.Y., Tsukada, K., Chu, H.H., Siio, I.: Persuasive technology to improve eating behavior using a sensor-embedded fork. In: Proceedings of the 2014 ACM International Joint Conference on Pervasive and Ubiquitous Computing, pp. 319–329. ACM (2014). https:// doi.org/10.1145/2632048.2632093
31. Joi, Y.R., et al.: Interactive and connected tableware for promoting children's vegetable-eating and family interaction. In: Proceedings of the the 15th International Conference on Interaction Design and Children, pp. 414–420. ACM (2016). https://doi.org/10.1145/2930674.2930711
32. Deterding, S., Dixon, D., Khaled, R., Nacke, L.: From game design elements to gamefulness: defining "gamification". In: Proceedings of the 15th International Academic MindTrek Conference: Envisioning Future Media Environments, pp. 9–15. ACM (2011). https://doi.org/10. 1145/2181037.2181040
33. Zhao, Y., et al.: FunEat: an interactive tableware for improving eating habits in children. In: Extended Abstracts of the 2021 CHI Conference on Human Factors in Computing Systems, pp. 1–5. ACM (2021). https://doi.org/10.1145/3411763.3451682
34. Ganesh, S., Marshall, P., Rogers, Y., O'Hara, K.: FoodWorks: tackling fussy eating by digitally augmenting children's meals. In: Proceedings of the 8th Nordic Conference on Human-Computer Interaction: Fun, Fast, Foundational, pp. 147–156. ACM (2014). https://doi.org/ 10.1145/2639189.2639225

Sundial: Assist Children Learning Time with a Shining Ball Shaped Device

Yi Chun Hsieh[1] and Chenwei Chiang[2]([✉])

[1] National Taipei University of Technology, 10608 Taipei, Taiwan
[2] National Taipei University of Business, 10608 Taipei, Taiwan
chenwei@ntub.edu.tw

Abstract. Time is a complex concept having been developed and built gradually over years. An 18-month-old toddler has started developing rough cognition of time, yet most of children still cannot understand the concept completely until getting entering elementary school. In the long process of learning time, the range of communication in daily life becomes challenging and restricted, and even cause the situation that people misunderstand and fight with each other, which could have been avoided at first place.

The study is focusing on "Sundial", which is a shining ball-shaped learning device, and enables assists children to acquire the idea of duration of time and to know how to read the time corresponding to it. Children can learn the concept of time in the place where they are familiar with by utilizing with the device with tangible user interface.

The research is aims to discuss the following issues. Firstly, whether "Sundial" help children learn the concept of time effectively? Secondly, whether the device distract children's attention from learning or decrease the rate of physical activity? Lastly, how do children feel about the device when learning and what are their expectation? By quantifying and doing qualitative data analysis with the observation data, which would be compare with learning performance and the later interview materials, during the experiment. The effect of the device on arousing children's interest on learning can be evaluated. The expected result from the study would be based on the current prototype of "Sundial". I would improve and fix the test result, a leading to the experimental results and in turn redesign device that can be utilized in our daily lives and assist parents to teach their children the concept of time effectively.

Keywords: Tangible user interface · Education · Interface with children

1 Introduction

In the ever-changing era when people interact with each other more often, "time" has become essential in our daily lives, and it is necessary to utilize the concept of time, and period to communicate and to describe the situation. For example, solve a math question in 10 min, arrange the curfew time, or remind an important forthcoming meeting, etc. "Time" not only represent the present moment, but also stand for the board line between

M. Kurosu (Ed.): HCII 2022, LNCS 13302, pp. 582–593, 2022.
https://doi.org/10.1007/978-3-031-05311-5_41

the events. The capability of time management improves work efficiency; therefore, It is a crucial issue to cultivate and to teach children the concept of time at a young age.

For children, it is difficult to comprehend the concept of time because it takes several years to fully understand the idea. Moreover, it does not rely on one single cognitive ability but several skills, such as counting, read and write, memorizing, and spatial ability [7]. For preschool children, most of the above-mentioned skills are immature. They cannot perceive the lengths of time or grasp the ability of mathematics. Moreover, they have difficulty comprehending the positioning of the hands on the clock and fail to connect these skills. Time skills would not be fully acquired until the age of 10 [4], and even for children in grades 2–5, passed time is a thorny issue in communication [5]. Children will increasingly anticipant fixen-time activities, such as studying, having meals, or playing, in their growth, and it has already become a tricky problem for parents to set the timeline with their children. For example, if the parents communicate with children for the usage time of electronic products by warning or countdown, it may be prone to lead to dramatic conflict [2], witch reveals that it is challenging for child to deal with the time issue.

To improve the above-mentioned situation, lots of researchers have launched interesting and tangible interaction devices, assist children to learn the concept of time through their daily in activities family or kindergarten. These research define the ability of time reading and cognition as independent skills, which influences the design to focus on the concept of duration of time rather than that of time reading [3, 6, 9].

"Sundial" invented in the study is designed for learning the concept of duration of time and time reading on the clock by LED light. Through operating with Sundial, parents carers and children can enhance the degree of communication related to the concept of time, while they can understand the connection between time and the corresponding events via learning how to read time in our daily lives.

2 Related Work

2.1 Development of the Concept of Time

According to Jean Piaget, a Swiss psychologist, the concept of time is not a sort of transcendental idealism. The development of "time" at young age constantly reconstructs with children's ever-changing and forms gradually, and it takes years of learning to grasp the notion [13]. Several research aims at the process of how children acquire the concept of time [12, 17]. Most children develop the idea of chronological order at 2–3 years old, and express themselves verbally by using adverbs of time in present, past, or future tense. At 4–5 years old, children could ponder over the time with independent thinking and recognize the connection of timing and the progress of time. Kids aged 6 are able to develop the cognition of clock and calendar system, repetitive period (including day, week, and month) and a particular time, such as birthday. The vast majority of children don't begin learning time measurement units such as seconds, minutes, and hours until they are 8–9 years old. At that time, they can use the habitual time to measure the intervals of time, and they can completely understand the units of any period of time around 11 years old [18].

2.2 Children's Time Teaching

Based on the past research, it takes a long way for children to acquire the system of clock and calendar. They need to entirely understand the system so that they make the decision more flexibly according to the situation.

The regular time to teach the concepts of time would be arranged after entering primary school. Before that, some parents would conduct time enlightenment teaching before their children reach school age. For children, it is difficult to understand about "time". Therefore, when teaching the concept of time, whether it is formal education or enlightenment teaching, teachers and parents prefer to utilize the tangible devices such as the clock teaching aids with pointers, which allows children to simulate the flow of time by operating the hour and minute hand.

In the study, it was found that giving children blank paper clocks as an aid for the time test was not helpful for most children, which shows that children who have not yet grasped the concepts of time would find it more difficult to use paper clocks to learn or think [5]. However, Ali and the others further found that, learning with, the clock teaching aids with pointers is more preferred for children, and is more favorable for demonstrating the continuity of time and the numeral system among minutes, seconds, and hours [8]. However, it needs parents company and instruction to facilitate the learning process, or children's interest in studying will decrease due to deficiency in interactivity. In terms of the situation, Plass and others point out the choices on colors, materials, shapes, interactivity levels of the teaching aids would affect the performance on learning [14]. Therefore, how to enhance the interesting element among the teaching aids and orientate children towards learning actively with the help of teaching aids are essential issues for teachers and parents to teach the concepts of time.

2.3 Tangible User Interface

Compared with current teaching aids, tangible devices with user interface emphasize the digital operation in the physical environment. It is accessible to be moved, fetched, and rotated by users instinctively and responds with sound, light, and vibration, which solves the insufficiency in current teaching aids.

Karimi and others created a task-based time learning devices [3] called "Time-Me" for pre-school children at 4–7 years old. It is composed by three cubes in different length, representing 2, 5, and 10 min. The users would be asked to accomplish various tasks labelled by diverse stickers, and the devices would manifest the tasks and duration accordingly, by which children can learn how to build the connection between the activities and the duration of time. "Timelight" designed by Müller and others is also inspired by the similar concepts [9]. Through attracting children's attention moderately with the amount of lighting cubes and colors, children's recognition on duration of time would be formed. When nearly running out of time, the lighting from cubes becomes stronger to remind children. Bakker and others consider that the devices with tangible user interface is suitable for the lessons in the elementary school so that they create "Cawclock", a clock with pointers, which reacts with various colors of light and animal sounds to represent different phases in class. The features help the teachers communicate with children easier and manage the class [15]. Hayashi and others said that the devices for children are accessible and user-friendly. Moreover, "TimeBlocks" is the device made of cubes in the same size in denomination 5 min and shows different duration of time stacking and diverse colors [6]. Although these studies had the positive result about children's recognition toward time, the issue whether children can read the clock still leave something to be desired. For example, whether children are capable of utilizing the devices with user interface to learn how to read the time while connect certain events with duration.

The study is inspired by the concepts used in "Cawclock" and "TimeBlocks". The proper way to connect the concepts of time and events in our daily lives is to encourage children to consider time in different situations every day and to attempt to teach them the concepts of time in specific method witch would provoke children to think independently and learn from what they have experienced. Thus, the teaching aids should be designed as the format of the clock with pointers and can be operated by children, which make it more effectively to learn. On the basis of the above-mentioned, the study create "Sundial", a shining ball-shaped device that helps children understand time. By experiencing all categories of events in virtual lives, children can gradually acquire the concepts of time reading and understanding with the assistance of the devices.

3 Sundial—The Interactive Device Assists Children Understand Time

3.1 Overview

"Sundial" is an interactive device that assists children to explore and learn about time. It evolves from current clocks carrying the pointers and displays the duration of time that corresponds with the pointers so as to help children understand the concepts of time and read the time on clock face. Gelderblom and others found that it is important to help children connect formal representations and dynamic visual representations [10]. The device is designed for children to learn in general environment and to inspire them to consider about time in their everyday lives. Sundial adopts the visual and tangible approach to help children connect time reading and understanding its duration by utilizing its ability to recognize events and visual, and creating relationships between everyday activities and short time periods.

The research aims to discuss the following issues: Firstly, could children operate "Sundial" on their own? Secondly, does the device distract children's attention from learning or decreasing their physical activities? Lastly, summarize children's experiences and expectation toward the device.

3.2 Design Process and Rationale

Prior to the development of the designs about Sundial, we have conducted in-field research by interviewing experts within the secondary target audience to know how children learn. We interviewed a primary school teacher, a parent class teacher, and two parents of kindergarten students who all work with young children.

An important insight was that children would tend to learn certain activities that they are already familiar with. According to these findings, we determined that Sundial would be primarily used to connect duration of time and daily activities by means of a tangible user interface that adopts shapes already familiar to children.

According to the interviews, preschool children usually take advantage of objects that they are familiar with so as to learn counting (such as blocks, spheres or some basic geometric shapes). In terms of preschool or kindergarten, parents and teachers usually teach children the concepts of quinary (1, 2, 3… on the clock face represent 5, 10, 15… minutes respectively) [16] with the numbers on the clock or the same shape and size of objects. Time Machine launched by Ahmed and others is equipped with physically interactive as well as auditory functions and ambient display. Stacking marbles serves as a way to display time and to represent that Time Machine is to enhance the faculty of memory and reduce cognitive load by providing a tangible representative for time management [1]. Considering the designs and the mode of operation of Sundial, we referred to Ahmed's design and in turn we decided to use a glass ball with good light transmission as a tool for time setting and management and followed the teaching mode that children are used to setting a ball with five minutes.

At the same time, the research into Sundial's design is also referred to the theory of peripheral interaction, which emphasises that both perception of information and interaction with digital systems might shift between the focus and periphery of attention [4]. This type of Human-Computer Interaction (HCI) is based on the observation in our everyday lives. Since people are prone to be distracted due to various activities, we hope that children would pay more attention to the job at hand with the help of Sundial while they only check time when needed. Consequently, we adopted the most common clock shape regarding the design of the teaching aids and employed recognizable lights as a display of time so that they can smoothly switch their attention without overload in cognition.

3.3 Use Case

"Sundial" is made for children to acquire the concept of time in family and school activities. The following is the description of the ways to use and the circumstances suitable for usage.

The teacher managed the class time with Sundial to facilitate the group arrangement. Firstly, he/she explains to children that each ball represents the duration of 5 min and the light would be turned off every 5 min. It is 3 p.m. and the teacher would appoint students to conduct group discussion within 15 min.

1. At this time, the time has not been set on the device, and there is no response except for the rotation of the hands (as shown in Fig. 1).

2. Then the teacher instructs the students that 15 min is equal to three "5 min", so they should take 3 balls and put them into the corresponding holes according to the position of minute hand (as shown in Fig. 1).

3. The balls begin shining and timing after settled. When it comes to 3:05 p.m., the first 5 min have passed. At this time, the first ball will change color and go out after five seconds (as shown in Fig. 2).

4. In the process of group arrangement activity, students could confirm how much time has left with the help of the device. The light of all balls would go out at 3:15, and students would stop discussing and pay attention to the teacher (as shown in Fig. 2).

Fig. 1. Use example diagram

Fig. 2. Use example diagram

3.4 The Prototype

The main part of "Sundial" contains a standard clock with hour hand and minute hand, and the outside is surrounded by 12 holes, which respond to the numbers 1 to 12 and are available for children to insert the balls. The different number of balls represents different lengths of time, and the passage of time is displayed by the on and off of LED lights (Light Emitting Diodes).

To use Sundial for daily activities, we have to set up Sundial before the activities, lead children to select the number of balls corresponding to the time required for the activity, and place them in the grooves in sequence. The device counts down from 20 s once it senses the balls being put into holes. In the period, the position of balls can be changed depending on the need. The device would not function the determination system until 20 s later. And according to time, a sphere would go off in the corresponding position every five minutes. After completing the countdown, the device will turn off the light and stop functioning. It also represents the end of the activity, during which children can check the remaining time through Sundial at any time.

The hardware of "Sundial" includes 12 RGB LED lights, 12 micro switch and the Arduino controller board that commands main function. And use ordinary glass spheres are provide for children. The micro switch will be activated based on the weight of the spheres, and there are RGB LED lights settled in the groove. When the ball is placed in the groove, the spheres can emit light and create a scene that the ball glows (as shown in Fig. 3).

Sundial is the unconventional use of connecting time to physical objects. In order to make it easier for children to gain easy access to this teaching aids. As a result, this method of setting time is regardless with direction or order, which allows young kids to operate the device easily. Children may initially need to use Sundial with parents to help them more easily communicate time in a collaborative way based on daily activities. According to Vygotsky's findings, children are able to complete tasks better with some help from an adult than on their own, showing that social support is a critical factor in children's learning [16].

Fig. 3. Sundial's appearance design and internal configuration

4   User Study Setup

4.1   Study Design

To study the overall effect of Sundial on children's learning in the concepts of time, in addition to ensuring that the experiment is carried out in the common and virtual places, the target events should also be tasks that children are familiar with or daily routines in order to achieve "establishing the concepts of time from daily activities." In the meanwhile, we confirm the acquisition of knowledge of time for each child before they employ the devices, and the current environment when they use the devices, which avoid individual or environmental errors affecting the results of the research.

In order to simulate the environment in children's daily lives and ensure that the participants can use Sundial smoothly, the experiment was carried out in kindergartens or children's houses while some tasks were set in the process, such as jigsaw puzzles, painting, and homework, etc. Participants would execute those tasks with the use of Sundial amid the process. This experiment is a one-time experiment. Only one participating child, one companion and one researcher will be present in every experiment to reduce the interference of external factors. The experiment would last around one hour and the whole process would be recorded (as shown in Fig. 4).

Fig. 4. The detailed field configuration in the study

4.2 Participants

We recruited five participants, two males, and three females who are aged 5–6 (m = 5.4, sd = 0.55). Three of the children were from the same kindergarten, and the others were from the community. All children have received preschool education and they were immune to diseases or developmental retardation. The average level of their parent's education was bachelor's degree (Table 1).

Table 1. The participants' information

Number of children	Age
P1	6 years old
P2	5 years old
P3	6 years old
P4	5 years old
P5	5 years old

4.3 Procedure

Prior to the study, we contacted the principal of the kindergarten in person. We explained the content of the study and demonstrated the use of Sundial. We distributed the study information and later collected the informed consent. The teachers helped us collect the forms from parents taking part in our study in the kindergarten.

After confirming the participants, we arranged a two-week experiment, divided into five parts conducted separately. Those who are qualified for the experiment must take a pre-test with a time questionnaire adapted from the TKQ counterparts before using Sundial [17] so as to ensure the data from all participants would be proper. Sundial learning begins after the pre-test. The experiment should be carried out in an environment that the subjects are familiar with and deter from interference. Plus, a parent or teacher will accompany the tester without interfering with the experiment. Appropriate guidance will be adopted, and the whole process will be observed and recorded.

The process of the experiment can be subdivided into three stages. First, the testers would illustrate the detailed functions and the way to use Sundial. Next, children will be asked to operate Sundial and set 15 min, 10 min, and 5 min respectively (take three times). Then the children perform one task within fixed time and they would be required to notify the tester at the end of the time. The entire experiment would end after the third task; at the end, a semi-structured interview will be conducted to probe the participants with a simple quiz and asked the participants for their thoughts and suggestions during the process.

5 Discussion

5.1 The Use of Sundial

We evaluate whether children can control sundial on their own, and whether they understand the time meaning it represents. After the test, we can roughly divide the children into three types. First, two children were able to use this teaching aid independently after being explained by the tester, accounting for 40% of the total number of people tested. After the two children were explained, they still needed the intervention of the tester, and timely guidance to complete the operation, accounting for 40% of the total number of people tested. Finally, one of the children needs the assistance of testers to perform most of the operations, accounted for 20% of the total number of people tested. Among them, the main reason why children cannot use this teaching aid independently is that they have not been able to clearly locate the position of the minute hand, resulting in the inability to correctly place the ball in the appropriate hole. The other reason is that they have not yet acquired the mathematical ability to count five and one, so the correct number of balls cannot be selected.

Regarding to the meaning of time, after using sundial, one child can clearly understand the time experienced by the task, and can correctly read the clock face time before and after the task. While three children can't completely correct in the interpretation of the clock face time, there was a significant improvement and a clear understanding of the time elapsed for their task. The only child, who could not read the clock face time nor understand the elapsed time of the task, although not yet able to acquire time knowledge by sundial, this teaching aid gives good time prompts in the process of performing tasks, which can effectively help children manage time in daily activities.

5.2 Sundial and the Periphery of the Attention

The intention of Sundial is to help children manage time at home and classroom environment, and to think and build the concepts of time. While using it, people should be able to smoothly switch between attention and the edge of attention, and avoid negative effects such as distraction.

With above mentioned, we specially evaluated the attention of children when performing tasks. All children observed Sundial more frequently when they used Sundial for the first time, and couldn't fully concentrate on the things at hand, but this situation only lasted for two minutes. Four of the children can correctly perform the assigned tasks after getting used to the operation of this device. They will only check Sundial when they look up or when the things at hand reach a paragraph, and the frequency does not exceed three times per minute. There's only one child watched Sundial more frequently, but didn't overly affect the efficiency of its tasks; the frequency of attention shifts is about six to eight times per minute.

5.3 Findings

At the end of the experiment, we conducted a semi-structured interview to summarize the children's feelings and expectations about the teaching aid. We hope that the substantial feedback can be used as the basis for subsequent revision and optimization of Sundial. The following is a brief description of what the children mentioned in the interview. Content and recommendations.

In terms of appearance design, P1 and P3 highly affirmed. P1 said that he knew how to read the time on the clock face as soon as he saw Sundial, because, in appearance, it was not much different from the teaching aids that teachers usually use in teaching. P5 said that he sometimes could not distinguish between long needles and short needles. If he could make a more obvious difference, it would help him understand more easily. P4 said that he likes the current Sundial very much, and it would be better if he could add a little more color to the appearance.

As for overall operation, all children have a high interest in Sundial. P1 said that compared with ordinary clocks, Sundial displays the time in a luminous way, which can make him pay more attention to the remaining time, and set the time with a ball. The way it works is interesting to him. P2 said that the hole on the clock face made him intuitively know to place the ball in the hole, and the form of taking the ball at the same time helped him calculate the time. P3 believes that setting the time with the ball will remind him of playing with toys, which is much more interesting than buttons or touch controls. P5 said that while he still can't understand how many balls to take and where to place them, he likes the ability of Sundial to glow, which, in addition to its specificity, helps him understand how much time is left.

Finally, in terms of time learning and reminders, all children indicated that using Sundial for daily learning is less stressful or serious for them, and more beneficial in a familiar and relaxing environment, compared to time teaching in the classroom think about them. In addition, P1 and P3 believe that the way the ball glows is beneficial to reminding them of time, but it will not affect their concentration, and it will not make them feel pressure like an alarm clock. In this regard, P2 and P5 put forward different views. They believe that although Sundial's light gives a good time reminder, it is still easy to ignore the reminder when you are very focused on the things at hand. Adding some audible cues might make it easier for them to identify.

6 Conclusion

6.1 Limitations

As a work in progress paper, our research exists several limitations including the insufficient number of participants and deficiency in consideration regarding children's learning ability.

6.2 Conclusion and Future Work

In this paper, we presented an exploratory study that an ambient light was used to help children better understand the passage of time and duration of various activities. We created a shining ball-shaped learning device called "Sundial," which assisted children to acquire the concepts of duration in their daily lives and the capability of time reading. The design did not aim to encourage children to learn the concepts of time passively but try to combine it with everyday life. The result suggested that the system was readily accepted by children and integrated well into their daily activities. The device supported them to keep track of time rather than deprived them of their powers of concentration.

While children tend to fail to come by comprehensive understanding regarding Sundial, they possessed great interest in the prototype and could tell that the pre-set time period. In the foreseeable future, we would like to run Sundial with more younger participants. Through employing larger scale for user testing, we would understand the learning conditions and effects among children of all ages and further observe the difference that children utilize Sundial under diverse circumstances. Specific research objectives involve finding out how effective the timer is, and which age group is suitable to operate the device. Eventually, we would refine the design step by step and invent an effective learning device with a view to helping children learn the concepts of time without provoking distraction in their daily lives. The availability and adoption from various suggestions and feedback would also be necessary by conducting survey.

References

1. Ahmed, R., Chambers, A., Frontz, M., Voida, S.: A tangible approach to time management. In: Proceedings of UbiComp 2014 Adjunct, pp. 207–210 (2014)
2. Hiniker, A., Suh, H., Cao, S., Kientz, J.A.: Screen time tantrums: how families manage screen media experiences for toddlers and preschoolers. In: Proceedings of the 2016 CHI Conference on Human Factors in Computing Systems. ACM (2016)
3. Karimi, A., Liang, B., Nip, A., Nowroozi, S., Pang, C.: Time-Me: helping children understand time. In: Proceedings of the 11th International Conference on Interaction Design and Children (IDC 2012), pp. 268–271. Association for Computing Machinery (2012)
4. Bakker, S., van den Hoven, E., Eggen, B.: Peripheral interaction: characteristics and considerations. Pers. Ubiquit. Comput. 19(1), 239–254 (2014). https://doi.org/10.1007/s00779-014-0775-2
5. Kamii, C., Russell, K.A.: Elapsed time: why is it so difficult to teach? J. Res. Math. Educ. 43(3), 296–315 (2012)
6. Hayashi, E., Rau, M., Neo, Z.H., Tan, N., Ramasubramanian, S., Paulos, E.: TimeBlocks: mom, can i have another block of time. In: Proceedings of the SIGCHI Conference on Human Factors in Computing Systems, pp. 1713–1716. Association for Computing Machinery (2012)

7. Burny, E., Valcke, M., Desoete, A.: Towards an agenda for studying learning and instruction focusing on time-related competences in children. Educ. Stud. **35**(5), 481–492 (2009)
8. Ali, H., Singh, G., Sandnes, F.E.: Towards accessible representations of time: learning from the preferences of children and adults. In: Proceedings of the 12th ACM International Conference on PErvasive Technologies Related to Assistive Environments (PETRA 2019), pp. 317–318. Association for Computing Machinery (2019)
9. Müller, H., Pieper, C., Heuten, W., Boll, S.: TimeLight: helping children understand and learn time durations. In: Proceedings of the 2016 CHI Conference Extended Abstracts on Human Factors in Computing Systems (CHI EA 2016), pp. 3738–3741. Association for Computing Machinery (2016)
10. Gelderblom, H., Kotzé, P.: Ten design lessons from the literature on child development and children's use of technology. In: Proceedings of the 8th International Conference on Interaction Design and Children (IDC 2009), pp. 52–60. Association for Computing Machinery (2009)
11. Labrell, F., Mikaeloff, Y., Perdry, H., Dellatolas, G.: Time knowledge acquisition in children aged 6 to 11 years and its relationship with numerical skills. J. Exp. Child Psychol. **143**, 1–13 (2016)
12. McCormack, T., Hoerl, C.: The development of temporal concepts: learning to locate events in time. Timing Time Percept. **5**(3–4), 297–327 (2017)
13. Piaget, J.: The Child's Conception of Time, 1st edn. Routledge, London (2006)
14. Plass, J.L., Heidig, S., Hayward, E.O., Homer, B.D., Um, E.: Emotional design in multimedia learning: Effects of shape and color on affect and learning. Learn. Instr. **29**, 128–140 (2014)
15. Bakker, S., van den Hoven, E., Eggen, B., Overbeeke, K.: Exploring peripheral interaction design for primary school teachers. In: Proceedings of the Sixth International Conference on Tangible, Embedded and Embodied Interaction (TEI 2012), pp. 245–252. Association for Computing Machinery (2012)
16. Vygotsky, L.S.: Play and its role in the mental development of the child. Sov. Psychol. **5**, 6–18 (1967)
17. Friedman, W.J.: Development of time concepts in children. Adv. Child Dev. Behav. **12**, 267–298 (1978)
18. Friedman, W.J.: The development of children's memory for the time of past events. Child Dev. **62**, 139–155 (1991)

Scan Buddy: A Gamified App to Prepare Children for an MRI Scan

Privender Saini[1]([envelope]), Chelsey Koehn[4], Annerieke Heuvelink[1], Ozgur Tasar[2], Elizabeth van Vorstenbosch-Lynn[3], Sanne Nauts[1], and Andrew T. Trout[4]

[1] Philips Research, High Tech Campus 34, 5656 AE Eindhoven, Netherlands
privender.saini@philips.com
[2] Philips Experience Design, High Tech Campus 33, 5656 AE Eindhoven, Netherlands
[3] Philips Healthcare, Veenpluis 6, 5684 PC Best, Netherlands
[4] Department of Radiology, Cincinnati Children's Hospital and Medical Center, 3333 Burnet Avenue, MLC5031, Cincinnati, OH 45229, USA

Abstract. Undergoing an MRI scan can be a stressful experience for young children. For this reason, pediatric patients are often scanned under general anesthesia or sedation, which is costly and may carry health risks. By preparing children for their scan, anesthesia may be avoided; however, existing preparation solutions are generally hospital-specific and not easily scalable. We describe the iterative design process and feasibility test of the Scan Buddy app: a scalable app to prepare children 4–10 for an MRI scan.

Interviews and Questionnaire: Interviews with 19 healthcare practitioners (US and EU) revealed a desire to reduce anesthesia for imaging through better patient preparation. A questionnaire administered to 73 caregivers of children who recently had an MRI scan exposed the need for well-designed tools to explain the MRI procedure as well as caregivers' willingness to invest time in at-home preparation if it could increase the likelihood of an awake scan.

Design Rationale: We developed a learning framework based on Informing, Familiarizing and Training children for MRI (FIT-for-MRI), and designed a gamified app with 7 learning goals.

Method: Scan Buddy v1 was used in the weeks prior to an MRI examination by 28 children in a feasibility test at Cincinnati Children's Hospital Medical Center.
Results: Scan Buddy prepared the children for their MRI: learning goals were met, children enjoyed playing with the app, awake scanning was successful, and parents felt it supported their child in their preparation. Scan Buddy v2 was subsequently developed, and the rationale for design is detailed.

Keywords: Pediatric patient preparation · MRI · Serious gaming

1 Introduction

For physicians, Magnetic Resonance Imaging (MRI) is a powerful tool to create detailed images of the inside of a patient's body. For young children, however, undergoing an MRI scan can be a stressful experience. Children need to lie down on a table that moves

© The Author(s), under exclusive license to Springer Nature Switzerland AG 2022
M. Kurosu (Ed.): HCII 2022, LNCS 13302, pp. 594–612, 2022.
https://doi.org/10.1007/978-3-031-05311-5_42

into a large, unfamiliar machine. A scan can take anywhere between 10 and 90 min, and the highest diagnostic quality is achieved when the child lies perfectly still for the duration of the scan. During the MRI scan, the machine makes loud clicking or banging noises (ranging 82–138 dB; Li et al. 2011) that start, stop, and change throughout the scan.

Unfamiliarity and fear of the unknown can lead to anxiety in young patients, who do not understand what is required of them as part of a medical encounter (Marshall et al. 1993, Tyc et al. 1995). Children can become anxious and have trouble keeping still for an extended period of time, leading to scans with insufficient diagnostic quality, or the need for costly repeat scans. For this reason, many young children require sedation or general anesthesia (GA) to undergo an MRI scan, and many hospitals err on the side of sedating children to ensure high quality images. Using sedation/GA has several disadvantages, such as longer waiting lists (Vanderby et al. 2010), more time spent in the hospital, post-scan irritability (Walker et al. 2008) and potential adverse health effects (see Artunduaga et al. 2021 for a review). Moreover, using sedation/GA is costly; a scan with GA is approximately 9 times more expensive than an awake scan; (Vanderby et al. 2010).

The known disadvantages of sedation/GA have prompted various approaches to scan children awake (for an overview see Janos et al. 2019; Harrington et al. 2022). Many hospitals have created a child-friendly MRI room, e.g., by using colored lighting, changing the appearance of the scanner (making it look like a castle or submarine), or allowing children to watch a movie during the scan. Another common approach is to prepare and practice with patients in the imaging facility, for example with an educational video (Hogan et al. 2018) or face-to-face training using a mock scanner or simulated scanning sessions (e.g., Barnea-Goraly et al. 2014; Jaimes et al. 2021; Nordahl et al. 2016). Some hospitals offer solutions to prepare children at home such as preparatory videos, brochures and hospital-specific mobile apps (e.g., McGlashan et al. 2018; Runge et al. 2018; Törnqvist et al. 2015). Other imaging facilities combine preparation at home and in the hospital, sometimes in addition to adjustments within the MRI room (e.g., Barnea-Goraly et al. 2014; Rothman et al. 2016; Runge et al. 2018). Evaluative studies suggest that many of these approaches can improve the scan experience for pediatric patients, while increasing the rate of successful awake scans. This suggests that it is possible to reduce sedation/GA rates in pediatric MRI through preparation and guidance.

Creating and maintaining facility-specific programs and content requires substantial effort and expertise on the part of a hospital. After introduction, many programs require continued time and resources from specialized hospital staff. As a result, not all hospitals are able to provide these types of programs to patients. An additional constraint is the large number of children who undergo MRI imaging, and the fact that it can occur at all times of day and across multiple physical locations. As a result, even specialized children's hospitals who have access to certified child life specialists (CLSs) or other dedicated professionals may not be able to continuously provide in-person training to *every* child due to constraints in time and resources. Put differently: there are many initiatives and programs that are highly effective, but these programs are currently only available to a very small group of pediatric patients worldwide.

To allow more children to be scanned awake, there is a need for a scalable, broadly applicable solution that many different hospitals can easily implement within their existing workflow. One potential solution is a vendor-agnostic mobile app to prepare children for their MRI at home. Such a solution extends availability of patient preparation to facilities that do not have the time, resources, or expertise to create and maintain their own programs. It could also be added to existing programs to allow specialized children's hospitals to prepare those patients that they currently cannot prepare due to practical constraints (e.g., the availability of certified Child Life Specialists). Although a ready-to-use patient preparation solution has advantages in terms of scalability, a challenge is that it needs to optimally prepare children while fitting into variable clinical workflows. The specific experience of one pediatric patient may be completely different from the experience of another patient in terms of scan length (will a scan take 10 min or 60?), equipment (can the child watch a movie in the scanner or not?), procedure and accessories (will the child receive an IV for contrast? Will they need to hold their breath at moments in the scan?), etc.

With Scan Buddy we aimed to create an app that effectively prepares patients for their MRI scan, in a way that is suitable to variable clinical workflows. To achieve this, we carried out three steps, described in Sects. 2, 3 and 4 respectively. First, we gathered input from stakeholders by interviewing healthcare providers from various hospitals and conducting a questionnaire with parents/caregivers of children who had recently had an MRI scan. This served to provide background information on needs and the current workflow in different hospitals. Second, based on insights from the interviews and questionnaire, we created a learning framework (the FIT-for-MRI framework) and defined learning goals that are important for children to master, and that are relevant to the variety of clinical workflows. Third, we created a gamified mobile app (Scan Buddy v1) and tested if pediatric MRI patients met the learning goals, and if stakeholders (children, parents/caregivers, and healthcare providers) felt the app helped them to be well-prepared for the scan. In Sect. 4 we also discuss the implications of the work for the final design of the app (Scan Buddy v2). In Sect. 5 we discuss the possibility to embed the app in a larger patient coaching solution that guides children at home, in the waiting room, and in the MRI scanner. Figure 1 contains an overview of the different steps in the process of designing and testing the Scan Buddy app.

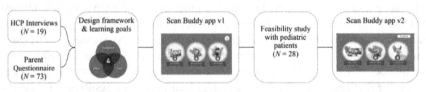

Fig. 1. Different steps in designing and testing the Scan Buddy app.

2 Stakeholder Interviews and Parent Questionnaire

2.1 Methods

We aimed to get more insight into healthcare providers' (HCPs) needs with respect to pediatric patient preparation using a semi-structured interviewing method. The first part of the interview concerned HCPs' opinions, current way of working, and future needs with respect to pediatric patient preparation for MRI. Next, we showed interviewees a video prototype of an app solution. The prototype itself was a non-functional video mock-up that looked like an app, with the intent to stimulate conversation on the topic. In this second part of the interview, we were interested to find out if such an app for preparing patients could be useful and a valuable tool for HCPs. As the focus of the interviews was to expose opinions, challenges, needs and desires, the interviews were analyzed qualitatively within the themes of the interviews.

In parallel to the interviews, we sent out an online questionnaire to parents whose child had recently undergone an MRI scan. Data collection and recruitment was done by a recruitment agency with respondents in the Netherlands. The questionnaire contained questions about the period before the scan: did parents receive material to prepare themselves or their child? If they did, how did they prepare their children, how much time did they spend, what difficulties did they think they would encounter? We also asked them what could have potentially helped them to better prepare their child. The surveys were analyzed qualitatively, by examining the percentages of answers given to get a flavor of parents' needs and experiences.

2.2 Results

Interviews with HCPs
Nineteen interviews were conducted with healthcare professionals involved in pediatric radiology. Interviewees worked as child life specialists, radiologist, department manager, or account manager across fourteen hospitals in the US and Europe. Interviewees all expressed that preparing young children is important to achieve a smooth procedure. Many interviewees emphasized that high-quality, timely preparation is important to enable as many children as possible to undergo an awake scan. All facilities reported having a certain age range that qualified for GA, although this age range differed across hospitals. Some healthcare providers indicated that 4 was the minimum age at which they believed an awake scan would be possible. All interviewees voiced a desire to reduce sedation and GA frequencies at their hospitals.

Next to preparing children, interviewees mentioned that it is equally important to prepare parents/caregivers, as the behavior of accompanying parents/caregivers can have a large impact on the patient's behavior. If the parent is anxious, or is showing other signs of distress, this affects the child's anxiety level. Preparation can affect the anxiety level of parents/caregivers, as well as their willingness to attempt an awake scan.

When it comes to current practices in patient preparation, many hospitals called a parent/caregiver several days before the scan to provide basic information. On the day of the scan, children were sometimes guided by a professional trained to work with children (e.g., a child life specialist), who interacts with the child and explains the procedure using a variety of resources, such as books, leaflets, digital media, or even a mock scanner. Sometimes, a 'tour' was given of the MRI room. Many hospitals provided in-bore entertainment (e.g., movie goggles) to distract children during the scan. The availability of these services, as well as the exact workflow steps, differed between hospitals, hospital locations, and other factors (e.g., the availability of equipment/child life specialists).

Many healthcare providers voiced having a lack of high-quality materials to prepare patients, especially at home. Several interviewees voiced lacking the time to provide comprehensive preparation for all pediatric MRI patients; even specialized children's hospitals indicated that support from a child life specialist is only available to a minority of patients. Interviewees mentioned that ideally, training could occur in a simulated environment, and help them identify children that need additional attention. This could help them allocate their limited resources (e.g., the time of child life specialists) more effectively.

Interviewees' opinions about the video prototype were generally positive. Many respondents mentioned that it would be important for them to be able to customize such an app, for branding purposes and to maximize familiarity for the child (e.g., by including the hospital logo as well as pictures of their reception desk, waiting room, or personnel). Concerns around internet access, smart tech ownership, smart tech usage comfort, and cost were raised as potential barriers to adoption. Additionally, it was mentioned that it would be optimal if an app could connect to or be integrated into the *existing* hospital workflow or tech platform to promote adoption and endorsement by hospital staff.

In summary, all interviewees expressed a desire to reduce sedation/GA in pediatric MRI within their hospital. All agreed that proper preparation is key to scanning children awake in a pleasant way, and that preparing parents/caregivers is as important as preparing patients. The desire to extensively prepare children was thwarted by a lack of resources, and all agreed that an at home-app could help them prepare more patients.

Questionnaire with Parents
Seventy-three questionnaires were completed. Almost all parents were provided some form of information about the MRI examination by the imaging facility. 40 out of 73 parents mentioned that they had a conversation with a healthcare professional about the scan prior to the scan. 24 received a brochure with general information about the scan, and 33 received a brochure that was tailored to children. Only 6 parents mentioned receiving other information (e.g., a link to the hospital website).

Most parents talked to their child prior to the imaging encounter and explained what was going to happen during the MRI scan. About 20% of parents spent less than 15 min talking with and preparing their child for the MRI scan, around 60% spent 15 to 60 min, and the remainder (20%) spent more than an hour discussing the topic. About 60% of parents mentioned preparing their child for their scan beyond just talking to them. Parents provided minimal information about what they did beyond talking, but most often mentioned was using a brochure as an aid to walk the children through the upcoming procedure as well as look for helpful videos online and reassure their child that everything was going to be alright.

What parents found most helpful for them and their child was the conversation with their physician and explanation of the MRI procedure by an operator. They also found it important that the MRI personnel made efforts to put the child's mind at ease.

In summary, parents spent time discussing the upcoming scan with their children. The willingness to invest significant time on such conversations, was evident. Most commonly, parents use material that they have been provided as a source of information or as reference in the discussion with their child. What parents would appreciate most is the explanation of the procedure to the child by someone knowledgeable. Although we did not explicitly ask their opinion about an app to support at-home preparation in this specific questionnaire, answers suggest that if such an app were provided by their hospitals parents would use it.

3 Design of the Scan Buddy App

The design of the Scan Buddy app was based on the findings from the interviews with healthcare providers and questionnaire with parents; the intended target group is pediatric patients who need an MRI aged 4 to 10 years.

3.1 Learning Goals

As a basis for the Scan Buddy app, we defined learning goals describing things children would need to know or practice to be able to undergo an awake scan.

We initially identified 13 goals, which we put forward for scrutiny during in-depth conversations and workshops with specialists at partner hospitals around the globe, and at conferences and customer visits. Based on their feedback, we concluded that some learning goals were too workflow specific and did not generalize across hospitals. Nothing new was mentioned in all the feedback to add to the list of 13 (i.e., we did not miss anything crucial in our initial list). After filtering 7 learning goals were formulated (see Table 1) that applied to almost all MRI scans, regardless of the specific hospital.

Table 1. Learning goals of the Scan Buddy app

#	Learning goals	Explanation
1	Understanding the procedure	Understanding the entire journey of arriving at the hospital, checking in, meeting the staff that are involved with the MRI, getting changed, hopping onto the table and getting geared-up and having the scan
2	Getting acquainted with accessories	Understanding the need for, and role of accessories (e.g., earplugs, headphones, coils)
3	Understanding metals	Understanding that the MRI is a big magnet, and that metal is a hazard
4	Getting familiar with MRI sounds	Familiarizing children with MRI sounds and explaining that they will be heard throughout the scan
5	Getting familiar with the size of the MRI scanner	Familiarizing children with the MRI machine and its size, to prevent feeling overwhelmed at first sight
6	Experience that a scan takes time	Experiencing the duration of the MRI scan, and being able to cope with that while in the scanner
7	Practice lying still	Practicing lying still under difficult circumstances: in a narrow bore, with high sound exposure, for long periods

3.2 Design Framework

In the next step of the design process, we tackled the question: how will we ensure proper app design to convey the 7 learning goals? We opted for a gamified mobile app to allow children to learn and experiment in a playful, fun and safe environment. To optimally support the various learning goals, a learning framework was defined based on explicit, implicit, and procedural learning. Three components were defined: *Inform* the child about topics that can be discussed in conversation (explicit learning), *Familiarize* the child to characteristics that can be perceived as overwhelming (implicit learning), and *Train* the child to acquire skills that are necessary to undergo an MRI scan awake (procedural learning).

Inform. Foremost, we needed an informational component to teach children what MRI is and what procedural steps and accessories are involved. This *Inform* component relies on explicit learning and is equivalent to existing paper leaflets or informational movies. Storytelling and immersion are the main techniques we employ to inform the child.

Familiarize. In addition, we identified the need for an implicit learning component: learning while focusing on doing something else or learning without explicit instructions. We call this the *Familiarize* component, with the important role in Scan Buddy to expose children to MRI sounds throughout the app. This is done in a playful manner, with the sounds appearing in different ways (in the foreground, in the background, softly, and loudly, but ever present), preparing the child for the full-life experience. Similarly, through play we familiarize the child with the size and shape of the MRI scanner. Immersion, habituation, graded exposure, and normalization are the main techniques we use to familiarize the child.

Train. The final component (*Train*) is intended to teach children new skills through procedural learning. Most importantly, training is used to teach children to lie still during the scan, as this is a skill that is difficult to acquire through explicit/implicit learning alone. The training component only comes after informing and familiarization. In other words, a basic idea of what will happen and exposure and habituation to sounds and the particulars of the MRI machine is needed before we can work on skills training. Biofeedback, progress feedback, and rewards are the main techniques we utilize to train the child.

Taken together, these three components make up the FIT-for-MRI framework (Familiarize-Inform-Train; see Fig. 2) and form the theoretical basis for the design of Scan Buddy and other pediatric coaching solutions we work on.

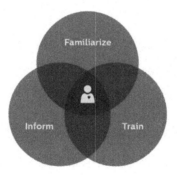

Fig. 2. FIT-for-MRI framework

3.3 Scan Buddy App Modules

The Scan Buddy app consists of four modules: three for the pediatric patient and one for parents/caregivers (see Fig. 3). The modules for children are: 1) an educational video, 2) a scan game, and 3) a game in Augmented Reality. The module for adults provides general information, an FAQ about MRI and suggests fun activities to do with children to prepare them for their scan.

The first time the child plays, the modules unlock one at a time, if the previous module is completed. This is to ensure that the games are played in the desired order to cover all learning goals. After all the modules are unlocked, the child can access them in any order.

Fig. 3. The three games in Scan Buddy, and parent module (button top right)

What is MRI? The first module is a video, with the main goal to *Inform.* As depicted in Fig. 4, the movie displays two children having their MRI, covering all the steps from sitting in the waiting room to being picked up, removing metal, getting accessories (headphones, coils), to completing the MRI. In the first version of the app (Scan Buddy v1), the movie featured one child and procedure; in the final version (Scan Buddy v2), the movie was improved by adding a second child to ensure diversity in procedures (brain scan vs. abdominal scan; with and without contrast) and emotional responses (with one child not knowing what to expect and another child being very confident).

Fig. 4. Sample images from the intro video

MRI Scan Game. The second module is an interactive game in which the child helps to scan a young cartoon elephant (see Fig. 5). The main goal of the scan game is to *Familiarize* children with the sounds, scan procedure/accessories, and the fact that it takes time to complete a scan. Another goal is to *train* children to keep still.

At the start of the scan game, children remove metal objects from the cartoon elephant (top left) before it can enter the MRI room. Next, the elephant climbs onto the scanner table and the child selects the right accessories (headphones, coil etc., top-right) and holds the phone still while the scan takes place (bottom row). During the scan, a progress bar is visible, and a cartoon MRI image is slowly exposed to simulate the passing of time, and to indicate that the scan can take a while. If the phone is moved too much during scanning, there is a yellow warning (bottom left), which turns into a red warning (bottom middle) if the child continues to move. In the case of continued movement, the scan starts over, just like in real life. During the entire game, the background sound of the MRI scanner (the so called *cryopump sound*) is audible in the background. While

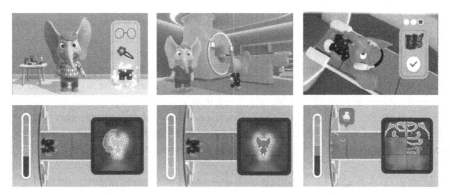

Fig. 5. Sample images from the scan game. Top row: removing metal and gearing up. Bottom row: the scanning game with color coded warnings that trigger when the child moves the phone.

the elephant is being scanned, the MRI sounds (*acquisition sounds*) are played louder, in the foreground.

For purposes of re-playability, every time the game is played a slightly different looking young elephant is introduced with different metal objects to be removed.

In Scan Buddy v1, only one scan type (head scans) was displayed; v2 was improved by adding more types of scans (head, stomach, knee), either with or without contrast fluid and an IV drip (bottom right). Additionally, the lying still training was added to Scan Buddy v2 to further solidify this important learning goal.

Explore in AR. The third module is a game deploying Augmented Reality (AR); see Fig. 6. The goal of this game is to achieve *Familiarity* with the MRI machine by exploring it up-close in AR. While doing so the *Inform* goal is met by providing bite-sized information in the form of audio-visual educational material during a sticker hunt.

Fig. 6. Sample images from the AR game.

The game starts with the child virtually placing the MRI scanner in their home, so they can walk around it and get a good look from all sides (top left). Next, there is a short animation in which a cartoon elephant slides into the scanner, after which the scanner becomes transparent, and the inside of the scanner is visible (top middle). When finished exploring, the child can continue with an interactive sticker hunt. Stickers appear on all sides of the MRI machine (top right), and the child is encouraged to find and collect them. After a sticker is found (bottom left) it reveals additional content (pictures or a video) that help inform the child about MRI (bottom middle). The sticker game ends when all stickers are found (bottom right) and form a poster. For re-playability, there are 5 different sticker hunts with different educational material embedded. This game was added in the final version of the Scan Buddy app; Scan Buddy v1 contained a lying still feedback game using VR goggles, which was abandoned in v2.

4 Feasibility Study

We tested the initial version (v1) of the Scan Buddy app at Cincinnati Children's Hospital Medical Center (CCHMC) in Ohio, USA. Scan Buddy v1 was designed around the same considerations and learning goals of Scan Buddy v2 but differed in several ways. The biggest differences were: 1) an early version of the intro movie, and 2) an early version of the scan game, and 3) did not have the AR game, but included a lying still game which used Virtual Reality (VR) goggles (Fig. 7). For the lying still game, the child would watch a short movie clip while lying down with the VR goggles on. Movement of the head was captured by the smartphone accelerometer, and feedback about movement was provided to the child, similar to Fig. 5, bottom row. Scan Buddy v1's modules catered to all 7 learning goals (Table 1), but we emphasized learning about the following for the study: a) understanding metals, b) getting familiar with MRI sounds, c) getting familiar with the size of the MRI machine (and space in the bore), d) experience that a scan takes time (or duration), and e) practice lying still.

Fig. 7. The menu of Scan Buddy v1

Our primary objective of the early test of the app was to 1) investigate whether the app prepared children for an MRI scan. Secondary objectives were to: 2) learn how much the child played with the app and their opinion about game content, 3) characterize parents' opinions about the app.

4.1   Method

Study Design. As this was a feasibility study for Scan Buddy v1; our intention was to recruit 30 patients with their parent/caregiver ('parent'). Institutional Review Board approval was obtained for this study. Parents and children participated on voluntary basis with written informed consent obtained from the parent. No randomization was performed due to the explorative nature of the study. Parents received monetary incentives for participation: $20 USD at study entry, and $30 USD at completion ($50 USD total). Children received a coloring book, and stickers (with characters from the app). They also received an MRI scan completion certificate after the scan.

Recruitment, Materials, and Procedure. The children recruited were patients cared for at CCHMC. Children in the study completed their MRI scan at CCHMC or at a satellite imaging facility.

Patients were screened about a week before the scan to identify patients aged 5 to <10 years scheduled for awake brain MRI examinations. Potential participants were contacted by phone by a study team member to gauge interest in the study. Interested participants were invited on short notice to attend an enrollment visit (T0) at the main hospital during which they provided Informed Consent, filled in the baseline questionnaires and picked up the study kit.

The study kit consisted of an Android smart phone, commercially available VR goggles, a short instruction booklet, a short questionnaire for the children to fill out after using the app but before their MRI scan, as well as contact information for the study coordinator. Parents were asked to walk through the study kit at home and let their child play with the app as often and as long as they saw fit. There was a short questionnaire that was to be filled out by the child, with or without parental assistance, prior to coming to the hospital for the MRI scan (T1).

On the day of the MRI, parent and child were met by a study team member. A study team member accepted the filled-out questionnaire and study kit. After scanning, radiology staff recorded qualitative assessments related to the child's ability to participate in the scan and difficulties performing the scan (T2). A post-scan questionnaire and interview were also conducted with the child and parent, asking questions about usage and engagement with the app (T3).

Measures. As we wanted to ask children to fill in questionnaires, we needed the questionnaires to be short. Based on user experience research with children, and the experience of CCHMC's child life specialists (CLS), we decided on 5 questions maximum on paper per topic, and no more than 10 per session. Answering options were either three- or four-point visual scales using child-friendly answering options in the form of smiley faces.

To get insight in our main objective, whether the app prepared children for an MRI scan, we took the following measurements:

T0 - Pre-study visit (baseline questionnaires) at hospital - 1) General anxiety level of child (two questions on paper filled in by child: I am worried about my MRI exam and I am looking forward to my MRI exam) and 2) Anxiety of child and parent related to scan (six questions on paper filled in by parent, about anticipated level of child's anxiety and their own).

T1 - Post-app-play questionnaire at home - 3) General anxiety level of child (same two questions as above). 4) Expectation of child (two questions on paper as part of study kit: Have you had an MRI exam before? And I know what my MRI exam is going to be like) 5) Achievement of learning goals (five questions that tested the knowledge that was potentially gained from playing, the app quiz: I need to check my pockets before having my MRI exam, I need to hold very still during my MRI exam, There will be lots of room in the MRI scanner, The MRI scanner will be loud, and My MRI test will be very quick and short).

T2 - Questions for radiology staff about the scan - 6) Quality of scan and duration and 7) Patient's readiness for scan (anxiety and ability to lie still).

T3 - Exit interview - The exit interview contained questions to the child related to how well they thought they did and how well they were able to lie still. It also asked about content appreciation: what did they like/dislike about the app. The parent part of the exit interview contained questions about how well they thought the app helped prepare the child for the MRI as well as their general opinion of the app.

App data - Usage logs of the app served to provide information on duration and frequency of interaction with the various app modules.

4.2 Results

A total of 28 parent-child dyads were enrolled in the study. Twelve boys and 16 girls participated aged 5–9 years (M = 7.21, SD = 1.40). For 12 participants, it was their first MRI scan. The other 16 had previously had one or more MRI scans.

Complete data were available for 20 participants. For 7 participants app usage data were unavailable, and for 5 participants, one or multiple questionnaires were missing. As such, N differs per analysis.

Did the App Prepare Children for an MRI? Children were quite positive when it came to answering questions about the MRI scan after playing with the app, and at the exit interview. 71% ticked the option *yes* to the question 'I know what my MRI exam is going to be like' (after playing the app). 81% thought the MRI scan went well, and 96% indicated they were able to lie still. Most parents (89%) indicated that, in their view, their child was well-prepared for their scan thanks to the app.

The learning goals that were very explicitly present in the app (e.g., lying still, MRI sounds), were met: 96–100% had the answers in the *app quiz* correct relating to these learning goals and children were able to put into their own words why they had to lie still or could not bring metal with them (mentioned in the exit interview). Learning goals that were present less explicitly in Scan Buddy v1 (e.g., duration, narrowness of bore), were met 42–50%. These data suggest that most children mastered the learning goals that were emphasized in the app.

MR technologists indicated that children in the study were able to lie still very well: on a scale from 1 (could not lie still at all) to 5 (could lie still very well), the average score they gave was a 4 ($N = 26$, $SD = 1.27$). Image quality was good ($M = 4.38$ on a

5-point scale; $SD = 0.77, N = 24$). This suggests that patients were able to keep still for their scan, and image quality was high.

The mean anxiety level (reported by the child, on a 4 point scale) at baseline (T0) was 1.63 (SD = 0.75), and after app-play was 1.91 (SD = 0.85), which was not a significant difference[1] (t(23) = 1.06, p = 0.45). However, a greater proportion of children (37%) reported lower anxiety after app play (Fig. 8).

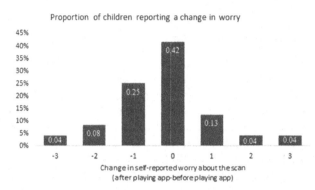

Fig. 8. Change in self-reported worry from before to after playing with Scan Buddy v1

App Usage. On average the intro movie (03:55 min) was fully watched 3 times (M = 2.6), and on average partially watched an additional 5 times (M = 5). The scan game was fully played approximately 9 times (M = 8.7) and partially played once (M = 0.9). The lying still game was on average fully played 4 times (M = 3.8) and partially played an additional 3 times (M = 3.3). Children moved approximately 18 times (M = 17.8, range = 6–51 times) while watching the animated movie (07:28 min) embedded in the lying still game. Unfortunately, it was difficult to ascertain from the patterns whether the movements were voluntary (on-purpose to trigger the warnings) or involuntary (inability to lie still). Next to that, there was too much variability in the measurements to reliably extract a learning trend. The parent module was only accessed 3 times in total.

Participants' Opinions. The scan game was the most popular game, and in the exit interview it was mentioned as the most liked game. In fact, when asked what they liked most about the app, the most popular answer was 'smartphone' and 'VR goggles', third came 'the scan game'. One child mentioned s/he liked the intro movie best, and no child liked the lying still game itself, even if they liked the goggles. To the question what they liked least about the app, the most common answer was the 'lie still game', followed by the 'goggles', and 'the movie' on the third spot.

Overall, parents and children had a favorable impression of the app (see Fig. 9 for quotes). 85% of children enjoyed playing the games in the app, the other 15% were 'neutral'.

---

[1] The study was not designed to be powered. We inspected trends and interesting patterns.

Fig. 9. Quotes of parents and children who used Scan Buddy v1

4.3 Implications for Final App Design

The results of the feasibility study had implications for the final design of the Scan Buddy app (v2). Here we discuss the rationale for the changes.

Scan Buddy v1 embedded an early version of the intro movie which featured one child undergoing a head scan, and an early version of the scan game focused on the young elephant character undergoing an MRI scan of the head. While this was sufficient for the feasibility study, it would not be for the app as the goal was to prepare children for all types of MRI exams. For Scan Buddy v2 we extended the first two modules to include multiple scan types, including head, abdomen, and knee, and exams done with and without contrast.

Intro Movie. The final intro movie was updated to 1) stronger emphasize various learning goals and 2) be more inclusive. In support of the learning goals, it also features additional content on the procedure from arrival at the hospital to completing the MRI scan, the duration and the sounds of the MRI, and the various accessories possibly encountered. To be more inclusive of the various experiences pediatric patients may have, we embedded a broader representation of possible scan experiences by adding a second child undergoing a body scan with contrast. Last, it was explicitly pointed out that *every scan is just a little bit different*, and theirs too will be a little different from what they see in Scan Buddy.

MRI Scan Game. We learned that the scan game was a favorite. Even the limited version embedded in v1 was played often. Given these insights and the strengths of an interactive experience to *Familiarize* children with various aspects of a scan, this game was extended and upgraded to 1) again emphasize stronger various learning goals and 2) be more inclusive for the various scan experiences. In particular, we strengthened the learning goals of understanding metals and getting acquainted with the various accessories by broadening the set of metal items to remove, and by adding different MRI coils to choose from.

The introduction of contrast and various scan types not only introduced more accessories, but also the possibility for a feet-first position on the table, see Fig. 5. Adding contrast to the scan game was an outcome of additional interaction with stakeholders as is generally considered a challenging aspect of undergoing an MRI. By featuring a different type of scan (head, abdominal, extremity, and with or without contrast) each time a new game is started, we enable a more varied and therefore engaging game-play experience, promoting replays.

VR/AR Game. The biggest change from prototype v1 to final version v2 of Scan Buddy was the third module. The lie still game featuring VR goggles was replaced by an AR game. The feasibility study showed that the lie still game was played less often than the scan game, and the exit interview gave insight into some of the contributing factors. We conclude that the complexity of the game, involving having to put the phone into the VR goggles requiring adult assistance and having to lie down on the ground or couch to practice lying still, was a barrier to playing. This, and the fact that VR goggles were required to play which would either exclude players or introduce unnecessary difficulties with workflow logistics to include VR goggles as part of MRI preparation package, led to the decision to abandon the VR game.

To ensure sufficient attention to the lying still learning goal, we extended the scan game so that children needed to hold the phone very still while the cartoon elephant is being scanned. When they move during this scene, they receive biofeedback and immediately experience the effects of motion on the scan.

By removing the VR game, we opened the spot for a new game. We developed an AR game and offered children the opportunity to familiarize themselves with the scanner up-close, e.g., with the narrowness of the tunnel, and its accessories. We expect the 'coolness' factor of AR to equal that of VR (children indicated in the exit interview that the phone and googles were the most liked) to promote play.

Parent Module. One element that was mentioned by HCPs in the interviews was the importance of preparing parents. The Scan Buddy app contains a separate module for parents/caregivers, containing general information and FAQ about MRI, and suggestions for fun, preparatory activities; yet, in the feasibility study, the parent module was opened just a few times. We believe that the set-up of the study may have contributed to that, namely the provision of a smartphone for the child to use for the study. When parents need to install the app on their phone, we expect a higher level of engagement with the 'For parents' module. Additionally, the small 'i' icon in Scan Buddy v1 was replaced by a clear 'For parents' button in v2.

5 Discussion

Literature suggests that there are many ways to prepare children for an awake MRI scan. Many existing solutions have proven effective in research and in practice. However, they are often developed *in-house* to fit the workflows of one facility (or even one specific group of patients within a facility), are often labor intensive or costly to develop and manage over time. At home preparation, using digital technology, appears to be viable solution. We developed Scan Buddy to do a *good-enough* job of preparing pediatric patients at home, without affecting hospital workflow, and with the potential to be adopted easily by radiology departments, as well as the end users: children and parents.

Our learning framework and the gamification approach facilitated the design of three app modules that showed promise in preparing children for their MRI scan. The feasibility study demonstrated that Scan Buddy could engage and support young children in overcoming and handling a potentially overwhelming and scary situation.

Children were able and willing to play with an app on a smart phone, which is not surprising in this era, but would the app be engaging enough to instill some knowledge as well as rudimentary skills needed to lie still in a noisy MRI machine? Although we cannot definitively answer this question based on data, promising patterns and parent, MR tech and child *perception* tentatively point towards a *yes*. The study also showed that parents support the approach of using an app at home and are happy to facilitate the child in working with it. They felt it educated and supported their child in undergoing an awake scan.

We made a decision to abandon the VR lie still game for the sake of simplicity and removing any barriers to use for the child and hospital. This decision also meant that we replaced a game that served an important learning goal: practicing lying still. Although we introduce and playfully stimulate the child to consider this important behavior in other ways, we acknowledge that we made a compromise. The *train* component in the learning framework is currently underrepresented in Scan Buddy v2; a caveat we intent to rectify in future releases of the app. We continue to explore, ideate, prototype, and test solutions to this end.

We invested considerable effort in designing an app for children, and one module designed specifically for caregivers. We did not yet take into consideration needs of another important stakeholder: the hospital. A next step would be to allow hospitals to customize the app to their requirements, such as branding. But also offer the option to provide Scan Buddy through their own channels, such as the hospital website or the opportunity to easily 'find' and download the app at the hospital, to anticipate and remove barriers that caregivers may have with respect to internet access and inexperience with technology.

The Scan Buddy app is our first solution for preparation of pediatric patients at home. On its own, it will have a role in teaching the child the basics about having an MRI scan. However, a multifaceted approach starting from referral to end of scan is expected to have a bigger impact on the whole experience of the hospital and the child. There are many solutions in existence, as is evident from literature and our interviews. And in fact, many hospitals are combining interventions that they develop with existing solutions into a multifaceted approach. For example, a Children Centered Care approach included an interactive app, toy scanner, and entertainment in the MRI room (Runge et al. 2018); another approach combined an instructional movie, booklet, and practice session in an MRI simulator (Rothman et al. 2016). In these studies, the multi-faceted approach proved to be more effective than an approach that addressed a single facet. Such a holistic approach could greatly benefit the pediatric radiology departments of hospitals and is a need that we are addressing with a suite of solutions spanning from referral, to home, to end of scan.

Finally, having a multifaceted approach could inform the hospital of different journeys the patient may receive. The at-home component – like the Scan Buddy app – should ultimately inform the hospital about which child may need some extra attention before the scan (e.g., a personal training session with a CLS), and which child did so well that they may take a more expedited journey. Equally important is the identification of children that despite training, may not be able to cope with an awake scan. Timely and accurate prediction would facilitate proper allocation of resources and a better patient experience.

6 Conclusion

We developed an app to prepare children for an awake MRI scan. We took an iterative user-centered centered approach of looking into the literature, talking to stakeholders in the hospital and at home, as well as test a prototype with end-users.

The results of the feasibility study provided us with sufficient confidence to take the app to the next phase. Scan Buddy v2 was developed after the study. The *final* design of the app was presented in the appropriate section of the paper, but more research is needed to test the efficacy and make further improvements.

Acknowledgements. We would like to thank Janneke Verhaegh and Edwin Heijman for kick-starting this project and their contributions in the initial phase.

References

Artunduaga, M., et al.: Safety challenges related to the use of sedation and general anesthesia in pediatric patients undergoing magnetic resonance imaging examinations. Pediatr. Radiol. **51**(5), 724–735 (2021). https://doi.org/10.1007/s00247-021-05044-5

Barnea-Goraly, N., et al., Diabetes Research in Children Network (DirecNet): High success rates of sedation-free brain MRI scanning in young children using simple subject preparation protocols with and without a commercial mock scanner–the diabetes research in children network (DirecNet) experience. Pediatr. Radiol. **44**(2), 181–186 (2014)

Harrington, S.G., Jaimes, C., Weagle, K.M., Greer, M.-L., Gee, M.S.: Strategies to perform magnetic resonance imaging in infants and young children without sedation. Pediatr. Radiol. **52**, 374–381 (2021). https://doi.org/10.1007/s00247-021-05062-3

Hogan, D., DiMartino, T., Liu, J., Mastro, K.A., Larson, E., Carter, E.: Video-based education to reduce distress and improve understanding among pediatric MRI patients: a randomized controlled study. J. Pediatr. Nurs. **41**, 48–53 (2018)

Jaimes, C., et al.: Success of nonsedated neuroradiologic MRI in children 1–7 years old. Am. J. Roentgenol. **216**(5), 1370–1377 (2021)

Janos, S., Schooler, G.R., Ngo, J.S., Davis, J.T.: Free-breathing unsedated MRI in children: justification and techniques. J. Magn. Reson. Imaging **50**(2), 365–376 (2019)

Li, M., Rudd, B., Lim, T.C., Lee, J.H.: In situ active control of noise in a 4 T MRI scanner. J. Magn. Reson. Imaging JMRI **34**(3), 662–669 (2011)

Marshall, G.N., Hays, R.D., Sherbourne, C.D., Wells, K.B.: The structure of patient satisfaction with outpatient medical care. Psychol. Assess. **5**(4), 477–483 (1993)

McGlashan, H.L., et al.: Evaluation of an internet-based animated preparatory video for children undergoing non-sedated MRI. Br. J. Radiol. **91**(1087), 20170719 (2018)

Nordahl, C.W., et al.: Methods for acquiring MRI data in children with autism spectrum disorder and intellectual impairment without the use of sedation. J. Neurodev. Disord. **8**, 20 (2016)

Rothman, S., Gonen, A., Vodonos, A., Novack, V., Shelef, I.: Does preparation of children before MRI reduce the need for anesthesia? Prospective randomized control trial. Pediatric Radiol. **46**(11), 1599–1605 (2016)

Runge, S.B., Christensen, N.L., Jensen, K., Jensen, I.E.: Children centered care: minimizing the need for anesthesia with a multi-faceted concept for MRI in children aged 4–6. Eur. J. Radiol. **107**, 183–187 (2018)

Törnqvist, E., Månsson, Å., Hallström, I.: Children having magnetic resonance imaging: a preparatory storybook and audio/visual media are preferable to anesthesia or deep sedation. J. Child Health Care **19**(3), 359–369 (2015)

Tyc, V.L., Fairclough, D., Fletcher, B., Leigh, L., Mulhern, R.K.: Children's distress during magnetic resonance imaging procedures. Children's Health Care J. Assoc. Care Children's Health **24**(1), 5–19 (1995). https://doi.org/10.1207/s15326888chc2401_2

Vanderby, S.A., Babyn, P.S., Carter, M.W., Jewell, S.M., McKeever, P.D.: Effect of anesthesia and sedation on pediatric MR imaging patient flow. Radiology **256**(1), 229–237 (2010)

Walker, B., et al.: Parent perspectives and preferences for strategies regarding nonsedated MRI scans in a pediatric oncology population. Support. Care Cancer **26**(6), 1815–1824 (2017). https://doi.org/10.1007/s00520-017-4009-9

A Learning Support System of Acquiring Four Skills to Succeed a Fundamental Trick of Kendama Named as "Around Japan"

Yu Shibuya[✉] and Riku Yasui

Kyoto Institute of Technology, Kyoto, Japan
shibuya@kit.ac.jp
https://www.hi.is.kit.ac.jp/en/

Abstract. The kendama is a traditional Japanese skill toy. It has been played for a long time in Japan. In addition, it is also well-known to foreigners, e.g. people in United States, Denmark, and Taiwan. Playing kendama might be an ice breaker between players and non-players and induce communication among them. In this study, we propose a learning support system of acquiring four skills to succeed a fundamental trick of kendama named as "around Japan". The system measures the acquisition degree of each skill of users. When users do wrong movement during measurement, the system shows it by a voice message. In addition, after the measurement, the system shows graphs which express the acquisition degrees of each skill of users and shows text messages about the evaluation of each skill. As a result of experiment, it was not able to demonstrate that the system raised the success rate of "around Japan" significantly. However, the system made users keeping their motivation to acquire "knee bending and stretching skill" and "keeping hole insight skill".

Keywords: Kendama · Skill acquisition · Learning support

1 Introduction

In Japan, there is a skill toy called kendama, which has been familiar to Japanese people for a long time. The kendama is the Japanese version of the Cup & Ball game. It consists of a handle with several cups and a spike with a ball connected by a length of string. The physical benefits are many including hand-eye coordination and exercise. It is played by both men and women of all ages [2]. The kendama has been played for a long time in Japan. In addition, the kendama is also well-known to foreigners, e.g. people in United States, Denmark, and Taiwan.

In some cases, playing kendama might be an ice breaker between players and non-player audience and induce communication among them. For example, when one of authors went abroad and he was asked to teach a trick to a guy. Then he taught the guy a skill, started to talk about something, and they have

M. Kurosu (Ed.): HCII 2022, LNCS 13302, pp. 613–622, 2022.
https://doi.org/10.1007/978-3-031-05311-5_43

been friend until now. Not only overseas but also in Japan, the kendama is an instrument of starting conversation between young players and older players.

So, where should you start to play with the kendama? You can learn from people who have experience with the kendama, or you can watch books and videos to practice. If you know someone who is experienced in the kendama, you can learn from her/him. If there are no experienced kendama players near you, you can go to a kendama class, but it takes time and money to find a kendama class. However, it is difficult for a beginner to judge which move is wrong if he cannot learn the move or if he learns it incorrectly.

Therefore, in this study, we propose a system to help a beginner of kendama to succeed in a representative kendama move. The system detects the movement of the kettle and the user, and teaches them to correct the wrong movement, so that they can learn the necessary skills to succeed in the technique.

This study proposes a learning support system for the player to acquire four skills to succeed a fundamental trick of kendama named as "around Japan". The reason for choosing "around Japan" as the representative kendama technique in this study is as follows. It is considered to be one of the most representative techniques of kendama, as it is used to certify the kendama class and rank. In addition, "around Japan" is the easiest of the continuous stabbing techniques for kendama.

2   Related Works

In order to learn a kendama technique, the user generally learns how to perform the technique and the tricks to make it successful by reading reference books or watching videos, and then the user challenges the technique. However, it is impossible to tell users how to improve their movements because reference books and videos only tell users the tricks and do not detect the user's movements.

Another related product of kendama is "Dendama" [3], which Otani et al. started to sell in 2016. Dendama, which consists of a kendama with a built-in sensor and a smartphone application, detects the movement of the kendama from the sensor and judges which moves are successful. However, this product is not intended for kendama beginners to learn kendama skills, but for experienced players to play against other kendama players around the world on the Internet through a smartphone application. Also, because of the built-in sensor, the texture and weight of this product are different from normal kendama.

3   Four Fundamental Skills

The words "small cup", "big cup", "cup body", "sword", "spike", "string", "ball", and "hole" in the following articles refer to the parts as shown in Fig. 1, respectively. The following four skills are important for a successful "round Japan" trick, according to the well known web site [1].

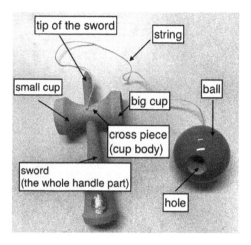

Fig. 1. Parts of kendama

Sword Grasping Skill: As shown in Fig. 2, in order to hold the sword steadily, hold the lower part of the sword with the thumb and forefinger and hold the it also with rest of the fingers firmly together.

Knee Bending and Stretching Skill: It is important to raise the ball with bending and stretching knees. Figure 3 shows the initial posture to raise the ball. As shown in Fig. 3, bending knees is required to raise the ball by stretching knees. Bending knees is also required to to raise the ball from the cup as shown in Fig. 4. It is also important to bend the knees when placing the ball on the cup. Beginners may raise and put the ball with the snap of their wrist without bending and stretching their knees and fail the trick by making the ball unstable

Keeping Sword Horizontally Skill: It is also important to keep the sword horizontally during the ball is on the cup.

Keeping Hole Insight Skill: In order to insert the ball into the sword at the end of "around Japan", it is necessary to keep the hole position in sight. When raising the ball from the position shown in Fig. 5, the ball should be raised by pulling the sword diagonally forward with appropriate force, so that the position of the hole can be seen when the ball is placed on a small cup.

4   Proposed System

In this study, we proposed and implemented a system to measure the learning level of users and to give them appropriate advice. Based on Daniel's study [6], in which the user successfully improved his turning skill by providing real-time

Fig. 2. Correct form of grasping "sword"

Fig. 3. Initial posture to raise the ball

notifications during snowboard turning, our system also provides real-time audio notifications when the user makes a wrong move during the measurement. After the measurement, a graph showing the user's level of mastery of each skill and text messages about the evaluation of each skill are presented so that the user can easily check the level of mastery of her/his own skills. We aim to help the user learn each skill efficiently while keeping her/his motivation.

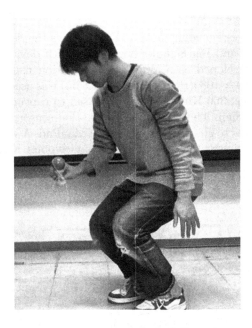

Fig. 4. Posture to raise the ball from the cup

Fig. 5. When stabbing the tip of sword to the hole of ball, the player should turn one's wrist as shown in the figure.

4.1 System Configuration

Figure 6 shows the system configuration, Fig. 7 shows the device and equipment used in the system, and Fig. 8 shows how a user with devices and equipments. The system was developed as a Windows application using C++. A display (resolution: 1920(W) × 1080(H) pixels, size: 21.5 in.) was used to show a feedback to the user. An Xbox 360 Kinect sensor was used to capture the movements of the ball and the human. The ENLIVEN 3D motion sensor was attached to the user's hand and knees to get the user movement via iPad. A web camera attached to the headband was used to acquire the user's viewpoint image.

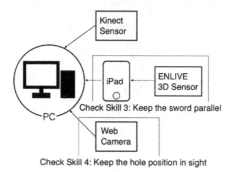

Fig. 6. System configuratin

4.2 Sequence of Learning Skills

Four kinds of acquiring skill are divided into following three learning parts in the proposed system.

1. "sword grasping skill" learning part
2. "knee bending and stretching skill" and "keeping sword horizontally skill" simultaneously learning part
3. "keeping hole insight skill" learning part

Fig. 7. Devices and equipments

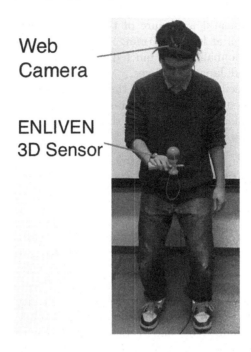

Web
Camera

ENLIVEN
3D Sensor

Fig. 8. A user with devices and equipments

5   Experiment

5.1   Purpose

The purpose of the experiment is to verify the following items.

Hypothesis 1: The success rate of the "around Japan" is higher when practicing with the advice system than when practicing without the advice system.
Hypothesis 2: Practicing with advice makes the user more careful to acquire skills than practicing without advice.

5.2   Participants

There were fourteen participants and they were asked to do a preliminary experiment in which they were asked to challenge the "around Japan" 10 times after watching a video that summarized the "around Japan" method and points to be careful about. Ten participants could not succeed anytimes and other four participants succeeded one time.

5.3   Procedure

Half of participants were asked to do following experimental procedure. Other seven participants were asked to follow the same procedure except exchanging the order of 1 and 4.

1. Read the experimental procedure of the with-advised system and use the with-advice system at longest 30 min.
2. Answer the questionnaire "How much did you focus on acquiring each skill?".
3. Try to do "around Japan" 10 times.
4. Read the experimental procedure of the without-advised system and use the without-advice system at longest 30 min.
5. Answer the questionnaire "How much did you focus on acquiring each skill?".
6. Try to do "around Japan" 10 times.

6 Result and Consideration

6.1 Hypothesis 1

Figure 9 shows the success rate of the "around Japan" before and after the system was used. As shown in Fig. 9, it could not be demonstrated that "Hypothesis 1: The success rate of the "around Japan" is higher when practicing with the advice system than when practicing without the advice system". One of the reasons for the lack of significant difference is the difficulty of learning the hole position visualization skills. The comments such as "I think it is more difficult to keep the hole position in sight" and "I want to know how to turn my wrist when I put the ken in the hole at the end" were commonly found in participants. This indicates that some participants were not able to learn "keeping hole insight" skill by using the system. In the system with advice, users were informed whether they could see the position of the hole or not, but they were instructed how to move their bodies. Therefore, it is thought that the success rate of "around Japan" will be increased by adding a function that judges not only the position of the hole but also the location of the hole and notifies the user how to move the body based on the judgement result.

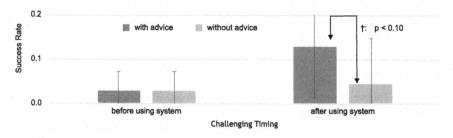

Fig. 9. Success rate of "around Japan" before and after using the proposed system

6.2 Hypothesis 2

After using each system, the participants were asked to answer the questionnaires. The questionnaires were asked the motivation about to acquire four fundamental skills. The results of the questionnaire are shown in Fig. 10.

As shown in Fig. 10, "Hypothesis 2: Practicing with advice makes the user more attentive to acquire skills than practicing without advice" can only be demonstrated for "knee bending and stretching skill" and "keeping hole insight skill". The reason why there was no significant difference in the "sword grasping skill" was ease of learning the skill. After using the system, all participants were able to grasp the sword correctly. The reason why there was no significant difference in the "keeping sword horizontally skill" was not-enough advice about the skill.

Anyway the system needs further experiments with more participants, clearing the problem, and improving the functions and user interface.

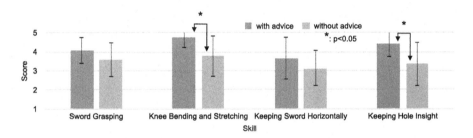

Fig. 10. Results of questionnaires

7 Conclusion

In this study, we proposed a system to support the acquisition of four skills necessary for a trick of kendama named as "around Japan". As a result of the experiment, we could not demonstrate that the system increases the success rate of the "around Japan". However, it was found that the participants were able to focus on acquiring "knee bending and stretching skill" and "keeping hole insight skill".

References

1. JAVE Association : Let's have fun playing with kendama! (in Japanese). http://yume.javea.or.jp/kendama/. Accessed 30 Jan 2022
2. JK Association: Kendama. https://en.wikipedia.org/wiki/Kendama. Accessed 30 Jan 2022
3. Axell Inc.: Dendama. https://axell.tokyo/dendama_en.html. Accessed 30 Jan 2022
4. Microsoft: Kinect for windows. https://developer.microsoft.com/en-us/windows/kinect/. Accessed 30 Jan 2022

5. OpenCV: Opencv. https://opencv.org. Accessed 30 Jan 2022
6. Spelmezan, D.: An investigation into the use of tactile instructions in snowboarding. In: Proceedings of the 14th International Conference on Human-Computer Interaction with Mobile Devices and Services. MobileHCI 2012, pp. 417–426. Association for Computing Machinery, New York (2012). https://doi.org/10.1145/2371574.2371639

The Color Analysis of "Lolita" Fashion Style in Japan

Peeraya Sripian[1]([✉]), Keiko Miyatake[2], Tipporn Laohakangvalvit[1], and Michiko Ohkura[1]

[1] Shibaura Institute of Technology, 3-7-5 Toyosu, Koto-ku, Tokyo 135-8548, Japan
{peeraya,tipporn}@shibaura-it.ac.jp,
ohkura@sic.shibaura-it.ac.jp
[2] Kyoritsu Women's University, 2-2-1 Hitotsubashi, Chiyoda-ku, Tokyo 101-8437, Japan
kmiyatake@kyoritsu-wu.ac.jp

Abstract. Nowadays, the Japanese word "Kawaii" has been officially recognized internationally and used in many studies. Fashion is one of the top industries that is seems associated with "Kawaii" in Japan. This work focuses on Kawaii fashion that can be observed at Harajuku, the place that is popular for teenagers in Japan to show off their outfit coordination. Japanese Lolita is a unique fashion style that can be seen at Harajuku. It is empirically known for some distinct features such as the usage of pastel color. However, the style has never been objectively clarified yet. In this study, we objectively clarify the Lolita fashion style using color feature extraction method, i.e., the calculation of Colorfulness and the dominant color in the HSV color space.

Keywords: Kawaii · Lolita · Colorfulness · Fashion

1 Introduction

Kawaii has been officially recognized worldwide since Japan's Ministry of Foreign Affairs has appointed "Kawaii Ambassadors" in 2009 to promote the Japanese pop culture. The authors have been conducting collaborative research on Kawaii fashion since 2018. We investigated Kawaii fashion trends in Japan and suggested that the Kawaii fashion observed at Harajuku can be classified into Lolita fashion and Harajuku-type Kawaii fashion (HK) [1].

We made the hypothesis that HK is somewhat high saturation and colorful. We successfully verified that HK contains statistically higher saturation and more Colorfulness than the street fashion observed at Harajuku and Shibuya [2–5]. In our recent work, the Colorfulness of HK was compared with other Kawaii fashion: "Classic Retro Doll" (Classic), Orthodox Pretty and Cute" (Orthodox), and "Street Kawaii" (Street) [6]. The comparison results still showed that HK is very much distinct from other Kawaii styles. In this work, we focus on the other Kawaii fashion observed at Harajuku, the Lolita fashion style such as "BABY, THE STARS SHINE BRIGHT", [7], or "Angelic Pretty" [8], the well-known fashion brands that have their branch stores outside of Japan.

M. Kurosu (Ed.): HCII 2022, LNCS 13302, pp. 623–633, 2022.
https://doi.org/10.1007/978-3-031-05311-5_44

"Lolita" fashion that is seen in Japan is perceived differently in the West than in Japan. Originally, the term was originated from the novel *Lolita* by Vladimir Nabokov in 1958, which was often used to describe sexualized dress by young girls, or middle-aged men's pedophilic attachment to such girls [9]. Therefore, it was seen in the mainstream Western media that the perception of Lolita was negative concept of femininity. On the other hand, the subcultural Lolita in Japan was perceived as part of acceptable mainstream fashion. Especially *GothLoli* or the combination of Gothic and Lolita expression, was seem to has no direct reference to Nabokov and his novel [10], and it was related to fashion with no sexual connotations.

The study by Yahata and Watanabe [11] described the summary and arguments for the changes of Japanese Lolita's fashion rules in time as follows:

> It is argued that today's Lolita fashion originated from the prosperity of street fashion in the 1990s and became generalized after the periods of subdivision in the 2000s. During the period of subdivision in the early 2000s, the trend focused on classical items with the theme of the Rococo world, while in the late 2000s, the trend focused on items with the theme of princesses in stories. The style we recognize as Lolita fashion can be thought of as a style that incorporates the characteristics of post-2000 styles described so far.

> To excerpt only the color characteristics along the timeline, in the early 2000's subdivision, "Sweet Lolita" was mostly in shades of white, red, pink, and sax, but even black could be included in "Sweet Lolita" if the styling did not include gothic elements. "Classical Lolita" is less flamboyant, with shades of brown and smoky pink. "Decorated Lolita" is a style that uses pastel colors such as pink, saxe blue, lavender, and mint green.

> In the late 2000s, printed items became the main trend, with illustrations of various themes such as animals, sweets, ribbons, and fairy tales printed on colorful fabrics such as pastel pink, mint, saxe blue, and pastel purple. The styling also includes blouses in white, black, and pastel colored.

> In the latter half of the 2000s, the casual style of Lolita became popular, and slightly casual designs with less volume skirts that can be worn in everyday life such as dresses, skirts, salopettes, and hoodies appeared. Classic style categorized in this study is based on this taste and is a style that can be worn more casually. On the other hand, there are many devoted fans who continue to follow the styles of the early 2000s. An example of this is the Lolita fashion brand that reprinted popular original prints and sold them years later.

2   Research Purpose

Although Lolita fashion style is widely known, there is no objective analysis of the colors used in Lolita's clothing. The purpose of this work is to objectively clarify the Lolita fashion style based on the color characteristic of the fashion. We collect data of Lolita fashion, preprocess the data, and analyze the color of each image.

3 Proposed Method

3.1 Overview

Fashion images are selected from the Lolita fashion brands' websites. All images are full-body photos with the brand's clothing combinations. The background of each image was removed using Photoshop before the data analysis. The full list of Lolita fashion brands used in this work with the number of images collected per brand is shown in Table 1. For the analysis, we employ three indicators:

- Colorfulness [12]
- Dominant color

  – Saturation (saturation of the HSV color space)
  – Brightness (value of the HSV color space)

We employ Colorfulness because it is useful to distinguish Kawaii fashion in our previous works [2, 5, 6]. We also employ dominant color and analyze the combination of Saturation and Brightness because pastel colors are defined as colors with high value and low saturation in the HSV color space [13]. Therefore, these indicators may be useful to objectively distinguish Lolita fashion from other fashion style.

Table 1. List of brands that represent Lolita fashion style, presented with number of collected images and the website URL.

Brand	Number of images	Website URL
Angelic Pretty	27	https://angelicpretty-onlineshop.com/
BABY, THE STARS SHINE BRIGHT	27	https://www.babyssb.co.jp/
Enchantlic Enchantilly	2	https://enchantlic-enchantilly.com/
Innocent World	10	https://innocent-w.jp/onlineshop/
Juliette et Justine	3	https://juliette-et-justine.com/
Mary Magdalene	3	http://www.marymagdalene.jp/
Metamorphose temps de fille	15	https://metamorphose.gr.jp/
Millefleurs	3	https://millefleurs-noirs.com/catalog.html
Victorian maiden	10	https://www.victorianmaiden.com/
Total images	**100**	

3.2 Colorfulness

Colorfulness is a holistic interpretation of color in an image. To quantify the variety of colors in an image, a Colorfulness metric is proposed by Hasler and Süsstrunk [12] in the context of image compression quality evaluation. The Colorfulness of an image can be calculated by defining the opponent color values using Eqs. 1 and 2 with R_p, G_p, and B_p are the values in the Red, Green, and Blue channels accordingly. For each image, we calculate Eqs. (1) and (2) of each pixel. The results of u and v for all pixels are stored in one-dimensional array accordingly.

$$u_p = R_p - G_p \tag{1}$$

$$v_p = \frac{1}{2}(R_p + G_p) - B_p \tag{2}$$

Then, μ_{uv} and σ_{uv} are computed using Eqs. (3) and (4). In the equations, μ_u and σ_u are the mean and the standard deviation of u_p, while, μ_v and σ_v are the mean and the standard deviation of v_p. Equation (5) shows the calculation of the final Colorfulness: C.

$$\mu_{uv} = \sqrt{\mu_u^2 + \mu_v^2} \tag{3}$$

$$\sigma_{uv} = \sqrt{\sigma_u^2 + \sigma_v^2} \tag{4}$$

$$C = \sigma_{uv} + \alpha \cdot \mu_{uv} \tag{5}$$

We use $\alpha = 0.3$ in our work, similar to Hasler and Süsstrunk [12]. The Colorfulness for images (a), (b), and (c) are shown in Table 3.

3.3 Calculation of Dominant Colors

Saturation defines the brilliance and intensity of a color. High saturation colors appear to be rich and full, while low saturation colors appear to be dull and grayish. We extract saturation of the top dominant color from each image based on the method in [14, 15]. To calculate the dominant colors, the following steps are performed:

(1) Convert the color space from RGB to HSV.
(2) Perform color quantization by K-Means (N = 72).
(3) Create a histogram with 72 bins.
(4) Normalize the values of the histogram.
(5) Sort the histogram in the decreasing order.
(6) Obtain the HSV color values from the first bin as the top dominant color of that image.

4 Result and Discussion

We compared Lolita fashion style to other four Kawaii fashion styles: HK, Classic, Orthodox, and Street, which were collected in our previous work.

4.1 Colorfulness Comparison

We show the boxplot comparison of Colorfulness of each data set of fashion style in Fig. 1.

A Kruskal–Wallis test showed a statistically significant main effect of Colorfulness in the fashion styles, $(H(4) = 188.176, p < 0.0001)$.

Pairwise comparisons with adjusted p-values revealed statistically significant differences in Colorfulness between HK to all other styles: HK vs. Orthodox $(p < 0.0001)$, HK vs. Classic $(p < 0.0001)$, HK vs. Street $(p < 0.0001)$, and HK vs. Lolita $(p < 0.0001)$. The difference of Colorfulness between Street and Orthodox was also significant $(p < 0.05)$, but not between other group combinations. Colorfulness of each style are ranked in descending order as follows, HK (80.61), Street (31.42), Classic (30.07), Lolita (28.99), and Orthodox (26.72).

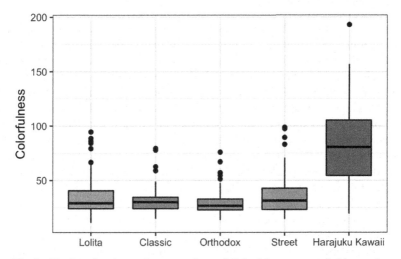

Fig. 1. The boxplot shows the comparison of Colorfulness across fashion styles.

Figure 2 shows violin plot of Colorfulness of each fashion style. The red dot shows the median Colorfulness for each data set. The data set's ratio of images is indicated by the width of the area at each level of Colorfulness. From this figure, HK is very distinctively different from the other data sets. It is noted that the violin plot of Colorfulness of Lolita and Street are quite similar, with the medians a little higher than the widest area of the plot.

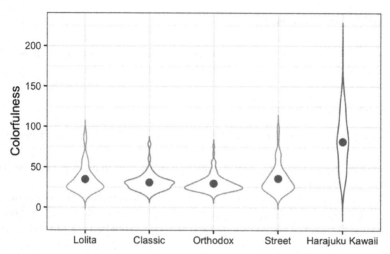

Fig. 2. The violin plot of Colorfulness for each fashion styles. Regions: 1-top, 2-median, 3-widest, and 4-bottom are illustrated by dashed grey box on the plot for further analysis.

4.2 Saturation and Brightness

Since the pastel color is defined as a less saturated but brighter color [13], we analyze by investigating the saturation and brightness of the image. The top dominant color accounts for the most region in an image, therefore, it is reasonable to employ as the representative color for a fashion image. We plot the saturation and value (brightness) of the top dominant color for all fashion images, separated by fashion style for visualization in Fig. 3. Each point on the graph is a representative of one fashion image. From this figure, Lolita's data points are gathering toward the highest left, indicating that most Lolita images have very high value (almost 1.0) and very low saturation (toward 0.0), while other data sets are scattering somewhat toward the lower right, or to the middle of the plot. Moreover, for Harajuku-type Kawaii fashion, the points are scattered throughout the whole plot, indicating that each fashion image has its own unique brightness and saturation, and they tend now to form a visible group (Figs. 3).

We performed Kruskal-Wallis H test to test if there were significant main effects of saturation and brightness between fashion styles. The median values, shown in Table 2, of saturation and brightness of all fashion styles were not statistically significantly same, $H(4) = 772.583$, p < .0001 and $H(4) = 187.677$, p < .0001 for saturation and brightness, respectively. Subsequently, pairwise comparisons were performed using Dunn's (1964) procedure with a Bonferroni correction for multiple comparisons. Adjusted p-values are employed. This post hoc analysis revealed statistically significant differences between most of the comparison pairs for saturation and value, as shown in Table 3. We show the boxplots for saturation and brightness of the top dominant color in Figs. 4 and 5 accordingly.

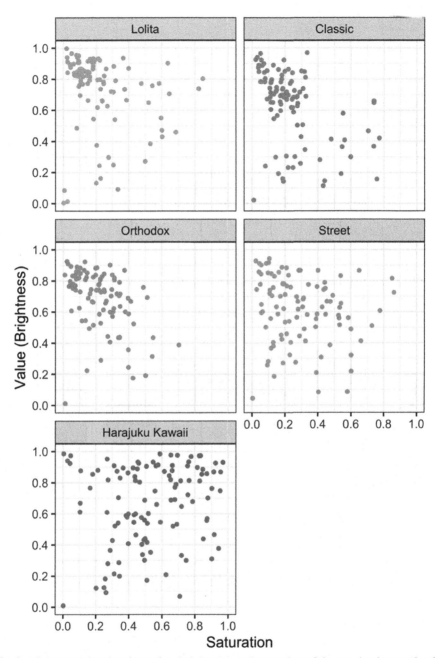

Fig. 3. The scatterplot showing value (brightness) and saturation of the top dominant color for all fashion styles. Each point represents a fashion image.

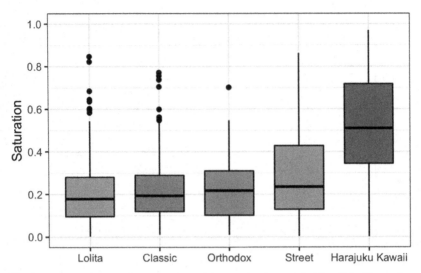

Fig. 4. The boxplot showing saturation of the top dominant color for all fashion styles.

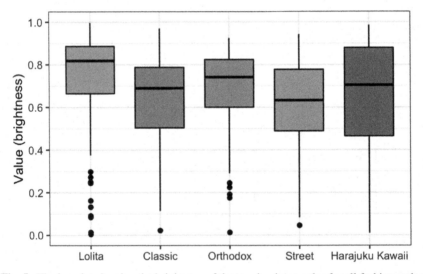

Fig. 5. The boxplot showing the brightness of the top dominant color for all fashion styles.

Hence, by employing the visualization of saturation and value of the top dominant colors, we can clarify the characteristic of the fashion styles, especially for Lolita. The scatterplot of saturation and value of Lolita shows that many images of the Lolita fashion use pastel colors.

Table 2. Median saturation and Median value of the top dominant color for all fashion images in each fashion style

Fashion style	Saturation	Value
Lolita	0.182200	0.782100
Classic	0.210500	0.679450
Orthodox	0.231250	0.707050
Street	0.252550	0.632650
Harajuku Kawaii	0.432850	0.698200

Table 3. Adjusted P values from the post-hoc comparison. P < 0.05 is displayed in bold and underlined.

Comparison pairs		*p values*	
		Saturation	Value
Lolita	Classic	**0.017**	**0.000**
Lolita	Orthodox	**0.000**	**0.000**
Lolita	Street	**0.000**	**0.000**
Lolita	Harajuku Kawaii	**0.000**	**0.000**
Classic	Orthodox	1.000	**0.010**
Classic	Street	**0.000**	**0.023**
Classic	Harajuku Kawaii	**0.000**	**0.002**
Orthodox	Street	**0.003**	**0.000**
Orthodox	Harajuku Kawaii	**0.000**	1.000
Street	Harajuku Kawaii	**0.000**	**0.000**

4.3 Further Analysis

The result of the comparison of Colorfulness from both boxplot and violin plot confirmed that HK is distinctively different from other Kawaii fashion styles, including Lolita. Meanwhile, the violin plot in Fig. 2 showed that Lolita and Street are similar. For further analysis, we investigated the images of Lolita and Street data set for a particular Colorfulness region. We selected fashion images from Lolita and Classic that are in the top (region 1), median (region 2), widest area (region 3), and bottom (region 4) area of the plot, ten images for each region. When comparing the Lolita and Street images, Lolita shows more "pastel" colors. Pastel pink, mint, and saxe blue can be particularly seen from Lolita fashion images in regions 2 and 3. These colors are not found in the Street. As stated in the previous study [8], these colors are one of the characteristics of Lolita fashion and are still supported as its core colors. They are considered colors that are generally recognized as the traditional colors of Lolita fashion.

Lolita fashion images in region 1 are often styled in bright, deep shades rather than royal pastel colors. It is also characterized by the use of red. This is a different color style from the traditional pastel colors mentioned above. Lolita's fashion images in region 4 are mostly white. There are several styles in region 4 where the overall impression of the color is "whiteish." These are styles that have not been seen in Lolita fashion until now. In recent years, the trend has been toward one-tone coordination, and in the spring/summer of 2021, there were many designs in which the entire outfit was white. It can be assumed that this is the influence. In addition, Lolita's fashion images at regions 3 and 4 show black and dark blue styles.

Although Street's fashion images at region 1 show a lot of red, like Lolita, Lolita is bright red, and the Street is deep red. Street's fashion images at regions 2 and 3 are mostly in neutral colors and do not show any color characteristics. In region 4, Street's fashion images show the same whitish coordination, similar to Lolita. It can be implied that this is also a trend. Since the Street is more affected by the trend than Lolita, it is reasonable that white coordination is being adopted. In addition, the deep color coordination observed in Street's fashion images of region 4 (violin plot) is not seen in Lolita. We had assumed that streets with elements such as rock and sports would use bright colors, but the results were different. The different result is that the bright colors are presented only in the pink trend, which could be observed from Street's images in region 1. In summary, there are many neutral colors in Street's fashion image. This may be due to the fact that the designers designed the clothes with selling as the primary goal.

5 Conclusion

In this work, we objectively clarify the Lolita fashion style using Colorfulness, Saturation, and Value. From the comparison of Colorfulness with other Kawaii fashion styles, we found that Lolita and Street Kawaii are very similar in terms of Colorfulness distribution. From the further investigation of images at each distribution region, we found that pastel colors are observed in most Lolita images but not in Street images, which is empirically recognized for Lolita fashion [8].

From the comparison of Saturation against Value of each style, Lolita accumulates at a higher Value and lowest Saturation, while other styles are more distributed toward the center of the plot. We were able to show that Lolita is distinct from other Kawaii styles by using Saturation and Value.

In summary, we objectively proved what had been empirically known by employing Colorfulness and the combination of Value and Saturation from the image processing research field.

Acknowledgement. This work was partially supported by JSPS KAKENHI Grant Number 20K12032.

References

1. Miyatake, K.: Japanese Kawaii fashion-historic changes in trends and styles. In: Spring Conference of Japan Society of Kansei Engineering, Nagoya (2018). (in Japanese)

2. Sripian, P., Miyatake, K., Ohkura, M.: Study on color feature of Harajuku Kawaii fashion. In: The 14th Spring Conference of Japan Society of Kansei Engineering (2019)
3. Miyatake, K., Sripian, P., Ohkura, M.: Study on style of Harajuku Kawaii fashion (1st report) - design features. In: The 20th Annual Meeting of Japan Society of Kansei Engineering, Tokyo, Japan (2018). (in Japanese)
4. Sripian, P., Miyatake, K., Ohkura, M.: Study on style of Harajuku Kawaii fashion (2nd report) - color features. In: The 20th Annual Meeting of Japan Society of Kansei Engineering, Tokyo, Japan (2018)
5. Sripian, P., Miyatake, K., Ohkura, M.: Study on the color feature of Harajuku-type Kawaii fashion comparison with street snap images using colorfulness. TNI J. Eng. Technol. **8**(1), 63–72 (2020)
6. Sripian, P., Miyatake, K., Ohkura, M.: Study on style of Kawaii fashion (11th Report) –the colorfulness comparison of various Kawaii fashions. In: The 16th Spring Annual Meeting of Japan Society of Kansei Engineering, Online 2021 (2021)
7. Baby the stars shine bright online store (2021). https://www.babyssb.co.jp/en/
8. Angelic Pretty Online Shop. https://angelicpretty-onlineshop.com/. Accessed 12 July 2021
9. Merskin, D.: Reviving Lolita? A media literacy examination of sexual portrayals of girls in fashion advertising. Am. Behav. Sci. **48**(1), 119–129 (2004)
10. Monden, M.: Transcultural flow of demure aesthetics: examining cultural globalisation through Gothic & Lolita fashion. New Voices **2**(2008), 21–40 (2008)
11. Yahata, M., Watanabe, A.: The roots of Lolita fashion - focus on street fashion after the 1980s - (in Japanese). Annu. Bull. Dept. Sci. Living, Kyoritsu Women's Univ. **56**, 11–31 (2013)
12. Hasler, D., Suesstrunk, S.E.: Measuring colorfulness in natural images. In: Proceedings of SPIE 2003 (2003)
13. Gilbert, B.: Beaded Colorways: Freeform Beadweaving Projects and Palettes. North Light Books, Cincinnati (2009)
14. Yamada, A.: MPEG-7 Visual part of eXperimentation Model version 9.0. ISO/IEC JTC1/SC29/WG11/N3914 (2001)
15. Forczmański, P., Czapiewski, P., Frejlichowski, D., Okarma, K., Hofman, R.: Comparing clothing styles by means of computer vision methods. In: Chmielewski, L.J., Kozera, R., Shin, B.-S., Wojciechowski, K. (eds.) ICCVG 2014. LNCS, vol. 8671, pp. 203–211. Springer, Cham (2014). https://doi.org/10.1007/978-3-319-11331-9_25

Author Index

Printed in the United States
by Baker & Taylor Publisher Services